Alan Palmer was educated at Bancroft's School, Woodford Green, and at Oriel College, Oxford. He was head of the History Department at Highgate School from 1953 to 1969 when he gave up his post to concentrate on historical writing and research. Alan Palmer lives in Woodstock, Oxfordshire.

Alexander I

Tsar of War and Peace

Alan Palmer

A PHOENIX GIANT PAPERBACK

First published in Great Britain by Weidenfeld and Nicolson in 1974
This paperback edition published in 1997 by Phoenix,
a division of Orion Books Ltd,
Orion House, 5 Upper St Martin's Lane,
London WC2H 9EA

A CIP catalogue record for this book is available
from the British Library.

ISBN: 1 85799 866 9

Printed and bound in Great Britain by
Butler & Tanner Ltd, Frome and London

To Veronica

Contents

List of Illustrations and Maps		xii
Author's Note		xiv
Preface		xvi

CHAPTER 1	THE CROW IN PEACOCK FEATHERS	1
	The Bronze Horseman	1
	Alexander's Childhood	6
	Betrothal and Marriage	13
	The Last Years of Catherine II	21
	The Succession in Doubt	24

CHAPTER 2	EMPIRE ON PARADE	27
	The Grand Duke Comes to Town	27
	Doubts of a Tsarevich	32
	Suvorov in Italy and Switzerland	37
	Mounting Tension in the Capital	39
	Murder at the Mikhailovsky (March 1801)	42

CHAPTER 3	THE CRACKING OF THE ICE	47
	A Promise of Reform	47
	The Secret Committee and its Enemies	50
	Alexander's Coronation in Moscow (September 1801)	56

CHAPTER 4	'THE EMPEROR WANTS IT THUS'	62
	Foreign Affairs: Isolation or Alignment?	62

Governmental Reform and the Primacy of
   Vorontsov   67
Alexander, Elizabeth and Maria Naryshkin   73

CHAPTER 5   SHADOW OF WAR   78
Alexander Disillusioned with the First Consul (1803–4)   78
Czartoryski, Novosiltsov and the Grand Design of
   1804   82
Military Plans and the Polish Question   87
Alexander at Pulawy and Berlin (October–November
   1805)   91

CHAPTER 6   AUSTERLITZ AND AFTER   95
Alexander and Kutuzov in Moravia   95
Peace Parleys   100
The Battle of Austerlitz (2 December 1805)   103
Alexander Humiliated   110

CHAPTER 7   ANATHEMA   115
Inquest on Austerlitz   115
The End of Government by the Tsar's Friends   117
Across the Bridge   120
Preparing for War on Two Fronts, 1806   122
Eylau and Friedland   127

CHAPTER 8   TILSIT   132
Alexander and Napoleon Meet in Midstream   132
The Fine Phrases of Tilsit   136
The Tilsit Settlement (July 1807)   139

CHAPTER 9   AS DESTINY DEMANDS   145
The Effects of Tilsit Abroad   145
Alexander's Throne in Danger?   147
Caulaincourt arrives in St Petersburg (December 1807)   151
The Death of Lisinka (May 1808)   154
Erfurt   155

CONTENTS

CHAPTER 10   THE PRIMACY OF SPERANSKY   164
             The Rise of Michael Speransky   164
             The Reforms of 1808–9 and their Critics   168
             The Council of State at Work   174

CHAPTER 11   THE VICEROY   177
             Caulaincourt: The Prussian Royal Visit; and the
                 Marriage of Catherine   177
             Russia and Napoleon's 1809 Campaign   182
             A Russian Empress for the French?   185

CHAPTER 12   'BLOOD MUST FLOW AGAIN'   193
             Alexander at Tver and Gruzino   193
             Personal Sorrows, 1810   195
             Alexander takes Russia out of the Continental
                 System   197
             The War Scare of 1811   199
             Discomforted Diplomats   203
             Portents and Military Plans   206
             The Fall of Speransky and Alexander's Departure for
                 the Army   210

CHAPTER 13   CAPTAIN IN THE FIELD   216
             The Pleasures of Vilna   216
             The Eve of Invasion, 1812   219
             Resolution and Retreat   224
             From Vilna to Drissa   228

CHAPTER 14   THE RAZOR-EDGE OF FATE   234
             Alexander in Moscow (July 1812)   234
             The Clamour for Kutuzov   237
             Bernadotte; General Wilson; and Germaine de Staël 240
             Borodino and its Consequences   244
             Plain Speaking from a Sister   247
             Alexander refuses to make Peace   250

CONTENTS

CHAPTER 15 TSAR WITH A MISSION   257
            Vilna Again (December 1812–January 1813)   257
            The Liberation of Prussia   260
            The Changing Fortunes of War (Spring 1813)   262
            Diplomatic Interlude (June–August 1813)   267
            The Battles of Dresden and Leipzig and the Race for
                Frankfurt   270
            The Campaign in France, 1814   275
            Alexander Enters Paris (31 March 1814)   280

CHAPTER 16 PARIS AND LONDON   282
            The Tsar, Talleyrand and Caulaincourt (April 1814)   282
            Peacemaking in Paris   286
            Catherine Blazes an English Trail   291
            Alexander in England (June 1814)   293

CHAPTER 17 THE PANORAMA OF EUROPE   302
            Preparing for the Vienna Congress in St Petersburg
                and at Pulawy   302
            Alexander in Residence at the Hofburg   306
            Congress Diplomacy (October 1814–February 1815)   310
            Alexander's Change of Heart   316
            Napoleon's Return from Elba and the Close of the
                Vienna Congress   319

CHAPTER 18 HOLY ALLIANCE   325
            The Heilbronn Prophetess   325
            Peacemaking in Paris once more   327
            Julie von Krüdener at her Prime   330
            The Treaty of the Holy Alliance, 26 September 1815   333
            Disillusionment?   337

CHAPTER 19 CONTRASTS   339
            Alexander in Congress Poland (November 1815)   339
            St Petersburg Once More   342
            The Arakcheev System and the Military Colonies   344
            Imperial Weddings   348
            Alexander continues his Spiritual Quest   351

Disarmament and Foreign Affairs (1816–18) 354
The Congress of Aix (1818) 358

CHAPTER 20 THE ABSENTEE TSAR 362
Sad News from Stuttgart (January 1819) 362
Government by Post Chaise 363
The Tsar Goes to Troppau 369
Mutiny in the Semeonovsky Regiment (October 1820) 372
Laibach and the Re-opening of the Eastern Question 375
Alexander's Dilemma over the Greek Insurrection 378
Vienna and Verona (1822) 381

CHAPTER 21 'AN ISLAND BATTERED BY THE WAVES' 384
Procrastination 384
Alexander's Illness; His Reconciliation with Elizabeth; and the Ascendancy of Photius 387
The Flood of 1824 394
The Decision to go to Taganrog 397

CHAPTER 22 TAGANROG 400
To the Sea of Azov 400
Alexander in the Crimea 403
The Last Fourteen Days 405
The Aftermath 409
Legends 412

Genealogical Table 418
Reference Notes 421
Select Bibliography 462
Index 471

Illustrations

1   The six eldest children of Paul and Marie Feodorovna (*Mansell Collection*)
2   Catherine the Great by Lampi (*photo Alinari-Giraudon*)
3   The Mikhailovsky Palace in 1807 (*Collection Viollet*)
4   Tsar Paul I shortly before his death. Engraving by Wolf (*Radio Times Hulton Picture Library*)
5   Alexander from the painting by Monnier, 1806 (*Radio Times Hulton Picture Library*)
6   Empress Elizabeth in 1814 (*The Wallace Collection*)
7   Prince Adam Czartoryski after an engraving by Soliman (*Radio Times Hulton Picture Library*)
8   Arakcheev as a young man (*Radio Times Hulton Picture Library*)
9   Queen Louise of Prussia by Grassi in 1802 (*Mansell Collection*)
10 Maria Naryshkin, Alexander's mistress (*Radio Times Hulton Picture Library*)
11 The meeting between Alexander and Napoleon on a raft at Tilsit in 1807 (*from* Imperator Aleksandr *by N. K. Shilder*)
12 A contemporary English cartoon satirizing the new-found friendship between Russia and France (*photo Françoise Foliot*)
13 Marshal Kutuzov (*Novosti Press Agency*)
14 Michael Speransky (*Novosti Press Agency*)
15 The historic letter from the Grand-Duchess Catherine to Alexander informing him of the loss of Moscow
16 Letter from Alexander to the Grand-Duchess Catherine
17 The Allied leaders in Hyde Park, 1814 (*reproduced by gracious permission of Her Majesty the Queen*)

18 The Grand-Duchess Catherine Pavlovna. An engraving of 1814 (*Mary Evans Picture Library*)

19 The Dowager Empress Marie Feodorovna. An engraving by T. Wright from a painting by George Dawe (*Mary Evans Picture Library*)

20 The Imperial villa on Kammionyi Island where the Tsar spent the anxious weeks after the burning of Moscow in 1812 (*photo by Victor Kennett*)

21 The river front of the Winter Palace in St Petersburg (*photo by Victor Kennett*)

22 Baroness Julie von Krüdener (*Radio Times Hulton Picture Library*)

23 Alexander in 1818. Engraving by V. Bromley from a drawing by Igleson (*Novosti Press Agency*)

LIST OF MAPS

The Europe of Alexander I   xviii
St Petersburg in the Early Nineteenth Century   3
The Battle of Austerlitz   105

Author's Note

Throughout the narrative and reference notes of this book my practice has been as follows:

Dates. Unless specifically stated otherwise, all dates are given according to the Gregorian Calendar, common to western Europe and the Americas, rather than to the Julian Calendar which was followed by the Russians until the Bolshevik Revolution. In the eighteenth century the Julian Calendar was eleven days behind the Gregorian Calendar and in the nineteenth century the difference was twelve days.

Spelling of Foreign Words and Names. So far as possible, I have tried to follow the currently fashionable system of transliteration except when common English usage commends an alternative spelling more naturally acceptable to the general reader. For arbitrary distinctions of this kind I ask the indulgence of linguistic purists.

Place-Names and First Names. The names used for places are normally those which were current in Alexander's reign; I have at times added modern alternatives to assist the reader to identify them on a map. First names have been anglicized: thus 'Catherine' for 'Ekaterina'. The only occasion upon which I have used a foreign form is to distinguish a person from somebody with a similar name who has already appeared in the text.

Titles. I have used the word 'Tsar' where contemporaries would have said 'Emperor' so as to distinguish Alexander from Napoleon and Francis of Austria. I have, however, referred to Alexander's wife as the Empress Elizabeth, his mother as the Dowager Empress Marie Feodorovna and his grandmother as the Empress Catherine II. This is a totally illogical personal foible caused by the fact that I do not like the English rendering 'Tsarina'. Moreover reigning Empresses, unlike their husbands, do not crowd out the page.

I would like to acknowledge my debt to the authors of the specialized studies cited in the bibliography and to express my gratitude to the staffs of the London Library and the Bodleian Library, Oxford, for their kind assistance and courtesy. It is also a pleasure to thank Miss Gila Curtis for the care she has taken in editing this book for publication, and I wish particularly to thank Mrs M. D. Anderson who once again prepared the Index with such remarkable speed and skill. I am especially indebted to my wife, Veronica, who accompanied me on both my trips to Russia and who read and discussed every chapter with me in detail as it was written.

A.W.P.

Preface

Alexander I, ruler of Russia for the first quarter of the nineteenth century, is remembered today mainly on three counts: as the Tsar who refused to make peace with the French when Moscow fell in 1812; as the idealist who sought to bind Europe's sovereigns in a Holy Alliance in 1815; and as the Emperor who died – or gave the impression of having died – at the remote southern seaport of Taganrog in the winter of 1825. Recent interest has concentrated, perhaps excessively, on the third of these dramatic episodes although it is natural that the epic years of the struggle with Napoleon should continue to excite the historical imagination.

There was, however, much of significance in Alexander's life and reign besides these events. 'A more virtuous man, I believe, does not exist, nor one who is more enthusiastically devoted to better the condition of mankind,' declared President Thomas Jefferson six years after Alexander's accession; and Castlereagh, the British Foreign Secretary, writing a private note to his own brother eleven years later, was prepared to assert he knew 'of no Sovereign in history who has had so rich a harvest of glory'. Napoleon and Metternich, on the other hand, both complained that Alexander was inconsistent and untrustworthy; and there were numerous occasions when he puzzled, or exasperated, contemporaries. Was he sincere in his principles of government? Did he understand how to manage the armies he delighted to see on parade? Were his hours of religious devotion an escape from the responsibilities of Empire or a necessary means of finding strength and inspiration? Could he ever be relied upon to follow through logically a line of thought or action?

The questions, and the doubts, accumulated readily enough in his own lifetime. It was the answers which posed difficulty then, and the passage of a century and a half has made them no easier to attain. Alexander was a remarkably complex personality. There remains about the nature of his reign and his character sufficient mystery for him to have been dubbed, in retrospect, 'the enigmatic Tsar'. This present book attempts to assemble clues to understand him as a man and as a sovereign; it does not pretend to present a final and definitive answer, for that is impossible. Pushkin once declared Alexander was 'a Sphinx who carried his riddle with him to the tomb'. There are some who say that tomb is empty.

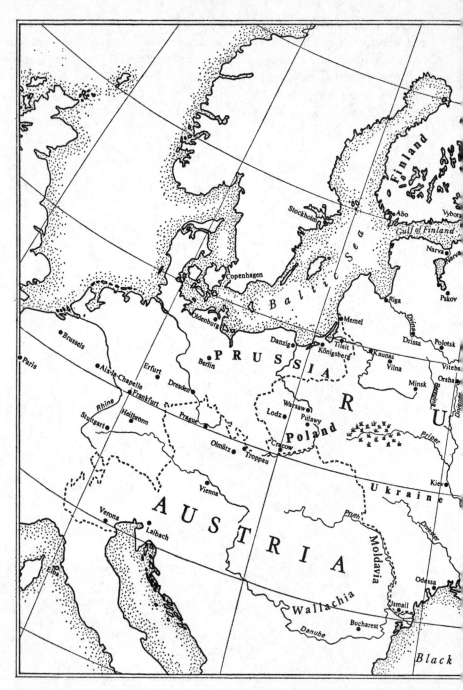

The Europe o

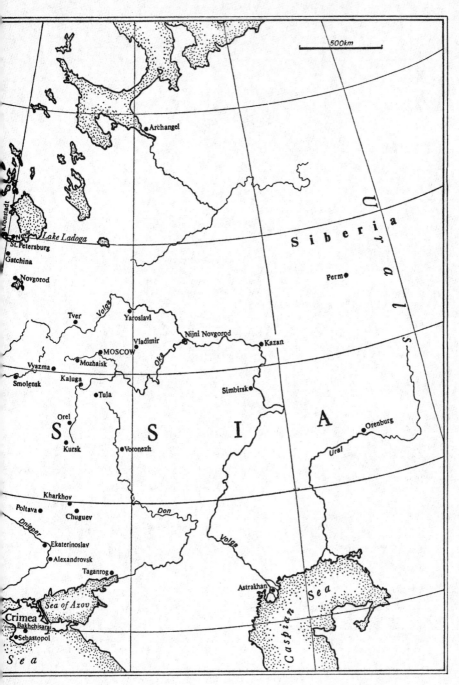

500km

Archangel

S i b e r i a

Kronstadt

Lake Ladoga

St.Petersburg

Gatchina

Novgorod

Perm

Tver

Volga

Yaroslavl

Nijni Novgorod

Vladimir

Kazan

MOSCOW

Vyazma

Mozhaisk

Oka

Smolensk

Kaluga

U r a l s

Tula

Simbirsk

Orel

S   S   I   A

Kursk

Voronezh

Orenburg

Ural

Kharkhov

Poltava

Don

Chuguev

Dnieper

Ekaterinoslav

Volga

Alexandrovsk

Taganrog

Astrakhan

Caspian Sea

Sea of Azov

Crimea

Bakhchisarai

Caspian Sea

Sebastopol

Sea

Alexander I

1

The Crow in Peacock Feathers

The Bronze Horseman

The city of St Petersburg awoke early in the summer sunshine. It was
Wednesday, 7 August 1782, and from soon after dawn the long avenues of
the Russian capital echoed with all the anticipatory bustle of a grand
parade. Bugles sounded in the fortress of St Peter and St Paul; cavalry
hooves rang out sharply on the Nevsky Prospect and down the granite quays
along the left bank of the river Neva; bands led the Guards past the ordered line of public buildings – the green and red of the Preobrazhensky
Grenadiers, the green and white of the Izmailovsky, the blue and white of
the Semeonovsky. By mid-morning eight regiments were drawn up facing
outwards in a circle at the centre of the huge square between the Admiralty
and the Senate House. From ornamented windows to east and west the
great families of the Empire waited and watched. Less privileged onlookers – masons, carpenters, minor government officials and their wives,
foreign traders and seamen, peasants come to town from the island villages
or the fields to the south – jostled each other along the new embankment
above the Neva. Some labourers clambered among the foundations of St
Isaac's Cathedral: they felt at home there, knowing every stone after ten
years' or more work, sleeping during the summer months in a cantonment
at the foot of the church's massive walls. Off the quay, a dark flotilla of
warships rode at anchor, dressed overall. In the clear northern light flags
and bunting were caught so sharply that the smooth grey river gleamed
with rare colour. Someone had calculated that, over the previous decade,
the citizens of the capital had enjoyed bright sunshine on only one day in

I

four and that on almost half the days of the year it either rained or snowed. This morning they were fortunate. An artist who sketched the scene shows cloud rolling in from the Gulf of Finland, but the weather was good. Oddly enough, the elements always treated Catherine the Great's days of public spectacle with proper respect.

At last the long French windows of the Senate House opened; the troops sprang to the salute; and Catherine II, Empress of All the Russias, came out on the balcony. Eyeing her with wonder from a room above was her eldest grandson, Grand Duke Alexander Pavlovich, four months short of his fifth birthday. It was unusual for members of the Imperial family to be in St Petersburg during July and August, but the Empress had insisted on bringing Alexander and his younger brother, Constantine, with her when she left the summer residence at Tsarskoe Selo on Monday morning. This was an occasion for associating the future with the past, as well as with the present. Attention that day was to be focused for once not on the Empress herself but on the most renowned of her forerunners. In the centre of the square Falconet's massive equestrian statue of Peter the Great was ready to be unveiled, after fifteen years of dispute and weary labour. To the sound of ceremonial cannon the last wooden palisades were knocked away and, as the smoke and dust cleared, the Bronze Horseman stood revealed to St Petersburg in all his majesty, the animal prancing wildly on a granite pedestal while its master, with arm outstretched towards the river and the Gulf, commands the waters on which he had dared to build his city to keep their distance. An eloquently simple inscription was carved in the rock base of Finnish stone – *Petro Primo Catharina Secunda*. Thus one great autocrat hailed another in comradely greeting, projecting herself to twenty million subjects as his true and undoubted successor.[1]

Yet Catherine was not a Russian Empress by inheritance but a Germanic usurper, converted from Lutheran Protestantism to Orthodoxy as a convenience of marriage and thrust on the throne in a palace revolution. She was born in April 1729 at Stettin on the Baltic coast, the eldest daughter of Prince Christian of Anhalt-Zerbst. At sixteen she was married to her first cousin, Peter the Great's grandson and namesake, who succeeded his aunt (Elizabeth) as Peter III in the first days of 1762. Both as husband and sovereign Peter was ineffectual. According to Catherine's memoirs, the marriage was never consummated. A son, Paul, was indeed born in September 1754 but his paternity has always been in doubt and Catherine herself indicated that the father was Prince Serge Saltykov, a not unattractive member of an old Russian family. Peter III reigned for only twenty-seven weeks, alienating the nobility and Church dignitaries by his

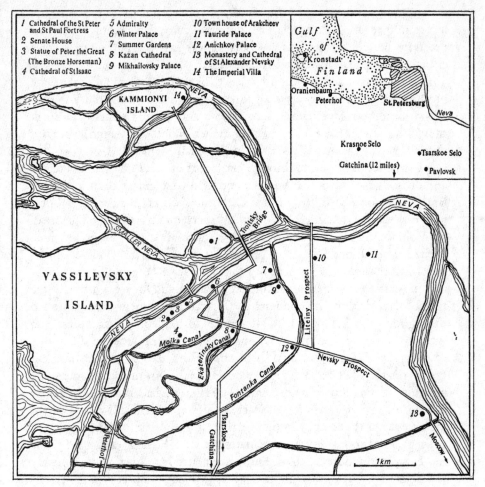

1 Cathedral of the St Peter and St Paul Fortress
2 Senate House
3 Statue of Peter the Great (The Bronze Horseman)
4 Cathedral of St Isaac
5 Admiralty
6 Winter Palace
7 Summer Gardens
8 Kazan Cathedral
9 Mikhailovsky Palace
10 Town house of Arakcheev
11 Tauride Palace
12 Anichkov Palace
13 Monastery and Cathedral of St Alexander Nevsky
14 The Imperial Villa

St Peterburg in the Early Nineteenth Century

contempt for the customs and interests of the Empire he had inherited. By contrast, Catherine's attachment to Russian traditions won her a following in the capital. During the last week of June 1762 the Guards Regiments shifted their allegiance from Peter III to his consort, forced the Tsar to abdicate and proclaimed Catherine his successor. Peter was banished to Ropsha, some twenty-five miles from St Petersburg. A few days later there was a drunken brawl around the dinner table at Ropsha and, in the confusion, the ex-Tsar was strangled. His custodians went unpunished and his widow announced he had died from a sudden attack of colic. Within three months she was solemnly crowned by the Metropolitan Archbishop of Novgorod in the Uspensky Cathedral, Moscow. 'The Lord has placed

3

the crown upon thine head,' the Metropolitan declared, with the comforting assurance of inner revelation. Foreign envoys, watching Catherine prostrate herself before Russia's holy relics, knowingly discounted her chances of survival in such a barbaric land.[2]

Twenty years later, in August 1782, their successors saw her salute the most illustrious of past Tsars as an equal. She had shown an ability to play off one ambitious favourite against another and to bend rather than break those who would have schemed against her. The most frightful peasant revolt for many centuries, the rising of Emelian Pugachev in 1773–4, had sent a shudder of revulsion through her Court but had failed to shake her authority. Russia's frontiers were extended to west and to south, and more lands were soon to follow. Now Catherine was credited with political genius by all the statesmen of Europe and acclaimed 'Catherine the Great' by Voltaire. Yet it was not merely the statecraft of the Empress which excited admiration. She drew up a scheme of reform so radical in its liberalism that the government of Louis xv sought to prohibit its circulation in France for fear that it would create a demand for recognition of the rule of law within the monarchy. Capital punishment was restricted throughout the Empire, formal torture forbidden. The Empress had written of the virtues of toleration, of the responsibilities of the nobles towards the peasants who were their serfs, of the need to rest government policy on the 'dictates of Nature and Reason'. No one could deny the imaginative magnitude of her enterprise. Peter I had turned Muscovite Tsardom away from Asia so as to face the West; Catherine II watched over the growth of that empire, while, at the same time, safeguarding Peter's conception of monarchy by vaccinating it with French ideas against the more dangerous political ills of Europe. Much in her policy was ultimately self-defeating, but in that summer of 1782 success still crowned her endeavours. The young Grand Duke Alexander thus stood by his grandmother's side at the very zenith of her reign. No other sovereign outside Asia enjoyed such absolute power; and already Catherine was preparing Alexander for the heritage she would bequeath. By contrast Paul, her own son, had always counted for little in her eyes. He had an estate at Pavlovsk, only a short distance from her palace at Tsarskoe Selo, but it could well have been several hundred miles away for all the contact between them.

Grand Duke Paul was not present when the Bronze Horseman was unveiled. With his mother's encouragement, he had set out in the previous autumn on a tour of the European Courts. He had visited Vienna, Florence, Naples and Paris, and by the beginning of August 1782 he was journeying at a leisurely pace through Picardy and into the French-speaking provinces of the Austrian Netherlands. With Paul travelled his second wife, a Württemberg Princess whom he had met in Berlin and married in the autumn of 1776. She took the names Marie Feodorovna on being received into the Orthodox Church. The Grand Duchess was tall and well-built, distinguished in appearance rather than pretty and noted, during those early years in Russia, for her patience and modest bearing. 'Sweetness of disposition is her chief characteristic' wrote Frederic Masson, one of the many French tutors employed at St Petersburg by aristocratic families in these years.[3] There is no doubt that Grand Duchess Marie loved her husband dearly; she always described him in affectionate terms in her letters. It cannot have been easy for her to comfort and honour a man of such temperament, soured by years of neglect, distrusting every move which his mother made, and convinced he was haunted by Peter the Great, the apparition accompanying him through the streets of the capital and murmuring sadly, 'Paul, poor Paul.'

Nor were Marie's relations with her formidable mother-in-law always happy. Marie was only eighteen when, on 24 December 1777, she gave birth to her first child and named him after St Alexander Nevsky, the warrior prince of the thirteenth century. Catherine, delighted at the event but inclined to criticize the choice of name for its hint of grandeur, declared that Marie was too young to look after the boy.[4] From earliest days she determined the details of Alexander's life. He was not to be coddled: his mattress should be filled with hay; his room should always have a window open, even in the Russian winter; he was to sleep in the wing of the Winter Palace beside the Admiralty so that he should grow accustomed to cannon fire from the ceremonial salutes. No one can be sure of the psychological effects of these experiences in infancy. It is not surprising that he began to suffer from deafness of the left ear.

The Empress was no less possessive towards Marie's second son, born in May 1779. She insisted not only on how he was to be reared but on the name he should carry. He was baptized Constantine; for Catherine, whose armies were sweeping the Turks into the Black Sea, had convinced herself that this second grandson would one day reign on the Bosphorus as Emperor of a new Byzantium. No thought was given to the mother's wishes. Any ordinary girl would have been swiftly crushed by the mere shadow of Catherine's presence in her children's nursery; but Marie Feodorovna was far from ordinary. Her character gained in strength from the battles she lost at Court; so, in other times, had Catherine's.

As yet, however, it was solely the will of the Empress that counted. Hers was a strange personality, as full of paradox as the Russian Empire itself.

There was Catherine the proud, surfeited with flattery and seeking more, a person 'to be approached with all the reverence due to a divinity', as an English diplomat commented soon after arriving in Russia.[5] But there was also Catherine the modestly diffident, gently suggesting to Frederick II of Prussia that her vaunted intellectual powers were exaggerated, that she was no more than 'a crow in peacock feathers'.[6] Then there was Catherine the passionate lover, soul aflame for the sensuous and dramatic, half afraid of her paramours but playing out such a fantasy of conjugality with the greatest of them, Prince Potemkin, that many believed they were secretly married. And again there was Catherine the lost literary idol, fingers made restless – so she said – by the sight of a newly cut quill, the woman who dashed off nine plays in four years and then launched a periodical to satirize society in her own capital. Nor were these Catherine's only roles. Others emerge from the memoirs of the time: a business woman bound to a routine of daily administration; a devout high priestess, on pilgrimage to the Troitska monastery or the relics of St Dmitri in Rostov; a rationalist exchanging ideas with Voltaire and Diderot; an imperialist partitioning Poland and looking out greedily from the hills above Sebastopol towards the Turkish shores of the Black Sea. Sadly, in the end, there was another Catherine: the disillusioned tyrant who sent Alexander Radischev in chains to Siberia for publishing an honestly bitter indictment of serfdom which once she would have praised for its compassion. Each of these several Catherines was respected or feared by her contemporaries; and each, indeed, has become part of her legend. One side of her character was less readily revealed because it ran counter to so much that was known of her; and yet, in the last nineteen years of her reign, she emerged as an adoring grandmother. She bestowed on all eight of her grandchildren the affection she had denied their father in his childhood. But none possessed her heart as much as Alexander.[7]

Alexander's Childhood

Catherine confided her hopes for her two eldest Grand Dukes in an unlikely adviser, Melchior Grimm, a German-born critic of the French literary scene. Grimm, who was long a friend of Jean-Jacques Rousseau, had visited St Petersburg in 1773 and the Empress found his conversation so stimulating that, for the rest of her life, she continued to send him letters, mingling political comment with social gossip and flippant humour. In return, he acted as her agent for obtaining books in Paris and other centres of western culture. Inevitably Catherine's correspondence contained anecdotes of her grandchildren, especially Alexander; and Grimm was shrewd enough to ask the type of questions to which a doting grandmother was pleased to reply.

If Catherine's account may be believed, Grand Duke Alexander was remarkably precocious. At the age of two years and three months he was sending her notes from his bedroom, and she wrote proudly to Grimm, 'Now, at this very moment, he knows more than a child of four or five.'[8] And when he was indeed four years old she reported that he could find on his globe any town which she mentioned to him. On the eve of his fifth birthday she recorded a touching scene when he said that he wished to meet someone of whom he had heard, one 'Alexander the Great', and he was most unhappy when informed that an introduction could not be arranged.[9] Grimm was told of Alexander's good looks, of his interest in tilling the soil, and of the cleanliness and simple good sense of his nurse (who was an Englishwoman, Pauline Hessler, married to a footman in the household of the Empress). With the slightly coy playfulness which she affected in her domestic correspondence, Catherine wrote, 'I feel certain that should Monsieur Alexander have a son of his own brought up by this same Englishwoman, the throne would rest secure for over a century to come.'[10] At times Catherine's matriarchal enthusiasm carried her into trivialities which Baron Grimm must surely have found a trifle perplexing. Thus, in the early summer of 1781, Catherine sent him a letter from Tsarskoe Selo commenting on two German poems she had particularly enjoyed and giving him instructions for purchasing books for her in Paris; but between these items she included details of a special one-piece costume which she had herself designed for her grandson so that it could easily be put on and taken off. Alexander, she explained, had worn this type of dress ever since he was six months old: 'The King of Sweden and the Prince of Prussia have asked for and obtained the pattern', she added; and she was so pleased with 'my stroke of genius' that she sketched the child's dress in order that Grimm might admire it from afar.[11] There is no doubt that Alexander's grandmother was, on every count, a remarkable woman.

She had theories of her own on education, some of which she certainly owed to *Emile* although, typically, she tempered Rousseau's zeal with natural common sense. Her grandsons, she insisted, were to be observed at play as well as during times of formal tuition and their teaching was to follow, so far as possible, the interests revealed by their active imagination. They should learn to maintain their self-respect in the presence of their elders without an excess of abject docility. On the other hand, towards those of less fortunate birth, the boys must be taught to show compassion and sympathy rather than the arrogance of pride.[12] Her precepts were admirable; and so long as Catherine herself could spare time to attend to her grandchildren, they benefited from her tolerant counsels. But when Grand Duke Paul returned to Russia from his visit to the Western capitals, the Empress gave him the estate of Gatchina, a grim square-towered fortress twenty-eight miles from St Petersburg; and the mood of Paul's circle of intimates at Gatchina was totally at variance with the enlightened education which Catherine had decreed for his sons. The disturbing contrast between life at the Winter Palace or at Tsarskoe Selo and life at Gatchina broke the even tone of Alexander's mental training far more than his grandmother suspected. He learnt, as an early lesson, the art of dissimulation: it had not figured on Catherine's programme of instruction.

There was another grave weakness in her method. Who in Russia was sufficiently skilled to tutor Alexander in the way the Empress wished? The boy must be taught, she wrote to Grimm, by someone of 'the highest integrity, with liberal views and with known excellence in history, geography, mathematics and philosophy'.[13] She was forced to admit that there was no such educational paragon within the borders of her own Empire. Grimm came to her rescue. There was, he said, in Switzerland a brilliant scholar of unquestioned ability as a teacher: he was convinced that it would be right for the Empress to entrust Alexander's education to the discretion of Frederick Caesar La Harpe. In the spring of 1783, when he was twenty-nine years old, La Harpe came to Russia, originally as a tutor to the brother of one of Catherine's favourites. Although aware that La Harpe was living in St Petersburg, the Empress at first kept him 'in reserve', as she wrote to Grimm.[14] Either she was reluctant to introduce a man of advanced views into the entourage of the Grand Duke or – more probably – she sensed that Alexander, despite the praise she had lavished on him, was not yet sufficiently mature for regular tuition. Ever since their parents had first gone abroad, Alexander and Constantine had been placed under the supervision of one of her ladies-in-waiting, Countess Sophia Benckendorff, who was in effect their governess. Catherine was reluctant to end an arrangement which still permitted her to see much of the boys' progress. The Empress, as she grew older, became increasingly irresolute and this characteristic extended from matters of state to her own family circle.

But on 19 September 1783 Sophia Benckendorff collapsed and died while in attendance on the Empress at Tsarskoe Selo; and Catherine, however much she might wish to temporize, could do so no longer. She would not accept Grimm's advice outright and send for La Harpe. The Grand Dukes, she decided, should have not a mere tutor, but a Governor; and for this post she chose General Nicholas Ivanovitch Saltykov, younger brother of the man who she maintained was Paul's real father. She sent the General an able directive on the principles of education, and selected a team of tutors who were to work together under Saltykov's direction.[15]

La Harpe was one of the tutors, but it was not until the autumn of 1784 that Catherine referred to him in a letter as 'being at Alexander's side'. He was to share responsibilities with Frederic Masson (the French writer of memoirs of the Court) and with three Russians, Muraviev, Protassov and Samborsky. Apart from Muraviev, to whom everyone willingly left instruction in Russian grammar, there was no clear distinction of teaching functions. Protassov, an officer in one of the fashionable regiments, kept a diary of his years in attendance on the Grand Duke: he complained that Alexander was inadequately trained in specifically Russian traditions and was made to look towards Europe too much. Samborsky, by contrast, was an unconventional priest, sent by the Empress to England as a young man in order to study English farming methods. He married an English girl and acted as chaplain to the Russian diplomatic envoys in London before returning to St Petersburg. To the horror of the Church hierarchy, the Empress permitted him to wear ordinary clothes and remain beardless. He taught Alexander the basic Church catechism and the English language, in which he rapidly became proficient. Like the eldest sons of George III, the two Grand Dukes were expected to cultivate a strip of land and it was Samborsky who showed them how to use a harrow and a plough in the fields around Tsarskoe Selo. Inevitably Samborsky and La Harpe formed a progressive faction among the Grand Dukes' tutors and were opposed by Masson (who was particularly envious of La Harpe's European reputation) and by Protassov. Alexander tended to attach himself to the progressives. On the other hand, Constantine, who did not take easily to any form of tuition, was invariably rude to La Harpe, was never able to master the English language – he had been assigned a Greek and not an English nurse in infancy – and was criticized by Protassov for his temper rather than his methods of study.[16]

All the tutors seem to have despised poor General Saltykov; and this was unjust. The General had an unenviable task, which he discharged well. Clearly he was a man of limited sympathies and no scholar; but neither was he a militaristic bigot. His family had moved forward with the fashion and he personally always kept up with them. When Society looked for enlightenment to France, the Saltykovs duly imported a French tutor into their home circle: his name was Marat, and a few years later his brother achieved some notoriety in revolutionary Paris; but no whisper of libertarian sentiment overtaxed Saltykov minds. The General had at least absorbed the idea that Frenchmen are natural pedagogues; and, though he did not understand all that the Empress had to say about education, his wife explained what she thought he needed to know, leaving him to see that the Grand Dukes remained smartly turned out and in good health. He possessed an instinctive tact for retaining favour: glowing reports went regularly from him both to the Winter Palace and to Paul at Gatchina; and he succeeded in making himself acceptable to the Empress and equally to Paul and Marie Feodorovna. Whatever others might think of his abilities, Alexander himself always continued to treat the General with respect. It is significant that during the crisis years from 1812 to 1815 it was to Saltykov that Alexander looked when he needed a Chairman for his Committee of Ministers; for he knew, from what he had seen as a child, that Saltykov of all men would stand above quarrels and disputes, discreetly magisterial and impressively remote.[17]

Yet, in later years, people barely remembered Saltykov as one of the formative influences on Alexander's mind. It was La Harpe whom they commended, or condemned, for the Tsar's generous principles; and, in his moments of enlightened liberalism, Alexander himself was ever ready to acknowledge the debt. From La Harpe he learnt of ancient Greece and Rome, the culture of the Renaissance, the contractual theories of Locke (and how the Americans were interpreting them) and what it was that his grandmother had found fit to admire in Voltaire. When, in June 1792, an envoy from Paris was surprised to find Alexander discussing the Rights of Man and the French constitution, the voice may have been the Grand Duke's but the thoughts were La Harpe's.[18] Yet such a breadth of understanding did not come easily to Alexander. He was remarkably slow in picking up the French language. It was not until April 1785, when he had experienced a year's teaching from both Masson and La Harpe, that Alexander risked a note in French to his 'chère Grand Maman' and it was hardly a message of elaborate construction: 'Comme Maman vous écrit,' he wrote, 'je veux vous écrire aussi et dire que je vous aime de tous mon coeur.'[19] Eighteen months later he managed some seventy words in French to the Empress, letting her know how much he had enjoyed a performance of Beaumarchais's *Barbier de Seville* – in Russian. Catherine, at any rate, was impressed and, at the end of 1787, she told Grimm that La Harpe had the highest hopes of her grandson's intelligence. Characteristically the Empress added the comment that since La Harpe was a Swiss republican, there was no reason why he should make flattering remarks about Alexander's progress; and she therefore assumed his judgement was sound.[20]

Like any other pupil, Alexander's mental development was determined as much by what he saw and heard outside the classroom as within. His grandmother's Court was still as brilliant as any in Europe and the Empress had ensured that Alexander made an early appearance as a princely figure. By the age of thirteen he was accepted as a young dandy, for Catherine insisted on her elder grandson having brocade coats from France, buckled shoes from England, Italian coloured waistcoats, lace ruffles from the Netherlands. Alexander was handsome and the Empress's enthusiastic comments on his appearance at state occasions in her letters show how justified she thought her indulgence to have been. But neither Protassov nor La Harpe felt such extravagance good for the Grand Duke's character; and they may well have been right in their private strictures.

Life at Gatchina with his father and mother was markedly different. Grand Duke Paul ran his estate as a miniature kingdom of its own, owing more in style to Prussia than to France. He was not an eccentric hedonist. Although every minute of their lives was regulated by his orders, the peasants around Gatchina were well cared for, with churches, hospitals and schools of their own. But Paul delighted in military masquerade. He built up a private army, dressed in Prussian uniforms and drilled by the codes introduced in Peter III's brief reign. The whole region around Gatchina rang with the harsh commands of army discipline. Reveille was at four in the morning, there were ceremonial drill parades or field exercises throughout the day, formal entertainments in the evening, a curfew by ten at night. Routine was varied by a church parade on holy days and by an occasional mock naval battle on the lake whenever the Grand Duke remembered that he was an honorary Admiral of the Russian fleet. Guests from St Petersburg seem, for the most part, to have found Gatchina boring though to some it appeared ominously sinister. Alexander and his brother enjoyed their visits. They had far less freedom than at their grandmother's Court, they had to wear the tight-fitting green uniform of the Gatchina regiment, but they were treated with exaggerated respect by the officers of their father's household.[21] There was no rift between Alexander and his father in these days; and the young Grand Duke gave the impression of being as much at home in the soldierly encampment of Gatchina as in the ballroom elegance of the capital.

Sometimes the suspicions of Paul towards the Empress led to open conflict between Gatchina and the Winter Palace. At the end of 1786

Catherine accepted an invitation from Potemkin to visit southern Russia and the Crimea so as to see for herself the lands in which he had fought his Turkish campaigns. Since these rich territories were now part of the Russian Empire he hoped to inherit, Paul asked to accompany his mother. Catherine refused; but she proposed to take with her Alexander and Constantine. Paul was very angry, and Marie Feodorovna joined him in protesting; for a region so recently freed from the Tatars and the Turks did not seem to them a fit place in which boys of nine and seven should pass the winter months. Eventually Providence intervened: on the eve of Catherine's departure, Constantine went down with measles and it was anticipated (wrongly) that Alexander would catch it from him. Their physicians insisted they remain in St Petersburg. Foreign visitors found the Empress sulking over the way in which her will had been thwarted.[22] When, that autumn, war was renewed against the Turks Paul begged to be allowed to lead his troops into action; but Catherine would have none of it. While Potemkin and Suvorov were winning fresh laurels from their campaigns in the south, Paul and his regiment remained at Gatchina, with manoeuvres every Wednesday and some interesting experiments with artillery to pass the time. Although it is true that the Gatchina troops were helping to protect the capital against a threatened invasion from Sweden, this was not sufficiently heroic for Paul. He bitterly resented his mother's veto, swore vengeance on her favourites and barely hid his envy of the military commanders on the Turkish Front.[23]

But in these years of triumph against the Turks there was little that Paul could do, except send congratulations to his mother. The end of the 1780s saw the influence of Gregory Potemkin, Viceroy of New Russia and Prince of Taurida, at its zenith. He was Catherine's most faithful lover – for fifteen years tactfully seeing that she had a substitute 'admirer' whenever he was absent from the Court – but he was also Russia's most effective colonial entrepreneur, adding thousands of miles to the Russian Empire; and it was on this count that Catherine wished Alexander to honour him. Alexander dutifully did what was expected of him, and the Empress could hardly restrain her pleasure at the compliments which Potemkin paid the Grand Duke: he had, so Potemkin told his grandmother and she informed Grimm, 'the appearance of Apollo combined with great modesty and much character' and he added that 'if you could choose from a thousand candidates for his position, it would be difficult to pick an equal and impossible to find someone better.'[24] On 28 April 1791, Potemkin gave the last and greatest festival to Catherine at the Tauride Palace. Three thousand guests attended the celebrations which included, not merely dancing and a massive banquet, but a performance of two plays and two ballets and a choral cantata in honour of the Empress. More than two hundred crystal candelabra lit the three great halls of the palace; and to her delight the Empress noted Alexander leading the first quadrille. But extravagance on this scale encouraged extraordinary notions of luxurious living in the mind of a lad of thirteen. Protassov commented tartly in his diary on Alexander's constant quest for pleasure and he was especially irritated to find the Grand Duke amusing himself with mimicry, one of the social accomplishments which the Empress had always found most endearing in Potemkin.[25] Perhaps it was as well for Alexander's adolescence that the celebrations proved to be Potemkin's final gala. Soon afterwards he set out for the southern provinces and caught malaria. To Catherine's grief he died on 5 October.

Betrothal and Marriage

Catherine was frightened as well as saddened by Potemkin's sudden death. She was sixty-two, ten years older than her favourite, and although gossip still credited her with sexual adventures, there was no doubt that she was, in many ways, prematurely aged. At times her legs were so swollen that she was confined to a wheel chair; and her letters no longer reflected the intellectual curiosity of earlier years. Naturally she recoiled from news of revolution in Paris: it seemed as if her whole creed of enlightenment was betrayed. But she rejected other forms of speculation as well as dangerous thoughts from France. She could not, for example, read Gibbon and it does not seem as if she appreciated the power of Burke's reasoning. Sadly her legend condemned her to a lustre she could no longer burnish.

Conscious of her failing powers, Catherine increasingly turned her thoughts towards her family and the dynasty. Already she had convinced herself that Alexander, with his good looks and charming manners, was warming the hearts of all the young ladies in St Petersburg society; and she may well have been right, even though he only celebrated his fourteenth birthday at the end of the year. But, in that bleak winter which followed Potemkin's death, she resolved to push Alexander precipitately into manhood. A bride must be found for her favourite grandson. She would establish him with a Court of his own, near to her at Tsarskoe Selo: it would be gratifying to live long enough for great-grandchildren to visit her at the palace.

There was, moreover, another problem nagging at her mind. What she knew of Paul and his armed camp at Gatchina disquieted her. 'I can see into what hands the Empire will fall after my death', she once grimly remarked, after a meeting with her son, 'We shall be converted into a province dependent on the will of Prussia.'[26] It was as if her husband's ghost had come to mock her. But was it necessary for Paul to succeed her? Ever since Peter the Great's day, it had been accepted that the sovereign possessed the right to determine to whom the crown should pass: a formal decree of February 1722 had abolished primogeniture as a principle of succession. Were Alexander to marry and consolidate his hold on the affections of the people, there was every reason for Catherine to publish an edict which would debar Paul from the throne and proclaim her eldest grandson as heir to the Empire. The thought had already occurred to many at Court, and indeed to Paul himself. Rumour said a proclamation would be made on the day Alexander was married: but the Empress was slow to give any sign of her intentions.

In August 1792 Catherine, commenting in a letter to Grimm on the way in which so many European thrones were threatened by the revolutionary virus, allowed herself to paint a brief and idyllic picture of Alexander married, crowned and assured of his future whatever might happen in other lands. A few weeks later she sent the Countess Shuvalova, one of her ladies-in-waiting, to southern Germany with instructions to escort two daughters of the Crown Prince of Baden to St Petersburg: Louise celebrated her fourteenth birthday that autumn and her sister, Frederika, was only eleven. They arrived in St Petersburg on the evening of 31 October. Catherine was delighted with Louise, and told Grimm that she hoped Alexander would not let the opportunity slip, although she acknowledged that 'people are unaccustomed to marriage so young here'. Alexander, she added, 'does not think of it. He is an innocent at heart and it is a devilish trick I am playing on him, for I am leading him into temptation.' She seems to have relished the prospect.[27]

Alexander, quite clearly, did not. Poor Louise, overawed by the Empress and all the splendours of St Petersburg, later admitted in her journal that the first meeting with her proposed husband had not gone well: 'He gave me an unfriendly look', she wrote.[28] Everyone else welcomed the two girls, especially Louise. She reminded many people at Court of her aunt, who had been married to Paul in 1773 only to die in childbirth three years later. But this tragic echo from the past was not seen as any impediment to the new marriage, not even by Paul (who had much loved his first wife). The only doubt was whether Alexander at fourteen was ready for married life. Protassov confessed sadly in his diary that he was not, but he consoled himself with the thought that in temperament

Louise would prove an ideal partner for his pupil. He admired her beauty and her voice, commenting favourably on her grace of movement and 'quite remarkable modesty'.[29]

Catherine was too ruthless a matchmaker to share Protassov's uneasiness. She could see, readily enough, that Louise was soon completely infatuated with Alexander, and she brushed aside her grandson's manifest lack of ardour as natural reticence. There was no cause for worry. Five weeks after Louise and her sister arrived in Russia, Catherine sent the inevitable progress report to Melchior Grimm:

Monsieur Alexander will behave very sensibly and with prudence: that is to say, at this moment he is just beginning to show some tender affection towards the elder princess from Baden, and I do not doubt that it will be fully reciprocated. Never was there a pair more suited to each other – as lovely as the day, full of grace and spirit. Everyone takes a delight in smiling on their budding love.

If some of the ladies of St Petersburg confided in their journals and letters that, on closer acquaintance, they found Princess Louise a little shy and retiring, who can wonder why?[30]

To be transported from sober and respectable Karlsruhe to the palaces of Petersburg was in itself a bewildering experience for a girl of fourteen. Nearly half a century ago Catherine herself had made a similar transition, and she sympathized with Louise in her moments of home-sickness. This seemed the regular fate of German Princesses: it was not many years since Alexander's mother had been fetched over from Stuttgart. To Catherine there was, of course, no comparison between her own wretchedly contrived betrothal and the opportunities awaiting Louise; nor did she see the difficulties posed for the Princess by the rival Court at Gatchina. The Empress invariably minimized the importance of Paul's wishes, and her exchanges with Marie Feodorovna had always ended with such a courteously phrased letter from her daughter-in-law that Catherine assumed she, too, might be ignored. Neither Paul nor Marie Feodorovna was consulted over Catherine's marriage project for their son though both travelled up to St Petersburg from Gatchina two days after the arrival of the Badenese Princesses. Marie Feodorovna was, indeed, as enthusiastic about Louise as the Empress herself: 'The eldest seemed charming to me', she wrote, 'I found her not merely pretty but possessing such an attractive figure that even the most indifferent person would love her'[31]; and she added that she was particularly pleased by her affability and candour. Paul, too, welcomed Louise and was at first amused by the high spirits of the two girls. But what was acceptable in the capital seemed out of place at Gatchina; and, although Louise endeavoured to please Alexander's parents, it was difficult for a child of her years not to find the atmosphere of a military camp oppressive, and even harder for her not to show her real feelings. The fact that Alexander himself appeared untroubled by the contrast puzzled her; but she was too much in love with him – and too accustomed to an affectionate family circle – for this to worry her deeply.

By the following spring all was settled. At Easter Protassov noted in his journal a conversation with Alexander in which the Grand Duke said that he had a 'special feeling' for the Princess, that he felt conscious of it as soon as she came into a room or happened to be standing near him. On Easter Day itself, seven months after their first meeting, the two young people at last dared to embrace each other – twice. Louise dashed off a letter home which was dewy with rapturous innocence: 'These are the first two times I have kissed him', she told her mother, 'You cannot imagine how funny I found it embracing a man who was neither my father nor my uncle. And what seems odder still is that it feels different from when Papa kisses me: he was always scratching me with his beard.'[32] More solemn occasions soon occupied her attention. In the second week of May 1793 Louise was received into the Orthodox Church and took the names Elizabeth Alexievna; and on the next day she was formally betrothed to Alexander, and created Grand Duchess. Once more the Empress rushed into rhapsody over the event: 'Everyone said they were two angels pledging themselves to each other. You could not see anything lovelier than this fiancé of 15 and that fiancée of 14.' And she added, with a typical lapse into litotes, 'Besides that, they do not love each other at all badly either.' ('Outre cela ils ne s'aiment pas mal.')[33]

There followed several days of festivity. Grand Duchess Elizabeth was happy, confiding amused comments to her young sister. Alexander found that he did not spend so much time at his studies, a development which saddened him little; and no one had seen the Empress so pleased with herself since Potemkin's death. The high point of these celebrations was a production of Sheridan's The School for Scandal which one of Alexander's tutors, presumably Samborsky, had translated the previous summer. Catherine enjoyed the performance at her private theatre in the Hermitage, but she was startled to find her grandson popularly given credit for the adaptation and she demanded an explanation. Alexander, 'blushing deeply', was forced to admit that though the translation was undoubtedly his tutor's, certain sallies written into it had been modified at his own suggestion. The Empress poured out the whole story to Melchior Grimm;

but she does not appear to have been certain whether to chide the tutor for encouraging Alexander in such frivolities or to be amused by the reputation which the Grand Duke had acquired in St Petersburg as a student of English.[34]

Unfortunately there were other forms of self-pretence in his life that summer. Protassov found him appallingly ignorant of what was happening elsewhere in the Empire; and La Harpe complained he had been entrusted with a system of education which required several more years of concentrated work. Saddest of all, poor Elizabeth began to see flaws in Alexander's character: a caustic edge to his agreeability; an impatient, almost bored, dismissal of the high romantic note she sought for their relationship; a negative insensibility to the foolish things which delight an adolescent girl. She did not, for one moment, doubt she had found the love of her life, as she assured her mother by almost every postbag; but she confessed to being worried by 'a nothingness in his attitude' and, as the summer months went by, she became lonely and miserable.[35] In the first days of August her sister was packed off to Baden, apparently because she had caught the eye of the last favourite of the Empress, Platon Zubov, a twenty-six-year-old exquisite improbably commissioned in the Preobrazhensky Guards; but Elizabeth's sorrow at the injustice to her sister soon gave way to indignation at tales of her own conduct. It was said that, while staying in Pavlovsk, she had pressed her charms prematurely on Alexander, climbing into his room through the window. Gossip travelled even as far as Baden and the much maligned Elizabeth was forced to write a hot denial to her mother. Jealous tongues, as the young Grand Duchess soon perceived, made mischief with ugly ease. But what did they find to envy? The simplicity of her grace and charm at a Court which was raising splendour to vulgarity? Or was it, perhaps, her unresponsive suitor with his slender figure and fresh-blown complexion? Most likely it was more selfish interests, the thought that he and she might reign after Catherine's death and a whole generation be thus robbed of its span of sovereignty. There is little doubt that those who gambled on Paul's speedy accession, clustering around him at Pavlovsk and Gatchina, had no particular desire to see Alexander's marriage prosper too happily too soon.[36]

The Empress knew something of these intrigues but paid them little attention. When at midsummer it was rumoured Alexander would be sent on a grand tour of Europe and the marriage delayed, Catherine testily denied the story: 'The wedding will be here and it will take place before Christmas', she wrote on 5 August. It was, she insisted, 'a love match' and she continued to praise Elizabeth's beauty – the clarity of her blue eyes, the classic line of her profile, the quiet melody of her voice. The Empress had, in fact, decided that Elizabeth's appearance closely resembled her own in those distant days when she had herself arrived from Germany. Portraits of half a century ago were hunted out to prove the point. The likeness was not immediately apparent and some at Court were embarrassed. A dreadful doubt began to steal into their minds: the Empress had such a waspish sense of humour.[37]

As summer passed into autumn, Catherine speeded the arrangements for the wedding. She had declared her intention of having 'a simple yet lofty' palace built for her grandson and his bride in the park at Tsarskoe Selo; it would be close to her own favourite residence and no more than fifteen miles from St Petersburg itself. But the building could not be finished for more than a year. There was no need to wait for it: Alexander and Elizabeth could set up a miniature Court of their own in St Petersburg that winter. And there was no need either to wait for the Grand Duke to complete his studies: he would have a household of fifteen dignitaries, but he would still receive tuition and Protassov would keep a record of his academic progress. By the end of September everything was ready, but for Elizabeth there was another disappointment. A sudden illness prevented her father from setting out from Germany and her mother chose to remain with him, perhaps from wifely concern but just possibly because she had once been a contender for the hand of Grand Duke Paul, and Russia did not have for her the pleasantest of associations.

The marriage was celebrated on 9 October 1793, in the Court Church. The bridegroom was eleven weeks short of his sixteenth birthday and the bride ten months younger. Three ladies-in-waiting and their maids were expected to inform both Catherine and Marie Feodorovna of the relations between the newly married couple. Not that Catherine had any doubts: 'The dearest children were *so* happy', she wrote effusively to Elizabeth's mother in Baden. And to one of her oldest friends, the Prince de Ligne, she was just as enthusiastic: 'It is a marriage of Cupid and Psyche', she declared contentedly.[38] While Juno was thus preening herself at the Hermitage, her grandson and his bride were moving in as neighbours along the Quay. With fifteen hundred rooms from which to choose in the Winter Palace, it was not difficult to find a suite for them. They spent the first winter of married life in rococo splendour, far removed from the real Russia which neither of them as yet knew. From their windows they could look out across the frozen Neva to the tall slender spire of St Peter and St Paul, a church within a fortress, soul and symbol of the city.

Alexander and Elizabeth were, indeed, far too young to assume the responsibilities of married life. They were intelligent children well-tutored but badly schooled, for neither had experienced any consistent formal education. Their temperaments were remarkably similar, as General Protassov had noted soon after Elizabeth's arrival in Russia. Both possessed an endearing charm of manner and a spirit of obstinate independence which tended to be weakened by excessive trust in the loyalty and judgement of a favourite companion. In his tutor's eyes, Alexander was a naturally kind young man with many virtues though inclined to indolence and prevarication.[39] Protassov permitted himself to hope in his journal that Elizabeth might impart some of her own energy and live-liness to her husband; but this, of course, was asking too much from a girl of fifteen already intimidated by the unconventional conventions of an alien Court. It was easier for her to share Alexander's delight in trivialities, and far more natural. To dance the polonaise and the mazurka and to discover the excitement of the new waltzing made every ball during Elizabeth's first winter as a Grand Duchess the occasion for a letter home to Karls-ruhe. There were evenings when she would sing, Alexander play the violin, his elder sisters join in duets, and the great Empress nod approvingly; while on other nights a play, an opera or a ballet would be presented in the little theatre at the Hermitage, with two generations watching Catherine uncertainly before venturing to applaud. Not all the moments of amuse-ment were so public or so inhibiting. Alexander, to the consternation of his tutors, would waste hours playing with his newest toy, a marionette theatre: and there is a refreshing innocence in some of Elizabeth's frolics. In a letter written to her mother when she was three months short of her sixteenth birthday, the newest Grand Duchess describes the fun she found in sitting up late at night with two of her ladies-in-waiting as they scared each other silly with tales of ghosts and haunted rooms. In Catherine's palaces such a pastime required strong nerves indeed.[40]

St Petersburg Society was puzzled by this second Grand-Ducal Court. Alexander's domestic household contained more dignitaries than Paul's had ever done: did this, then, mean that he was now heir-apparent? It was an important question. If Paul's claims to the succession were to be ignored, good sense recommended cultivating the friendship of Alexander and his young wife. On the other hand, neither Paul nor Marie Feodorovna was likely to accept exclusion without a bitter struggle, and Catherine seemed in no hurry to make public her intentions. It would be rash to fall foul of Paul's temper and, as yet, Alexander lacked the outward assurance of a prince at the foot of his throne. There was no general transference of loyalties away from Paul's Court to the new Court; and many of Alexander's own advisers believed any decree of succession which denied hereditary right would weaken the Crown for generations.

Yet rumours persisted in the capital that the Empress was about to proclaim Alexander her successor. It was thought that the most likely time for an announcement of this kind would be as soon as he became a father. Throughout the summer of 1794 the unfortunate Elizabeth was embarrassed by pointed enquiries about her health, and at one moment Marie Feodorovna asked Alexander outright if his wife was pregnant; but there was no immediate prospect of any child being born to the young couple. As if to mock poor Elizabeth's expectations, Marie Feodorovna herself gave birth to a seventh baby in January 1795, a girl baptized Anna; and within eighteen months she had yet another child, the future Tsar Nicholas I. Even the Empress began to show more interest in the growing family at Pavlovsk and Gatchina than in Alexander and his wife.[41]

It is not surprising that, at times, Elizabeth's letters home seem low spirited. To many in St Petersburg she now appeared a person of little significance. In her loneliness she became pathetically attached to the wife of the marshal of the Court, Countess Varvara Golovina, a woman twelve years her senior with whom she established an indiscreet relationship. Within less than twelve months of her marriage, Elizabeth was writing passionate notes to the Countess, apparently with Alexander's complaisance. Child-husband and child-wife remained emotionally immature so long as Catherine lived, although each was genuinely fond of the other.[42]

La Harpe and Protassov both saw the danger for Russia and for Alexander personally of a deep conflict between the two Grand-Ducal Courts. They did what they could to prevent it. Yet, by the end of 1794, Catherine had become so suspicious of La Harpe's 'Jacobin' teachings that she decided to put an end to his services in Russia and encourage him to return to Switzerland. He had, however, one last task of importance to perform. In May 1795, on the eve of his departure La Harpe drove out to Gatchina. He later described how he had 'an interview of two hours' with Paul 'in his study, during which I unburdened my heart', urging a re-conciliation between the father and his sons. Paul was moved by the occasion. Unexpectedly he invited La Harpe to stay at Gatchina for a ball which was to be given in Constantine's honour, even lending the much-abused tutor a pair of white gloves so that he might join in the polonaise without embarrassment (a gift which the Swiss republican preserved for the rest of his days).[43] It is not clear how much La Harpe revealed of Catherine's intentions over the succession, a subject on which she had spoken to him several times in the preceding eighteen months; but Paul took his advice to heart, and made a point of seeing more of Alexander and Constantine in the following year.

Even without La Harpe's intervention, Alexander would almost certainly have sought to improve relations with his parents. Catherine still did not speak directly to him of her plans for the future, but she had already tried to enlist the support of Marie Feodorovna and some councillors of state for a decree of exclusion. Alexander disliked the project. He was terrified of his father and unwilling to become a talisman of contention. Moreover, at heart, filial respect and a sound measure of common sense made him loyal to his father's claims. He diligently attended the manoeuvres at Gatchina throughout the summer of 1795 and on into 1796. Although there was much in Paul's way of life which he found onerous, he preferred the members of the Gatchina officers corps to the sycophants around his grandmother in St Petersburg; and once he was at Gatchina or Pavlovsk, he submitted readily enough to his mother's influence. Only Elizabeth fared badly from the family reconciliation, for she found it difficult to hide her dislike of Paul's mania for parades and was too high spirited not to resent Marie Feodorovna's domineering manner.

There was another question which drew Alexander and Paul closer together. Both were critical of Catherine's Polish policy, which by 1794 had encroached so ruthlessly on traditional liberties that it produced the first modern patriotic revolt against Russia, with Warsaw emerging as the revolutionary capital of eastern Europe. Although Russian troops dealt drastically with the Polish rebels and Catherine seized the opportunity to advance her Empire's frontier to the rivers Niemen and Bug, both Paul and Alexander felt that the final destruction of the old Polish Kingdom was morally wrong and politically injudicious; and they sympathized with the Polish patriot leader, Tadeusz Kosciuszko, who was captured and imprisoned by the Russians in October 1794. Yet Catherine was not unduly troubled by their disapproval. She was convinced that Alexander harboured no treasonable thoughts, and she had long since given up caring what Paul said to the troops of his shadow army within the walls of Gatchina.[44]

The Last Years of Catherine II

Strangely enough, it was Catherine who by accident ensured that Alexander's interest in Poland became more than a mere passing sympathy for a romantic cause. For, eighteen months after her grandson's marriage, she brought to St Petersburg two members of the Polish nobility, the Princes

Adam and Constantine Czartoryski. It was inevitable that two charming and courteous newcomers, with topics of conversation fresh to him, should immediately attract the young Grand Duke's attention. He was, at that very moment, beginning to find friends outside the narrow circle prescribed for him by his family and tutors. Naturally the Czartoryski brothers found themselves brought more and more into Alexander's company. A close friendship rapidly developed between Prince Adam Czartoryski and Catherine's eldest grandson, and the Polish aristocrat became in effect a successor to La Harpe as Alexander's principal mentor and confidant.

This was certainly not the Empress's intention. The Czartoryskis were one of the most enlightened Polish aristocratic families, inclined in the past to co-operate with the Russians.[45] But in 1794 they had supported Kosciuszko, and were now therefore liable to lose their estates. Catherine II, however, gave an undertaking that if the two young Princes of the family, Adam and Constantine, would come to St Petersburg and enter the Russian service as a guarantee of the family's good behaviour, the Czartoryski estates would not be forfeited. Adam Czartoryski, who had been abroad during the revolt and had not actively assisted Kosciuszko himself, arrived in St Petersburg in the spring of 1795. He was seven years older than Alexander. He had travelled widely in western Europe, spending several months in Paris and Vienna and a whole year in London. His understanding of foreign affairs was remarkable in a man of twenty-five. Already he could look back on Mirabeau 'in his most brilliant days' and he was a great admirer of Charles James Fox and the British parliamentary system. It is easy to see what Alexander found attractive. He had never been abroad nor even visited the new Russian territories in the west and the south; and here was a man who knew the salons of Paris and the clubs of London and who had felt for himself the menacing thrill of new ideas in a free society. Alexander envied Czartoryski his wide experience, and sought to harness the Pole's abilities for his own ends.

More than half a century later Czartoryski looked back in his *Memoirs* at these early days of friendship with his future sovereign. It was in the spring of 1796 that Alexander invited Prince Adam to walk with him around the gardens of the Tauride Palace and, in three hours of conversation, explained to him his political hopes and principles. Czartoryski was surprised by the Grand Duke's liberal sentiments, which he may have taken rather more seriously than was warranted. Alexander declared that he did not approve of the policies of the Government and of the Court, especially towards Poland:

He added that he detested despotism everywhere, no matter in what way it was exercised; that he loved liberty, to which all men had a right; that he had taken the strongest interest in the French Revolution and, while condemning its terrible excesses, he wished the French Republic success and rejoiced in its establishment . . . The Grand Duke told me he confided his thoughts to his wife and that she alone knew and approved his sentiments.[46]

Not unnaturally, Adam Czartoryski was deeply moved by Alexander's show of confidence. Privately he rejoiced in the hopes it seemed to hold for Russia, for Europe and, above all, for Poland. Later that year, though still expected to show penitence for his countrymen's political sins, he was appointed chief aide-de-camp to Alexander. It was a good beginning to a remarkable career.

Two other men besides Czartoryski influenced Alexander's development in these last years of Catherine's reign, Count Victor Kochubey and Colonel Alexei Arakcheev. They differed markedly in background and personality. Kochubey was a nephew of Prince Bezborodko, one of Catherine's chief ministers, and had spent much of his youth abroad. Before entering the Russian diplomatic service he had already stayed for several years in Sweden and made what was fast becoming the recognized grand tour of the Russian aristocracy, to London, Vienna and revolutionary Paris. Like Czartoryski and his friends, Kochubey accepted many of the ideas of the Enlightenment, acquiring – so a colleague said – 'a certain European varnish and grand manner which made him a favourite in society'.[47] Arakcheev, by contrast, was a professional soldier who came from a small provincial landowner's family and whose vision never looked beyond the limited horizon of a serf community. As a cadet Arakcheev worked so conscientiously at the school of artillery that he was seconded in 1792 to Paul's Gatchina Corps (a unit which had little appeal to members of the more aristocratic families). At Gatchina he won rapid promotion, partly because of his efficiency but also because his strict sense of discipline appealed to his master. When in 1795 Alexander and Constantine began to attend their father's parades and field exercises, Arakcheev was entrusted with the duty of introducing them to military service – or, rather, to Paul's ideas of what an officer should do. Arakcheev's close attention to parade punctilio and the details of field exercises saved Alexander from committing unmartial solecisms which would have aroused Paul's anger.[48]

It was a curious basis upon which to build a lasting friendship. But, in this period of his life, Alexander needed Arakcheev more than the young liberal-minded aristocrats. They might widen his perspective, but

Arakcheev had a more urgent task: he taught Alexander how to simulate soldierly attributes he did not possess. Ever since childhood Alexander had been deaf in the left ear. Now he was also becoming slightly short-sighted and, although his height gave him a natural dignity and presence, he moved awkwardly because once he had fallen from a horse and injured his hip. These disabilities, slight in any private individual, were a potential source of humiliation in his father's militaristic society. It says much for Arakcheev's patient tuition that Alexander was able to conceal from Paul, and from other officers in the Gatchina garrison, the full extent of his afflictions.

The Succession in Doubt

Psychologically, however, all this pretence was bad for Alexander. By the summer of 1796 his character was vitiated through and through by a strong element of make-believe. In a sense it had always been there, asserting itself in those childish games which had delighted Catherine and taking command in the difficult moments when he moved between the Courts of his grandmother and his father, letting his individuality lose itself in their shadows. But self-deception at nineteen has more range than in boyhood. Now he spoke the language of the Enlightenment with Czartoryski and his liberal friends, and failed to understand it; he played at officering in an army corps which was itself shadow-acting past campaigns; and he sought to fulfil a marriage in which love flickered but never flamed. The prospect ahead seemed even more daunting, and he shrank from it. In May 1796 he wrote to Kochubey, who was serving as a diplomat at Constantinople:

There is incredible confusion in our affairs. In such circumstances, is it possible for one man to rule the State, still less correct abuses within it? This is beyond the strength not only of someone endowed with ordinary abilities like myself, but even of a genius; and I have always held to the rule that it is better not to attempt something than to do it badly. My plan is to settle with my wife on the banks of the Rhine, where I shall live peacefully as a private person finding happiness in the company of friends and in the study of nature.[49]

It is hard to say what was in Alexander's mind. Was he genuinely considering renouncing his rights, or merely indulging in romantic escapism? Probably he was allowing his pen to create yet another dream-world in which he could project his passing enthusiasms, and his words should not be taken too seriously. But it was not the last time that he was to contemplate, if only momentarily, a flight from reality.

Within five months an unforeseen event posed questions he had wished not to answer. On 22 September 1796 the Empress Catherine, belatedly thwarted in a plan to marry her eldest grand-daughter Alexandra Pavlovna to the young King of Sweden, suffered a slight apoplectic stroke. Although a few days later she assured Melchior Grimm that she was once more 'as busy as a bird', she knew a decision over the succession could not be delayed much longer: and on 26 September a peremptory order was despatched to Gatchina requiring the immediate presence of Alexander in the capital.[50]

He came at once, and had a long discussion with the Empress. What exactly was said is not known, for no one else was present. Almost certainly Catherine at last formally told him of her wish that he should succeed her on the throne. She entrusted him with a number of state papers, including explanatory memoranda which she had herself drafted. It is probable that among the documents he received was an outline of the proclamation in which she would indicate both the future status of Paul and her decision in Alexander's favour. None of these papers have survived, but Alexander's reply to Catherine's proposals gives a clear indication of their significance. Sent on 4 October, it is an interesting exercise in diplomatic dissimulation:

Never shall I be able to express gratitude for the confidence with which Your Majesty has graciously honoured me and the kindness with which you have written in your own hand a commentary to clarify the other papers. I hope Your Majesty will see by my zeal that I am worthy of this inestimable trust, the true value of which I perceive. [*J'espère que Votre Majesté verra, par mon zèle, à mériter ses precieuses bontés, que j'en sens tout le prix.*] I can never repay, even with my blood, all that you have done and still wish to do for me. These papers clearly confirm all the thoughts which Your Majesty has been so kind as to communicate to me, and which, if I may offer an opinion, could not be more just. Once more assuring Your Imperial Majesty of my deepest gratitude, I take the liberty to remain, with profound reverence and indissoluble attachment, Your Imperial Majesty's most humble and most obedient servant and grandson,

Alexander.[51]

The Grand Duke thus neither accepted nor rejected whatever proposal had been made to him, and Catherine may well have been puzzled over his attitude. No proclamation was made, even though Alexander remained for most of the following month in the capital. It is possible that he still did not know precisely what he wanted. There was another wild moment when he told some friends he was thinking of casting away all his privileges and settling as a private citizen in America; and yet, on the day before sending this reply to the Empress, he permitted himself a slip of phraseology in a letter to Arakcheev, referring to his father with anticipatory respect as 'His Imperial Majesty'.[52] Alexander was developing masterly skill at concealing his innermost feelings. At times he hid them even from himself.

❧2❧

Empire on Parade

The Grand Duke Comes to Town

Six weeks later St Petersburg was in turmoil. On the morning of 15 November 1796 the Empress suffered a second stroke; she collapsed while seated on her commode and at once lost consciousness. Neither her son nor her grandson were in the Winter Palace at the time: Paul was at Gatchina; and Alexander, though resident in the capital, was that morning visiting Constantine Czartoryski. General Saltykov sent a messenger to fetch Alexander to his grandmother's sick-bed and he came at once. As soon as he reached the palace he realized Catherine was gravely ill. Significantly he made no attempt to claim succession for himself but immediately ordered a courtier to ride out to Gatchina and inform Paul he would await him in the capital. For this mission Alexander chose Theodore Rostopchin, a young landowner from Moscow who had fallen from grace with Catherine by an unauthorized marriage with a maid of honour but who remained attached to her son's miniature Court. It is an interesting commentary on Alexander's sense of filial duty that, at this moment, he should have turned for assistance to a trusted confidant of his father rather than to one of his own friends.

Rostopchin was not, however, the first messenger to leave St Petersburg that morning for Gatchina. The initiative was seized by the last of all Catherine's favourites, Platon Zubov, who had ordered his brother Nicholas to head for Paul's estate with news of the Empress's illness while Alexander was still at Czartoryski's house. Nicholas Zubov reached Gatchina in the early afternoon, but Paul was not there. He had ridden out to a distant corner of his estate to watch cavalry manoeuvres. In his absence the bodyguard at Gatchina treated Zubov with suspicion, for it was known that the Grand Duke was on the alert for a Court intrigue which would deprive him of the succession and no one trusted the Zubovs. A horseman was sent to inform Paul that the Count had arrived from St Petersburg with a message he would communicate only to the Grand Duke in person. This seemed to Paul such an ominous development that he discussed with his escorting officers the wisdom of placing Zubov under restraint and defying the mischief plotted against him in the capital. When Paul heard the reason for the Count's journey, he showed no emotion. At once he ordered his carriage and with a small escort set out for St Petersburg.[1] Although he hated the Zubov family, he found an early opportunity of rewarding the Count with a high decoration.

Paul's carriage should have made the journey from Gatchina to the capital in a few hours, for it was less than thirty miles away. But this was no ordinary day. Allegiance was shifting visibly around him. First he was stopped by Rostopchin, with Alexander's message. 'Ah, Your Highness, what a moment this is for you!' Rostopchin remarked as the Grand Duke warmly gripped his hand. 'Wait, my dear fellow, only wait,' Paul replied. 'I have lived forty-two years and the Almighty has given me His help. Maybe He will now endow me with strength and willpower to measure up to my Destiny.'[2] More than twenty other courtiers hailed Paul on his progress northwards. By the time the Grand Duke's carriage reached the outskirts of St Petersburg his escort had multiplied so that it looked like a cavalcade of the men of yesterday and tomorrow, spurred and jackbooted for the occasion. The night was frosty but clear, with no snow to muffle the sound of the procession as the racing wheels of the carriages thundered across the cobbles into the great square of the Winter Palace. There, on the steps, Alexander and Constantine awaited their father's coming. They were dressed in the cumbersome dark green uniforms of the Gatchina Corps, never before displayed on a public occasion in the capital. Silently they fell into step behind their father as he was ushered into the Palace. Paul was received, as Rostopchin noted, as though he were already Autocrat of All the Russias.

Yet he was not. So long as Catherine breathed there was still a possibility she might recover her power of speech, signify whom she wished to succeed her, perhaps even indicate where a draft proclamation could be found. For the next twenty hours there were extraordinary scenes at the Palace. Paul moved into a small study on the far side of the Empress's bedroom so that, as the senior officers hurried to the Palace, they all had to pass the dying Empress on her bed in order to report to Paul in the inner room, where he sat hunched over official documents, eager to discover her secrets of government. At one moment Arakcheev arrived and Paul entrusted arrangements for his own security jointly to Alexander and this favourite 'Corporal' from Gatchina. Arakcheev's horses had set such a pace on his journey to the capital that his collar was spattered with mud, and Alexander – who was genuinely sensitive over such matters – insisted on taking him to his own rooms and supplying him with a clean shirt, a gesture which deeply affected the hard-bitten artillery man.[3] There were few such spontaneous actions during these tense hours of interregnum.

It was not until the evening of 17 November, two and a half days after her collapse, that Catherine died. An epoch ended overnight for St Petersburg and for all Russia. Whatever her faults she had reigned in the grand manner, her follies and failures on a scale commensurate with her greatness. She was succeeded by a petty tyrant eager to impose on civil society the archaic order he had already introduced in the regulation of his regiments. Within hours of Catherine's death, St Petersburg was left in no doubt that Russia had a new master. Formal decrees from the Palace began to regulate social custom: neither round hats nor tail coats might be worn; the number of horses harnessed to a single carriage would be subject to standard regulation, which would vary according to the status of the person who owned the vehicle; large receptions or private parties might, in future, be held only with permission from the Imperial Household or (outside the capital) from the provincial Governor; and, at all times, officers would appear in uniform. Strict control was imposed on the importing of foreign books and on the activities of the academic institutions which had flourished in Catherine's earlier years. The Winter Palace was ringed by a hideous line of new sentry-boxes within days of Paul's accession. Nothing seemed to matter to the new Tsar but his daily exercising of his soldiers. As Masson, Alexander's former tutor, wrote a few years later,

The guard-parade became for him the most important institution and focal point of government. Every day, no matter how cold it might be, he dedicated the same time to it, spending each morning in plain deep green uniform, great boots and a large hat exercising his guards ... Surrounded by his sons and aides-de-camp he would stamp his heels on the stones to keep himself warm, his bald head bare, his nose in the air, one hand behind his back, the other raising and falling a baton as he beat time, crying out '*Raz, dva – raz, dva*' ['one, two – one, two'].[4]

It was a bleak prospect for an Empire of forty million.

Alexander had anticipated revolutionary changes once his father came to the throne, but, like everyone else, he was puzzled and worried by Paul's behaviour. It was natural that, after more than thirty years of humiliation and neglect, Paul should feel embittered towards his mother and her policies. Yet, although he ousted Catherine's favourites from St Petersburg, he did not impose harsh penalties on them, even though some might justly have been condemned for peculation. So far as he could, he avenged himself on his mother's renown rather than on her admirers.[5] The summer palace at Tsarskoe Selo was left empty so long as Paul was on the throne, weeds spreading through the English gardens in which Catherine delighted to sit. The Tauride Palace, rich with memories of her love for Potemkin, was turned into a cavalry barracks, with horse droppings heaped on the marble floor of the ballroom. Yet the strangest gesture of all was made at the very start of Paul's reign, to the private consternation of his family. Two days after Catherine's death the new Tsar ordered the abbot of the monastery of Alexander Nevsky to disinter the coffin of her murdered husband, Peter III. The embalmed remains were then transferred to a richly decorated sarcophagus and laid in state beside Catherine's body. Finally Paul supervised arrangements for a joint burial of 'Their Imperial Majesties' and summoned Count Alexei Orlov, who had played a sinister part in Peter's murder, to carry the crown through the streets immediately behind his victim's bier.[6] National mourning 'for the late Emperor and Empress' was ordered to last for twelve months.

This display of macabre theatricality raised fresh doubts over Paul's sanity. Undoubtedly his mind was warped and yet he was by no means unintelligent. He spoke French and German better than either of his eldest sons, possessed some skill in applied mathematics, and understood the Old Slavonic language used by the Orthodox Church in its liturgy. Moreover he had some inkling of the weaknesses in Russian society, even if the drastic remedies he favoured were inappropriate and essentially superficial. Though harsh, he was not persistently cruel and there were moments when he showed kindness and generosity, above all towards the Polish patriots who had suffered for defying his mother's policy. But the Russian nobility, especially the army officers, were terrified by Paul's sudden fits of rage over trivial affronts. So, for that matter, were his two sons. Week after week they were expected to remain at Court fulfilling the duties of regimental officers. Although to some extent both Alexander and Constantine inherited their father's delight in parade-ground choreography, much of the drill and the garrison duties was tedious. Moreover, with their father's uncertain temper, it was frequently humiliating. And, at times, once off the parade-ground Alexander collapsed in tears of frustration and bewilderment.

Life was harder still for the young Grand Dukes' wives. Alexander's consort, Elizabeth, had at least come to know Russia before the sudden shock of Paul's accession. Constantine, on the other hand, had married only a few months previously and his wife, Anna Feodorovna, hardly had time to accustom herself to the great contrast between life in Saxe-Coburg (where she was born) and in Imperial Petersburg before everything was made even stranger by Catherine's death. Though Constantine was too boorish to feel for Anna the sympathetic affection which linked Alexander and Elizabeth, the uncertainties of their father's whim temporarily acted as a bond bringing together both brothers and their wives. Adversity fostered an especially deep friendship between Elizabeth and poor Anna.

Elizabeth's letters to her mother provide a vivid commentary on the new reign, although she had to be certain she could rely upon the courier, for it would have been disastrous had her messages fallen into Paul's hands. Ten weeks after his accession she risked committing her first impressions to paper:

I am certain, dear Mother, that the death of the good Empress affected you deeply. As for me, I can assure you that I cannot cease thinking of it. You have no idea how every little thing has been turned upside down. All this made such a wretched impression on me, especially in the first days, that I scarcely recognized myself. Oh, how awful those first days were! Anna was my only consolation, as I was hers. She practically lived with me, coming here in the morning, dressing here, having dinner on most occasions and remaining all day until we would go together in attendance on the Emperor. Our husbands were hardly ever at home and we could find little to do with ourselves, the way of life not having been regulated in every respect. It was necessary for us to hold ourselves ready to be summoned to the Empress [Marie Feodorovna] at any moment. You have no idea of the terrible emptiness that there was, of how sad and gloomy everybody seemed, except the new Majesties [les nouvelles Majestés]. Oh, I have been so shocked by the Emperor's lack of grief. It would seem as if it were his father who had just died and not his mother, for he speaks only of the former, providing every room with his portrait and saying not a word of his mother, except to condemn and roundly abuse everything that was done in her day.[7]

The Tsar's conduct was bad enough: his daughters-in-law also resented their treatment by Marie Feodorovna. They were expected to behave as though they were ladies-in-waiting, while Paul's recognized mistress, Catherine Nelidova, was treated with courtesy and respect at Court, even

by the new Empress herself. Yet let either Elizabeth or Anna show independence and they would be sternly rebuked. 'That kind of thing will
never do on a parade occasion', Marie Feodorovna remarked icily as she
tore roses from a buckle with which Elizabeth was seeking to relieve the
severity of a formal gown.[8] 'What silly things Mother does', Alexander
confessed to Elizabeth, 'she really has no idea at all how to conduct herself.'[9] With so much tension in the family circle Alexander and Elizabeth
drew closer together in spirit than at any time since those first days of their
marriage. But Elizabeth wept for the privacy and self-respect they had
lost when 'the good Empress' passed away.

Doubts of a Tsarevich

In April 1797 Tsar Paul travelled to Moscow for his coronation, accompanied by his sons and all the Court. His mother's coronation in
1762 was already enshrined in popular legend. She had spent several
months in residence at the Kremlin, entertaining so prodigiously that life
in retrospect seemed an endless carnival, with gifts distributed to every
class in society. By contrast, the coronation of Paul was an austere religious
ceremony which was followed by formal acts of homage and the inevitable military review.[10] Later in the week, the customary coronation
balls and receptions were held – for Paul was not the person to break
tradition. But no one enjoyed themselves. Strict etiquette was enforced on
all the Imperial Family, who were expected to wear throughout the
Moscow visit their ceremonial robes or full-dress uniforms. It was
exhausting and dispiriting, especially as so many of the younger generation had never before seen the wonder of the old capital. The nervous
strain was too much for the eighteen-year-old Elizabeth: she collapsed on
returning to St Petersburg and spent the early summer recuperating.

For Alexander, however, his father's coronation was important in two
respects, dynastic and personal. On the day he was crowned (24 April)
Paul published a decree formally superseding Peter the Great's ruling of
1722 by which the Tsar and Autocrat had been entitled to nominate his
heir.[11] Henceforth the Imperial crown was to pass by the normal rule of
primogeniture to the eldest son and, should he have no male offspring, to
his brothers in order of seniority. Alexander was now officially recognized
as Tsarevich, principal Grand Duke in the Empire, a status enjoyed by his
father in Catherine's reign only during those months when he was permitted to travel abroad. The immediate effect was to enhance Alexander's
standing among his brother officers. Yet the most interesting consequence

of his visit to Moscow was a widening of his circle of friends. It was there for the first time that he met Paul Stroganov and Nikolai Novosiltsov his cousin.[12] Both young men (Stroganov was twenty-five and Novosiltsov ten years older) were close acquaintances of the Czartoryski brothers, sharing their liberal sympathies and cultural interests. They were pleasantly clubbable men who enjoyed gambling and amusing themselves as much as anybody else at Court, but they imbued conversation with a mental vigour new to Alexander and refreshingly different from the small talk of fashionable society, or the even smaller talk of Paul's Gatchina officers. Although far more warm-hearted than the sceptical intellectuals of the West, Alexander's new friends had interests which were free-ranging, rational and cultivated. They provided him with that sharpening of the mind normally associated with a university education. Inevitably many of the ideas he picked up were superficial, a digest of current thought rather than the real thing; but at least his intellectual sights were raised above the level of a parade ground.

Unfortunately Alexander was soon thrown back into an entirely military environment. Immediately after the Moscow coronation, the Tsar set out upon a grand progress through the western provinces of his Empire and he ordered Alexander to accompany him.[13] Paul believed, perfectly correctly, that it was essential for the heir to the throne to discover for himself the character of the Russian lands and get away from the artificial constriction of life in the capital. The region through which the Tsar and his party planned to travel had considerable strategic significance. From Moscow, which they left on 14 May, they went first to Smolensk and then entered territories which had belonged to the Polish Kingdom before the partitions of Catherine's reign. They visited Orsha, Mogilev, Minsk, Vilna, Grodno, Kovno and Mitau before crossing back into Russian Courland (Latvia) at Riga and proceeding to Paul's summer residence at Pavlovsk by way of Narva. This was the most extensive journey through the Empire which Alexander had as yet undertaken, and it should theoretically have been of considerable educational value.

It was not. Paul's obsessive interest in military affairs meant that the expedition became primarily a tour of inspection, and Alexander saw little of the way in which his future subjects lived. All that Paul wished to know was whether or not the army was being drilled and exercised according to his own standards. At Kovno there was a frightful explosion of wrath when it seemed to the Tsar that the Tavrichesky Grenadiers, stationed on the Prussian frontier, had not absorbed the Germanic spirit he was seeking to instil into the older regiments; and Arakcheev was seconded from the Tsarevich's bodyguard to put the Grenadiers through their paces.[14] But for most of the time, both during the journey through the western provinces and back at St Petersburg on garrison duty, Alexander needed Arakcheev's assistance. 'Please do me the good service of being here when my guard is mounted so nothing goes wrong', he wrote in a characteristic note to the General that summer.[15] And that autumn, with the Court once more in the capital, 'good Alexei' began to assume responsibility for other military duties nominally discharged by the heir to the throne. He even drafted reports for Paul which Alexander signed without bothering to read. Time and time again the General saved Alexander from making a fool of himself on parade. Over military matters he did not question Arakcheev's advice.

It was, of course, unwise for the Tsarevich to become so dependent on a General who was far from popular with his brother officers. Alexander, conscious of the uneasiness in the army at his father's imposition of Prussian customs, sensed the widespread contempt felt for Arakcheev and, though he never in these years doubted the General's competence or good faith, there were moments when it was obvious that the two men failed to understand each other. Occasionally Alexander censured Arakcheev for acts of harsh discipline, but more frequently he told the General of the quarrels he was having with his father and of the difficulty he was finding in enforcing reforms which the officers disliked and of which he could not see the value. In September 1797 Alexander was so depressed that he confided to Arakcheev his longing to shed responsibilities and retire abroad with Elizabeth.[16] But this was not the future which Arakcheev envisaged for him; it was a mood with which he felt little sympathy.

Nor indeed did it correspond with the wishes of Alexander's liberal friends in the Czartoryski circle. That autumn they encouraged the Grand Duke to formulate other plans, which are preserved for us in unexpected detail. Novosiltsov had sought, and received, permission to leave Russia and visit England, where he already possessed influential connections. Before he set out from St Petersburg the Tsarevich entrusted him with a letter which was to be forwarded from Sweden to La Harpe. In it he clearly showed the extent to which he had become disillusioned by less than a year of his father's rule.

The letter was written at Gatchina on 8 October 1797. Alexander began by admitting that in the last years of the old Empress abuses of government multiplied as she herself became physically weaker. He continued:

When my father came to the throne he wished to reform everything. The beginning of his reign was indeed bright enough, but its continuation has not fulfilled expectations. Everything has been turned upside down ... You have always known my thoughts about leaving my country ... Now the wretched condition of my fatherland makes me look differently at my ideas. I think that if ever the time comes for me to reign, rather than go into voluntary exile myself, I had far better devote myself to the task of giving freedom to my country and thereby preventing her from becoming in the future a toy in a madman's hands. I have been in touch with enlightened people who, on their side, have long thought in the same way. In all we are only four in number, that is to say, M. Novosiltsov, Count Stroganov, the young Prince Czartoryski, my aide-de-camp (a young man in a million) and me. Our idea is that during the present reign we should translate into the Russian language as many useful books as is possible, of which we would print as many as would be permitted, and we will reserve others for a future occasion ... Once my turn comes, then it will be essential to work, little by little, of course, for a method of representing the nation ... let it be by a free constitution, after which my authority will end absolutely and, if Providence seconds our endeavours, I will retire into some place and I will live contentedly and happily observing the good fortune of my country and rejoicing in it.

Alexander ended by hoping that La Harpe would support the scheme and give the four liberal enthusiasts his advice.[17]

Few documents show so clearly the confusion of purpose and muddled idealism in Alexander's mind. Had the letter been intercepted, it would have aroused Paul to take strong measures against his son's friends and almost certainly against Alexander himself, for the Tsar held independent thought to be treasonable and all talk of constitutions indistinguishable from rank Jacobinism. But in content the letter seems harmless enough, more a fairy tale with a happy ending than a revolutionary manifesto. The idea of educating Russians to govern themselves by translating a series of unspecified foreign works was a nostalgic reminiscence, an echo from the earlier 'Enlightened' years of Catherine II: it was unrealistic and, in the rigidly anti-intellectual mood of Paul's reign, impracticable. A leading Russian scholar, Nikolai Karamzin, was severely reprimanded by the Tsar for translating the letters of that dangerous republican, Marcus Tullius Cicero;[18] and it is unlikely that the printing of any of 'the useful books' which Alexander had in mind would have been permitted. For Alexander, the proposal had another purpose, although he may not have been consciously aware of it. As his letters to Arakcheev show, the Tsarevich was sufficiently Paul's son to thrill at the sight of well-drilled troops moving in blind obedience across the parade-ground. In gloomier moments of self-analysis this reaction depressed him as much as it worried his liberal aristocratic friends. By showing willingness to encourage the translation of academic works frowned upon by the authorities, Alexander was strengthening his own resistance to that obsessive paradomania which Adam Czartoryski feared he inherited from his father. The fact that nothing came of the project is immaterial: its chief value for the heir to the throne was therapeutic.

There remains, however, one peculiar feature of Alexander's letter which suggests he was already haunted by a possibility he dared not admit, even to himself. In the autumn of 1797, when Alexander first began to discuss future policy with his friends, Tsar Paul was still only forty-three years old. Apart from the alarming vagaries of his mind, his health was good and there was no physical obstacle to prevent him from fulfilling his natural life span, reigning in Russia for another quarter of a century or more. Why, then, was his son already planning the programme he would follow upon his own accession? It is not difficult to guess the reason. Alexander sensed that his father's behaviour was courting disaster. On three occasions in the previous sixty years the Guards Regiments had staged a palace revolution in St Petersburg to rid themselves of a ruler in whom they lacked confidence. Yet no previous Tsar had deliberately flouted traditions as Paul was doing day after day. Many distinguished officers either resigned their commissions or were compulsorily retired from active service, among them the great Marshal Suvorov, hero of the wars against the Turks. It seemed, that October, only a matter of months before some exasperated member of the nobility once more led the Guards against their sovereign's throne. Where would Alexander's loyalty place him in such a situation? Natural respect for the autocratic principle, and genuine affection for his father and mother, made him dislike the prospect of such a conspiracy, and yet he sympathized with the grievances of many young aristocrats and officers. He, too, was conscious of wasted opportunities. From the letters he exchanged with Arakcheev it is clear be believed there was a risk of army revolt, but he took no counter-measures.[19] He did not wish to contemplate hypothetical dilemmas. Waiting upon events better suited his temperament than anticipating them.

Others, besides Alexander, were alive to the danger. In two private letters written at Pavlovsk in August 1797 Marie Feodorovna mentioned her fear of a Guards mutiny, and in a more revealing note sent from St Petersburg four months later she described how worried she had become when a false fire alarm brought all the troops in the capital hastening to one side of the Palace while Paul was left, momentarily isolated, on the other.[20] The Tsar himself had few illusions over his unpopularity with the veterans of Catherine's wars. He continued to rely on the loyalty of the officers who had been closest to him at Gatchina and Pavlovsk in the old days, but he knew that he needed more protection than they could offer. The Winter Palace was huge and rambling, as easy to break into as the Tuileries in Paris. He therefore decided to build a new fortified palace in the capital, with moats, drawbridges and turreted courtyards, a natural citadel as much as the home of the sovereign. Work began on the foundations towards the end of 1797 and the first stone was laid on 8 February 1798, the day on which Marie Feodorovna gave birth to the last of her nine children. Both son and palace were named in honour of the Archangel Michael, long revered in the Church as a protector of soldiers, and a saint after Paul's own heart.

Suvorov in Italy and Switzerland

It was impossible to build the Mikhailovsky Palace in less than three years. To many it seemed unlikely Paul would reign long enough to reside within its walls. That he did so at all – though only for a few weeks – was largely a consequence of a change in Russia's relations with the other European Powers. An active foreign policy postponed the final and decisive confrontation between the dissidents in the army and their sovereign.[21]

Hitherto the Russians had stood aside from the great struggle on the continent between the French Republic and the defenders of the old order. Shortly before her death Catherine had agreed to plans for despatching an expeditionary force to assist the Austrians against the French in the Rhineland. But, partly from uncertainty over the efficiency of his army and partly from his desire to break with his mother's policy, Paul had held back his troops. In the summer of 1798, however, Paul decided that his fleet and army should enter the war, associating themselves with Great Britain and the traditional enemy, Turkey, in an effort to curb Bonaparte's growing strength in the Mediterranean. The reason for Paul's change of policy was almost absurdly trivial, a claim on the part of the Tsar to champion the rights of the Maltese Order of Knights, who had been deprived of their island by the French:* but, for most of the Russian

---

* The Knights of St. John had long possessed a priory in one of the regions of Poland incorporated in Russia by the partitions. On his accession Paul confirmed the rights of the Order within his Empire and even made a personal contribution to the running expenses of

officers, the cause of hostilities mattered less than the prospect of resuming Catherine's expansionist adventures. An expeditionary force needed veteran commanders rather than Paul's parade-ground martinets. Hence Generals and Colonels who had passed into retirement during the first year of Paul's reign were recalled to their regiments. When, in the early months of 1799, the Second Coalition came into being, Marshal Suvorov himself was reinstated by the Tsar and given command of an Austro-Russian army which challenged the supremacy of France in the Italian peninsula.

Alexander would have liked to see active service under Suvorov. Paul refused to permit him to leave the Empire, although he allowed Constantine to go to Italy. To his chagrin, Alexander was forced to remain on garrison duty in the capital while Suvorov's army enacted one of the most brilliant episodes of Russian military history, clearing the enemy from the Lombard Plain and threatening to cross the Alps and make Paris its ultimate objective. Friction between the Russians and their Austrian allies caused Suvorov's grand strategic plan to fall short of its expectations, and, after a grimly resolute advance into the Swiss Alps, he was ordered to disengage and return to the homeland. Militarily the campaign brought no lasting gains to Russia. But the prestige of having served in regiments which entered Milan and Turin in triumph and scaled the heights of the St Gothard was considerable. The 'sons of Suvorov' were an honoured band of brothers: it grieved Alexander not to be among them.

His father at first identified himself closely with the war, vicariously sharing Suvorov's days of triumph. He heaped honours upon the old Marshal, creating him 'Prince of Italy' and Generalissimo of all the armies of the Russian Empire. The mood soon passed. Envy and suspicion began to eat into Paul's mind and in the end he turned against Suvorov with a callous insensitivity which alienated all who had fought in Italy and Switzerland. The Marshal returned to St Petersburg at the end of October 1799, a dying man worn out with his exertions. His officers had expected him to receive a triumphant reception. But, at the last moment, Paul cancelled the arrangements. He had heard that Suvorov ignored army regulations when selecting his staff, and the Tsar's petty spirit insisted on

---

the priory. When, in June 1798, Bonaparte occupied Malta itself, the head of the priory offered the Grand Mastership of the whole Order of Knights to Paul, even though he was Orthodox and not Catholic in religion. The Tsar accepted the Grand Mastership and demanded that the French evacuate Malta. When they ignored his intervention he authorized a naval squadron to attack the French outposts in the Ionian Islands as a preliminary to general war in the Mediterranean. In the following year Russia joined the Second Coalition.

making an example of his greatest commander. A few months later Suvorov died, still officially in disgrace. His burial in the crypt of the Annunciation at the Nevsky Monastery in St Petersburg became a silent demonstration by his officers of their contempt for the Tsar. Paul did not attend the Prince of Italy's funeral.[22]

Mounting Tension in the Capital

There had been another cause for official celebrations in the capital during the spring of 1799, quite apart from Suvorov's victories in Italy. For on 29 May the Grand Duchess Elizabeth gave birth to a girl, baptized Maria Alexandrovna. The baby was unusually dark, with black hair and features which seemed to correspond neither to her mother's nor to Alexander's. Aristocratic gossip maintained that the child's father was not the Grand Duke but his friend, Adam Czartoryski.[23] There is no doubt the Polish Prince had become passionately attached to the Grand Duchess and that their warm friendship was encouraged by Alexander. The fact that Czartoryski was hurriedly sent on a diplomatic mission in August 1798 and remained in exile until after Alexander's accession was accepted in some contemporary memoirs as evidence that Paul had discovered the truth about the Pole's romance with Elizabeth and was determined to keep the lovers apart. But although Paul may have decided that Czartoryski was an unfortunate influence both upon his son and his daughter-in-law, he cannot have suspected the Prince had fathered a child on Elizabeth. For Czartoryski left St Petersburg on 22 August 1798, nine months and one week before the baby's birth, almost certainly too early for Elizabeth (let alone anyone else) to have discovered she was pregnant. The Tsar treated Elizabeth with kindness rather than displeasure during her confinement and distributed honours to her personal household when the baby was born. Tragically little Maria died from convulsions when she was only fourteen months old, but during her brief life there is no suggestion of coolness between husband and wife. If Czartoryski was indeed the baby's father, it did not lessen Alexander's personal regard for him. On the other hand, Marie Feodorovna hardened her attitude towards Elizabeth and made no effort to disguise her dislike of the Czartoryskis. Throughout her life she tended to distrust Poles on principle.

Meanwhile Alexander's day-to-day existence changed little. As heir to the throne he was kept in close attendance on his father. More than any other individual he was thus able to perceive the terrors of a darkened mind often tangled in shadows but never enveloped in them. For, though foreign observers might write glibly of the Tsar's 'madness' in their confidential reports, the truth was more complex.[24] George III at Windsor in 1788–9 had suffered from bouts of incoherent loquacity and at times used personal violence on those around him: stripped of authority so long as his mind was wandering, he became an object of pity and sympathy and in a matter of months he recovered his mental health. Paul's case was different. There was never any moment of complete collapse, and his general vitality prevented his delusions from totally dominating his behaviour. It is questionable whether he was as 'mad' as his idol, the founder of St Petersburg; certainly he was not so cruel as Peter. The most terrifying aspect of Paul's character was the capricious ease with which his mood would change. One day he would honour someone at Court: and on another banish him to his estate in disgrace or order him into Siberian exile. Even his close advisers from Gatchina fell sudden victims to his suspicion, and other people's tales: thus both Arakcheev and Rostopchin were peremptorily dismissed from service in St Petersburg. And on one extraordinary day Alexander, to whom his father had been especially gracious at a ball the previous night, was visited by one of Paul's aides who arrived with instructions from the Tsar to read aloud to the Grand Duke a passage from a Russian chronicle which described the sufferings and death of the Tsarevich Alexis, whom Peter the Great believed had plotted against him.[25] The psychological intricacies of Paul's mental condition remained beyond Alexander's comprehension. In his leisure hours he began to read Roman history: it gave him little comfort.

Alexander remained loyal to his father, though at times it took hard nerves to brazen out life in St Petersburg. But from the moment of Suvorov's disgrace conspiracy was in the air, and by the spring of 1800 it had begun to assume a definite shape.[26] Its leaders were Admiral Ribas and Count Nikita Panin, nephew and namesake of one of Paul's tutors and himself a trusted adviser on foreign affairs. Panin appears to have discussed his plans with the British ambassador, Lord Whitworth, who had never been a friend of Paul or his policy. Arakcheev's successor as military commandant of the capital, Count Peter von Pahlen, also knew of the plot and sympathized with Panin. It was on Pahlen's suggestion that Panin met Alexander about the time of Suvorov's funeral and did his best to persuade him that the hour had come to depose his father. Exactly what was said is not clear; but the Tsarevich gained the impression that Panin intended Paul to be placed under restraint while Alexander himself was proclaimed Regent. If this was indeed Panin's plan then it was clearly a constitutional device owing more to Whitworth's recollections of

George III's illness than to Russian experience. Nothing, however, came of the project. Alexander declined to commit himself. Indiscreet behaviour led Whitworth to be sent home to London in June; Panin incurred Paul's displeasure for giving disagreeable advice on foreign policy and was banished to his estates; and a heart attack removed Admiral Ribas in December. By the end of 1800 there remained of the would-be conspirators in the capital only Pahlen – and the wavering figure of Alexander.

By now the need to curb Paul's impetuosity was greater than ever. Foreign policy no less than social conventions had become dependent on personal whim. Consul Bonaparte, Paul believed, was a man he could respect, a soldier who would tame the revolutionary beast in France and impose good order on Europe. In December 1800 and January 1801 the Tsar wrote three personal letters to Bonaparte, proposing a meeting at which they could discuss the prospects for a general peace and ways of putting pressure on the British, whom Paul was now convinced were the greatest menace to a lasting settlement in Europe.[27] At the same time Paul imposed an embargo on British trade with Russia and ordered a force of twenty thousand Don Cossacks to set out from Orenburg and advance by way of Khiva and Bokhara to the Indus, where they would form the advance-guard for a projected Franco-Russian invasion of India. The Tsar's commercial policy was unpopular in the Baltic ports, while the expedition to the Indus was regarded by the army commanders as the height of folly, for there was no hope of supplies in the Central Asian wastes and much of the route beyond Khiva remained unmapped.[28] Grand Duke Constantine, not by nature inclined to aphorisms, was heard to remark, 'My father has declared war on common sense, firmly resolved never to conclude a truce.'[29]

In these final months of his life every facet of Paul's character became grossly exaggerated, as in some hideous caricature. He had always suspected hidden conspiracies among officers he saw talking together. Now his paranoia extended even to his wife and his former mistress, Catherine Nelidova, two women who remained devoted to 'our dear Emperor' and who longed to help him.[30] He seemed at times to shake at the shadows he had himself conjured up, peering anxiously at his sentries to make certain the Guards had not been changed without his knowledge. On 13 February 1801 Paul took up residence in the Mikhailovsky Palace. There, so he told his new mistress, he felt safe, and he installed her in an apartment immediately beneath his own rooms.[31] He had himself supervised the security arrangements – the double doors, the water defences, the drawbridges. The Mikhailovsky would be the Kremlin of St Petersburg. He expected the imperial family and their households to share it with him. How else could he be certain what Alexander and Constantine and Marie Feodorovna were plotting?

The two Grand Dukes and Grand Duchesses moved into their apartments, unenthusiastically, on 5 March. The building was so new that when the stoves were fired the walls steamed with damp. Paul had always been impervious to home comforts but his sons and daughters-in-law, though hardly Sybarites, were certainly not Spartans and there was about the Mikhailovsky an air of austerity which it shared with the best prisons. Elizabeth, however, was not unduly downcast and two days after moving in she sent a hopeful letter back to her mother at Baden. 'I await the Spring with more impatience than ever', she wrote, 'Since our rooms are bounded on one side by a canal and on the other by the Summer Garden, springtime here will be pleasant.'[32] But by the time spring came at last, the Grand Ducal suites at the Mikhailovsky were grey with dust-sheets, silent and deserted.

Murder at the Mikhailovsky (March 1801)

At the end of February Alexander had a meeting with Count von Pahlen.[33] There was no reason why they should not have come together as often as they wished, since they shared responsibility for security in the capital. Yet on this occasion they met discreetly, if not exactly in secret, for Pahlen was again anxious to sound Alexander over the possibility of deposing Paul. But Alexander was not helpful. He was genuinely troubled by the oath of fealty he had sworn in the coronation ceremony and he could not therefore approve any conspiracy which had, as its principal purpose, the abdication of the sovereign. Pahlen, however, persevered and eventually secured from Alexander verbal consent to a plan for placing Paul under restraint and establishing a Regency. The Grand Duke insisted that no harm should come to his father. He thought it would be possible to confine him in one of the Imperial palaces near St Petersburg, much as George III had been at Windsor in 1788–9. Since everything would be done in the Tsar's name, the conspiracy did not appear to involve any breach of the coronation oath.

It is incredible that Alexander and Pahlen should ever have thought that Paul, of all people, could be induced to surrender his rights, even temporarily. Probably at heart neither man believed it. Pahlen was too ruthless to care about such niceties while Alexander possessed a strange quality of self-deception which allowed him to foresee half an event but not its consequences. He always lacked the courage to think logically of what he most dreaded. Although Pahlen kept him informed of the progress of the conspiracy, even of its timing, he remained convinced his father's life would be spared. This error of judgement racked Alexander's conscience for the remainder of his days.

Most of Pahlen's fellow conspirators were recruited from the Guard Regiments, who had always resented Paul's contemptuous disregard of their traditions. There were others with old scores to settle, favourites from Catherine's reign like the Zubov brothers, aristocrats like Prince Yashvil and Prince Viazemsky whom Paul had insulted; but the brain behind the conspiracy was the Hanoverian-born General, Levin Bennigsen, a professional soldier who at fifty-five had spent nearly half his life in Russian service. His quarrel with Paul came, not from the heart, but from the intellect: he despaired of a commander-in-chief who could throw himself into such rages of pique; he feared for an empire in which the Autocrat could cut free from foreign alliances on the whim of a moment. The conspirators were men of courage but not of noble ideals. None of their leaders were personal friends of Alexander although they included officers from the Semeonovsky Regiment whom he knew well as he was their Colonel-in-Chief. Several prominent conspirators, notably the Zubovs, Alexander had long detested.

In the second week of March Paul picked up the scent of the conspiracy. Unexpectedly he challenged Pahlen at their next meeting, even though he had continued to show a blind confidence in the city commandant ever since his appointment eighteen months previously. Pahlen admitted that officers were plotting against the Tsar and claimed that he had penetrated their movement so that, in due course, he would be able to denounce them. 'Don't waste time, then!' Paul screamed at him, 'Remember that my father was murdered in 1762.'[34]

Paul went through the motions of taking Pahlen at his word, but he was alarmed. He regretted the way in which he had banished those two stalwarts from Gatchina days, Arakcheev and Rostopchin. Secretly, on Saturday 21 March, Paul ordered a messenger to ride out to Arakcheev's estate at Gruzino (eighty miles away) with a note for the General, 'I need you: come at once.' But Pahlen was a good security man. He intercepted the courier, confiscated Paul's note and confronted the Tsar with it telling him that he assumed it was a forgery intended to embroil Arakcheev in the plot, since it had been despatched without Pahlen's knowledge. By now the Tsar was too terrified to fly into a rage. He insisted that the messenger be sent on to Gruzino and at the same time made an effort to get a similar note through to Rostopchin.[35]

But the knowledge that Paul was seeking to rally support from 'the men of Gatchina' precipitated the crisis. On Sunday evening (22 March) Pahlen summoned the principal conspirators to a meeting in the house of Countess Zherebzova, sister of the Zubovs. There it was agreed that a battalion of the Semeonovsky Guards should take over palace duties for the following evening, that General Bennigsen would take six conspirators to the Tsar's bedroom at midnight, that Paul would then be placed under arrest and conveyed across the river to the Fortress of St Peter and St Paul.

Alexander does not seem to have been informed that action was imminent until Pahlen visited him at six o'clock on the Monday evening. Once more the Grand Duke was assured that no harm would come to his father and that he would be permitted to live in an Imperial residence within the Petersburg boundaries. Pahlen left Alexander's apartments and went at once to the home of General Talytzin, commander of the Semeonovsky, where some sixty officers were plied with more wine than was good for them on a cold night. One of the older conspirators, more sober than the others, pertinently asked the question which Alexander had always ignored: what would happen if the Tsar offered resistance? 'Gentlemen,' Pahlen replied calmly, 'you cannot make an omelette without breaking eggs.'[36] It was an ominous remark, difficult to reconcile with his assurance to Alexander.

Meanwhile, in the Mikhailovsky, Paul had seventeen guests to dinner that night.[37] Both his elder sons and their wives were present and so was his fourteen-year-old daughter, Marie. The visitors were mainly senior officers from the garrison, the most distinguished of them being General Kutuzov, who was accompanied by his wife. Apart from Alexander, no one at table knew what was planned for later that night. Paul, who had been morbidly suspicious all day, was now in a genial mood and was especially pleased with a new porcelain dinner service which depicted views of the Mikhailovsky on every plate and dish. He noticed that Alexander had little appetite and suggested he should see his doctor, a Scots physician, James Wylie. But when the meal was over the officer of the Guard brought Paul the regulation nightly report and at once the Tsar's guests saw him turn purple with anger. For the Guard duties were being carried out, not by his regular bodyguard, but by the Semeonovsky Regiment whose officers he held to be crypto-Jacobins. Pahlen, he insisted, should have known better than to replace his men by the Semeonovsky.

The dinner party, not surprisingly, broke up early. Alexander, pleading indigestion, retired to his apartment facing the Summer Garden. Paul went upstairs to his own suite of five rooms, diagonally opposite to his eldest son's across the courtyard. Every door was locked, including the one which communicated with Marie Feodorovna's apartments. Two personal valets remained on guard in an ante-chamber, looking impressively alert in full Hussar uniform.

There are several accounts of what happened that night, some of them in marked contradiction to others.[38] It was bitterly cold, a strong wind sending scurries of sleet through streets lined with snow which had begun to melt by day but was now once more frozen. By eleven o'clock the city was deserted. An officer of the Preobrazhensky Guards admitted the conspirators to the outer courtyard. Pahlen headed at once for Alexander's rooms, although he moved quietly and made no attempt to wake the Grand Duke. Bennigsen led his group, swollen to eighteen officers directly to the Tsar's apartment. The two valets were overcome, the door broken down, and the bedroom entered. A single candle was burning but there was, at first, no sign of the Tsar. Bennigsen, however, holding the candle above his head, saw Paul crouching in terror behind a screen. 'Sire,' he declared, 'you have ceased to reign and we are arresting you on the orders of the Emperor Alexander.'[39] As if uncertain whether this was reality or nightmare, Paul remained silent. Then he began to argue; but the officers, heavily fortified with drink, were in no mood for talk. There was a confused scuffle and Paul cried out for help. Nicholas Zubov, whom Paul had wrongly thought to be the herald of disaster at Gatchina on the eve of his accession, picked up a heavy snuffbox and struck Paul violently on the left temple. When he fell to the ground one of the other conspirators seized a silk scarf and began to strangle him, and yet another officer held a malachite paperweight against his windpipe until he stopped breathing. No one could be certain who actually murdered him. It was some minutes short of one o'clock in the morning of 12 March by the Russian calendar, 24 March 1801 by the Gregorian calendar of western Europe.

Pahlen woke Alexander with the news that his father was dead. He told him that the threat of detention had thrown Paul into an apoplectic fit, from which he never recovered. Alexander was not deceived. The new Autocrat of All the Russias collapsed with grief. 'I cannot go on with it', he sobbed, 'I have no strength to reign. Let someone else take over from me', he declared, resting his head on Elizabeth's shoulder.[40] But she, though startled by the news, remained magnificently resolute. She begged her husband to steel his nerves, to show himself to the troops so as to

45

prevent further mischief. At last, reluctantly and hardly able to move his legs for shock, he agreed to leave at once for the Winter Palace and assume his responsibilities as sovereign of the Empire.

There were still terrible hours ahead of him that day, and often he seemed to walk in a daze, barely conscious of what was going on. He told the troops that his father had died and that he would reign according to the spirit and principles of the Empress Catherine. James Wylie came to the Mikhailovsky Palace and certified that Paul had indeed died from apoplexy, a fiction officially maintained for more than a century. Few believed it even at the time. Marie Feodorovna collapsed in hysterical sobs as soon as she was told of Paul's death.[41] At first she denounced Alexander for conniving at his father's death and she refused to receive him in her apartments. Momentarily, in her hysteria, she even claimed the throne for herself, insisting that the night's crime made a mockery of Paul's coronation and therefore invalidated every pronouncement made on that occasion, including the decree regulating the succession. By noon, however, she was sufficiently recovered to talk sensibly to her eldest son, whose grief convinced her he had not known his father's life was in danger. Outside, wrote Princess Lieven in later years, 'a superb sun broke over this great and terrible day . . . There were shouts of deliverance and of joy.'[42] Inside the Winter Palace a young man of twenty-three was stunned into silence, his broad shoulders still shaking with convulsive sobs.

Alexander's nerves were shattered. For weeks on end he could bear to dine only with Elizabeth at his table, back in the familiar surrounds of the Winter Palace. She believed it was the manner of his father's death, the sordid scuffling by candlelight, which troubled his mind: 'His sensitive soul will remain tortured by it for ever', she wrote to her mother a fortnight later.[43] Yet as the months passed into years, with the murderers themselves going unpunished, it became clear that Alexander was haunted, not by a crime he never witnessed, but by the conspiracy of which he had known too much and too little. Until the end of his life there would come, now and again, black days of despair when he was unsure of himself or his purpose; alone with his doubts and reflections, his conscience would begin to turn round upon itself and the Tsar of Russia became a squirrel in a cage, thrown into torment by the shadows of parricide.

3

The Cracking of the Ice

A Promise of Reform

The mood of the people of St Petersburg in that spring of 1801 was a strange compound of mixed emotions. Most of them greeted with relief the accession of a young and handsome Emperor, but their joy was tinged at first with an odd sense of doubt and uncertainty as though they could not entirely accept the fact that the grotesque tyranny of the past four years was ended. Paul met his death on the Tuesday of Passion Week and his embalmed body lay in state at the Mikhailovsky Palace from the following afternoon until the evening of Good Friday: during those nine days more than one hundred thousand men and women – half the population of the capital – filed past the catafalque.[1] Few showed signs of sorrow, only of curiosity. They needed to convince themselves that the ruler whom they had learnt to fear was really dead and not spirited off to some distant fortress from which he might one day return to take vengeance on those who hailed liberty with such rash jubilation. Experience had taught them circumspection.

Yet once certain that Paul's reign was indeed ended, they slipped easily back into old habits and customs. The weather helped them welcome Alexander's accession. Springtime came with astonishing rapidity that year, the ice on the Neva cracking and melting rapidly under bright sunshine, a good omen to the superstitious. Although Court etiquette imposed many weeks of mourning on the country, Alexander lifted all excessive restrictions for the traditional revels of Easter Week. People found a simple pleasure in doing what had been forbidden under the austere code

47

of previous months. Nobody bothered any longer over the shape of a hat or the cut of a coat, and the wealthier families were able to hold parties and receptions without first having to seek police permission. Streets previously deserted long before dusk were made lively by onlookers eager to watch the carriages drive up to the Winter Palace or to catch a glimpse of their sovereign as he rode out in the dark blue uniform of the Semeonovsky. Paul had always expected dignitaries summoned to the Court to arrive on foot or, if the weather were bad, in little sledges; and he had ordered the citizens of the capital to prostrate themselves whenever their Tsar and his consort passed by. But Alexander rejected such outward manifestations of authority. He felt no need to make his subjects abase themselves in his presence: they respected him for what he was and for the promise of a new era which his accession held out for them.

The sudden exhilaration of the capital fascinated foreign observers and it was the Austrian Consul who best caught the spirit of the times. Returning to St Petersburg from Riga at the end of April after an absence of several weeks, he was amazed by the contentment and 'vivacity' he found around him and commented on the affection which his subjects felt for the new Tsar: 'People of every rank, sex and age are delighted ... to be living under ... a sovereign who is good, just, merciful and worthy of respect for showing the qualities which make a Great Monarch', he declared in a happy flow of rapturous anticipation.[2]

The Russians were asking too much from a young man of twenty-three, who had seen little of his Empire and nothing of the world beyond its frontiers. Alexander was fully aware he was expected to do great things, and he found the prospect daunting. In a proclamation issued within a few hours of his father's death he pledged himself 'to rule the people entrusted to us by Almighty God in accord with the laws and spirit of our august deceased grandmother, Catherine the Great, whose memory will ever be dear to us and to the entire fatherland.'[3] His words were greeted with enthusiasm in the streets of St Petersburg and later in Moscow. But it was easy enough to win cheers by wrapping fine abstractions in exalted language: the difficulty was to translate them into action. The men around Alexander at Court were not reformers at heart but conservative, jealously coveting privileges wrung from his grandmother in moments of weakness for the Crown and subsequently threatened by his father's arbitrary decrees. They were glad for their new sovereign to pardon those who had been unjustly disgraced in the previous reign and to rescind senseless measures of petty oppression. But Alexander knew well enough that there were limits to what they would accept as desirable for the structure of Tsardom. None of the close friends to whom he had confided his nebulous dreams of constitutional rule were in or near St Petersburg that Easter. However much he might hate Pahlen and the regicide conspirators, it was difficult for him to avoid dependence upon them. Though the people might demonstrate their loyalty and affection each time he rode through the city, Alexander and Elizabeth felt wretchedly isolated in that agonizing week and a half between Paul's murder and his burial.*

Yet, though the Palace was full of self-seekers, there were still young idealists close to the centre of affairs who believed the only logical policy for an enlightened autocrat was the abolition of autocracy itself. Ten days after Paul's death Alexander was unexpectedly made aware of their existence. Returning to the Winter Palace that night, he found someone had left upon his desk an anonymous letter, more than 2,500 words in length. He read it with elation, for it echoed sentiments he had often expressed privately to his friends in earlier years. 'Is it possible', the letter asked, for the Tsar 'to set aside the hope of nations in favour of the sheer delight of self rule? . . . No! He will at last open the book of fate which Catherine merely perceived. He will give us immutable laws. He will establish them for ever by an oath binding him to all his subjects. To Russia he will say, "Here lie the bounds to my autocratic power and to the power of those who will follow me, unalterable and everlasting".'[4]

Alexander, his nerves tense with the shock of accession, was deeply moved by this strange burst of rhetoric. Here, he felt, spoke the true voice of the Russian people. He sent at once for Dmitri Troschinsky who, as Procurator of the Senate, was principal administrative official in the Empire and ordered him to discover the identity of the person who had written the letter and to bring him to the Tsar. Since only a limited number of civil servants were permitted to enter the Tsar's apartments and leave documents on his desk, Troschinsky's task was relatively straightforward. By the following morning he was able to inform Alexander that the letter had been written by one Vassili Karazin, a twenty-eight-year-old

---

* To assist Elizabeth to recover from the shock of the events at the Mikhailovsky, Alexander invited his father-in-law and his mother-in-law to Russia. They arrived in St Petersburg on 23 July 1801, accompanied by Elizabeth's brother Charles (aged fifteen) and her sisters Amelia (twenty-four) and Marie (nineteen). The Badenese royal family remained in Russia throughout what was left of the summer, and Amelia stayed on as a companion for Elizabeth for several years. The remainder of the party travelled to Sweden in September. On 16 December Elizabeth's father died as a result of injuries received when his sledge overturned near the Swedish town of Arboga.

member of the chancery staff who held a civilian rank equivalent to a colonelcy in the army.

There followed an episode which anywhere except Russia would have seemed fantastic. When summoned to the Tsar's presence, Karazin feared a severe rebuke for his presumption. But Alexander was effusively magnanimous. He embraced Karazin warmly and commended his sense of patriotic duty. Karazin, for his part, knelt in tears at Alexander's feet, pledging his personal loyalty. Then the two men talked at length about the problems facing the Empire, of the need to safeguard the people from acts of arbitrary tyranny and to educate them so that they could assume in time the responsibilities of government. Finally Karazin swore a solemn oath that he would keep his sovereign informed of what ordinary Russian men and women were thinking. For more than three years after this first encounter, Karazin basked in the Tsar's favour, although he was never given an official appointment at Court.* He was not a popular figure with members of the nobility or the administration; advancement by means of an anonymous letter was a rare phenomenon, even in St Petersburg.[5]

Yet, whatever its consequences, the Karazin incident heartened Alexander at a moment when his spirits were low. Cautiously he summoned back the young liberal aristocrats whom Paul had banished and he sent an invitation to La Harpe in Paris to return to Russia. At the same time he took care not to rely exclusively on any particular faction. Barely a month after his accession he established a Permanent Council of state dignitaries, most of them veterans from his grandmother's reign with Troschinsky at their head. And a few weeks later Alexander announced he was setting up a committee to review the powers of the Senate, a nominated body with administrative and judicial authority originally created by Peter I in 1711 but ignored by Catherine in her last years and only partially reinstated by Paul.[6] The prospect of increased Senatorial influence pleased the landed nobility and ensured their willingness to accept Alexander's lead in any administrative reforms he might wish to impose.

The Secret Committee and its Enemies

Every person of rank in St Petersburg, whether a native-born Russian or a foreign observer, knew it was essential for Alexander to modernize

* Karazin subsequently became the first Administrative Secretary of the Directorate of Schools (established in 1803) and played a considerable part in securing governmental support for a University at Kharkov, which was opened in January 1805. He owned estates in Kharkov Province.

the institutions of his Empire: how otherwise would it be possible to meet the challenge of the new century? But there were wide differences of opinion over what should be done.[7] In 1801 Russia was a land of more than forty-one million people, half of whom were bound in some form of personal serfdom to individuals or to the State. Alexander himself had written of 'the misery and misfortune' in which 'the slave peasants' of Russia were forced to live: ought this abuse to be swept aisde before any other question was tackled? On the other hand, it could be argued that the problem of serfdom was only the most dramatic aspect of Russia's social backwardness. With less than seven out of every hundred people living in a town and with trade and commerce still predominantly in foreign hands, economic life in Russia remained primitive: ought Alexander to mobilize the material resources of his Empire and re-shape the day-to-day existence of his subjects, much as Peter the Great had sought to do a century before? But only a gifted and enlightened ruler, sure of himself and of what he wished to achieve, could prescribe so drastic a remedy. There were many in the capital who, like Karazin, believed that the first necessity was a guarantee of constitutional progress, some device by which the Tsar would recognize the political maturity of the aristocracy. For on one point only everyone was agreed: the degree of reform must depend upon Alexander's courage and foresight, and upon his willingness to break with the established order.

To bring clarity and common sense to the government of Russia had long been Alexander's cherished ambition. He was not, however, a jurist; nor had he acquired more than a superficial acquaintance with the language of political science. At times, like many of his subjects, he used a fashionable jargon which he could never fully comprehend. Popular sovereignty meant nothing to him and although he had heard of the doctrine of separation of powers he understood it to imply a mere functional division of administrative offices for the sake of convenience. He wrote and spoke of 'a constitution' but thought in terms of the rule of law rather than of a new and comprehensive ordering of society.[8] Like Bonaparte, he approached all questions of government with the mind of a soldier who was accustomed to regimentation within a recognized hierarchical system; but while Napoleon was prepared to take a personal initiative in drafting political and legal codes for France and her dependencies, Alexander lacked the qualities which would have made him a Russian Justinian. Although he buried himself in work during the spring and summer of 1801, he was too inexperienced to have real insight into his country's problems. He encouraged the discussion of administrative reform; he pleased the merchants by proposing the immediate relaxation of the high protectionist tariff of 1797 and all other trade restrictions imposed by his father; and he showed his concern for the least fortunate of his subjects by publishing a decree ordering the newspapers of St Petersburg and Moscow to abandon the practice of advertising serfs for sale. These measures were, however, only palliative gestures. Since he did not possess the patience and persistence of the enlightened reformer, fulfilment inevitably fell short of expectation. He preferred to leave the detailed mechanics of a project either to members of the Senate or to his circle of liberal-minded friends; and all too frequently their knowledge of what they were seeking to achieve went little deeper than his own.

Within a few weeks of his accession Alexander established an informal council of advisers, the *Neglassny Komitet* ('Secret Committee'), complementary to the official Permanent Council of State and to the Senatorial Committee of reform. The first meeting of the Secret Committee was held on 6 July 1801.[9] It consisted of only four members, the three friends whom Alexander had mentioned in his letter to La Harpe of October 1797 – Czartoryski, Novosiltsov and Paul Stroganov – together with Victor Kochubey (who had been abroad at that time). When La Harpe himself returned to St Petersburg in the late summer of 1801 he was sometimes consulted by the Committee and so, too, were a number of other prominent figures at Court, but only the four original members and the Tsar took part in the Committee's deliberations. Basically its meetings remained a gathering of friends. The four men would dine with Alexander and Elizabeth at irregular intervals in these first months of the reign, often twice a week. They then adjourned to a separate room for discussions where, later in the evening, Alexander would join them, occasionally listening and saying little but at other times intervening in the general exchange of ideas and projects. He had high hopes of the Secret Committee: all its members were intimates who understood his point of view and whose experience he respected; it possessed the informality of an eighteenth-century cabinet and yet (apart from Kochubey, who was placed in charge of foreign affairs in October 1801) its members had no particular ministerial responsibilities; and, unlike the Senate, it was not bound to any sectional interest by the memory of past contests for power. In 1801-2, to some extent, the Secret Committee was to Alexander what the Brain Trust became for Franklin Roosevelt a hundred and thirty years later, a body which by some mysterious collective sympathy would provide him with a new deal for the people. At the same time Alexander also expected the Secret Committee to establish guiding principles upon which foreign policy could be based throughout his reign. It was a formidable assignment for 'the Emperor's young friends', as people called them at Court.

Ultimately, of course, the task was beyond them. Most of their decisions were negative ones. They resolved that conditions in Russia were too varied for the introduction of a formal constitutional law binding in all regions, that the nobility was too selfish to be entrusted with executive power, and that serfdom was too fundamental to the Russian economy for it to be abolished in a massive social revolution, even though it was a wasteful and unproductive system. They discussed, and rejected, the idea of a unified government with a prime minister at its head; they turned down proposals from a Senatorial Commission that the Senate should become a legislative assembly and that some Senators should be elected;[10] for they knew that Alexander would never allow his autocratic prerogatives to be trimmed in order to benefit any one class or faction among his subjects. At times they found Alexander a difficult master to please. Kochubey once complained that the Tsar followed no systematic plan of action, that 'he kept knocking at every door';[11] and, after a particularly trying conference in the second week of September 1801, Paul Stroganov noted that since it was impossible to persuade Alexander by logical argument, the only way of overcoming stubborn objections to a policy was to introduce the subject in a different form on a later occasion and trust that his mood had changed.[12] Even so, they found him obstinately reluctant to authorize any major innovations. It was difficult for him to reconcile an avowed faith in constitutionalism and reform with his instinctive respect for hierarchy and order. As Czartoryski early perceived he was happiest when absorbed in the minutiae of military ceremonial: for, though he might invoke the 'dear memory' of his grandmother, he was also a son of Paul.

But these long evenings spent in discussion with his friends on the Secret Committee did more to train Alexander's mind than he acknowledged or appreciated. From the very beginning of their meetings, the four members of the Committee realized the opportunity awaiting them. In correspondence with each other – and, indeed, with Alexander himself – they maintained that their principal task was to help him discover what was the wisest policy for an enlightened autocrat to pursue. This was no fictitious convention on their part. Marginal comments each made on the others' written memoranda, together with the unofficial minutes kept by Paul Stroganov, show the extent to which they examined alternative panacea for Russia's ills.[13] They proposed remedies, but did not seek to impose them. Nor were they in a hurry to settle delicate questions: consultations over codification of the laws, for which a commission was established in the summer of 1801, were still in progress in January 1809;[14] and it was not until 1832 that the laws of Russia were at last codified. But, for Alexander, speed of decision did not matter. The Committee sessions provided him with an opportunity to think aloud: hence the need for secrecy and informality. He was not bound to act upon what he said when seated in private with his friends at the Palace.

Unfortunately not all the consequences of the Committee's meetings were of benefit to Alexander's character, nor to his method of government. Increasingly he showed an emotional and personal response to problems with which he was confronted, as though he were acting out a role for the sake of his friends. He tended, moreover, to acquire the habit of examining, at considerable length, matters great or small rather than delegate to subordinates, who could have settled affairs with less delay. As Alexander gradually grew accustomed to exercising his autocratic powers, these traits became more and more marked: they provided a poor basis for rational administration.

However some important reforms were initiated in the first years of Alexander's reign: a major change in the administrative machinery of the State; a project for a system of public education; amelioration of conditions for the serfs; and definition of the rights and duties of Senators.[15] All these developments owed much to the discussions of the Secret Committee, but their final form was shaped by others. The Tsar rejected proposals from Stroganov for partial emancipation of the serfs and from Kochubey and Czartoryski for a ban on the sale of serfs without a corresponding transfer of land to support them. On the other hand, he accepted a measure first put forward by Count Peter Rumiantsev by which landowners might voluntarily free their serfs, if they so desired; but Rumiantsev was head of a family long distinguished at Court and he was never a member of the Secret Committee. Alexander was also reluctant to put into practice the Committee's recommendations for a central executive body, an embryonic cabinet in which governmental ministers would share joint responsibility with their sovereign for a common course of action.[16] He still preferred to entrust office to men of conflicting sympathies and temperaments rather than to the representatives of any one party or faction in the capital. No doubt there was good sense in seeking a balanced administration, but at times it seemed as if Alexander favoured the conservative 'Senatorial' party. In the last resort Alexander did not dare to take the reins of government away from the old oligarchic families who had welcomed his accession as a return to the normal pattern of political life.

To see the politics of 1801–2 as an internal power game between the Secret Committee and the Senators is, however, an over-simplification. Some of the Senatorial party were as reformist in spirit as the Tsar's 'young friends', notably the Vorontsov brothers who corresponded regularly with Kochubey and Stroganov. Moreover, both groups were conscious of a threat from two opposing extremes at Court, the circle around the Dowager-Empress Marie Feodorovna, and the regicide conspirators who looked for a lead to Count von Pahlen. Ultimately, as Kochubey noted early in the reign, the more serious danger came from Marie Feodorovna whose powerful personality for a time over-shadowed Alexander, playing ominously with his doubts and hesitations.[17] But the Tsar himself was more troubled by Pahlen, for Alexander perceived easily enough that he could never keep the confidence of his subjects if they once began to see him as the mere puppet of a regicide oligarchy.

For the first three months of his reign, there was little he could do to free himself from Pahlen's over-bearing authority. Then a curious incident in June gave Alexander his opportunity. Early in the month Pahlen discovered that a priest in St Petersburg was claiming to have received a miraculous ikon from the Holy Virgin on which was inscribed the ominous threat, 'God punishes all the murderers of Paul I.' Pahlen at once interrogated the priest and had him flogged; but he maintained he was acting with Marie Feodorovna's blessing and that she, too, had experienced a spiritual revelation which cried out for vengeance. At this point Pahlen raised the question with Alexander, who found his mother already incensed by Pahlen's behaviour and demanding his dismissal. The Tsar sent a message to Pahlen asking for suggestions on how to ease the tension at Court. At once Pahlen offered to surrender all his official posts, confident that Alexander was still too inexperienced to let him go. 'That is a very good solution he has found', Alexander commented. 'Now let him make it perfect by a quick departure from the city.'[18] Within hours Pahlen was on his way to Riga. It was announced in the official gazette on 22 June that, because of ill-health, Count Pahlen had resigned and was leaving St Petersburg to seek a spell of convalescence on his estate at Eckau in Latvia. The hardy climate seems to have benefited him: he lived for another quarter of a century, but took no further part in public affairs.

Most of the other conspirators found it discreet to retire from the capital at the earliest opportunity and fade into provincial obscurity. Some were later entrusted by Alexander with high office: thus General Bennigsen, after serving a term as Governor-General of Lithuania, was appointed an army commander in 1806; while Prince Peter Volkonsky, who had taken a smaller part in the conspiracy, became an aide-de-camp to Alexander and remained a close friend for the whole of his life. But the terrible drama at the Mikhailovsky so played on Alexander's conscience that he wished, as much as possible, to avoid contact with any of the men who had plotted the palace revolution.[19] Count Panin was in a different position, for though he had first spoken to Alexander of the need to remove Paul from the throne, he had been absent from St Petersburg on the night of the murder and was less implicated than Alexander himself. Panin's father and uncle had been influential figures at Catherine II's Court and, in his desire to associate the new reign with his grandmother's achievements, Alexander turned to Panin at the beginning of April 1801 when he wished to find a respected dignitary who would take charge of foreign affairs. In practice, Panin was far too reactionary for Alexander's policy of conciliating France; and Panin, for his part, openly expressed his dislike of Alexander's 'liberal opinions or the prejudices which La Harpe inspired in his youth'.[20] By mid-summer of 1801 it had become clear that the two men were so different in temperament and attitude that they could not work together, but Panin possessed remarkable talents in organizing the routine business of a government department and it suited Alexander to retain his services until order was achieved in the diplomatic services. He remained in office until after the Tsar's coronation.

Alexander's Coronation in Moscow (September 1801)

Within the Court itself there was throughout the summer a strong desire for the Tsar to travel south to Moscow and be crowned in the old capital as soon as possible. Alexander shared this sentiment: he knew he would only be recognized as undoubted 'Emperor and Autocrat of All the Russias' when he had accomplished the elaborate ritual of coronation in the Uspensky Cathedral. Etiquette demanded the lapse of a reasonable length of time from his father's burial, but common sense dictated that the ceremony should take place before winter. Eventually it was agreed that the coronation should be celebrated in mid-September by the Russian calendar (27 September by the calendar of western Europe), and, as the first rains of autumn came to Russia, the great nobles and their retainers set off from St Petersburg for Moscow, four hundred miles away. Only four years and five months had passed since they made similar journeys for Paul's coronation.

Alexander and Elizabeth left St Petersburg on 11 September and travelled by easy stages to Novgorod and thence on to Tver.[21] As he came nearer to Moscow, however, Alexander's impatience mounted. The Imperial carriage and their escort clattered into Tver on the evening of 16 September, still a hundred miles from Moscow. To the consternation of his aides – and, indeed, of his wife – Alexander decided to snatch a hurried meal, stretch out for a couple of hours on a couch, and then resume his journey at two in the morning. His restless energy was a strain on everyone's nerves. The road was extremely primitive, little more than a dirt track, and Alexander insisted on covering the hundred miles in sixteen hours, including a break for a light meal in the afternoon. 'At dinner', wrote Elizabeth to her mother on the following morning, 'we were able to have a quick wash, of which we had a great need for I believe I have never been so filthy in my life. During all the journey we raised a frightful cloud of dust.'[22] At six in the evening of 17 September Alexander and Elizabeth reached the Petrovsky Palace, on the north-western approaches to Moscow. There, in the neo-classical elegance of one of Catherine's later palaces, they rested for three days before making their solemn entry into the old capital. Even Elizabeth was puzzled why her husband should have been in such a hurry; but it was not the last time that he forced his horses to be driven recklessly for no logical reason, a spontaneous gust of temperament governing his senses.

The coronation ceremonies of the Tsars always emphasized the close relationship between ecclesiastical authority and secular sovereignty in 'Holy Russia'. For nearly four centuries Moscow had been accorded a unique status as the repository of the soul of Russian Orthodoxy, a national shrine to millions of devout believers. In 1801 Moscow was still a city of glittering domes and cupolas, its streets filled with the constant pealing of church-bells; one man in every fifty of its inhabitants was a priest, and there were more basilicas within its walls than in Rome.[23] But the city was not only a spiritual centre: it was the traditional home of the Tsars and the solemn entry of a new sovereign through the Tver Gate and down the long avenue to the Kremlin was a moment of deep significance for each of his subjects, an assertion of continuity between the heritage of Muscovy and the empire which Peter had created from his artificial capital in the Northern marshes. Hence, although the climax to the ceremonies was the formal act of crowning within the Uspensky

Cathedral, the coronation was preceded by a week of elaborate spectacle hallowed for every true Russian by history and convention.

For Alexander the ceremonies began on Sunday, 20 September, when he left the Petrovsky Palace and rode slowly astride a white horse along a four-mile route to the Kremlin. It was a gloriously fine autumnal day and the city streets were filled with thousands of people, who knelt and made the sign of the cross in blessing as their 'Little Father', their 'Dear Angel', passed before them. Some tried to kiss his riding boots or even, very dangerously, the legs of his horse. He acknowledged their devotion as though in a dream, a carved smile lighting his face with the spirituality of an idol. Ahead of him rode the cavalry of the Guard regiments, their horses caparisoned in red and gold, and the nobility of Moscow wearing braided costumes far older in cut than anyone would see in Petersburg. The Empress Elizabeth followed her husband in a golden coach drawn by eight greys: she was less at ease than Alexander, perhaps because she could not identify herself as he could with Moscow's deep sense of the past. The coach reminded her of a lantern on wheels and she felt slightly ridiculous as it trundled her slowly into the city with four small pages perched precariously on the coach-board facing her. But, apart from the formal procession into the city, the day's events were not unduly taxing. The Imperial couple entered the principal cathedrals and churches, kissed the sacred ikons and took up residence in the Slobodsky Palace. There were more exhausting occasions ahead.[24]

Throughout the following week there was a succession of banquets and solemn receptions, and both Alexander and Elizabeth were thankful for each day's task completed. The Tsar's training in self-control and his gift in dissimulation enabled him to greet people with an open affability on which they commented with extravagant warmth – 'the cloudless sun of his smile', 'the coming of Spring casting from the mind the dark anguish of Winter.'[25] Elizabeth, who had been unhappy in Moscow during Paul's coronation festivities, was not at ease with the gentry of the old capital: 'Not knowing their names or their families, I am hard-pressed what to say', she confessed to her mother after the first big reception; and she added that she had been happier dining with the Governor-General of Moscow, 'the greater part of his circle being from Petersburg'.[26] By the end of the week she was complaining, too, of the 'constant moving around': three nights when they arrived from Tver at the Petrovsky, five nights in the Slobodsky, five more in the Imperial apartments of the Kremlin, and then the prospect of returning to the Slobodsky for the remainder of their stay in the city.[27] The truth was that both husband and wife were beginning to suffer from intensive stage-fright as the protracted theatricals of the Moscow visit approached their climax. Czartoryski wrote later that 'the young and handsome couple who were to be crowned did not look happy', and he added that Alexander 'had never more strongly felt remorse at having contributed, against his intentions, to his father's death.'[28] The Act of Succession, which Paul had issued on his coronation day, was preserved in a casket among the holy relics behind the altar-screen of the Uspensky, and Alexander felt his father's spiritual presence around him in the Kremlin. At times the burden of self-criticism drove him to tears; and on this occasion his wife was little comfort to him, for on the very eve of the coronation she was forced to retire to her room with 'a bilious fever'.[29] The thought of the five-hour religious ceremony was agony to both of them.

The weather remained fine for coronation day itself.[30] Heralds rode through the streets soon after dawn proclaiming that this day – Sunday, 27 September 1801 – an Emperor would be crowned within the city. Tables spread with food and drink for the townsfolk were set up along the thoroughfare from the Krasnyia Gate through the poorer districts to the Nikolsky Gate in the Kremlin wall; but few of the ordinary people saw anything of the ceremony itself. Alexander and Elizabeth were robed in their apartments and passed in procession through the Hall of St Vladimir, with its black and red silk banners, to the 'Beautiful Stairs' – often translated as 'Red Staircase' – where briefly their subjects could see them beneath a golden baldichino as they moved slowly to the porch of the Uspensky Cathedral, less than a hundred yards away. The atmosphere within the church was heavy with centuries of accumulated piety, reflected candlelight flickering mysteriously from frescoes around the walls and ceiling, catching the jewels of the ikonostasis and the gold of vestments and banners. Alexander was escorted by the higher church dignitaries past a raised dais in the nave to a throne encrusted with nearly a thousand precious stones; and Elizabeth was seated beside him on an ivory throne, originally carved for the daughter of the last Byzantine Emperor. Although Metropolitan Platon of Moscow presided over the Liturgy, the Tsars by tradition were not mere recipients in their coronation service. It was Alexander who said the Orthodox Confession and who knelt on his knees to pray aloud for his empire and his subjects. After being anointed with Holy Oil by the Metropolitan, Alexander swore a solemn oath to preserve the integrity of the Russian lands and the sacred concept of autocracy; and he was then permitted, as one blessed by God, to pass through the Royal Doors into the Sanctuary where the Tsars had, on this one occasion of their lives, the privilege of administering to themselves the Holy Sacrament. But Alexander felt unworthy to exercise the priestly office in this way; and, as Platon offered him the chalice, he knelt to receive communion as a member of the laity. Although only the higher clergy and their acolytes witnessed this gesture of humility, it was soon known in the city at large and created a deep impression of the new Tsar's sense of spiritual discipline.[31]

At last the Metropolitan led Alexander back from the Sanctuary and up to the coronation platform. He handed him the Imperial crown made originally for his grandmother in 1762. Alexander lifted the crown and held it high for a moment, a nine-pound weight of gold and diamonds. Then he lowered it firmly on his head. He next crowned Elizabeth and when sovereign and consort had received the Metropolitan's blessing, they returned to their thrones and accepted homage from the members of the Imperial family. Finally they were robed in special vestments of rich brocade, escorted back up the Beautiful Stairs and formally presented to the people, to whom they bowed three times in honour of the Trinity. At once the bells of the Kremlin towers and the ceremonial roar of cannon let Moscow, and all the countryside around, know that Alexander was, indeed, the crowned Emperor and Autocrat of All the Russias.

The Imperial couple remained in Moscow for a full month after the coronation ceremony. There were banquets for several hundred guests, masked balls to attend, a huge open-air feast for the townsfolk, plays, concerts and military parades. Now that the most solemn purpose of the visit was safely accomplished Alexander's spirits began to rise. His good humour spread to all his attendants and friends, so that they commented on the change of mood as though it were a transition from Lent to Easter. To some it seemed as if he were already ensnared by the charms of Maria Naryshkin, a sultry Polish-born Countess who pursued him relentlessly from one social evening to another, and it is probable that her predatory activities account, in part, for Elizabeth's weariness with Moscow.[32] But much of Alexander's high spirits were spontaneous, he always enjoyed a waltz and the polonaise, even the restrained orderliness of a quadrille. So, one suspects, did Elizabeth for, although she continued to complain of having to go to 'ball after ball', her letters listed the delights of the various entertainments: at Madame Apraxine's there were few people present and one could dance freely; so one could, too, at Count Saltykov's, though the company was duller; and at Count Chremetiev's villa, two miles beyond the city limits, there were fireworks and illuminations; while there was another nobleman – unspecified, and therefore presumably anxious for recognition – who was organizing an afternoon horse race, a novelty which Elizabeth was determined not to miss.[33]

But not all the events of the coronation visit were frivolous. On the eve of their eighth wedding anniversary Alexander and Elizabeth went on a pilgrimage to the shrine of St Sergius at the Troitsa Monastery, forty miles from Moscow on the road to Yaroslavl; and there was another day when the Imperial couple had a chance to distribute gifts to the foundlings of the city. Moreover, by tradition, the coronation was a moment for bestowing titles, gifts, and land on faithful courtiers; but Alexander gave only a few honours and refused to hand over Crown peasants in serfdom to the nobility and gentry who had given him their support. Though he might not be sure how to remedy the miseries of serfdom, at least he was determined that the institution should not be allowed to grow while he was on the throne. In a negative way, his decision was a portent. The landowners were not sure how to interpret it; and there were many at the coronation who looked in surprise at the medal they were given for their services. On one side it showed Alexander's profile, austerely proud as a Roman Emperor, and on the obverse was engraved a pillar, bearing the word 'Law', surmounted by a replica of the coronation crown and the inscription 'Such is the guarantee of universal happiness.'[34] It could mean much, or nothing: who was there to read the young Tsar's mind?

The Moscow visit outlasted autumn. Rain swept in from the east and with it the threat of sleet and snow. At last, on Tuesday, 27 October, the Imperial calvalcade set out along the road towards Tver and the northern capital. The route, which had been dry and dusty six weeks before, was now thick with mud. It made no difference to Alexander's madcap haste. 'The Emperor was absolutely determined to complete the journey in less than five days', wrote Elizabeth afterwards; and in consequence they had only a few hours' sleep on the first two nights and drove throughout the fourth, arriving in St Petersburg late on the Saturday evening. They were mud-stained and exhausted, relieved (as Elizabeth said) to have a moment to clean their teeth – but they were thoroughly happy in laughing at the misfortunes they had brought on themselves.[35] For, though he was now crowned sovereign of the largest empire in the world, Alexander was still some weeks short of his twenty-fourth birthday; and, despite Countess Naryshkin, Elizabeth at twenty-three remained his chief companion and sole confidante.

4

'The Emperor wants it Thus'

Foreign Affairs: Isolation or Alignment?

Alexander returned to St Petersburg with a new sense of elation and inner confidence. During the summer of 1801 people had noticed how, from time to time, he would appear distracted, walking diffidently with stumbling steps: now, in November, he strode rapidly, shook hands with an iron grip and looked as if he had a purpose in all he was doing.[1] It was not difficult to find a reason for this change of mood. The coronation ceremonies were safely behind him and he had seen for himself the depth and warmth of his subjects' loyalties. They received him as a sovereign in his own right, not as a usurper or a parricide. For the first time since his accession Alexander could convince himself that his father's ghost was laid. Cautiously he was beginning to assert his individuality. A week before leaving Moscow he granted Count Panin three years' leave of absence 'for reasons of health', thus freeing the administration from the last of the men who had conspired against Paul. For, though he might wish to modify the structure of government, Alexander was determined to exercise his absolute will over questions which – as he said later – 'sovereigns alone are capable of deciding'.[2] Foremost among such matters was the conduct of international affairs. With Panin 'resting' on his estate at Marfino, the Tsar would find it easier to make his début on the diplomatic stage.

Yet at first it was by no means clear what role he should play. When

Paul was murdered the war of the Second Coalition, which had begun two years before with Suvorov's remarkable performance on the battlefields of Lombardy, was dragging its way through an inconclusive final act. French victories against the Austrians at Marengo and Hohenlinden re-established Napoleon's mastery of northern Italy by the end of 1800 and forced the Austrians to sue for peace; and Paul himself, in the closing months of his reign, was co-operating with Denmark, Sweden and Prussia in a League of Armed Neutrality, a combination calculated to put pressure on the British in northern Germany and the Baltic. But this alignment was short-lived. Five days after Paul's murder the British naval action against the Danish fleet at Copenhagen led to the dissolution of the League and intensified the desire of the new Tsar's advisers to reach an understanding with Addington's Government in London (which had itself already approached the French with an offer to open negotiations for a general peace settlement). There were accordingly four courses of action open to Alexander: he could work closely with the French; he could ally with the British; he could offer his services as a general mediator in Europe's affairs; or he could ignore the disputes and rivalries of other Powers and concentrate on domestic reform in a golden era of peace for his Empire. Each of these possibilities had supporters in St Petersburg, and until after his coronation Alexander continued to hesitate over which course to pursue.

So long as Panin remained in effective control of Russian policy, it was the Anglophile party which flourished. The British ambassador, Lord St Helens, found Panin agreeable company and the British Foreign Secretary, Lord Hawkesbury, even induced King George III to send a friendly letter to the new Tsar.[3] Since most disputes between Britain and Russia arose from the attempts of the Royal Navy to maintain a blockade of France and her dependencies, it was not difficult to reach an understanding. The Anglo-Russian Convention of June 1801 duly ended all immediate risk of hostilities in the Baltic. But Alexander, despite the gracious words of His Britannic Majesty, was less inclined than Panin to be conciliatory. He did not trust the British, especially after the raid on Copenhagen, and much that Consul Bonaparte was achieving in France appealed to his own political instincts. Provided Napoleon had no territorial ambitions in the Balkans or the eastern Mediterranean, Alexander could see no reason for a clash of interests between France and Russia. The Emperor's 'young friends' on the Secret Committee agreed in general with him rather than with Panin, and when Alexander discussed foreign affairs with them during the late summer of 1801, they received the impression that he favoured settling differences with France as a preliminary to a policy of passive isolation.[4] As St Helens wrote to Hawkesbury shortly before Alexander's departure for Moscow, 'The members of the Emperor's Council, with whom he is particularly connected ... have been ... zealous in promoting the intended peace with France, it being their professed System to endeavour to disengage the Emperor from all foreign Concerns ... and induce him to direct his principal attention to the Affairs of the Interior.'[5]

The events of the following month appeared to confirm the ambassador's analysis. At the end of the first week in October a treaty was signed by Russia and France in Paris which formally restored peace between the two countries: the French recognized Russia's interest in the eastern Mediterranean and conceded the principle that Alexander should be consulted over re-shaping the territorial boundaries of the German states.[6] When, a few days later, it was announced that Panin would retire to his estates and hand over responsibility for the conduct of foreign affairs to Prince Kochubey, most of the diplomats in St Petersburg believed the Tsar and his minister would pursue a simple policy of external peace and internal reform. They were convinced that 'this zealous and talented nobleman', with his knowledge of Europe and understanding of his sovereign, would be the real arbiter of Russian policy for several years ahead.[7]

So, indeed, thought Kochubey himself, even though he insisted he would rather have concentrated on administrative reform than on the frustrations of diplomacy. But Kochubey and the ambassadors underestimated Alexander. He was outwardly so full of charm and good intentions, so often lost in the enthusiasms and uncertainties of a protracted adolescence, that it seemed impossible he should seek to rule as an autocrat. Yet increasingly in the winter of 1801–2 the Tsar was behaving as though he were his own foreign minister. By the Spring his interest in European affairs was sufficiently marked for him to spurn the advice of the Secret Committee. Paul Stroganov noted on 28 March that Alexander 'appeared very determined in his outlook' and a week later there was a head-on clash between the Tsar and his friends, with Alexander actually proposing that Russia should seek to weave a network of alliances rather than isolate herself from what was taking place in western and central Europe.[8]

Kochubey was puzzled. The Secret Committee tended privately to blame Marie Feodorovna for any intractable mood on the part of her son, who made a point of dining with his mother once a week during the first winter of his reign;[9] and no doubt at times her iron hostility to the new men entered into his soul. But there was another reason for Alexander's attitude. On his return from Moscow the Tsar received a letter from King Frederick William III of Prussia proposing that the two monarchs might meet and discuss the affairs of the German states and central Europe.[10] Early in the New Year the King repeated his suggestion and invited Alexander to come to Prussia; and on 8 February the Tsar sent Frederick William a personal note in which he made it clear that he would welcome a meeting of this kind.[11] Alexander did not inform Kochubey of his correspondence with the King until the middle of April, when it was far too late for any change to be made in the arrangements, and the Secret Committee only heard of the projected meeting a few days before the Tsar's departure. Understandably Kochubey was angry: 'Imagine a minister for foreign affairs who had no knowledge at all of this escapade', he wrote in a private letter to Simon Vorontsov, the ambassador in London.[12] And, although both Kochubey and Novosiltsov accompanied Alexander when he crossed the frontier to meet Frederick William III at Memel, he made it embarrassingly clear to both of them who was in the saddle. It was rare for a Tsar and Autocrat of All the Russias to undertake a state visit: on such an occasion Alexander reckoned he should seek advice from neither friends nor ministers.

Although Alexander had never met Frederick William or his consort Queen Louise, there was already a close friendship between the royal families of Berlin and St Petersburg. Alexander's second sister, Helen, had married the Prince of Mecklenburg-Schwerin and the young couple often visited Berlin, where Helen was a particular favourite of both the King and the Queen. Helen had encouraged Alexander to go to Memel, convinced that her brother and Frederick William were kindred spirits. Politically a meeting made good sense to both sovereigns: each was concerned over Napoleon's encroachments on central Europe; Alexander rated highly the Prussian army; and Frederick William believed the Tsar had some influence on Napoleon because of the clause in the Franco-Russian Treaty of the previous October which placed the two emperors on an equal footing if it were necessary for outsiders to mediate on the future of the German lands. But ultimately the question of 'joint mediation' proved far less important than the personal consequences of this first meeting between the Tsar and the Prussian King and Queen.

Alexander arrived at Memel on 10 June and spent nearly a week there.[13] Although it was only a few miles from his own Lithuanian territories, the town possessed a special fascination for Alexander on these long summer days. Never before had he been guest at a foreign Court, and the Prussians did all they could to flatter his vanity. Every evening there was a ball, at which he danced with the beautiful Queen who was twenty-one months his senior. He enjoyed flirting with Louise, and she for her part was over-whelmed with admiration for his kindness and nobility. Alexander was impressed by all he saw but especially by the army, the Potsdam regiments marching and counter-marching on the parade ground with that rigid precision which poor Paul had once tried to impose on his own Guard battalions. To Kochubey's alarm it seemed almost as if Alexander were assuming the character of his father, impatient and short-tempered when he was not with his host and hostess, endlessly fussing over the trivia of uniforms and military decorations. The air was heavy with faint echoes of old triumphs and half-forgotten conflicts: each morning the Tsar of Russia would ride out beside the King of Prussia deep in conversation, the grandson of Catherine II and the great-nephew of Frederick II holding forth on soldiery and politics, determining the fate of a continent in their saddle-talk as though they, rather than Bonaparte, were the true masters of the central European plain. 'The two sovereigns settled matters person-ally', wrote Kochubey four days after reaching Memel, and he added wryly, 'In such a state of affairs, I am often reduced to silence.'[14]

But what matters could they settle? French military successes ensured it was in Paris that the map-makers would first outline the new frontiers of Europe, not in Berlin or St Petersburg, and certainly not in remote Memel. All that the two sovereigns could decide was how to assert claims based on past habits of thought in a revolutionary era. Inevitably they exaggerated their own influence and minimized the awe in which others held the First Consul. So pleased was Alexander with the attentions paid to him at Memel that he would certainly have championed Prussia's claims to leader-ship in Germany, had Napoleon been prepared to listen to him. But, as yet, nobody except Frederick William especially wished to consult a young and inexperienced Tsar of Russia. The other German Princes preferred to settle directly with Napoleon, as he had always anticipated that they would do; and in consequence the original formula of 'joint mediation' became a simple process by which the Russians were invited to approve what the French had already determined to impose. In time, Alexander came to resent such treatment by the French and rejected a policy which required Russia to encourage others to shore up the Bonaparte State. But in 1802 he still hoped Russia and Prussia could enjoy freedom of ma-noeuvre within the new European order; and the tearful leavetaking of the two sovereigns on 16 June made it easy for him to believe that the pleasan-tries of Memel would possess a lasting significance.

So, indeed, they did. A commemorative medal, struck in honour of the visit, showed on one side the Emperor and the King in profile and, on the obverse, two hands clasped in eternal friendship.[15] In later years Alexander looked back with affection on the warmth of Frederick William's companionship and the limpid beauty of Queen Louise recollected in tranquillity, and there is no doubt that the Tsar's emotional response to political questions afforded Prussia generous treatment. But these imponderables lay in the future, and when he arrived back in St Petersburg Alexander found there were those who questioned the value of his trip to Memel.[16] His actions won warm approval from Marie Feodorovna, to whom so close a bond between Russia and Prussia appeared almost as a diplomatic triumph from beyond the grave. Others in the capital were less happy. The Empress Elizabeth, with family attachments to Baden, did not welcome the prospect of close collaboration with Prussia (nor, one suspects, was she pleased at the constant eulogies of Prussia's Queen). Kochubey was anxious to prevent Alexander abandoning his self-imposed obligations as an impartial umpire of Europe's affairs, and Czartoryski's Polish patriotism made him distrust all signs of cordiality between the Romanov and Hohenzollern dynasties. The Tsar, on his return to the capital, was ready with assurances of good intent: he insisted to Kochubey that he would not sign any Russo-Prussian alliance nor become an active participant in the European squabbles.[17] Yet by now the honeymoon period of the reign was over; Kochubey was far from convinced Alexander was keeping faith with his professed principles.

At the end of July the Foreign Minister was even contemplating resignation. He found that Alexander would give him orders which he was expected to execute without disputing their wisdom or timing. 'I am reduced to saying "The Emperor wants it thus",' he explained in a private letter. 'And to the question "Why?" I am forced to reply, "I know nothing about it – such is his supreme will."'[18] Although Alexander still retained at Court the pleasant informality of manner which so marked off his reign from that of his father, after fifteen months on the throne he was hardly less autocratic than Paul had been. The growing resemblance between Alexander and his father was ominous. So, too, was the Tsar's failure to invite the Secret Committee to resume its meetings in the Palace.

Governmental Reform and the Primacy of Vorontsov

It was, however, at this very moment when Alexander appeared to be turning his back on domestic reform that plans were completed for the establishment of a new bureaucratic system in Russia. A decree published in the Tsar's name on 20 September 1802 set up eight government departments, Foreign Affairs, War, the Admiralty, the Interior, Finance, Justice, Commerce and Education.[19] Each department was to be headed by a minister and a deputy minister appointed by the sovereign and directly responsible to him. Proposals for governmental reform had, of course, long been in the air and the September Decree was less revolutionary than the scheme discussed by the Secret Committee and by the Senatorial Commission in the previous year; it made, however, for more orderly administration, at least on paper. Detailed regulations subsequently set out the organization and procedure of each of these new departments, sometimes with admirable clarity but occasionally with an impracticable precision which only converted chaos into confusion. Some aspects of life in Russia benefited considerably from the reform: the Ministry of Education established a Directorate of Schools which set up a surprisingly effective system of instruction in the larger cities and, during 1803 and 1804, founded universities at Dorpat, Kazan, Kharkov and Vilna; and in the Ministry of the Interior matters of public welfare were entrusted to a young and able departmental executive, Michael Speransky, who was soon to achieve greater distinction than any of the ministers whom he served. But several government departments were so hide-bound with convention that they fitted awkwardly into the new system: chief among these was the Ministry of War, an institution over-burdened with Generals and over-shadowed by the Tsar himself.

The September Decree also established a Committee of Ministers.[20] Although purely an advisory body and not an embryonic cabinet on the British model, the Committee served as a convenient centre for discussion. Normally its sessions were presided over by the Tsar, who intended the Committee to be a means of co-ordinating policy while avoiding all notions of collective responsibility. Originally Alexander took the work of the Committee of Ministers seriously; he insisted that it should meet frequently, and he attended all but three of the sixty-five sessions held in the first fifteen months of the Committee's existence. He gave orders that the ministers should come together at five in the afternoon on every Tuesday and Friday and that he should receive an agenda on the morning of every day the Committee was to sit. This, of course, was far too rigid and exacting a plan to be effective. Ministers began to suggest to Elizabeth and others at Court that the Tsar was working too hard; and in due course they approached Alexander himself. By the end of 1804 his enthusiasm for the Committee was on the wane; and in the following year it met no more than sixteen times, with Alexander present at only the first four sessions.

To a limited extent the Tuesday and Friday meetings of the Committee of Ministers provided Alexander with a safety-valve for his autocratic inclinations. But otherwise the value of the Committee's work during these years is questionable. By temperament Alexander was able to co-operate closely only with one individual at a time and he was therefore unsuited to preside over any council, least of all one in which he was seeking to keep a balance of interests between 'conservatives' and 'liberals'. Alexander was also suspicious of any potential challenge to his prerogatives, especially one caused by excessive reliance on a single minister or adviser. In consequence, the principal power game within the Committee consisted of attempts to alert the Tsar to the alleged pretensions of the favoured man of the moment. It was a game which broadened rather than narrowed the differences between the political factions, and it could hardly help the Committee to become an efficient instrument of government.

The September Decree had the incidental effect of providing Kochubey with an opportunity to leave the Foreign Ministry with dignity. In the reshuffling of governmental responsibilities Alexander appointed him as Minister of the Interior and assigned him another member of the Secret Committee, Paul Stroganov, as a deputy. The Tsar turned, for a new Foreign Minister, to Count Alexander Vorontsov, a sexagenarian who began his diplomatic career forty years before when he presented his credentials as ambassador to the young George III in London. Subsequently he had gained considerable experience of administrative problems during the reign of Catherine II; and more recently his wise moderation in the Senate had earned him respect from the younger generation, even though Vorontsov outwardly possessed more of the attributes and graces of an elder statesman than any other leader of the Russian nobility.[21]

It was an interesting appointment. At times Vorontsov seemed almost a Whig in his sympathies. In the summer of 1801 he had been principal sponsor of a draft 'Charter for the Russian People' which he had wished Alexander to publish in Moscow on coronation day as a pledge of liberal reform.[22] The Tsar, after sounding out the Secret Committee, had declined so radical a break with tradition but he held the Count in deep respect and, when he proposed that Vorontsov should become Foreign Minister, he coupled the offer with a promise of the rank of State Chancellor. Such a title was only rarely accorded to those who supervised the diplomatic activities of the Empire, and the foreign community in St Petersburg assumed that its bestowal proved the Tsar's concern to magnify Russia's status as a European Power.

There was, however, little likelihood of the new Chancellor becoming a Russian Richelieu or a Kaunitz. Age and temperament inhibited Vorontsov from initiating a positive policy of his own; had it been otherwise Alexander would hardly have appointed him. For, though Vorontsov was an unconventional representative of the landowning class within Russia, the changes he had witnessed in the relative status of other governments made him look upon European affairs with caution and distrust. He knew Russia could not face a major campaign abroad so long as her economy depended on free passage of the Baltic and he shared many of the instinctive doubts of his predecessor, Kochubey. Indeed there was no real change in policy, although Vorontsov's years of office under Catherine enabled him to handle her grandson with greater tact. Everyone in St Petersburg looked upon Vorontsov as an Anglophile but he never listened so readily to the British as his brother, Simon, ambassador in London and close confidant of the younger Pitt. If forced to choose between alliance with Napoleon or George III or Frederick William of Prussia, then he would opt for the British connection before any other. He preferred, however, to steer clear of foreign entanglements and, soon after becoming Chancellor, declined to respond to tentative proposals from London for a closer understanding on future policy. Alexander did not always agree with Vorontsov any more than he had with his predecessor, but he treated his judgements with greater respect. Privately the Tsar preferred to work with the man whom he had appointed as Vorontsov's deputy, Adam Czartoryski; but he was well aware of the hostility which the continued presence of a Polish Prince at Court aroused among many of the older landed nobility; and it suited Alexander to have a respected Russian nobleman as the formal head of the Foreign Ministry, even if his achievements in office belied his reputation.[23]

The beginning of Vorontsov's Chancellorship in the autumn of 1802 coincided with the first respite from war which Europe had enjoyed for a decade. In March 1802 the Treaty of Amiens ended open hostilities between France and Britain while three months later peace was concluded between France and her forgotten enemy, Turkey. For a few months Europe seemed strangely normal. The British flocked to Paris, with the more adventurous spirits travelling farther east, crossing the Rhine to the German cities and Vienna, and some even reaching St Petersburg. The Russian aristocracy, too, found it easier to move freely on the continent now the armies were no longer on the march. Thus, at the very moment when Alexander and his ministers were committed to an isolationist policy, the European Courts and capitals were drawing closer together than they had been since the downfall of the French monarchy in 1792. But, as diplomats and travellers alike soon perceived, it was easier to silence the guns than make peace. The problems of Germany and Italy, the future of Malta (held since 1800 by the British, but promised to be restored to the Knights of St John), and the uncertain fate of distant colonies testified to the hollowness of treaty obligations. By the closing months of 1802 it was clear the contest between the Powers would soon be resumed. In each of the European chancelleries the diplomats began to assess the prospects of keeping out of war; and most of them found the outlook gloomy.[24]

Even had he wished to do so, Alexander could not ignore the succession of crises in Europe. The French had treated Russia with scant respect since the conclusion of the Peace Treaty of Paris in October 1801, and scoffed at Memel and its display of sentimental diplomacy. But when the details of the new German settlement were ready for presentation to the Austrians at the end of 1802, the French found they needed Russian support in order to persuade Emperor Francis in Vienna to accept such a diminution of the traditional Habsburg rights. Alexander, for his part, was prepared to follow the French lead in such matters: he asked only that Napoleon would treat generously German Princes who had close dynastic links with Russia and show sympathy for the rulers of states to whom Russia had assumed especial obligations. This, of course, was a tall order. Napoleon was willing for Elizabeth's homeland, Baden, to receive the towns of Heidelberg and Mannheim and he also gave additional territory (and a new Electoral dignity) to Alexander's first cousin, Frederick of Württemberg; but he was not inclined to admit that the Tsar had any right to protect the interests of Sardinia (whose sovereign had once been his father's ally) nor to concern himself with the affairs of Switzerland out of loyalty to an ex-tutor.[25] Moreover, the Russians continued to show what was to the French a tiresome obsession with the Mediterranean. Napoleon, like everybody in Europe, was puzzled at Alexander's attitude over Malta. Since the Knights of St John had conferred the Grand Mastership of their order on his father, Alexander claimed to be the rightful protector both of the Knights and their island. At first, the Maltese Question brought France and Russia closer together, for it was in both their interests to encourage Britain to evacuate the island. But in the first weeks of 1803 there were widespread reports of intrigues by French agents in the Levant and in the Balkans. The possibility that Napoleon might be about to embark on a forward policy in regions to which Russia was so sensitive induced Alexander and Vorontsov to modify their original attitude over Malta: better the British stay in the island than that it should become the advanced base for a second French expedition to the East.[26]

In England the rumours of a Franco-Russian rift over Mediterranean questions encouraged the critics of the Peace of Amiens. Already, at the Foreign Office, Lord Hawkesbury was thinking in terms of a new defensive coalition of Russia, Austria and Britain. This optimism was, however, premature. Whatever views Simon Vorontsov might express at the embassy in London, his brother the Chancellor was still hesitant about involving Russia in a major land campaign, and when war was resumed between Britain and France in May 1803, Tsar Alexander was angered by a new series of naval incidents in the Baltic.[27] By now, however, Alexander accepted the fact that he might have to abandon the principle of passive isolation. He was ready to pursue a vigorous foreign policy, although he was uncertain how or when he should intervene and whether he should concentrate on neutralizing Napoleon or on building up a powerful combination against him. All the Tsar wished was assurance that, should war come, the Russian army would be able to hold its own against the inspired soldiery of the Bonapartist levies. No one, unfortunately, could offer him encouragement from among the senior commanders: the army seemed short of muskets, short of cannon, short of ideas, and even short of men.

In Alexander's judgement there was one person capable of knocking the army into shape; and this was his old companion-in-arms, Alexei Arakcheev. Since October 1799 Arakcheev had remained on his estate at Gruzino, some eighty miles south-east of the capital. It was there, on 9 May 1803, that he received a message from the Tsar: 'Alexei Andreevich, I need you and I ask you to come to St Petersburg.'[28] Within a few days the General was back in the capital, still wearing the pattern of uniform laid down in Paul's regulations and with his hair knotted above the neck in the Gatchina fashion of old. His arrival caused consternation among the liberals. Discreet approaches were made to the Tsar in the hope he might be dissuaded from reinstating a man so closely associated with the tyranny of the previous reign. To Alexander, however, Arakcheev remained the friend who had once initiated him into the mysteries of garrison duty and the Prussian drill code. It was as natural for him, when faced by a military problem, to turn to Arakcheev for guidance as it was for him to look to La Harpe in constitutional matters. Once Alexander made up his mind that Arakcheev could bring order and efficiency into the training and preparation of an army for battle, nothing would prevent him from summoning the General back to active service. On 26 May he informed Arakcheev that he was appointing him Inspector-General of Artillery. It would be his prime task to build up gunnery and establish effective systems of supply and command, travelling through the Empire spurring on casual officers as he had once done the Tavrichesky Grenadiers at Kovno. If it came to war with Napoleon – the greatest artillery commander of his age – the concentrated fire-power of the French would be answered, not by horsemen and infantry with guns in support, but by new regiments and the heavy cannon from the Tula Arms Works, provided always that Arakcheev had time to accomplish his task before the muster-drums began to roll once more.

Alexander, Elizabeth and Maria Naryshkin

Throughout the winter of 1802–3 and the following summer Alexander was increasingly concerned with military affairs and the problems of a grand European policy. His zest for the social life of St Petersburg flagged: the Empress had considerable difficulty in inducing him to participate in the Carnival balls and theatrical presentations preceding the Lenten abstinence of 1803; and, when he attended any major Society occasion, he continued to complain afterwards how tedious he had found it – 'All the next day I have to listen to his self-pity for having been there', wrote Elizabeth to her mother on 26 February.[29] Unfortunately, it was a year which required a special effort, for in May the city of St Petersburg celebrated its centenary with a combination of ceremonial pomp and popular rejoicing, which continued through much of the summer. There was a long *Te Deum* in the Isaac Cathedral on 28 May, followed by a grand parade in which regiment after regiment filed past the Tsar as he stood beside Falconet's statue of Peter the Great; and at night the city was illuminated, while Society amused itself with masked balls, with concerts and private theatrical performances.[30] There was a carnival atmosphere, too, for the general populace including a fashionable diversion which invariably caused wonder, the ascent from the centre of Petersburg of an air balloon. Yet, though willing enough to take the salute from his Guards or from one or other of the military academies, Alexander did not share the festive spirit. The self-assurance he had shown after the coronation was dissipated. Once more he was sunk in youthful melancholy, as in the black days which followed his father's murder. Then he had at least found consolation with Elizabeth. Now she sensed he was turning away from her. As she confessed in a letter to her mother that spring, life was fast becoming 'an endless winter'.[31]

The truth was that Alexander could no longer summon the will-power to fight against his infatuation with Countess Maria Naryshkin, the Polish-born beauty who had attracted him two years previously in Moscow. At the end of 1801 affection for Elizabeth – together, one suspects, with awareness of the political inconvenience of a Polish mistress – led him to break formally with the Countess. One of the chamberlains of the Court conveyed to her a final message of renunciation.[32] But it was difficult for Alexander to avoid meeting a vivacious and designing character who was married to one of the wealthiest men in the capital; and he probably did not try very hard. Maria Naryshkin was certainly no ordinary courtesan. By 1803 Society was already calling her 'the Aspasia of the North', a title which flattered her wit and culture and, indeed, her companion's gifts of statesmanship. For though in later years there were some who hailed Alexander as the new Agamemnon, it was hard to see him as Pericles. His love for Maria Naryshkin was in a lower key. The complexities of government, the failure of Elizabeth to provide him with an heir, the amorous vagaries of his brother Constantine, possibly even the growing authority within his counsels of the Pole, Czartoryski – all these influences and others, too, prompted Alexander to turn more and more to the passionate Maria for sensual satisfaction.

In that spring of 1803 Alexander would slip away again and again to her palace by the Fontanka Canal and in the summer evenings he followed her to a villa on the islands. She had the power to indulge the coquetries and caprices of a siren and always found ways of attracting those whom she wished to bemuse. Sometime that July she became pregnant and, with heartless lack of compassion, flaunted herself before Elizabeth, not disguising the fatherhood of the child she was expecting. Perhaps she believed Alexander would induce the Orthodox hierarchy to annul his marriage and her own marriage, and make her his wife and Empress. But, if she did so dream, she failed to understand the complexities of Tsardom or the ties which still bound sovereign and consort.[33]

No one in St Petersburg was shocked or surprised that the Tsar should have a recognized mistress, least of all his mother, who had always tended to treat Paul's courtesans as personal friends and companions, if he would permit her to do so. But Elizabeth was in a different position: she had no surviving children of her own; she remained a lonely un-Russian figure, never entirely assimilating the ways of her country of adoption; she was constantly upstaged by the Dowager Empress, to whom Court etiquette assigned precedence at every public occasion; and, above all, she continued to love her husband for himself rather than for the stature bestowed on him as ruler of All the Russias.[34] To Elizabeth 'the Naryshkin woman' was simply a harlot bent on destroying what was for her still a romance, after nearly ten years of marriage. She would not follow the example of her friend, the Grand Duchess Anna, who, weary of Constantine's rages and infidelity, had returned (also childless) to Germany; and she was prepared to show patience, though at times resignation gave way to tears of despair. For, ultimately, Elizabeth possessed one advantage denied to any other woman who sought to captivate Alexander. She alone knew the full emotional confusion of her husband. Occasionally, instinct even helped her to understand it. And she therefore counted on him in the end to return the love which she felt towards him.

This belief was no mere hopeful flicker lightening the gloom of life within the Palace. For Alexander could not be constantly inconstant. It was impossible for him to be certain of his illusions, least of all those which sprang from the heart rather than from the mind. Though he rightly sensed he needed Maria Naryshkin, he was by nature too conscious of guilt to gain from his newest love the relaxed contentment of genuine happiness. The Countess might prattle inconsequentially of fashion and clothes and the impossibility of not receiving or giving pleasure; her moods might range from light flirtation to heavy passion; but she was breathing warmth into an artificial atmosphere, not firing the hopes and despair of real existence. Though too often Alexander treated Elizabeth as a companion rather than a wife, there was a depth in their relationship which no exercises in insolent allurement could dispel. It was solely with Elizabeth that Alexander might share retrospective delight in old amusements and sense once more the comforting bond of sympathy first forged in Paul's reign. Yet it was in the very moments when some mirror from the past caught this present posturing in all its insincerity that Alexander sought to hide himself from public ceremony, victim to what Elizabeth herself called 'a fit of indolence terrible for Society'.[35] When sensitivity thus tortured his conscience there was no joy left in anything which they undertook, only recrimination and complaint; but equally, in such a mood, stolen hours with Maria could not bring him lasting satisfaction. Although in public policy the Emperor might expect his will to be obeyed (as Kochubey had complained), he was as unsure how to seek private happiness as in the days when his loyalties had been torn between grandmother and father.

A tragic episode in the following year revealed once more the extent of

Alexander's dependence on Elizabeth.[36] In January Maria Naryshkin bore her lover a daughter. Alexander could not hide from Elizabeth the pride he felt in fatherhood. A few months later, however, the little girl died. Countess Maria hardly allowed the tragedy to disturb the flow of her life. It was Elizabeth, rather than Maria, who perceived the depth of Alexander's grief and who gave to him reassurance and comfort. And this is not surprising; for it was only she who knew how, with each successive personal sorrow, the Tsar felt the cumulative burden of guilt weigh more heavily on his shoulders.

Had the Naryshkin affair been the only source of emotional confusion to Alexander during these years of mounting foreign menace, it is likely that husband and wife would speedily have found reconciliation. But Alexander could never resolve the problems of affection towards his own family. He was the eldest child in a brood of four boys and five girls; but, apart from his brother Constantine, he had seen little of the other members of the family in their infancy. As a young boy, visiting the Grand-Ducal Court almost as a stranger, he showed special devotion to his eldest sister, Alexandra, five and a half years his junior. In the winter of 1799–1800 Alexandra Pavlovna married Archduke Joseph, the Palatine of Hungary, but she died in child-birth in March 1801, in the same week as her father's murder. The coincidental timing of these two deaths preyed heavily on Alexander's mind.[37] Soon after coming to the throne he began to find in his fourth sister, Catherine, who had been born in May 1788, a consolation for the loss he had felt. He always made a point of travelling to Pavlovsk for Grand Duchess Catherine's birthday and he regularly observed the feasts of her name-day, with an attention he did not accord to other younger members of the family. By the coming of spring in 1803 Marie Feodorovna was looking for a suitor for Catherine. She had always liked Archduke Joseph, and she now invited him to make another journey to Russia where, though this was left unsaid, it was felt he could well find a second wife from within the same family.

The moment was ill-timed, for Alexander at least. He was, that April, already deep in melancholy. So disturbed was he at the thought of losing once again to the Archduke Joseph a sister whom he loved that, on the day of the Palatine's arrival, Alexander took to his bed and remained unwell for nearly a week.[38] On this occasion, however, he need not have worried: there were too many obstacles, political and religious, to the marriage, and Joseph returned to Hungary without any prospect of a bride. But the episode appears to have intensified Alexander's affection for his sister. She became for him, as he wrote in an excess of brotherly endearment, 'the light of my eyes, the adored of my heart, the polestar of the age'.[39] The Empress Elizabeth, though fond of her own sisters and brother, could not abide Catherine Pavlovna. In this instance at least, she found it difficult to understand the intensity of Alexander's feelings. She was not alone in her doubts. And as Catherine grew prettier – as dark as Maria Naryshkin but (so Alexander wrote) with 'a dear nose I take pleasure in flattening and kissing'[40] – so the intimate friendship of brother and sister became closer. Since Catherine also developed the will-power and much of the ambition of her grandmother and namesake, these bonds of affection gradually assumed political significance.

Outwardly, there was little to show the tensions which troubled Alexander's spirits in the course of 1803, apart from the days when he felt unwilling to join in the dances which had given him such pleasure a few years before. Alexander and Elizabeth continued to attend most of the formal functions together, as they had been accustomed to do, even before his accession. On 30 July, for example, both were present at what nowadays would be called a passing-out parade of military cadets in St Petersburg. Watching them that day was Martha Wilmot, a young Anglo-Irishwoman, newly arrived in St Petersburg on her way to stay with the Princess Dashkov; and Miss Wilmot wrote back to her mother in Cork giving her impressions of the Imperial couple: 'He is a tall, fair handsomish looking Young Man – she tall, fair, and would be very pretty, only for a dreadful scurvy she has on her face; her dress was a lilac round Gown of slight Silk always flowing on the ground which is *quite Russian*, a Shawl and a lace Veil thrown over her head which was all the covering it had.'[41] It seems as if the strain of her husband's unpredictability was beginning to ravage Elizabeth's good looks, for others besides the gimlet-eyed Martha Wilmot noticed the nervous eczema from which she was suffering that year; and yet the Tsar himself remained as impressive in appearance as ever.[42]

Certainly Alexander had lost none of his popularity with the mass of his subjects in the capital. But was his temperament changing? Liberal friends among the younger nobility privately expressed disappointment that the reforming zeal with which the reign had opened was yielding such small returns. Alexander still rarely missed a meeting of ministers, but he was interesting himself more and more in military affairs. That autumn the unfortunate Elizabeth complained light-heartedly in one of her letters that life in the small palace of Krasnoe Selo was so dominated by the army and its needs that she felt inclined to write 'From General Headquarters' as a heading to every sheet of paper. Almost always nowadays Alexander seemed booted and spurred. It was an ominous development.[43]

5

Shadow of War

Alexander Disillusioned with the First Consul (1803–4)

By midsummer 1803 the shadow of general war lay heavily across the continent. There was uncertainty over French intentions in Germany, in northern Italy and in the eastern Mediterranean: and already the British had resumed the conflict. Yet for the moment no one was eager to join them. Experience of two previous coalitions against France showed the folly of entering lightly into military engagements, and the possibility that a political crisis might explode prematurely into war held back each of the Great Powers. They were as afraid of the peace terms which would follow a campaign as of the outcome of the battles themselves, for twice already Napoleon, in victory, had shown scant regard for Europe's traditional frontiers and institutions. The Empire of the Habsburgs and the sprawling kingdom of the Hohenzollerns were too fragile to risk defeat and, though distance afforded the Russians greater immunity, Alexander and his advisers did not wish to see fresh successes consolidate French mastery over central and south-eastern Europe.[1] In St Petersburg it seemed more sense to build up the army as a diplomatic weapon held in reserve than to gamble on a triumph against so perfect a military machine. More than two years elapsed before the marching columns tramped once more westwards to their war stations.

During this uneasy interlude Alexander never contemplated a retreat into the self-imposed isolation which Kochubey had earlier favoured. The Tsar was by now far too conscious of his empire's prestige to accept voluntary exclusion from Europe's affairs. Yet at first Alexander remained unsure of his sympathies. Both Chancellor Vorontsov and the deputy foreign minister, Adam Czartoryski, were more convinced of the need to be on guard against Napoleon's ambitions than the Tsar himself. Indeed, in the first months of the renewed Anglo-French war, Alexander treated the British ambassador in St Petersburg coolly and did not hesitate to blame the Addington Government in London for the breakdown of the Peace of Amiens.[2] In June 1803 Alexander even seemed momentarily to have recovered his old admiration for the First Consul, for Napoleon invited the Tsar to mediate in the conflict, a suggestion which pleased Alexander considerably.[3] He saw himself accepted by the rival combatants as an impartial arbiter, imposing wise and disinterested counsels upon a grateful continent. This unfortunately was not precisely the role for which Napoleon had cast him. Failure to distinguish between an invitation to mediate and an appeal to arbitrate left Alexander making expansive gestures which nobody but himself took at their face value.

The whole confused episode of Russian mediation lasted barely six weeks. It was on 19 July 1803 that Alexander put forward his proposals for a general settlement.[4] They caused consternation in Paris: the British were invited to establish themselves on the Mediterranean island of Lampedusa, having handed over Malta to a Russian garrison, and the French were assured of their natural frontiers and of a predominant position in nothern Italy; but Alexander's proposals also included establishing a belt of neutral states across the continent which would have robbed Napoleon of the mastery he had achieved in Germany, Switzerland, Holland and the Italian peninsula. So radical a re-adjustment of the European map was acceptable neither to Paris nor to London. Napoleon himself was righteously indignant with Alexander: he complained, with justice, that he had never invited the Tsar to distribute the prizes of his own campaigns; and he concluded, with far less justice, that if the Russians really believed they could put forward proposals of this nature, they must already have sold themselves to the English. On 29 August the First Consul formally rejected Alexander's good offices; and thereafter he began to speak of the Russians as potential enemies.[5]

Alexander was naively puzzled by Napoleon's attitude. His vanity smarted at the revelation that he was not, after all, to determine the structure of Europe. Soon he had other grievances too. For several years the vicissitudes of Russian policy had been interpreted at the French Court by Count Arkady Morkov, an ambassador whose record of service was impressive but in whom Alexander personally felt little confidence. Nor, it would appear, did Napoleon. For, at the end of September 1803, the

First Consul subjected the unfortunate Morkov to one of those melodramatic moments of public abuse which, from time to time, invigorated diplomatic receptions in the French capital. On this occasion, Napoleon openly accused Morkov of conspiring with his domestic enemies in Paris and of showing sympathy for the royalist émigrés and their British patrons.[6] There was some justification for the complaint, but when the Tsar learnt of the incident he was angry: though long critical of Morkov, he was not prepared to permit a foreign Head of State to subject his accredited spokesman to such humiliating rebuff. Rather than await a formal demand from Napoleon for the ambassador's recall, Alexander summoned Morkov back to St Petersburg immediately and, on his arrival home, made a great show of awarding him one of the Empire's highest decorations.[7] Within a few days of Morkov's return, Chancellor Vorontsov was putting forward in St Petersburg a proposal for an approach to the British. Although in earlier months Alexander had invariably frowned on all talk of an English alliance, he now made no effort to hold Vorontsov back.[8]

The Morkov affair, trivial though it was in form, completed Alexander's personal disillusionment with the character of Napoleon's government. His attitude towards the French hardened at the close of 1803; and in the following months events both in St Petersburg and Paris confirmed all his suspicions. More and more in this period the Tsar turned for advice to Adam Czartoryski, partly from inclination and partly because Vorontsov's health was rapidly deteriorating.[9] Czartoryski had never placed much faith in Napoleon's fair words and promises, and he used the Morkov incident to draw the Tsar's attention to French intrigues in an area to which the Russians were especially sensitive. Throughout the year of 1803 the Foreign Ministry in St Petersburg had received reports from its diplomatic representatives within the Turkish Empire of the growing activity of French agents in the Balkans and among Greek residents in Constantinople itself.[10] If the French embarked on a forward policy in south-eastern Europe, Russia's Black Sea trade would be challenged and it was even possible that the territories acquired in Catherine's wars against the Turks might be in jeopardy. The bogey of French intervention in the Eastern Question aroused lively apprehension in St Petersburg: French gun-running on the Adriatic coast and among the Aegean islands, French money bribing the clans of Montenegro, French memoranda planning the establishment of client dependencies throughout the Balkan peninsula; all such tales – true, half-true or false – were certain to provoke a reaction from Alexander. By the autumn of 1804 he had despatched 11,000

Russian soldiers to Corfu, making use of a protectorate over the Ionian Islands claimed by his father during the war of the Second Coalition.[11] It was in these waters, rather than on the land mass of the continent itself, that the rival interests of France and Russia came nearest to conflict.

Vorontsov left St Petersburg to recuperate on his estates in the second week of February 1804, though he continued to draft instructions and despatches on foreign affairs for another eighteen months.[12] Effectively, however, Russian foreign policy throughout the year of 1804 was determined by Alexander himself and by Czartoryski. They were soon faced by a major crisis. Within little more than a month of Vorontsov's withdrawal from St Petersburg, the capital was shocked by the news from Paris: the Duc d'Enghien had been seized by French agents on the neutral soil of Baden, conveyed to Vincennes, placed on trial before a French military court, and summarily executed as a traitor in the pay of a foreign country pledged to invade the territories of the French Republic. Not since the days of the Terror had an event in Paris aroused such widespread horror in the capitals of Europe. At St Petersburg it was seen as proof that a new Jacobin spirit was at large in France.[13]

Alexander was enraged by the crime. The Duc d'Enghien was a member of the French royal house. By conniving at his kidnapping and execution the First Consul became, in Alexander's eyes, a regicide. Nor was this the only cause of the Tsar's indignation. He regarded the abduction of the Duke from Baden as a particular insult to Russia, for Napoleon had been repeatedly reminded that Alexander expected the French authorities to respect the lands of his wife's family. His response was swift and dramatic. A meeting of the Council of State was convened in mid-April at which it was resolved, with only one dissentient voice, to break off all diplomatic contact with France.[14] The Russian Court went into official mourning and a solemn note of protest was despatched to Paris.

But the French paid little regard to Russian susceptibilities. Napoleon interpreted Alexander's complaint as unjustified interference with the domestic affairs and internal security of France. He entrusted the reply to Talleyrand, his Minister of Foreign Affairs, and a bland statement appeared in the official *Moniteur*: 'If, when England prepared the assassination of Paul I, the Russian Government had discovered that the organizers of the plot were no more than a league from the frontier, would it not have seized them at once?'[15] No allusion could have been better calculated to wound the Tsar than this deliberate reference to the circumstances of his own accession. It was a rhetorical question which he found hard to forgive or forget. A month later news came from Paris that the First

Consul had accepted from the French Senate the title of Emperor.[16] Now, to all his other transgressions, Napoleon had added contempt for the dynastic principle. Resolutely the successor of Peter the Great refused to acknowledge the newest of empires.

Czartoryski, Novosiltsov and the Grand Design of 1804

The execution of the Duc d'Enghien and the proclamation of the French Empire had the incidental effect of consolidating Czartoryski's position in St Petersburg. Indignation at the enormities of the French silenced his opponents. When anger subsided and tempers cooled, all the old suspicion of Czartoryski as a non-Russian and a Roman Catholic returned to the forefront of people's minds and most of the factions in St Petersburg united against him; but for the moment his disabilities seemed of minor importance provided that he denounced with appropriate firmness the Carolingian make-believe of Paris. Alexander, for his part, gave the Polish Prince his confidence, even though caution made him keep in reserve the full dignity of ministerial rank. Titles, however, mattered little to Czartoryski. Although he signed himself 'Assistant Minister' he knew he was enjoying greater freedom of initiative in shaping policy than any adviser on foreign affairs in Russia within living memory. He made good use of his opportunities, never forgetting his loyalty to Alexander personally nor to the Poland of his birth.[17]

Basically Alexander and Czartoryski were at one on the course Russia must follow: the Tsar would weld together a formidable alliance against the French. If possible, he still wished to avoid a general war and, though more favourably disposed to the British now that Pitt had succeeded Addington as head of the government, he preferred to act independently, building up a defensive league of which Russia, Austria and Prussia were to be the principal members. Once agreed between themselves, the three autocracies would present Napoleon with terms for a general settlement. Only if he rejected their proposals would the league make common cause with his old enemy across the Channel and confront the French Empire with a Third Coalition of the European Powers. Czartoryski placed more emphasis than Alexander on the need for a preliminary understanding with the British, and his Polish patriotism made him suspect the intentions of the Prussians; but he was prepared to support approaches to both Vienna and Berlin so long as there remained general agreement on war aims, and he also encouraged the beginning of conversations between the Russians and the Swedes. Throughout the summer of 1804 Russian diplomats were active in every capital not already under the dominance of the French; and in St Petersburg all thoughts of domestic reform were abandoned in favour of a positive foreign policy.

By the autumn it was clear that one at least of Czartoryski's reservations was correct: the key to future action lay in London, if only because of the need for subsidies to bring the armies of the remaining independent Powers into the field. In September it was accordingly resolved to send Novosiltsov to England to negotiate an alliance.[18] The choice of Novosiltsov as a special emissary was significant: he had been a member of the Secret Committee and therefore a close associate for many years both of Czartoryski and Alexander himself; and he had contacts in London, not only with Pitt and the Tories, but with Fox and the Whig Opposition as well. It was intended that he should be the Tsar's personal representative, capable of giving to the British statesmen a more direct assessment of Alexander's intentions than the ambassador, Simon Vorontsov, could ever have made. Not unnaturally, Vorontsov resented Novosiltsov's intervention. The tension between the two men was so evident to the British ministers that it hampered negotiations and increased the suspicion with which Alexander's overtures were received.[19] In London it remained difficult to understand the Russians.

Novosiltsov's instructions were drafted by Czartoryski and based upon memoranda which he had submitted to his sovereign in the previous year.[20] Their combination of high-sounding idealism with a realistic attempt to attain Russian primacy in central Europe and the Balkans appealed so closely to Alexander's temperament that he appropriated Czartoryski's proposals and made them his own. The instructions to Novosiltsov of 23 September 1804 therefore represent the earliest draft of the Tsar's general plan to establish a new order in Europe; they are, in consequence, of considerable significance in the evolution of his thoughts on international policy. The moralistic phrases which puzzled and irritated Pitt and his ministers in 1804–5 re-appeared in a new guise ten years later: concern for the collective security of Europe and its identification with the imperial future of Russia became the characteristic feature of Alexander's diplomacy, at once both the most responsible and the most pretentious of his historical innovations.

The Grand Design of 1804 was indeed staggeringly comprehensive. Alexander and Czartoryski assumed the allies needed an ideological appeal which, to the peoples of Europe, would counter the attractions of France's revolutionary principles. No attempt would be made to impose discredited régimes from the past on lands liberated from French military rule. The French people themselves were to be told that the Coalition was fighting, not against their natural rights, but against a government which was 'no less a tyranny for France than for the rest of Europe'. The new map of the continent must rest on principles of justice: frontiers would be so drawn that they coincided with natural geographical boundaries, provided outlets for industries, and associated in one political unit 'homogeneous peoples able to agree among themselves'. Novosiltsov's instructions were often vague but they contained three specific proposals of considerable originality: the establishment of a German Confederation independent of both Austria and Prussia; the conclusion of an agreement between Britain and Russia to determine the eventual partition of the Ottoman Empire if the Sultan's rule collapsed from internal strains or from excessive dependence upon French patronage; and the acceptance of a revised code of maritime law to safeguard the commerce of neutral states from British naval interference in any future war. Yet it was hoped there would be no occasions for a major conflict in the years ahead: the new Europe was to rest upon a careful balance of power between potential rival states; and, once peace was established, it was proposed that the European governments in concert should put forward 'a new concept of law among nations' based upon 'an obligation not to wage war unless all means of mediation had been previously exhausted'. The principle of 'reasonable freedom' guaranteeing 'the sacred rights of humanity and the true interests of lawful government' must be an absolute condition for 'close and cordial union between Russia and England'.

Alexander's emissary was courteously received in London. He spent much of November and most of January in discussion with Pitt and with the outgoing Foreign Secretary (Lord Harrowby) and his successor, Lord Mulgrave.[21] Novosiltsov's vanity and arrogance of manner left a bad impression and it was tactless of him to hold long and frequent conversations with Pitt's domestic enemies, the Prince of Wales, Charles James Fox and Lord Moira. But Pitt made allowances for Novosiltsov's inexperience and youthful enthusiasm: he was more interested in him as the spokesman for Russia's idealistic sovereign than for himself. There was much which Pitt found totally incomprehensible in the Russian proposals, especially the suggestion that the two governments would find it easy to agree on a common policy over the Ottoman Empire. Pitt respected Alexander's desire for a comprehensive statement of war aims but he had no wish to transform a war against France into a crusade for ill-defined 'sacred rights' in which he did not himself believe. He rejected out of hand all talk of revising maritime law and he made it clear that Britain was unwilling, at this stage of the war with France, to be drawn into the intricacies of the Eastern Question. All this fell far short of Novosiltsov's hopes. But at heart Pitt was as eager as Czartoryski and Alexander to build up another coalition to challenge France. It seemed to him, however, unlikely that the Tsar's proposals would be acceptable to either of the other great European Powers, Austria and Prussia; and he was therefore prepared to counter Alexander's design for peace with a programme of his own. This he discussed at length, not only with Mulgrave, but with other members of his cabinet.[22]

Although the British counter-proposals of January 1805 avoided precise commitments they sought to bring Alexander's idealism down to earth.[23] Pitt wanted the establishment of a 'system of public law' among the European nations, whereby the governments of all states on the mainland of Europe would pledge themselves to uphold the settlement, which would also remain under the special protective guarantee of the two Great Powers on the fringe of the continent, Britain and Russia. The assumption that Britain would continue to have a European policy after the restoration of peace was a revolutionary concept and clearly showed Pitt's desire to please the Tsar. But detailed proposals conveyed to Novosiltsov and Simon Vorontsov showed a marked divergence of interests between the British and Russian governments, especially over the future of Germany and Italy and the frontiers of France in the east and the north. When, early in February 1805, the despatches from London reached St Petersburg it was obvious that, as yet, the two countries were not ready to conclude a binding alliance.[24]

Czartoryski, however, was not prepared to admit that the Novosiltsov mission was a failure. The news from London came at a bad moment for him. By now his opponents at Court had rallied after the shocks of the previous spring: the conservative Senatorial party warned Alexander that Czartoryski was pro-British and anti-Prussian; and Marie Feodorovna urged him not to stake the future of Russia on a policy determined by the son of a Polish rebel. Alexander, too, was having second thoughts: were not the British potentially more serious rivals to Russian interests on the Black Sea and at Constantinople than the French? If Czartoryski was to retain his sovereign's confidence he had to convince Alexander that their friend, Novosiltsov, had charmed the English into support for the Tsar's Grand Design, for nothing so pleased Alexander as the thought that he was respected as a philosopher-king with a mission.

Fortunately for Czartoryski, Pitt's counter-proposals began with the slightly surprising statement that King George III was 'happy to perceive that the views and sentiments of the Emperor ... correspond so entirely with his own'.[25] It was therefore possible for Czartoryski to maintain to Alexander that the distinctions between British and Russian policy were slight and that they could be overcome by negotiations in St Petersburg with the British ambassador. There followed two months of confused discussion with both the Austrian and British representatives in the Russian capital before it was agreed to submit a draft treaty to Napoleon as a virtual ultimatum. The French were to be informed that they must withdraw their troops behind the line of the Alps, Pyrenees, Rhine and Moselle, that a new arrangement must be made for the future of Italy, and that Britain, as a gesture of goodwill, would hand over Malta to be protected henceforth by a Russian garrison; and the treaty also stipulated that there should be a congress summoned to 'settle the public law in Europe'. It was Alexander's intention that Novosiltsov should be sent to Paris in order to present Napoleon with the Allied terms.[26]

The Tsar so misunderstood the British point of view that he genuinely believed Pitt would accept these proposals and endorse the decision to present them to the French. But Pitt refused outright to approve, and he regarded the suggestion that Malta should be left in the custody of a Russian garrison as a remarkable piece of diplomatic chicanery.[27] To Alexander's dismay the British insisted that, under such conditions, it would be impossible for them to collaborate with Russia and her allies in seeking to impose armed mediation on Napoleon. It now seemed unlikely that there would be any agreement over the grand strategy of a Third Coalition, let alone over its war aims.

Yet at this point, in June 1805, Napoleon inadvertently healed the rift between Britain and Russia. For some months he had been strengthening his grip on northern Italy, a process which reached a dramatic climax in the third week of May when he crowned himself 'King of All-Italy' in Milan, nominating his stepson Eugene Beauharnais as Viceroy; but on 6 June he went even further and annexed Genoa and the Ligurian coast to metropolitan France. Alexander was now convinced that the terms he had proposed to offer Napoleon would be treated with contempt. There was no sense in quarrelling with Britain over the hypothetical disposal of Malta or the future of the Italian peninsula when the real master of Italy was encroaching further and further to the south. The Tsar accordingly countermanded his order to Novosiltsov and summoned him back to St Petersburg. The Anglo-Russian Alliance, long under discussion and already drafted in April, was at last ratified on 28 July. The British promised an annual subsidy of £1½ million for every hundred thousand men Russia put into the field, but the controversial questions of Italy and Malta were omitted from the final treaty.[28] Twelve days later the Austrians, even more alarmed than the Russians or the British at French activity in the Italian peninsula, added their signatures to the alliance. The Third Coalition was at last in being: but what had started out as an elaborate attempt by the Tsar to inspire an ideological challenge to Bonapartism became, in the end, a mere hurried instrument for waging a particular campaign.

Alexander's first sustained diplomatic initiative thus reflected small credit either on his sense of what was practicable or on his understanding of European affairs. Clearly Czartoryski was to blame for much of the confusion and vacillation in Russian policy; but the Tsar associated himself so closely with his Polish friend's programme of action that the final responsibility was unquestionably his own. He had wished to impress Europe with a sense of mission: he succeeded only in winning a reputation for insincerity and dissimulation. His handling of diplomatic questions was all too frequently a response to an emotional instinct rather than the product of careful reasoning or reflection. Unfortunately, in the months ahead, this tendency to allow his decisions to be determined by personal impressions and sympathies became more and more marked. These are not the qualities which fill either allies or subordinates with confidence in a war leader.

Military Plans and the Polish Question

Although the diplomatic preparations for the war of the Third Coalition had dragged on unconscionably long, agreement was speedily reached on a plan of operations.[29] On paper it seemed masterly. Napoleon's Empire was to be attacked from the east, the north and the south. The Austrians would begin hostilities by a thrust into southern Germany and would be supported by a Russian advance force, with the main body of men to follow within a few weeks. The British undertook to send 26,000 men to the mouth of the Weser and link up with a joint Russo-Swedish expeditionary corps which would strike into Hanover and march westwards to the old battlefields of the Netherlands. Finally the whole French position in Italy would be threatened by a massive pincer movement: an Austrian attack upon Venetia and Lombardy in the north; and a joint Russo-British invasion of Naples from the south, using the much disputed bases of Malta and Corfu and relying upon pledges of support from the army of the Kingdom of Naples, which numbered some 40,000 men.

There remained, however, one weak point in the plan. No one in St

Petersburg, London or Vienna could be sure what part the Prussians would play in any campaign; and in each of these capitals it was suspected, with good reason, that equal uncertainty prevailed in Berlin itself.[30] Personal sympathies linked Frederick William III, Queen Louise and Tsar Alexander in an indissoluble bond of friendship, but political necessity was at times cruelly unsentimental and many of the Prussian King's advisers felt more might be gained from collaboration with Napoleon than with his enemies. There was a marked repugnance to support any enterprise which depended upon maintaining Swedish forces in Pomerania or which invited the Elector of Hanover to land troops on the Weser, for these were territories which every good Prussian coveted for the Hohenzollern Crown. Frederick William himself possessed a laudable desire to keep war away from northern Germany and saw nothing contradictory in giving assurances to the Russians one week and to the French the next. But a neutral Prussia, potentially hostile to the allies, straddling northern Germany was a serious military obstacle to the operational plan agreed in London and St Petersburg. As early as March 1805 the British Foreign Secretary, Lord Mulgrave, had sent a fiery despatch to the ambassador in St Petersburg complaining of 'the crooked policy of the Court of Berlin' and suggesting that the Tsar might be invited to mobilize an army along the Prussian frontier in Poland which would force Frederick William to decide whether to resist the allies or march with them against the Corsican usurper.[31]

Mulgrave's despatch delighted Czartoryski but confounded Russian preparations for war in a way which its author had failed to foresee. For Czartoryski used the doubts over Prussia's attitude as an excuse for inviting Alexander to assume the leadership of the Polish national cause. The plan which he outlined to the Tsar was ingenious.[32] Assuming that Frederick William remained recalcitrant, a Russian army corps would advance across the frontier from Brest and occupy Warsaw, then the administrative centre of what was known in Berlin as 'Southern Prussia'. With Warsaw in Russian hands, the Polish nobility would offer Alexander the crown of a Polish State to exist henceforth in dynastic union with the Russian Empire. Subsequently it was anticipated that the Austrians might cede the former Polish lands in Galicia in return for compensation elsewhere, probably in Silesia. The Polish people, grateful to the Russians as liberators, would rise against the Tsar's enemies and supplement the allied armies in their march to the West. Czartoryski made contact with the Polish patriots outside the Russian Empire and received approval for his plan from national leaders normally hostile to Russian pretensions.[33] In particular Czartoryski was given assurances of support in Warsaw from Prince Poniatowski, a nephew of the last Polish King and his own cousin, who was later to serve Napoleon and die a Marshal of France at the battle of Leipzig. Never before or after was there such enthusiasm among the Polish aristocracy for a ruler of Russia as in this summer of 1805; but it is extremely doubtful if Russia's Austrian ally was prepared to accept a re-opening of the Polish Question at such a time.

Alexander alternately blew hot and cold over Czartoryski's project. He was too cautious to approve his friend's plans in their entirety; but he always held that the restoration of Poland, in a form acceptable to the leaders of both the Russian and the Polish nations, was one of his cherished ambitions and he was accordingly reluctant to neglect such an opportunity. On the other hand, Alexander was acutely sensitive of his commitments to make war on France. He continued to hope he could reach an agreement with Frederick William III which would allow Russian troops free passage across Germany, even if it did not bring Prussia into the Coalition as a belligerent. Sponsorship of Polish nationalism clearly ruled out such understanding. Czartoryski deceived himself into believing that Alexander had decided to give his support to the project: he wrote to Simon Vorontsov, in mid-August, 'Once he has taken a great decision, he knows how to adhere to it with unshaken firmness.'[34] But, whatever assurances he may have given in private conversation at the council table Alexander still shirked the 'great decision' on the Polish Question; and he continued to do so even after the armies were massed along the frontier.

By now the opposition at Court to Czartoryski had found a natural leader in Prince Peter Dolgoruky, descendant of a great *boyar* family and one of the few representatives of the old Russian conservative tradition on terms of personal friendship with Alexander (who was his exact contemporary). Dolgoruky, who had once been Arakcheev's adjutant, had impressed Alexander during Paul's reign by the efficiency with which, as a colonel, he had modernized the fortifications of Smolensk. After his accession Alexander appointed Dolgoruky a principal aide-de-camp and regarded him as a military expert. It was in this capacity that he attended meetings of the Council of State where, partly from genuine conviction, he was hostile to every proposal which came from the members of the old Secret Committee. He warmly supported the idea of Russian participation in a war against Napoleon but he thought little of the attempts to co-ordinate grand strategy with the British and preferred a continental league of Russia, Prussia and Austria. Although Dolgoruky did not know the full details of Czartoryski's Polish projects, he suspected that they would commit the Tsar to military operations peripheral to the main campaign. There was a stormy occasion at the Winter Palace when Dolgoruky interrupted a detailed exposition by Czartoryski with the comment: 'By your leave, Prince, may we have rather less of these Polish affairs? You are still in the service of the Tsar of Russia.'[35] The point was not lost on Alexander.

One aspect of Dolgoruky's reasoning especially appealed to Alexander; for the young Prince was convinced he could win Frederick William of Prussia over to the Allied cause, despite unfavourable reports from Novo-siltsov, who was in Berlin at the beginning of July. On 7 August the Tsar sent a letter to Frederick William urging him to allow Russian troops to pass through Prussia and for the following nine weeks secret messages, highly charged with emotion, were exchanged between the two monarchs with Dolgoruky's collaboration.[36] Alexander also insisted on modifications in the original plan of operations, which delayed the concentration of the principal Russian army by more than a fortnight. The slowness of communications across Europe meant that the Austrians launched their initial offensive against the French positions in Bavaria on 2 September without realizing the confusion and hesitancy in the Russian High Command. General Kutuzov, with the Russian advance guard, did not begin to march westwards until 12 September: he was, even then, five hundred miles from the battle zone; and the main Russian armies were still trundling slowly towards the frontier, their commanders uncertain if they were to invade Prussia, cross Prussian territory as friends, or strike south-westwards (as Kutuzov had done) avoiding Prussia entirely. It was an inauspicious beginning to the campaign.

Alexander meanwhile was in a fever of excitement.[37] Most of August he spent in St Petersburg, striking appropriately martial attitudes. Against the advice of Czartoryski and the diplomatic envoys of his Austrian ally, he had decided to follow his armies into the field and share their fortunes in battle. The prospect of war both thrilled and sobered him. He seems to have seen little of Countess Naryshkin and spent some happy weeks with Elizabeth in the Tauride Palace before leaving on his journey to the frontier. On his last full day in St Petersburg – Friday, 20 September – he consulted a much revered holy man, the hermit Sevastianov, who urged him not to be in haste to destroy 'the accursed Frenchman'; and early on the Saturday morning he attended a service at the Cathedral, kneeling for a long time in silent prayer. By half-past eleven his carriage was moving slowly south-westwards down the road that led to Vitebsk, Moghilev and the frontier at Brest; and back in the Tauride Palace Elizabeth was writing an almost incoherent letter to her mother, full of the proud sorrow with which she had watched her Emperor and husband set out for the wars.[38]

Alexander at Pulawy and Berlin (October–November 1805)

There followed anticlimax. Eight weeks separate Alexander's departure from his capital and his arrival at the field headquarters of his army. During this period Napoleon checked the Austrian thrust into Bavaria and penetrated three hundred miles down the Danube to the outskirts of Vienna, which was in French hands long before Alexander saw the first flash of cannon-fire on the hills of Moravia. It is as if the Tsar had interpreted too literally the inspired advice he received from Sevastianov for, while the Emperor of the French was adding fresh lustre to his reputation, the Emperor of All the Russias lingered hesitantly among the fields and forests of his Polish lands.

The truth was that Alexander had become ensnared by his preoccupation with Prussia. At the beginning of September he sent a letter to Frederick William repeating his request for free passage for his troops and urging the King to come and meet him so that they might discuss their problems together. But it was not until Alexander reached Brest on 27 September that he received an answer: Frederick William, though pathetically willing for the Tsar to visit him, obstinately clung to a rigid interpretation of his pledges of neutrality.[39] But Alexander was not entirely discouraged: he sent Dolgoruky to Berlin to see if a personal emissary could overcome the King's reluctance; and, to the delight of the Poles in his entourage, he decided to await further reports from Berlin at Pulawy, the Czartoryski family estate, only seventy miles from the 'Southern Prussian' capital of Warsaw.[40] He did not inform Czartoryski of Dolgoruky's mission.

Alexander arrived at Pulawy at dead of night on 3 October. His carriage had snapped a shaft and he finished the journey on foot, following a local peasant with a lantern along forest paths. He was so exhausted when he reached the house that he refused to allow the porter to awaken his hosts and was content to throw himself fully dressed on to a bed, where he slept until seven in the morning.[41] Despite this unorthodox beginning to his period of residence at Pulawy, the Czartoryski estate soon assumed the dignity of an improvised Court. The Tsar was attended by many of his ministers and generals and by some of the diplomatic corps and for a fortnight this remote château in a Polish forest was the effective capital of the Russian Empire.

For most of his sojourn at Pulawy Alexander was in buoyant spirits. He approved, and immediately cancelled, orders for an advance on Warsaw; he explained by letter to the Austrian Emperor how much he was hoping for an understanding with the Prussians while assuring the head of the Austrian military mission, by word of mouth, how determined he was 'to make the Poles rise against Prussia'; he let his hosts think that the pro-clamation of a new Polish Kingdom was imminent and proceeded to examine maps so as to see whether, after all, it was essential to move across Prussian territory.[42] His inconsistencies baffled strangers and exasperated those who, like Czartoryski, knew him well. Yet the possibility that he was contradicting himself troubled Alexander little. For now he was about to do great things he found he loved the anticipation of action more than the deed itself. It was exhilarating to feel one's word could send the Guards marching to the Vistula and a nod of approval awaken the nation of Sobieski. Indeed it was so gratifying that Alexander dared not risk disillusionment by either saying the word or giving the nod. Confident he was champion of their cause, the Polish aristocracy flattered the Tsar, and he was charmed by their courtesies. Thoughtfully Princess Radziwill let Empress Elizabeth know how happy everyone was at Pulawy;[43] and Alexander himself found time to dash off seven notes of affectionate nonsense to his sister Catherine in the dozen days which it took Napoleon to lead an army from the Rhine to the Danube.[44]

Oddly enough, it was the movement of French troops elsewhere which at last decided Alexander on his course of action. For, on the Tsar's third day in Pulawy, Marshal Bernadotte's corps marched through the Prussian enclave of Ansbach in its haste to join the force which Napoleon was concentrating in Bavaria. When news reached Berlin that the French had thus violated Prussian territory, Frederick William was so infuriated by this cavalier disregard for his neutrality that he consented to the Russian request for a right of passage across Prussian Silesia. So sudden was Frederick William's change of mood that Dolgoruky had actually begun his return journey to Poland convinced his mission was a failure when he was overtaken by a messenger summoning him back for another audience. The King was now anxious to meet the Tsar in Prussia as soon as possible, preferably at a secret rendezvous near the frontier.[45]

Reports of the French incursion into Ansbach also provoked a reaction in Alexander. On 16 October he suddenly informed Czartoryski he was leaving Pulawy for military headquarters at Kozienice: he would not now be going to Warsaw, nor making a visit to Poniatowski on his estates in southern Prussia, as was at one time planned.[46] The Tsar's decision convinced Czartoryski that he had, after all, decided against the Polish project. Now he was primarily interested in going to Berlin, for he intended that all Europe should see that Prussia had broken with the French; and hence he had no liking for Frederick William's proposal of a clandestine exchange of views in a remote corner of his kingdom. Once he had reached Kozienice Alexander gave all his confidence to Dolgoruky, who had travelled with news from Berlin; and on 21 October – the day on which the fleet of his British ally gave battle to the French and Spanish squadrons off Cape Trafalgar – Alexander announced he would go in person to the Prussian capital and settle matters with Frederick William.[47] He ordered Czartoryski to be in attendance as assistant minister for Foreign Affairs. Bitter at heart and conscious of the disillusionment felt by his fellow Poles, Czartoryski rode westwards in the Imperial cavalcade as his sovereign headed for Berlin across the dreary rainswept plain, listening to Dolgoruky's briefing on the conflict of factions at the Prussian Court. When Dolgoruky paused there were long silences.[48]

Alexander's entry into Berlin on 25 October was an impressive exercise in ceremonial, for though Frederick William would have preferred a less ostentatious encounter, he was determined to please the Tsar by receiving him with all the respect due to Imperial dignity.[49] As at Memel three years previously, all the external trappings were brought out for the occasion: fireworks, displays, splendid receptions and banquets, reviews of regiments which had so nearly found themselves having to resist a Russian invasion. Alexander, as usual, stole the scene in every moment of pageantry, confident in himself and confident of the defeats his armies would soon inflict upon the French. Here was a conqueror-to-be in whom it was hard to recognize the wavering dreamer of Brest and Pulawy. Only to a few observers did there seem something unreal in the certainty with which he predicted Napoleon's coming defeat. The Austrian ambassador, Clement von Metternich, whom Alexander met for the first time on 29 October, was flattered by the Tsar's gracious comments; but he shrewdly sought to bring Alexander's enthusiasm for his royal hosts down to earth.[50] What was needed was a military alliance not lofty sentiment.

By 3 November a draft secret treaty had been drawn up for signature between the two monarchs. It fell far short of what Metternich had wished and it seemed 'calamitous' to Czartoryski; but Alexander and Dolgoruky were well satisfied with its terms. If France refused to accept proposals for peace from Frederick William based on the agreements reached between the Russians, Austrians and British, then Prussia would enter the war against Napoleon by the end of the year; and should

Frederick William be able to bring an army of 180,000 men into the field within the following six weeks, Alexander undertook to seek from his English ally the eventual cession to Prussia of the Electorate of Hanover. Only pessimists doubted if there would still be a war for Prussia to enter in six weeks time.[51]

There remained for Alexander one last gesture of theatricality before he resumed his protracted departure for the wars. Late at night, on 4 November, the Tsar, the King and Queen Louise left the palace at Potsdam and went on foot to the garrison church. Descending in weirdly flickering candle-light to the tiny crypt, the two monarchs faced each other across the wooden coffin in which Frederick the Great had been laid to rest. With tears of emotion running down his cheeks, Alexander embraced Frederick William as each sovereign swore an oath of eternal friendship, pledging that never again would the interests or the fate of Prussia and Russia run in conflict.[52] Next day the Tsar's carriage headed south for Wittenberg, Leipzig and reality.

6

Austerlitz and After

Alexander and Kutuzov in Moravia

Despite the knowledge that Napoleon had embarked on a full-scale invasion of the Austrian lands, Alexander was still in no hurry. He left Potsdam on the morning of 5 November: he did not arrive at allied headquarters in Olmütz (Olomouc) until the evening of 18 November. By then it had taken his carriages nearly a fortnight to cover 320 miles – an instructive contrast to his speed when returning to St Petersburg from his coronation four years before. Some of the delay was accidental: winter came early, snow followed by a thaw leaving the roads of Bohemia heavy with slush; and confusion over the precise siting of headquarters ruled out the shortest routes to Moravia. But Alexander himself added four or five days to the journey by suddenly deciding to make a westward detour and pay a visit to his eldest surviving sister, Marie Pavlovna, who had married the Crown Prince of Saxe-Weimar in the previous year. Marie, an intelligent nineteen-year-old girl with much artistic talent, insisted on presenting to her brother the great literary figures who so enriched the cultural life of Weimar at this time. Alexander enjoyed the intellectual stimulus of conversations with Goethe, Herder and Wieland and stayed longer in Weimar than good sense warranted.[1] On the same day that Alexander said his farewells the Emperor whom he had set out to fight was installing himself in the Habsburg summer palace at Schönbrunn and the tricolour flag flew over Vienna. Small wonder if, when his carriages clattered at last into Olmütz, Alexander was received by his Austrian ally with a formality as frigid as the weather.

The preceding month had brought the heaviest blows to Austrian arms for over a century. When hostilities began in the first week of September the Allies assumed they would take Napoleon off his guard and strike westwards before the Grand Army could concentrate on the Rhine; but the French moved with far greater speed than their enemies, and the principal Austrian army was encircled at Ulm in mid-October and forced to capitulate. After this disaster Emperor Francis relied primarily upon the Russian advance-guard to stem the French thrust down the Danube while he re-grouped the remaining Austrian forces to the north and the south and awaited the arrival of the Russians in full strength. It proved an expensive strategic manoeuvre, at least in terms of prestige. For, after the capitulation at Ulm, effective control of the armies on the Danube devolved upon the commander of the Russian advance-guard, General Mikhail Kutuzov, who had no intention of wasting the lives of his men in order to keep the French out of the Austrian capital.

Kutuzov was the most distinguished surviving veteran of Catherine the Great's reign.[2] He had learnt the science of war on the vast plains of southern Russia where armies moved across the emptiness of steppe-land with the freedom of battle-fleets at sea. His principal mentor was the legendary Suvorov beside whom he had fought at Alushta in 1774 (where he lost the sight of his right eye) and at the siege of Ismail in 1791. It was after this final Turkish campaign that Suvorov had said of Kutuzov, 'He commanded my left flank but he was my right arm.' Yet, though he possessed some of Suvorov's qualities, he owed many of his strategic ideas to another of Catherine's generals, P. A. Rumiantsev, who had once declared, 'The objective is not the occupation of a geographical position but the destruction of enemy forces.' This maxim dominated Kutuzov's thinking in the wars against Napoleon. Hence, although in 1805 the Russians fought tenacious actions to delay the French cavalry whenever it threatened the main column of retreat, Kutuzov systematically evacuated the string of small towns along the Danube as soon as they came under attack and it was natural for him to order his men to retire north-eastwards across the river rather than make a show of defending Vienna. While refusing to offer the French a set-piece battle with inferior numbers, he could claim he was luring Napoleon eastwards so as to expose his line of communications to flank attack from the north and south.

Even so, the long retreat across an unfamiliar countryside in the depths of winter imposed a heavy strain on Kutuzov's men. Sometimes they had to go more than twenty-four hours without food for themselves or fodder for their horses. By 19 November, when they made contact with the main Russian army in Moravia, they were utterly weary and exhausted, but they had denied Napoleon the decisive early victory he needed to complete the triumph of Ulm. When Kutuzov reported to Alexander in Olmütz he was a tired but satisfied man.[3] Now that the allied armies had at last come together, they possessed a numerical advantage over the French which, though slight at the moment, would grow considerably as further reinforcements arrived from Poland. Time, so Kutuzov argued, was on the side of the Russians and Austrians: Napoleon, whose troops were also under severe strain, was unlikely to attack; once the Russians had rested, re-organized and received fresh supplies from the East, they would be ready to launch a counter-offensive, but for the moment it was important to stand on the defensive and allow the thrusts and skirmishing of recent weeks to die away in the worsening weather.

Kutuzov's advice made such sound sense that Alexander might well have heeded it had it come from any other commander. But he personally never felt sure of Kutuzov: there was so much about the man which ran counter to the Tsar's image of an ideal officer. For Kutuzov never possessed the romantic fire of a hero on horseback. Though only sixty he had begun to show the failings of old age without its redeeming serenity: he would not commit himself to final verdicts on the assessments of other officers nor – if he could help it – did he go so far as to add his signature to any formal orders. He fussed over matters of personal comfort: soft beds; easy chairs; good food and wine; the opportunity to sleep long hours at night and in the afternoon. On the other hand he disliked the parade uniforms affected by the Tsar and his entourage at every military occasion: they might wear cocked hats trimmed with plumes of feathers; but he was content to place on his carefully powdered white hair a flat round cap, not unlike a sailor's, with a red ribbon encircling it to match the red lapels on his old green greatcoat. Since the cap carried no mark of distinction it was the most distinguished article of headgear in the Russian army. He was shrewd enough to use the legend of his own indolence as a means of avoiding decisions which he preferred others to take and to hide from those who opposed him the resilience and tenacity which had held Suvorov's regard in earlier years. Like Suvorov he tended to express his judgements verbally rather than on paper, showing a peasant's flair for proverbs and fables and a gift of imagery which appealed to the common soldiers but perplexed gentlemen who had learnt strategy and tactics from some manual of instruction. Alexander had known Kutuzov for more than a decade and appointed him as commander of the army he despatched to aid the Austrians because he was, to outward appearances, so much the heir of Suvorov. But Alexander never fully understood Kutuzov and sensed that there must always be a strained reserve between the General and himself: for Kutuzov and his wife had dined as Paul's guests at the Mikhailovsky in March 1801, on that last evening before his murder. Though tact might ensure silence, memory imposed a barrier between the two men.

But there were other reasons why, at Olmütz, the Tsar should have rejected Kutuzov's advice. Alexander arrived in Moravia with a swollen retinue of friends, courtiers and experts.[4] Dolgoruky and Czartoryski were still with him, each suspicious of the other's next move. Paul Stroganov and Novosiltsov were also in attendance; and so, too, were Peter Volkonsky and Arakcheev (who, like Alexander, was seeing active service for the first time). And, as well as these close associates, there were several senior officers who owed their promotion to the young Tsar's favour: General Buxhöwden, who commanded the corps which had linked up with Kutuzov on 19 November; Count Wintzingerode, a Württemberger General whom hatred of Napoleon had driven into Russian service and who had already acted as the Tsar's personal envoy on diplomatic missions; General Sukhtelen, a bearded giant of Dutch descent appointed Quartermaster-General by Alexander on the eve of the campaign; and the Comte de Langeron, royalist émigré from Provence and now a commander of a Russian division. None of these men agreed entirely with Kutuzov although, since Dolgoruky was impatient for action, Czartoryski favoured a general policy of waiting upon events. Alexander confirmed Kutuzov's position as commander-in-chief and then proceeded, throughout the remaining days of November, to ignore any proposal he made. Langeron, more sympathetic to Kutuzov than most of the non-Russians in Alexander's circle, was indignant at the treatment accorded to him. 'The young men around the Emperor', he wrote later, 'referred to him as General Dawdler and he was left without authority and without influence.'[5]

It had been anticipated that the arrival of their sovereign would fire the Russian rank and file with enthusiasm. But, as Langeron noticed, they remained largely indifferent to his presence and resented the intrusion into camp-life of parade martinets like Arakcheev. Friction between the new arrivals and the veteran commanders was so marked that Czartoryski even claims to have advised the Tsar to give the army his blessing, leave his Generals to fight the enemy, and return to St Petersburg to govern his Empire. Alexander, however, had no intention of allowing others to claim credit for defeating Napoleon. Dolgoruky encouraged him with bursts of contemptuous anger towards 'the usurper Bonaparte and his horde'; and messages from St Petersburg strengthened his resolve to remain with his army, for it was clear the people of his capital daily expected news of their beloved sovereign's triumph.[6]

Alexander, though flattered by these signs of confidence, inwardly knew he was too inexperienced to make detailed dispositions for battle. Clearly, if Napoleon was to be successfully challenged on the Moravian plateau, it was essential for the operational planning to be entrusted to someone who knew the terrain; and accordingly Alexander turned, in the first instance, not to one of the favourites he had brought with him from St Petersburg, but to an Austrian, General Weyrother, chief-of-staff to the Emperor Francis.[7] This gesture towards an ally, whose troops were outnumbered in Moravia five to one by the Russians, did much to break down the reserve with which the Austrians had treated Alexander and his senior officers. Weyrother, whom Alexander met briefly at Pulawy early in October, possessed none of the prestige of Prince Schwarzenberg or Prince Johann von Liechtenstein, who were with Emperor Francis at Olmütz; but in 1804 Weyrother had conducted manoeuvres in this part of Moravia and he claimed to know every stream and every undulation in the fields. Both Emperors, Francis and Alexander, thought themselves fortunate to have so meticulous an expert to brief their corps commanders.

Alexander's Generals were, however, less sanguine. Two of them had indeed good reason to remember Weyrother from Suvorov's last campaign. For in September 1799, when the old Marshal was nearly encircled by the French in the Swiss Alps, Colonel Weyrother, a geographical specialist on the Austrian staff, had shown Suvorov on a map a route from Altdorf to Schwyz.[8] When the Russians had fought their way across the St Gothard Pass and reached the town of Altdorf, they found a precipitous wall of mountain where the Colonel had so confidently drawn his pen. Among the officers who took to the narrow Alpine tracks on that occasion was Prince Bagration; now, in 1805, he commanded Kutuzov's cavalry and was a hero of the retreat along the Danube valley. And General Mikhail Miloradovich, who fought with the Aspheron Regiment under Suvorov in the Alps, still had the regiment under his command in Moravia six years later. Neither Bagration nor Miloradovich felt much faith in the expert geographer who had so impressed the two Emperors; both were men of high standing among their brother officers.

Peace Parleys

One at least of Kutuzov's predictions was soon shown to be correct. On 20 November Napoleon entered Brünn (Brno), principal city and provincial capital of Moravia, and there he was content to remain for a week, resting and re-organizing his forces. While French patrols scouted the rolling plain to the east and south of Brünn, the Russians and Austrians stayed inactive around Olmütz, a fortress town forty miles north-east of Brünn and nestling beneath forested foothills of the Carpathians and a southern outcrop of the Sudeten Mountains, known as the Jeseniky Range. The small town was appallingly overcrowded and distribution of food was chaotic. Had it not been for the cold weather, disease must have spread rapidly from the inadequate sewers, and Kutuzov wisely insisted on the bulk of the Russian army remaining in bivouacs outside the ramparts. The Emperor Francis took up residence in the episcopal palace while Alexander and his retinue occupied the citadel, where the wells were thought to be purer than in the town. Even so, soon after leaving Olmütz for the battle zone, Alexander was struck down by a bad fever and was forced to spend the last days of the month in bed; but before the illness attacked him he had already carried out tours of inspection and presided over long sessions around the conference table.

The most important of these conferences was held on 24 November.[9] On that occasion it was finally decided the Allied armies should launch a counter-offensive at the earliest opportunity, the immediate objective being to cut off Napoleon in Brünn and thus facilitate the recovery of Vienna. All the reports in the following three days seemed favourable: patrols in the Moravian countryside indicated that the French were withdrawing advance-posts from commanding positions along the road to Vienna from Olmütz, as if Napoleon wished to remain close to the shelter of Brünn itself. There seemed to be confusion in the Grand Army: why otherwise should so great a commander have ordered his men to evacuate the high land west of the Kaunitz family estates at Austerlitz? Anyone could see that the Pratzen Plateau, as it was called, formed a pivotal point in any attack to the east: could it be that the Emperor of the French was worried, that he feared for the long and slender supply line back to his bases? Hopefully Alexander ordered his carriage to drive him twenty miles south to the small town of Wischau (Vyskov) where he was close enough to the enemy to perceive any further signs that Napoleon knew he was a beaten man.

They were not long in coming. On two occasions during the retreat down the Danube there had been parleying between the French and Bagration's rearguard, and each time a temporary truce had been agreed. Napoleon had viewed these activities with disfavour, but now he decided to turn them to his own advantage. A hint of an armistice, if conveyed by an experienced messenger who kept his eyes open, would have the double merit of lulling the Allies into a false sense of security and of gathering information about their strength and probable intentions. From Brünn on 25 November Napoleon accordingly despatched a letter to Alexander assuring him of his good wishes and the hope of finding an occasion to give proof of his goodwill; and one of his most trusted aides-de-camp duly set out for the Russian advance-posts to seek an audience with the Tsar.[10]

Napoleon's choice of emissary showed a sound contempt for past quarrels. He selected General Savary, who as chief of gendarmerie in 1803–4 had played a sinister part in the kidnapping and condemnation of the Duc d'Enghien. Now, twenty months later, Savary was courteously received in Wischau and entrusted by the Tsar with an answer to Napoleon's letter. The reply was pleasantly phrased; it spoke of Alexander's sole 'desire to see the peace of Europe re-established with fairness and on a just basis'; and it contained an assurance of the Tsar's wish 'to oblige you personally'; but, with childish pedantry, it was addressed to Napoleon as 'Head of the French Government' rather than as Emperor, an insult which momentarily exasperated its recipient.[11] Yet Napoleon was curious about this extraordinary young man who was risking the armies of two empires on these remote plains of central Europe; and he sent Savary back to the Russian lines with an invitation to Alexander for a personal interview on the following day at any time which was convenient to him. Napoleon had already selected the region where he hoped the Allies would give him battle but he did not want an engagement until he had been reinforced by the arrival of Marshal Davout and the Third Corps from Vienna; and he hoped a meeting with Alexander would at least postpone action for another twenty-four hours. Nor was he being entirely insincere in proposing such a meeting: for, with Vienna in his hands and the Austrian lands split in two by the Grand Army, there were no material gains awaiting him. If the Allies would accept peace on his terms, so much the better. The humiliation of Mack's army at Ulm had been a necessity: there was no need to destroy the Russians and the rump of the Austrians in Moravia. While despatching outriders to hustle up Davout, Napoleon left Brünn and turned eastwards along the Olmütz road to await, with an open mind, the outcome of Savary's second mission.[12]

By the time Savary returned to the Russian outposts, the Allied army was already moving ponderously forward and Bagration delayed him all night, on thin excuses, before sending him under escort to Wischau. There he was received, early in the morning of 29 November, by Dolgoruky who conveyed Napoleon's invitation to the Tsar. A meeting between the two Emperors was, in fact, out of the question because Alexander was unwell; but he, too, would willingly have spared his men the ordeal of battle provided the enemy accepted peace on Russia's terms. He therefore ordered Dolgoruky to accompany Savary back to the French lines and sound out Napoleon.

Dolgoruky was left under guard in a French bivouac while Savary rode ahead and reported to Napoleon. By now the Emperor was impatient and he wasted few words on Savary before mounting his horse and galloping off for his interview with Dolgoruky. Both men subsequently gave accounts of the meeting, and it was clearly not the happiest of encounters.[13] This is hardly surprising, for Dolgoruky was convinced that the French were afraid of the military might facing them and he chose to gratify his egotism by a show of flamboyant arrogance which left Napoleon's judgement seared with rage. To Dolgoruky, Napoleon appeared as 'a little figure, remarkably dirty and ill-dressed' (and he had, indeed, found no opportunity to change his shirt for four days); while Napoleon described the Russian envoy as 'an impertinent young puppy ... who spoke to me as he would have done to a boyar he wished to send to Siberia'. Dolgoruky made no effort to conceal his assumption that fear of defeat was prompting Napoleon to put out peace feelers, and he appears to have offered Napoleon the choice of immediate withdrawal from the Austrian lands and the Italian peninsula or of a renewed war which would only end when the French retired behind the frontiers of 1789. To threaten Napoleon with the loss of Belgium and Savoy when he was encamped at the head of an unbeaten army less than forty miles from Hungary and eighty miles from historic Poland showed either astonishing confusion over strategic geography or a strange assessment of the realities of power. But, whichever the fault, it made little difference to Napoleon. As Savary had already told him, Alexander was clearly surrounded by rogues: if the Russians could do no better than entrust negotiations to 'this perfumed booby Dolgoruky', then nothing would be gained by prolonging the meeting. Savary conducted the Russian to Bagration's forward posts and Napoleon rode back to the village of Bellowitz where he set up his field headquarters five miles east of Brünn.

The Battle of Austerlitz (2 December 1805)

There was little daylight in Moravia during the early days of December. Hence final plans for the clash between the two armies were drawn across maps lit by candles while, outside, camp fires of wood and straw protected chilled limbs from the frozen ground. The wintry weather made the prospect of a bloody encounter seem even grimmer. Although a slight thaw had left the marshy banks of the stream across the plain muddy and slippery, there was still a deceptively thin film of ice on the lakes and ponds nestling at the edge of the plateau. And when, on 1 December, the Tsar emerged from his quarters in Wischau in the misty half-light and mounted his chestnut mare, the escort moved off slowly down the treacherous roads. Even so, once his horse stumbled and he was thrown from the saddle, though he got away with a shaking and some bruises. After two days confined to bed, Alexander looked pale and unsure of himself; but in the early afternoon he was well enough to ride over to the village of Krzenowitz with the Emperor Francis and his personal aides. There Alexander decided to spend the night, sleeping in the largest house in the village, with giant guardsmen from the Semeonovsky Regiment patrolling the solitary track. His physician, James Wylie, remained within easy call in case the fever returned.[14] Kutuzov and his staff were a mile and a half away, housed in the slightly smaller village of Birnbaum; and five to six miles to the west Napoleon and his Marshals were gathered in a third cluster of abandoned homes, the hamlet known as Schlapanitz. The chateau of Austerlitz, which was to give its name to the forthcoming battle, was three miles to the rear of Russian headquarters and that night offered shelter to some members of the Austrian aristocracy who had hunted over these meadows in happier days.

Soon after six in the evening – though it was by then a dark and misty night – Weyrother rode into Birnbaum to go over the final details of the battle plan with the Russian leaders.[15] Not all were there: the Tsar himself was at dinner and had been joined by his brother, Constantine, who was to command the Reserve on the following day; and Prince Bagration, having little taste for a lesson on tactics from a man he despised and distrusted, excused himself on the pretext of keeping watch for enemy movements. Kutuzov was, of course, present, silent and half-asleep, and most of the other Russian commanders were content to follow his example. Langeron, the émigré from Provence, remained alert and has left his record of Weyrother's briefing: 'He read his dispositions to us', he wrote, ' in a tone of uplift and an air of pride which proclaimed his certainty of his own merit and our unworthiness. He was like an usher in a high school reading a lesson to the young pupils. Perhaps we were indeed pupils; but he was by no means a good teacher.'[16] Yet it was the lesson their Tsar had approved, and none of Weyrother's class had the courage to criticize the basic curriculum.

Essentially Weyrother's plan was sound – provided that Napoleon did exactly what he was expected to do. The main Allied force would move southwards across the Pratzen Plateau to the village of Telnitz, where only a thin line of French outposts protected the crossing of a stream known as the Goldbach. Meanwhile, to the north of the battlefield, Bagration would engage the French near the Brünn-Olmütz road, where it was assumed Napoleon most feared a determined attack. Once across the Goldbach, the Allied columns would wheel to the right, encircling the principal French force as it resisted Bagration. The French would then retire towards Brünn and be destroyed by cavalry on their right flank as they fled for safety.

Langeron claims that when Weyrother finished the three-hour exposition, he asked what would happen should Napoleon forestall the Allied move by an attack across the Pratzen Plateau; and he maintains that Weyrother dismissed the point with a shrug of the shoulders as an irrelevant excursion into the hypothetical.[17] But the other Generals resigned themselves to accepting a plan devised by the man to whom Alexander had given his confidence. Weyrother had spent the day in the saddle reconnoitring the region and he delivered his briefing with meticulous attention to detail. It was far too late to modify the operational orders; and Kutuzov, for one, believed that the prime need at the moment was a sound night's sleep. Shortly after midnight the conference abruptly broke up. Only Weyrother and Dolgoruky held high hopes for what would happen when daylight came.

That night there was little sleep for officers or men in either of the opposing armies. Around one o'clock someone in the French camp noticed that the temperature was six below freezing (Centigrade). Outside, hundreds of camp-fires formed parallel avenues of light across the rolling meadows between the villages. There was a crisp breeze and, down to the south, mist drifted over the ponds and swamps beyond Telnitz but elsewhere a good moon picked out the gentle slope running down from the Pratzen Plateau to the Goldbach stream. The stillness of the night magnified every sound, so that the exchange of shots between an Austrian patrol and a Franco-Italian outpost four miles from the centre of the

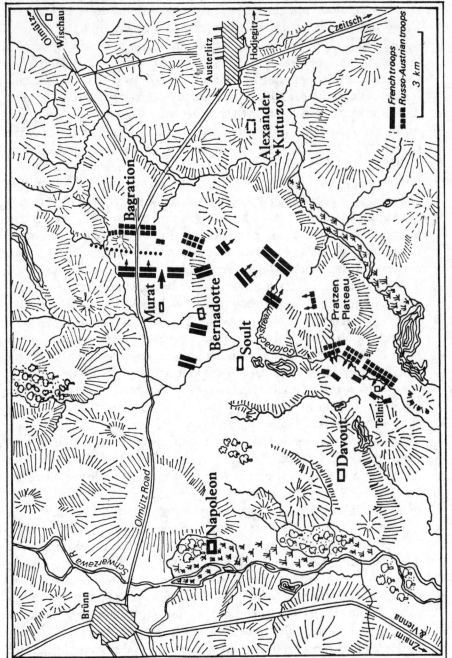

The Battle of Austerlitz

armies was loud enough to put Napoleon on the alert and disturb Dolgoruky, at Russian headquarters across the valley.

An hour later the breeze had dropped and thickening mist blotted out the moonlight, playing weird tricks on strained eyes watching for movements in the opposing line. Even Napoleon was anxious, especially for his weak position around Telnitz, and he rode out to some of the more distant bivouacs, once narrowly missing an encounter with a Cossack patrol. At one point, he dismounted and, while walking towards sentries of one of the French infantry regiments, caught his foot in a tree root and stumbled. Immediately, there was a commotion among the French infantrymen, who rushed forward with torches and shouts of *Vive l'Empereur.* Someone remembered it was the anniversary of Napoleon's coronation and the cry was taken up by other troops in the French line. So great was the noise and excitement, especially among the men of the Guard, that the alarm was sounded, three miles to the east, in the village of Krzenowitz, where Dolgoruky awoke Alexander and one of the Austrian aides hurried off to get the Emperor Francis into his uniform.[18] No one troubled to ride to Birnbaum and awaken Kutuzov. Before either sovereign could mount into the saddle, Bagration had come across from the right wing of the Allied army, and urged everyone to snatch a few more hours' sleep: it was only the French steeling themselves for battle with a show of loyalty at three in the morning.

At half-past six, strictly according to Weyrother's plan, the first infantry – Austrians attached to Buxhöwden's largely Russian army corps – attacked the Franco-Italian outposts before Telnitz. Nearly five miles away Alexander and his aides-de-camp were in the saddle waiting for news. By now, with the slight rise in temperature which preceded dawn, there was a grey fog everywhere; and, for more than an hour, the little group of men at Krzenowitz saw nothing of the battle apart from the constant passage of cavalry and guns moving to the south, spectral columns in the mist. Confused reports seeped through: progress against Telnitz was slow, but by eight o'clock it was clear the Allies had established themselves across the Goldbach, even though Prince Johann von Liechtenstein had mistaken his objective in the fog and sent his Hussars forward to the wrong village. Slowly, surrounded by a guard from the Semeonovsky Regiment, Alexander and his retinue, with the Emperor Francis in attendance, began to ride up the slope to the village of Pratzen. Suddenly, beginning in the east behind the Russian positions, the sun broke through and the fog dispersed. It rolled back as if it were a drop-curtain revealing to the French as it ascended an almost deserted stage, for by now most of the Allied units had moved off to the south, intent on encircling Napoleon's army. At the same time, the mist continued to shroud the principal French positions. Perhaps for as long as half an hour, Alexander and those around him remained unaware how dangerously exposed they were to an enemy attack.

Russian survivors, looking back on the battle of Austerlitz once the campaign was over, found memory playing tricks when they sought to distinguish the events of the following five hours.[19] On the eastern edge of the plateau, between Pratzen village and the approaches to Austerlitz itself, dramatic episodes followed each other with such disconcerting speed that we are left with a record of isolated incidents, scenes sharply defined as in a Shakespearean chronicle and with all the dramatist's imprecision over the passage of time. No one is certain, for example, when precisely Alexander rebuked Kutuzov for his inactivity. It cannot, however, have been long after eight o'clock, as the exchange of words themselves show. Why, asked Alexander was Kutuzov retaining General Miloradovich's division beside him in front of Krzenowitz rather than riding with them across the Pratzen Plateau? 'I am waiting, Sire', replied Kutuzov patiently, 'since not all the columns have yet formed up.' But it was not a good enough explanation for Alexander, who exclaimed haughtily, 'Come now, Mikhail Ilarionovich, we are not on the parade-ground where a march-past does not begin until all the troops are assembled.' 'Exactly, Sire,' responded Kutuzov. 'It is because we are not on parade that I am waiting. But if you wish me to go forward . . .'[20] And thus the whole column moved across the Plateau, with the Marshal slowly following Miloradovich. Kutuzov was still worried over what orders Napoleon would give when he saw the main Russo-Austrian force wheeling round his right flank. But, since the Tsar would not permit his commander-in-chief to wait longer, the Marshal set out for Pratzen with Alexander watching, erect and motionless astride his chestnut mare.

Within minutes, it seems, Napoleon's answer to the Allied manoeuvre was revealed, not only to Kutuzov but to Alexander and his retinue also as they looked towards the plateau. For at eight-thirty Marshal Soult's cavalry bore briskly down the slope beyond Pratzen and against the weakened centre of the Allied line. Soon Kutuzov was wounded in the cheek by a glancing shot and both Alexander and Francis came under fire. The two Emperors, reining in their horses, watched from a knoll as Miloradovich's division caught the impact of the French assault. Later, Czartoryski wrote down the impressions he received as he stood beside Alexander:

I saw very distinctly the two lines of enemy cavalry execute in succession several charges ... There was an outcry for the Tsar's safety: the horses were turned and we galloped off ... A large battery of Russian guns, with its commander totally distraught, was being led in the opposite direction from the field of battle. I forced him to turn back and assist the columns hard-pressed in front of us. By good fortune I was constantly meeting the Tsar as he visited in succession different firing-positions and he often sent me forward to see what was happening.[21]

The panic cannot have lasted long, but soon all the Allied centre was falling back to the woods and pheasantries of the Austerlitz estate. Despite his wounds, Kutuzov sought to restore some order into the retreat and sent urgent messages to Bagration, on the Brünn–Olmütz road, summoning him back so that his men might form defensive squares and check the French thrust. By half-past nine the fighting had died away between Pratzen and Austerlitz, but further to the south the main Austro-Prussian army which had taken Telnitz was hopelessly isolated. With Napoleon pouring more and more men into the breach which Soult had made, the troops around Telnitz were now themselves threatened with encirclement. 'I saw', says Czartoryski, 'the wretched Weyrother wandering from place to place bravely risking his life in an effort to redeem the disaster of which he was one of the chief causes.'[22] Yet, though the Allies could not win the day, all was not lost: Bagration was still holding out and Miloradovich performing feats of valour under the Tsar's admiring eyes. Provided the weather held, there remained the possibility of a counter-attack which might at least dislodge the enemy: an inconclusive stalemate was preferable to total defeat.

For two hours the fighting continued on either flank. At eleven Kutuzov sent orders to Buxhöwden, commanding at Telnitz, to retire across the Goldbach Stream and link up with the Guard regiments around Austerlitz itself; but Kutuzov's outrider could not get through the enemy screen and it was three in the afternoon before the Marshal's instructions reached Buxhöwden. The crucial decision on whether or not to counter-attack had to be taken soon after midday, with no news reaching either Kutuzov or Alexander from the left flank. The weather was rapidly deteriorating: no more sunshine, only an icy wind and grey rolling clouds threatening snow. About half-past twelve, the counter-attack came.[23] But by whom was it ordered? Not, it would appear, by Kutuzov nor by Alexander; and certainly not by the Austrians, for it cut almost across Johann von Liechtenstein's cavalry as they sought to move in a crablike progression northwards to make contact with Bagration. The counter-attack was led by the commanding General of the Reserve, probably on his own initiative. For the Reserve – ten battalions and eighteen squadrons of the Russian Imperial Guard – had been entrusted to the Grand Duke Constantine. Alone of all commanders in the field, the brother of the Tsar might risk with impunity the consequences of independent action. It was the bravest and most tragic gesture of the day; and it cost the two finest regiments in the Russian army more than 500 dead and 200 prisoners.

Napoleon, who had seen little of the morning's fighting at close hand, personally witnessed the charge of the Russian Imperial Guard – more than a thousand horsemen galloping up the slopes of the Pratzen Plateau towards the French cannon and a glinting wall of wavering bayonets. The sheer impetus of the assault inevitably broke the French line, but, as Napoleon's reinforcements closed in on the attackers, the awful futility of the charge was made clear to observers in the two opposing camps. Constantine himself, indistinguishable from his brother officers in cavalry helmet and breastplate, charged bravely at the head of one of his squadrons and was nearly captured by Mamelukes, who seized the squadron standard. Within half an hour it was all over. The survivors regrouped around Constantine in the village of Krzenowitz, where Alexander had spent the previous night, but they were given no respite. As the snow began to fall Marshal Bernadotte sent in his weary cavalry against Krzenowitz, and by two o'clock what was left of the Imperial Guard was falling down the mile-long avenue of chestnuts and past the château of Austerlitz in search of their defeated Tsar. 'There are many fine ladies who will weep tomorrow in Petersburg', declared Napoleon, as he saw the slope of the Plateau strewn with the hideous aftermath of Constantine's charge.[24]

The battle was over, but not yet finished. Marshal Davout's Third Corps – for whose arrival from Vienna Napoleon had delayed engaging the enemy – had the wretched task of pursuing Buxhöwden's men as they sought escape from the trap at Telnitz. It was not a glorious feat of arms, for many of the Russians were drowned as hot shot rained down from the French guns on the thin ice of frozen ponds across which they were seeking to make their way towards Austerlitz. Ultimately, however, it was decisive. The Russian troops were hungry, wet and cold. Though fewer perished than the Bulletins of the Grand Army were subsequently to claim, those who survived had lost their will to resist. Some 20,000 men, more than half of Buxhöwden's corps, emerged unscathed physically from the battle, but they could no longer be described as a fighting force. By half-past four, with all daylight gone, they were tramping eastwards without any clear purpose, except the instinct to live.[25] The tracks were deep in mud and slush, and sleet scudded down from a night sky in which there was no sign of moon or stars. Somewhere beyond Austerlitz were the young Tsar and the old Marshal; but nobody in the defeated army was certain where they had found refuge. At the moment it did not seem to matter very much; for at least they were away from the treacherous plains of Moravia and nearer to the Russian homeland, still almost four hundred miles distant.

Alexander Humiliated

Theoretically General Buxhöwden knew where he should find Alexander and Kutuzov. For, on the previous evening, the Marshal had privately instructed the army commanders and the Tsar's aides-de-camp that, if Weyrother's plan failed to put the French to flight, the Russians must fall back on the river Morava.[26] The first rallying point would be a cluster of wooden huts marked on the map as the village of Hodjegitz, little more than two miles east of Austerlitz.

Around five o'clock on 2 December Alexander duly arrived at Hodjegitz, with the smallest of escorts.[27] His usually flaccid face was strangely taut and tears of humiliation ran down his cheeks. There was no sign of Kutuzov, nor of any other senior commander. For, though the Marshal had foreseen the probable need to retreat, he had never anticipated a rout, in which the survivors would be spread out in jostling columns across five or six miles of rolling countryside. The surprising fact was that Alexander's aides should have shown such sense of order as actually to find Hodjegitz. Kutuzov himself, along with Constantine, Miloradovich and what was left of the Imperial Guard, had reached the hamlet of Wazan, four miles from Hodjegitz; but the triple combination of inadequate maps, bad weather and French patrols prevented any of the commander-in-chief's couriers from getting through to the Tsar. One of Alexander's aides, reconnoitring around Hodjegitz, did however encounter an Austrian officer who told him that Emperor Francis was in the small town of Czeitsch, eight miles to the south. Since it was clear Alexander was still too close to Napoleon for safety, he announced to his aides in the early evening he would set out at once for Czeitsch and a conference with the Austrian Emperor.

The decision was a bad one. Alexander was forced to travel on foot or in the saddle, for his carriage had become a casualty of the battle. It was hard going and he was desperately weary and at times feverish. Soon it became clear he could not manage the eight miles to Czeitsch.[28] He collapsed in one of the villages on the way and was helped into a peasant's hut, where he was able to rest under a makeshift quilt of straw. Fortunately James Wylie had remained with him continuously since leaving Wischau, but the position was serious. The ruler of Russia, with five or six men around him, was isolated in a remote clearing in the Moravian woodland, where there were neither comforts nor medicaments for a sick man. At three in the morning he was seized by such a violent cramp in the lower intestines that Wylie feared for his life (or so the Empress Elizabeth was told three weeks later).[29] Leaving Czartoryski at Alexander's bedside, Wylie rode on to Czeitsch and begged an Austrian officer at the headquarters of Francis to let him have some red wine to warm his patient's stomach. The Austrian – still according to Elizabeth's account – refused the request and Wylie was forced to bribe a servant so as to secure 'half a bottle of poor red wine'. By the time Wylie returned to the Tsar, the attack of stomach cramp seems to have passed, for at seven in the morning Alexander was well enough to clamber back into the saddle.

Later that morning Alexander was re-united with the Emperor Francis and with Kutuzov. Although the Allies had lost between 25,000 and 30,000 men killed, wounded or captured at Austerlitz, they still possessed an army of nominally 60,000 men, with the prospect of reinforcements from Bohemia and from the army of the Archduke Charles, which had retreated from Venetia to Styria. Moreover there was the certainty of further levies arriving from Russian Poland and, above all, the hope that Prussia would honour the treaty which Alexander and Frederick William had signed in Potsdam only a month ago. Alexander certainly had no intention of suing for peace, though he had lost some of the finest horsemen in his cavalry squadrons and a hundred and thirty-three pieces of field artillery, more than half the guns with which Arakcheev had equipped the army. But to Francis and his ministers the situation seemed almost hopeless: they had little faith in Prussia's word, especially as Haugwitz, one of the leading 'pro-French' counsellors in Berlin, had already arrived at Napoleon's headquarters and been sent on to negotiate with Talleyrand in Vienna. It seemed absurd to the Austrians to continue a war in which there was no immediate prospect of ousting the invader from their capital city; the longer the campaign dragged on, the harder would be the peace terms. Francis resolved to send Prince Johann von Liechtenstein to Napoleon in Austerlitz and seek an armistice, a personal meeting and a separate peace. Hostilities between Austria and France duly ended on the following day (4 December) and it was agreed that the conditions of armistice should apply to the Russians as well, provided that they evacuated the Habsburg lands and retired across the river Bug to their own territories.[30]

The Russian army was already plodding back eastwards and, as soon as his conferences in Czeitsch were over, Alexander joined the homeward trek. He made good speed, up the valley of the Vah to Trencin, through the western Beskids to Teschen and then along the upper Vistula to Lublin and across the frontier to Brest. On 6 December he despatched Dolgoruky with a letter of explanation to Frederick William in Berlin: the Tsar indicated his intention of continuing the campaign until he could establish a just and lasting peace with Napoleon and he renewed an offer to support the Prussians by two army corps.[31] He also informed Frederick William that he was sending Grand Duke Constantine to supplement Dolgoruky's efforts or (as the Tsar himself more tactfully phrased it) to serve 'as an eye-witness of all that has taken place'.[32] With the Grand Army still deployed in central Europe, a resolute advance by the Prussians and the two Russian army corps might seriously embarrass Napoleon and counter some of the humiliation of Austerlitz.

But, while Alexander was hurrying back to his capital, Frederick William had taken stock of the situation. The oath sworn over Frederick's tomb now seemed somehow a little less valid than in the emotive Gothic twilight of November. Besides, Talleyrand was treating Haugwitz with courtesy and generosity: if Prussia ceded the French those two tiresome enclaves of Ansbach and Neuchatel, Frederick William could receive the cherished prize of Hanover. Hence on 15 December, the very day on which by Alexander's calculations the Prussians should have gone to war, Frederick William's envoys put their signatures beside Talleyrand's in the palace of Schönbrünn and Prussia became a beneficiary of Napoleon's latest round of map-making.[33] It was not what Dolgoruky or Constantine had anticipated and it rendered their Berlin mission pointless. The news reached Alexander as the horses hastened him across the bleak Polish plain where two army corps were ready for a war which would not now be fought. If he was surprised he did not show it: there were so many betrayals and disappointments on which he might ponder. 'Everything I have sought to undertake has turned disastrously against me', he remarked;[34] but he spoke with resignation rather than self-pity. Full details of what had happened at Austerlitz only reached St Petersburg on Wednesday, 18 December, more than a fortnight after the battle. The capital had been so long without news that, as the Empress Elizabeth wrote to her mother, 'everyone was trying to keep up their spirits by persuading themselves that speculation one way or the other could not be true'.[35]

There was, in consequence, some relief at first that neither the army, nor the Tsar himself, had been wiped out and the magnitude of the disaster was not immediately apparent. Since the Russians were still at war while the Austrians had sued for peace, it was assumed that the battle had been lost through 'the infamous conduct of the Austrians'. Even Elizabeth, who was normally generous at heart, could write, 'the name "Austrian" is and must be a term of abhorrence, not only to every Russian but to every being who has a soul.'[36] And, as soon as she heard Alexander was coming directly to his capital, she ordered her carriage to take her to Gatchina. There she had to spend a tense day and a half with Marie Feodorovna as the two Empresses awaited the return of their husband and son, each subject to strong emotions which neither could hide from the other.

Alexander arrived at Gatchina shortly after midnight on 21 December.[37] He exchanged no more than a few words with his mother and then insisted, with some of his old restlessness, on changing horses and driving through the night over the last thirty-odd miles to the Winter Palace. He talked endlessly to Elizabeth of the frustration and disappointments of the campaign. As ever when he was over-burdened with inner conflicts, he found in her the perfect listener, one who burned with anger for every slight he had sustained. Two days later she wrote, 'What I suffered in that coach from hearing of all these indignities will never be erased from my memory.'[38] The horses clattered into the great square behind the Palace at five o'clock on a Saturday morning. Alexander thought he could not face the ordeal of a public return in daylight. He would carry his sorrows silently to his room, with only guardsmen to see the heaviness of his step.

Yet he had forgotten the faith of his devoted Petersburgers.[39] They heard on the Friday evening that the Tsar was expected back at any hour. It was enough for them that 'their Angel' had returned unscathed from the wars. Throughout the bitterly cold December night they kept a vigil in the square; and they were there in hundreds to salute his carriage as it ended the long journey home. Deeply moved he went, as soon as possible, to the Cathedral where he had knelt in prayer on that other Saturday morning, three months and an eternity before. As he tried to make his way back from the Cathedral to the Winter Palace the collective emotion of the crowd thrust it forward and he became once more a God among his subjects, as in Moscow at his coronation. 'Everyone pressed towards him, so tightly packed that he could make no progress', wrote Paul Stroganov's wife afterwards, 'They prostrated themselves, seeking to kiss his feet and hands, even his uniform; and they were delirious with joy.'[40] Tears ran down Alexander's cheeks, and he was heard to assure those around him that such a demonstration 'so dear to his heart' healed 'the suffering of his soul'.[41] It could not, however, bring back the regiments lost on the Moravian plain nor mend the broken limbs of wounded captives left in French care. Those who understood events would neither forget nor forgive the humiliation of Austerlitz.

7

Anathema

Inquest on Austerlitz

'Let us not mention Austerlitz, Mamma. There is so much to say on that inexhaustible subject that there is no point in beginning to set it down on paper.'[1] So wrote Elizabeth a month after Alexander's return; and it is easy to understand her reluctance. For by mid-January 1806 the mood of demonstrative sympathy and relief had evaporated and, at Court and in the fashionable salons, people were seeking to understand what had gone wrong.[2] As more and more survivors arrived home with blurred tales of confusion and chaos it became clear the battle had been an overwhelmingly Russian disaster, not to be explained away by facile accusations of Austrian incompetence. Long and painful analyses posed awkward questions. Why was there no co-ordination between infantry, gunners and cavalry? Did the Tsar's friends induce their sovereign to scorn the advice of his field commanders? And why, for that matter, did the Tsar rely so heavily for his counsellors on favourites of the parade-ground, un-schooled in battle? It was all too easy to find answers which cast doubts on Alexander's judgement. Small wonder if Elizabeth preferred to talk of other things.

Alexander knew very well he had failed. For two years he had willed himself to think and act as a soldier, the supreme commander of the future, leading his armies westward and imposing territorial boundaries upon a grateful continent. At Austerlitz that dream was shattered, along with many other illusions of his youth. But he could not immediately abandon either the Coalition or the policies which had carried Russia into war, and obstinacy made him at first retain the very men against whom his critics railed: Czartoryski was instructed to prepare memoranda on what might still be gained in the Mediterranean, Paul Stroganov was sent to London to reassure the British; Dolgoruky continued to hold secret talks with the Prussians; and Arakcheev, who was alleged to have been seen riding hastily eastward on the morning of the battle, was appointed head of a commission to enquire into the failure of the artillery on that decisive December day.[3] Outwardly there was no change in men or measures at St Petersburg. The Tsar had little wish to make personal friends scapegoats: they knew him and his policy too well. Though he was conscious of their deep sense of loyalty so long as they remained close to the throne, he could not be certain if, in adversity, they would continue to observe the same reticent silence. There had been some moments at Olmütz and Austerlitz, perhaps even earlier, when Alexander's conduct had fallen short of the occasion and (as one of his more responsible friends wrote in a private letter) 'he listened only to a few giddy-headed young men.'[4] Now that his own prestige in the capital was sinking rapidly, he had no desire to strengthen the hands of his critics by a public breach with advisers so recently in his confidence. Who, after all, would take their place? Better seek to live down the disaster of Austerlitz with ministers of one's own choice than risk dependence on narrowly Russian nationalists from the Senatorial party or on the small group who hankered after a French alliance despite the humiliations of the past year.

Yet, in pressing new responsibilities on his friends, Alexander reckoned without the hostility of his own family. When her eldest son had returned from the war, Marie Feodorovna rejoiced as thankfully as any Russian mother. Though she always disliked and distrusted Czartoryski, she insisted on presenting him with a personal gift 'for not having left her son's side during the battle or afterwards'.[5] But as soon as the Grand Duke Constantine reached Gatchina from his abortive Prussian mission, the Dowager Empress became herself once more, and tart letters of reproach were despatched to the Winter Palace, upbraiding Alexander for his vacillations and cautioning him against the intrigues of the Pole. For Constantine had acquired in Moravia a high regard for his own valour which, when added to his skill in showing off and his jealousy of his elder brother, made him an irresponsible nuisance at Court. He made it clear he believed Czartoryski's conduct of foreign affairs to be little short of treason and maintained that Arakcheev had supplied the artillery with lightweight guns which disintegrated under the strain of rapid fire. Whatever others might think of Constantine's soldierly qualities, his mother –

and the younger members of the family – were suitably impressed; and by the middle of February Alexander was under almost daily pressure to cut himself free from the last ties linking him with his friends of the Secret Committee.

The End of Government by the Tsar's Friends

Unfortunately this crisis in government, following so closely on the traumatic shock of Austerlitz, sapped what remained of Alexander's confidence while leaving his determination to rule as an autocrat un-diminished. Throughout most of the year 1806, his conduct of affairs was again weak and dilatory: meetings of councils and committees were un-duly protracted; there were long discussions on alternative policies and no business was settled. Czartoryski was bitterly disappointed.[6] 'The Emperor is always the same, mingling fear with weakness to the highest degree', he wrote confidentially in mid-February,

We are afraid of everything, we can no longer take vigorous steps; it is not even possible to advise him because he will not take advice. The Emperor still prefers to keep us [i.e. Czartoryski, Kochubey and Novosiltsov] in order to avoid the embarrassment of making a change, but he would like to act only according to his own fancy. Misfortune has not strengthened his powers of logical analysis: he has become more arbitrary than ever before. Such accumulation of weakness, uncertainty, fear, injustice and extravagant gestures fills one only with gloom and despair.[7]

And Paul Stroganov, who was by nature far more patient and staid than Czartoryski, was almost as critical. He confided to his wife in a note on 18 February[7], 'I love our Emperor as much as is humanly possible but I pity him for possessing such a character. What kind of future will there be for those on whom he calls to govern? In the Emperor's mind they would be destined as mere blind instruments of his will.'[8]

A policy of balance and careful trimming – even occasionally of procrastination – has its merits in times of peace, with ministers sharply divided over measures of domestic reform. But it is an impossible line of conduct for any government at war, least of all in one seeking to save its face after crushing military defeat. By February 1806 the contests with Napoleon had come virtually to a standstill. The only point of contact between the French and Russian forces was in the Adriatic where Admiral Dmitri Senyavin's naval squadron waged an enterprising campaign against French outposts in southern Dalmatia. Czartoryski, increasingly exasper-ated at the inertia in St Petersburg, tried to persuade Alexander to support

Senyavin by a forward policy in the Balkans, rousing the Greeks and the southern Slavs against Russia's traditional foe, Turkey, and her present enemy, France. It was all in vain. Alexander thought only of security, of some observation platform beyond the range of Napoleon's armies where he might watch and wait. Now that Pitt had died, the Tsar had little interest in the English alliance or in what was left of the Third Coalition. Czartoryski, who had worked as much as any man to bring the Coalition together, reminded Alexander of Peter the Great's warning. 'We have nothing but honour, and to renounce it is to cease to be a monarch.'[9] But such solemn words from the past failed, for once, to evoke a response in Alexander. As a young man Peter, too, suffered defeat and waited nine years for his revenge; and Alexander felt able to insist that he was in no hurry. 'Let us remain totally passive and not make any move until the time when we are attacked upon our own soil,' he declared.[10]

For Czartoryski it was all too much. In the fourth week of March he sought to resign, only to be told that his sovereign still needed him. In April Czartoryski changed his tactics. He sent the Tsar a letter, several thousand words in length, in which he reviewed foreign and military policy over the previous three years.[11] It is a remarkable document, a rare indictment of a sovereign by his minister: Alexander, it maintained, had wasted time between the original breach with France and the start of the campaign; he had allowed personal sentiment to shape his policy towards Prussia; he had hampered conduct of the campaign by joining the army in the field and insisting on giving Napoleon battle. 'Your presence at Austerlitz was of no value', wrote Czartoryski with icy candour. 'The rout was most immediate and complete at the point where you stood. Your Imperial Majesty participated in it and was forced to retire rapidly, an embarrassment you should never have risked.'

Oddly enough, Alexander accepted this lesson in statecraft and soldiery with pained forbearance rather than anger. He was honest enough with himself to see that most of what Czartoryski wrote was true. By now, moreover, he was well accustomed to receiving hectoring notes from his mother at Gatchina or Pavlovsk, none of them so cogently argued as this letter from someone whom he was still glad to acknowledge as 'a devoted friend'. Throughout the spring he pressed Czartoryski to stay in office, though privately he began to sound out possible successors in April. Inevitably Tsar and minister met almost every day; and it was with Czartoryski's agreement that Alexander sent a special emissary to Paris in the hope that a general peace might replace the indeterminate state of no-war between the two countries.[12] In the second week of May Czartoryski drew up clear and detailed instructions for Oubril, whom the Tsar had selected for the mission: he was not to sacrifice Russia's interests for transitory gains. But subsequently Alexander informed Oubril orally of his own personal desire for a settlement, and confidentially made it clear that Czartoryski's ministerial appointment would soon be ended.[13]

The final breach came in the closing days of May. The two men found themselves engaged in 'several heated controversies', as Czartoryski wrote at the time. Once more he went through the familiar ritual of tendering his resignation; and on this occasion – perhaps a little to his surprise – he found Alexander prepared to accept it.[14]

Czartoryski's departure was not made public until the beginning of July, when it was announced that General Andrei Budberg had been appointed Minister of Foreign Affairs (a title never formally accorded to his predecessor). The news was received with mixed feelings both in St Petersburg and Moscow.[15] There was little personal sympathy for Czartoryski; the old Russian families still maintained that, however loyal to the dynasty he might be, his Polish patriotism inevitably conflicted with the true needs of the Empire; and they were glad to see him go. But everyone was alarmed at the appointment of Budberg, a Baltic baron whose diplomatic experience was limited to a disastrous spell at the Swedish Court, whence he was hurriedly recalled at the Swedes' own request. From his estate near Moscow, Theodore Rostopchin – who could never quite understand why he was not himself offered preferment – let it be known that Budberg had just sufficient intelligence to make a capable foreign minister of San Marino; and most of the diplomats in St Petersburg soon came to agree with Rostopchin.[16] There was indeed little to be said in poor Budberg's favour: his Estonian origin made him unacceptable to the true Russian conservatives among the nobility and his ignorance of Europe aroused the intelligentsia to derisive contempt. Twelve years ago he had been an amiable and conscientious instructor to the Tsar, teaching him the rudiments of military science; but he had refused all later advancement, partly on the grounds of bad health, but also because he genuinely doubted his own abilities. Even now, only the formidable insistence of Marie Feodorovna browbeat him into accepting the Foreign Ministry. What did Alexander gain by thrusting into high office a man of such limited capacity? Could it be that, after three years of Czartoryski, Alexander wished for a servant rather than a master? So at least believed the Austrian ambassador.[17]

Some people, both foreign residents and native Russians, regretted the Pole's departure for another reason. So long as he was able to influence the

Tsar, Russian policy could champion an alternative programme to the new ideology of the French. Now that was no longer possible, and the mood of the government both in home affairs and over war aims became cautiously conservative. Czartoryski's fall marked the final dispersal of the Secret Committee. Though as a body it never met after 1803, its members remained close to Alexander until his return from Austerlitz. But, with Czartoryski gone, neither Novosiltsov nor Paul Stroganov wished to retain responsible posts in the administration, and both soon resigned.[18] Although they remained members of the Senate, they faded from the public eye. Kochubey alone continued in office, at least for another fifteen months, but he never succeeded in capturing Alexander's interest for any of his reform projects. For the moment little was left of the ideals which fired the Tsar's enthusiasm in earlier years. The visionary had lost sight of his apocalypse; and in doing so he became hardly distinguishable from the frightened autocrats of Berlin and Vienna, uncertain of themselves in a world which outpaced their imagination.

Across the Bridge

Throughout the year 1806 the people of Russia saw little of their sovereign. The Tsar remained close to St Petersburg, venturing out occasionally as far as Pavlovsk or Gatchina, but taking little part in the life of the capital.[19] He showed no interest at all in what took place in Moscow (where they feted Bagration) or in Kiev (where they heaped honours on a convalescent Kutuzov). Inevitably Alexander's remoteness encouraged gossip and rumour. It was said that his character was coming more and more to resemble his father's: unpredictable moods of anger and suspicion descending with the suddenness of a summer storm; black days when he wished to hide from the public eye; and hours of deep remorse when (so they said) the memory of Austerlitz left him broken with tears. Once more, people caught a fleeting glimpse of a barouche hurrying out in the evenings, across the bridge of boats, past the Fortress of St Peter and St Paul, and along the straight avenue towards the Greater Neva and Maria Naryshkin's villa; and they knew their Tsar was escaping from the cares of government and the strain of life in the Winter Palace.

The Tsar's behaviour provoked censorious comment in unexpected places. A mischievous 'letter from St Petersburg' was printed in Le Publiciste, a Parisian newspaper, on 12 February: the political life of the Russian capital was, it said, dominated by the Dowager Empress, while 'the reigning Empress has only the modest ambition of finding means to recapture her husband's heart', and it went on to paint a sensational picture of the scandal caused by 'the constant favours and gifts' bestowed by the Tsar on 'Madame de Naryshkin ... a beautiful Polish woman'.[20] *Le Publiciste* already had a tradition of gutter journalism, going back at least eight years to the Congress of Rastatt when it had reflected piously on the deplorable reputation of the Metternich family (father and son) who were among Austria's representatives;[21] but it was a publication which enjoyed wide readership in France and the Bonapartist dependencies, and eventually a copy reached Alexander's mother-in-law in Karlsruhe. The Margravine cannot, in all honesty, have been surprised at the relevations. Only two months previously Napoleon himself had said to her, 'Your son-in-law is surrounded by Poles – his minister and his mistress come from that nation, and the last-named is a worthless woman.' But the Margravine could not ignore the gossip. Strictures on moral rectitude from the Emperor of the French might be dismissed with an ironic sigh of disbelief; prurient pillorying in the public press was another matter. On 3 April 'with pain', the Margravine sent the more damning extracts from the French newspaper to her daughter in St Petersburg.[22]

As Elizabeth well knew, the report was not far removed from the truth. Never before had the Dowager Empress and her whims carried such weight in the affairs of the capital; while Alexander's flirtations (which were by no means limited to Countess Naryshkin) had become notorious. But Elizabeth was too proud and too tolerant to turn her marriage into a dog-fight. She resented the masterful manners of Marie Feodorovna and the flaunting insolence of the Polish courtesan, just as she had done two years before; but now she knew – as no journalist suspected – that she was better fitted to meet a challenge to her domestic happiness. For by the day she received her mother's letter she had discovered that, for the first time in seven years, she was pregnant. At last she hoped to present Russia with an heir to the Imperial title. If St Petersburg saw little of Elizabeth that summer, it was not that she frowned on her husband's behaviour but that she needed long hours of rest in the quiet of Kammionyi Island. There, at the small gem of a palace which Bezhenov had built for Paul, she could look out on the pallid stillness of the Finnish waters and find the tranquillity the city denied her. Alexander, for all his waywardness, was most solicitous for Elizabeth's well-being.[23] Kammionyi Island was only three miles from the Winter Palace itself; and sometimes that summer and autumn, as the Imperial carriage swept across the River Neva, it was carrying the Tsar, not to the voluptuous Maria, but to his wife in Bezhenov's villa above the reedy shallows of the Gulf.

On 15 November, 1806, Elizabeth duly gave birth to her child. Three days later she sent a brief note to Karlsruhe, 'I am doing fine, my darling Mamma, and so is my little Elise who asks you to forgive her for not being a boy.'[24] Salvoes of rejoicing were fired in St Petersburg and Moscow; and Alexander was relieved at Elizabeth's safe delivery. Characteristically he insisted on doubling the number of physicians in attendance upon her, and then ordered her to remain in bed for one day longer than the nine which the most cautious of her doctors recommended.[25] Alexander still had no son to succeed him; but, if pangs of regret troubled him, he hid his anguish with comforting reassurance and was delighted to be, once more, the father of a baby daughter.

Preparing for War on Two Fronts, 1806

By November 1806, when the child was born, Alexander had again become deeply involved in the European conflict. To outside observers Budberg's foreign policy seemed hardly distinguishable from his predecessor's, except that it lacked long-term planning. Within four months of Czartoryski's resignation the Russians were engaged in the two-front war which he had long anticipated: a campaign against Turkey on the lower Danube; and a renewed campaign against the French on the plains of Poland. Neither enterprise showed, however, the offensive spirit which Czartoryski had sought eagerly to encourage in Alexander and his more conservative advisors; and in both instances the decisive move towards war was taken by foreign sovereigns rather than by the Tsar.

In June Napoleon sent a note to his foreign minister, Talleyrand, in which he declared, 'The ultimate object of my policy is to make a triple alliance of myself, the Porte [i.e. Turkey] and Persia, aimed against Russia directly or by implication.'[26] Ever since the defeat at Austerlitz, the Turks had shown suspicion and hostility towards their Russian neighbour and the Sultan welcomed French overtures in Constantinople, hoping that Turkey might recover her old mastery of the Black Sea if joint operations with the French and the Persians made the Tsar sue for peace. The Russians, however, were disinclined to stand idly by and watch a hostile combination form against them. There was a formidable war party in St Petersburg which had long desired to resume the Russian march southwards, and as soon as the Turkish attitude stiffened, the Russians began to concentrate an army of 35,000 men between the lower Bug and the Dniester. When, at the end of August, the Sultan replaced the Governors of the two Danubian Principalities (Moldavia and Wallachia) by agents of the French, there was an explosion of wrath in St Petersburg, intensified by the Sultan's refusal to allow Russian warships through the Bosphorus and Dardanelles to join Senyavin's squadron in the Adriatic; and early in November Alexander authorized his troops to cross the River Dniester and invade the Roumanian regions of the Sultan's Empire.[27] Thus, almost as a sideshow, a war began with Turkey which was to drag on intermittently for five and a half years. It tied down trained troops whom the Tsar could ill spare from the north.

These developments coincided with the resumption of hostilities in central Europe. In July 1806 it seemed to Napoleon – and indeed to many Russians – as if there was a good prospect of establishing peace between the two empires. Oubril had arrived in Paris convinced his sovereign was eager for a settlement; and on 20 July he signed a treaty with Talleyrand in which the French conceded many of the points for which Alexander had pressed.[28] But the Tsar subsequently refused to have the Oubril treaty ratified: he maintained that it sacrificed the interests of Russia in the Adriatic while acknowledging Napoleon's right to determine the political structure of the German lands without reference to the other European Powers. For several months Russia and France thus continued to eye each other suspiciously, still locked in that curious state of suspended belligerency which had prevailed ever since the Tsar's return from Austerlitz.

Napoleon was irritated by the cavalier way in which the Oubril treaty was cast aside.[29] He attributed Alexander's change of heart to private exchanges with Frederick William in Berlin. In this he was perfectly correct. The King of Prussia, whose good German soul was almost as conscience-torn as Alexander's, was alarmed by the reflection that after Austerlitz his country's pusillanimity was hardly in accord with the macabre pledges the two sovereigns had made at Potsdam; and he continued throughout the summer of 1806 to keep in contact with Alexander.[30] By midsummer there was a more prosaic reason for Russo-Prussian collaboration: the creation by Napoleon of a new Confederation of the Rhine, from which Prussia was excluded, lost Frederick William any opportunity he might have had for dominating northern Germany and made him believe that Hanover (which he had so long coveted) would become yet another French dependency. A secret Russo-Prussian declaration was signed in Berlin precisely one week before Oubril's empty triumph in Paris.[31] By the second week in August the Russian ambassador in Berlin was collaborating so closely with the Prussian ministers that Frederick William was justified in assuming he could rely on Russian military assistance if war with France came in the autumn.

The pace of events in Germany was, however, much too rapid for Alexander. Despite commitments on the Turkish Front, he believed he could raise an army of 60,000 men to concentrate in Lithuania and Russian Poland by the end of October, with a further force of comparable size arriving within the following fortnight; but it was impossible for the Russians to be ready for operations in the German lands before the weather broke. For, quite apart from normal difficulties of mobilizing an army, Alexander was confronted by a problem peculiar to the conditions of Russian service: he had to find a commander-in-chief acceptable to the majority of his senior officers, to the Dowager Empress and, above all, to himself.[32] He refused to consider Kutuzov or Bagration, resisted the claims of his brother Constantine, and thought it impolitic to choose anyone not of Russian origin. At the top of his short list were two veterans from the wars of his grandmother and father, Marshal Kamensky and Marshal Prozorovsky, whom it would have been kinder to leave vegetating in retirement. Since Prozorovsky's eyesight was so bad that he could not even recognize his Tsar, Alexander eventually appointed Kamensky, who was said to suffer from so many ailments that he was never sure which was troubling him at any one moment. Effective control of the army in the field was entrusted to Bennigsen, a far abler soldier than either of the old Marshals but a man whose role in the conspiracy against Paul had earned him the implacable hatred of Marie Feodorovna. There was so little sense of urgency in St Petersburg that Kamensky did not even set out until 22 November, more than six weeks after the opening of the campaign.[33]

Frederick William, on the other hand, acted with foolhardy impetuosity. At the end of September, the Prussian Prime Minister in Paris delivered an ultimatum demanding the immediate withdrawal of French troops from Germany east of the Rhine. There was never any possibility that the French would accept such imperious conditions, and war followed on 7 October. The Prussian high command hoped to surprise the French, inflict an initial defeat before the coming of winter, and then rely on Russian aid to tip the balance finally against Napoleon. But the French had anticipated Prussian action. Within a week of the outbreak of war, Frederick William's army was routed in the twin battles of Jena and Auerstadt.[34] The route to the Prussian capital lay open even before Alexander had begun to concentrate the vanguard of his army. Napoleon arrived at Potsdam on 24 October and entered Berlin itself three days later. The Prussian ministers, broken and cowed by the experience of defeat, urged Frederick William to sue at once for peace. It began to seem as if the Russians would not, after all, be required to march westwards that winter.

There followed, however, a strange intrusion of private affairs into public policy. When the French armies were approaching Berlin, Frederick William and his Queen fled eastwards towards the Vistulan fortress towns and the comparative security of Königsberg; but they left so hurriedly that most of their personal belongings remained in the Charlottenburg Palace. As soon as Napoleon reached the city he ordered a search to be made among the archives and confidential papers for evidence of the diplomatic policy which his two enemies were pursuing. Diligent civil servants accordingly handed over to him copies of the correspondence between Alexander and Frederick William earlier in the year; and he thus received confirmation of what he had long suspected, that the Tsar was encouraging the King to resist the French at the very moment when, in Paris, they were negotiating the abortive treaty with Oubril. This revelation of Alexander's duplicity made Napoleon unreasonably angry.[35] He decided that, for the moment, he had no time for fair words and promises. Better to force the Russians to fight now as a means of imposing a general European settlement rather than to agree the limited peace which Frederick William desired. War with Prussia continued; and war with Russia would now begin in earnest.

French snooping at Charlottenburg also led to another discovery. In the Queen's private apartments, among her most cherished possessions, the French came across portraits of the Tsar, along with endearing letters and all the trifling mementoes of affection. Once again Napoleon was informed of what his servants had found, and he was unchivalrous enough to ridicule openly the romantic attachment between Louise and Alexander. He even amused the barrack-rooms of the Grand Army by inserting into several of the official Bulletins derisive invective intended to destroy the Queen's reputation.[36] It was now the turn of Frederick William and Alexander to be enraged. The Tsar spoke grandly of a war 'for the finest and most just of causes', though it remains uncertain whether the ideal which merited such superlatives was the defence of the Russian homeland, the honour of Queen Louise, or the sanctity of private correspondence.[37] Orders went out from St Petersburg to the landowners for twice as many serfs to be conscripted for military service as in the previous years; and Alexander began to envisage a front-line army of some six hundred thousand men.

Although as yet the danger from the French appeared remote to most of the Russian gentry, it was already posing a serious political problem for those members of the aristocracy who possessed lands in the Polish territories of the Empire. For, on 27 November, French troops entered Warsaw, ejecting a Russian Corps which had advanced tentatively across the frontier a week before. Many Poles welcomed Napoleon as a liberator, although the patrician families hesitated to commit themselves irrevocably to the French cause. Ought Alexander to forestall Napoleon by proclaiming a Polish Kingdom, issuing a guarantee of Polish liberties, and linking the crowns of Russia and Poland in a dynastic union similar to the bond between the Habsburgs and Hungary? So at least argued Czartoryski; and he was not the only great landowner in St Petersburg to do so.

Alexander was tempted. In December he began once more to exchange views with his old friend. There was talk in St Petersburg of Czartoryski's imminent return to office, with a free hand to wave the Polish flag enthusiastically whenever Napoleon seemed about to make concessions in Warsaw.[38] But in the last resort Alexander's nerve failed him. He did not wish to offend his Prussian ally at such a moment, nor would he risk a breach with Austria. The Polish Question had always been a matter of joint concern, not for unilateral action. If Napoleon became the patron of Polish patriotism, then at least it would be possible to see whose treachery merited reprisals when retribution fell on the invader. Czartoryski's loyalty did not waver; but in what had been Prussian Poland the magnates waited no longer. Poniatowski entered French service and most of the great families followed his example; by the middle of January Napoleon was ready to set up a provisional Polish administration in Warsaw – and, despite his avowed concern over Alexander's moral lapses, he too had by now acquired a Polish mistress, Maria Walewska.

Yet while Alexander was reluctant to appear as a champion of Polish national sentiment, he needed to appeal to some feeling of exalted pride if he was to give his army a collective spirit capable of challenging the fervour of Bonapartism. He believed he had found it in the Church: let all Holy Russia condemn Napoleon as the Antichrist and to the peasant masses of his Empire the war with France would become a crusade. At the end of the year the Holy Synod duly pronounced a solemn anathema stigmatizing Napoleon Bonaparte as the accursed foe of Christendom. The thunder of denunciation rolled through every cathedral and church in the Russian lands as priests, richly robed before their altars, declaimed the six-hundred-word proclamation: let no one now doubt the turpitude of the monster who dared to call himself Emperor of the French. His sins were made known to the faithful in all the pomp and piety of Orthodoxy; and the scornful abuse of the Grand Army Bulletins was answered with the awe-inspiring cadence of accumulated authority. He was, declared the voice of the Church, 'The principal enemy of Mankind, one who worships idols and whores'. Nor had he as yet completed the enormities of which his soul was capable: 'he is planning to bring together every Judas in the World . . . in order that the Church of God may be destroyed'; and, moreover, 'surpassing in wickedness every terrible crime he has already committed, he intends that he shall be hailed as the Messiah'.[39] To make certain of invoking God's blessing in the war against the Evil One, three additional prayers were inserted in the Liturgy: one in the Office of Preparation; one in the Litany of the Word; and one in the Post-Communion. Not since the early days of Muscovy had the Russian Church with such intensity called on all believers to render service to their Little Father in his struggle with the forces of darkness.

Eylau and Friedland

A winter war in eastern Prussia and the Polish lands could never rise to the climax of a crusade for either belligerent; and, once established on the Vistula, Napoleon for his part sought to halt all campaigning until the spring. The Russians, however, needed a triumph of arms, not only to offset the memory of Austerlitz twelve months before, but to hearten troops toiling slowly westwards through the interminable plains. There had never been much prospect of a victory from Marshal Kamensky; but he, poor man, found the journey to the frontier so exhausting that he took to his bed on reaching headquarters and only rose from it a week later in order to resign his command. During his seven days of almost active service Kamensky gave so many contradictory orders from his sickbed that he left the Russian Generals floundering in confusion. More remarkably, he also succeeded in confounding the enemy, who had no idea where the Russians were concentrating or whether they planned to advance or retreat. Kamensky's departure left General Bennigsen with more freedom of action than anyone had anticipated, least of all the Tsar; and the Hanoverian was not the man to waste opportunities for swelling his own prestige. On 26 December the French attacked Bennigsen's position at Pultusk in the mistaken belief that they had stumbled on Kamensky's rearguard. Since the Russians outnumbered their assailants by more than two to one and had fifty field-pieces of artillery, the French were repulsed. Immediately, Bennigsen sent news to St Petersburg that he had thrown back Napoleon (who was over forty miles from Pultusk that day) and had defeated 60,000 Frenchmen (in reality 20,000); he omitted to add that he had subsequently abandoned Pultusk and was retiring northwards.[40] But the details did not matter for Alexander. He had a victory to celebrate. The year 1807 was opening for Russia full of hope; and Bennigsen – past crimes forgiven in the intoxication of Pultusk – was confirmed as commander-in-chief against Napoleon.

Disillusionment followed all too soon. Bennigsen genuinely wished to bring the French to battle and he made a number of tentative probes towards the garrison city of Thorn, but it was impossible to make any progress in the appalling conditions, the snow and ice worse than in Moravia before Austerlitz. At the end of the first week in February the two armies stumbled against each other, almost by accident, around the town of Preussich-Eylau – rolling countryside in which numerous lakes and marshes lay treacherously hidden beneath three or four feet of snow, indistinguishable from the fields between the villages. The battle of Eylau was fought on 8 February, almost in darkness and, with snow squalls swept down from the north by a strong wind, nearly fifty thousand men (French, Russian and Prussian) perishing in an indecisive conflict. Bagration and the rear-guard fought as valiantly as on the Danube a year previously but they could achieve nothing.* For years afterwards Russian officers remembered Eylau as the most senseless bloodbath in all the wars which they had fought; and when Napoleon dictated the Bulletin of the Grand Army in which he described his visits to the battlefield after the armies had retired, he said quite simply, 'Such a sight as this should inspire rulers with love of peace and hatred of war.'[41]

Technically, however, Eylau was reckoned a Napoleonic victory. The Russians fell back on the city of Königsberg, where the King and Queen of Prussia were still in residence; and the French were left masters of the field of battle. But Napoleon was deeply conscious that Eylau was no Austerlitz or Jena. He was grimly impressed by the courage and tenacity of the Russian troops and worried by problems of waging a winter campaign along the eastern fringe of Europe. Bennigsen even claimed Eylau as a strategic victory for the Russian command, since the French made no attempt to exploit their gains by threatening Königsberg, and asked for prayers of thanksgiving to be offered throughout the Empire for this second success of Russian arms. Alexander was willing enough to praise Bennigsen's initiative: ceremonial salutes greeted the news of the

---

* After the Second World War the Eylau region was annexed to the Soviet Union. Thereupon Preussich-Eylau, a frontier post on the road from Königsberg (Kaliningrad) to Warsaw, was re-named Bagrationovsk in patriotic association with the corps commander of the Russian rearguard in 1806.

battle in St Petersburg and the Tsar attended a *Te Deum* in the capital.[42] But inwardly Alexander was troubled by fears of what would happen in the spring and summer. He was anxious to settle future military and diplomatic policy with Frederick William; and he longed to set out again for his armies.

By mid-March there were signs of an early spring and Alexander became increasingly restive. He still faced difficulties with his own family, especially his mother. For Marie Feodorovna disliked the whole campaign, fearing that Russian lives were being sacrificed for the benefit of Prussia. She warned her son not to allow his sympathies for the Prussian royal family to warp his judgement; and she begged him not to assume command in the field himself. Alexander was indeed conscious of the dangers she stressed. But his mind was made up. He attended the religious services marking the sixth anniversary of his father's death and his own accession; then left St Petersburg on the morning of 28 March. No one this time should accuse him of tardiness and inactivity. He forced his coachmen to drive the horses so hard that he covered the 320 miles to Riga in a mere forty-eight hours; and two days later he was once more in Memel, where Frederick William and his Queen were waiting to talk of the past and plan the future.[43]

For Alexander it was a sad reunion. When he saw Louise, here at Memel in the summer of 1802, her ethereal beauty and her sense of life cast a spell upon him which he enjoyed far too deeply to resist. No other Queen of Prussia, before or after, radiated such bewitching qualities: in her presence even an honest dull-dog husband like Frederick William gleamed momentarily with refracted vitality. But now, less than five years since that first meeting, she was a tired and sick woman. To fight the apathetic despair of the Prussian Court she needed to draw on all her reserves of will-power and courage. Strained lines on her face told of the inner humiliation she felt at insults in the French bulletins. Yet suffering accorded her an almost saintly nobility and, though moved by her frailty, Alexander found the outward magic of her personality undimmed by disaster. Despite all the cautioning from his mother and his friends, Alexander had never felt his fortune so closely intertwined with the honour of the Prussian Royal House.

From Memel the Tsar insisted on accompanying Frederick William into the battle zone of the two armies and, in the last week of April, both monarchs signed a convention at Bartenstein as a supreme gesture of Russo-Prussian unity.[44] The Tsar swore that in any peace with the French he would insist on the restoration of Prussia's 1805 boundaries or the provision of equivalent compensation for Frederick William elsewhere in Germany. At the same time the two monarchs undertook to work for the establishment of a German federation, under Austro-Prussian protection, and with a military frontier along the line of the Rhine. Since all Germany was under French occupation, the Convention displayed an optimism which bordered on folly. Nor did its terms accord with the intentions of the Austrians, the British or the Swedes for the future of the German lands. Like the Potsdam Oath of November 1805 it was a token of Alexander's romanticism rather than a tribute to his political sense.

The sole justification for the Bartenstein Convention was a hope that, after two indecisive engagements at Pultusk and Eylau in the winter, a major battle fought over gentler terrain in midsummer would result in a Russian victory. The French, on the other hand, were determined to complete the defeat of Prussia by capturing the one remaining Prussian city, Königsberg. Bennigsen had reconnoitred most of the area south of Königsberg and he was anxious to relieve pressure on the city by forcing the French Sixth Corps, under Ney, to retire from its position some fifty miles to the south-east. Throughout the first ten days of June there was intermittent skirmishing over a wide area. Napoleon correctly interpreted Bennigsen's movements and planned to draw him further away from the city in order to strike at it along one of the other roads; but Bennigsen, in his turn, spotted the French ruse and sought to offset it by retiring on a fortified camp in a commanding position on the river Alle. Although with so much marching and counter-marching the military situation remained strangely fluid, no one doubted a decisive battle was imminent – unless, of course, the Russians were prepared to abandon Königsberg and sue for peace.

Such a possibility had been out of the question at the end of April; but by early June it seemed not unlikely. Alexander withdrew from the exposed area around Bartenstein and established himself in the town of Tilsit, on the river Niemen, where communications with St Petersburg and the interior of the Empire were easier than in the eastern Prussian salient.[45] He was joined by his brother Constantine and by General Budberg. Alexander hoped for news of a military diversion by the British or even of a threat of intervention against the French by the Austrians. But all the information Budberg brought to him was gloomy. It was clear that no help, military or diplomatic, was forthcoming. Budberg himself was by no means despondent: he believed Russia possessed greater resources than the Napoleonic Empire and was therefore better prepared for a war of attrition, irrespective of what happened in front of Königs-berg. But no one else in Alexander's circle shared this opinion. Some were strongly in favour of an immediate approach to Napoleon, so as to prevent waste of lives in a battle which, at best, could in their eyes only benefit the Prusians. Among Budberg's strongest critics was Prince Kurakin, long a favosurite of the Dowager Empress, with whom he kept in contact by letters from Tilsit.[46] Alexander was thus under considerable pressure to authorize negotiations: he knew that, despite attempts to magnify Bennigsen's successes, most of the army command lacked zest; and he was painfully aware that not even the thunder of the Church had 1oused the interest of his subjects in the war. He hesitated, offsetting in his mind the commitments he had made at Bartenstein against the weight of feeling around him; and once more Budberg pressed him to continue the struggle. On 14 June, while Alexander was still undecided between peace and war, the opposing armies clashed at last in the small town of Friedland, on the banks of the Alle seventy miles west of Alexander's headquarters. After initial success against one of the columns on Napoleon's flank, the Russians were caught by converging attacks from the whole of the Grand Army in the late evening of a long day. By ten o'clock that night, as summer twilight hung over the smouldering remains of the town, Bennigsen began to fall back towards the Niemen with a mere five thousand men still capable of offering effective resistance. The major battle for which all Russia waited throughout the spring had come in the end; but victory rested once more with Napoleon.[47]

8

Tilsit

Alexander and Napoleon Meet in Midstream

Friedland was a more decisive engagement for the Russians than Austerlitz eighteen months before. Although a greater number of men perished
in the earlier battle, the defeat was never accepted in St Petersburg or
Moscow as a conclusive verdict on the whole war; and, in those winter
months of 1806, many Russians in authority were ready to prepare, with
reasonable confidence, for a resumption of the struggle against Napoleon
in the following spring. But after Friedland there could be no such
comforting pretence: the war was lost. The finest regiments in the Tsar's
service were trundling back, exhausted and demoralized, to the frontiers
of the Empire; and the last Prussian strongholds were falling into the
hands of the French. There was no promise of help from Russia's British
or Swedish allies, and no patriotic response from the heart of Alexander's
Empire. The levy of serfs, which should have raised a reserve army of
over half a million men, had as yet yielded a militia of little more than
30,000 raw recruits. The choice facing Alexander was starkly clear
to all around him: either he allowed the campaign to drag on across the
great estates of Russian Poland and Russian Lithuania; or he sought an
immediate armistice. Apart from Budberg, there were by now few fire-
eaters in the Russian camp.[1]

Alexander was still on the Prussian side of the river Niemen, at Tilsit,
when he heard details of Bennigsen's defeat. He perceived at once the
terrible finality of what had taken place that summer evening along the
banks of the Alle. Naturally he was bitterly depressed by the catastrophe,

but since it was not a personal humiliation – as Austerlitz had been – he kept a tight grip on his nerves and took rapid decisions of policy without awaiting the advice of his ministers. With Bennigsen's army beaten, Alexander hesitated no longer between peace and war. He began immediately to draft proposals for an armistice and only when he had committed his first thoughts to paper did he notify Budberg of the sad state of the army. The Foreign Minister was to be given no opportunity of presenting his case. 'Here, General, is the fatal news I have just received', the Tsar wrote. 'It is useless to dwell on the arguments to be made. You can conceive all the difficulty of my position.'[2] An emissary would be sent to Napoleon to sue for an armistice. Meanwhile, since Bennigsen feared an enveloping movement on Tilsit by the Grand Army, the Russians evacuated the left bank of the Niemen and set fire to the wooden bridge across the river. Alexander withdrew a few miles to the east, and at the village of Olitcha established field headquarters almost on the borders of his own Empire.

As peace emissary Alexander selected a soldierly diplomat, Prince Dmitri Lobanov-Rostovsky, a member of a distinguished Muscovite family who was serving as a Lieutenant-General under Bennigsen's command. The last military spokesman sent by Alexander to the French during a campaign had been the egregious Dolgoruky, whose attitude had so displeased Napoleon on the eve of Austerlitz. But Lobanov was a totally different type of man, tactful and courteous where Dolgoruky was arrogant. He arrived at the French outposts on the evening of 18 June and was escorted to Berthier, Napoleon's chief-of-staff, who sounded him out for almost an hour in order to be sure his mission was sincere.[3] It was only on the following afternoon that Napoleon himself reached Tilsit, and he sent for Lobanov as soon as he had established himself in the town. Napoleon, too, wanted peace in eastern Europe so as to concentrate his efforts against Britain and complete his re-organization of the German lands and Italy. He welcomed Lobanov's proposals for putting an end to the fighting and, on the following day, he sent General Duroc to Bennigsen's headquarters to agree on final terms. An armistice of a month's duration was concluded on 21 June, the two armies facing each other along the winding course of the Niemen as far as Grodno and thence down the old Russo-Prussian frontier to the river Bug. If the armistice broke down Napoleon knew that, within a few days, his troops could occupy Vilna, which was at the time the third largest city in Alexander's dominions.

But Napoleon did not want to send his army into Russian Poland and

Lithuania. 'It is essential that all this ends with a system of close alliance,' he declared to Talleyrand, who was still his Foreign Minister.[4] A reliable ally on the east of the continent would prevent French resources from being over-stretched. Talleyrand himself preferred an Austrian alliance; but Napoleon had always favoured a Russian connection, if only because the vastness of the Tsar's dominions threatened the interests of his arch-enemy, Britain, in so many different parts of the world. Now at last there was a prospect of dictating the peace settlement he desired and of conclud-ing an understanding with Russia on his own terms. On 22 June Napoleon invited Lobanov to dine with him in Tilsit, proposed a toast to the Tsar's health, and assured the Prince he had never taken a hostile attitude towards Russia. 'The reciprocal interest of the two empires calls for an alliance between them', he declared; and, to make his views even clearer he pointed to the line of the Vistula on a map and said, 'Here is the boundary of our two empires. Your master must dominate one side and I the other.'[5]

Alexander was intrigued by Lobanov's reports of his reception. If Napoleon showed such expansive generosity it might yet be possible to emerge from the war with credit, Russian diplomacy winning the triumph which had eluded Russian arms. Moreover, here was an opportunity for the Tsar himself to shine as a master-statesman, settling the affairs of Europe personally with Napoleon as Emperor to Emperor. On the after-noon of June 24 Lobanov arrived back at Tilsit with a message from his sovereign to Napoleon. 'Alliance between France and Russia has always been a particular wish of mine [*l'objet de mes desirs*] and I am convinced that this alone can guarantee the welfare and peace of the world', Alex-ander declared; and he proposed a personal meeting of the two rulers who, he believed, would reach an understanding without difficulty.[6] Hopefully Alexander left Olitcha and found new quarters in the village of Amt-Blauben, only a couple of miles from the banks of the Niemen.

'The Emperor of Russia has come a league from here and I am told he wants an interview', Napoleon wrote to Talleyrand after seeing Lobanov, 'I care only middlingly for the idea [*Je m'en soucie mediocrement*] but I cannot turn it down.'[7] Elaborate arrangements were made for the meeting, despite Napoleon's lack of enthusiasm, and General Duroc was sent to Amt-Blauben in order to assure Alexander of the Emperor's good wishes. Since there was no neutral territory where the two sovereigns could come together Napoleon proposed the interview should take place in midstream. There is little darkness on the Niemen in the last week of June and through-out the night hours the French were able to work on the construction of a raft, bearing on it two pavilions made of wood draped with canvas and white linen. During the morning of 25 June the raft was towed into midstream and secured to the piles of the ruined bridge, an operation directed rather unexpectedly by General La Riboisière, commander of the Guard Artillery. Spectacular improvisation decorated the larger pavilion with the two Imperial monograms, elegantly curved and painted green because there was no other colour available in the artillery stores. The letter N faced the left bank, the letter A the right: over such details the Guard was always meticulously tidy.[8]

Alexander arrived on his bank of the river at eleven o'clock, far too soon for the French.[9] He had set out from Amt-Blauben accompanied by his brother Constantine as well as by Bennigsen, Lobanov, and his principal aide-de-camp Count Paul Lieven. They attended, however, as curious observers rather than as participants in the meeting since it was clearly understood that no one would join the Emperors during their first exchange of views. Hovering in the background and uncertain of his status was the unfortunate Frederick William, titular sovereign of Tilsit. By now all his kingdom, except the city of Memel and its hinterland was occupied by the French; and he counted for little in Napoleon's eyes. If anything were saved from the wreck of Prussia, it would be by the grace of his powerful neighbours. Riboisière's artists had not bothered to paint the King's monogram on the side of the pavilion.

For nearly two hours Alexander waited, with growing impatience, at an inn by the water's edge in the village of Picktupöhnen. Across the river the Russian party could clearly observe all the bustle in Tilsit itself. Shortly before one o'clock Lieven spotted Napoleon riding down to the boat which would carry him out to the raft. The sound of cheering was borne across the Niemen (which, as Napoleon himself was to write, 'is here as wide as the Seine'). Alexander and his retinue at once went aboard their ferry and were rowed slowly across the water. Napoleon, who was accompanied by Berthier, Duroc and General Armand de Caulaincourt, reached the raft first and welcomed Alexander as host to guest when the Tsar's boat pulled alongside. From the bank observers saw the two men shake hands, Alexander's six-foot frame towering over Napoleon who was some six or seven inches shorter and who still retained the lithe figure of an active man. Then, alone, the two Emperors entered the larger pavilion. They remained in conversation for an hour and three-quarters while their attendants sheltered from the sunshine (and later from the rain) in cramped discomfort on the far side of the raft. Along opposite banks men who had fought each other at Friedland eleven days ago watched the strange meeting-place of their sovereigns rising and falling gently on the gleaming waters and speculated on what they were saying.

Nobody knows the precise words they used; and the general drift of their conversation was soon distorted by embellishment, much of it added in all sincerity when memory began to rationalize what was, at the time, a highly emotional occasion for both participants.[10] For, though Napoleon had met Francis of Austria briefly after Austerlitz, he had never before mounted a grand ceremony for a foreign Head of State prepared to accept him as a brother sovereign; and he became to some extent a captive of his own grandeur. Alexander, too, was overwhelmed by the drama of the moment, inspired by that consciousness of mission which always served him as a substitute for logical analysis. Even at this first encounter Alexander, so often unsure of himself, was fascinated by the magnetism of Napoleon's decisiveness.

It was, allegedly, Alexander who opened the conversation. 'Sire,' he declared, 'I hate the English no less than you do and I am ready to assist you in any enterprise against them.' 'In that case', Napoleon is said to have replied, 'everything can be speedily settled between us and peace is made.'[11] These phrases, however, do not ring true; for the Tsar was never so direct in his conversational habits. Nevertheless, whatever words were used, their talk convinced Napoleon that Alexander had little love for his former ally and was willing to work with the French in forcing a settlement upon the English; and that, for Napoleon, was quite enough. His plans ranged over the whole of Europe's affairs and into other continents as well. The magnificent sweep of his vision excited the romantic idealism in Alexander. When the two men emerged from the pavilion each had on his face a smile of contentment. They agreed that half of Tilsit would be neutralized and that the Tsar and the Russian Imperial Guard would cross the river and occupy part of the town; for it was clear that there would be long conversations between the two rulers and their advisers in the days ahead. Meanwhile, each Emperor presented members of his suite to the other before crossing to his respective bank of the river. It was a memorable day, as neo-classical in form as one of David's canvases.

The Fine Phrases of Tilsit

The Tsar landed at Picktupöhnen dazed and subdued but by the time he arrived back in Amt-Blauben he was intoxicated with enthusiasm. No superlatives were too strong for Napoleon. 'If only I had seen him sooner!'

he mused and added, with a stylistic echo from across the Niemen, 'The veil is torn aside and the time of error past.'[12] Alexander, declared Constantine later, was in a seventh heaven of delight. Napoleon, too, was pleased though less exuberant. That evening he dictated a hurried note to the Empress Josephine, grand in condescension: 'My dear,' he said, 'I have just seen the Emperor Alexander. I am well pleased with him: he is quite a handsome and good young Emperor. There is more spirit in him than one usually imagines. Tomorrow he is coming to lodge in the town of Tilsit.'[13] And he sent an urgent message to Talleyrand, who was on his way from Warsaw to Königsberg, to come immediately and help draft treaties of peace and friendship.[14]

Next day (Friday, 26 June) there was one more meeting on the raft before it was dismantled.[15] Alexander, belatedly remembering that Frederick William, too, had some self-respect, presented the King to the Emperor of the French (who treated him with scant sympathy). For the sake of convenience it was agreed he might be fitted in at some spare house in Tilsit, though there was little chance of making room for him for a couple of days. No such delay was allowed to hamper Alexander's movements. On the Friday evening he crossed the Niemen and was received with full military honours. That night he dined with Napoleon at French headquarters. The password issued by Napoleon to his Guard was 'Alexander, Russia, Greatness'. On the Saturday evening Alexander repaid the courtesy and Russian Guards responded to the improbable – and slightly ambiguous – challenge of 'Napoleon, France, Courage'. Yet apart from Alexander himself, who was childishly flattered by the attentions lavished on him, the quality of friendship between the rival army commanders showed a dignified constraint.

For over a week the two Emperors followed a regular pattern of dinners, military parades and inspections, with frequent excursions on horseback into the countryside around Tilsit. Generally they would meet in the middle of the day, at one or other of their lodgings, and talk at length over world affairs, sometimes pacing the salons deep in thought and sometimes standing in front of maps on which Napoleon would outline the new Europe of his vision. The prospect of remote horizons and distant perspectives stirred Alexander almost as much as a grand parade. It was encouraging, after the bitterness of a lost war, to find a triumphant soldier who shared his delight in ranging over such splendid vistas. They would talk again, long into the night, with no one to record what they said ('the fine phrases I dropped around at Tilsit', as Napoleon remarked a year later, half laughing at himself). 'In one hour', Napoleon had boasted at an early meeting, 'we shall achieve more than our spokesmen in several days. I shall be your secretary and you mine.'[16] If it was a confidence trick, Alexander enjoyed every minute of it. He even exchanged cravats and decorated handkerchiefs with Napoleon.

Occasionally the two Emperors would invite Frederick William to dine with them. He seemed, however, unable to rise to the inspired sublimity of their verbal exchanges, probably because he was worried over the fate of his kingdom; and they were always glad when he left them. ('A nasty king, a nasty nation, a nasty army', said Napoleon to Alexander one night after Frederick William had gone back to his temporary home.) Once or twice Frederick William accompanied the Emperors on their rides through the East Prussian countryside but he was not such a good horseman and often he would trail at their heels like some puzzled and faithful dog, left dazed and uncomprehending by the sudden shifts of fortune. In desperation he sent a letter to Memel imploring Queen Louise to come to Tilsit and charm Alexander back into his senses, or, if that were impossible, at least remind him of the Potsdam Oath and the solemn pledges of Bartenstein a mere two months ago.[17]

The King was not the only person who failed to understand all that was happening. Formal military orders reminded the Russian soldiery to be civil to the French whenever they met them and refer to their leader as the Emperor Napoleon rather than as 'Buonaparte'. Senior officers were called to make harder sacrifices of conscience. It was all too much for General Budberg, whose health conveniently gave way shortly before the arrival of Talleyrand so that the duties of Foreign Minister had to be undertaken by Prince Kurakin (who, in his turn, promptly confined himself to bed in the vain hope of acquiring a high fever so as to avoid any responsibility for the negotiations).[18] To others it seemed as if Alexander, in his desire to keep Napoleon's confidence, was in danger of losing his dignity. As the days went by with no clear news from Tilsit, the cities of the Empire were again filled with alarming rumours, as they had been after Austerlitz: was Holy Russia to be sold to the Antichrist? For, whatever the fashion on the Niemen, in St Petersburg and Moscow the Church still thundered on Sundays against Bonaparte, that 'worshipper of idols and whores'. The Holy Synod was unaccustomed to diplomatic revolution.

Among the Tsar's severest critics were those members of his family who had most urged him to make peace. Alexander sought to justify his behaviour in letters to his mother and to his sister Catherine, now almost nineteen. To Marie Feodorovna he wrote: 'Happily Bonaparte, for all his genius, has a vulnerable side; this is his vanity. And I have decided to sacrifice my own self-respect for the salvation of the Empire.'[19] But this explanation sounded too fine to be true. Nor did it accord with Constantine's accounts of the pleasure Alexander was finding in Napoleon's company. Marie Feodorovna remained unconvinced; and Kurakin's letters, which emphasized the personal nature of the Tsar's policy, were hardly likely to mollify her.[20]

With his sister, Alexander was more honest. In the small hours of 29 June he sent Catherine a note written when he was too weary to dissimulate:

God has saved us: instead of having to make sacrifices, we have emerged almost gloriously from the struggle. But what do you think of all these events? Just imagine my spending days with Bonaparte, talking for hours quite alone with him! I ask you, does not all this seem like a dream? It is past midnight and he has only just left me. How I wish you could be an invisible witness of all that was going on! Adieu, my dearest friend, I do not write often to you but, on my honour, I have hardly a minute in which to breathe.[21]

The questions may have been rhetorical but they received from Catherine a response which could have left Alexander in no doubt of his favourite sister's feelings:

We shall have made huge sacrifices and for what? . . . I wish to see [Russia] respected not in words but in reality, since she certainly has the means and the right to be so. While I live I shall not get used to the idea of knowing that you pass your days with Bonaparte. When people say so, it seems like a bad joke and impossible. All the coaxing he has tried on this nation is only so much deceit, for the man is a blend of cunning, ambition and pretence . . . He does himself honour by being with you . . . Forgive the flow of words, my friend, but it is only from the well of my heart that the mouth speaks. Adieu, Alexander, my sincere devotion will end only with my life.[22]

There had at one moment in the exchanges of Napoleon and Alexander been a suggestion that the Bonaparte family might provide Catherine with a husband, presumably the twenty-two-year-old Jerome. It is, perhaps, as well nothing more was heard of the project. She was becoming a woman of too strong character for a Bonaparte in full Imperial plumage.

The Tilsit Settlement (July 1807)

By the time Catherine's fiery reply reached her brother everything was settled in Tilsit. Six days of conversations enabled the two Emperors to focus their eyes on immediate issues rather than on the distant horizons to which each felt more naturally attracted.[23] Even so, the range of problems they discussed was remarkable: the way in which Britain might be forced into peace; the boundaries of the new Germany and, in particular, of Prussia; the future of Poland, now that the French held Warsaw; and the likely fate of Turkey, where the Janissary Corps had recently dethroned the Sultan. Occasionally, especially when Napoleon and Alexander considered the evident weakness of the Ottoman Empire, their talk was flavoured by old ambitions until it seemed as if they were preparing to partition the civilized world, assigning provinces to one another like the triumvirs in the closing years of the Roman Republic. But in such matters neither ruler could afford to be honest with the other and there remained a studied vagueness over detail.

The problem of Britain gave them little trouble. Alexander was justified in complaining that the London Government had done little for Russia during the previous two years and had shown some hostility to Russian activity in the Balkans and eastern Mediterranean. The Tsar was willing to halt all trade with England, summon her to make peace by surrendering her colonial conquests and recognizing freedom of the seas, and to declare war if she ignored his mediation. Napoleon was gratified but he wanted other states besides Russia to make a clear break with England: all the continent must come together and stifle this nation of higglers and hucksters. He accordingly proposed that pressure should be applied to Denmark and Sweden (and, indeed, Portugal) to induce these countries to enter his economic system and Alexander agreed to support the diplomatic initiative of the French. If necessary, Russia would even undertake a campaign in the Baltic against the Swedes: successes on the shores of the Gulf of Finland might strengthen the future security of St Petersburg; and a new Northern War against a traditional enemy would help the army recover its lost prestige. The Tsar's willingness to commit his Empire to the Napoleonic 'Continental System' was a major miscalculation. He had no idea of the damage which a breach with Britain and a war in the Baltic would inflict on Russian commerce. For the merchants of Petersburg and Riga his secret pledge at Tilsit was an error of judgement they found hard to forgive.

Over Germany Alexander was less acquiescent. He was prepared to recognize French hegemony west of the Elbe and the establishment of an impromptu throne for Napoleon's brother, Jerome, in Westphalia but towards Prussia his mood changed from hour to hour. Marie Feodorovna had, for months past, begged him not to sacrifice the needs of his own Empire for the sake of the Hohenzollerns; and now Napoleon was at hand to remind him that Frederick William was 'utterly ruined, a man without character and without means'.[24] It was tempting to let the French have their way and see Prussia wiped from the map of Europe, especially when a share of her Polish lands might strengthen Russia's own position on the Vistula. But treachery of this magnitude overstretched Alexander's conscience. He was deeply moved by the reproaches of Queen Louise, who arrived at Tilsit on 6 July. 'You have cruelly deceived me,' she complained to the friend from whom she had expected so much.[25] Even Napoleon likened her to a great tragedienne acting Corneille and, though he might claim to have resisted her blandishments, the Tsar's sensitive soul was easily subjected to such a show of emotion. He insisted that the throne of the Hohenzollerns should be preserved and that two-thirds of Frederick William's hereditary territories be returned to him. A phrase in the final treaty between France and Prussia made it clear that the restoration to Frederick William of the heart of his kingdom was 'from consideration of the wishes of His Majesty the Emperor of All the Russias'. To Queen Louise this phrase was yet another instance of the humiliation to which Napoleon constantly exposed her; but her husband remained for the rest of his days sentimentally grateful to his 'divine friend' Alexander for the special favour which his intercession had won from the victor of Jena. 'I have done everything humanly possible,' the Tsar declared in a private note to Frederick William, 'but it remains cruelly disappointing for me that I should now have lost even the hope of serving you as my heart would have wished.'[26] And the King of Prussia, with a heavy indemnity imposed on his people and with what was left of his land permanently occupied by French troops, took Alexander at his word. He had no option if he wished to comfort himself with any illusions for the future.

The disposal of the Prussian lands was closely involved with the fate of Poland. The landed gentry of the region around Warsaw welcomed the French as allies as soon as Murat entered the city, and had established a provisional government in the hopes that Napoleon would undo the wrong of the Partitions. But the Emperor of the French as yet felt no especial obligation towards any of the Slav peoples, least of all to a nation so loyal in its Catholicism as the Poles. He was prepared at first to hand over to Alexander the areas his troops had occupied, provided that the Tsar recognized the cession of Prussian Silesia to Jerome Bonaparte as King of Westphalia and that Alexander restored a Polish State in personal union with the Russian Crown, for Napoleon was determined at all costs never to allow the Prussians back in Warsaw. This solution corresponded in many respects with the proposals which Czartoryski had put forward in 1805 and, once again, Alexander was tempted to accept Napoleon's offer. He declined it allegedly from 'what was left of my regard for unfortunate Prussia'; but it is probable that, once having made the offer, Napoleon had second thoughts.[27] For when the Tsar remarked that the Vistula was the natural boundary for Russian Poland – a suggestion corresponding closely to the ideas Napoleon had expressed to Lobanov a few days previously – he found that the French were openly alarmed at the prospect of seeing a Russian garrison quartered opposite Warsaw. In the end, Alexander's conscience permitted him to accept one fragment of formerly Prussian territory, the province of Bialystok. The rest of what had been Prussian Poland (apart from a small area around Danzig, left to Frederick William) was established as the Grand-Duchy of Warsaw, nominally ruled by the King of Saxony but in practice under the personal protection of Napoleon and garrisoned by 30,000 French troops. Poland thus appeared resurrected by grace of the French Emperor; and Warsaw, the city which his young friends had urged Alexander to seize two years before, was now the eastern outpost of the Grand Army, the natural base for an attack on Russia should all these protestations of friendship ring hollow in later years. To most Russians, it did not seem an ideal solution of the Polish Question.

Alexander, however, believed he was extricating himself adroitly from the pains of military defeat. Despite Russia's disastrous record in the German campaigns, he lost no territory to the French on his western frontier and by the annexation of Bialystok even added a new town to his Polish lands. But Napoleon, as a true son of the Latin South, was far less accommodating over the Russian presence in the Mediterranean. Though he appeared to encourage Russia to resume the traditional policy of expansion around the shores of the Black Sea, Napoleon in reality set distinct limits to what Alexander might acquire in south-eastern Europe. The Tsar was obliged to renounce all the Empire's recent gains in the southern Adriatic and the Ionian Sea, ceding to the French both Cattaro (Kotor) and the strategically important string of islands from Corfu to Zante. Napoleon suggested he should mediate between Russia and Turkey so as to end the war which had begun in the Danubian Principalities during the late autumn of the previous year, and he induced Alexander to promise that the Russian forces would evacuate the Principalities on condition that the Turks did not re-occupy them until a peace treaty had been signed. But it was also agreed between the two Emperors that, should the Sultan decline to make peace within three months, the French would assist the Russians to expel the Turks from most of the Balkan peninsula and thereby establish an entirely new order in south-eastern Europe. Once again that old elusive dream of ousting the Turks from Constantinople fascinated a Russian ruler.

But Napoleon never intended Alexander to become master of the Bosphorus and Dardanelles. Though he did not have any clear idea of what he sought in the Balkans, he was occasionally attracted by the fantasy of himself entering in triumph the old gates of Byzantium. 'Constantinople', he remarked to Meneval, his principal secretary, during his stay in Tilsit, 'is the centre of world empire.'[28] It therefore followed that so rich a prize could not fall to a mere latterday neophyte, like the Tsar of Russia. A compromise was essential, preferably one which would bind Alexander to the virtue of self-denial. Accordingly the two Emperors solemnly agreed that when the time came to partition the Ottoman Empire, the Sultan might retain his capital and most of Thrace. At heart neither seriously believed the other would be bound by such an undertaking and assented to the compromise with inner reservations of conscience. Each was perfectly well aware that over Constantinople it was impossible for them to remain in step; but for the moment it was better not to permit unworthy doubts to mar the delights of Tilsit. Outwardly agreement had been reached over the future of the Ottoman Empire and old ambitions were restrained by the need to act in concert.

By the end of the first week in July agreement was, indeed, close at hand on most matters. It only remained for Talleyrand and Kurakin to draw up suitable documents for signature: a public treaty of peace between Russia and France and a secret treaty of alliance. Then, while a suitable engagement was hurriedly prepared to bind Prussia to the Napoleonic system, the whole pageant of Tilsit could be brought to an end with appropriate ceremonial. Both Emperors were by now in a hurry to return to their capitals: Napoleon had been absent from Paris for ten months and wished to turn his attention to other problems of government; and, though Alexander had been away from St Petersburg for a much shorter period, it was becoming pressing for him to show the people of the capital who was really in the saddle. It was difficult to hold Empires together from the obscurity of East Prussia.

On Tuesday, 7 July, just three weeks and two days after the futile slaughter of Friedland, the Franco-Russian treaties were ready for signature. With both sovereigns present the formalities of ratification were settled within forty-eight hours and on Thursday, 9 July 1807, the French and Russian Empires were formally linked in alliance.[29] The whole of Wednesday was spent in farewell courtesies. Napoleon visited Alexander's lodgings and bestowed on him the Grand Cross of the Legion of Honour, and at the same time decorated Grand Duke Constantine, Bennigsen and all the other senior Russian commanders. The Tsar duly conferred on Napoleon the highest of the Russian orders of chivalry, the Cross of St Andrew; and there then followed the famous incident in which Napoleon gave his own cross of the Legion to a Russian Grenadier as a gesture of admiration for the valour of Alexander's army. The two Emperors dined together for the last time at Tilsit and talked, as on so many previous days, long into the night.

But they had still not made their formal farewells. At noon on the Thursday the Tsar, wearing the scarlet ribbon of the Legion of Honour, left his residence on horseback and rode down the main street of Tilsit to meet Napoleon, who was decorated with the blue cordon of St Andrew. On Alexander's left, the street was lined by a battalion of the Preobrazhensky Regiment in ceremonial green and red; and on his right was a long line of tall bearskins as the French Imperial Guard presented arms for its sovereign's newest ally. The Emperors returned to Alexander's lodging to seal the treaties and spent another couple of hours in conversation, each assuring the other of his lasting friendship. Then, in mid-afternoon, Napoleon accompanied Alexander down to the banks of the Niemen, embraced him amid cheers and salutes from the two armies, and watched as the enemy who had now become so close a friend was rowed back across the river, the familiar tricorn hat raised in a last gesture of farewell. That night Alexander's carriage began the journey to Riga and St Petersburg; and Napoleon, not wishing to waste any time on the King and Queen of Prussia now that the Tsar had gone, set out down the long road to the West. Frederick William and Louise travelled slowly and disconsolately to Memel, for with French garrisons parading in Berlin they had no desire to return to the heart of the kingdom. For the French and Russians a war may have ended at Tilsit: but for the Prussians what followed was hardly peace.

9

As Destiny Demands

The Effects of Tilsit Abroad

The first reports of the Tilsit talks began to circulate in Europe even before the two Emperors arrived back in their capitals. Everyone accepted that Tilsit was a grand occasion, but there was uncertainty over its significance. Recent history showed Russian policy capable of startling vacillation and there seemed no good reason for assuming Alexander would be any more successful than his father in reconciling the great Russian families to French mastery of the continent. On the other hand, it was felt that Napoleon had admitted the military impossibility of a successful invasion of the Russian lands and that the tide of French conquest had at last reached its natural limits. In despatches to Paris Napoleon insisted that the Tilsit Peace should be presented as a diplomatic triumph, a dramatic recognition of the victories gained by the Grand Army in its long march across the continent;[1] but behind all the excitement and celebration there lingered a suspicion that the Tsar of Russia, though vanquished on the field, had shown his Empire, by its very size, to be the equal of Napoleon's. Only in the smaller German cities and in neutral Vienna was there genuine alarm at the reversal of alliances, a sense of abandonment and isolation. Metternich, now in his second year as Austrian ambassador in Paris, declared that 'the day when the French and Russian Emperors will fall out is inevitable, and, according to my innermost feelings, much nearer than many people suppose.'[2] But, with Austria deprived of all influence in the German lands, in Poland and in the Balkans, there were few in Vienna with such confident optimism.

Yet in London the news of the Tilsit meeting caused little consternation. Newspapers and periodicals which had lavished excessive praise on the Tsar in the early months of the Third Coalition found it expedient to condemn him as a dupe of the French, 'weak and thoughtless' and 'fundamentally devoid of principle', but among the English Tories there was a measure of understanding for Alexander's dilemma after Friedland.[3] George Canning, who had become Foreign Secretary in the new Portland Ministry in March 1807, admitted privately that he could not blame the Tsar for seeking to end a struggle in which his British ally had brought him so little assistance or encouragement.[4] No member of the British Government believed Tilsit to be a final settlement of Europe's affairs and most public figures would have agreed with Metternich that Franco-Russian friendship would not survive long. Eventually, it was felt, the Russians would come back into the war on the side of the righteous; and meanwhile it was essential for the British to discover the true nature of the commitments assumed in Tilsit and to frustrate French intentions in the Baltic.

The British had some grounds for their high hopes. Budberg returned from Tilsit still nominally in charge of Russia's foreign relations and, in conversations with the British ambassador, he went out of his way to minimize the extent of his country's commitments to the French. The settlement, he told the ambassador, 'must be considered as a momentary respite and by no means as affording any prospect of permanent tranquillity'; and he added the significant explanation, 'We must employ this moment of repose in preparing the means of resistance against another attack.'[5] A similar impression was received by Sir Robert Wilson, a young British General attached to the Russian army during the campaign in Prussia who now found himself feted in every salon in the Russian capital. So convinced was Wilson of the basic goodwill at the Russian Court that he hurried back to London early in September in order to reassure Canning of Alexander's intentions.[6] He had dined at the Tsar's table and heard for himself the generous feelings of the Russians for everything English. Even the British expedition to seize the Danish fleet need not necessarily lead to a rupture. Canning, though impressed by Wilson's pleading, remained sceptical. He was sure that Alexander had no wish for a breach with Britain so long as Admiral Senyavin's vessels – Russia's finest naval squadron – were still sailing back painfully slowly from the Adriatic to the Baltic; but it was an open question what would happen if Senyavin sought protection from the French. British policy was acutely sensitive in the balance of sea-power.

Alexander's Throne in Danger?

Until the middle of September Alexander hesitated to commit himself openly to the French cause. At the end of July he had personally welcomed to St Petersburg General Savary, whom Napoleon sent as an envoy pending the formal resumption of diplomatic relations. Alexander showered courtesies on Savary, entertaining him privately at Kamennoi Ostrov where life was more relaxed than in the greater palaces of the capital. Savary dutifully reported to Paris all Alexander's fine words, his willingness to act against England without prompting from Napoleon, his happy memories of Tilsit, his hope that he might one day visit Paris as guest of the Emperor of the French. 'I shall never forget the tokens of friendship afforded me by the Emperor Napoleon', Alexander declared, 'The more I think of them, the more happy I am to have known him. What an extraordinary man!'[7] But honesty compelled Savary also to inform Paris of his own unpopularity in the capital, of his frigid reception 'lasting for less than a minute' by Marie Feodorovna, and of the way in which Russian Society insisted on 'observing an astonishing silence over every political question'.[8] Little effort was made to conceal the contempt by Russians of high standing for Savary personally and for the sovereign he represented. They had longer memories than their Tsar.

Alexander was fully aware of the mood in the capital, and his natural instinct for survival led him to tread cautiously. For the first time since his accession he found it difficult to trust ministers and advisers, nor was it easy to find new men to replace those who had lost his confidence. He knew that, as ever, he could rely on Arakcheev but to entrust him with ministerial responsibilities would increase dissatisfaction in the capital, especially among the officers of the Guards Regiments. Of Alexander's old friends from the Secret Committee only Kochubey still held office in 1807 and he frequently absented himself from meetings of the Council that summer and autumn on grounds of ill-health. Each member of the former Secret Committee felt their common hopes and ideals already betrayed. But the ministers on whom Alexander had most closely relied in the preceding twelve months were equally ill at ease. Almost every week between July and September Budberg wrote to Alexander requesting to be relieved from his post as Foreign Minister, while Kurakin sought, and obtained, the embassy in Vienna.[9] The only minister who unreservedly supported reconciliation with Napoleon was Count Nicolai Rumiantsev, who had been in charge of commercial affairs since 1802 and over the years exasperated each successive Foreign Minister by consistently opposing war with France at the council table. Early in September the Tsar personally went to Rumiantsev's office and begged him to take over foreign affairs from Budberg.[10] Significantly Alexander also insisted that Rumiantsev should remain Minister of Commerce. There was no one else to whom he could turn for support of an economic policy so unpopular with the merchants.

The first six months which followed the Tilsit meeting imposed on Alexander a strain as great as in any military campaign. In meeting Napoleon personally as Emperor to Emperor he assumed autocratic powers which it was difficult for him to delegate once he returned to the capital. Inevitably he had to take a greater share in the effective running of government, much as he had in the early months of his reign; but, at the same time, he had to appear more and more in public so as to let his subjects see their Tsar had not abandoned them nor given himself up to despair. In later years people remembered the Petersburg season of 1807 as particularly brilliant, with Alexander and Elizabeth attending more balls and receptions than ever before.[11] Slowly he sought to recover the popularity he had enjoyed in happier times, over-taxing in these efforts both his charm and his patience.

The Empress Elizabeth once again loyally supported her husband. Although unhappy over many aspects of the new policy, she sympathized with Alexander and understood him better than he did himself. But even Elizabeth found the tension almost unbearable, and on 10 September she wrote a long letter to her mother in which she made no attempt to conceal the anger she felt towards the other members of the Tsar's family:[12]

You know, Mamma, this man [Napoleon] seems to me like an irresistible seducer who by temptation or force succeeds in stealing the hearts of his victims. Russia, the most virtuous of them, has defended herself for a long time; but she has ended up no better than the others. And, in the person of her Emperor [Alexander], she has yielded as much to charm as to force. He feels a secret attraction towards his enticer which is apparent in all he does. I should indeed like to know what magic it is that he [Napoleon] employs to change people's opinions so suddenly and so completely ... Unfortunately it is only the Emperor and a tiny group of people whom the seducer has conquered. The more the Emperor shows attachment to his new ally and accords favours to Savary, the louder the outcry until by now it has reached frightening proportions. The Dowager Empress, inspired by the colossal vanity which leads her to curry support from the toadies, has been the first to set an example of discontent and to speak openly against the policy of her son ... The Dowager Empress, who as a *mother* should have upheld the interests of her son, is now virtually a rebel leader. All the dissidents gather around her and praise her to the skies. Never has her Court been so well attended: never has she attracted so many members of the nobility to Pavlovsk as this year. I cannot express to you how indignant this has made me feel. At such a moment as this, when she must know to what a point the public is exasperated with the Emperor, is it for her at such a time to entertain and flatter those who most vehemently abuse him? I do not know; but I cannot find anything praiseworthy in such conduct, especially on the part of a *mother* . . . They tell us that the Grand Duke Constantine, as soon as his brother's back is turned, makes as much fuss as anyone else about what has happened and what is happening. I do not know his opinions, for we are not on a sufficiently familiar footing to exchange confidences, but knowing the full baseness of his character, I believe him capable of it. In short the good Emperor, who is the best of all his family, seems to me to be sold and betrayed by his own kinsfolk. He is certainly unfortunate but the more painful the situation becomes, the more I feel for him, perhaps to the point of making me unfair towards those who do not treat him kindly . . .

As for [the Grand Duchess Catherine] . . . I have never seen a stranger young woman. She is on the wrong path because she takes as a model for her opinions, her conduct – and even her manners – her dear brother Constantine. She has a style [*un ton*] which would not suit a woman of forty, let alone a girl of nine-teen, besides putting on an act of twisting her mother round her little finger (and sometimes succeeding) . . . At the present time she is hand in glove with Prince Bagration who, for the last two summers, has been in residence at Pavlovsk where he commands the garrison.

. . . If she were not so plain, she would run a risk of ruining herself by this liaison, but her plainness saves the Grand Duchess.

Although Elizabeth's letter was enlivened by a waspish dash of gossip, it is clear she was alarmed by Alexander's isolation; and in a briefer note a month later she again referred to the dangers of a sudden ill-considered act by 'the public' of the capital.[13] Nor was the Empress alone in her fears: both the Swedish ambassador and the minister of Sardinia-Piedmont sent ominous reports back to their governments;[14] and in the fourth week of September General Savary even broached the possibility of a hostile conspiracy in conversation with the Tsar. But Alexander refused to take the situation seriously. He urged Savary not to pay too much attention to those in the capital who played at intrigues, even in his own family circle. 'General', he said, 'I have made my choice and nothing will change it. Let us say nothing more about it, and we will see what happens.'[15]

Alexander's fatalistic self-confidence at this crisis is remarkable and, at first sight, out of character. Yet he was not putting on a bold front for the benefit of Napoleon's envoy: once he had decided to entrust foreign affairs to Rumiantsev his mind was made up; and in the closing three months of 1807 he took surprising risks. On 11 October he set out for a ten day tour of inspection of garrison towns in Byelo-Russia (Polotsk, Vitebsk and Minsk) as though inviting conspirators in the capital to strike in his absence.[16] Nothing serious happened apart from clumsy efforts by General Wilson (who arrived back from London on 17 October) to mobilize the Anglophile party against Rumiantsev's policy of appeasement. During the last days of October the Tsar determined to put an end to Wilson's mischievous intrigues and he ordered the General to be expelled from his Empire. On 7 November an official bulletin was published in St Petersburg which denounced the British Government for interfering with Russian vessels on the high seas and formally broke off diplomatic relations between the two countries, who were now virtually in a state of war.[17] Although the official value of the rouble fell dramatically and there were complaints from the merchants of Petersburg and the other Baltic ports, once again there was no open sign of defiance. Finally, in the last days of the old year, Alexander dismissed his insignificant War Minister (General Vyazmitinov) and appointed as his successor Alexei Arakcheev.[18] Foreign observers in the capital held their breath and waited for the explosion of anger from the army. It never came. 'From among the oligarchy of military favourites', wrote Joseph de Maistre, the Sardinian minister, at this time, 'General Arakcheev has suddenly, without any warning signals, risen out of the ground. He is cruel, stern and unshakable ... It remains to be explained why his Imperial Majesty has decided to acquire a vizier, since nothing is more alien to his character and way of governing ... I suppose he wanted to have a more frightening bogeyman by his side because of the domestic ferment which prevails here.'[19] None of the diplomats, apart from Savary, welcomed Arakcheev's appointment; but they were impressed by the way in which the Tsar was facing the challenge from the malcontents.

In retrospect it is hard to believe that Alexander's throne was ever seriously in danger. The violence of Russia's internal history over the previous century and a half haunted people's memories. Because the Guards Regiments had made a palace revolution on four occasions, it was assumed they would strike again rather than resign themselves to a humiliating period of personal rule by a Tsar who had lost his popularity with the citizens of the capital. Even Joseph de Maistre wrote cryptically of seeking an escape from 'this dangerous situation' by what he euphemistically termed 'the Asiatic remedy'.[20] But there was no real parallel between the discontent of 1807 and any of these previous crises. It is unlikely the army would have wished to put Constantine on the throne: they regarded him as an empty-headed braggart, no less susceptible to Napoleon's flattery than his brother and primarily interested in the welfare of the French actress he had taken as a mistress (who, at this time, was about to bear him a child). No one in Society ever took Constantine too seriously.

The only possible threat to Alexander was a conspiracy involving the Grand Duchess Catherine and Bagration who, as Savary reported, was a popular hero 'sullen, ambitious and with no love for the French'.[21] But there were three good reasons why such a plot was unlikely: the Grand Duchess was too young and wilful to be thrust upon a throne; she was too fond of both her brothers to deny them their rights, unless they wished to renounce them; and, though Bagration might seek glory on the field of battle, he was not by nature a political schemer, nor did he show any desire to play the kingmaker. Alexander understood better than outside observers – and, for that matter, better than Elizabeth – the real purpose of the opposition centred on Marie Feodorovna's court. The Dowager Empress had been informed of what was agreed at Tilsit, but she was never consulted in advance. Russian Court etiquette already gave the mother of a Tsar precedence over everyone in the Empire except the reigning sovereign; and now Marie Feodorovna was seeking to match convention with reality so that in future she might let her will be known ventriloquially through the words of her son. Alexander was thus faced, in those closing months of 1807, not with an immediate palace revolution but with a power contest against his mother. There was nothing new in such a challenge – the Tsar's 'young friends' had tactfully warned him of the danger within a few weeks of his accession – but after Tilsit it was harder to master than in the days when Alexander could feel all the capital was behind him. Yet, though often tense and wearying, the contest in it-self did not endanger the stability of the throne. Hence the confidence with which Alexander sought to allay Savary's fears of subversion.

Caulaincourt arrives in St Petersburg (December 1807)

In December 1807 General Armand de Caulaincourt, an aristocrat from Picardy who had once served in Louis XVI's finest cavalry regiment, arrived in St Petersburg as ambassador of France.[22] His cultured interests and good breeding made him popular in Society and he was rapidly on even friendlier terms with the Tsar than Savary had been, despite the fact that he too was implicated in the d'Enghien affair. Savary duly returned to Paris early in the New Year and reported to Napoleon. The Emperor was not entirely satisfied with the development of Russo-French relations.[23] He was pleased with Alexander's moves against the British and with the extent of Russian participation in the Continental System; and he welcomed Alexander's willingness to mount a military expedition against Sweden, whose King had refused to follow the other states of northern Europe by breaking off all trade with England. If Alexander wished to annex Finland to his Empire, then such matters were of no concern to the French. On the other hand, the Russians were being difficult over Germany and over the Eastern Question. Napoleon was not as yet prepared to evacuate his troops from Prussia and, so long as the French flag flew in Berlin, Alexander showed a similar reluctance to pull his army out of the Danubian Principalities as a preliminary to a general settlement with the Sultan. Napoleon's first compromise suggestion that Russia should keep the Principalities pending a new disposal of Prussia's lands was rejected out of hand by Alexander and Rumiantsev. But at the beginning of February 1808 Napoleon proposed a far more attractive scheme by which he hoped to harness Russian ambitions for Turkish territories to his cherished plan for a French march into Asia.

On 2 February 1808 Napoleon dictated a remarkable letter for despatch to Alexander.[24] He wished for closer collaboration with Russia against the 'pigmy power' who denied the world a lasting peace. Though he disguised the blatantly acquisitive intentions of his design with fine words, what he had to say was in itself sufficiently attractive for Alexander to be thrown once more into an ecstasy of personal admiration:

Will Your Majesty listen graciously to the advice of someone who claims that he is honestly and affectionately attached to you? Your need is to remove the Swedes farther from your capital. Let your frontiers be extended as far as you wish in that direction. I am ready to assist you in this with all the means in my power.

A Russo-French army of fifty thousand men, including perhaps a few Austrians, marching via Constantinople into Asia, would no sooner appear on the Euphrates than it would throw England into panic and force her to seek mercy from the continental powers. I am within striking distance in Dalmatia, Your Majesty on the Danube. Within a month of our plans being settled, this army could be at the Bosphorus. The blow would be felt in India and England would be on her knees. I should reject no preliminary agreement which might enable me to achieve so magnificent a result. But the mutual interest of our states must be counter-balanced and combined ... Everything could be settled and signed before 15 March. By 1 May our troops could be in Asia and

Your Majesty's army in Stockholm ... Wisdom and policy dictates that we must do as destiny demands and keep pace with the irresistible march of events ... What was decided at Tilsit will determine the destiny of the World.

The letter reached St Petersburg on 25 February and was immediately conveyed by Caulaincourt to the Tsar. Alexander read it in the ambassador's presence, 'his expression gradually becoming more and more animated', as Caulaincourt at once reported back to Paris.[25] 'This is the way it was at Tilsit,' Alexander commented, as his eyes ran down the page. 'There's the man in all his greatness.' Napoleon had suggested they might once again meet to discuss the future division of Asia; and Alexander immediately declared to Caulaincourt his willingness to journey westwards into Germany for fresh discussion with Napoleon as soon as the Emperor wished. Meanwhile Rumiantsev and Caulaincourt would discuss means of reconciling the conflicting interests of the two empires in Turkey and the Near East.

These problems, and especially the fate of Constantinople, could not be speedily settled over a glass of tea, as Alexander knew full well. But while the diplomats were studying the map of south-eastern Europe there was no reason why the Generals should not recover lost prestige by a successful campaign against Sweden's Finnish provinces.[26] Even before the arrival of Napoleon's letter, Alexander had authorized General Buxhöwden to cross the Finnish frontier with a force of some 24,000 men; and, at the time of Caulaincourt's audience, the Tsar and his ministers were anxiously awaiting first reports from Finland. They knew that the army consisted of a small corps of regular veterans supplemented by hastily levied serfs, badly equipped and ill-trained; and success depended on taking the Swedes by surprise. At first all went well for Buxhöwden. The Swedes had only a thin line of defenders stretched along an extensive frontier and they offered little serious resistance. Within three weeks General Sukhtelen's corps was in Helsinki; but there the Russians were faced by the formidable island fortress of Sveaborg, its guns commanding the seaward approach to the city. Once Sveaborg was in Russian hands then Alexander knew he could proclaim the annexation of Finland. But for nearly two months Sveaborg defied the invader. Alexander's wish to present his subjects with a victory before Easter was frustrated. At last, on 3 May, with no sign of a relief force breaking through the Russian blockade, the fortress surrendered. And six days later the Tsar proclaimed the incorporation of the Grand-Duchy of Finland in his Empire. A Te Deum was sung in the Kazan Cathedral and a victory parade ordered in the streets of the capital.

But, though Sweden was a traditional enemy, this latest war failed to capture the public imagination. It completed the ruin of Baltic trade, and seemed to many a wastage of men and material. Few onlookers lined the streets for the victory procession. Even the weather was against Alexander. The day was bitterly cold and gusty squalls off the Gulf blew around the prancing statuary along the quays 'to the discomfiture of everyone, especially the ladies', as Joseph de Maistre wrote.[27] It was a hollow triumph nor did it even mark the ending of the war, for Finnish guerrillas continued to resist in the woods and forests and the Swedes showed no inclination to make peace.

The Death of Lisinka (May 1808)

Within three days of the parade, tragedy enveloped the Tsar's private life. Early in the morning of 12 May his eighteen-month-old daughter died from convulsions in her mother's arms as Alexander and Elizabeth stood helplessly beside her cot. They had known as they watched the troops filing past that she was suffering from a dental infection and onlookers noted the anxiety on Elizabeth's face as she waited for the parade to end so that she could resume her long vigil; but no one in the family thought that the child's life was in danger. Momentarily the shock unnerved Alexander and he saw his loss as a penalty of retribution. Wylie sought to console him; there was every hope that he and Elizabeth would have other children. But Alexander was not to be comforted. 'No, my friend', he said sorrowfully, 'God does not love my offspring.'[28]

For Elizabeth the death of 'Lisinka' was an even greater wound, one from which her spirit never fully recovered. Throughout the preceding year she had resented 'each moment that takes me away from my little angel', as she had written before the child's illness. Lisinka had been a bond strengthening her love for Alexander, enabling her to ignore all those hours he chose once more to pass with Maria Naryshkin, steeling her loyalty to him in the hard tussle with his family. Now that Lisinka was gone the pleasures and quarrels of the world seemed ephemeral and for more than two years Elizabeth remained in mourning, appearing on state occasions sombre behind the magnificence of Alexander and Marie Feodorovna, as though she were a spectral figure from a hidden past. It was not that she wished to draw attention to her wretchedness. She accepted the burden of duty mechanically, weaving into the tapestry of daily life a thin thread of spiritual vision, which those close to her sensed but could not themselves perceive. Sometimes alone and sometimes with her sister, she would find understanding, walking silently in the gardens of Tsarskoe Selo or beside the reeds off Kammionyi Island or beneath the trees surrounding the Nevsky Monastery, where both her babies were buried. In later years, other tortures of the mind led Alexander himself to seek similar consolation; but for the moment, though sympathizing at first with Elizabeth's anguish, he could not share her sensitivity and became impatient with her protracted sorrow. It seemed enough to him to lose himself in the ordered pattern of government. Being too busy to weep for long and readily indulging his passion for others, he failed to recognize for more than a decade the inner loneliness of his consort. His imagination, terrifyingly gloomy whenever he lost confidence in his public mission, never fully comprehended her depths of private grief; and the breach between husband and wife became wider with every month that passed, as everyone at Court could see.

Erfurt

The early summer of 1808 brought Alexander a succession of political disappointments. The talks between Rumiantsev and Caulaincourt made little progress; for, as Napoleon himself demanded, 'Who was to hold Constantinople?'[29] The war with Sweden dragged on; and it was clear that the Finns were not as yet ready to enjoy the benefits of Tsarist rule. The French remained in Prussia and continued to court the Polish gentry. And the meeting with Napoleon, first projected in early March, was postponed because national insurrections by the peoples of Spain and Portugal kept him at Bayonne. It was difficult to conjure up armies to march down the Euphrates when one's attention was focused on the Ebro and the Tagus.

Yet by August it was clear that Russia stood to gain from the embarrassments of the French in the Iberian Peninsula. If Napoleon needed to mount full-scale military operations south of the Pyrenees, he would have to withdraw troops from Prussia; and once he weakened his position in Germany, he would depend upon Russian goodwill to maintain the existing order and to restrain the Austrians from taking advantage of the Spanish crisis to seek revenge for Austerlitz. So long as Russian friendship was essential for French security, Alexander might reasonably expect a free hand against the Turks. Hence, while continuing to shower compliments on Napoleon personally each time he met Caulaincourt, Alexander now began to determine the pace of events in a way which had seemed impossible during the patronizing exchanges at Tilsit a year before. In the last week of the month Alexander wrote to Napoleon informing him that, unless he heard otherwise from the French, he had every intention of setting out for central Germany on 13 September and he hoped to meet Napoleon a fortnight later in Erfurt, the small town in Thuringia where the two Emperors had agreed, in the spring, that they would gather in conference.[30]

The Tsar's message arrived in Paris on 5 September. The news from Spain and Portugal continued to be bad, and there was ample evidence that many prominent Austrians were seeking to encourage Emperor Francis to strike once more at the French. Napoleon was accordingly determined to strengthen his alliance with Russia and to let the Habsburgs show how little they counted in Europe's affairs. On the very day he received Alexander's letter, Napoleon ordered Marshal Lannes to set out for the Vistula and escort the Tsar westwards to Thuringia.[31] At the same time Napoleon's court dignitaries were instructed to plan entertainments and festivities for the Erfurt Congress so as to present the Emperor of the French as a second Charlemagne. Everyone of cultural eminence in Germany was invited to Erfurt, provided he was neither a Prussian nor an Austrian subject; and all the tributary kings and princes of the new European order were expected to attend, though not the King of Prussia and certainly not the Emperor of Austria. Moreover, to stress the links between metropolitan France and Napoleon's German dependencies, it was decreed that the *Théatre Français* – a company of thirty-two actors and actresses, with the great François-Joseph Talma at their head – should set out for Thuringia and honour their sovereign's guests with a heavy programme of classical tragedy. Alexander should thus see for himself the panoply of French majesty, and measure it in his mind against childhood memories of his grandmother's Court. How could such a pageant fail to gratify his vanity?

Napoleon left St Cloud for Erfurt on 22 September convinced he would again be able to charm and flatter Alexander. On the day before he set out, he visited a special panorama of Tilsit in the Boulevard des Capucines, as though seeking to rekindle the emotional fire which had ignited so readily in the Prussian borderlands the previous summer.[32] Over fourteen months the exchange of courtesies, gifts and letters had dulled Napoleon's natural suspicion of a man who had already once veered from collaboration with France into open hostility. Then, in 1803, the Tsar had depended for advice on Czartoryski, with his strongly anti-French bias; but now, if Alexander turned to anyone, it was to Rumiantsev, whom Napoleon knew to be 'strongly convinced' that Russia's 'best interest is to remain united with France'. As he travelled to Erfurt Napoleon consistently undervalued Alexander's political astuteness and exaggerated both his dependence on Rumiantsev and his attachment to the French connection. 'Tell the Emperor he can count on me just as he can on you', Alexander instructed Caulaincourt as they prepared for the Erfurt Congress; and both Caulaincourt and Napoleon took him at his word.[33]

People far closer to Alexander than Napoleon or his ambassador were equally convinced of the Tsar's loyalty to his Tilsit engagements. Throughout the summer of 1808 Marie Feodorovna and the Grand Duchess Catherine tried to persuade him of his folly in seeking another meeting with 'Bonaparte'. In an almost hysterical letter a week before the Tsar's departure from the capital, his mother urged him not to go to Erfurt: he should not risk his person by associating himself with so unscrupulous a ruler deep in Germany; and he should turn back from his foolish policy of bolstering the French at a time when it was becoming clear that 'the idol was about to topple'.[34] Patiently the Tsar replied, carefully explaining his policy: Russia, he said,

needs to breathe freely for a time and, during this valuable interlude, must build up her material and her forces . . . Only in deepest silence must we work and not by making known our armaments nor our preparations, nor yet by loudly denouncing the one whom we are defying . . . If such be the will of God, we shall see his fall with calmness . . . The wisest of all policies is to await the right moment to act.[35]

The Dowager Empress was not convinced. She made abundantly clear her strong disapproval of Alexander's journey to Thuringia and the policy which she assumed he still intended to pursue: but she did not try to prevent her second son, Constantine, from attending the Erfurt Congress as well as his brother.

Alexander sent his retinue ahead of him and travelled lightly in a calèche, a four-wheeled carriage with a falling top, so that he could cover the seven hundred and fifty miles from Petersburg to Erfurt 'faster than any courier'.[36] He broke his journey for a couple of days in Königsberg, where Frederick William and Louise offered him such hospitality as they could afford.[37] Louise, like his mother, warned Alexander not to trust Napoleon and begged him to seek the early evacuation by the French of the Prussian lands. As ever, Alexander was deeply moved by her entreaties; but he contented himself with vague assurances, pledges of personal devotion and counsels of patience. He also had talks with Baron vom Stein, Prussia's chief minister and a relentless foe of Napoleon. Stein urged Alexander to take the lead in organizing, together with the Prussians and Austrians, a concerted front against the French hold on Europe. Alexander was impressed by the forcefulness of Stein's personality but had no wish to involve himself at that moment in diplomatic intrigues. After an affectionate farewell to Louise, he hurried on to Bromberg (Bydgoszcz), where he crossed the Vistula, and Kustrin (Kostrzyn), where he turned south so as to avoid the embarrassment of passing through occupied Berlin. In Paris Napoleon's agents kept him well informed of the general mood at Königsberg and he was far from pleased to hear that 'these wretched Prussians' had been 'interfering once more' in his affairs.[38]

But everything that Marshal Lannes reported to the Emperor was pleasantly reassuring. Lannes had greeted Alexander, in Napoleon's name, as soon as he crossed into the Grand-Duchy of Warsaw. He found him full of goodwill and impressed by the attentions accorded him as he journeyed westwards. From Bromberg to Erfurt, a distance of more than 350 miles, the towns were occupied by French troops and Alexander found he was constantly being saluted by Guards of Honour from some of the finest regiments that had fought against his army. But Alexander's thoughts were racing ahead of him. 'If everything goes well as I hope it will', he told Marshal Lannes more than once, 'I greatly wish to see Paris and spend a long time there with the Emperor Napoleon.'[39]

Such news was gratifying to Napoleon; but he was suddenly confronted by an unexpected problem. Alexander's calèche was bowling along at such a pace that it began to seem as if he would arrive in Erfurt before his host. Napoleon had not minded keeping him waiting on the right bank of the Niemen before the famous meeting on the raft. But the Erfurt Congress was intended to be a magnificent spectacle in honour of France's friend and ally, and the opening scene of this living pageant would be ruined should the Tsar make his entry too soon. Napoleon, who had twice stopped in the Rhineland to review brigades of cavalry on his way from St Cloud, was now forced to drive his horses so hard that he covered the 150 miles between one breakfast and the next. Even so he would have lost the undignified race had not Alexander – or was it the resourceful Lannes? – proposed a break in Weimar to take rest, refreshment and a bath before setting out on the final lap to Erfurt. Napoleon arrived in time to check with the King of Saxony and with General Oudinot (who commanded the citadel) that all was ready to awaken Gothic Erfurt from its two centuries of sleep. Then, once sure the triumphal arches were in position and the artillery almost primed for the salute, Napoleon rode out towards Weimar to greet the Tsar.[40]

They met in the village of Münchenholzen, a few miles east of the town, early in the afternoon of 27 September, the seventh anniversary of the Moscow coronation. Alexander stepped down from his carriage and the two men embraced and exchanged pleasantries before the Tsar mounted a horse provided from the French imperial stables and saddled with white ermine in his honour. Side by side Napoleon and Alexander rode slowly into town: the crowd, unused to such occasions, marvelled at the colour of the uniforms, at the burnished glint of steel from swords and helmets as the escort trotted past, and at the tall, erect figure of the Tsar, who seemed so much more impressive on horseback than the Emperor of the French. Many onlookers recorded their impressions that day, for it was not often that History rode down their streets; and yet most felt stunned by the sheer noise as much as by anything they saw – bells pealing from towers and steeples, the low hills on either side of the town throwing back the thunder of Oudinot's guns and the less predictable salvoes of the city's own cannon ranged along the ramparts. And down in the narrow streets themselves, there was the constant iteration of drums, the rattle of troops springing to attention as the procession moved by, the roar of 'Vivent les Empereurs'. Napoleon looked contented, Alexander beamed affably (for he was too deaf to be troubled by the din). That night the town was illuminated, the two sovereigns remained talking until ten o'clock, Napoleon declared the townsfolk exempt from paying for the festivities, and everyone joined in the celebrations, even if a little doubt remained over what precisely was their purpose.[41]

Napoleon's good humour continued for most of the next week. They talked of political questions in the morning, rode in the afternoon, dined with the rulers of Saxony, Bavaria, Württemberg, Weimar and Westphalia, and in the evening attended the theatre or a concert. 'I am well pleased with Alexander and he must be with me', Napoleon wrote back to the Empress Josephine. 'If he were a woman, I think I would make him my mistress.'[42] On 4 October the Emperors, and all the attendant royalty, were present at a production of Voltaire's Oedipus; and when Talma reached the verse 'The friendship of a great man is a favour from the Gods', Alexander stood up and shook Napoleon's hand vigorously while all the audience cheered this spontaneous act of live theatre.[43] Two days later the royal cavalcade moved to Weimar where Alexander's sister, Marie Pavlovna, helped to entertain her father-in-law's guests. The Tsar had the doubtful pleasure of being escorted around the battlefield of Jena by Napoleon himself, who showed Alexander exactly how he had defeated Frederick William; but more to Alexander's taste was a Grand

Ball in Weimar, where he partnered the Queen of Westphalia. 'The Emperor danced', reported Napoleon to Josephine, 'but not for me – after all, forty *is* forty.'[44] No doubt at thirty Alexander might be excused such lightness of foot.

All these episodes, whether spontaneous or dramatically posed, were uniformly trivial, and it is hardly surprising if Napoleon felt Alexander to be the same immature hero-worshipper whom he had bewitched at Tilsit. But he was not. The more exaggerated his gesture, the less sincere were his expressions of goodwill. Napoleon, though himself gifted with a sense of theatre, did not have a sharp eye for pretence and affectation in others. There is no evidence he realized that, at Weimar, Alexander was acting the role of a simple dupe; and yet it was from Weimar that the Tsar sent his sister Catherine a significant comment: 'Napoleon thinks I am no better than a fool, but he who laughs last laughs longest' (*Napoleon pense que je ne suis qu'un sot, rira mieux qui rira le dernier*).[45] When, after the interlude at Weimar, the two sovereigns returned to Erfurt and sought agreement on their general policy, Napoleon was startled from his complacency by clear signs of obstinacy in the Tsar's attitude; could it possibly be that, after all, they were not brothers in destiny?

Napoleon's prime concern at Erfurt was to use the threat of Russian power to keep the Austrians quiet while he disposed of the Spanish and Portuguese troubles. The Erfurt Congress had begun, as he wished, with a graciously cold acknowledgement of Emperor Francis's representative by the assembled Princes of the French Empire and Germany, with the Tsar supporting them.[46] But there was all the difference in the world between humiliating the unfortunate Baron Vincent and agreeing to joint Franco-Russian action against the Austrians, so as to force Francis to order total disarmament of the troops along his frontiers. Alexander preferred to invite the Austrians to a conference where all members of the Continental System would thrash out the problems that might otherwise menace the stability of the new European order. Protracted talks of this nature did not suit Napoleon's timetable; and the idea of having to listen to the grievances of the Austrians and Prussians as well as of his German satellites threw Napoleon into a fit of rage. Furiously he seized his hat, hurled it on the floor and then trampled on it. Alexander, who like Napoleon was pacing the length of the room in which they were talking, paused and fixed his companion with a calm smile: 'You are violent', he said 'and I am stubborn. Anger will gain nothing with me. Let us talk, let us reason – or else I shall go away.'[47] Hastily Napoleon recovered his temper and the interminable discussion was resumed, but it made no progress. Later

Napoleon complained testily to Caulaincourt, 'That Emperor Alexander of yours is as stubborn as a mule: he turns a deaf ear to anything he does not want to hear.'[48] It was all sadly disillusioning.

Alexander convinced himself that he resisted Napoleon's blandishments from his own sense of what was good for Russia and for Europe. Perhaps so: but it must be admitted that his judgement over such questions was helped by advice from an unexpected quarter. Talleyrand, whom the Tsar first met at Tilsit, had handed over the French Foreign Ministry to Champagny in August 1807 but he retained considerable influence as Grand Chamberlain and Vice-Grand Elector, third highest state dignitary in the Empire, and he was invited to Erfurt by Napoleon because of his experience in 'speaking the language' of diplomacy. Throughout Alexander's visit to Erfurt, Talleyrand was one of a group of visitors to the drawing-room of the Princess de Thurn-Taxis (a sister of Queen Louise) where small talk lacked sympathy with Napoleon and where there was an opportunity of more serious conversation with the Tsar.[49] Exactly what words were exchanged between the two men remains unknown: but it is clear that Talleyrand emphasized the need for Russia to co-operate with Austria in restraining Napoleon rather than participating in any campaign to destroy the last vestiges of Austrian power in central Europe. Talleyrand later claimed to have told Alexander, 'Sire, it is in your power to save Europe, and you will not succeed by giving way to Napoleon. The French people are civilized, their sovereign is not. The sovereign of Russia is civilized, his people are not. The sovereign of Russia must therefore be the ally of the people of France.'[50] Whether or not these words were used, it was certainly on the basis of some such syllogism that Talleyrand and Alexander came to work together. The understanding they achieved at Erfurt outlasted the Napoleonic Empire itself.

The general affairs of Europe were settled – in so far as they were determined at all – by a secret Franco-Russian treaty signed on 12 October by Champagny and Rumiantsev.[51] Its provisions were a disappointment for Napoleon: the two Emperors re-affirmed their alliance and undertook to make a fresh personal approach to George III for peace; Finland and the Danubian Provinces of Moldavia and Wallachia were to be annexed to the Russian Empire; all the Turkish lands, apart from the Danubian Provinces, were to remain under the Sultan's rule and were to be respected by both Emperors; and, should Austria launch an attack upon France, the Russians would 'make common cause' with the French. Nothing was said of the grand partition of the Ottoman Empire or of the march into Asia or, indeed, of putting pressure on the

Austrians to disarm. Equally, however, there was no mention in the treaty of evacuation by the French of their garrisons from Prussia. The Tsar assured Napoleon he would let the Austrians know that Russia had commitments to France in the hope of dissuading Emperor Francis from consenting to war; and Napoleon similarly gave verbal pledges of his intention to withdraw all his forces from the Prussian lands, apart from a small token army under Davout. There was still sufficient goodwill between the two Emperors for each to carry out his undertaking.

The Erfurt Congress did not dissolve until two days after the signing of the secret treaty; for there remained a delicate question which had not as yet been raised and which Napoleon wished to discuss in his private meetings with the Tsar. Ever since Napoleon's return from Tilsit rumours had circulated in Paris and other capital cities maintaining that the Emperor wished to divorce Josephine and seek a new wife capable of bearing him a son. Only thus, it was said, would the position of the Bonaparte dynasty be consolidated on the throne. Most frequently these reports mentioned the Grand Duchess Catherine as Napoleon's likely choice, but Alexander, who had raised objections to three or four other suitors (including Emperor Francis), did not wish his favourite sister to be installed in the Tuileries; and Marie Fcodorovna, with whom all questions of marriage finally rested, was resolutely opposed to a link between the Romanovs and the Bonapartes. Napoleon remained officially silent on the matter but Caulaincourt – apparently on his own initiative – went to considerable pains to let Paris know of the Grand Duchess's favours and interests; although when, at the end of February 1808, he solemnly noted that 'The Grand Duchess Catherine is going to marry the Emperor for she is learning how to dance French quadrilles' one suspects the ambassador was salting his despatches with dry humour.[52]

At Erfurt Napoleon hoped Alexander would mention the rumours. But the Tsar, no doubt thinking of coming domestic battles with the Dowager Empress, tactfully kept silent. At last, prompted by Napoleon, both Talleyrand and Caulaincourt privately pressed Alexander to raise the delicate question in general terms.[53] At one of their final meetings, Alexander duly expressed his hope that Napoleon would crown his work by a new marriage and the foundation of a dynasty. The possibility of a family alliance was considered: Catherine's name was not mentioned, although there was a brief reference to the future prospects of the Grand Duchess Anna Pavlovna, Alexander's youngest sister, who was then aged thirteen. But Napoleon was not prepared to commit himself to an engagement: there were fifteen other Princesses on his list of possible consorts; and he was still so affectionately attached to Josephine that he was reluctant to take any irrevocable step towards a divorce. The conversation with Alexander turned to other matters; and the Tsar prepared to set out for home, without having compromised his family. Within a month it was announced that the Grand Duchess Catherine would marry Prince George of Holstein-Oldenburg, her second cousin, who was already serving in the Russian army and had every intention of settling in Russia.

Outwardly the Erfurt Congress ended on a high note of festivity, with the relations of France and Russia as cordial as ever. On 14 October the two Emperors rode out together along the route towards Weimar, with all the noisy ceremonial which had accompanied their arrival two and a half weeks before. At Münchenholzen they dismounted and remained, for a time, deep in conversation. Yet nothing was agreed about any visit from Alexander to Paris, still less for Napoleon to come in state to St Petersburg. They embraced each other, Alexander climbed into his coach and started back on the long journey to his capital.[54] Napoleon watched the dust of his escort disappearing, turned his horse towards Erfurt, and throughout the ride back to his residence remained silent, his face sad and grim. For eighteen days of festivity and talk, his material gains were slight; and the fabric of friendship with Alexander was worn transparently thin. They were never to meet again.

10

The Primacy of Speransky

The Rise of Michael Speransky

Most of the dignitaries who accompanied Alexander to Erfurt were members of families distinguished through several generations of service to the Russian Empire. Their names – Volkonsky, Golitsyn, Rumiantsev, and so on – were familiar enough to the Germans and the French. In many cases they were themselves personal acquaintances, sometimes even related by marriage to the famous dynasties of western and central Europe. Yet among this closely knit group there was one unexpected newcomer, a sharp-featured man in his mid-thirties, prematurely bald and coldly courteous. His origins were so unaristocratic that he had been baptized quite simply, 'Michael, son of the priest Michael'; but for a career these days one needed a patronymic and in its absence he had chosen, as a student, a surname of impeccably Latin origin; hence he was now known as Michael Speransky.[1] It was a happily prophetic inspiration.

Technically, in 1808, Speransky was merely a high grade civil servant, head of the Second Department in the Ministry of the Interior, released from his desk to act as secretary to the Tsar. But outside observers perceived in him an influence greater than his modest rank. At Erfurt the French, always inclined to search among the shadows for advisers who really mattered, readily accorded him respect. Napoleon studied him with a shrewd eye; Talleyrand encouraged him to talk.[2] They found Speransky too intelligent to reveal inner thoughts and aspirations; and this discovery therefore convinced them they were right in judging him to be a figure of substance. He was, they thought, not just an administrative bureaucrat but a personal assistant to his master, someone who understood Alexander's intentions better than the Foreign Minister, Rumiantsev. And Caulaincourt, the French ambassador, who had first met Speransky at a private dinner-party given by the Tsar early in the previous July,[3] returned to St Petersburg determined to watch his progress with lively interest.

Speransky was, indeed, an unexpected person to find in the circle of Alexander's closest advisers. He was nearly six years older than the Tsar and, like most of his generation, had absorbed the ideas and the philosophy fashionable in the cultural outposts of Catherine II's Empire. But there was a difference between the way in which Speransky had trained his mind and the intellectual dabbling of the nobility, so many of whose thoughts were rendered giddily unrealistic by the Enlightenment. He was the eldest son of a village priest in the province of Vladimir and was himself originally educated at a seminary and trained for the priesthood. His natural intelligence carried him to what was, in effect, the central theological faculty of the Russian Orthodox Church at the end of the eighteenth century, a seminary attached to the Alexander Nevsky Monastery in St Petersburg. Some of Speransky's tutors there showed an intellectual comprehension which was far broader than the traditional academic disciplines of seminarists; and the young student was introduced to the ideas of Descartes, Locke, Leibnitz, Newton, Voltaire, Diderot and Kant as well as to the new sciences of men like Benjamin Franklin and Joseph Priestley. He developed such remarkable gifts of logical analysis and synthesis that, like many other able members of the seminary, he was seconded to the lay world before completing his theological studies; and he served as principal secretary to Prince Kurakin, who was entrusted with high office early in Paul's reign. Kurakin, for his part, was deeply impressed with Speransky; and in the spring of 1797 the Prince secured the permanent transference of the brilliant young seminarist to the civil service.[4] It was, almost certainly, his natural vocation.

Ten years passed before Speransky attracted the attention of Tsar Alexander. But from 1802 onwards his remarkable memoranda on the opportunities and limits for reform within the Russian social system began to supply ideas for Kochubey, and other members of the Secret Committee as well.[5] It is therefore probable that Alexander was familiar with many of Speransky's projects long before they ever met, though he cannot have known their origin. Speransky's language and processes of thought would inevitably appeal to someone who still valued the precepts and teachings of La Harpe.

Alexander first became aware of Speransky as a person largely by chance. Shortly after the Tsar's return to St Petersburg from Tilsit, Kochubey (who was at that time still Minister of the Interior) fell ill and was unable to make his regular oral report to the sovereign. In his place Kochubey sent Speransky who, as the most competent of his departmental chiefs, was a natural deputy for the minister. Like everyone else who met him, the Tsar was impressed by Speransky's air of efficiency and his authoritative mastery of detail. Some public figures – including Arakcheev and Alexander's sister, Catherine Pavlovna – resented Speransky's manner, finding something alien in the rigid austerity of his bureaucratic mind.[6] But, at that particular moment, Alexander was desperately short of reliable advisers and acutely conscious of the unpopularity of Tilsit in many sections of society. He needed someone who understood the causes of discontent at home, who could explain why the purchasing power of the paper rouble was only a quarter the purchasing power of the silver rouble, who could distinguish between the real and theoretical obligations of serf-owners, and who knew the ways in which legal practice varied from province to province and district to district. Above all, Alexander wanted someone new around him, a person unassociated with the hopes and disappointments of the past five years, and a man of peace rather than a soldierly pensionary. The qualities in Speransky that put General Arak-cheev and the Grand Duchess on their guard were the very ones which most appealed to Alexander. If the Tsar were once again to encourage internal reforms, Speransky would be as valuable a servant for him as any-one in St Petersburg. Instinctively Alexander sensed the genius of the man who gave him such clear and comprehensive reports. He insisted on re-taining him in his own service rather than allowing him to continue at the Ministry of the Interior; and in October 1807 Speransky accompanied Alexander on his short tour of inspection in Byelo-Russia.[7] By the follow-ing autumn he had become so indispensable to the efficient working of the Tsar's chancery that it was natural for Alexander to command him to make the long journey to Erfurt, even though he was primarily concerned with domestic matters. When he returned to St Petersburg he was appointed Assistant Minister of Justice, receiving in January 1810 the rank and title of State Secretary. Throughout the three and a half years which followed Erfurt he remained Alexander's most trusted political confidant. As Joseph de Maistre (who did not like him) was to write in the spring of 1812, Speransky was 'virtually prime minister . . . great and all-powerful'.[8]

For the orphaned son of a poor country priest such advancement was meteoric, and in Russia unique. During the preceding half century men of insignificant birth occasionally climbed the social ladder with astonishing rapidity, yet they were always helped upwards either by tales of manly courage in battle or by a graceful skill in polished compliment, and sometimes by both. Even Arakcheev, uncouth though he was in many ways, knew when to fawn and how to flatter. But Speransky possessed none of these social gifts. He was uncompromisingly honest, ascetically cold and reserved, almost non-Russian in his faceless personality; he lacked all ambition for customary rewards, seeking neither a fortune nor the prestige of enhanced status. It was difficult to find in his conscientious devotion to governmental service any lust for power; nor was there any suggestion of opportunism in his earlier career for, though he was at one stage under the patronage of the well-known Court chaplain Andrei Samborsky, he never made use of any contacts in society for his own betterment. The aristocrats of the cities and the great landowners on their estates did not easily accustom themselves to government by a bureaucrat of whom it was said that 'his heart was fragrant with fresh, clean air'.[9] They had disapproved of Czartoryski as a Pole and Budberg as an alleged Swede and many of them continued to frown on the coarse-fibred arrogance of Arakcheev, but they could not even begin to understand why Alexander placed so much trust in this thick-skinned Puritan from Vladimir. Years afterwards one of Speransky's fellow-seminarists recalled how in 1792 the future State Secretary (who was then aged twenty) was authorized to preach a practice sermon at the Alexander Nevsky Monastery on the Last Judgement. It was 'delivered . . . with such enthusiasm that the signs of conviction visibly spread on the faces of his listeners.'[10] Russia's rulers had not hitherto looked to the pulpits to supply them with government ministers.

Naturally scandal-mongers scoured Speransky's private life for morsels, but they did so in vain. When he was twenty-six he had married an English girl, Elizabeth Stephens, the daughter of a widowed governess whom he met at Samborsky's home, where many members of the English colony in St Petersburg were accustomed to gather. But Elizabeth did not live long enough to influence her husband's ideas: she died from tuberculosis less than twelve months after her marriage. The tragedy ravaged so deeply Speransky's reason that he was forced to impose a barrier on every emotion. Only by tireless employment of the mind was he able to dissipate his grief. He scorned the diversions of high society, preferring to seek mental relaxation in spiritual exercises. Thus during the years he was State Secretary (and for long afterwards) Speransky was engaged in completing the first Russian translation of Thomas à Kempis. It was an unexpected pursuit for the chief minister of a Tsar; and, against the glittering back-cloth of Petersburg fashion, an anachronistic one.[11]

The Reforms of 1808–9 and their Critics

Alexander saw Speransky's chief task in 1808 as the modernization of the structure of Tsardom, in much the same way as his new Italian architects were remodelling the outer fabric of palaces first erected half a century ago. He did not want Speransky or anybody else to institute some dramatically radical upheaval, but rather to shepherd the State through a series of gradual innovations. If Speransky could unravel the complexities of accumulated legal confusion and substitute for them civil and commercial codes for all the provinces of the Empire, so much the better; but, above all, Alexander wished him to concentrate on ways of sparing his ministers the chronic embarrassment of crippling financial crises.[12] Speransky was to be the Colbert of Russia, building up her strength as a world power by calculated plans for economic development and seeing to it that the abilities of her administrators were harnessed in a rational system of advancement. The phrases – like the problems – were familiar: but there is no reason to believe that in reverting to them Alexander was assuming a hypocritical pose. Balanced budgets, codified laws, efficient government were as much in the interests of the Tsar as of his people, provided of course that no well-meaning reformer was rash enough to fetter the sovereign's authority.

Speransky's plans were more ambitious than his actual achievements (at least during the reign of Alexander). They always looked impressive on paper. He wished to define the precise limits of the legislative, administrative and judicial functions of government, believing that a clear separation of powers was a safeguard against irresponsible tyranny and therefore a guarantee of stable progress for the community as a whole. Although he insisted that the legislative initiative must remain with the Tsar and a Council of State nominated by the sovereign, he foresaw a pyramid of elected representative assemblies in central and local administration, primarily advisory in character. He proposed a gradual transition from the autocratic oligarchical constitution of the eighteenth century to what he personally termed the 'monarchical government' of western Europe, although he seems to have had primarily in his mind the new Napoleonic structure of France.[13] As a specialist in financial matters he also drew up a comprehensive scheme which was intended to base the Russian taxation system upon the agricultural wealth of the country while at the same time proposing a uniform method of governmental accountancy, related to an annual budget approved by the Tsar and the Council of State. Finally, in his capacity as Assistant Minister of Justice, Speransky presided over meetings of a commission which sought to replace the confused mass of Russian laws by a single code inspired by the revolutionary models of the Napoleonic Empire and, to a lesser extent, by enlightened reforms in Prussia and Austria.[14]

Alexander was intensely interested in each of these projects and Speransky himself calculated that in 1809 he held 'perhaps a hundred talks and discussions' with the Tsar, amplifying and explaining his memoranda, occasionally modifying his views.[15] Almost every morning when Alexander was in residence at the Winter Palace, Speransky was summoned for an audience. Occasionally, too, he dined privately with the Tsar on Kammionyi Island although he took no part in the ceremonial functions of government, fading more and more into the background as his influence and importance increased.* Alexander's own notions of enlightened absolutism made him naturally receptive to many of Speransky's proposals. Neither man was ever a 'liberal' in the western European or American sense of the term. Whenever the Tsar failed to understand a problem, he applied to it a militaristic appraisal: if he saw a solution which was orderly, rational and based upon a hierarchical structure of command and responsibility, he believed in it; if it showed excessive originality or independence and stressed rights rather than obligations, he distrusted it. Since Speransky favoured government by strict regulation and decree his attitude of mind made him put forward ideas which Alexander found, for the most part, readily acceptable. There were no basic differences of principle between the two men. It was only when Speransky tried to translate ideas into legislative acts that the Tsar began to suspect his right-hand man was alienating all the social classes of Russia at one and the same time: and his political instincts placed him on guard against mounting opposition.

Like most autocrats, Alexander was reluctant to delegate matters of substance even after he had approved the terms of reference for any particular sub-committee. To some extent, the experience of 1802–3 was

---

* From October 1809 until April 1813 the United States were represented at St Petersburg by John Quincy Adams, son of the second President of the Union (and who was himself to become in 1824 the sixth President). It is significant that, although Adams kept a full diary of his mission to Russia, the printed version does not once record any meeting with Speransky, despite the obvious similarity of interests between the architect of Russia's reform programme and an ex-Senator who knew by experience the faults and virtues of the finest product of eighteenth-century constitutional thought.

repeated in 1809–10: Alexander insisted to Speransky (as earlier he had to Stroganov and Novosiltsov) that he should be consulted over everything, however trivial; and decisions were thus postponed over questions of importance simply because the Tsar needed more time to weigh their significance. It is, of course, true that Speransky was attempting to formulate a new system at a time of chronic crisis for Europe as a whole and therefore Alexander could never concentrate on domestic affairs to the exclusion of diplomatic and military questions. Moreover, occasionally Alexander certainly used these other problems as an excuse for procrastination, especially if he saw that a particular reform was likely to arouse opposition from the conservatives at his Court, with the Dowager Empress and the Grand Duchess Catherine as their champions. Speransky found – again as Stroganov had done – that Alexander's vacillations of mood made him a difficult master, one who at times could drive any minister into the depths of despair: 'He is too weak to rule and too strong to be ruled,' Speransky once complained in a fit of exasperation.[16] Yet, at least until the autumn of 1811, Speransky continued to enjoy Alexander's confidence in a way which his old friends on the Secret Committee had never known; and, although most of his projects were left unsanctioned, he achieved more in his brief spell as the Tsar's principal adviser than any other reformer in Russia during the first half of the nineteenth century.

The range of Speransky's reforms illustrates clearly the extent to which Alexandrine Russia was still only superficially westernized. Most of the Tsar's earliest confidants – Czartoryski, Paul Stroganov, Novosiltsov and even the young idealist Karamzin – had emphasized to Alexander the urgent necessity for improving the educational structure of his Empire, and it was a task to which he gave serious attention throughout the first decade of his reign. Speransky was placed by the Tsar on a commission which he established in the winter of 1807–8 to propose legislation for modernizing the curriculum of the Church schools in Russia, and in the following year he was made a formal Administrator of (secular) Schools. Speransky's educational reforms coincided closely with the earlier ideas of Kochubey, who wrote to his former protegé, 'It is not universities, especially universities on the German model, that we need when there is no one to study at them; what we need are primary and secondary schools.'[17] In June 1808 Speransky was largely responsible for drafting a law which served as the basic regulation for ecclesiastical schools until the eve of the Revolution and he played an active part in encouraging the Orthodox dioceses to set up educational institutions in the more remote regions rather than merely concentrating them around St Petersburg and Moscow. Speransky himself subsequently claimed to have drawn up the statutes for the famous school which Alexander established in 1811 at Tsarskoe Selo on the model of the French lycées (an institution fortunate enough to include in its foundation class of thirty boys the twelve-year-old Alexander Pushkin); and, although other civil servants are officially credited with organizing the Tsarskoe Selo *Litsei*, it is known that Speransky prepared for Alexander a paper on the educational principles involved in secondary school teaching of this type.[18] His plea for recognition of the need to mould character rather than merely to convey factual knowledge shows clearly enough what both the Tsar and his minister had in mind – the creation of an intellectual élite who would give guidance and moral leadership to the next generation of Russians in Church and State. Yet even these activities of Speransky won him enemies: traditionalists maintained that the only appropriate education for men of quality in Russian life was at military academies, such as Catherine II's Land Cadet Corps College and the school for artillery cadets; and there was also a powerful Roman Catholic group among the nobility (which originated with emigrés like Joseph de Maistre) who had already established a Jesuit school in St Petersburg and who maintained that the *Litsei* was a dangerous source of rationalistic ideas from abroad, alien to every good Russian.[19]

Alexander took little notice of these criticisms. He also supported two decrees, drafted by Speransky in April and August 1809, which swept aside cherished privileges permitting the more rapid advancement of members of the nobility within the civil service and insisted that applicants for the higher ranks of state services should be appointed only after sitting for a written examination.[20] In spirit both of these measures fulfilled earlier ideas of Peter the Great, and Alexander thought they made good sense. They aroused, however, furious indignation among the aristocracy, especially those who were seeking to promote the interests of their sons by careers in the administration at St Petersburg. Many members of the petty nobility still on the lower rungs of the social ladder were now prevented from climbing to greater eminence by the awkward fact that they could never pass an examination in Russian and mathematics, let alone in such strict disciplines as French and Latin (a subject of particular complaint). Only a priest's son who had risen from the very dust of Vladimir would, it was felt, seek to mortify honest Russians in such a way. Once again Speransky had stirred up that xenophobic patriotism which was never far below the surface in Russian minds.

Grand Duchess Catherine left her brother in no doubt of the hostility aroused by these decrees; and Alexander became uneasy.[21] He had already taken the first steps to implement some of Speransky's constitutional proposals and his financial plan. But in the closing quarter of 1809 the Tsar lapsed into caution. Although he had insisted Speransky should keep both his ultimate objectives and his palliative measures strictly secret, alarming reports of pending changes were circulating in St Petersburg; and there were even more fantastic rumours in Moscow and among the land-owners on the great estates around the old capital.[22] Hence Alexander resolved he would first establish Speransky's proposed Council of State, a nominated body whose members would subsequently initiate and consider the drafts of all laws and statutes before submitting them for final sanction to the sovereign. By this means it would, of course, be possible for the Council of State jointly to accept responsibility for financial measures which everyone realized were bound to be unpopular. Despite the mounting criticism of Speransky, Alexander had no wish to see so able a civil servant hounded out of office by conservative landowners.

There had already been several State Councils in the modern history of Russia: a small inner body of nine under Catherine the Great; an Imperial Council to assist Paul to draft legislation; and an inaptly named Perman-ent Council, established by Alexander at his accession, to advise him 'on important state affairs'.[23] Moreover, in September 1802, it will be remembered Alexander had enthusiastically instituted a Committee of Ministers, whose functions were also purely advisory and tended, after Austerlitz, to be replaced by special commissions which were given specific tasks by the sovereign. The new Council of State was to be more highly organized than any of its predecessors and was to have direct supervision of the most important aspects of governmental business. There would be, within the Council, subordinate departmental councils which would review the work of the Ministries; and the whole Council itself was assisted by a Chancellery headed by a State Secretary (Speransky himself). Since the State Secretary was to co-ordinate the work of the various departmental councils and supervise all the drafting operations for the Council of State, his position was one of real power even if the last word over all decisions rested with the Council's President, the Tsar.[24]

Alexander discussed the final form of the Council of State with only four other dignitaries besides Speransky, and his choice of confidants is significant. First among them was Kochubey, a friend since the last year of his grandmother's reign and a former member of the Secret Committee as well as Minister of the Interior. Then there was General Saltykov, Alexander's moral tutor when he was a boy; and Rumiantsev, the

Foreign Minister, who was accorded the title of Chancellor in the autumn of 1809, partly because Alexander wished to acknowledge his long service to the State and partly to reassure the French, who regarded him as the principal champion of Franco-Russian friendship at the Tsar's Court. Finally Alexander consulted Prince Lopukhin, an elderly member of the Senate, naturally conservative in temperament.[25] They agreed that the Council would be established on the Russian New Year's Day of 1810 and that the Tsar himself should open its first session with fitting pomp and ceremonial.

There was, however, one person in St Petersburg of considerable importance whom Alexander virtually ignored. General Arakcheev had improved his reputation as an administrator in two years as Minister of War; and the Tsar personally paid tribute to his services in the war against Sweden; but he never took him into his confidence.[26] With rumours circulating that the military administration was to be subject to civil control, Arakcheev naturally asked the Tsar for information and found him sympathetic and conciliatory. He promised that, before the proposed reform was made public, the General would be consulted.

On 24 December by the Russian Calendar (5 January 1810 in western Europe) Arakcheev was informed the Tsar would send for him that evening. The General waited at his house in Liteiny Prospect for a summons to the palace, less than a mile away across the snow-muffled squares. At last, very late, a visitor arrived. It was Speransky, sent by Alexander to explain to the War Minister what the reforms were all about. Arakcheev felt slighted and lost his temper. Ten minutes later Speransky made a hurried departure, leaving memoranda for the minister to study. As soon as conditions permitted, Arakcheev set out for his estate at Gruzino, furious with Speransky, indignant at his own treatment by Alexander, and determined to resign.[27]

There followed an exchange of letters between the General and his sovereign which reveals much about each man's character. Arakcheev began by explaining that he had read through the documents left by Speransky but did not feel competent to comment on the reasoning behind them. He continued:

Sire, you know the kind of education I received in my youth . . . I feel that, at my age, I am no more than a competent officer, able to administer correctly our military affairs . . . In order to put your wise proposals into effect, you need a minister who has received a comprehensive and general education. Only a man with this background will be of use to this important new institution and able to uphold the first military responsibility in the State which I assume to be defence of the Council itself, since without military defence the best provisions made by the Council may be frustrated. I cannot do this, Sire, and since I am not able adequately to fufill these duties, I would be a discredit [as Minister].[28]

Alexander wrote a frank reply:

For what reasons must I search in order to see why you intend to leave the post you occupy? ... I cannot accept your explanation ... Nobody will understand it. Everyone who has read the new proposals finds that the Council will be good for the Empire. Only you, on whose co-operation I especially relied and who have so often said that apart from a sense of duty to the nation you are moved by personal affection for myself, only you ... hasten to give up the duties you direct at a time when your conscience must be telling you how impossible it will be to replace you. If you ask yourself sincerely what your real motive is, and are honest with yourself, you will not be proud of it ...[29]

Naturally, after such a stern missive, Arakcheev could not retire into the country. Alexander offered him the choice of remaining Minister of War or of becoming Chairman of the Military Department in the Council of State; and Arakcheev, believing that the Council would ultimately control the ministries, chose the new Military Department. He was soon to find he had made a mistake. The Council proved too cumbersome to function smoothly in an emergency; and, under the threat of another war it was Arakcheev's successor as Minister, General Barclay de Tolly, who decided how the army should meet this gravest of all challenges.

The Council of State at Work

When Alexander stood godfather to Speransky's brain-child he certainly intended the Council to share the burden of administrative responsibility. The Empress Elizabeth twice mentioned his desire to make innovations in letters to her mother, though she was commenting on relaxations in Court etiquette and ceremonial rather than in government.[30] It is as though he felt the whole machinery of state needed overhauling; and there is no doubt he would have welcomed ways of shedding irksome tasks, provided nothing encroached on his autocratic prerogative. For the first half of 1810 the new system worked well enough. The Council cleared the agenda Speransky drew up with astonishing rapidity. Within five weeks the first decrees on financial reform were sealed and published; and, although it took another four months to float a domestic loan and to stabilize the values of silver and copper, Speransky was optimistic he would be able to check what would now be called the 'galloping inflation' of the

Russian economy. Work began anew on codification of the laws and some progress was made in defining the delicate relationship between the departments of the Council and the various ministries. With Alexander's approval, the Council moved on to other questions: the need to set up a new government agency to develop transport and internal commerce; and proposals for the eventual establishment of a Ministry of Police, which would safeguard the life and property of individuals as well as maintaining the internal security of the State.[31]

All these changes were of lasting value to Alexander's Empire, and indeed to his successors. But the Tsar never fulfilled Speransky's hopes. His enthusiasm for reform declined during the course of the year, partly because of the pressure of foreign affairs but also because he could not ignore the mood of the nobility on whose services he necessarily relied for national defence. Speransky became more and more unpopular. Despite the attempt to associate all members of the Council of State with the financial plan, the State Secretary inevitably became the scapegoat for every grievance; for there were many of the nobility only too pleased to remember that the constitutional reform was drafted by Speransky and that it was according to his financial plan that the new taxes were being levied. As Speransky himself ruefully admitted a year or so later, nobody is ever grateful to a man who imposes taxes. He became to some extent the victim of his own desire to escape the limelight: his public anonymity aggravated those at Court who wanted, for their own well-being, to discover a sinister influence behind the throne. It was widely rumoured, by the end of the year, that Speransky was proposing to introduce an income tax to set alongside the heavy stamp duties which his reforms had already introduced.[32]

Speransky was in an unenviable position. He could claim that public accountancy had improved, that there was even a prospect of balancing the budget, eventually. But in the second half of the year 1810 he found it increasingly necessary to remind Alexander of the purpose and principles which lay behind the Council of State, of the danger in setting up *ad hoc* committees to give speedy advice on specific problems, and of the way in which the Council had been planned as the apex of a pyramid of elected representative assemblies.[33] Alexander, probably correctly, believed the external menace to Russia was too grave to authorize legislation for further internal reforms. At the end of the year Speransky wished to resign his post of State Secretary so as to concentrate on the legal complexities of codification, which now seemed to him the most important task for the future. But Alexander was always reluctant to accept the resignation of men in whom he had confidence. He still needed Speransky as State Secretary and he appears to have hoped to return to a policy of reform once the foreign situation eased again. Certainly he blamed the limited implementation of Speransky's projects on the recurrent international crises. Hence he pressed Speransky to keep office rather than abandon the post created only twelve months previously. Like Arakcheev, Speransky felt bound in loyalty to do as the Tsar wished; and, like Arakcheev, he was soon to regret his decision.[34]

Speransky's enemies, unable to oust the State Secretary from his position of primacy through legitimate complaints, had one old weapon to hand; they could smear his reputation by alleging he was an agent of the French. This particular tale had begun as soon as the Tsar returned from Erfurt, for it had seemed to some in attendance on Alexander that Speransky was unduly impressed by the institutions of French government during the Congress (though how he had found the time to study them in such unnatural surroundings nobody troubled to explain). From this story it was easy enough for jealous tongues to maintain Speransky had been persuaded (or, according to some, bribed) to introduce into Russia alien ideas of government which were deliberately based upon the constitutional usage of France and which were therefore surrounding the Tsar with dangerous revolutionary notions. Speransky, it was said, was morally guilty of treachery to the ancient ideals of Russia; and it was essential for someone to expose to the well-intentioned Tsar the viper which had infiltrated his throne-room.[35] Throughout the years 1810 and 1811 the campaign against the State Secretary continued, but it was not until the following March that a mood of fear and exaggerated patriotism swept it to triumph; and its victim into exile from the capital.

11

The Viceroy

The witch-hunt against Speransky was to some extent a method of easing individual consciences. For while there is no evidence the State Secretary or any other public figure received bribes from Napoleon, there was in St Petersburg hardly a member of the conservative aristocracy who had not, in some way or other, enjoyed French hospitality during the years of nominal alliance between the two Empires. General Armand de Caulaincourt, Duke of Vicenza, Master of the Horse to the Emperor of the French and Ambassador Extraordinary to the Emperor of All the Russias, held a position in Society worthy of his high-sounding titles and eminence. When Napoleon first sent him to Alexander's Court four months after Tilsit he insisted Caulaincourt should take pains to impress the Russians by a show of lavish entertainment and, in particular, he urged him to cultivate the personal friendship of the Tsar. A generous allowance was placed at the ambassador's disposal and increased after Erfurt, where Caulaincourt confessed that life in the Russian capital was running him heavily into debt.[1] So eager was Napoleon for his mission to succeed that he would have granted him a fortune.

The ambassador fulfilled his instructions to the letter. There was no carriage in the Nevsky Prospect so smartly burnished as Caulaincourt's, no horses so elegantly groomed. The gourmets of St Petersburg delighted in the creations of his chef, the intellectually fastidious admired the good taste of his social evenings, the ladies (and their consorts) thrilled to the glamour of masked balls which he mounted in quasi-royal splendour. 'I was virtually the Viceroy of the Emperor at St Petersburg', he wrote later.[2] As well as a palace near the Hermitage, Caulaincourt had a country house on the road to Peterhof and a villa on Kammionyi Island, strategic-ally placed between the Tsar's retreat and Madame Naryshkin's. A small supper party on the island would be planned for fifty guests, an embassy reception for three, four or five times that number.[3] Though now and again some twist of French policy hardened feeling against Caulaincourt, the great families were too envious of his social ingenuity to maintain for long any self-denying censure. Those who remembered to disapprove of him as the velvet glove of a foreign tyranny attended his dinners and purged their patriotic souls by drawing up a mental inventory of the expenses. The results were startling: pears provided at a banquet for four hundred guests cost 300 francs each (about £13); festoons of candles illuminated every room; the finest vintage wines trundled across Europe in protective casks. In the twelve months following Erfurt it was calculated that the French ambassador's expenses 'amounted at least to four hundred thousand roubles' and 'probably to more than a million'.[4] Whichever the figure, it was far in excess of his allowance from Napoleon.

For such lavish spending Caulaincourt expected, and received, pre-ferential treatment among the foreign envoys. Though not the doyen of the diplomatic corps he asserted a precedence which nobody challenged. 'The French ambassador took his station nearest the door and the Corps Diplomatique stood in succession after him', Adams recorded in his journal when he attended his first ceremonial reception in December 1809. A few days later, at a New Year dinner in the Hermitage, Adams was intrigued to note that Caulaincourt was seated at the table 'in the centre appropriated to the Imperial family', while other foreign ministers had the second table to themselves. And similarly, while most envoys watched the annual blessing of the waters of the Neva from the windows of the palace, Caulaincourt throughout the ceremony remained in attendance on the Tsar as though he were a member of Alexander's own suite.[5] No one was allowed to forget the special relationship binding together the Russians and the French.

But did Caulaincourt really obtain anything of value for his money? Alexander showed him genuinely personal affection and the two men understood and sympathized with each other's public and private prob-lems. But Caulaincourt had few illusions over his influence: Alexander, he wrote to Napoleon, 'appears to be weak but is really far from being so ... Beneath all his natural benevolence, honesty and natural loyalty, beneath all his exalted ideas and principles, there is a strong element of royal dissimulation born of an obstinacy that nothing can conquer.'[6] For most of the eighteen months which followed the Erfurt Congress, Caulaincourt was unable to exert any effective pressure whatsoever on Russian policy, even though this was the period in which he appeared to be at the height of his social eminence in St Petersburg. Alexander rode with him, dined with him, listened to his accounts of Napoleon's policy, replied equably to the honeyed words and veiled threats from Paris – and proceeded to use every report of French embarrassment, whether in Spain and Portugal or later in Austria, as an opportunity for asserting Russia's freedom of action. Thus the war with Sweden was pressed to a victorious conclusion with a remarkably daring crossing of the frozen Gulf of Bothnia; and the war with Turkey was allowed to flare up once more in the summer of 1809, with the Russians improving their position in Wallachia and, across the Black Sea in the forgotten Caucasus, establishing new bases in Georgia. Caulaincourt could not fail to see that reports of victories in the south, though often exaggerated, improved morale in St Petersburg; for the Turkish War was always far more popular than the campaign against the Swedes, which was interpreted as a non-Russian enterprise imposed on Alexander by the French.

Yet the first clear indication of Alexander's independence in foreign affairs had come far closer to Erfurt than the resumption of the Turkish War. In January 1809, only twelve weeks after bidding Napoleon farewell, Alexander was host to Frederick William of Prussia in St Petersburg.[7] Foreign residents in the capital noted with amazement the elaborate and expensive preparations ordered by the Tsar for the visit of the King, who was accompanied by Queen Louise and by two of his brothers. It was the first time a reigning sovereign of Prussia had ever come to the Russian capital; and, as if to compensate the Hohenzollerns for the humiliations they had suffered since Tilsit, Alexander entertained his friends with a hospitality as generous as his grandmother had bestowed on her favourites a generation ago. For three and a half weeks there was constant festivity at the Court – balls, banquets and theatrical presentations which soon outshone for Alexander the fading memories of Erfurt. Society, which in the recent past had been critical both of the Tsar and the Prussians, warmly supported Alexander, believing that in honouring the victims of Napoleon's malice it was striking a gesture of defiance against the French. Even the Empress Elizabeth, though still wretchedly miserable in spirit, was cheered by the spate of entertainments and showed a sincere affection towards Louise, who she well knew had stirred her husband's heart so deeply over the preceding six years. By now, too, the tension was less acute between the Court and Marie Feodorovna's establishment at Pavlovsk, for Alexander had convinced his mother that he was playing a deep game with Napoleon; and the Dowager Empress co-operated readily with the reigning Empress in showing favour to the Prussians.

Caulaincourt was vexed by the hospitality which the Imperial family was so ostentatiously lavishing on the Hohenzollerns, a dynasty against whom Napoleon had never ceased to caution Alexander. At one of the aristocratic salons the ambassador's customary tact deserted him. In a rash moment he brusquely declared: 'There is no mystery about this visit – the Queen of Prussia has come to sleep with Tsar Alexander.'[8] The remark, which was almost certainly an unjustified slander, was ill-received by those around the ambassador, and it was soon being repeated in tones of decorous prurience from one scandalized group to another. The unfortunate Caulaincourt felt his social position slipping. Belatedly he decided that before the royal couple set out for Königsberg he must honour their presence in the capital. It was, wrote Elizabeth in a letter to her mother, 'a very fine ball'; and well it may have been, for Napoleon's ambassador had the privilege of spending some thirty thousand roubles on entertaining two sovereigns whom his master's troops were still preventing from returning to Berlin.[9]

Politically, of course, the visit of Frederick William had no immediate significance. Prussia was too weak to count for much in anyone's calculations at the beginning of 1809. Alexander was at pains in his conversations with the French ambassador to insist that for him the visit was primarily a social occasion. 'I did not talk politics with the King more than twice', he assured Caulaincourt;[10] and he added that, even then, he had concentrated on stressing to Frederick William the wisdom of seeking good relations with Napoleon. The visit was, indeed, essentially a winter frolic; and towards the end poor Louise found the pace of entertainment so exacting that she had to retire, with Elizabeth, for several days of rest at Tsarskoe Selo while the indefatigable Alexander took Frederick William and his brothers to Kronstadt, Oranienbaum and Peterhof.[11] Yet, though disappointed she had seen 'too little' of the Tsar and sad that there seemed no immediate prospect of improving Prussia's status among the nations, Louise was able once again to bring down the curtain with a dramatic flourish, even if only Alexander was aware of her action. For, while journeying back to Königsberg, she dashed off a message which was intended for Alexander's eyes alone. In the note, she spoke of the love which bound her to the Tsar 'beyond all expression' and, as though conscious that this was truly a valediction, she commended to his care 'the interests of the King, the future happiness of my children and of all Prussia'.[12] Within eighteen months Louise was dead; and Alexander, who had sometimes wavered from the pledges of Memel and the oath of Potsdam, felt bound to honour the plea she had sent him for all the remaining years of his reign. Her hold on Alexander's heart was more powerful from beyond the grave than ever in life.

All this, however, lay far in the future during those first months of 1809. Alexander's immediate concern was with a family matter which distracted his thoughts until it seemed to him more pressing than even the latest communication from Napoleon. For while the Prussian royalty were in St Petersburg the formal betrothal of the Grand Duchess Catherine to George of Holstein-Oldenburg had taken place;[13] and now Alexander was trying to accept the marriage of the sister whom he had, for so long, come to regard as his own companion and confidante. He liked George well enough; but the prospect of Catherine's marriage again affected his health and he was forced to take 'days of rest' that spring. But the marriage took place quite happily in the first week of May, although Elizabeth, who could never bring herself to love her sister-in-law, found the ceremony 'overweighted with grandeur'.[14] As an official residence in the capital the Grand Duchess and her husband were assigned the Anichkov Palace, a delightful mid-eighteenth-century building newly remodelled by Quarenghi and standing at the point where the Nevsky Prospect crosses the Fontanka Canal. It only remained for Alexander to find for Prince George some post in the Russian administration which would neither deprive the Empire of Catherine's services, nor himself of her occasional company.

He found what he wanted for George at Tver, the old city on the Upper Volga a hundred miles along the Petersburg road from Moscow. The Prince was solemnly appointed Governor-General of the provinces of Tver, Yaroslavl and Novgorod. It was agreed that George and Catherine would move into the palace of Tver, which had been originally constructed for Catherine II forty years previously. The Grand Duchess, however, expected finer accommodation and, throughout the summer, there was an extensive re-building project in Tver, supervised by Carlo Rossi (who was later to use his genius for classical unity to enrich the architecture of the capital). By the autumn Rossi's workmen had made sufficient progress for Catherine to set out for Tver; and on 26 August she left the Tauride Palace amid scenes of tearful farewell, as though passing into lasting exile.[15] In fact, however, as her brother soon realized, by establishing the Grand Duchess between St Petersburg and Moscow, the Tsar was indirectly strengthening the influence of the dynasty in a vital region of the Empire. Until now Alexander had not once visited Moscow since his coronation; but with his sister and brother-in-law in Tver he found it expedient to make tours now and again to the ancient capital, beginning that very December, for, as Alexander himself remarked, 'when I have a mind to go to Moscow I have only to take her in my pocket, and can then go without any of the expense and parade of an imperial journey'.[16] Probably Catherine would not have found Alexander's pragmatism flattering. She took her position at Tver very seriously and immediately began to try to emulate her sister Marie in Weimar by establishing a literary salon; but Catherine's real interests remained in political intrigue, and at Tver she was sufficiently close to the estates of the Moscow nobility to make contact with all those conservative aristocrats who resented Speransky's reforming zeal as much as she did. She had no intention of permitting the Empire to be robbed of her abilities.

Russia and Napoleon's 1809 Campaign

While Alexander was fussing over the details of Catherine's establishment, his nominal ally had to meet in Bavaria the Austrian challenge which he had long anticipated. As early as February a courier arrived in St Petersburg from Napoleon's headquarters with messages which were intended to enable Caulaincourt to convince Alexander the Austrians were about to begin a preventive war in Germany. To the delight of the French ambassador, the Tsar immediately recognized that he had to honour the obligations he had assumed at Erfurt: 'He has never spoken so cordially to me since first I had the privilege of treating with him,' reported Caulaincourt to Paris.[17] The Austrian ambassador was at once summoned to the Winter Palace and notified by Alexander personally that he had commitments to the French and would keep faith with his word. Eagerly Caulaincourt awaited news that the Russians were mobilizing an army in Poland so as to menace the Austrian position in Galicia; he hoped the Russian force would supplement the Polish brigades of Poniatowski, already raised under Napoleon's auspices from among the population of the Grand-Duchy of Warsaw. But, for all his assurances, Alexander was reluctant to commit his troops to a campaign in central Europe and Francis's military counsellors in Vienna were threatened from the east by nothing more formidable than words of reproof.[18] In the second week of April the Austrians, untroubled by the thought of the Russians in their rear, crossed the River Inn and offered their challenge to the French. At

St Petersburg that day they were celebrating a bitterly cold Easter, with the ice still on the Neva and the Gulf.[19] Once the Easter festivities were over, Prince Golitsyn was assigned an army corps which was to assemble in southern Poland. By then the French and Austrians were already engaged in battle, with Napoleon once more advancing down the Danube Valley. Despite the brilliant generalship of Archduke Charles it soon became clear the Austrians would not be able to fight a long and sustained campaign. The French had no need of Russian assistance, but Alexander was resolved to fulfil the letter of his treaty obligations.

Not that he was in any hurry to do so. Orders for Golitsyn to enter Galicia were only sent on 18 May, five days after Napoleon had entered Vienna itself. And even then another seventeen days were to elapse before Golitsyn's corps began to move forward, showing, it seemed, more interest in securing the towns of the province than in giving battle to the Austrians.[20] An unprejudiced observer might well have thought the Russian army was primarily engaged in containing Poniatowski's Polish brigades, nominally its ally. Caulaincourt, who was by nature far from unprejudiced and by training a cavalry commander, had no doubt at all of Golitsyn's intentions and he complained of them to Rumiantsev.[21] But, where Polish questions were concerned, the Russians tended to assume treaty obligations were subject to liberal interpretation; and Caulaincourt received little satisfaction. As if to emphasize the tacit understanding between the two dynastic Empires, in mid-July the Austrian commander of Cracow, who had defied Poniatowski for nearly two months, handed over the city to Golitsyn's Russians rather than surrender to a Pole. During the whole campaign the Russian army corps suffered only two casualties. Small wonder if the French felt their ally was scorning all the fair words of Tilsit and Erfurt.

In St Petersburg prominent Russians made little effort to hide their sympathies. Normally the Empress Elizabeth avoided commenting on international affairs in her private letters, presumably for fear they might be intercepted; but in May she did not hesitate to let her mother know how 'the bad news of Austria's misfortune' had saddened her and Alexander too.[22] Rumiantsev, whom everyone in the capital regarded as an arch-Francophile, emphasized to Caulaincourt his determination to protect the Empire against resurgent Polish patriotic pride; and the French ambassador, though angered by Russia's derisory rejection of her commitments, faithfully reported the mood of St Petersburg to Champagny, Napoleon's Foreign Minister, who had followed the army to Vienna.[23] Confidentially, in reply, Caulaincourt was informed that

Napoleon himself 'no longer believes in the Russian alliance'; but he was instructed not to modify his behaviour in any way, nor give Alexander any excuse for letting Europe see how fragile were the bonds between the Empires.[24] Caulaincourt, as a good soldier, dutifully obeyed orders, though he found the warmth of Alexander's friendship increasingly embarrassing at such a time.

Napoleon's changes of mood did not make Caulaincourt's task any easier. For, even after the hollow mockery of Russian participation in his campaign, Napoleon was unwilling to break finally with Alexander. The peace settlement imposed on the Austrians that autumn showed some evidence of Napoleon's concern for Russian sensitivity over Poland; for, though the Austrians were forced to make extensive sacrifices on the Adriatic, they were allowed to retain all those regions in Galicia acquired in the first Polish Partition (1772), ceding to the Grand-Duchy of Warsaw only the much smaller area annexed in 1795.[25] And the Russians were even awarded compensation for this territorial addition to the Grand-Duchy, for Alexander was now permitted to annex the two Austrian districts of Czartow and Tarnopol, districts in eastern Galicia where the inhabitants were predominantly Ukrainians rather than Poles, but which had for centuries been reckoned an integral part of the Polish State.[26] Thus, for the second time in three years, Russia extended her western frontier in Poland by grace of the Emperor of the French. Yet when Caulaincourt informed Alexander of the final peace terms at an audience on 27 October, he found the Tsar unusually cold and distant: he was alarmed at the extent to which the French were strengthening their foot-hold in western Croatia and Dalmatia, along the borders of the Turkish Empire; and he was disappointed that Russia had not received the city of Lemberg (Lvov), which now passed once more under Polish rule.

Ten days later Caulaincourt had another audience with the Tsar. On this occasion the ambassador told him that Napoleon was willing to discuss with the Russians a final settlement of the Polish Question so as to ease the tension between the two Empires. As a start, the French proposed an undertaking that no use should be made, for the present or in the future, of the term 'Poland'. This was a gesture Alexander understood and appreciated. He purred with contentment: it was, he said 'something really in the spirit of the alliance'.[27] For the next three months he left Caulaincourt and Rumiantsev to thrash out an understanding.

It is impossible not to feel deep sympathy for Caulaincourt. He had no idea of Napoleon's motives and he was hampered in the following weeks by the sudden departure of Alexander on the first of his journeys to Tver and Moscow, where he was received so rapturously by the people of the old capital that he returned to St Petersburg determined to let the French sense in his person the residual authority of the Princes of Muscovy.[28] During Alexander's absence the ambassador was startled by fresh instructions from Paris, which completely transformed the nature of his mission. For, on 14 December, Caulaincourt received a letter from Champagny (which had taken more than three weeks to cross Europe) in which he was told to find out if Alexander would sanction a marriage between Napoleon and his youngest sister, Anna Pavlovna.[29] The Tsar's absence in Moscow made it impossible for Caulaincourt to take any action for another fortnight. Life had been simpler for him when he was a mere General.

A Russian Empress for the French?

Alexander arrived back at the Winter Palace soon after ten at night on 26 December. Two evenings later he entertained Caulaincourt privately to dinner. It was only after he had listened to an enthusiastic account of the visit to Moscow that the ambassador was able to sound out Alexander on Napoleon's proposal. Though Anna's future was mentioned briefly at Erfurt, the Tsar does not appear to have given the question any further thought. She was still a few days short of her fifteenth birthday and there seems to have been some doubt in her brother's mind whether she had yet reached puberty. The long delay in communications with Paris made Caulaincourt unusually pressing. He wanted a reply within forty-eight hours; but the Tsar was far too elated from his journey to take any decision couched in so peremptory a manner. He courteously acknowledged Napoleon's request but explained that, by the will of Tsar Paul, all such matters depended upon the sanction of the Dowager Empress who was in residence at Gatchina. Alexander asked for ten days in which to consult Marie Feodorovna and other members of the family.* Caulaincourt tactfully indicated that he understood the Tsar's difficulty and that he would let Paris know the reasons for the delay.[30]

There followed three weeks of confused farce and prevarication. On the day after his interview with the Tsar, Caulaincourt entertained fifty members of the diplomatic corps to a sledging party on the ice-hills in

---

* Marie Feodorovna arrived at the Tauride Palace from Gatchina on 4 January 1810 with the intention of remaining in the capital for the (Russian) New Year and Epiphany celebrations. She did not leave for Gatchina again until 31 January and was therefore able to discuss matters with Alexander at great length. These were the same weeks in which the Tsar was inaugurating the Council of State and persuading Arakcheev not to retire to his estate at Gruzino (see previous chapter).

the gardens of his villa on Kammionyi Island. Although Napoleon's overture was strictly confidential, the possibility of a Bonaparte-Romanov marriage somehow became a principal topic of conversation during the New Year festivities; and everyone enjoyed watching Caulaincourt in the hope of detecting on that inscrutably sardonic face some estimate of the odds in the dynastic marriage stakes. He revealed nothing; and yet by 9 January Six d'Oterbeck, the Dutch minister, was roundly declaring that it was 'certainly not a Russian Princess that the Emperor Napoleon is to marry'; and it was generally agreed that in such matters the Dutch minister, having little to do but listen to palace gossip, was rarely wrong.[31]

Officially, however, no reply had as yet been made to Napoleon. The Russian Court moved slowly. It was not until 4 January (which, by the Russian Calendar, was 23 December) that Alexander informed his 'dear sweet friend' at Tver of what was proposed for their sister, and his letter to Catherine shows the uncertainty of his mood:[32]

I send this to you to let you know of one of the most disagreeable plights in which I have ever found myself to be. Napoleon is seeking a divorce and casting eyes upon Anna. This time it is a real and lasting idea and I refer you to the details which Mother is giving you. It is difficult to choose the right course. My own view is that because of all the trouble, annoyance, bad-feeling and hatred aroused by that person it is easier to deny him his wishes than accept with a bad grace. I must do Mother justice to add that she showed far more calm over it than I should have thought possible. She wishes, anyhow, to consult you and I think she is perfectly right to do so. I too seek your advice with that confidence which I place in your reason and your heart.

This letter was mildly disingenuous; for the whole problem was much more complicated than Alexander revealed. Reports from Paris (and indeed Caulaincourt's whole bearing) left him in little doubt that the marriage proposal and the Polish negotiations were closely linked in Napoleon's mind.[33] This development was awkward for Alexander: even though he might care little these days for the prospect of a Bonaparte brother-in-law, the bait of a Polish settlement was too tempting to be ignored; and he certainly had no wish to see exchanges between Rumiantsev and Caulaincourt over the future of the Grand-Duchy of Warsaw prove as fruitless as their talks on the Eastern Question, before Erfurt. It would be politically injudicious to offend Napoleon at such a time. But what was he to do? Though the Dowager Empress had not exploded in anger at the news of the French proposal, she rapidly began to see in it a worthless and cumbersome insult. Indeed, on the same day that Alexander was letting Catherine into the secret, Marie Feodorovna acquired her second wind and expressed herself with vigour on the Bonapartes, on France, and on the sufferings of Russia in general and her younger children in particular.[34] She maintained that she was convinced economic necessity would drive Alexander to break with France, marriage or no marriage; and she roundly declared that, if she accepted Napoleon's request for Anna's hand, she would be 'sacrificing a daughter to a man of vile character, for whom nothing is sacred and who knows no restraint because he does not believe in God.' Nevertheless, she would not positively turn down the proposal: like Alexander she waited on a judgement from Tver.

It was therefore left to Catherine Pavlovna to suggest a tactful compromise, which was framed so discreetly that one suspects it owes more to her husband's good sense than to her own impetuous tongue.[35] At the end of the first week in February Alexander at last gave Caulaincourt an audience in which he imparted the decision of the family: the ambassador was to inform Napoleon of the sense of flattery experienced by the Dowager Empress at the prospect of a marriage between her younger daughter and the illustrious Emperor of the French but he was to explain that, though 'for some five months now her figure had been filling out', the Grand Duchess Anna had only recently celebrated her fifteenth birthday and since the Dowager Empress 'had already been forced to mourn the loss of two daughters through premature marriages, no consideration could permit her to risk endangering the life of the Grand Duchess by contracting matrimonial obligations so young'; and the Russian Imperial family hoped that the Emperor Napoleon would thus perceive the wisdom of postponing marriage with the Grand Duchess for another two years.[36]

Alexander can hardly have put forward this compromise as a serious proposition. He had himself heard from Napoleon personally at Erfurt that the sole argument for separation from Josephine was need of a son to preserve the dynasty and it was therefore unreasonable to imagine that Napoleon, of all people, would be prepared to wait for a Grand Duchess, whom he had never seen, to grow into a mature woman. The Tsar hoped that marriage negotiations, becoming more and more hypothetical, would continue at least until the Russians had extracted from the French an acceptable treaty over Poland. He was, however, to be doubly disappointed. While letters were travelling from Petersburg to Tver and Gatchina and back again, the salons of Paris were filled with rival partisans of a Russian or an Austrian marriage; and as the only messages from Caulaincourt indicated hesitancy and delay, so the pro-Austrian party took heart and pressed the claims for attention of the Archduchess Marie Louise.[37] Napoleon become impatient; and before details of Alexander's compromise reached Paris, everyone knew that the man who had twice in half a decade seized Vienna would soon be marrying the daughter of the Emperor of Austria, a girl three years older than Anna Pavlovna and physically far more mature. The news reached St Petersburg on 23 February; and with it came a clear indication that Napoleon was no longer interested in concluding any paper agreement on Polish affairs.[38]

Since Alexander had virtually rejected the marriage proposal, he had no grounds for disappointment at Napoleon's decision to seek a Habsburg bride. But he was, in fact, intensely irritated at the turn in events and did not trouble to hide his displeasure from Caulaincourt. There were three principal reasons for his anger: the discovery that an approach had been made to the Austrians before the French received final word from St Petersburg on the original proposal of a Russian marriage; the apparent willingness of Napoleon to find in Austria a new political ally for his European schemes; and the revelation that the discussions over Poland were, as the Tsar had feared, only incidental to Napoleon's dynastic ambitions. It was this frustration of his hopes for Poland which most stung Alexander. The Russians had prepared a draft treaty which included, in its first article, the categorical statement that 'the Kingdom of Poland shall never be restored'.[39] Now Napoleon refused to accept any such commitment: 'Divinity alone can speak as Russia proposes', he declared.[40] Worse was to follow. The French began publicly to refer to the Grand-Duchy of Warsaw as 'the Duchy of Poland'. With eight Polish provinces still within his Empire, this overt patronage of Polish national sentiment filled Alexander with genuine alarm and suspicion. He determined to gain a clearer impression of Napoleon's policy than he could obtain either from his Francophile foreign minister or from Caulaincourt; and he turned for support to the two most dissimilar men among his confidants, Prince Adam Czartoryski and State Secretary Speransky.

It was during the closing months of 1809 that Society in the Russian capital began to amuse itself in speculating why Czartoryski was to be seen once more at the Winter Palace and on Kammionyi Island. Gossips assumed he had returned from foreign travel to console the Empress Elizabeth; and it is true that, whatever her feelings may have been, he always remained as romantically attached to Elizabeth as Alexander did to Queen Louise. But on this occasion it was primarily Alexander who sought the Prince's advice, hoping to discover from him the extent of loyal sentiment within the Grand-Duchy of Warsaw to its patron in Paris. After the Austrian marriage, Alexander's conversations with his old friend became more frequent and recaptured much of the intimacy of their youth. More than once Alexander looked back regretfully to the abortive plans for a restored Poland with which he had toyed at Pulawy in 1805; and at their meeting on 5 April 1810, Czartoryski was startled to hear the Tsar predicting there would be a crisis in Franco-Russian affairs 'nine months from now' and to note on Alexander's face that haggard expression of self-pity he had last observed on the day following Austerlitz. Czartoryski himself felt a conflict of loyalties between the Empire he had served and his compatriots; but he knew Alexander too well to encourage him to expect Polish support merely on a show of sentimental nostalgia. He asked the Tsar for details of the negotiations with Napoleon over the Polish Question; and when Alexander became evasive, Czartoryski for his part spoke of other things.[41]

Yet these talks between the Tsar and his former director of foreign affairs had some significance for the future. Although Czartoryski doubted Alexander's sincerity and suspected him of wishing to perpetuate the division of the Polish nation, he recognized a hardening of the Tsar's mind against Napoleon's policy. It was a phenomenon he had already seen in earlier years; and, although he had little doubt what his compatriots in the Grand-Duchy would tell him, he continued to sound out the aristocratic families.[42] Unfortunately his conclusions brought Alexander small comfort: only a pledge to grant political unity to the Polish nation and the promise of constitutional government would make it possible for the Tsar of Russia to solicit Polish support so long as there remained a centralized administration in Warsaw dependent for its composition and character on the goodwill of the French. But Alexander was not prepared to give up hope of winning over the Poles; for what would happen to the Grand-Duchy once Napoleon's position in Europe began to weaken was anyone's guess. Historical tradition and geographical common sense mocked the chances for survival of any Bonapartist creation on the Vistula; and it was half as far again from Warsaw to Paris as from Warsaw to St Petersburg.

Speransky was a less obvious consultant than Czartoryski on international questions for, until the spring of 1810, the responsibilities of the State Secretary stopped short of foreign affairs. Yet there were good reasons why Alexander should turn to Speransky at this time of crisis; for he alone knew how far the Continental System was hampering Russian trade and, in the last resort, only he could tell the Tsar whether the Empire's precarious financial structure would collapse under the strain of re-armament or war. Alexander had encouraged Speransky to meet Caulain-court from time to time in order to discuss commercial relations between the two Empires and, at his own discretion, he occasionally showed Speransky reports from Russian agents and representatives in foreign countries. Hence, although Speransky was less well-informed than Czartoryski about conditions in Europe, he had some knowledge of the economic state of the Napoleonic Empire. Moreover at Erfurt he had met Talleyrand and other great names in the Bonapartist establishment; and he knew as well as anyone in Russia the extent to which the new European order was an autocracy tempered by corruption.[43]

In February 1809 Talleyrand himself had suggested to Alexander, in a personal message, that Speransky might serve as a valuable intermediary for communications from Paris which needed to be franker than the formal despatches of accredited diplomats.[44] For a year the Tsar does not appear to have acted on Talleyrand's proposal; but, soon after Napoleon's betrothal to Marie Louise, Speransky recommended to the Tsar a change in the form of diplomatic representation in France, by which commercial arrangements would be entrusted to a specialist who would report directly to Speransky on the possibility of obtaining from France a financial loan. For this task Alexander selected Karl von Nesselrode, a thirty-year-old Westphalian nobleman whose family had entered Russian service during the early campaigns of the French revolutionary wars and who had already been employed on several delicate diplomatic missions. Between March 1810 and August 1811 Nesselrode sent useful information to St Petersburg, not only on the economic structure of France but on the general trends in Napoleon's policy.[45] Much of what he said was interest-ing; and this is hardly surprising, for many of Nesselrode's comments and suggestions originated with a gentleman described in the secret corre-spondence as 'Cousin Henry', a person of wide experience and many identities (among them the Prince of Benevento and Citizen Talleyrand). It was Cousin Henry who urged the Russians to keep on good terms with Vienna so that the two governments might keep the peace of Europe 'by imposing an obstacle to the encroachments of France'.[46] Sometimes, it must be admitted, Cousin Henry's counsels consist of truisms wrapped in mystery so as to give them an air of genius; and Speransky's memoranda on foreign affairs lack the profundity or originality of his analyses of Russia's internal problems; but there is no doubt that the Nesselrode-Talleyrand link strengthened Speransky's position in Alexander's circle of close advisers at a time when resentment over his administrative reforms was widespread among the conservative aristocracy. Although Speransky was not himself aware of the importance of his intrusion into foreign affairs,* the fresh prestige he acquired in the Tsar's eyes may well have enabled him to maintain his influence for as much as eighteen months longer than Alexander would otherwise have permitted.

There was one man in St Petersburg who had no illusions at all over the change in his personal status. By the spring of 1810 Caulaincourt's antennae were well-attuned to the moods of the Russian capital and its master; and he could see the Austrian marriage and the failure of the Polish negotiations had cost him his privileged position at Court. In vain he hoped for an early summons back to Paris: France, he believed, needed a different type of representative, one who would not find loyalty strained by friendship for the sovereign to whom he was accredited. But Napoleon had no understanding of such niceties of temperament and, for a whole year, he ignored the ambassador's request.[47]

The unfortunate Caulaincourt was thus left to waste his own funds on maintaining a social position to which he had aspired solely on his Emperor's orders. He behaved with remarkable dignity: only occasionally did members of his staff or the spokesmen of other governments perceive the strain. On 23 May 1810, he gave the finest ball of his term of residence in St Petersburg to celebrate the marriage of Napoleon and Marie Louise.[48] It was a splendid occasion attended by the Imperial family (including the Dowager Empress), by ambassadors, ministers and envoys, and by the greatest names in Russia. The ball began at nine in the evening, while (according to the American minister) 'it was daylight as at noon'; and the Imperial party was still joining in the celebrations at 'past two in the morning'. The Tsar, wrote Adams in his journal, 'was gracious to everybody beyond his usual custom, which is remarkable for affability'; and he danced a polonaise not only with Mrs Adams but with her young sister, Catherine Johnson, who had not as yet been presented at Court. But, Adams himself noted, 'a very small part of the company took real pleasure in the fête'.[49] By now everyone sensed the hollowness in the feigned friendship between the two Empires of France and Russia, and feared for the future. Caulaincourt duly informed Paris of the 'graciousness and condescension' with which the Imperial party had 'deigned to

---

* Speransky also established an agent in Vienna, Joseph Mallia, who supplied him with information on the policy of the new Austrian Foreign Minister, Metternich; but, since 'secrets' leaked as readily from Vienna as from a sieve, Mallia's value to Speransky and Alexander was on a far lower level than Nesselrode's. (For the Mallia–Speransky connection, see Schilder, *Alexsandr*, Vol. III, p. 494.)

stay' and honour Napoleon's marriage.[50] Yet it is a rather different Caulaincourt who finds his way into Adams's journal: 'I heard the Ambassador himself say to some one that he gave this ball because he was obliged to do it – it gave him no pleasure.'[51] The words might almost have been an epitome of 'the Viceroy's' whole mission.

'Blood Must Flow Again'

Alexander at Tver and Gruzino

For Alexander the summer and autumn of 1810 were months of mingled elation and sorrow, a fitting prelude to the years of widening apprehension which lay ahead. They began happily enough. In the second week of June his carriage sped rapidly southwards to Catherine at Tver, who was then in the sixth month of pregnancy and bored by her relative isolation. The seasons were wretchedly late and Alexander was surprised by 'a very considerable flight of snow on the road'; but the warmth of his reception soon compensated for any earlier discomfort.[1] Catherine, irritated beyond reason at alleged slights by Speransky as State Secretary, was determined to impress her brother: she let him know the views of the Moscow conservatives who flocked to her soirées; she gave him a book list of improving titles she wanted from St Petersburg for her library (which he promptly lost); and, more effectively, she saw to it that 'her ladies', as Alexander called them, attended to his needs. He was particularly charmed by her principal maid-of-honour, Catherine Muraviev-Apostol, 'a heavenly creature', as he remarked in a later letter to his hostess. Although Alexander knew his sister too well to pay undue attention to her political strictures, he listened with sympathy, said nothing, and enjoyed himself. It was good to shake off the bustle of the capital for a week. 'They were delightful days I spent at Tver', he wrote afterwards.[2]

From his sister's miniature Court he travelled due north by way of Novgorod to Arakcheev's estate at Gruzino, which he had never visited before. He spent a night as the General's guest and was impressed by the tidiness and symmetry of everything around him. 'It really is a charming place', he wrote back to Catherine, 'but it is the order which reigns here that is unique . . . The streets of the villages have precisely that quality of cleanliness I have been trying so hard to establish in the towns'; and he urged both his sister and her husband to visit Gruzino as soon as they had the opportunity and observe for themselves the wonders wrought there by 'the corporal of Gatchina'.[3]

Alexander's enthusiasm was not merely an expression of delight at seeing villages trimmed up as though on parade. Already that spring he had begun to consider the establishment of pioneer settlements, in which a battalion of troops would cultivate neglected fields and, together with their families, establish a new community, agriculturally self-supporting and socially constructive as life in a barracks could never become. If Arakcheev was able to convert the flat and often flooded marshland around Gruzino into a model agrarian settlement, then great tasks must await him in the Empire as a whole; and the Tsar returned to St Petersburg convinced he should be assigned responsibility for setting up these 'military colonies'. The General, tired of abortive paper-work in the military department of the Council of State, welcomed the chance to control a project in which the Tsar himself was clearly so interested.[4] No time would be wasted on long-term planning. Within twelve weeks of Alexander's visit Arakcheev had requisitioned land between Smolensk and Minsk and sketched out regulations for the first military colony; and, before the coming of the winter frost, a battalion of musketeers found itself, a little surprisingly, building new villages and cultivating fields in this colony near the upper Dnieper. It was not exactly what Alexander originally had in mind – for the region was already showing a good yield of crops before the army moved in – but Arakcheev was too experienced a showman to set himself an impossible task. Provided there was neither a drought nor a foreign invasion, the experiment had no reason to fail. Unfortunately, in successive summers, there was both.

Yet, in those white nights of June 1810, such hopes and disappointments were still far ahead in an uncertain future. Good news followed Alexander back to the capital from Gruzino. The war with Turkey, so often delayed by diplomatic parleying, was at last going well. On the Sunday after the Tsar's return a bulletin from General Kamensky reported he had taken the fortress of Silistria on the Danube. Alexander was excited to learn of Kamensky's success and promptly ordered the priests in his chapel to stop singing the Liturgy in order that Barclay de Tolly, the Minister of War, might read Kamensky's message to the distinguished congregation (which he did so badly that most of what he said was incomprehensible).[5] Other victories followed in August and October, celebrated in a more conventional manner; and before the coming of winter it was possible for the Tsar and his ministers to consider moving troops away from the Danube to the new danger zone along the Niemen and the Bug. Now that they no longer had to consider French sensitivities the Russians were able to recover the initiative in foreign affairs.

Personal Sorrows, 1810

But, swiftly offsetting the Silistria triumph, came personal tragedies which plunged Alexander once more into deep depression. His principal mistress, Maria Naryshkin, had given birth to two more daughters since the death of the first child she bore Alexander in 1804. Now, in June 1810, the eldest of these girls, Zinaida, suddenly and unexpectedly died, and Alexander was left to mourn 'the passing of some of the happiness I possess in this world', as he wrote to his sister.[6] A month later an emissary from Berlin brought Alexander further sad news: Queen Louise, permitted at last to return to Prussia's capital, died suddenly on 19 July while visiting her family home in Mecklenburg. Officially it was said she had died from damaged lungs and a polyp in the heart but it was generally accepted that her life had been shortened by the strain of maintaining Prussia's liberties against the encroachments of Napoleon. According to the Prussian envoy to St Petersburg, Major von Wrangel, Alexander was so distressed by the news that he promptly declared, 'I swear to you that I shall avenge her death and shall make certain that her murderer [Napoleon] pays for his crime.' The Tsar is reported to have told Wrangel that in four years' time he would have an army powerful enough to march against the French and liberate all Germany. Although Wrangel's story could well have been manufactured later, a melodramatic and anticipatorily boastful response of this kind was certainly consistent with Alexander's character.[7]

Under this double blow Alexander responded as when Elizabeth's daughter had died. He shut himself in his study, absorbed in the minutiae of administration, not always bothering to inform ministers or counsellors precisely what he was doing. Though no doubt such behaviour was therapeutic, it did not make for efficient government and exasperated both the State Secretary and Chancellor Rumiantsev. Speransky's private comments (eagerly seized upon by his enemies) were less sympathetic than experience or tact dictated. Even Adams, one of the least perceptive foreign envoys, noted the confusion at Court and predicted the early resignation of the Chancellor, although in this instance he proved to be wrong.[8]

Naturally these personal sorrows had their greatest effect on the Tsar's private life. When Maria Naryshkin's first child died Elizabeth consoled Alexander with all the tenderness of a starved heart. But that was six years ago. Since then she had suffered the tragic loss of 'Lisinka' and a series of vexatious affronts heaped upon her both by the Polish courtesan and by the Grand Duchess Catherine. The burden of sustained grief, often misunderstood by her husband, seemed gradually to dry the wells of compassion in Elizabeth's soul. She cared, as ever, for Alexander; but her tone now was firmer than in earlier years. When it was rumoured among her ladies that Alexander was having a suite of rooms prepared in the Winter Palace for one of his favourites, Elizabeth let it be known that should he seek to install a mistress in any of the official residences (as his father had done at the Mikhailovsky) she would move out and return to Baden.[9] In fact, Alexander never inflicted on Elizabeth so public a humiliation, if only because he had too deep a sense of dignity to endure an open breach with his wife.

Yet in the last days of July 1810 Elizabeth did, temporarily, leave Kammionyi Island and take a long holiday at the seaside village of Plöen, on the Gulf of Riga.[10] Her doctors had recommended for several years that she should seek to strengthen her frail constitution by bathing in the salt sea (as opposed to the almost fresh waters of the Gulf of Finland). But one wonders if she chose those particular weeks purely by chance. For a few days before her departure from St Petersburg the Dowager Empress arrived at the Tauride Palace to meet the Grand Duchess Catherine and escort her back to Pavlovsk to await the birth of her first child. Throughout August and early September Alexander was thus subjected even more than usual to earnest advice from his mother and sister; and it was, from Elizabeth's point of view, a good time to absent herself. The Grand Duchess tended to accord Countess Naryshkin a privileged status as the mother of her brother's children; and this was an affront which Elizabeth found hard to forgive.

At Plöen Elizabeth's health improved rapidly. She enjoyed the sunshine, rare in that wretched summer, and the novelty of almost immersing herself in the waves ('There are few sensations so pleasant as sea-bathing, even when the water is cold . . .'); and there is no doubt that she was happily fêted by her small suite of friends and ladies-of-honour.* She returned to the capital in the first week of September and, with some apprehension, journeyed out to Pavlovsk for the baptism into the Lutheran Church of the 'little Oldenburg', to whom the Grand Duchess gave birth on 28 August. But Elizabeth's nerves were less strained than earlier in the summer and the visit was not such a social ordeal as she feared. Although, as usual, she had to accord precedence to Marie Feodorovna, some attempt was made to acknowlege her existence as a person. During the evening festivities a short ballet was mounted, based upon Elizabeth's favourite waltzes; and it was still possible, by such trivial gestures, for Alexander to win back Elizabeth's loyalty and reconcile her to his mother and sister.[11] The month's absence from St Petersburg (the first holiday she had taken since Alexander's accession) had a remarkable effect upon her standing at Court: and there was even a letter to the Tsar from an eccentric German émigré scholar, whom Alexander had met some years previously, which proposed that the Tsar should put himself at the head of his army, challenge the might of Napoleon, and proclaim Elizabeth the Regent of Russia. It is unlikely Alexander showed this letter either to his mother or his sister, each of whom naturally assumed she alone possessed the qualities and standing of a Regent.[12]

Alexander takes Russia out of the Continental System

The general situation did not, however, yet require such drastic steps. Napoleon was still troubled by the intractable problems of the Iberian peninsula; and he was now stung by the back-lash of his own Continental System, with banking-houses failing first in his Germanic dependencies and subsequently in Paris itself. The French harvest of 1810 was poor and the price of corn rose so steeply that Napoleon feared he might soon be faced by agrarian troubles, especially in Brittany. During August Alexander was disturbed by reports that three French divisions had been moved from southern Germany to the Baltic coast and that 50,000 new muskets had arrived in Warsaw for Poniatowski's Polish brigades.[13] But

* The Empress Elizabeth's suite was headed by Prince Alexander Mikhailovitch Golitsyn (the bereaved husband of one of her oldest friends) and by Prince Alexander Naryshkin, a somewhat high-spirited member of the family into which the Tsar's mistress had married. Like her husband, Elizabeth retained the same physician for many years, Dr Stoffregen, who – in the fashion of medical advisers to the English royal family at this time – strongly believed in the curative powers of sea-water bathing.

the Tsar did not believe there was any immediate danger, for he was well-informed about Napoleon's difficulties by Nesselrode and the impenitent 'Cousin Henry'. Indeed, in the late autumn, Alexander received clear evidence of financial embarrassment at the French Court by a sudden request from Talleyrand for fifteen hundred thousand francs, which he was sure the Tsar 'with his richly endowed qualities of generosity' would despatch to him. Although Alexander felt 'compelled with regret to forgo the pleasure of obliging' Talleyrand on this occasion, he was ironically amused by the blatant cupidity of so influential a figure in Paris.[14] There might well come a time when benevolence to the needy rich would prove a useful political investment.

But neither Alexander nor his ministers could afford to be complacent over the economic ills of the Continental System. The Tilsit commitments had produced severe dislocations of commerce in the first eighteen months of alliance with France, although trade began to pick up again during the year of 1809. But inevitably the Russian merchants and their credit institutions were hit by the failure of the Rodda Bank in Lübeck and other signs of commercial panic in the old Hanseatic cities. Moreover, at this very moment, all the old resentment at French interference with traditional Anglo-Russian trading arrangements was revived by the Trianon and Fontainebleau Decrees, which tightened the blockade against English goods. There was much talk in St Petersburg of seeking release from a system that prevented Russia exporting hemp, grain and flax or from receiving English manufactured goods while permitting the Empire to be flooded with French luxuries, perfumes and wines. Chancellor Rumiantsev might maintain to the Senate in mid-October that the Continental System was stimulating industry within Russia and helping the merchants to find new markets; but few people found his arguments convincing. Trade restraint remained the most unpopular aspect of the French alliance, as Alexander himself well knew.[15]

Yet what precisely should be done? The Council of State considered ways of gradually easing Russia out of the Continental System, and the question was also discussed between Alexander and his ministers. Rumiantsev opposed any change in tariffs, primarily because he did not want to force a crisis of diplomacy with the French; Speransky, leaning heavily on the theories of Adam Smith, favoured freer trade and the Minister of Finance supported him; but the Tsar was unable to make up his mind. Tentatively, in the third week of December, he approved a decree allowing the landowners freedom to export grain;[16] but hardly had this measure been published when rumours reached St Petersburg that

Napoleon had incorporated all the northern coasts of Germany into metropolitan France and was proposing to annex the Duchy of Oldenburg.* This sudden activity by Napoleon in a region of political and dynastic concern to Alexander hardened his wavering resolution. On 31 December 1810 he approved the famous tariff decree which imposed heavy duties on goods coming overland while removing restrictions on imports by sea and allowing almost complete freedom to Russian exports. In practical terms, this measure was seen as a blow against French luxuries and in favour of renewed trade with the maritime powers, including Britain. Small wonder that at the Tsar's New Year ball a few days later Caulaincourt was 'seized with a swimming in the head' and left early.[17]

The War Scare of 1811

Alexander knew well enough the gravity of the steps he was taking; but it was the fate of Oldenburg which was uppermost in his mind. A week after publishing the Tariff Decree he unburdened some of his thoughts to Catherine and her husband (who was heir to the threatened Duchy). 'Everything is beginning to look intensely gloomy', he wrote. 'It seems that blood must flow again, but at least I have done all that is humanly possible to avoid it'; and he then proceeded, in a style markedly distinct from the usual tone of his Tver correspondence, to list fifteen topics which he intended to discuss with George and Catherine when he next visited them.[18] Although three of these headings related to Speransky and his institutions, more than half of them were directly concerned with military affairs, including the siting of reserve depots and the organization of a defensive militia. Alexander was thus prepared to recognize even in the first days of January 1811 the probability of invasion; but, as he was not proposing to travel to Tver and discuss these matters for several weeks, he clearly did not anticipate an early breach with the French.

It is, however, difficult to discover exactly what Alexander did wish to do. Even before receiving confirmation that Napoleon was annexing

---

* In 1810 the Duchy of Oldenburg covered an area of some 2000 square miles on the left bank of the Weser, where it enters the North Sea. The ruling dynasty was a branch of the Holstein-Gottorp family who had, of course, made a successful takeover bid for the Russian Romanovs in 1762. Even before the marriage of Catherine Pavlovna to an Oldenburg prince, Alexander regarded the Duchy as a distant fief of the Russian Crown and had, he thought, safeguarded the rights of its sovereign under the Treaty of Tilsit. Napoleon's subsequent offer to compensate Duke Peter of Oldenburg by according him the principality of Erfurt (which was hardly a sixth the size of Oldenburg) seemed to Alexander almost a derisory gesture.

Oldenburg, he had once again written to Czartoryski and urged him to sound out the Polish aristocrats to see if their allegiance to the French was any less loyal than in the previous spring.[19] And yet, as late as 2 February, Alexander personally drafted instructions for a new envoy he was sending to the King of Sardinia in Cagliari and used precisely the same phrases which he would have included at any time in the preceding three and a half years: an assertion of the value to Russia of her French alliance; and a careful denunciation of the predatory activities of the British on the high seas.[20] Although by his actions in Germany Napoleon had broken the terms of Tilsit, Alexander was still outwardly conforming to the spirit of friendship between the two Empires.

Yet that spirit was rapidly running dry. Alexander was certainly tempted by an alternative policy, which he had first sketched in the letter to Czartoryski. He calculated that, with the French military effort primarily concentrated in Spain, Napoleon had in Germany a mere 46,000 regular troops, commanded by Davout. Even with the auxiliaries from the Grand-Duchy of Warsaw and from his ally in Dresden, Napoleon could put into the field scarcely more than 100,000 men, many of indifferent fighting quality and experience. By contrast, Alexander could rapidly concentrate along his western frontiers two armies, totalling in all a quarter of a million. A speedy Russian invasion of Germany might lead to a Prussian rising against the French and possibly to Austrian intervention: the armies of the three Eastern autocracies would thus roll back the limits of Napoleon's Empire before its master could mount a counter-offensive. But the success of such a strategy depended to a large extent upon the attitude of the Poles: if the Grand-Duchy of Warsaw remained loyal to its French patron, Poniatowski's men would endanger the Russian left flank and might delay the Russian advance into Germany long enough for Napoleon to strike back. Hence, on 12 February, Alexander wrote for a second time to Czartoryski and offered to proclaim a Polish Kingdom, to which he would guarantee a liberal constitution as well as a national government and army, provided that the principal political and military figures in the Grand-Duchy would give Czartoryski written pledges of support for the Russian plan. 'I cannot start a war against France until I have received guarantees of Polish co-operation', Alexander told Czartoryski bluntly.[21]

This latest grand design was potentially disastrous, militarily and politically. Like the Prussian plan of 1806 and the Austrian three years later, it took no account of Napoleon's skill in improvising armies and moving them speedily to points in the battle zone where he could seize the initiative. But was Alexander in earnest? In the third week of February he wrote to Frederick William III, taking him partly into his confidence, and to Emperor Francis of Austria, to whom he offered to hand over most of the territory captured from the Turks in Moldavia and Wallachia, provided the Austrians ceded to Russia what remained of their Polish lands.[22] By thus recklessly advertising his intentions to Warsaw, Berlin and Vienna, Alexander totally destroyed any chances of taking Napoleon by surprise. For his diplomatic initiative Alexander had selected three cities from which he could be certain French intelligence would hear of his plans within a matter of days. Yet, as if to give credence to his change of policy, five divisions were removed from the Turkish war-zone and set out for Poland; 180 heavy cannon were ostentatiously sent westwards from St Petersburg; General Kamensky was summoned back from his triumphs against the Turks 'for a more important command' (or so the foreign envoys in Petersburg were told); and orders were given for the arms factories at Tula and Alexandrovsk to continue to turn out weapons and munitions each day of the year rather than close on the great festivals of the Church.[23] Even Holy Russia, it seemed, was girding herself for war.

If Alexander really hoped for partners in his enterprise he was swiftly disappointed. Frederick William was blandly non-committal. Czartory-ski found the Polish magnates bound to Napoleon by sentiments of 'loyalty, gratitude, confidence and fear'. Emperor Francis made it clear he thought more highly of Galicia than of Moldavia or Wallachia, and his Foreign Minister, Metternich, was as yet too dependent upon Napoleon's goodwill to countenance independent bargaining with a potential enemy of the French.[24] The most Alexander could achieve was some strengthening of his relations with Vienna; the status of the Austrian and Russian ambassadors in the respective capitals was raised; and a young diplomat, Ludwig von Lebzeltern, was despatched by Metternich to St Petersburg with orders to establish personal contact with the Tsar and find out what he wanted, as opposed to the official policy of Chancellor Rumiantsev. Although Lebzeltern's mission was of service to Alexander in the crisis months a year later, he was hardly a substitute for the phantom army conjured up in Alexander's original plan.

Yet if, on the other hand, the Tsar had merely intended to threaten Napoleon at a time when the French economy was under strain so as to call a halt to further encroachments in east-central Europe, then he did indeed have some success. The French were already puzzled by the change in Russia's tariff policy. By the last week in February there was genuine disquiet in Paris over Alexander's attitude. On the final day of the month

Napoleon sent for General Chernyshev, one of the Tsar's aides-de-camp who was attached to the Russian embassy in Paris, and entrusted to him a special letter for speedy communication to his sovereign.[25] It was a remarkably subtle document, couched in terms of pained surprise rather than of anger and holding out some prospect of negotiation in order to remove the misunderstandings which had sprung up in recent months between the two Empires.

It took Chernyshev eighteen days to travel from Paris to St Petersburg and another three weeks to complete his discussions in the capital and make the return journey.[26] During Chernyshev's absence, the war scare in Paris intensified rather than diminished. Poniatowski informed the French of Czartoryski's activities and further reports came in from Berlin, Dresden and Vienna, all of which confirmed the seriousness of Russian preparations for a campaign. Napoleon was sufficiently alarmed by the news to have a contingency plan drafted: if the Russians attacked, Poniatowski should evacuate his troops from the Grand-Duchy of Warsaw and subsequently collaborate with Marshal Davout in a holding operation on the Oder, preparatory to a grand counter-offensive by the main French army which would be assisted (or so Napoleon believed) by the Austrians. It is significant that Davout's troops in Germany, together with the armies of the Grand-Duchy and the German dependencies, were kept on the alert from mid-March until the beginning of May.[27]

Tension relaxed in St Petersburg as soon as Chernyshev arrived from Paris on 17 March. Within twenty-four hours of his coming, it was being said among foreign diplomats that Napoleon's letter to Alexander showed a warmth of friendship more cordial than any communication exchanged between the two men for many months.[28] Rumiantsev, with Alexander's written approval, drafted a long despatch to Kurakin (the ambassador in Paris) which held out some prospect of revising the Russian tariff so as to maintain the fiction of a Continental System; and Alexander himself handed Chernyshev a pleasantly phrased letter for Napoleon personally.[29] After attending the annual requiem on the tenth anniversary of his father's death, Alexander set out on his long-projected visit to Tver; and there was widespread relief among the foreign community in the capital.[30] With Alexander turning his carriage southwards rather than towards the frontier and with his aide-de-camp speeding back to Paris, it was generally accepted that the prospect of another campaign against the French had receded. As St Petersburg basked in a warmer and finer Easter than its sovereign could ever remember – or so Alexander assured the American minister – it became increasingly difficult to take the war scare too seriously; and at the start of May Caulaincourt, writing to Napoleon, could report that Alexander had described the Franco-Russian alliance as 'better able than any other possible combination to maintain the peace of Europe'.[31]

Discomforted Diplomats

Yet though pretty phrases might flow like honey between St Petersburg and St Cloud, the old special relationship of the two Empires was at an end, as Caulaincourt himself had long sensed. On 8 May the Marquis de Lauriston arrived in Russia to take up his duties as French ambassador, Napoleon at last having agreed to re-call Caulaincourt 'for reasons of health'.[32] Significantly Caulaincourt had been forbidden to leave Russia until the coming of his successor since it seemed to Napoleon vital for France to have a responsible spokesman at St Petersburg during these weeks of alarming rumours and uncertainty. Now it only remained for 'the Viceroy' to make a dignified exit.

On the morning of 18 May, the day before his departure, he was received in a farewell audience by the Tsar.[33] It was a touching occasion, with Alexander treating Caulaincourt as a personal friend and even shedding tears. But if the ambassador's account is genuine, the Tsar appears to have spoken with prophetic insight:

Should the Emperor Napoleon make war on me, it is possible, even probable, that we shall be defeated. But this will not give him peace ... We shall enter into no compromise agreements; we have plenty of open spaces in our rear, and we shall preserve a well-organized army ... I shall not be the first to draw my sword, but I shall be the last to sheath it ... I should sooner retire to Kamchatka than yield provinces or put my signature to a treaty in my conquered capital which was no more than a truce.

Whether or not Alexander used these particular words, the audience left no doubt in Caulaincourt's mind of the new spirit of determination in St Petersburg; and when he reached Paris at the end of the first week in June, he attempted to convince Napoleon he was no longer dealing with the affable young charmer of Tilsit and Erfurt. But, although Napoleon was prepared to complain that Alexander was 'feeble and fickle', 'untrustworthy' and 'ambitious to achieve some hidden purpose through war', he would not admit that the Tsar was ever likely to prove a serious adversary. 'Puh! You speak like a Russian', he told Caulaincourt. 'One good battle will see the end of all your friend Alexander's fine resolutions – and his castles of sand as well!'[34]

Throughout the early summer of 1811 talks continued between Lauriston and Rumiantsev over possible compensation for the annexation of Oldenburg; and in Paris Kurakin continued to give hints of a modification in the tariffs. But, almost imperceptibly, the two Empires were drifting into a position where each accepted the inevitability of war and maintained the forms of diplomacy from mere habit and convention. By mid-July Alexander was writing privately to his sister Catherine about Napoleon's utter unreasonableness: 'Is he a creature who may not be expected to loosen his grip on any prize unless compelled by force of arms? And do we have the force of arms to compel him?' he asked in a burst of gloomy rhetoric. 'It seems to me', he added, 'most hopeful to look for time to aid us, and even to the very size of this evil . . . In one way or another, this state of affairs is bound to come to an end.' And, with a marked lack of charity towards the brother sovereign he had saluted so ardently at Erfurt, Alexander told Catherine of the rumour that a young man had recently tried to assassinate Napoleon, a deed which, he added, 'will have admirers and imitators'.[35]

On 15 August Napoleon celebrated his forty-second birthday. In St Petersburg Lauriston gave a dinner for some fifty or sixty guests which followed closely the pattern determined in previous years by Caulaincourt. But this time everything was as formal as on a ceremonial occasion: 'The dinner was short', Adams remarked, 'and the company all very soon afterwards retired.'[36] In Paris, too, the birthday was celebrated in customary splendour, the Emperor receiving congratulations from the diplomatic corps, with ambassadors and ministers lined up in the throne room at the Tuileries, as though they were a guard of honour ready for inspection. Three years previously Napoleon had used the occasion to rebuke Metternich, who was then Austrian ambassador in Paris, for the military preparations which led, within a year, to the Wagram Campaign.[37] Now Napoleon accorded precisely the same treatment to Alexander's representative, Prince Kurakin. For half an hour, speaking so rapidly that Kurakin could say little in reply, Napoleon poured out all his complaints against Alexander's policy – his championship of Oldenburg, his intrigues in Poland, his willingness to become enmeshed once more in the wicked machinations of the English, his secret military preparations along the Polish frontier. He threatened Russia with another campaign in which she would be left to fight without allies and would suffer defeats just as Austria had done in 1809. Finally he proposed that all these difficulties might yet be solved if the Russians were prepared to sit down with the French and draft a new treaty of alliance; and when Kurakin explained that he had no powers to conclude so important a document, Napoleon brusquely dismissed the objection as irrelevant. 'No powers?' he exclaimed. 'Then you must write at once to the Tsar and request them.'[38]

There was in this embarrassing scene a considerable amount of poor play-acting. Napoleon himself hinted as much when, soon afterwards, he tried to soothe the ruffled feelings of the unfortunate Caulaincourt, who had been present at the Tuileries reception and had thus heard his own views misrepresented by the Emperor for Kurakin's benefit.[39] In speaking as he did, Napoleon was relying on his conviction that he understood Russia and its sovereign better than any of the envoys he had sent to the Court in St Petersburg. He believed he could count on Rumiantsev to champion the interests of France in any discussions with the Tsar; and he was confident that Kurakin, who had been the chief negotiator with Talleyrand at Tilsit, would readily accept a new draft treaty if given the authority. Moreover, Napoleon knew that the incident with Metternich three years previously had created a major diplomatic sensation abroad (especially in Russia) and that all formal receptions thereafter were treated with particular respect by the ambassadors at his Court. No one would miss the significance of what he had said. But if Napoleon really imagined he could bully Russia back into nominal friendship, he was wrong. He failed to realize Alexander could never risk another blow to his popular reputation by a surrender to French hectoring, nor did he allow for Kurakin's affronted pride and the decline in Rumiantsev's influence on Alexander. Both Maret (Napoleon's foreign minister) and Lauriston sensed that this scene in the Tuileries harmed Franco-Russian relations; and each man independently sought to explain away the Emperor's threats.[40] But without success. Alexander was not interested in drawing up another paper treaty with the French. Napoleon's boorishness convinced him that for the French, as for the Russians, what had been signed at Tilsit was now essentially a historical relic, merely a collector's item for the muniments room.

And so, in a sense, it was. For on the day following the diplomatic reception at the Tuileries, Napoleon ordered Maret to bring him all the papers on Franco-Russian relations over the previous four years.[41] Together the two men pored over the files of the Polish problem and the blockade, the blueprints for partitioning Turkey, and the claims of compensation for Oldenburg. It was a depressing task. That evening Napoleon held a Council of State. There could be no Russian campaign now in 1811, for it was already too late in the year; but the winter months must be used for preparation and for making certain of Austrian and Prussian co-operation.

Although as yet Napoleon would take no final decision over whether or not to march to the East, work was beginning already on planning the greatest military enterprise of his career, an invasion of the endless Russian plains.

Portents and Military Plans

In St Petersburg the autumn of 1811, like the summer which had preceded it, was pleasantly warm and free from dangerous alarms. Society was more interested in celebrating victories against the Turks than in rumours of tension with the French, although fairly accurate reports of Napoleon's tirade were circulating before the middle of September. The principal occasion that month in the Russian capital was the solemn consecration of the massive new basilica on the Nevsky Prospect, dedicated to Our Lady of Kazan.[42] For over ten years craftsmen and labourers had been toiling on the neo-classical cathedral, with its arc of 136 Corinthian columns, monoliths of Finnish granite bringing to Alexander's capital the dignified grandeur of St Peter's in Rome; and the Tsar and all the members of the Imperial family were present at the consecration on 27 September, the tenth anniversary of Alexander's coronation. The service, which was preceded by a brief parade of troops, lasted for three and a half hours; and Alexander, together with the two Empresses and the Grand Duke Constantine, followed the Metropolitan Ambrose in procession as the sacred ikon of the Virgin was borne out of the richly decorated central portal and around the great square, with its crescented colonnade. There was an 'immense crowd' of worshippers and onlookers. Not for many years had the people of St Petersburg witnessed so solemn a ceremony symbolizing the inter-dependence of Church and State, for this essential bond of Tsardom was customarily emphasized in Moscow rather than in the newer capital. To some it seemed, both at the time and later, that the act of consecration served Alexander as a moment of re-dedication and renewal, linking the pledges he had given at his crowning in Moscow with the mounting challenge from across the frontier. For the rest of the century, the Kazan Cathedral remained associated in people's minds with the high drama of its early years, so that it became in time a shrine for the heroes of the Napoleonic wars.

The final quarter of this year, 1811, was indeed heavy with portent. Everywhere in Europe, from Moscow to Glasgow and south as far as Lisbon, simple souls watched a comet blaze in the heavens and turned, in fear, to their devotions. Some, especially in St Petersburg, believed they saw two comets at the same time. Alexander, 'though no astronomer' (as he admitted), was fascinated; and in the second week of December he discussed the phenomenon both with Lauriston and with John Quincy Adams.[43] The Tsar was inclined to mock the superstitious who seemed so willingly to read disaster in the night skies, suggesting light-heartedly in conversation that if there were really two comets (as he himself believed) then 'their mischief will operate mutually against each other' and so offset any evil they might foreshadow. But his subjects were not so ready to dismiss these manifestations with a private joke; and the enormous comet, with its 'white radiance and long uplifted tail' passed into folk legend – and ultimately into the prose of Leo Tolstoy.[44]

Alexander had no need of such metaphysical omens to convince him his Empire was approaching a climacteric in its history. He was impressed by sober warnings from Nesselrode in October and, even more, by noting movements of French troops as reported each fortnight in the 'Summary of the Situation', a highly confidential document which a clerk in the Department of War Administration in Paris regularly sold to Chernyshev until his discovery and arrest in February 1812.[45] Moreover in November Kurakin, once such a patron of the French alliance, confirmed the war preparations which Nesselrode and Chernyshev had already reported: 'The time has passed', Kurakin wrote, 'when we could delude ourselves with vain hopes. The time is fast approaching when, with courage and resolution, we must preserve our national heritage and the present limits of our frontiers.'[46] Alexander took all these gloomy messages to heart. He informed Catherine in November that he remained 'on constant guard' in St Petersburg, unable to escape for even a few days to Tver. And in the following month, on his birthday, he wrote to his sister: 'All this devilish political business is going from bad to worse, and that infernal creature who is the curse of all the human race becomes every day more and more abominable.'[47] This was the language of the Anathema once more, rather than the apologetic self-justification he had sent Catherine from Tilsit and Erfurt.

Words, however, were not enough to prepare Russia for war. Throughout the winter of 1811–12 Alexander and Rumiantsev sought to improve the Empire's international position, combating the isolation which Napoleon had predicted to Kurakin would await the Tsar's armies if the fate of Poland led to new campaigns. Naturally, in the first instance, Alexander continued to appeal to the Prussians and Austrians, but with only limited success: for, while a comprehensive Russo-Prussian military convention was actually drafted in St Petersburg in the third week of

October, Napoleon made it clear a month later he would abolish the Kingdom of Prussia entirely unless Frederick William co-operated with Davout;[48] and, though the Austrians gave verbal assurances that the Tsar need not fear more than token participation on Napoleon's side in any campaign, Metternich could not risk losing the privileged position he had obtained among France's clients by overt collaboration with the Russians. Prussia concluded a humiliating alliance with France on 24 February 1812 (which induced almost a quarter of the officer corps to resign their commissions) and Austria signed a far less rigid commitment with the French less than three weeks later.[49] Alexander was left to win diplomatic triumphs elsewhere. In order to free his southern armies from pressure, the Tsar authorized General Kutuzov, who had succeeded Kamensky as commander on the Danubian Front in the spring of 1811, to begin peace talks with Turkish representatives at Giurgiu.[50] He also found an opportunity to strengthen the northern flank of his armies by improving relations with Sweden where the Gascon-born Bernadotte wished to demonstrate his change of loyalties by opposing the spread of French influence along the southern shores of the Baltic.* Talks between a Swedish emissary and the Russians began in the third week of February and ended with the conclusion of a limited form of alliance, signed in St Petersburg at the beginning of April.[51] It was, however, far harder for the Russians to pin down the Turks to any written undertaking, and military operations were resumed on the Danubian Front at the start of January 1812 in the vain hope of inflicting a decisive defeat on the Turks before the summer months.

In addition to all this diplomatic activity, Alexander was busy in the final weeks of 1811 with military plans for the future campaign. By now St Petersburg was rapidly becoming a refuge for statesmen and soldiers exiled from their homeland by hostility to Napoleon. Among the earliest military commanders to seek sanctuary in St Petersburg was General von Pfuehl, one of the original three joint chiefs-of-staff in the Prussian army

---

* In March 1809 the Swedish aristocracy overthrew King Gustavus IV (who was held to be an imbecile) and placed his uncle, Charles XIII, on the throne. The Peace of Friedrichsham in September 1809 formally ceded Finland to Russia, but left relations between the two countries tense. When the heir to Charles XIII died suddenly at the end of May 1810, the Swedish parliament elected Marshal Bernadotte Prince-Royal of the Kingdom. With Napoleon's hesitant consent Bernadotte accepted the title, much to the dismay of the Tsar who feared a Swedish war of revenge for the loss of Finland. Once in Stockholm, however, Bernadotte took charge of Swedish military and foreign policy and was determined to show his independence of Napoleon. When, in January 1812, Davout was ordered to occupy Swedish Pomerania so as to strengthen the French hold on the Baltic, Bernadotte at once put out feelers for a Russian alliance.

and a specialist in the military history of ancient Greece and the Roman Republic. Pfuehl enjoyed a considerable reputation in St Petersburg society, not least because of his ability to describe the campaigns of Lysander, Hannibal and Philip of Macedon as though he had himself fought in them. When John Quincy Adams attended his first 'great diplomatic dinner' a month after his arrival in Russia in 1809, his neighbour drew his attention to General von Pfuehl, speaking of him with awe as 'one of the ablest men in the world'.[52] Naturally Alexander, always inclined to favour any armchair strategist with a strong German accent, was impressed by Pfuehl. When the General suggested that the Russians should prepare an entrenched fortress between Riga and Smolensk in order to delay any invader, the Tsar gave orders for thousands of labourers to be sent to the town of Drissa on the river Dvina, where they were to construct a formidable defensive encampment which would require investment by the French before they could advance on the major cities of Russia. The plan did not appeal to Russia's military leaders (nor to Pfuehl's gifted compatriot and fellow exile, Colonel von Clausewitz) but it made sense to Alexander – just as Weyrother's ideas had done on the eve of Austerlitz.[53]

By now, however, Alexander was sufficiently experienced not to rely exclusively on Pfuehl or any other single adviser. There was, as yet, no concept of a General Staff in Russia but, since all plans required approval from the Ministry of War, the minister himself inevitably had greater influence than any commander in the field. Hence, almost by chance, Alexander found he was giving more and more weight to the opinions of General Barclay de Tolly, a fifty-year-old Baltic baron of Scottish descent who had acquired a sound knowledge of warfare on the shores of the Black Sea and in Finland.[54] Barclay's appointment as Minister of War in the first weeks of 1810 owed something to his administrative abilities and even more to the fact that Arakcheev had thrown his fit of pique at the wrong moment. He was not, in any sense, an original thinker nor did he ever reflect the glamour of a military hero; but he was in many ways an ideal man to prepare armies for a massive campaign. Whatever his deficiencies, he possessed a sense of order and an understanding of Russia's strategic needs, broad in geographical compass. A memorandum on the need for an all-European concept of policy which he submitted to Alexander on 3 February 1812 is repetitive and clumsily expressed, but its basic points are sound enough: peace with Turkey was desirable to relieve pressure in the South, irrespective of what terms the Sultan granted; an anti-French diversion in the Mediterranean would remove Napoleon's troops from the vital war zone in Prussia; and a solution of the Polish problem would ease the path of the Russians in their early battles.[55] Here, indeed, was a more enterprising war plan than Pfuehl had to offer.

Barclay was a sound product of the military academies, with none of the personality of Suvorov, Kutuzov or the current idol of the soldiery, Prince Bagration; but this absence of flair well suited Alexander. In many respects Barclay's qualities complemented his own. If war came, Alexander was prepared to leave to Barclay de Tolly all the tedious problems of keeping an army in the field while he, once more a soldier Tsar in the saddle, would inspire his troops with the will to win their battles. For strangely enough, despite the traumatic recollection of Austerlitz, Alexander was still able to convince himself he was born to lead his armies to victory – provided, of course, that Barclay could supply the men, the horses and the guns of which such armies are composed, and provided too that his officers would follow him against Napoleon.

The Fall of Speransky and Alexander's Departure for the Army

Early in the New Year Alexander left St Petersburg for a tour of inspection of border fortresses.[56] Since the frost that winter was particularly severe and all Russia's western provinces lay deep in snow, the effectiveness of the Tsar's visit was minimal. There were ironical comments in the Petersburg salons. Speransky, who possessed an astringent tongue, could not resist making a pun on the name of that most famous champion of barrier fortresses, Marshal Vauban, and referred to the Tsar as '*notre Veau Blanc*'.[57] When the joke was repeated to Alexander by mischief-makers at Court, it failed somehow to appeal to his sense of humour; and a certain coolness which had begun to mark the Tsar's relations with his State Secretary over the preceding six months was intensified. Speransky was a little surprised to discover in February that Alexander was too busy to accord him an audience or to go through with him the papers which needed signing; but the State Secretary assumed that he was pre-occupied with military affairs and, though he grumbled to his colleagues at the delay, he was not alarmed. Eventually, on the morning of Sunday, 29 March, a messenger from the Winter Palace informed Speransky that the Tsar would receive him that evening.[58]

When Speransky reached the anteroom of the Tsar's study shortly after half-past eight, he found it crowded with important dignitaries awaiting an audience with the sovereign. But Speransky was summoned into Alexander's presence ahead of everybody else. For more than two hours the others waited, puzzled by the length of what was normally a formal occasion. At last about eleven at night Speransky emerged, visibly upset, and began to put his papers into his briefcase, without a word to those around him. Suddenly the Tsar's door opened again and Alexander came out, tears coursing down his cheeks. He embraced Speransky, declaring melodramatically, 'Once more, Mikhail Mikhailovich, farewell'; and then he retired just as abruptly to his room. Speransky hurried home, found the Minister of Police awaiting for him with an official carriage, and departed that same night for exile at Nizhni Novgorod, the great trading centre on the Volga. At the palace Alexander instructed an attendant to inform those waiting for an audience that, to his regret, he would not be able to see any more visitors that night.[59]

The fall of Speransky created a sensation in Russia and abroad, as one suspects the Tsar intended when he staged it in so dramatic and mysterious a way. No one knows precisely what was said between the two men during those two hours on the Sunday evening: Speransky left no record of the conversation; and, although Alexander subsequently indicated to Novosiltsov he had urged the State Secretary to escape from St Petersburg as excited patriots were accusing him of treachery, this is clearly not the whole story. For several weeks Alexander had allowed Balashov, the Minister of Police, to trail Speransky (and had also instructed a special agent of his own to trail both Balashov and Speransky). Yet, apart from his unfortunate tendency to make injudicious verbal asides, there was little enough evidence on which to damn Speransky.* Nor does it seem as if Alexander wished to discover anything against him, for there is no doubt he was genuinely distressed at having to dismiss a man on whom he had relied so heavily for the past four years. On that Monday morning Prince Golitsyn – one of the dignitaries denied an audience the previous evening – visited Alexander and, as an old friend, asked him why he was looking so wretched. 'No doubt you too would lament and cry with pain if someone amputated your hand', replied Alexander bitterly. 'Last night they took Speransky from me, and he was my right hand.'[60] On Tuesday Nesselrode, too, was received by Alexander. He found him

---

* Alexander was also irritated to discover the extent of Speransky's correspondence with members of the Russian diplomatic service in foreign capitals, although he had earlier encouraged the State Secretary to have his own sources of information on economic problems. The link with Talleyrand declined in importance, partly because of the return of Nesselrode to St Petersburg but also because Talleyrand was excluded from the centre of affairs in Paris at the start of the year 1812 since Napoleon was alarmed by his 'verbal indiscretions'.

deeply moved by what had happened and mourning the departure of someone 'whose character he liked and whose talents he respected'. 'Only the present exceptional circumstances could induce me to make such a sacrifice to public opinion', Alexander declared. Nesselrode, who regarded himself as one of Speransky's friends, commented sadly in his journal, 'It is clear he is the victim of an intrigue'.[61] And so, indeed, he was.

The agitation against Speransky, already active among conservative backwoodsmen in 1810, had grown in intensity as the foreign crisis mounted and the burden of taxation increased to keep pace with the expanding army. To his old enemies he had recently added many of the foreigners who were seeking to enter the service of Alexander, for it was difficult for them to infiltrate a system of government controlled by someone as rigid over appointments and preferment as the State Secretary. Yet his most formidable adversary remained, as ever, the Grand Duchess Catherine Pavlovna, who could never forgive him for insisting that her husband's reports as Governor-General should pass through the normal departments of the administration rather than receive direct and preferential treatment from his brother-in-law on the throne. It was Catherine who forwarded to Alexander a powerfully written memorandum by the distinguished historian Karamzin, which was a plea for strong autocratic government rather than the hesitant deliberation in committee which, it was assumed, the State Secretary's methods encouraged; and it appears to have been Catherine who, generalizing from the mood of her salon at Tver, insisted to Alexander that the sacrifice of Speransky was essential if the Tsar wished to rally his nobility and gentry in a patriotic front of resistance to the French.[62] It is significant that, on the very Sunday Speransky was dismissed, the most articulate and ambitious of the Muscovite landowners, Rostopchin, was forwarding to Alexander a petition from the patrician families of the old capital begging the Tsar to protect 'his loyal subjects' from the hardships of the State Secretary's policy. The intrigue which ousted Speransky certainly had its agents in St Petersburg, but the pressure to get rid of him came above all from Moscow and Tver.[63]

Speransky was succeeded as State Secretary by Admiral Shishkov, against whom little was known, even at Tver. And, as though to reward Catherine and her vigilantes, Alexander agreed to appoint her nominee, Rostopchin, as Governor-General of Moscow when the post fell vacant in the spring of 1812. It must be admitted that the Tsar was reluctant to give such responsibilities to Rostopchin, for he had distrusted the man ever since the days when he had fawned on Paul at Gatchina, some twenty years ago. At first Alexander did his best to persuade Catherine to change her mind. 'He's no soldier', Alexander complained, 'and the Governor of Moscow must bear epaulettes on his shoulders'. But his sister was not to be thwarted. 'That', she replied grandly, 'is a matter for the tailor'; and Alexander capitulated.[64] When, however, the Grand Duchess went further still and began to press for her exiled father-in-law, Duke Peter of Oldenburg, to be entrusted with high command in the Russian army, Alexander dug in his toes. It was one thing to find room for distinguished foreign soldiers from abroad, but rather a different matter to persuade naturally xenophobic troops to accept an ageing German Prince, who happened to be a first cousin of Catherine the Great.[65] Russia would venture much for Oldenburg, but not the fate of an army. Alexander's brotherly affection stopped short of endorsing the ridiculous; and, as she came to know her father-in-law better, Catherine readily perceived Alexander was right.

Even before the coming of the thaw the Russian capital had the air of a city preparing for war. 'Seven or eight regiments have already marched from St Petersburg within the last three weeks for the frontiers, and others are following twice or three times each week', wrote John Quincy Adams in his journal on 19 March.[66] In Paris Kurakin continued to put forward proposals for a settlement, and the Tsar held out some hopes of a compromise in his talks with Lauriston. But privately Alexander knew he was facing the reality of war: 'I have done everything to prevent this struggle but thus it ends', he observed to Adams when they happened to meet walking along the quay by the Neva ten days before Speransky's dismissal.[67] Every possible solution for easing tension between the Russians and French broke down on two basic questions: the refusal of the French to permit Russia total freedom of trade by land and by sea; and the French insistence on retaining armies of occupation on Prussian territory, even as far east as the line of the Niemen. No one doubted in St Petersburg that Napoleon was preparing for a campaign on an unprecedented scale: there were reports of troops on the move northwards from Spain and Italy, of great collections of food and fodder at centres in Danzig and Königsberg, of thousands of horses moving eastwards from Holstein. At times it seemed as if Napoleon regarded the Russian operation as a preliminary to something far grander (such as a march on India), in which Alexander's hostility was a mere matter of form, easily brushed aside by the first troops to cross the frontier: 'You may assure the Tsar', Napoleon told Chernyshev in the last days of February, 'that should Fate ordain we must fight each other, I shall make war on him in a chivalrous spirit, without hate and without rancour. And if circumstances permit, I will even send an invitation for him to dine with me among the advance posts.'[68]

Alexander, however, was no longer inclined to treat the tragedy of war as though it were some personal duel. He had accepted the principle which Barclay had pressed on him for several weeks: he would encourage unrest within Napoleon's Empire, and prepare a rising in the Adriatic to divert troops from the North. In the second week of April he wrote to Baron vom Stein, the Prussian reformer whom Napoleon had driven into exile in Bohemia, suggesting he might like to come to Russia and work for the liberation of the German lands from across the frontiers.[69]* And Alexander also drafted a directive recommending Admiral Chichagov to study the possibilities of carrying war to the French (and, if necessary, Austrian) outposts in Dalmatia and Croatia.[70] If there was to be another contest with the French, Alexander saw it in terms of Europe as a whole and not merely a dispute over Russia's own frontiers. Yet, in his final audience with Lauriston on 20 April, Alexander limited himself to specific demands for relaxing tension on his borders. He would accept an indemnity for Peter of Oldenburg, he would even modify the Russian tariff to the benefit of French trade; but he insisted on the total evacuation by the French of Swedish Pomerania and of all Prussia; and he warned Lauriston that if the French continued to concentrate armies east of the Oder and reinforced their bases on the Vistula, he would regard these dispositions as tantamount to an act of war against his Empire.[71] These proposals, virtually repeated by Kurakin to the French Foreign Minister a week later in Paris, were moderate; and, in private conversation, Lauriston declared that he had not yet given up hope that war might be avoided.[72] But Alexander was unwilling to wait any longer in his capital while the troops were massing. On the day after his audience with the Tsar, Lauriston was informed by Rumiantsev that Alexander had left for Vilna in order to prevent his army commanders from making any provocative moves in response to the massing of the French in eastern Prussia. Lauriston was to tell Napoleon that Alexander did not want a war, would seek to avoid it and that 'in Vilna, no less than in St Petersburg, he would remain a friend and loyal ally' to the French.[73]

The fiction that Alexander was leaving St Petersburg to carry out 'an ordinary review of his troops and the inspection of some of his provinces'

* Stein joined Alexander at Vilna on 12 June, less than a fortnight before Napoleon launched his invasion across the Niemen, but there is no evidence he had any significant influence on the Tsar's policy at this time. Subsequently Stein settled in St Petersburg.

was maintained in official communications from the Russian Foreign Ministry for several days.[74] But the people of St Petersburg had never doubted that the Tsar was once again off to the wars, following the regiments which had marched westwards so steadily over the preceding weeks. And on the afternoon of Alexander's departure (Tuesday, 21 April) his subjects pledged to him their loyalty and their sympathy, as they had done in such different circumstances after Austerlitz. The Empress Elizabeth, sensing what lay ahead for the country of her adoption, was uplifted with patriotic pride. Next morning she described the scene in a letter to her mother in Baden:

The Emperor left yesterday at two o'clock, to the accompaniment of cheers and blessings from an immense crowd of people who were tightly packed from the Kazan Church [sic] to the gate of the city. As these folk had not been hustled into position by the police and as the cheering was not led by planted agents, he was – quite rightly – moved deeply by such signs of affection from our splendid people! . . . 'For God and their Sovereign' – that was the cry! They make no distinction between them in their hearts and scarcely at all in their worship. Woe to him who profanes one or the other. These old-world attitudes are certainly not found more intensively anywhere than at the extremes of Europe. Forgive me, dear Mamma, for regaling you with commonplaces familiar to everyone who has a true knowledge of Russia, but one is carried away when speaking of something you love; and you know my passionate devotion to this country.[75]

13

Captain in the Field

The Pleasures of Vilna

Alexander arrived in the city of Vilna early on the following Sunday afternoon, 26 April. The old capital of the Lithuanian Kingdom was, in these days, the third most populous town in his Empire,* but few of its inhabitants were Russian in race or by religion.[1] Its churches were mostly Roman Catholic or Lutheran although for more than four generations the principal cultural influence in the city had been Jewish. Beyond the ramparts all the fields along the river Vileka were tilled by Polish or Lithuanian peasants and most of them were owned by families who regarded themselves as Poles, even though their racial origin and surnames were frequently Germanic. It would have been hardly surprising if the Tsar had received a cool welcome, for both Poles and Jews stood to gain much from incorporation in a Napoleonic dependency. Yet Alexander himself still hoped he could win support from the non-Russian peoples along his frontier, and before setting out from St Petersburg he seriously considered authorizing the proclamation of a Grand-Duchy of Lithuania which he would endow with representative institutions of its own. He rejected the idea in the end because he had no desire to alienate Polish sentiment by an appeal to specifically Lithuanian historical traditions and not to any common heritage.[2] So long as there was

* In normal times of peace Vilna had a population officially reckoned at 56,300 people but this figure was considerably swollen in the spring of 1812 because of the concentration of armies along the frontier. St Petersburg had 335,600 inhabitants in 1811 and Moscow 270,200. The only European capitals with more inhabitants than St Petersburg were London (1,009,546 according to the 1811 Census) and Paris (slightly over half a million).

an external crisis, he preferred to seek loyal support in a city close to the frontier by holding out the prospect of favours rather than by making gestures of reform benefiting one national group at the expense of others. He had only once in his reign briefly visited the Vilna region and he chose now to delay political decisions until he knew better the mood of this western fringe of his empire. This was not, perhaps, the most courageous of policies but against the darkening background of probable war it made good sense.

In one respect the Tsar need not have worried. His affability speedily conquered Vilna. Alexander was greeted with peals from the baroque belfries, with flags draped from windows and spring garlands festooned across the cobbled streets of the inner town. He responded to this unexpectedly warm reception with a refreshingly youthful geniality. There was, at first, some constraint on both sides, mainly because by the Russian Orthodox calendar it was still Lent while the Roman Catholics had celebrated Easter four weeks before the Tsar's arrival; but, once this awkward social distinction was overcome by the natural passage of time, the city took on the appearance of a capital in miniature – and enjoyed itself, as never before.[3] Many of the Tsar's ministers travelled out from St Petersburg, and so too did some of the diplomatic corps. 'His Majesty's choristers from the chapel of the Imperial palace' came to sing the Liturgy each Sunday. The Court, and the socially ambitious, treated the Tsar's period of residence in Lithuania much as they would have done had he decided on a protracted stay in Moscow or any other great city in the Empire. Ladies from St Petersburg society made the journey westwards to dance and gossip and flirt their way through the warm evenings and shortening nights of summer. Young officers frittered away hundreds of roubles in gambling, and the money-lenders of Vilna (like the innkeepers) found the Tsar's presence in the neighbourhood gratifyingly profitable. There were numerous balls, fêtes and formal receptions, while a surfeit of lighter entertainment strained the inventive ingenuity of the local nobility and ran many of them heavily into debt.

It was the daughters of the Polish-Lithuanian aristocracy who most welcomed all this excitement. Sixteen years later one of them, Countess Tiesenhausen, recalled the extraordinary summer in her memoirs: 'A storm was about to break over our heads', she wrote, 'and yet, feeling perfectly secure, none of us thought of anything but pleasure, and of the happiness in having the Emperor among us.'[4] The Countess, who had never seen Alexander before and who shared her father's suspicion of his political programme, was easily captivated by his personality. Her acute powers of observation missed little: the way in which he inclined his head to the right to catch a conversation, because of deafness in his left ear; the yellow morocco palliasse which his valet filled each night with fresh straw for his master's comfort; the small lorgnettes which the Tsar tucked into the sleeve of his uniform jacket, and often lost. She noted, too, his table-talk that summer: how he enjoyed travelling through the Lithuanian countryside; what beauty he found in the unexpected bends of the river Niemen; what problems he foresaw in farming the harvest that season; and how one evening, when someone anxiously touched on the proximity of Vilna to the frontier, he dismissed the whole subject with grand simplicity by declaring, 'I hope that all will be arranged'. At times, as others too noticed, Alexander seemed to treat the foreign menace as if it were a contemptible irrelevancy.[5]

The young Countess also tried to explain the fascination which Alexander kindled among those who were meeting him for the first time. She felt he was a man with so many shades of tone to his character that no artist could ever capture the subtleties of his nature for a portrait; and she therefore attempted to convey in prose some of the magic of his personality.

Despite the regularity and delicacy of his features and the bright freshness of his complexion, his physical beauty was at first sight less impressive than the air of kind benevolence which won all hearts and instantly inspired confidence. His tall, noble and majestic figure, often stooping graciously like the pose of an ancient statue, was already threatening to become stout, but he was perfectly formed. His eyes, alert and expressive, were blue and he was a little short-sighted. His nose was straight and well shaped with a small agreeable mouth. The rounded contours of his face resembled those of his august mother, as also did his profile. His forehead was slightly bald, giving to his whole countenance an open and serene expression, and his hair – which was a golden blond in colour – was carefully groomed as on the heads of classical cameos or medallions so that it seemed made to receive a triple crown of laurel, myrtle or olive.[6]

To Countess Tiesenhausen, and many other ladies of fashion as well, there was a friendly confidence in Alexander's manner which painted the future with bright colours of hope. Although the frontier along the Niemen was less than fifty miles from Vilna, nobody bothered much over what was happening elsewhere than in the city. 'We did not even know the French were crossing Germany, for no item of news was allowed to circulate in Lithuania', the Countess later wrote, almost apologetically.[7] No doubt much of what she says is exaggerated, for in reminiscence she was seeking to catch the fragrance of Alexander's charm and contrast it with the sorrow and suffering of the winter that was to come; but there is ample evidence from other sources to show the feverish self-confidence with which Vilna awaited the coming of war and the honours which its people heaped upon their sovereign.

The Eve of Invasion, 1812

It is, however, difficult to believe Alexander had much faith in the ability of his armies to contain the invaders, whatever remarks he may have made to his social neophytes in Vilna. He still appears to have favoured Pfuehl's planned withdrawal to Drissa, which implied the abandonment of all Lithuania and Byelo-Russia as well. But the Tsar was not totally convinced Pfuehl was right; and he was prepared to listen to Barclay de Tolly and to such veteran commanders as Bennigsen and Bagration. According to Lebzeltern (who had followed Alexander to Vilna, despite the strained relations between Austria and Russia), the Tsar 'did not place his entire confidence' in any one adviser, military or diplomatic. Alexander had developed a habit of letting 'many individuals know partially of matters uppermost in his thoughts while he was talking to them' but 'the result of these bursts of confidence is that nobody knows about general matters in their entirety'.[8] Lebzeltern's judgement is shrewd and more penetrating than the comments of any Russian observer, for few of the Tsar's own senior officers realized how muddled was the military thought at Imperial headquarters. Alexander was, at one and the same time, toying with at least four operational projects: he was willing to encourage Bagration, the commander of the Russian Second Army, to contemplate an advance up the Bug and the Vistula on Warsaw; he was prepared to approve two alternative contingency plans drawn up by Barclay de Tolly, one for a battle on the frontiers and the other for disengagement in depth; and he still gave the impression to foreign officers serving with him that he rated highly the value of Pfuehl's fortified camp at Drissa.[9] Alexander's mind was as confused over military affairs on the eve of invasion in 1812 as in the weeks preceding Austerlitz.

There was hardly any greater clarity of purpose in his foreign policy. Here, too, he relied increasingly on the advice of his latest discovery, the young Count Karl Nesselrode, who had already distinguished himself in Paris. Even before setting out from the capital Alexander informed Nesselrode of the responsibilities awaiting him should war come: 'I plan to place myself at the head of the armies', Alexander told him, 'I will need to have with me a young man capable of following me everywhere on horseback, to be in charge of my diplomatic correspondence . . . I have cast my eyes upon you and hope you will fulfil such a confidential post with loyalty and discretion.'[10] Technically Nesselrode was merely a high-ranking departmental secretary attached to the Foreign Ministry, but his importance increased when Chancellor Rumiantsev collapsed with an apoplectic stroke while travelling from St Petersburg to Vilna in May. Although Rumiantsev suffered only partial paralysis and remained nominally in charge of foreign affairs, Alexander used the Chancellor's ill-health as an excuse for ignoring him.[11] It was more convenient to consult Nesselrode, who had never been a Francophile but who understood the French political scene as well as anybody in the Russian diplomatic service. Moreover, Nesselrode had one particular advantage in Alexander's eyes: he was the first of the specialists in foreign affairs to be both younger and less experienced than the Tsar himself. Training and character alike thus made him naturally offer advice to Alexander rather than seek to dominate him. In a letter which he sent to his wife a month after arriving at Imperial headquarters, Nesselrode showed clearly enough the way in which Alexander intended foreign affairs to be conducted while he was in the field: 'I am summoned to him when I am needed', Nesselrode wrote, 'but otherwise I do not push myself forward so as to multiply these occasions. I am completely passive.'[12] With a departmental secretary who was prepared to interpret policy rather than initiate it, Alexander became in effect his own Foreign Minister. As with military affairs, there was uncertainty and vacillation in much he undertook.

At times during these eight weeks in Vilna Alexander appeared to support contradictory policies, especially towards Russia's neighbours. He could not, for example, decide if he should seek to perpetuate his private understanding with Metternich to limit Russo-Austrian hostilities or if he should encourage insurrection against the Austrians, as Napoleon's most powerful allies, by fomenting trouble in southern Hungary and the Tyrol. Similarly he was unsure how far he might trust the Swedes not to seek a war of revenge for the loss of Finland. Nor could he make up his mind about the British, whose exercise of sea power he still resented: ought he to conclude a genuine alliance with Lord Liverpool's new government in London, or would he benefit more from the independence that would be his through waging a parallel war against the French rather than becoming a partner in another coalition? Most of these questions remained unresolved when the invasion began at the end of June.[13] Paradoxically at the very moment when Alexander delighted in having control of foreign affairs under his own hands, he left vital decisions to ambassadors. To a growing extent, in that uncertain summer of 1812, he was prepared to wait upon events rather than seek to determine them himself.

This apparent taste for procrastination did not spring from mere idleness. He spent most mornings in Vilna discussing problems with his military commanders or his political advisers, and he studied carefully the reports brought to him by couriers from St Petersburg or directly from the principal European cities. The truth is that he was wretchedly overworked. He had left General Saltykov in St Petersburg with nominal responsibility for administrative problems but it was clear he expected every important decision in home affairs as well as over foreign policy to be referred to him in Vilna; for why, otherwise, would Alexander have insisted on Speransky's successor as State Secretary, Admiral Shishkov, coming to Lithuania rather than remaining in the capital?[14] Even before the war began, the Grand Duchess Catherine was seeking to induce her brother to give up his idea of commanding the army in the field, partly because she feared for his prestige should there be reverses, but also because she genuinely thought it essential to control the Empire from the centre of affairs rather than from the fringe: 'You must not only play the part of a captain but of a ruler as well', she wrote to him bluntly.[15] But he would not listen to her. He enjoyed his military role. As he wrote back to Catherine on 9 June: 'I scribble these lines to you having snatched forty winks after returning from a round of sixty miles, twenty of them on horseback, setting out at five in the morning . . . Despite that, I feel very fresh and am going to saddle my horse again for another reconnaisance.'[16] Vilna somehow brought out the eternal subaltern in him.

Yet if Alexander was half play-acting, so too was Napoleon; although his preference was for a pageant rather than an epic drama. He left St Cloud, with the Empress Marie Louise at his side, on 9 May, nearly a fortnight after the Tsar's arrival in Lithuania. Although from the Oder to the Vistula half a million men were moving relentlessly eastwards, Napoleon was still not irrevocably committed to war. He travelled not directly to the area where the armies were concentrating but to Dresden, where he was fêted by the King of Saxony and flattered by all the rulers of Germany including his father-in-law from Vienna and the unfortunate Frederick William of Prussia.[17] Napoleon decided to wait in Dresden until he could receive a report from one of his aides, Count Louis de Narbonne, whom he had sent from Berlin to the Tsar at Vilna in a last attempt to intimidate Russia back into the Continental System. Neither Napoleon nor his ministers believed Narbonne's mission would succeed;

but at least he would be able to let Napoleon know the mood of the Russian commanders; and the presence of an emissary of peace might prevent Alexander from ordering his vanguard across the frontier towards Warsaw before the Grand Army finally reached its war stations.

Narbonne's mission took the Russians by surprise. He arrived in Vilna on 18 May and was received by Alexander the same day.[18] The Tsar accepted a letter from Napoleon which emphasized yet again his desire for peace and assured Alexander that, even should the two Empires find themselves at war, his personal regard for the ruler of Russia would remain undiminished. Narbonne spoke airily of the power of the Grand Army and indicated that the Russians had only to close their ports to British trade for the war crisis to be over. But Alexander was not impressed. Napoleon, he complained, 'is ranging all Europe against Russia', and though as Tsar he had worked 'to uphold a political system which might lead to universal peace', he was prepared to risk an appeal to arms rather than 'besmirch the honour of the nation over which I rule'. He added, with a flourish of high rhetoric, 'If the Emperor Napoleon is determined on war, and if fortune does not smile on our just cause, his hunt for peace will take him to the uttermost ends of the World.'[19]

These sentiments were much more resolute than Narbonne had anticipated; but he was prepared to wait in Vilna, for he hoped the Tsar's ministers might well induce him to modify his proud tone. Narbonne was well treated. He was invited on 19 May to watch the Tsar review two regiments and to dine at his table. But, though Narbonne would have lingered in Lithuania as long as anybody, his visit was cut short by three members of the Tsar's suite who attended him on the following morning and informed him that, by early evening, his horses would be ready for him to set out for Dresden with Alexander's reply. Five days later Narbonne duly handed the Tsar's coldly polite letter to Napoleon and reported to him on his mission. Napoleon's secretary, Baron Fain, has left a dramatic account of Narbonne's audience: the Emperor paced up and down, deep in thought and suddenly exclaimed, 'So all means of understanding are at an end! The spirit which dominates the Russian camp pushes us into war! . . . There is no more time to lose in fruitless negotiations.'[20] Early on 29 May he set off across the Elbe for Danzig and the birch forests and marshes of Europe's borderland, through which he had last ridden on his way back from Tilsit.

Exactly five weeks separate Narbonne's departure from Vilna and the beginning of the invasion. For Alexander they were almost disturbingly free from incident. Life at Imperial headquarters was as much ridden by routine as in any garrison city in the provinces during time of peace. Alexander continued to combine his duties as commander-in-chief with his responsibilities of government, despite his sister's warnings. He inspected troops and fortifications along the rivers, and he studied anxiously the despatches from Bucharest, where Kutuzov was seeking a speedy ending of the war against Turkey so as to free another army either for service on the western frontiers or for that diversionary thrust towards the Adriatic which still appealed to many of the leading Russian commanders.[21] Occasionally reports of troop movements in Prussia or the Grand-Duchy of Warsaw raised a fresh alert at headquarters and sent couriers scurrying across the countryside, but even this excitement was becoming dulled by repetition long before midsummer.

The round of balls and banquets continued to provide entertainment far into the night. In order to repay hospitality from the local nobility and their families, Alexander's aides accepted an offer from General Bennigsen to give a grand ball on his estate at Zakret, some two or three miles east of the city. They selected the night of Wednesday, 24 June, when there would be only a few hours of darkness and when a full moon would show the English-style lawns and fountains of Zakret to advantage. Two days previously a specially constructed ballroom collapsed, but the officers went ahead with their plans for the entertainment, with the dances beginning on the lawns and only moving later to the house itself.[22] Unfortunately the fine moonlit nights that week favoured other enterprises, too.

The Countess Tiesenhausen (whom Alexander invited to partner him immediately after the wives of Generals Bennigsen and Barclay de Tolly) has left a vivid record of the evening:

The whole mansion ornamented with orange trees in full bloom, scenting the air ... the musicians of the Imperial Guard playing favourite passages of music in differing parts of the park ... the splendid uniforms with their diamond decorations ... old trees massively green over the Vileka, which reflected in its winding course the colours of the setting sun ... His Majesty wearing on that day the uniform of the Semeonovsky Guards, with light blue facings, which suited him well ... supper served without formality at small tables in the open air ... the weather so mild and still that the lights did not go out.[23]

Her account makes the occasion seem like a cross between a Cambridge May Ball and a garden party at the palace: there is no suggestion that Alexander knew Napoleon was already across the Niemen or even believed an invasion to be imminent. At least one Polish nobleman present at Zakret, Count Oginski, had seen for himself the activity of the French beyond the river little more than twenty-four hours previously and was surprised at the lack of concern in Vilna.[24]

Alexander learnt of the invasion while he was at the Zakret ball. There are slight variations in the reports of how he received the news. The Countess merely writes that he 'retired during the supper'. Oginski maintains he discussed a variety of topics with Alexander during the evening but never noticed any change in the Tsar's mood, even though (as he wrote) 'I discovered afterwards he was aware the French had just crossed the Niemen.' The traditional version, depending on the testimony of other guests at the ball, describes how Alexander's chief of police, General Balashov, brought him news of the invasion as the musicians were beginning to play a mazurka. But the accounts agree in two respects: Alexander was surprised to learn the campaign had begun without a declaration of war; and he insisted on leaving Zakret as unobtrusively as possible for the Episcopal Palace in Vilna, where he had established his personal headquarters. On that same night, Napoleon was sixty-five miles away, having arrived at a Russian Orthodox monastery outside Kovno at almost the same time as the Bennigsens received Alexander at Zakret.[25]

Resolution and Retreat

The precise order of events in Vilna over the following two days is hard to establish, not least because the whole region was swept by an almost tropical thunderstorm during the early afternoon of 25 June and the poor quality roads were turned into mud tracks within a matter of hours.[26] Communications were cut between vital outposts and messengers delayed in their journeys to Imperial headquarters. It is thus not clear when Alexander was informed that, in addition to Napoleon's crossing of the Niemen near Kovno, a second force had bridged the river eighty miles farther north at Tilsit and was advancing along the Petersburg road on Riga; but it is probable he knew of the Tilsit crossing before nightfall. There seems, however, to have been little contact with the Russian Second Army, under Bagration, which was concentrated nearly a hundred miles to the south-west of Vilna, around Brest, Bialystok and Volkovisk. The Russian Third Army, commanded by General Tormassov, was still assembling south of the Pripet Marshes and was almost as independent of Alexander as Kutuzov's army in Moldavia.

The Tsar spent the early hours of 25 June in conference with his chief aides-de-camp and with the State Secretary, Shishkov.[27] The reports which reached him indicated the invading army was far larger than any of the Russian Generals had anticipated when discussing war plans: in fact – though this did not become apparent until later – Barclay de Tolly's First Army was outnumbered four to one along the sector of the Vileka and the Niemen, between Vilna and Kovno. The mood at Imperial headquarters remained, however, resolute, despite disturbing rumours from the north and west. Alexander and Shishkov prepared a draft manifesto which was sent that evening to Saltykov in St Petersburg. It announced 'the invasion of the Russian territories by the French' in restrained and dignified language but it concluded with the solemn pledge, 'I will not make peace so long as a single enemy soldier remains armed within my Empire.'[28] And in a proclamation to his troops Alexander called down the wrath of God on 'the man who started the war'.[29] When the Tsar's words were published in St Petersburg on 30 June they made a great impression. From the old capital Rostopchin sent to Alexander a proud message of loyal encouragement – 'The Emperor of Russia will always remain formidable at Moscow, terrible at Kazan and invincible at Tobolsk.' This was to be no mere campaign along the frontiers of Alexander's vast Empire. Church, nobility and people were united with the sovereign in their determination to wage war relentlessly against 'the universal disturber of the world's peace'.[30]

Yet, in Lithuania, a lone voice pleaded for one last gesture of appeasement. On the same day on which the manifesto for Saltykov was drafted, Chancellor Rumiantsev wrote a hurried letter to the Tsar from the village of Nementschine, a staging post east of Vilna. It contained a strangely worded request: 'Would it, Sire', Rumiantsev asked, 'be too inconvenient for you to write yourself to the Emperor Napoleon indicating that you are too protective of the blood, not only of your own subjects but of all peoples to expose it to being spilt through a misunderstanding?'[31] And the letter went on to explain that messages from St Petersburg reported the French were angry because the Russian ambassador in Paris had asked for his passports twice in a single day, and this action was being interpreted by Napoleon as an indication that the Russians wanted war.

Alexander received Rumiantsev's letter that same evening. He was already considering sending an emissary to Napoleon, and the Chancellor's message finally determined his course of action. At ten o'clock at night he sent for Balashov and informed him that he was to undertake a special mission to the French camp.[32] In the letter to Napoleon Alexander incorporated a final plea based, in part, on Rumiantsev's initiative. For, though Alexander repeated his pledge not to make peace so long as the invaders were on Russian soil, he made it clear he was ready to negotiate once the Grand Army retired across the frontier: 'If Your Majesty will order a withdrawal of your troops from Russian territory, I am prepared to regard what has passed as though it had never happened, and an agreement is still possible between us', Alexander declared. With such a remarkable triumph as the crossing of the Niemen to his credit, there was never any prospect that Napoleon would order his troops to retreat purely through a faint hope of reconciliation. Alexander knew this as well as anybody: 'Between you and me,' he said to Balashov, 'I do not expect your mission will put an end to the war. But at any rate Europe will know we did not begin it, as this letter will once more prove.'

The Tsar was indeed much concerned over the response of his peoples, and other governments, to the coming of the war. He discussed with Shishkov the publication of a long manifesto which would explain the real causes of the breach with Napoleon so as to place responsibility firmly on the French.[33] A first draft was actually prepared which traced the intrigues of Napoleon in Poland, his aggression in northern Germany, his confiscation of the Duke of Oldenburg's possessions, and finally the unjustified grievances of the French at the changes in the Russian tariffs at the close of 1810. But this formidable apologia was never made public for, before Alexander could complete work on it, the campaign had acquired such momentum that it became an early casualty of the war against which it protested.

During the third night of the French invasion alarming rumours reached Vilna. Murat and the French cavalry were said to be heading for the city, some reports even alleging advanced patrols were scouring the countryside around Zakret.[34] Alexander had no wish to be surrounded in the first manoeuvres of the war. It was decided that Imperial headquarters should retire to Svencionys, forty miles to the north-east, a first stage in any retreat to Drissa. Meanwhile Barclay de Tolly would be left as commander-in-chief at Vilna with the responsibility of choosing either to make a stand against the French outside the city or to supervise the systematic withdrawal of his troops if this course seemed preferable. Alexander accordingly set out for Svencionys at three in the morning of 26 June, slipping unostentatiously through the streets of Vilna as dawn was breaking.[35] His escort saw no sign of the French: only the bad state of the roads impeded his progress.

Once it became known the Tsar had left Vilna, there was a near-panic in the city. All the civilians who had followed their sovereign to Lithuania during the previous two months were eager to flee from the advancing enemy. There was an acute shortage of horses, Barclay himself ordering the army to requisition animals so as to get guns and supplies away. 'I remember that one distinguished lady insisted on having her horses brought up to her room on the first floor so as to prevent anyone seizing them', wrote Count Oginski later.[36] Although Barclay did not finally announce his intention of abandoning Vilna until more than twenty-four hours after Alexander's departure, he never attempted to organize the defence of any part of the town except the gates and the bridges. Rather than risk battle with inferior forces, he chose to follow the traditional Russian policy of retirement in depth, much as Kutuzov had done in 1805 after the disaster at Ulm. The Russian troops filed out 'in good order and with a most impressive silence' (wrote Countess Tiesenhausen), after setting fire to the bridges and depots for such supplies as could not be loaded into wagons.[37] Vilna did not offer the enemy 'any advantageous positions', wrote Barclay's principal adjutant.

Nevertheless the abandonment of so important a city as Vilna without a fight caused heart-searching in Alexander's entourage and, indeed, in St Petersburg and Moscow. It was difficult to appreciate a strategy which necessitated the surrender of a fortified position so closely associated in the public eye with the Tsar himself over the preceding two months. Precipitate withdrawal seemed to mock the patriotic sentiments of the war manifesto. Shishkov expressed the general feeling of disillusionment when Alexander heard that Barclay had left the city: 'How terrible to lose Vilna only five days after the start of hostilities!' he wrote. 'To run away, to hand over so many towns and districts to the enemy and – on top of all that – actually to boast of such a beginning! What more could the enemy ask for? Nothing, except perhaps to be allowed to advance unhindered to the very gates of our two capitals! Oh Lord have mercy! Bitter tears stain the words I write.'[38]

Shishkov was prepared to place responsibility for the loss of Vilna on Barclay as commander of the First Army. Others, less closely associated with the Tsar, did not hesitate to blame Alexander himself; for it was he, they argued, who had always wished to resist Napoleon from the entrenchments of Drissa.[39] Already, in the first week of the campaign, his prestige was falling with the reverses of his troops, just as his sister had warned him in her letters. An Emperor of All the Russias was not expected to put himself at the head of regiments in retreat. If he could not lead them to victory, his place was in the capital not in the field. But it was anyone's guess how Alexander was to be convinced of this.

From Vilna to Drissa

Napoleon entered Vilna on the afternoon of Sunday, 28 June, during a heavy thunderstorm. He knew an emissary from the Tsar had arrived at Davout's headquarters on Friday morning and Alexander's letter was forwarded to him even before he left Kovno. But he had no desire to see Balashov until he was certain of his hold on Vilna and he therefore asked Davout to keep the Russian at his headquarters until the city was firmly in French hands. In fact, it was only on the following Wednesday evening that Napoleon consented to receive Balashov, the meeting taking place in the same room from which Alexander had sent his emissary to find the French five days previously.[40] Napoleon was worried, partly because of the strain the weather was imposing on his troops and also because the Poles and Lithuanians had not welcomed their liberation so warmly as he had anticipated. He could not hide from Balashov how ill at ease he felt, and much of his conversation consisted of alternate cheap jibes and boasting at Alexander's expense. This nervous uncertainty is reflected in the letter which he handed Balashov to take back to the Tsar. At great length Napoleon tried to justify his policy, roundly blaming Russia for ending the Tilsit alliance and charging Alexander personally with 'a lack of perseverance, trustfulness and (if I may say so) sincerity'. Yet in the final paragraph, Napoleon abruptly changed his tone. He was convinced the Russians planned only to offer token resistance and he therefore wished to give Alexander every opportunity to make peace swiftly, as after Friedland. Why, asked Napoleon, should not the two Emperors 'maintain direct communication' with each other during the campaign so that they would be able to exchange prisoners and decide in due course on a means of ending the conflict? Alexander should not regard the invasion of his empire as evidence of Napoleon's personal hostility. 'My private feelings towards you remain unaffected by these events', Napoleon wrote, 'and, should fortune again favour my arms, you will find me, as at Tilsit and Erfurt, full of friendship and esteem for your good and great qualities, and anxious only to prove it.'[41]

No other document shows quite so clearly Napoleon's total failure to understand either Alexander's character or the true nature of Tsardom. There could never be a second Tilsit so long as Alexander lived. Any sign of weakness now would imperil his throne, as he knew well enough. Moreover, he was not prepared to mock the pledges he had made when the invasion began by entering into any communications with the enemy. Caulaincourt, who was with Napoleon at Vilna, warned him not to minimize Alexander's tenacity of purpose, but his advice was wasted.[42] Napoleon, having twice met Alexander, believed he could read his mind better than the ex-ambassador. It was only when the summer weeks began to succeed each other with no sign of the Russians offering a decisive battle or a gesture of peace that Napoleon wondered if he had miscalculated the temper of his opponent; and even then he assumed it would never stand up to the loss of Moscow.

Certainly in this first fortnight of July Alexander was not an impressive national leader. No one was quite clear from one day to the next where the Tsar or his army commanders were establishing their headquarters. Between his departure from Vilna early on 26 June and his arrival at Drissa twelve days later Alexander was in no position to govern his empire effectively or to exercise decisive control over movements of the army he was nominally leading. He fell back on the river Dvina, halting briefly at the recognized staging posts – Svencionys, Vidzy and Zamosne. It was simple enough for him to send couriers with orders to Saltykov in St Petersburg or to Bagration's Second Army in Byelo-Russia, but he could not receive reports or despatches until he actually reached Drissa.[43] Fortunately the thunderstorms which slowed down Alexander's own movements hampered the French cavalry even more, for had Napoleon been able to exploit his capture of Vilna the relative isolation of the Tsar would have proved a considerable embarrassment. Russia was too vast and cumbersome to be ruled by a peripatetic prince any longer.

Alexander was geographically close enough both to Barclay and to the garrison commanders of Riga and Mitau to follow what was happening in the northern battle zone. But he could make no sense of the reports he found in Drissa from Bagration. Both the Tsar and his minister (Barclay) had assumed Bagration would fall back through Minsk and eventually establish contact with the First Army south of Drissa and west of Vitebsk. Bagration's reports indicated that he was proposing to march not north-eastwards but south-eastwards, through Bobruisk rather than Minsk. Alexander was angry at this apparent change in plan and sent a courier off to Bagration with a letter of stern rebuke as soon as he arrived at Drissa.[44] In reality, Bagration was striving desperately to avoid being cut off by Davout's corps (which entered Minsk on the very day the Tsar was dictating his letter of censure). Naturally, Bagration in his turn was incensed at the tone of Alexander's message. He assumed the reprimand had originated with Barclay de Tolly, whose position as minister he coveted and whom he had long ago come to regard as a personal enemy. In fact, Barclay did not arrive at Drissa until two days later. If anyone other than the Tsar himself inspired the letter, it would have been Arakcheev, whom Alexander had appointed 'Secretary to the Emperor for Military Affairs' on the eve of the invasion;[45] but Bagration had come to regard Arakcheev as a personal friend, and it was against the minister that his wrath was turned. 'I am not to blame for anything', Bagration wrote in a private note to Arakcheev. 'First they stretch me like a bow-string while the enemy breaks into our lines without firing a shot. Then we begin to retreat – nobody knows why . . . I cannot by myself defend the whole of Russia. The First Army should advance on Vilna at once without fail. What is there to fear? . . . I implore you to advance . . . It ill suits Russians to run . . . One feels ashamed.'[46]

The feud between Bagration and Barclay was only one of the conflicting currents of ill-feeling at headquarters. Since Bagration was still more than a hundred and sixty miles away, it was by no means the most serious cause of tension. Alexander was well-satisfied with Drissa and with the general course of events, apart from his disgust with the unfortunate Bagration. Four days after reaching Drissa, the Tsar sent an almost complacent letter to Admiral Chichagov, who had taken over command of the army in Moldavia from Kutuzov: 'We are now on 30 June' (12 July), Alexander wrote, 'and the enemy here has neither forced us to give a general battle nor cut off from us a single detachment of troops.'[47] But nobody else at Drissa shared the Tsar's confidence and contentment. Barclay was alarmed at the inadequate defences thrown up around the small town and all his old suspicion of General Pfuehl rapidly came to the surface. On one side of the entrenched camp there were, as yet, no fortifications whatsoever. To remain in Drissa was to risk encirclement and annihilation, Barclay argued; and although almost every other senior officer was involved in petty intrigues against the minister, for once they all agreed with him over this one question. By the middle of the month Alexander, too, had decided against Pfuehl and his whole plan.[48]

Rather surprisingly, the Tsar remained in Drissa for more than a week. There are two reasons for his protracted stay, military and political: before abandoning a camp equidistant from the main routes to both St Petersburg and Moscow, it was essential to discover which city was the more likely objective for the Grand Army's advance; and it was also desirable to complete outstanding business of government before once more setting out in the long caravan of command across the Russian countryside. Political questions were multiplying. At Drissa Alexander could take stock of the final terms agreed with the Sultan for ending the Russo-Turkish war at the end of May, and he was also able to consider the possibility of transforming the old enmity between Russians and Turks into a new alliance against the French.[49]* Then, too, there was a wealth of correspondence on Anglo-Russian relations for, although there had been exchanges between the British and Russian ministers in Sweden, technically the two Empires remained at war until a formal treaty was signed on 18 July.[50] Though still distrusting the British because of naval questions, Alexander needed to reach an understanding with London, if only to secure a subsidy. It was, in fact, from Drissa on 14 July that the Tsar wrote for the first time to the Prince Regent, expressing in his letter hopes for future co-operation and acknowledging the assistance of the British Minister in Constantinople (the young Stratford Canning) in negotiating peace with the Turks.[51]

Meanwhile hurried military conferences were held to improvise a new defensive strategy.[52] Barclay proposed to send an army corps under General Wittgenstein northwards to Pskov, where it would guard the road to St Petersburg while the remainder of the First Army would turn south-eastwards down the river Dvina to Vitebsk. There it would be due north of the 'Big One', the highway which Catherine the Great had ordered to be constructed from Minsk through Smolensk to Moscow. The Tsar approved this plan, even though it meant that Barclay would have no more than 75,000 men to place in the path of the French if Napoleon made his main thrust towards Moscow (as now seemed certain). Fresh orders were sent to Bagration: he was to turn northwards and establish contact with Barclay at Vitebsk, where it was assumed the minister intended to give battle to Napoleon.

Throughout 15 July preparations were in hand for resuming the retreat. But the Tsar's personal entourage were seized by a particular worry, hardly new to them but made acute by the rejection of the Pfuehl plan, to which Alexander had so markedly given his patronage in past weeks. To those who best knew the Tsar, it was clear that his understanding of military problems was far more limited than he could ever accept. His presence in the field was an embarrassment and a burden for his army commanders, and it was all too easy for unscrupulous careerists to use him as a means for their own advancement, filling his mind with prejudices

* The Treaty of Bucharest of 28 May 1812 was in many respects disappointing for the Russians after their military successes on the lower Danube in 1809 and 1811. It ceded Bessarabia to the Tsar but left the Danubian Principalities of Moldavia and Wallachia under Turkish control (although with limited autonomy). There was never much likelihood of the Turks assisting the Russians against the French in Dalmatia and the nebulous Balkan schemes of Alexander and Chichagov were shelved before the end of July. But peace with Turkey freed an army of 60,000 men for operations against Napoleon that autumn.

against Barclay and others in authority. On the other hand, in St Petersburg he could keep control of foreign affairs effectively in his hand while inspiring confidence in his subjects. Before leaving Drissa Admiral Shishkov had decided that, for the good of Russia, it was essential for Alexander to be persuaded back to his capital.[53]

Shishkov voiced his fears to Balashov, who agreed with him, and to Arakcheev, who was at first more hesitant, suspecting yet another political intrigue from which he could not see what he was himself to gain. But Shishkov and Balashov convinced him of the need to get the Tsar away from headquarters. Shishkov drafted a letter which the three men signed. Arakcheev then left it among the Tsar's papers of which, as personal Military Secretary, he was in charge. The letter was worded with tact: it explained how, since Alexander's crown was assumed by right and not by usurpation (as Napoleon's had been), the proper place for the sovereign of All the Russias was in the capital city of the Empire rather than in a military camp where he could concern himself with only one aspect of the struggle against the invader.[54] It powerfully reinforced the pleas from Catherine Pavlovna to her brother, urging him not to take command in the field; and, according to General von Loewenstern (one of the émigré Prussians in the Tsar's service), the letter coincided with Alexander's own belief that if he left headquarters, his departure would rally the ambitious officers around the commander-in-chief and thereby lessen the political intrigue so damaging to any army in the field.[55] But there is no evidence that Alexander had made up his mind to return to the capital before setting out from Drissa.

The First Army began to stream southwards from Drissa early on the morning of 16 July. Alexander rode in an open carriage, with an escort of the Semeonovsky Guards.[56] The roads were bad, the heat stifling and the whole Oriental caravan of pack-horses, droskys, britzas, powder-waggons, carts and cannon clogged the route between the forests, forcing marching regiments to wait for hours by the roadside as the paraphernalia of war trundled by. The Tsar's carriage was, of course, given priority and the halted foot-sloggers caught a sight of their sovereign and cheered as the racing wheels cut their way through the dusty tracks. By late afternoon Alexander's carriage had covered forty miles and reached Polotsk, still sixty miles short of Vitebsk.

When Alexander arrived in Polotsk he seemed at first inscrutably silent. Shortly after he stepped from his carriage he turned to Arakcheev and remarked brusquely, 'I have read your paper'.[57] If he looked pensive, it is hardly surprising. What ought he to do? Should he continue the journey to Vitebsk or was his presence with the army an embarrassment and a liability? He had always wished to serve at the head of his troops like his patron saint, Alexander Nevsky, and the Hellenistic conqueror whose name he proudly bore. Twice already he had set out for war only to return frustrated to his capital, burdened by the memory of Austerlitz and by the promise of a Peace which he found his subjects despised. If he did as Shishkov, Balashov and Arakcheev now proposed, there was a risk he would be blamed for deserting his troops. To a man of his sensitivities it needed more courage to accept the duty of turning his horses towards Moscow or Petersburg than to stay with the army in the field. But it was unlikely his critics would understand this inner conflict of loyalty.

That evening he had a horse saddled and rode out to Barclay's headquarters a couple of miles away. General Loewenstern describes the scene: 'He [Alexander] found him about to dine in a stable, for such was Barclay's modest and unconcerned manner that the external trappings of a lodging mattered nothing to him provided only it was near the army and its camp. After an hour's visit, the Tsar left Barclay, embraced him tenderly ... shook his hand warmly and said, "Goodbye, General, goodbye once more, *au revoir*. I commend my army to your keeping. Always remember it is the only one I have.' "[58]

Back in Polotsk, Shishkov heard from Alexander's chamberlain that orders had been given to make the Tsar's carriages ready for a journey to Moscow. 'My joy was indescribable', Shishkov said later, 'and the warmest prayer poured from my lips to the Bestower of all blessings, the Heavenly Creator.'[59] Next morning Alexander, with all his retinue of foreign military experts and his personal staff, left Polotsk and headed towards the upper Dnieper and the long road to the old capital. Five months were to elapse before Alexander again took command of his army in the field: in retrospect, it was to seem far longer.

14

The Razor-Edge of Fate

Alexander in Moscow (July 1812)

The abandonment of Vilna to Napoleon and the loss of Minsk to Davout led to a rapid fall in morale both at St Petersburg and Moscow. To many people it seemed ominous that, four weeks after the invasion, no bulletin had brought news of a major battle. Inevitably the self-important were busy disseminating defeatist talk in the salons of the capital: 'Rumours of disasters both to Prince Bagration's army and to the Emperor himself are circulating in whispers, but without any mention of particulars', John Quincy Adams noted in his journal on 22 July.[1] In Moscow Governor-General Rostopchin was not prepared to tolerate such sophisticated waywardness of temperament. He plastered the walls of the city with optimistic broadsheets and crude caricatures of Napoleon in an effort to harden the faint hearts around him, while he also threatened with exile to Siberia those whose patriotic faith remained unfashionably lukewarm. Even so there was at first widespread alarm when, on the morning of Thursday 23 July, the Muscovites learnt that the Tsar and an impressive array of dignitaries had arrived at Perhouskaya, a mere twenty miles to the east. If Alexander had left the army, it was felt he must either have been defeated already or have perceived he was facing so great a disaster that he wished to escape before the final blow fell. It needed all Rostopchin's gifts of showmanship to calm the people of the old capital and convince them that, in this crisis hour for Russia, their sovereign turned naturally to Holy Moscow for strength and inspiration.[2]

That Thursday evening a sixteen-year-old girl, Ververa Bakounina, saw Alexander ride into the city and recorded the event in her diary. She was impressed by the religious rapture with which the townsfolk knelt in the streets for the Tsar's blessing as his horses bore him, 'so sad and so beautiful' along the route he had followed on the eve of his coronation. He stayed for eight days in all within the Kremlin, and on that first Thursday night a huge crowd assembled outside its walls in loyalty to their sovereign, waiting almost silently, 'rippling under the moon like the sea in summer'.[3] For a young and romantic diarist it was a deeply moving experience.

So it was too for Alexander himself, though in a different way. He had come to Moscow wretchedly weary. The conflicts at Drissa between his advisers and his Generals, the agonizing doubts over the wisdom of leaving the army, the curious shadow-boxing of the first month's campaigning, all these uncertainties weighed heavily on his health. During his week on the road he ate little, sitting disconsolately in his carriage for mile after mile, wrapped in brooding silence. But once within Moscow his confidence revived and with it his vitality. He was spiritually uplifted by the *Te Deum* sung for the Bucharest Peace amid the relics and holy mysteries of the Kremlin cathedrals. The faith of his subjects in him and in their God re-charged the dynamism of Tsardom. On the very day after his arrival he wrote to Catherine Pavlovna, 'The mood of the people here is excellent . . . I cannot tell you what delightful memories of happy times . . . I have experienced at the sight of Moscow. It made me cry like a child.'[4]

There were, however, too many urgent problems for him long to indulge himself in bitter-sweet nostalgia. He needed troops and he needed money; and with Rostopchin's assistance he obtained both during his eight days in the city. On Monday, 27 July, he was received by separate assemblies of the merchants and the nobility. 'Sire, take everything, take our lives and our property', declared one of the more enthusiastic merchants, eager to assist any government ready to destroy the architect of the hated Continental System.[5] A subscription list was opened so that the merchants could show their patriotism by declaring at once the amount they would offer. The system was not exactly foolproof: one small tradesman, in an excess of generosity, wrote 5,000 roubles rather than 500 but was too proud and too excited to admit his error (which, since he could not afford even the original sum, was anyhow a largely academic question); but other merchants were ready to pledge amounts of money genuinely corresponding to their wealth which, it is safe to assume, they would only grudgingly have surrendered to any tax-gatherer. 'They wished to sacrifice a part of their fortune in order to save the rest', wrote Rostopchin later, with characteristic acerbity.[6] Yet, whatever the motive behind their actions, the contributions came flowing in – two million roubles in all – and Alexander was well pleased with the response.

At the second assembly of nominated representatives from the gentry and nobility of the Moscow region, Alexander sought, and obtained, more than mere money. He needed serfs for the militia and freemen volunteers as well, especially to organize and officer the new regiments. The first enrolment of militia recruits in Moscow took place on 29 July, while Alexander was still in the city. Within a month seven different regiments of militia from the area around the old capital were ready to augment the regular army, even though they were deficient in training and woefully short of weapons.[7] Whatever Alexander's faults as a supreme commander, no one could deny his effectiveness as a recruiting sergeant.

To appeal to the people for aid in throwing back the invader needed courage on the part of any Tsar. Rostopchin was uneasy, and so were others in Alexander's entourage; there was always a risk that the latest war with the French would be treated with apathy and that the sacrifices for which the Tsar called would be resented. Yet in relying on the loyalty of his subjects, Alexander showed a sound understanding of the new patriotic sentiments which had begun to penetrate all classes in Russia, even the serfs. It is impossible to tell how far this feeling for country was a response to an instinct of external danger and how far it was a xenophobic reaction to alien traditions of life and culture; but there is abundant evidence it was present in 1812, even before the months of crisis. Mme de Staël, who was travelling through the countryside south of Moscow at this very time, sensed 'the remarkable spirit' of the Russians and attempted to analyse it: 'The reputation for invincibility which their many successes have brought to this nation, the natural pride of the nobility, the inherent inclination towards devotion in the character of the people, the deep influence of religion, the hatred of foreigners ... which is ... rooted in the blood of the Russians and is occasionally roused, all these causes combine to make them a most energetic people', she wrote.[8] But she did not see how recent was this sense of nationhood. In proclaiming the struggle against Napoleon to be 'a national Holy War for the Father-land', Alexander was responding to a flowering of patriotism as deep as in the England of Elizabeth or the Britain of Nelson. It was fitting Alexander should make his call for a Holy War at Moscow. With six cathedrals and fifteen hundred churches, there was no better place in Russia from which to issue such a proclamation.

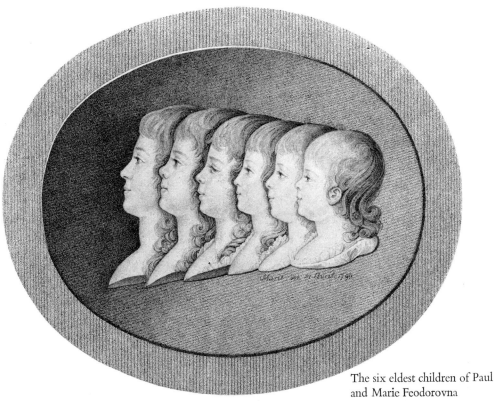

The six eldest children of Paul
and Marie Feodorovna

Catherine the Great by Lampi

The Mikhailovsky Palace in 1807

Tsar Paul I shortly before his death. Engraving by Wolf

Alexander from the painting by Monnier, 1806

Empress Elizabeth in 1814

Prince Adam Czartoryski
after an engraving by Soliman

Arakcheev as a young man

Queen Louise of Prussia
by Grassi in 1802

Maria Naryshkin,
Alexander's mistress

The meeting between Alexander and Napoleon on a raft at Tilsit in 1807
A contemporary English cartoon satirizing the new-found friendship between
Russia and France

Marshal Kutuzov

Michael Speransky

Jaroslaw ce 3 7b.
1812.

Moscou est pris! Il est des choses inexplicables. N'oubliez pas Votre réélection point de paix Et Vous avez encore l'espoir de recouvrer Votre honneur. Si Vous êtes dans la peine n'oubliez pas Ses Amis prêts à Voler vers Vous et trop heureux S'ils peuvent Vous être de quelque Secours, disposez d'eux. Mon Cher ami pas de paix Assurez Vous à Casan pas de paix

The historic letter from the Grand-Duchess Catherine to Alexander informing
him of the loss of Moscow, see p. 246

Lauban. Ce 10. May.

Chère Catherine recevez mes plus tendres félicitations sur la journée d'aujourd'hui, combien il m'en coûte de ne pouvoir pas vous embrasser moi même. Je vous envoie Wolchonsky pour porter ces lignes, il vous rendra un compte fidèle ainsi qu'à Maman des deux glorieuses journées qui se sont passées. Tout à vous de cœur et d'ame pour la vie. J'embrasse mille fois Maman.

Letter from Alexander to the Grand-Duchess Catherine

The Allied leaders in Hyde Park, 1814. Alexander is riding slightly ahead of the Prince Regent and the King of Prussia

Left The Grand-Duchess Catherine Pavlovna. An engraving of 1814
Right The Dowager Empress Marie Feodorovna. An engraving by T. Wright from a painting by George Dawe

The Imperial villa on Kammionyi Island where the Tsar spent the anxious weeks
after the burning of Moscow in 1812
The river front of the Winter Palace in St Petersburg

Baroness Julie von Krüdener

Alexander in 1818. Engraving by
V. Bromley from a drawing by
Igleson

The Clamour for Kutuzov

Alexander, having kissed Rostopchin farewell on both cheeks, left Moscow in the small hours of 31 July and hurried to Tver, which he reached late on that same Friday afternoon. He spent no more than a night at his sister's residence and there is no record of their discussions. Since Catherine was expecting a second child within a month it is likely much of their talk concerned trivialities. At all events the letters they subsequently exchanged show that Alexander did not then raise one of the problems uppermost in his mind – a warning he had received 'eight or ten days' before setting out for Vilna (i.e. in the second week of April) that Napoleon intended to discredit him in his family circle and to foment intrigues centred on the Grand Duchess herself.[9] Clearly Alexander decided not to tax his sister with such matters so near her confinement, and we learn of them only from a letter he wrote four weeks after Catherine had given birth to her baby son. But at least he was able to see there was no overt scheming at her Court. Troubled as usual by regrets that he could not spend longer with his 'dearest Catherine and George', he hastened back to the capital.[10]

He arrived in St Petersburg 'about two o'clock in the morning' on Monday, 3 August, slipping into the town almost unobserved: 'I walked before breakfast in the Summer Gardens', wrote Adams in his journal that day, 'and in turning round . . . I perceived the Imperial flag flying over the palace, which first gave me notice of the Emperor's return.'[11] This near-anonymity set the fashion for the remainder of the summer and autumn. Alexander made few public appearances and gave no balls or grand receptions: the Empire was at war and he was determined to emphasize the contrast with the halcyon days of the Tilsit Peace. Most of the following weeks he spent working in the small palace on Kammionyi Island. 'You can well imagine the endless jobs heaped upon me in Petersburg after so long an absence and especially under present conditions', he wrote to Catherine, and he added the significant comment, 'Here I have found a worse frame of mind than at Moscow or in the interior.'[12]

The truth was that people at Court and in Society were becoming more and more anxious over the way in which the war was being fought. While Alexander was in Moscow the rival armies had faced each other briefly outside Vitebsk but Barclay, painfully conscious of his inferior numbers, had declined to give battle and had fallen back eastwards overnight, closer and closer to Smolensk. The only good news reaching St Petersburg was from General Tormassov's Third Army in Volhynia.

Tormassov checked an incursion by a Saxon corps at Kobrin, near Brest, and went over to the offensive; but although Tormassov's victory was celebrated in St Petersburg, no one could disguise the fact that the Third Army's operations were essentially peripheral to the main arena of battle. What mattered was the vast concentration of 170,000 men – French, Germans, Italians, Poles, Croats and others – pressing inexorably forward towards Smolensk, an arrow thrust into the heart of Muscovy.

At times Alexander found the lack of reliable news intolerable. He no longer frittered away the hours with Maria Naryshkin. As in other moments of crisis he looked for support to Elizabeth, and she gave it to him. She remained magnificently resolute. 'How painful not to be able to tell you of what occupies my thoughts every moment of my day and my night, whether or not I sleep', she wrote to her mother a week after Alexander's return. 'Greetings from my dear and well-beloved Russia for whom I feel in this hour as for a darling child wretchedly sick! I am certain God will not abandon her but she will suffer and I with her, sharing every spasm of her anguish.'[13] So intensely was Elizabeth conscious of the perils facing Russia that she thus re-opened the deepest wound in her personal experience in order to identify herself with the tribulations of her adopted fatherland; while, as a practical gesture of sympathy, she established a fund for war orphans and handed over nine-tenths of her annual allowance to charities.[14]

Meanwhile from Russian headquarters there continued to come nothing but recrimination and excuses. Bagration, who at last linked up with Barclay in Smolensk, poured out pages of accumulated scorn in letters to Arakcheev. The Grand Duke Constantine penned bad advice to his brother, mostly at Barclay's expense. Barclay himself – 'the Minister', as his enemies insisted on calling him so as to detract from his military command – wrote directly to Alexander, patiently explaining how he was saving the army for the right moment; and that, after all, was the last order he had received from the Tsar at Polotsk.[15] But Alexander thought little of Barclay's explanations. 'There is', he wrote to Catherine, 'a great indignation here against the Minister of War who, I must confess, gives good grounds for it by indecision in conduct and by the chaos of his work.'[16] He was, however, reluctant to remove him from the high command: for who would take his place?

On 17 August Alexander received a letter from General Prince Shuvalov brought to him by his personal aide-de-camp, Prince Volkonsky. Shuvalov urgently begged Alexander to appoint another commander-in-chief 'or Russia will be lost'. That evening Alexander summoned a special committee of six generals, headed by Arakcheev and Saltykov. He left them to study the reports from the war zone and to advise him who should be given command of the armies. After three and a half hours of discussion they signed a resolution which unanimously proposed the appointment of Kutuzov, the popular idol of Moscow and St Petersburg and the true Russian father figure revered by the rank and file of the army at large.[17] Their choice did not surprise Alexander – 'I found everybody in Petersburg crying out to give old Kutuzov the chief command', he explained later[18] – but it could scarcely please him. It was hard to forget the humiliations of the Austerlitz campaign.

For three days Alexander hesitated. He seems to have considered appointing Bennigsen, or inviting Bernadotte to cross the Baltic and lead the armies against his old compatriots. Perhaps Alexander toyed again with the idea of once more putting himself at the head of his troops. His mind was made up by three letters: one from the Governor-General of Moscow; one from the Grand Duchess, who had moved from Tver to Yaroslavl for her confinement; and the third from her husband, George of Oldenburg. Rostopchin simply informed the Tsar that in Moscow, too, everyone was eager to see Kutuzov given the supreme command.[19] Prince George, having just received news from headquarters in Smolensk, supported the claims of Bagration whom, he insisted, 'the army longs to serve under, even if you do not like him yourself'.[20] Catherine agreed with her husband but her criticisms went deeper: 'If things go on like this', she wrote bluntly, 'the enemy will be in Moscow in ten days' time. George points out one way for you and there are others besides, but in God's name do not choose to command in person yourself. It is essential to appoint, without delay, a leader in whom the troops have confidence, and on that score you inspire none at all . . . I beg you to forgive me if my letter causes you displeasure and will only plead my good intentions and personal devotion which you can never hold in doubt.'[21]

Alexander forgave her; but nothing would induce him to give the supreme command to Bagration. He had long distrusted him and was still incensed by his apparent disobedience to the strategic plan in July. If it was really necessary to hand over the army to an Austerlitz veteran, better Kutuzov than Bagration, for at least the 'old fox' might delegate decisions of importance to Bennigsen. Hence, on 20 August, Alexander at last sent for Kutuzov who, since returning from the Turkish Front, had been organizing the militia in the capital. A decree nominating him commander-in-chief was signed that same day. Bennigsen would serve him as chief-of-staff, Barclay de Tolly and Bagration were confirmed in their respective army commands, and Barclay remained nominally Minister of War. It was a cumbersome arrangement, though a popular one with the men in the field. 'A true Russian exorcized the evil genius of the foreigners', wrote the Prussian Colonel, Karl von Clausewitz, with heavy irony.[22] But was it already too late? Kutuzov did not reach Barclay's headquarters until 29 August. By then Napoleon's Grand Army had passed through the burning wreck of Smolensk and captured Vyazma, little more than one hundred and fifty miles from Moscow. Time was running out for Russia: in less than seven weeks Barclay had retreated over five hundred miles.

Bernadotte; General Wilson; and Germaine de Staël

'People wanted his appointment: I named him. As for me, I wash my hands of it', Alexander is reported to have told one of his closest friends before Kutuzov left the capital.[23] These words show a lack of responsibility at variance with Alexander's whole approach to the campaign, yet there is no doubt he was angry at the pressures brought to bear on him, and he may well have made some such remark in a fit of pique. Certainly he did not wait to give the new commander-in-chief a detailed directive. He had already undertaken to make a visit to Finland for talks on the general situation in Europe with Bernadotte, the Prince Royal of Sweden, and he set out for the Gulf of Bothnia as soon as the decree nominating Kutuzov was published.

The meeting, which took place at Äbo (now Turku), created great interest. As usual on such occasions, it produced a fine crop of rumours.[24] It was said Alexander had offered Bernadotte a high Russian command with the possibility that, should he eventually liberate Paris from the Corsican, there would be no better candidate for the French throne. But, whatever may have been discussed in private, the public results of the meeting were meagre: an undertaking that the Swedes would not enter the war against Russia and would indeed ally with Alexander, provided the Russians assisted the Swedes with an attack on French-held Zealand and recognized the eventual cession of Norway to Sweden as compensation for the loss of Finland. Bernadotte also offered to police Finland with Swedish troops so as to relieve the Russian garrisons for service elsewhere, but the Tsar was not inclined to assist the Swedish army to return to territory seized from it by his own troops only three years previously. Alexander was accompanied to Äbo by Rumiantsev as well as by Nesselrode, but the principal discussions were conducted by the Tsar himself rather than his ministers. The main consequence of the Äbo meeting was thus the sealing of the friendship between Alexander and Bernadotte: the Tsar assured Lord Cathcart, the new British ambassador (whom Alexander first met at Äbo) that 'he was fully satisfied of the zeal and of the generous and loyal principles of the Prince Royal.'[25] This, as far as it went, was satisfactory; but it did not bring any Swedish aid across the Baltic to relieve the pressure on Kutuzov. Although it was no doubt valuable to be told by a Marshal of France that retreat in depth would 'exhaust the enemy' and 'worry the French soldier', some of Alexander's companions wondered not unnaturally in whose interest Bernadotte was tendering such sound advice. Loyalties and friendships changed these days with disconcerting rapidity.

The point was not lost on Alexander when he returned to St Petersburg on 3 September. Five years previously he had ordered the expulsion from his Empire of the British General, Sir Robert Wilson, who had repaid the Tsar's hospitality by clumsy patriotic intriguing against the Tilsit policy. Since then General Wilson had acquired a European reputation as an expert on Russia at war: his *Brief Remarks on the Character and Composition of the Russian Army* was published in 1810 and was studied by the military specialists of the age, including Napoleon himself. When, in the spring of 1812, it became obvious that war would be renewed between Russia and France, Wilson was sent by the British government from Turkey to the Russian Front, where he arrived in time to witness the fall of Smolensk But politics were always as fascinating to Wilson as war and within two weeks of returning to Russia he was again revelling in the intrigues of the high command.[26] He was sent to St Petersburg by officers at headquarters with a request he should inform the Tsar that 'if His Majesty would no longer give his confidence to advisers whose policy they mistrusted, they would testify their allegiance by exertions and sacrifices which would add splendour to the crown and security to the throne under every adversity.' When Alexander heard that Wilson had arrived in the capital during his absence in Finland, he at once invited him to dinner, asked his impressions of the army, and was duly given the message which the officers had entrusted to 'the English General' (as Wilson always referred to himself in his memoirs).[27]

Alexander treated this arrogant display of insolence with admirable restraint. Wilson describes how the Tsar went red in the face and stood in silence looking out of a window for several minutes. Then he calmly thanked Wilson for the message and told him he would consider it. It was clear to him that the officers (and no doubt the English General himself)

wished to get rid of the Chancellor, Rumiantsev, and other survivors
from the years of the Tilsit Peace. But Alexander had already bowed to
the popular will twice in five months: once when he exiled Speransky to
Nizhni Novgorod, and a second time when he appointed Kutuzov
commander-in-chief. He was not prepared to give way yet again, especially
since Rumiantsev's influence on affairs since his illness at Vilna was slight
and his duties as Chancellor purely formal. Alexander accordingly sent
next day for Wilson and asked him to return to headquarters: he was to
assure the officers of their sovereign's resolve not to make peace so long as
the French occupied any Russian territory. 'I would sooner let my beard
grow to the waist and eat potatoes in Siberia', the Tsar declared.[28] Meanwhile he declined to make any changes in his administration, and Rumiantsev remained nominally Chancellor for two more years.

Fortunately not all Alexander's visitors in that first week of September
were so importunate as General Wilson. Madame Germaine de Staël had two
audiences with him and found him 'a man of remarkable understanding
and information . . . modest in disposition.'[29]* Since Mme de Staël still
exercised some influence on the Prince Royal of Sweden and was about to
set out for Stockholm, Alexander used all his charm and grace on his
visitor. Her impressions of him must therefore be qualified by the fact that
he wished to enlist her services in winning over Bernadotte, but what she
says of Alexander on the eve of the great crisis of his reign is interesting
and reveals something of his character:

What first struck me in him was such an expression of goodness and dignity
that the two qualities appear inseparable, and in him form only one. I was also
very much affected with the noble simplicity with which he entered upon the
great interests of Europe, almost among the first words he addressed to me . . .
I do not believe that in the whole extent of his empire he could find a minister
better versed than himself in all that belongs to the judgment and direction of
public affairs . . . Alexander expressed to me his regret at not being a great
captain: I replied to this noble modesty, that a sovereign was much more rare

* Mme de Staël, then aged forty-six, was the only child of the great Jacques Necker,
finance minister to Louis XVI on the eve of the Revolution. The prestige of her salon in
Paris among French intellectuals earned her the early displeasure of Napoleon, intensified
by her novels and works of criticism, notably her book *De l'Allemagne* (of which he ordered
the seizure and destruction of the whole first edition in 1810). Although intensely loyal to
her concept of France, Germaine de Staël regarded Napoleon as a personal adversary and was
prepared to work with his enemies so long as they distinguished between the French people
and their sovereign. She crossed into Russia from Austria shortly before the beginning of
hostilities. Among her companions was her second son, Albert de Staël, whose real father
was Narbonne, the last envoy sent by Napoleon to Alexander.

than a general, and that the support of the public feelings of his people, by his example, was achieving the greatest victory, and the first of the kind which had ever been gained.[30]

Mme de Staël was also presented to the Empress Elizabeth, whom she describes as 'the tutelary angel of Russia', a rare 'instance of concord between power and virtue'. 'Her manners are extremely reserved', Mme de Staël wrote, 'but what she says is full of life.'[31] Small wonder if Elizabeth's behaviour seemed stiff and constrained. It cannot have been easy for her to exchange pleasantries with a French woman of letters at such a time. For, though Alexander might still enjoy escaping into grand-iose dreams, Elizabeth's feelings were more prosaic, nor was she so adept at pretending to a sentiment she did not genuinely experience. Not for her that elevated quest for perfectibility which carried Germaine de Staël sublimely from salon to salon across Europe. 'An imagination such as hers can truly find much to feed itself on here at this moment', Elizabeth reflected in a note to her mother; but she added the dry comment, 'She is spending the winter in Sweden.'[32]

Elizabeth's real thoughts were on more serious matters; for she knew that while her husband and his distinguished visitor were posturing for mutual compliments, the future of the Empire lay on the razor-edge of fate. She would not let it be believed abroad there was any weakening of will within Russia. It was difficult to get letters through to Baden but Elizabeth found a route, by way of a banking institution in Stockholm, and she kept her mother regularly informed of what was happening in Petersburg. Thus on 7 September, the day Germaine de Staël left for Sweden, Elizabeth wrote reassuringly to the Margravine:

I feel certain you are badly informed in Germany about what goes on here. Probably they have already convinced you we have fled to Siberia, while we have not in reality even left St Petersburg. We are ready for anything except negotiations. The farther Napoleon advances the less confidence he can feel in the possibility of peace. This is the unanimous view of the Emperor, of all the nation and of every class. In this respect there exists total harmony, thank God! That is something on which Napoleon never reckoned; he was wrong about that as about other matters! Every step he takes into this vast Russian land brings him closer to the abyss! We shall see how he manages to winter there![33]

Prophetic words – made especially significant by their timing. For at the head of her letter, Elizabeth wrote, '7 September, 1812, Monday at 11 o'clock in the morning'. At that very moment, nearly five hundred miles away, the armies of Kutuzov and Napoleon were locked in battle around a village 'at the twelfth verst from Mozhaisk'.[34]* His officers informed Kutuzov it was known as Borodino. Neither he, nor Alexander, had ever heard of the place.

Borodino and its Consequences

In later years Napoleon remembered the engagement west of Moscow as 'the most terrible of all my battles', a contest in which 'the French showed themselves worthy of victory and the Russians of being invincible.' At the time, however, Borodino was too tense and too close run for such a generous epigram. From six in the morning, when a hundred French cannon opened up on the left flank of the Russian defences, until four in the afternoon, when the Russians established a new line a thousand yards to the rear, the issue of the battle seemed uncertain. Indeed, at its close, both opposing commanders claimed a victory, Napoleon because his men had captured the Russian positions and Kutuzov because his army still barred the road to Moscow. Everyone was agreed on one particular only, that Borodino was a staggering shock, an artillery duel in which, for all their bravery, cavalry and infantry on both sides were no more than fodder for the cannon. The earth, people said, shook for a dozen miles around as a thousand guns thundered along the ravines. In no previous battle had there been so terrifying a volume of sound.[35]

That day over 30,000 soldiers of Napoleon's Grand Army perished. Possibly as many as 43,000 Russians died, one-third of Kutuzov's whole force. Napoleon lost ten Generals and ten Colonels, more high-ranking officers than his enemy. But among the Russians who were mortally wounded was Prince Bagration, struck by a splinter of grapeshot in the leg as he rallied the defenders within his entrenchments. Although his life lingered on for another seventeen days, the news that he had fallen spread dismay through the Russian left flank and gave the French the advantage for which they had been striving since daybreak. Yet no casualty statistics and no record of positions taken, re-taken or lost can convey the glory and horror of Borodino for both armies. When it was all over and mist and drizzle enveloped the crumpled plain, there was no elation in either camp – only weary relief mingled with apprehension that at dawn the futile folly would begin once again.

This, however, at least the troops were spared. Kutuzov dared not risk losing the rest of his men and guns by continuing the battle into a second

* A verst is 1060 metres, slightly more than five-eighths of a mile. Twelve versts were therefore approximately equivalent to 7½ miles.

day, as the Austrians had done, disastrously, at Wagram in 1809. Before the sun broke through, he began to pull back his troops towards Moscow, only seventy miles to the east. The retreat, originally planned by Barclay and reluctantly approved by the Tsar, was now confirmed by Kutuzov as the wisest course of action. To fall back on Moscow knowing it was unlikely there would be another chance to make a stand outside the city needed the calm courage and contempt for the opinion of others which Kutuzov had acquired from years of campaigning. It was as well for Alexander's reputation – and, indeed, for all Russia – that the Tsar was not present at army headquarters in these vital hours of crisis for his Empire.

News of Borodino did not reach St Petersburg until Friday morning, 11 September. It had, however, been known since late on Wednesday that a battle was imminent and Kutuzov's bulletins were awaited with lively confidence. The first report, sent on the Monday evening, was enthusiastically encouraging: there had been (so Elizabeth wrote to her mother) 'a great victory', inducing Napoleon to fall back seven miles.[36] That Friday was the feast of St Alexander Nevsky, and the Tsar announced the good news from Kutuzov in the monastic cathedral dedicated to his patron saint. St Petersburg celebrated well into the night, with peals of bells from all the churches, fireworks and chains of lanterns along the banks of the Neva and every vessel at the port illuminated for the occasion. Kutuzov was awarded a princely title, a hundred thousand silver roubles, and a Marshal's baton. At once speculation began on whether or not Napoleon was a prisoner: if so, would he be brought to the capital in an iron cage, like some captive wild beast? That, after all, was how Alexander's grandmother had treated Pugachev, who had raised the serfs in rebellion a third of a century ago.

It was only during Saturday evening that the first doubts began to spread through the city.[37] Rumour now said that Mozhaisk was in French hands. If this were true, then the invaders were heading for the low hills around Moscow. No fresh pronouncement came from the Tsar or his ministers, and elation rapidly gave place to gloom. At Court the battle of Borodino continued to be regarded as a Russian victory, one which (it was argued) would prove more costly to Napoleon as Marshal Kutuzov's manoeuvres lengthened the French line of communications. All this was very true: but it was asking much to expect the people of the capital to follow such sophisticated strategic reasoning. They could think only of the enemy pressing nearer to Holy Moscow with every day that went by. And after Moscow, would it be their turn next? Already the art treasures of the Hermitage were being packed up, as a precaution, and among the aristocrats there was a movement eastwards to lands on the fringe of Siberia, not the best of journeys in a cold and wet September with the prospect of winter to come.

According to John Quincy Adams, rumours that the French had entered Moscow began to circulate in St Petersburg on 21 September. He added, however, that it was also being said that the Grand Army was 'repulsed and the Emperor Napoleon mortally wounded'.[38] Alexander had a clearer picture of what was happening, but kept the knowledge to himself. Since despatches from Kutuzov were ominously slow in getting through to the capital, the Tsar learnt the fate of Moscow from his sister. A letter written by Catherine in Yaroslavl late on the very day Napoleon rode into the Kremlin (15 September) reached Alexander on the morning of 18 September, more than forty-eight hours before Kutuzov's personal aide, Colonel Michaud, arrived to explain the Marshal's movements.[39] The Tsar assured Catherine by letter and Michaud by word of his determination to fight on, but he would not permit the authorities to announce the fall of Moscow in an official bulletin. This was a mistake, for with private messages seeping through, the rumours grew more and more extravagant and morale rapidly declined. Several people were made to sweep the streets as punishment for spreading alarming tales about events in Moscow. But nobody was fooled by this heavy-handed activity, and the city sank into sullen silence.[40]

On Sunday, 27 September, Alexander was faced by one of the ceremonial occasions in the Court calendar, the eleventh anniversary of his coronation. This year he dared not risk riding on horseback to the Kazan Cathedral in the Nevsky Prospect. He accompanied Elizabeth in a closed carriage through streets which, to his attendants, had never seemed so ominously hostile. There was no greeting from the crowd as he descended from the carriage and climbed the granite stairway towards the huge portico through which he had passed in procession at the cathedral's dedication, exactly twelve months before. Now everything was silent, and the footsteps of the Imperial party resounded dully from the arc of the great colonnade. 'Never shall I forget those minutes', wrote Roxane Stourdza, one of Elizabeth's ladies-in-waiting. 'We ascended the cathedral steps between two ranks of onlookers who did not give a single cheer . . . I happened to glance at the Tsar and, sensing the agony of spirit he was undergoing, I felt my knees begin to tremble beneath me.'[41]

Two days later it was, at last, officially announced that Moscow had been evacuated although, as Adams wrote in his journal, 'it is attenuated into a circumstance of trifling importance as to the ultimate issue of the war.' And on the following Friday the people of the capital were told that St Petersburg was 'in no danger of being taken by the enemy' and that they should not be alarmed by the sight of packing cases outside the Hermitage 'and the public offices'.[42] This was hardly reassuring. The one person in society who seems to have breathed confidence wherever he went was Lord Cathcart, the British ambassador, who having survived the accidental overturning of his carriage on the last stage of his journey to the capital, was convinced his mission would be a success and promptly took a three-year lease on his official residence.[43] Few around him in the diplomatic corps shared his optimism: most, at the best, anticipated a negotiated settlement with the French.

Plain Speaking from a Sister

The four weeks which followed the strange scene at the Kazan Cathedral were, to a man of Alexander's pride and sensitivity, a period of prolonged mental anguish. He spent most of the month on Kammionyi Island, and for much of the time he was physically ill with erysipelas of the leg, a condition no doubt aggravated by nervous tension. He refused to consider peace feelers from Napoleon in Moscow, and would not even answer a letter from Napoleon which disclaimed French responsibility for the burning of the city: 'A single note from Your Majesty would have stopped my campaign, either before or after the last battle', Napoleon wrote.[44] But Alexander reiterated his pledge not to make peace so long as the enemy remained on Russian soil. 'My people and I stand united as never before', Alexander wrote to Bernadotte, 'and we would rather perish under the ruins than make peace with the modern Attila'.[45] And Elizabeth told her mother on 6 October, 'I can assure you the Tsar's resolution is unshakeable. Even should Petersburg suffer the fate of Moscow, even then he would never consider the possibility of a shameful peace.'[46]

Alexander, poor man, was not allowed to rest and recuperate on Kammionyi Island untroubled by his family. No accident of war had the good fortune to impede couriers hastening between the Grand Duchess Catherine in Yaroslavl and her brother; and, since the birth of her second son on 14 August, her masterly nature broke all restraint. Never, before or after, was she so markedly Catherine the Would-Be-Great. On 18 September she despatched one of her sterner letters of admonition to Alexander:

It is impossible for me to remain silent any longer despite the pain my words will cause you, dear friend. The capture of Moscow has brought the exasperation of the people to a head: discontent has reached a climax, and you yourself are far from being spared. If that is apparent to me, judge for yourself how it appears to others. You are openly blamed for the misfortunes of your Empire, for ruin general and particular, in fact for having lost your country's honour and your own. All classes combine to accuse you. Without listing what is said about our way of making war, one of the principal counts against you is that you broke faith with Moscow, which awaited your coming with desperate longing; you look as if you betrayed it. You need have no fear of a disaster of a revolutionary kind, certainly not! But I leave you to judge the state of affairs in a country whose ruler is despised . . . It does not come within my duties to tell you what you should do; but you must safeguard your honour which is under attack.[47]

And lest the Tsar failed to hear the bark of his twenty-four-year-old sister, good George yapped obediently at her heels: 'Hold fast to your people's respect', he wrote in a separate letter. 'Think of your glorious name.'[48]

Alexander replied to these extraordinarily brash communications with skill and dignity on 30 September. He dealt point by point with the matters which Catherine had raised: he knew his soldiers never doubted his courage and honour under fire; if he left the army after the Drissa episode, this was in part in answer to the entreaties of Catherine and her husband; and if he had not come back to Moscow after appointing Kutuzov, the reason was because of his commitments to meet Bernadotte and because Rostopchin and Kutuzov had asked him to delay his return until 'they were able to give me good news'. He then, at last, let Catherine know the warnings he received in April that Napoleon planned to use her in intrigues against himself, discrediting him in the eyes of his subjects and his family. 'The signal for all these conspiracies would be given on the day when one of the two capitals should fall into the hands of the enemy', he wrote. 'Here in St Petersburg I become every day more convinced of the accuracy of the warnings given to me and what you say in your latest letter contributes in no small measure to prove it.' Alexander did not specify whom he believed to be 'the real concoctors, Napoleon's tools'. He treated the whole affair with calm detachment: 'That people should be unjust to someone in misfortune, that they should overwhelm him with abuse and tear his reputation to shreds is only to be expected. I have never deceived myself on that point', he said, adding sadly, 'Perhaps I am even bound to lose friends on whom I most counted.' But he signed his letter, 'Yours in heart and soul, both of you, always', and he enclosed presents for the month-old baby.[49]

Catherine refused to be crushed. Though assuring her brother once more of her 'endless devotion', she claimed that had he come to Moscow the city would never have fallen to the French; and she told him sharply not to listen to slanderous tales by people eager to drag in Napoleon's name to cover their own surmises.[50] Why would he not send George to command an army at the Front? This, of course, was out of the question so long as both Alexander and Constantine were prepared to leave the war to the professional soldiers. Even Marie Feodorovna, so long Catherine's champion, was annoyed. 'I don't know what Katya wants', she remarked to Elizabeth, 'she has the finest provinces in Russia and still she is not content.'[51]

But suddenly Catherine's tone changed. On 25 September she heard that Bagration had died from the wounds he sustained at Borodino. Her memory returned to the days when she was nineteen and he the dashing commander of the Pavlovsk garrison. It was not, however, romantic sentiment that mellowed her mood. She had a request for her brother. 'You remember', she wrote to Alexander, 'the relations I had with him and that I told you he holds papers which could cruelly compromise me should they fall into strange hands. He swore to me a hundred times that he had destroyed them, but what I know of his character has always made me doubt it . . . I beg you have his papers sealed up and handed over to you so that I can recover those which belong to me.'[52] And Alexander, in the middle of his sorrows for gutted Moscow and his doubts of Kutuzov's strategy, was forced to attend to his sister's embarrassment. A special emissary was despatched to the province of Vladimir to secure Bagration's papers and preserve what was left of her good name.

At the end of the first week in October Alexander was able to reassure Catherine. 'Tell me, dearest friend, is it possible for anyone to love you more than I do?' he asked, with justifiable complacency, as he let her know he had carried out her request.[53] And four days later Catherine wrote back from Yaroslavl, 'It would be a sin in the eyes of God to doubt my devotion to you.'[54]* The intensity of their mutual affection ruled out further talk of plots to depose the one in favour of the other. Nor is there any evidence whom the Tsar suspected of being 'Napoleon's tool' in these alleged intrigues. Henceforth, however, both brother and sister shared an antipathy towards Rostopchin, formerly Catherine's protegé, and their prejudice may not entirely have sprung from the burning of Moscow.

* Catherine's panic was unnecessary. Her letters were not among Bagration's papers and she concluded he had indeed burnt them after her marriage.

Alexander refuses to make Peace

While these curious exchanges were passing between St Petersburg and Yaroslavl, Marshal Kutuzov and the main Russian army were encamped fifty-five miles south-west of Moscow around the twin villages of Tarutino and Letacheva. The Marshal intended to wait throughout the autumn for a favourable moment to attack the French: he was astride the old road from Moscow to Kaluga and was little more than sixty miles from Tula, the principal Russian ordnance centre. He had every hope of reinforcements in men and weapons reaching him from the south, while partisan detachments were beginning to raid the long line of Napoleon's communications back to his forward base in Vilna and his depots in Poland and Germany. Meanwhile, there was an unofficial truce around Moscow. Individual Russian commanders exchanged courtesies and gifts with Murat and Marshal Bessières. Napoleon himself did not approve of such fraternization, but he was gratified to learn from Murat that the Russians appeared eager for peace. This confirmed his own convictions. It seemed, however, strange to him that no messenger had as yet reached Moscow from Alexander with a proposal for negotiations.[55]

By the beginning of October there was still no word from St Petersburg and Napoleon was becoming increasingly uneasy at his position. He could not winter in Moscow for, quite apart from the destruction caused to the city by the fire, it would be impossible to continue governing the French Empire from improvised headquarters on what was to him the outer fringe of Asia. To his Marshals he proposed a re-grouping of the army which would enable him to shift his point of concentration northwards so as to threaten St Petersburg. They thought the project impracticable. More and more Napoleon was anxious to dictate peace while still holding 'the political position of Moscow', to use his own phrase. On 3 October he sent for Caulaincourt, who had accompanied him across Europe from Dresden, and asked him to set out for St Petersburg. 'You would see the Tsar Alexander. I would entrust you with a letter and you would make peace.' But Caulaincourt argued that his arrival in the Russian capital would merely convince the Tsar of the weakness of the French position, and he advised Napoleon not to place any confidence in the influence he had once enjoyed at Court as ambassador and friend. As an alternative, Napoleon sent for Caulaincourt's successor, Lauriston, and ordered him to go to Kutuzov's headquarters and seek a safe-conduct for St Petersburg. 'I wish for peace. I must have it. I need it at all costs except my honour', Napoleon declared to Lauriston.[56]

At midnight on 5–6 October Kutuzov received Lauriston. He said nothing about a safe-conduct to the capital (an idea Lauriston disliked as much as Caulaincourt) and he refused the French proposal for an immediate armistice pending negotiations, but he agreed to send Prince Volkonsky to St Petersburg with a copy of the letter Napoleon had written to the Tsar. Napoleon was well satisfied with what Lauriston had achieved. He was sure Alexander, like himself, was seeking peace with honour and that he had now taken the necessary diplomatic initiative to end the campaign. 'When they receive my letter in Petersburg, they will celebrate with bonfires', he declared.[57]

Once more, however, he was wrong. Volkonsky arrived in the capital on 16 October to find Alexander back in residence at the Winter Palace. The Tsar read Kutuzov's account of his talk with Lauriston and the copy of Napoleon's message. He was far from pleased. 'Peace?' Alexander declared to Volkonsky. 'But as yet we have not made war. My campaign is only just beginning.' He would not deign to acknowledge Napoleon's message, but sent Volkonsky back to Kutuzov five days later with orders that there should be no more parleying with the French: peace was impossible so long as the enemy was on Russian territory.[58]

As Caulaincourt and Lauriston had predicted, the knowledge that Napoleon was anxious for negotiations heartened Alexander, even if he rebuked Kutuzov for holding conversations with Napoleon's envoys without authority. 'The peace party about the Court' was said to be 'growing stronger', Adams noted in his journal on 21 October, though he thought 'this information . . . extremely questionable'.[59] After Volkonsky's report, however, Alexander was not in the least interested in seeking terms from the French. He was confident there would soon be good news from the battle fronts.

It began to reach him even before the end of the week. On 24 October the first reports arrived in St Petersburg of a substantial victory by Wittgenstein's corps at Polotsk, menacing the northern flank of Napoleon's main line of communication. On the same day came news that Kutuzov had resumed operations against Murat's vanguard south-west of Moscow and that Cossack patrols had even entered the streets of the old capital. Two days later there was an impressive *Te Deum* to celebrate this beginning of the counter-offensive. Adams noted in his journal that the storming of Polotsk had accomplished a 'change from despondency to confidence'.[60]

But the most welcome news of all only reached St Petersburg at noon on

27 October: for it was then that salvoes from the ceremonial cannon at the fortress of St Peter and St Paul let the people of the capital know that Moscow had been retaken by the Russians and Napoleon was in retreat.'At last God Almighty is leading us forwards', wrote Elizabeth that night to her mother.[61] Next day Alexander, Elizabeth, Marie Feodorovna, the Grand Dukes Constantine, Nicholas and Michael and the Grand Duchess Anna, together with all the ministers of the government and all the diplomatic corps, went once again to the Kazan Cathedral to give thanks to God for the deliverance of Moscow. 'The music of the *Te Deum* was remarkably fine', noted Adams, who was not by nature sympathetic to religious ceremonial, and he added in his journal, 'When the Emperor left the church to return to the palace, he was greeted with three shouts by the crowd of people who surrounded the church.'[62] It was only a month and a day since the terrifying silence of the Coronation anniversary.

Napoleon had, in fact, left Moscow on 19 October, originally striking south along the Kaluga road with the intention of inflicting a defeat on Kutuzov and, if the weather held out, destroying the arms centre of Tula before retiring on Smolensk. Although he was withdrawing from Moscow, he was not as yet technically in retreat and he was already considering how to regroup his armies for the assault on St Petersburg in the spring of 1813, assuming of course that the Tsar had not, in the intervening months, had the good sense to seek peace. For Napoleon the decisive day was yet to come. On 24 October a predominantly Italian Corps of the Grand Army, commanded by Napoleon's stepson Eugène Beauharnais, disputed possession of the small town of Maloyaroslavets with a force of some 15,000 Russians under General Docturov. In the end the town was captured by Eugène's men and Napoleon's bulletin subsequently claimed a victory. So, for that matter, did Kutuzov; and this time strategically he was fully justified in so doing.[63] For Maloyaroslavets showed the limits of Napoleon's power. He could not bring the main Russian army to battle for it was impossible to exploit Eugène's success. Instead, Napoleon's Marshals almost unanimously urged him to head at once for Mozhaisk and Smolensk rather than pursue the elusive Kutuzov along the Kaluga road. And on 26 October, he turned north-westwards, away from the Russians at last.

When, six days later, Alexander heard of Maloyaroslavets and of the French withdrawal he did not immediately assume the tide had turned. He had far too healthy a respect for Napoleon's military genius to make a snap judgement of this kind. Perhaps, too, he tended to treat Kutuzov's reports with discretion. He certainly seems to have given greater credence to bulletins from Wittgenstein's sector than from the commander-in-chief. For much of November Alexander was content to remain quietly in his study, assessing the reports and messages which came to him and running his eye over the maps which his staff provided. By now he had also a new occupation for the mind.[64] During the black weeks of October he had been impressed by the religious fortitude of three close companions: his wife, Elizabeth; his old friend, Prince Alexander Golitsyn, once a notorious rake; and young Rodion Koshelev, the cavalry officer he had employed on diplomatic missions to Vienna and who was now Grand Master of the Court. From these three friends Alexander discovered the comfort and inspiration of turning in hours of crisis to the Scriptures. He read the Psalms, he read the Old Testament prophets, he remembered the moments in Moscow when he had felt uplifted by a religious experience, and he grafted on to his Orthodox mysticism some of the zeal for truth in God of Protestant fundamentalism. It made a powerful combination. 'I simply devoured the Bible', Alexander said later, 'finding that its words poured an unknown peace into my heart and quenched the thirst of my soul. Our Lord, in His infinite kindness, inspired me in order to permit me to understand what I was reading.'[65] Thus it was with the prophecies of Isaiah, Jeremiah and Ezekiel before him that Alexander watched the Lord confounding His enemies on the freezing Russian plain.

For within a week of receiving Kutuzov's account of Maloyaroslavets, Alexander could see from the palace window great blocks of ice floating down the Neva. The temperature dropped suddenly in St Petersburg on the night of 7–8 November and, a couple of days later, sledges were passing over the snow in the streets and the canals were frozen over. The severity of the snowfall surprised people: winter was coming more than a fortnight earlier than in the two previous years.[66] Away from the Baltic zone, in the unbroken countryside west of Viazma, it was hard going for the armies. There the snow began to fall on 4 November and within forty-eight hours a blizzard was blowing on the retreating troops as they struggled to reach Smolensk. It was rarely possible to see more than a hundred yards ahead and there was always the danger of tumbling into drifts.[67] Conditions were terrifying, not only for Napoleon, but for Kutuzov, whose cavalry had been harassing the flank of the Grand Army constantly. Momentarily the blizzards put an end to operations. But to those who studied the map at headquarters or in St Petersburg, the suspension of fighting mattered little. For to Alexander and his staff it seemed as if Napoleon was stumbling back into a trap. In the north, Wittgenstein had already retaken Vitebsk, while to the south-west

Chichagov, with the combined forces of what had once been his 'Army of Moldavia' and Tormassov's 'Third Army', was advancing eastwards on Minsk. Three Russian armies were thus converging on Napoleon, heading for the long line of the river Berezina. There, surely, the French would be encircled – if, that is, they had not already been destroyed by the Cossacks and the cavalry, or by the ravages of winter.[68]

Momentarily Alexander thought he would himself once more take to the field. He told Catherine on 20 November that he intended to leave St Petersburg in a few days and join Wittgenstein who, he explained, 'according to the plan now being carried out, will link up with Chichagov's army and, facing about, will thus become the first line while the main army will become the second line'.[69] It is not clear why he gave up this idea. Possibly it was no more than an impulse. His leg was still troubling him and the blizzards made it difficult to get through to Novgorod, let alone to Wittgenstein's advance headquarters in Vitebsk. Moreover there was a real need for the Tsar to remain in touch with affairs at the centre of his Empire. By now encouraging reports were coming through from the battle area: it was clear that on 17 November, at Krasnoe, Napoleon had been nearly captured and that Ney and Davout had been badly mauled; and there were also strange rumours from beyond the frontiers. As Alexander was going to bed on 21 November he received a message from Kutuzov saying that his troops had captured a French General who told him a revolution had broken out in Paris, forcing the Empress Marie Louise to flee the capital. This tale was presumably based upon garbled reports of Malet's abortive conspiracy a month previously, of which Napoleon had been informed on 6 November.[70] Although these stories of dissension within France were vastly exaggerated, they excited Alexander considerably. With Marshal Davout's captured baton on display to the curious in the Kazan Cathedral there could no longer be any doubt that the enemy was in full flight towards the frontier. 'The Lord Almighty', he declared to Catherine in his new apocalyptic style, 'is sending down upon the head of Napoleon the very ills he destined for us.'[71]

By the first week in December there was once again a mood of exultant expectancy in St Petersburg. It seemed, wrote Adams, 'morally impossible' that the remnant of the Grand Army would escape the trap the Russians were springing on the Berezina.[72] But, as after Borodino, there was a sudden absence of news, which seemed ominous to the doubters. On 8–9 December the city was full of contradictory rumours: that the Russians had gained a striking victory over Napoleon, whose body was found on the field of battle; that two Russian armies had been utterly defeated; that Chichagov had been unable to halt Napoleon, who had out-paced his pursuers. At last it became clear that the third report was nearest to the truth. The French had deceived Chichagov by an elaborate diversion when they reached the Berezina near Borisov and between the afternoon of 26 November and 28–29 November some 50,000 men were able to cross the river and head north-westwards towards Vilna and the Prussian frontier. But Wittgenstein and Kutuzov were so close upon their heels that the improvised bridges over the river had to be destroyed before all the stragglers had made the crossing. Hence, although Napoleon had escaped, the French losses had been considerable: the Grand Army was now no better than a fugitive horde.

Alexander was disappointed that Napoleon had made his escape. He blamed Kutuzov for not having moved decisively both at Krasnoe and east of Borisov. But already by the time news of what had happened at the Berezina reached Petersburg, Napoleon had left the soil of Russia; he abandoned what remained of his army at Smorgonie on the evening of 5 December and set out on an eleven-hundred-mile journey to Paris, accompanied only by Caulaincourt and a Polish interpreter.[73] It was during these final days of the French retreat that the cold was cruellest, the temperature falling at times to twenty-five degrees of frost. Harassed by Cossacks and partisans, the residue of the Grand Army fell back through Vilna to the river Niemen. On 13 December the shattered rearguard under Marshal Ney finally crossed into Prussia at Kaunas: nearly half a million men of the Grand Army failed to return from Russia.

That same day Kutuzov entered Vilna. It was a city he knew well as he had twice commanded the garrison there but, though it had suffered little damage from the war, it was now scarcely recognizable. 'The town looked like some Tartar hell, everywhere appalling dirt and smells', wrote one of the Prussians serving on his staff.[74] The Marshal was acutely conscious of the danger of disease, but he was also anxious to find somewhere for his troops to recuperate after the pursuit through the snows. He had informed Alexander as early as 7 December of the total weariness of the regular troops, and his first despatch reporting the capture of Vilna again emphasized the privations which the Russian soldiers had endured in the previous five weeks.[75] Yet from St Petersburg it seemed to the Tsar as if Kutuzov must be exaggerating, and he could not hold himself back any longer. Even before Borodino he had resolved to carry the war across his frontiers and into Germany, as he had told the British ambassador at the end of August.[76] Now it was intolerable for Kutuzov to be complaining that the army needed rest and re-organizing. Clearly it was essential to see for himself the true state of affairs on the frontier. In the small hours of 19 December Alexander set out from the Winter Palace for Vilna once more. He was not to return to his capital for another eighteen months, and by then Napoleon would be immured on the island of Elba.

15

Tsar With a Mission

Vilna Again (December 1812–January 1813)

Travelling rapidly across the snows by sledge or by troika Alexander reached Vilna before daybreak on 23 December. 'It has cost me the end of my nose to come here', he remarked ruefully after the bitterly cold journey, but it was obvious to everyone around that he was glad to be back at headquarters.[1] He embraced Kutuzov, accepted from him the ceremonial surrender of captured flags and trophies, and bestowed on him the Star and Cross in diamonds of the Order of St George, highest of all Russia's military honours. Together sovereign and soldier shed tears of gratitude and relief. In public there was no sign of tension or mistrust between them. Whatever Alexander might say privately to his friends and ministers, he did not wish to lower Kutuzov's standing with the rank and file in the army. They needed a wise protector to idolize if they were to continue unflinchingly to wage the winter war.

Outwardly Alexander had changed little since he was last in the city. He still enjoyed taking tea with the ladies of the Polish nobility, even though almost all of them had fathers or brothers serving Napoleon. As in the summer he could on most days attend the principal parade in the city square, according his troops the traditional greeting, 'How are you faring, my children?' and receiving back a reply in unison, 'We are well, Sire, and Your Majesty?' So familiar was his pattern of life that it seemed natural to honour his birthday on 24 December by a ball in the Episcopal Palace, and Kutuzov duly instructed his aides to organize the festivities. Alexander himself did not wish to be the centre of personal celebrations at a time of national suffering. Yet he could not prevent the ball being held, and once there he seems to have had little difficulty in helping to make it a success. He danced again with the young Countess Tiesenhausen, whom he had last partnered at Zakret that memorable night six months before. 'You will be surprised ... to find me here at a ball', he remarked to her apologetically. 'But what could I do? I had to please that old fellow'; and he glanced towards Kutuzov, the nominal host for the evening. It was convenient, in small matters and great, to place the responsibility on shoulders long accustomed to changes of fortune. 'The old fellow ought to be contented', Alexander mused. 'The cold weather has rendered him a splendid service.'[2]

Yet in reality deep differences of outlook separated the Tsar and his Marshal. Alexander returned to Vilna determined to resume the role of Europe's liberator which he had sought to play prematurely seven years previously. He was now a Tsar with a sense of mission. Even Rumiantsev, appeaser though he was by nature, caught the new spirit: 'Heaven has chosen you to accomplish its designs', he wrote to his master from St Petersburg, 'revealing already your destiny, that you shall save Europe.'[3] But Kutuzov was cautious. He did not for one moment doubt continuation of the war would lead to the final downfall of Napoleon, but only if the Russians were strong in men and material. According to General Wilson, who was attached to Kutuzov's headquarters throughout the pursuit of Napoleon, the army suffered 45,000 casualties in the final four weeks before entering Vilna, and modern Soviet historians reckoned that only a third of Kutuzov's men were fit for active military service at the close of the year.[4] Kutuzov therefore wished to wait until the thousands of recruits marshalling in Russia had reached headquarters. He was not opposed to Alexander's mission, although he was naturally less interested in the general affairs of Europe than the non-Russians who had entered the Tsar's service; but he was convinced the army should not cross the frontier into Prussia in the depth of winter.

Alexander, however, had no intention of listening to Kutuzov. He was encouraged by the Prussian exile Stein who had already written urging him 'to deliver the human race from the most absurd and degrading of tyrannies', and he genuinely believed the Russians should strike while the enemy was still in confusion.[5] There was good sense in this argument, for the Cossacks and the militia units were better able to give battle under winter conditions than in the spring, when climate and terrain would favour troops from western and southern Europe. The Germans at Alexander's headquarters, both soldiers and civilians, argued that their compatriots were eager to change sides and turn against the French provided they could count on adequate Russian protection from counter-measures. Moreover, although Kutuzov was exhausted and anxious to rest both himself and his troops, Wittgenstein was still pursuing the enemy columns along the banks of the lower Niemen and had every intention of crossing into Prussia as soon as possible. Alexander warmly approved of Wittgenstein's initiative, as indeed he had done throughout the campaign: here at least was a General after his own heart. 'Thank Heavens everything here is going well', Alexander wrote to Saltykov once he had assessed the situation at Vilna. 'It is proving a little difficult to dispose of the Prince Marshal, but it is absolutely essential to do so.'[6]

Events played admirably into Alexander's hands. On 30 December General Hans von Yorck, commanding the Prussian contingent in what remained of the Grand Army, concluded a military convention at Tauroggen (Taurage) with the Russian General Diebitsch, a corps commander serving under Wittgenstein.[7] The actual terms of the convention were limited and precise: the Prussians would police the salient of territory around the mouth of the Niemen, southwards from Memel, and would offer no opposition to the Russian army; but the significance of this pledge of neutrality influenced events over a far larger area, for it made it virtually impossible for the French to retain any hold on East Prussia and they rapidly evacuated the city of Königsberg, though preparing to withstand a siege in Danzig rather than surrender so vital a port.

Alexander learnt of the Tauroggen Convention when one of Wittgenstein's aides arrived in Vilna on 4 January.[8] Immediately the Tsar decided to exploit the signs of weakness in the French hold on Germany. He sent the ardent Prussian patriot General von Boyen on a secret mission to King Frederick William with the offer of an offensive and defensive alliance, and he also encouraged Stein to issue an appeal to the King which urged him to break with Napoleon and call on his subjects to liberate themselves in partnership with the advancing Russians. Finally on 9 January Alexander left Vilna and prepared to carry the war into Europe. He established temporary headquarters down the Niemen at Meritz and it was from there that, three days later, he ordered his army westwards across the Niemen and into Prussia. By the Russian calendar it was the first day of the New Year, 1813; and a proclamation from Kutuzov called on Alexander's troops 'to liberate from oppression and misery even those nations who have taken up arms against Russia'.[9]

The Liberation of Prussia

For eleven weeks fortune favoured Alexander's cause. The French hurriedly retired westwards to shorten their lines. By the beginning of February Wittgenstein, in the north, was approaching the Oder while Alexander's headquarters were on the river Wrkra. Eugène Beauharnais, left in command by Napoleon, found it impossible to hold Poznan and by the second week in February was desperately trying to establish lines around Frankfurt-on-Oder, having retreated three hundred miles in a mere thirty days. But still the Russian advance went on: Wittgenstein sent off three small free corps to raid across Pomerania and into Mecklenburg, one of which startled all Europe by occupying Hamburg on 18 March. Meanwhile Eugène was forced to withdraw even from Berlin and fell back on Magdeburg and the central line of the Elbe. Politically this apparent collapse of the Napoleonic hold on central and eastern Germany led to a rapid strengthening of the Allies: the Prussians and the Swedes entered the war against France; and the Austrians (who had participated in the 1812 Campaign with as little enthusiasm as the Prussians) ordered their troops back to Galicia and concluded an armistice with the local Russian commanders. It seemed likely that the Austrians too would join the Allies, if, that is, Metternich could not induce the rival belligerents to accept an offer of mediation.[10]

Alexander went forward with his army in a state bordering on religious ecstasy. More and more he turned to the eleventh chapter of the Book of Daniel with the apocalyptic vision of how the all-conquering King of the South is cast down by the King of the North. It seemed to him as if the prophecies, which had sustained him during the dark days of autumn and early winter, were now to be fulfilled: Easter this year would come with a new spiritual significance of hope for all Europe. 'Placing myself firmly in the hands of God I submit blindly to His will', he informed his friend Golitsyn from Radzonow, on the Wrkra. 'My faith is sincere and warm with passion. Every day it grows firmer and I experience joys I had never known before . . . It is difficult to express in words the benefits I gain from reading the Scriptures, which previously I knew only superficially . . . All my glory I dedicate to the advancement of the reign of the Lord Jesus Christ.'[11] Nor was this mysticism confined to his private correspondence. At Kalisch (Kalisz) on the borders of the Grand-Duchy of Warsaw and Prussia the Tsar concluded a convention with Frederick William: the agreement provided for a close military alliance between Russia and Prussia, stipulating the size of their respective contingents and promising

Prussia territory as extensive as in 1806; but the final clauses went beyond the normal language of diplomacy to echo Alexander's religious inspiration. 'Let all Germany join us in our mission of liberation', the Kalisch Treaty said. 'The hour has come for obligations to be observed with that religious faith, that sacred inviolability which holds together the power and permanence of nations.'[12] Alexander was impelled across Germany by a girded energy which was almost Calvinistic in its intensity.

Those in attendance on him found it hard to understand their sovereign's extraordinary mood. Most of them were concerned with the simple task of translating vague aspirations into practical terms: Kutuzov, who possessed a peasant's uncomplicated religious faith, prepared military directives with brevity and precision; while Nesselrode (who was, rather unexpectedly, a baptized member of the Church of England*) had no sympathy for Alexander's pietism and only sought to prevent his sovereign's obsession with mystical revelation from obscuring his immediate political objectives. There was, at times, a danger that Alexander's confidence and enthusiasm would lead him to overreach himself, as Kutuzov foresaw. No one at Kalisch was able to restrain him once convinced he was obeying the will of the Almighty. When, in the second week of March, he travelled seventy miles westwards and joined Frederick William at Breslau (Wroclaw), Alexander's religious obsession became even more intensive and his correspondence was filled with as many Hosannas as the antiphons of Palm Sunday.[13] Frederick William and Alexander had not met since the death of Queen Louise and each was deeply affected, mourning her intensely while celebrating the triumphs of the new alliance against the old enemy.

Under normal conditions the one person who could have persuaded Alexander that the mantle of Elijah was cast uneasily on his shoulders was the Grand Duchess Catherine. But in these very months she was herself in a state of spiritual and physical collapse, which may in its turn have intensified her brother's introspective mysticism. For the unfortunate George of Oldenburg, Catherine's husband, had caught a fever at Tver shortly before leaving to take up the military command she had long badgered Alexander into giving him; and on 27 December he died. Catherine, a widow of twenty-four with two children, seemed at first overwhelmed with remorse, fearing that her 'restless ambition' had 'lost her everything': 'He was perfect but God in his mercy found this was too

* In the autobiographical section of his *Lettres et Papiers* Nesselrode wrote: 'My mother was a Protestant, my father a Catholic . . . I was baptized and became an Anglican for the remainder of my days' (Volume II, p. 17).

much for mortal existence, and He was right',[14] she wrote to Alexander on the day the corps which George would have commanded crossed the Niemen into Poland. And Alexander, always psychologically attuned to his sister's sweeps of emotion, felt deeply for her in these weeks of grief.

Fortunately, however, Catherine's powers of resilience were considerable. By the middle of February she was consoling herself with the thought that she always looked her best in black. A month in St Petersburg renewed her zest for intrigues, and her letters to Alexander once more show a healthy appetite for alleged slights. The Tsar, troubled by the problems of controlling foreign affairs from an obscure corner of western Poland, may even have found his sister's pleas vexatious; for on 7 March he replied to her from Kalisch with less than his customary sympathy. Patiently he informed his 'dear sweet friend' that he was not responsible for rulings over seniority at Court, the etiquette having been established by their father. He also took the opportunity to let her know why it was that in a previous note he had confessed to having 'scarcely a moment' in which to write his letters:

These last few days I have felt my head going round in circles under the burden of work that has fallen on me all at once: this alliance with the Prussians and the military rearrangements resulting from it; the arrival of General Scharnhorst and then the English ambassador; three couriers coming from Copenhagen, Stockholm and London; the arrival of the Austrian envoy, Lebzeltern, and the King of Prussia's aide-de-camp, Wrangel; finally the capture of Berlin. All these events are taking place at the same time so that I am either tied to my desk or in conference with these gentlemen. At last here I am with pen between my fingers, writing to you; and so that you may tell what things are like, I can say that it is half an hour after midnight, and that one of these men has only just left my room after having kept me talking since eight o'clock.[15]

Alexander was by now looking ahead, somewhat indistinctly, to a new ordering of the European system as well as co-ordinating military plans with Scharnhorst and the leaders of the Prussian officer corps. It was difficult for Catherine to appreciate the change in her brother's status and prestige over the past six months.

The Changing Fortunes of War (Spring 1813)

There was a grand ceremonial entry into liberated Berlin at the end of March and into Dresden on 23 April. Everywhere Alexander was greeted by cheers and by laurel wreaths, some of which he sent with suitably worded compliments to Kutuzov and his corps commanders. Nor, indeed, was all this adulation limited to the German lands. Public feeling in England and Scotland warmed to the Russians in the early months of 1813, manifesting itself both in the opening of charities for Russian relief and in less worthy enterprises, such as the publication of cheap coloured prints of 'the brave Cossacks' and the sale of an alleged 'Cossack love song'. This enthusiasm naturally sought a hero, and in popular imagination Tsar Alexander became a romantic figure who had defied the odious Bonaparte and scourged him across Europe. It was left to the widely read versifier and parodist Horatio Smith – who had amended his original Christian name 'Horace' in the year of Trafalgar – to celebrate the triumphs of Russia in a suitable metre:

> Rise children of Europe, march fearlessly forth,
> The pole-star of Liberty beams from the North,
> Be 'Vengeance' your cry, Alexander your trust,
> And Tyranny's sceptre shall crumble to dust.[16]

Such eloquence was heartening, at least to those who read English; but was it, perhaps, excessively optimistic? For to military experts it seemed unlikely that the Russians and their newly liberated allies on the continent would be allowed by the French to 'march fearlessly' much further. Napoleon was known to have given orders for the conscripts of 1813 to be summoned to the colours while he was still in Moscow; and in the second week of January he had called up conscripts for the following year as well.[17] By the spring it was therefore reasonable to anticipate he could be concentrating in Germany an army half as large again in numbers as the forces of the Allies. Who, then, would be crying 'Vengeance'?

Kutuzov foresaw this danger back in Vilna and continued to warn Alexander, even while the Russian advance seemed to be a cavalcade of victory. The crucial test came with the occupation of Berlin. Should the Allies cross the Elbe and march on Magdeburg or should they consolidate their positions and await the expected Napoleonic counter-offensive in prepared defences? Wittgenstein was certain he could penetrate deeply into Westphalia to hamper the concentration of the new French armies but Kutuzov, still commander-in-chief, wished him to leave a small defensive force between Magdeburg and Berlin, while bringing the main body of his troops into Saxony, where it was expected that Napoleon would strike his blow. 'We can cross the Elbe all right, but before long we shall cross it again with a bloody nose', Kutuzov said bluntly.[18] Wittgenstein, however, tried to combine both strategies. He crossed the Elbe successfully at Rosslau on 2 April and then swung southwards so as to link up with the Prussians under Blücher in Saxony, but the Russian casualties were heavy, and it was clear the enemy resistance was stiffening. By the third week in April both Wittgenstein and Blücher anticipated an attack by Napoleon personally in Saxony at any moment and were alarmed at their exposed position.

Alexander remained confident. He did not think Napoleon would attack until June and he doubted whether the new French levies would be capable of dislodging the Allies from the cities they had occupied earlier in the spring. So sure was Alexander of the general safety of the Allied positions that he welcomed the news that his sister Catherine was coming to Teplitz, at the start of May, to take the waters and he planned a family reunion there, with his elder sister Marie joining them from what he hoped would by then be liberated Weimar.[19] But in the last week of April Alexander was faced by what was to him, at least, a series of unexpected crises. Kutuzov suffered a stroke and died on 28 April at Bunzlau, in Prussian Silesia: the Tsar appointed Wittgenstein to succeed him as commander-in-chief but found two senior Russian Generals, Tormassov and Miloradovich, resented the promotion of a man of German origin junior in years of service to themselves; and Alexander was thus forced to put both of their corps under his personal command, leaving Wittgenstein with a predominantly Prussian force and separated from the remaining Russian units by the totally Prussian army of Blücher.[20] Such muddled dispositions invited confusion in command and ultimately disaster. It was at this point, on 30 April, that Napoleon took the initiative for the first time in six and a half months and sent the reconstituted Grand Army eastwards across the river Saale.

Napoleon's advance menaced both Leipzig and Dresden, where Alexander had celebrated the Orthodox Easter only a week previously. The two armies met on 2 May on high ground south of Lützen.[21] The position was nearly eighty miles west of Dresden but it was so strategically situated that the outcome of the battle would decide the fate of the whole of Saxony. In many respects it was an indeterminate engagement. The French suffered greater casualties than the Allies, but it was Wittgenstein and Blücher who were forced to retire and the battle was therefore technically a Napoleonic victory. Once the Russians were in retreat it was difficult for them to halt and turn about, although Miloradovich fought a brave delaying action against Eugène Beauharnais on 5 May at Colditz (where there was a fortress which was to gain notoriety in a later war). Wittgenstein hesitated on the right bank of the Elbe, for he knew that Alexander (back at headquarters in Görlitz) wished him to stand and fight with the river behind him. But Wittgenstein had no intention of repeating the mistake Bennigsen had made so disastrously at Friedland; and on 10 May the Russians re-crossed the Elbe 'with a bloody nose', as the old Marshal had predicted two months before. Napoleon was thus able to establish his advanced headquarters in Dresden, where King Frederick Augustus of Saxony, whose loyalties of late had been wavering, came down firmly and fatally on the side of the French big battalions.

The loss of Dresden chilled the faint hearts in the Allied camp. 'God in Heaven, does this then mean I must go back to Memel after all?' asked Frederick William of Prussia plaintively at the news of Napoleon's success;[22] and the Grand Duchess Catherine, who arrived in Teplitz (which is only twenty-five miles across the frontier from Dresden) on 7 May, decided she would be safer in Prague, and hurriedly had her horses re-harnessed, just in case Napoleon chose to pursue her brother into neutral Austria.[23] But in all this panic Alexander at least kept his nerve. He was furious with Wittgenstein for 'having re-crossed the Elbe . . . when we should have attacked since the enemy was near to rout'; but he did not think the general situation grave, for he was convinced the French could not exploit their gains.[24] The loss of Dresden helped him to resolve one problem. If Wittgenstein could not be relied upon to keep his head, there was no point in entrusting him with supreme command. The Tsar accordingly summoned back Barclay de Tolly, who was senior to any other Russian General in the field. Although the enemy as a whole had little respect for Barclay, he was less likely to arouse friction and resentment as commander-in-chief than anybody else now that his old rivals, Bagration and Kutuzov, were both dead.

There were, however, some anxious moments in the fourth week of May when Napoleon won another victory at Bautzen, thirty-five miles east of Dresden, and Barclay began to urge a retreat back into Poland.[25] But Alexander would have none of it. Peace was in the air. Metternich, eager to acquire status for Austria and himself, had sent two special envoys of considerable diplomatic experience to the rival headquarters in the hope that they would be able to induce Napoleon and Alexander to accept a compromise settlement, which would end the war for Europe as a whole.[26] Napoleon at heart was anxious to be rid of the whole folly of a campaign against Russia: he might have the men but he did not have the horses or guns, and supplies no longer came through from Paris with the regularity of his earlier enterprises. But Napoleon did not want to be dependent upon Austria. What he needed was a breathing-space in which he could see if it were possible to come to terms with the enemy. If it were not, he could reinforce tired regiments and replenish his ordnance. Once again he remembered Tilsit; and he sent for Caulaincourt. He was to go to Alexander's headquarters and 'rescue him from Metternich's clutches'. Napoleon was still convinced he was dealing with a man of easily impressionable character, whom anybody with a honeyed tongue could entice provided they treated him with sufficient flattery. 'If the Emperor Alexander and I could have just one talk together', Napoleon confided to Caulaincourt, 'I am certain we would end up agreeing with each other ... A single conversation at Russian headquarters and we could divide the world between us!' He was even willing to give Alexander public credit for bestowing peace on Europe, if that would please him.[27]

On 25 May Caulaincourt wrote to Nesselrode asking if he might pay his respects to Alexander and arrange an armistice between the opposing armies. But the Tsar had no intention of receiving Caulaincourt in audience. Armistice negotiations were carried on with proper diplomatic protocol between Caulaincourt and a Russian and a Prussian plenipotentiary, first at Waldstatt and later at Plaeswitz. On 4 June, after five days of bargaining, an armistice was signed: the French would retire to Liegnitz while the Allies held a line running south-westwards from Breslau to the Austrian frontier at Landshut, with a neutral corridor some thirty miles wide between the opposing armies; and all hostilities would cease for at least six weeks.[28]

Alexander was well satisfied. He preferred the pace to be set by Nesselrode rather than by the Austrians, whom he distrusted as much as did Napoleon. The Armistice of Plaeswitz was, to the Tsar, as good as a battle won, and without the cost in men and material. For the first time, in mid-summer, Napoleon had felt it necessary to halt the Grand Army short of its objectives. If this was not an admission of defeat, it was at least a concession that decisive victory was not in sight for the French; and there seemed at last a prospect of a compromise peace.

But was this what Alexander wanted? A patched-up Europe in which the French still exercised considerable power was far short of the ideals which had inspired the Tsar when his troops first entered Poland and Germany. The time had come for him to decide what sort of Europe he wished to see imposed on Napoleon when the fighting ended. The period of armistice now beginning was for Alexander – and as well for his brother sovereigns of Prussia and Austria – a hectic interlude of bluff and bargaining in which the diplomats rather than the generals held the centre of the stage.

Diplomatic Interlude (*June–August 1813*)

In earlier years Alexander had made clear his war aims with elaborate detail; but in 1813 he retained considerable freedom of action, and was reluctant to lose it. This independence was caused in part by accident: the nominal Chancellor, Rumiantsev, remained in St Petersburg 'for the sake of signing passports' (as he complained);[29] and Nesselrode was too self-effacing as yet to have a policy of his own, or to impose his opinions upon his master. Alexander was thus left to decide on policy to a greater extent than ever before in his reign. Since he had also to resolve questions of military strategy it is hardly surprising that he found no time to prepare an elaborate grand design for Europe. Necessity had induced him to offer no more than the vaguest statements on war aims; and with the British as well as the Austrians seeking to bind him to specific terms, it was natural he took advantage of his freedom from commitments to stand aside as long as possible.

He knew of course what he wanted in central Europe: expulsion of the French from Germany and the Grand-Duchy of Warsaw and the re-unification of the Polish lands under his own suzerainty. But what did he mean by 'Germany' and 'Poland'? He had at first encouraged Stein to proclaim a patriotic war for the German Fatherland, administering the territories liberated by his army; but on 25 March the Russians issued, in Kutuzov's name, an 'appeal to the princes and peoples of Germany' which, while calling for the abolition of the Napoleonic Confederation of the Rhine, fell far short of Stein's hopes for a unified German State. Similarly Alexander had given private assurances to the Austrians that he favoured restoration to Emperor Francis of the territories he had lost to Napoleon in successive wars and that he hoped the Habsburgs would again be recognized as the master dynasty in Germany once the French were expelled beyond the Rhine. All this was confusing enough: it was made no easier by the promise contained in the Prussian treaty of Kalisch that if Frederick William ceded his Polish lands to Alexander, he would receive territorial compensation elsewhere in Germany.[30]

Alexander's evasiveness irritated the British Foreign Secretary, Castlereagh, and perplexed Metternich (as he intended that it should). Castlereagh, seeking to pin down the Tsar, sent Cathcart a copy of Pitt's 'despatch on which the confederacy of 1805 was founded' in the hope that the ambassador would 'learn the bearings' of Alexander's mind on 'so masterly an outline for the restoration of Europe'.[31] The Tsar, however, had found it difficult to understand Pitt's principles at the time, and the passage of eight years did not make comprehension any easier. He was prepared to give an assurance that he would not sign a final peace with France without consulting his British ally; and now that Castlereagh was proposing a £2 million subsidy to Russia and another one of the same amount to Prussia, Alexander was willing to look favourably on the British efforts at defeating Napoleon, even ordering a *Te Deum* to be sung in honour of Wellington's triumph at Vittoria. But, though Cathcart and Alexander trusted and liked each other, not even sentiments of friendship could induce the Tsar to let Castlereagh have a clear statement of his war aims. A few months ago, when there was no immediate likelihood of Napoleon's downfall, Alexander had occasionally spoken of the need to find a new ruler for the French once 'Buonaparte' was overthrown, but now that the liberation of Europe had started in earnest Cathcart did not find him inclined to return to the subject.[32] It was all very exasperating.

With the Austrians Alexander had, in the end, to be more precise. Early in May Count Stadion, one of the most experienced Austrian diplomats and a former Foreign Minister, arrived at Russo-Prussian headquarters to discuss the terms under which Russia would accept peace from the French. Stadion was as much an avowed enemy of Napoleon as Stein and he made it clear to Alexander that if Napoleon rejected Austrian mediation Emperor Francis would enter the war on the Allied side.[33] In the second week of June Metternich himself travelled to Bohemia, met the Grand Duchess Catherine in Prague and let her know that he was anxious to co-ordinate policy with her brother.[34] Eventually it was arranged that Alexander should leave his headquarters near Reichenbach (Dzierzoniow) in Silesia on 16 June and cross the Austrian frontier to spend some days at a castle belonging to Count Colloredo at Opotschna, where he would be joined by his sisters Catherine and Marie – and by Metternich, who had travelled north to join Emperor Francis at the Austrian army headquarters in Gitschin.[35]

Alexander had only seen Metternich on one other occasion, his visit in November 1805 to Potsdam and Berlin, where Metternich was then serving as Austrian ambassador. Although they had remained in contact both before and after Napoleon's invasion of Russia, Alexander still tended to distrust Metternich as the man responsible for the Bonaparte-Habsburg marriage; and he was especially afraid that Metternich, unlike Stadion, wanted to secure reasonable peace terms for Napoleon precisely because the dynastic connection was his own first diplomatic triumph. When therefore the two men met at Opotschna on 18–19 June, Alexander was unusually reserved and gave Metternich the impression he believed him still to be 'totally on the side of the French'.[36] But real progress was made towards a general agreement. Alexander accepted four fundamental points as a basis for peace: an end to French military control of the Confederation of the Rhine and the re-constitution of Hamburg and Lübeck as Free Cities; the recovery by Prussia of the territory lost to French satellites in 1807; the return to Austria of her lost provinces on the Adriatic; and the formal dissolution of the Grand-Duchy of Warsaw. Napoleon was to be given the opportunity of accepting these terms as a basis for a peace conference; and had he not done so by 20 July, Austria would join the Allies and continue the war until Holland, Spain, Germany and all Italy were freed from French domination. These proposals, which had already been settled by Stadion and Nesselrode in discussion, became the minimum peace programme acceptable to Alexander; and they were formally incorporated in the Reichenbach Convention, concluded by Russia, Austria and Prussia on 27 June.

The Tsar returned to Reichenbach from Opotschna, delighted at his talks with his sisters, if not at those with Metternich. Now there was nothing to be done except await a response from the French. Metternich was summoned to Dresden for an audience with Napoleon almost as soon as he had left Alexander. There followed the famous interview of 26 June at the Marcolini Palace, in which Napoleon's histrionics revealed to Metternich the essential weakness of the French Imperial titles and their dependence upon continued military success.[37] After four days in Dresden Napoleon persuaded Metternich that he would accept the armed mediation of Austria and send a representative to a peace conference in Prague on 10 July provided that there were no military operations for another month after the conference ended. These conditions did not correspond with the points Alexander had made in the Opotschna talks or with the terms of the newly signed Reichenbach Convention, and Metternich had no right to extend an armistice of which Austria was not a signatory for another three weeks; but he was certainly not going to risk losing his position as arbiter by returning from Dresden to Gitschin empty-handed.

Alexander was angry at Metternich's apparent duplicity: this confirmed his worst fears of the man. He had no intention of going to Prague himself, nor was he prepared for Nesselrode to waste valuable days listening to Metternich pontificating in the capital of Bohemia. Russia, he decided, would be fittingly represented by an Alsatian émigré, Jean Anstedt, who hated Napoleon and was at the same time 'one of the most bitter enemies of Austria'.[38] Anstedt would certainly never allow Metternich to commit Russia to a compromise truce with the French, nor indeed – if he could help it – to show any diplomatic initiative whatsoever. At the same time Alexander proposed to his sister Catherine (who was enjoying herself in Prague when not taking the waters of Eger) that she might discover 'what is needed to make Metternich wholly ours', adding significantly 'I have the funds, so do not stint yourself';[39] but he did not specify precisely what Catherine was to do with the money, nor does she appear to have sent him a written account of her activities.

The Prague Conference in itself was unworthy of all this attention. Napoleon sent Caulaincourt, but permitted him only to sound out the Allied delegates, not to discuss the Reichenbach proposals; and Metternich was mainly concerned to let the Emperor Francis see how deeply his son-in-law was in the wrong, for there was still some reluctance on the Emperor's part to order the Austrian army to march against his favourite daughter's husband. It would have been wiser for Alexander to send Nesselrode, for Anstedt was unable (and unwilling) to discover from Caulaincourt so much about the war-weariness of the French as someone with a better knowledge of the Parisian pressure groups. As it was, Metternich gained much useful information from his talks with Caulaincourt, but he was disinclined to put it at the disposal of the Russians. He was, however, so convinced of the need for an Allied army to march speedily on France and dictate terms when poised on the frontiers that he delivered a virtual ultimatum on 8 August. Since no reply was received from the French, the Austrians joined Russia, Britain, Prussia and Sweden in the coalition against Napoleon on 12 August. The Armistice was at an end, and fighting was resumed in Silesia four days later.[40]

The Battles of Dresden and Leipzig and the Race for Frankfurt

Alexander was at that moment in Prague, meeting Emperor Francis for the first time since their harrowing encounter at Czeitsch on the day after Austerlitz. Today, as then, they were faced by an urgent military problem, although fortunately one dictated by strength rather than weakness. For there was now in Germany an allied force of more than 800,000 men, easily outnumbering Napoleon's army which, though almost twice as large as before the Armistice, contained many regiments filled by raw conscripts and some contingents from the remaining satellites (Bavaria and Saxony) of wavering loyalty. But who was to command this Allied army of liberation? Alexander had never thought any of his Russian Generals could co-ordinate so heterogeneous a force. For a time he favoured Bernadotte, who visited him at Reichenbach during the

Armistice and was now commanding a joint Swedish-Prussian force south of Berlin; and he considered both the Prussian Blücher and the Austrian Archduke Charles, who was, however, out of favour with his brother, Emperor Francis. Eventually, on 6 August, it was agreed that another Austrian, Prince Schwarzenberg, should serve as supreme commander. There was much to be said for Schwarzenberg: his generalship was respected by Napoleon; he knew his opponents, for he had been ambassador in Paris as well as commanding the Austrian auxiliaries attached to the Grand Army in 1812; and he was both personally brave and strategically ambitious, with the experience of a quarter of a century of warfare behind him. But no sooner had the Tsar given his approval of Schwarzenberg's appointment than he changed his mind – and requested the supreme command for himself.[41]

This proposal pleased nobody. Politically it would have confirmed the Tsar's status as leader of 'the Good Cause' against Bonaparte, to the chagrin of the ruler of Austria and his ministers. Militarily it would have been disastrous. Alexander had as yet been present only on one battlefield, Austerlitz. He remained impetuous and inclined to give undue weight to the theories of his discovery of the moment, thereby tending to favour a persuasive staff-officer at the expense of more taciturn men of greater experience. The Austrians flatly refused to give him the military authority for which he asked. Metternich threatened that Austria would withdraw from the coalition if the Tsar would not confirm Schwarzenberg's appointment; and he even hinted that they might put their troops at the disposal of Napoleon, enforcing peace with him rather than against him.[42] With a bad grace Alexander gave way: now he had yet another reason for resenting the Austrian minister.

In the fourth week of August Alexander sadly showed how limited was his knowledge of military affairs. The Allies were anxious to seize the initiative and advance on Leipzig before Napoleon could attack them. Alexander himself wished first to recover Dresden, a city to which he attached especial importance. Against the advice of the Austrians and with the reluctant consent of his own commanders, Alexander insisted that Schwarzenberg should make a frontal assault on Dresden from the hills to the south-west of the city.[43] The Tsar and Frederick William watched the battle from the Racknitz Heights on the afternoon of 26 August. At first the Allies seemed to make good progress. Then suddenly through his telescope Alexander saw the long dark line of the Old Guard sweeping into the city along the right bank of the Elbe and, behind them, what seemed endless columns of reinforcements streaming in from

Bautzen. The Tsar sensed the Allies had attacked too late and could not now gain a victory. He wished to break off the engagement at once. Unexpectedly Frederick William, standing beside him on the Racknitz Heights, took a tougher line: 'Why should 200,000 Allied soldiers give way before the Guard of one man?' he demanded. Alexander, perhaps already conscious he should not have insisted on an attack in the first place, acknowledged the validity of the King's objection and did not interfere again. Yet, although the battle continued well into the second day, it was no longer possible for the Allies to make any impression in the French defences, and before nightfall on 27 August they were falling back towards the mountains.[44]

Momentarily the battle of Dresden endangered the whole Allied position; for two days later French cavalry crossed into Austria and came to within five miles of the joint headquarters which the sovereigns had established at Teplitz. But on 30 August they were finally checked at Külm, and Schwarzenberg began slowly to build up his forces again for the thrust into western Saxony towards Leipzig. Although Alexander continued to give his opinions at the conference table the lesson of Dresden temporarily chastened him. He allowed the commander-in-chief to make his own dispositions, only complaining from time to time that Schwarzenberg was over-cautious and slow.[45]

At Teplitz the Tsar was soon distracted from military affairs to diplomatic questions once more. His partners were disturbed that there was still no formal understanding between the Allies on war aims. This was not a matter which especially worried Alexander since he still believed it was his mission to destroy the Napoleonic State and then seek revelation of what was to take place. But Metternich and Hardenberg (the chief minister of Prussia) were practical men, and so indeed was Nesselrode. Negotiations led on 9 September to the conclusion of three bilateral pacts binding Russia, Austria and Prussia, the basis of the continental alliance against Napoleon and indeed of the understanding between the three autocracies which endured for much of the next half-century. Collectively the pacts were known as the Teplitz Treaties. Publicly they announced the principal war aim as 'the re-establishment of a just equilibrium between the Powers'. Secret clauses expanded this vague intention a little more precisely, though not much: the Confederation of the Rhine and the Grand-Duchy of Warsaw were to be swept from the map as Napoleonic bric-à-brac; Austria and Prussia would recover 'as closely as possible' their territorial extent as in 1805; the smaller German states would enjoy 'entire and absolute independence'; and the future of Poland would be settled by amicable arrangements between the three Powers at a later stage. Far more issues were shirked by the Teplitz Treaties than were solved.[46] But at least Alexander could now count on the continued partnership of the Austrians in the grand march westwards.

The Allied advance began in earnest in the first week of October. Napoleon, who was painfully conscious of his inferiority in numbers, sought to shorten his lines and concentrate around Leipzig, while leaving garrisons to defend Dresden and other towns and cities in the east. After a preliminary skirmish outside Leipzig on 14 October the main battle for the city began two days later and continued intermittently for sixty hours. Alexander participated in the fighting more directly than in any previous engagement and was at one point in some danger when his escort had to throw themselves into the mêlée in order to check a French counterattack. By nightfall on 18 October it was clear to Napoleon that he would have to break off the battle, or risk annihilation. Leipzig was a battle in attrition, won by the Allies because they possessed the men and the material which Napoleon lacked; it was a triumph in determination rather than a victory of arms.[47]

A popular print circulated in England and Germany soon afterwards showed the three sovereigns of Russia, Austria and Prussia kneeling in prayer in the middle of the battlefield to give thanks to the Almighty for the success of their soldiery. The scene is no doubt apocryphal but the mood of pious thanksgiving genuine enough. In a letter to his friend, Golitsyn, on 21 October Alexander wrote:

Almighty God has granted us a glorious victory over the renowned Napoleon after a four day battle beneath the walls of Leipzig. The Almighty has demonstrated that in His eyes nobody in this world is strong or great except those whom He Himself exalts. Twenty-seven Generals captured, almost three hundred heavy cannon and 37,000 prisoners – such is the result of these four stirring days. And now we are no more than two marches away from Frankfurt-am-Main! You can well imagine what I am feeling and thinking![48]

The whole of Germany, right to the banks of the Rhine, lay open to invaders. Bavaria and Württemberg had deserted Napoleon before Leipzig, and Saxony during the battle itself. Now the French, routed and demoralized, were on their own. There was indeed good cause for thanksgiving.

The pursuit of the French across Germany trailed away as the weather broke and the roads turned to mud. But it was still possible to make an extra effort for any gain of particular substance. Thus in the first days of

November there was a dignified race for Frankfurt, the traditional corona-tion city of the old Holy Roman Empire. The race was won by Metternich who reached Frankfurt on the evening of 4 November, but Alexander arrived with the cavalry outriders next morning, having left the main body of Russian infantry far behind. Together Metternich and Alexander arranged a grand ceremonial entry for the Emperor Francis on 6 November. It was especially gratifying for the ruler of distant Russia to escort the last bearer of the old Imperial dignities to the doors of the church where he had received the German crown twenty-one years before.[49] Henceforth it would be difficult to banish a Tsar to the outer fringe of Europe or to settle the affairs of Germany without reference to St Petersburg as well as to Vienna.

There were, however, more urgent problems of policy which could not be resolved by grandiose gestures in historic places. While Alexander and the Austrians were racing for Frankfurt, the last troops of Napoleon's command re-crossed the Rhine at Mainz. Ought the Allies to press on at once into France or should there be a final attempt to achieve a general peace? And if so, on what terms? Alexander, as ever, wished to maintain the pursuit.[50] The Prussians and Austrians hesitated. Many of them, including Schwarzenberg himself, had marched on Paris in 1792 only to be checked by the patriotic spirit of the revolutionary army once its soil was sullied by the invader. The Allies could not risk a major defeat in a winter campaign when it would be difficult to bring up reinforcements and supplies. There was evidence that Napoleon wanted to negotiate, or rather that his marshals and ministers wanted him to negotiate. Among the prisoners taken in Germany was Caulaincourt's brother-in-law, Baron de St Aignan, and Metternich proposed he should be sent as rapidly as possible to Paris with an assurance to Napoleon that the Allies would offer generous terms to France, recognizing the right to retain 'her natural frontiers', including Belgium and the left bank of the Rhine. Alexander, perhaps preoccupied with military questions, approved Metternich's proposal although Nesselrode thought the Allies should, from the start of talks with Napoleon, insist on far stiffer terms.[51] It would certainly have been wiser to define their position more clearly; and, indeed, to have co-ordinated objectives with their ally across the Channel.

Outwardly relations between Alexander and Metternich were by now better than they had been in Bohemia: 'Prince Metternich has ready access to H.I.M. and he [the Tsar] certainly listens to his suggestions with confidence', reported Cathcart to London.[52] Basically, however, there remained a wide difference in their respective attitudes towards the problems of peace. Metternich's experience of three months' negotiating with the Russians convinced him Europe needed a strong, though not predominant, Bonapartist State to assist Austria to counter the Russo-Prussian combination in the post-war period. Alexander, on the other hand, still regarded himself as an instrument of divine retribution, seeking vengeance on Napoleon for the sufferings of 1812. The thought of entering Paris excluded all other considerations from his policy: by all means let there be talk of peace but let the advance continue; let it strike at the heart of France even as Napoleon had struck at the heart of Russia fifteen months before.[53]

Blücher and the Prussians agreed with Alexander: they urged the immediate crossing of the middle Rhine and a march through Lorraine. Schwarzenberg, unhappy at the pressures around the conference tables, hesitated to pit tired troops against the concentric fortresses long built to safeguard the old Kingdom of France. On 19 November, still in Frankfurt, Alexander accepted a compromise: the main army would wheel south through Basle and into the Belfort Gap while Blücher, with what had once been the 'Army of Silesia', would strike at Nancy and head for the upper Marne.[54] The Allies crossed the Rhine three days before Christmas, but the Tsar remained in southern Germany until the end of the first week of the New Year. While there was a possibility of an emissary from Napoleon arriving at Allied headquarters to seek peace, Alexander was determined not to allow Metternich a free hand. He would have preferred to be thrusting forward with the army but he was not prepared to leave Frederick William, Francis and Metternich to plot against him, especially now that the British Foreign Secretary, Castlereagh, was on his way to headquarters with plenipotentiary powers. Alexander had already heard of his own popularity in Britain. He awaited the coming of Castlereagh with lively curiosity.

The Campaign in France, 1814

In general, Alexander was as elated at the beginning of the year 1814 as twelve months previously at Vilna. From Freiburg, on 3 January, he sent a letter to his old tutor, La Harpe, which rang with an almost boyish enthusiasm for the winter campaign.[55] A week later he crossed into Switzerland and joined his brother sovereigns and Metternich at Basle. But he thought Schwarzenberg was making dismally slow progress and he grew restless. Metternich wrote to his friend Gentz on 13 January, 'Tsar Alexander believes it is his duty to Moscow to blow up the Tuileries:

they will not be blown up.'[56] This, of course, was an over-simplification of Alexander's intentions, for he did not wish to harm the city of Paris, only its ruler; but Metternich's remark caught faithfully enough the irrationality of Alexander's mood. His gusts of anger and impatience were exasperating to those around him. Even the pliable Nesselrode was out of sympathy with him: 'There are some men who want to push as far as Paris', he wrote obliquely to his wife on 16 January, 'but I only want to push as far as negotiations.'[57] It was on that day that Alexander felt he could contain himself no longer. Schwarzenberg had by now established field headquarters on the plateau of Langres, little more than 150 miles from Paris. Why was he waiting there? Alexander decided abruptly to leave Basle and go to stir him up. Poor Schwarzenberg! It is vexing to be unsure if one is to be visited by St George or by the Dragon.

Alexander found it increasingly difficult to separate these two roles. He thought there were good reasons why he should go to Langres rather than wait in Basle. The winter that year was colder and more intense than anyone could ever remember in western Europe, and the Tsar believed these conditions favoured his troops at the expense of the French (and, indeed, of the other Allied contingents). It seemed to him essential for Schwarzenberg to keep up the pressure on Napoleon's dwindling troops. In reality Alexander was misjudging Schwarzenberg and over-rating the mobility of his own army, and the achievements of the three Allied contingents in the appalling snow-drifts on the plateau were remarkable.[58] Militarily there was certainly no need for Alexander to go to Langres and politically the decision to leave Basle when he did was a serious mistake. Two days after his departure Castlereagh at last arrived and spent a week discussing war plans and peace terms with Metternich. Together they privately disposed of most of Alexander's projects: Castlereagh did not understand all the talk of Poland, but he indicated that he believed Metternich was right in fearing an exclusively Russo-Prussian solution of the problem; and when Metternich mentioned Alexander's inclination to see Bernadotte on the throne of France, he found Castlereagh agreeing with him that any such proposal would make nonsense of the dynastic principle upon which all good government must rest. By the closing week in January, when Metternich and Castlereagh crossed from Basle to Langres, they were united on almost every question of policy; and Alexander was starkly isolated.[59]

At the time, he did not care very much. On 1 February the Allies gained their first victory against the French on the soil of their homeland: Blücher, supported by Schwarzenberg, Barclay and Wittgenstein, attacked Napoleon and Ney at La Rothière and forced them to retire. Alexander urged the Generals to march at once on Paris and they agreed, sensing from the evidence of French desertions that morale was low. When therefore Metternich and Castlereagh tried to discover the Tsar's latest thoughts over peace terms, they found him too engrossed in military matters to give them particular attention. After five days of discussion he undertook to send a representative to Chatillon, on the upper Seine, for peace talks with Caulaincourt; but he indicated he had little faith in negotiating a peace settlement until Paris had fallen. On the other hand he raised no objections to a proposal by Metternich that the final form of the new Europe should be settled by a grand congress of the Powers to be held in Vienna. Meanwhile he encouraged Schwarzenberg to advance Allied headquarters to Troyes, only ninety miles from the French capital. Metternich decided to remain with Alexander; Castlereagh went to Chatillon.[60]

Within a week Castlereagh had been urgently summoned back to Troyes. Metternich found he could not hold the Tsar to any of his commitments with the Allies. Alexander had decided to order a direct march on Paris, to suspend all negotiations until after the fall of the capital, and then to summon an assembly of French dignitaries who would determine, in consultation with the Tsar, how France was to be ruled.[61] This was too much for his allies. On 13–14 February Alexander had two long and outspoken interviews with Castlereagh, having already exhausted Metternich. The Tsar refused to change his attitude, and Metternich once again tried to frighten him with threats of a separate peace.[62] But so great was Alexander's influence with the Generals in the field that he was not impressed by arguments or warnings: he took note only of the fortunes of war and the information which seeped through to headquarters from inside Paris.

Yet, at the very time when Alexander was behaving so intransigently towards Castlereagh, Napoleon was inflicting the first military reversals which the Allies had suffered since the end of August.[63] Blücher's Prussians were checked at Montmirail on 11 February and defeated again in the neighbouring village of Vauchamps three days later. Schwarzenberg, too, had encountered fierce opposition as he fumbled towards the forest of Fontainebleau and by 17 February the Allies were falling back and the sovereigns preparing to evacuate Troyes in order to establish new head-quarters at Chaumont on the upper Marne. These sudden signs of French determination to resist brought Alexander to his senses and he belatedly instructed Razumovsky, his delegate to the Chatillon Conference, to co-operate with the British and Austrians in seeking for a negotiated peace.[64] By now, however, Napoleon thought he could gain better terms and exploit Austro-Russian difficulties; and he, in his turn, was not prepared to accept the Allied proposals. There was never any hope that the Chatillon charade would lead to a settlement. Alexander was right in believing that it was the roar of the cannon rather than the persuasiveness of the diplomats which would bring the war to an end.

The chief effect of Napoleon's February victories was to unify the Allies at last. Under Castlereagh's lead the Russians, British, Austrians and Prussians signed on 9 March at Chaumont a treaty of Grand Alliance: no separate peace; an eventual settlement giving independence to the Netherlands and Switzerland, a confederated Germany and restitution of the old order in Spain and Italy (so far as was practicable); and continuance of this Quadruple Alliance for twenty years after the ending of the present war, so as to prevent a resurgent France from disturbing the peace of Europe for a generation.[65] Nothing was said of the future government of France – or, indeed, of other major problems, notably the fate of the Polish lands – but at least there was a prospect of the Allies remaining in concert rather than falling out among themselves before the fighting was even concluded.

But the war could not go on much longer. Napoleon had no resources apart from his own military genius. By the end of the first week in March both Blücher and Schwarzenberg had recovered the initiative and were prepared to resume their advance westwards. On 10 March an emissary arrived at Chatillon from within Paris with an unsigned letter for Nesselrode: 'You are groping about like children on crutches: make use of your legs and stride forward on stilts, for you can achieve anything you wish to achieve.'[66] There was little doubt in Nesselrode's mind that the message came, in the first instance, from Talleyrand and he hurried to let Alexander, Metternich and Castlereagh know what it said. Yet, for the moment, it was not possible 'to stride forward on stilts'. On that same day Blücher captured Laon but Napoleon began to move south-eastwards up the Marne as though threatening to take Schwarzenberg's army in the rear. No matter how eloquent Nesselrode and Alexander might be, it was impossible for them to induce the Austrian to risk encirclement and march boldly westwards.

In the fourth week of March fresh evidence came of internal discord. On 22 March a patrol of Cossacks intercepted a letter from Napoleon to Marie Louise which mentioned he was crossing the Marne so as to draw the invaders away from Paris.[67] Other captured messages confirmed the demoralization among the Napoleonic officials still left in the capital; and in the morning of 24 March Alexander summoned Frederick William, Schwarzenberg and the other leading Generals in the field to an informal council of war west of Vitry. Since Metternich and Castlereagh, with the Emperor Francis, were at Dijon there was no one prepared to argue with Alexander: he insisted that on the following day (Friday, 25 March) the main Allied army should march on Paris, a hundred miles away, leaving a Russian Corps under General Wintzingerode to keep watch on Napoleon's movements.[68] The Tsar and the King, together with the Grand Duke Constantine, went forward with Schwarzenberg's troops; and so, for that matter, did the King of Prussia's seventeen-year-old son, William, who was to make a similar journey with a conquering army fifty-six years later.

There was still some tough fighting ahead. On that very Friday Alexander came under heavy cannon fire at La Fère-Champenoise, where Constantine led impressive cavalry charges against a corps of brave but inexperienced young conscripts.[69] But the Allied weight of numbers was decisive and within three days the road to Paris was open, though there was a last show of resistance on the slopes of Montmartre. By Wednesday afternoon Alexander was only eight miles from the capital. That night he established final headquarters of the campaign in the Château de Bondy, and it was there that the Prefect of Paris came to negotiate surrender of the city.[70]

Next morning there was another unexpected visitor. Caulaincourt, appointed Foreign Minister by Napoleon on the eve of the invasion of France, had negotiated with the Allies intermittently for ten weeks, but the Tsar had always avoided receiving him, Now, however, he came on a mission directly from Napoleon, a last offer to negotiate peace before the fall of Paris; and Alexander, after some hesitation, agreed to see him. They had not met since their emotional farewell at St Petersburg in the spring of 1811. The Tsar greeted Caulaincourt warmly: he was 'the friend who is always welcome'; but no personal appeals could rob Alexander of the solemn entry into the French capital, for this was a moment he had cherished in anticipation throughout the hard days of two winters.[71] He explained to Caulaincourt that he came to Paris, not as a hostile invader, but as a liberator. He was convinced that France was as weary of the rule of Napoleon as was Europe and he had therefore resolved not to have any further dealings with Napoleon himself. The Seine was not the Niemen and Paris was a long way, in time and in space, from Tilsit.

Alexander Enters Paris (31 March 1814)

At eleven o'clock that same morning, 31 March, the first Russian cavalry reached the barrier of Pantin, on the eastern outskirts of Paris. They were followed by the Tsar's personal Guard in full parade uniform, and then by Alexander himself, riding slowly down the cobbled streets with Frederick William beside him and Constantine and other dignitaries immediately behind them.[72] Nobody appears to have noticed anyone in the procession apart from the Tsar, and this is hardly surprising. With the bright spring sunshine flashing on his golden epaulettes and collar, he looked the incarnation of one of the Gods in a classical myth. A smile of contentment was carved on his face as he acknowledged cheers by raising his right arm to his great green hat with its plume of cock feathers caught by the breeze. 'Long live the Allies! Hurrah for Peace! Hurrah for Tsar Alexander!' the onlookers called as the procession went by. No foreign conqueror had ridden into Paris for four hundred years. This was Alexander's hour of apotheosis, and he had every intention of savouring the experience to the full.

The Allied columns passed along the Rue du Faubourg Saint-Martin, through the old gate of Saint-Martin itself and eventually down the Rue Royale, past the place where the guillotine had stood during the Terror, and into the Champs Elysées. There Alexander halted at an improvised saluting base, beside the Marly Horses; the column turned and marched past the Tsar and the King before breaking ranks and finding bivouacs along the tree-covered mile to the (uncompleted) Arc de Triomphe or beneath the chestnuts of Chaillot. Guards were mounted at the city barriers for, although the fighting was no doubt over, Napoleon was still at Fontainebleau and there were other armies in the provinces. It was impossible to rule out completely a surprise assault on the city by the fallen Emperor.

The parade was not over until after five o'clock in the afternoon. Alexander had still not finally announced where he wished to stay in Paris. The Tuileries was out of the question, for he did not want to offend the Bourbons. At first he thought he would move into the Elysée Palace but during the parade Nesselrode received one of those mysterious anonymous notes which helped determine policy in these weeks of uncertainty. This particular message was a warning that the Elysée had been mined and that its occupants would be blown sky high once they took up residence there. This tale was nonsense and was probably invented by the person who had already privately offered hospitality to the Tsar, the egregious Talleyrand. At all events Alexander decided not to move into the Elysée but to turn to the man whom he was convinced best understood the needs of France at that moment. In the failing light of early evening Alexander rode to Talleyrand's residence at the corner of the Rue St Florentin and the Rue de Rivoli, diagonally across the Place de la Concorde from the Tsar's saluting base. 'Monsieur de Talleyrand,' Alexander said as he dismounted, 'I have decided I shall stay at your home since you possess the confidence of myself and of my allies.'[73] Talleyrand put the first floor of the huge house at Alexander's disposal and sentries from the Preobrazhensky Grenadiers mounted guard in the narrow Rue St Florentin. Perfect order and discipline reigned throughout the city. The candles shone through the windows of the large salon on Talleyrand's first floor and there was a comforting air of agreed improvisation. 'Hurrah for our liberators!' a few Parisians called as the Allied spokesmen gathered that evening to seek the advice of Alexander and Talleyrand.[74] It was a promising way for peace to break out: Moscow had experienced a more dramatic occupation.

16

Paris and London

The Tsar, Talleyrand and Caulaincourt (April 1814)

'I have come as a conqueror who seeks no other honour than the happiness of the vanquished', Alexander declared in a note to Golitsyn written within hours of reaching Paris. Such a remark would have seemed intolerably unctuous from any other public figure of 1814, a cant phrase satisfying a conscience excited beyond reason at receiving the surrender of the French capital. But from Alexander's pen the sentiment was genuine enough. For eighteen months he had seen himself as entrusted by the Almighty with a double mission: to rid Europe of the over-weening ambition of Napoleon; and to secure for the French people the benefits of an enlightened government, sufficiently stable to serve with Russia as a guarantor of peace in the new European order. With Napoleon isolated at Fontainebleau the first of these objectives was by now virtually achieved; but the second task was far from accomplished, not least because the Tsar himself remained uncertain how, in political terms, the vanquished were to be made happy.[1]

For the first fortnight of April 1814 Alexander enjoyed a predominance in European affairs which he had never envisaged. He was both the principal spokesman of the Allies and *de facto* ruler of France. Castlereagh, Metternich and the Emperor Francis remained in Dijon, unwilling to incur the blame for imposing on the French a form of government which would appear to have arrived in their own baggage-train. Bernadotte had halted his Swedes in the Low Countries; he did not wish to invade France, either from sentiments of nostalgic patriotism or because he felt the odium of

282

ousting Napoleon would damn his personal ambitions. Alexander therefore had with him in Paris only Schwarzenberg (who was concerned
solely with military matters), Nesselrode (who would do what he was
told) and Frederick William of Prussia (who had the instincts and interests
of a package tourist). It was therefore left to the Tsar to determine whether
or not the Bourbons should be restored to the throne of their ancestors
and what should be the fate of the Bonapartes. Over such matters
Alexander turned naturally for advice to his host, who had served every
régime in France for the past quarter of a century except the Jacobin
Committees; and he found, hardly surprisingly, that Talleyrand was
most helpful.[2]

There were, in Alexander's eyes, four possible solutions of the dynastic
question: a Bourbon restoration; a Regency for the three-year-old son of
Napoleon; a constitutional monarchy under Bernadotte; or, more
drastically, the passing over of all monarchical claims and the establish-
ment of a liberal republic, possibly with the Duke of Orleans as President.
It was unlikely the Austrians or the British would accept the last of these
four solutions and Alexander himself had become disenchanted with
Bernadotte during the winter campaign when he had displayed what the
Tsar considered to be a stubborn independence. Talleyrand had pressed on
Alexander the claims of the Bourbons from their first meeting in the
Rue St Florentin on the evening of 31 March, and the Tsar had undertaken to respect the wishes of the French Senate, a body of which Talleyrand as Vice-Grand Elector was the Chairman. The Senate – or rather the
sixty-four senators who answered Talleyrand's summons – proclaimed
the deposition of Napoleon on 2 April and 'freely called to the throne of
France' King Louis XVIII, who was at that moment recovering from an
attack of gout at the country house in Buckinghamshire where he had
spent his final years of exile. But Alexander did not regard himself as
bound to accept the decision of a Senate meeting at which more than half
the members were absent. He had no liking for the Bourbons. During his
father's reign Louis XVIII had, for a time, found sanctuary in Russia at
Mittau and exaggerated tales of dynastic sensitivities prejudiced Alexander
against the legitimist cause over the years. The Bourbons, he thought, were
arrogant, outmoded and incapable of winning the sympathy of a nation
which had recast its institutions in their absence. For the first ten days
which he spent in Paris Alexander considered he had avoided committing
himself over the dynastic question; and there were moments when he was
personally inclined to support a Bonapartist Regency.[3]

During the campaign in France Alexander repeatedly insisted to his allies he would not accept any personal dealings with Napoleon. Castle-reagh, though gratified by his assurance, was nevertheless worried over what he termed 'the chivalrous attitude of Emperor Alexander'; and he even warned London that the Tsar was 'only looking for the opportunity of entering Paris at the head of his valiant army in order to display the greatness of his soul in retaliation for the destruction of his capital.'[4] This was a shrewd analysis of the Tsar's character. Alexander, like Napoleon but to a different degree, was fired by an instinct of good theatre: now the fighting was over, a proud gesture of magnanimity towards the fallen giant would crown his mission with final nobility of purpose. He was not prepared for Napoleon to remain on the throne of France but he wished him personally to be treated with generosity and he saw no reason why the autocratic system he had created in France need be cast aside if a large section of the population remained Bonapartist at heart. It is significant that on the very evening he arrived in the Rue St Florentin as Talley-rand's guest Alexander found time to give Caulaincourt a further audience; and the same night officers of the Semeonovsky Regiment stopped royalist sympathizers from hauling down the statue of Napoleon from the column in the Place Vendôme.[5] The sentiment of friendship so ostenta-tiously displayed at Erfurt was not entirely dead; and it is anyone's guess what would have happened if Napoleon himself had contrived a meeting with Alexander during these days of uncertainty, for the combination of the fallen Emperor's personal magnetism and the Tsar's generosity of heart could well have deflected the intention of the Allies, even at this thirteenth hour. Small wonder so much store was set on keeping the two men apart.

The only link between them now, as in earlier years, was through Caulaincourt. During the first ten days of April he had, in all, four long discussions with Alexander, riding back and forth between Talleyrand's home and the palace of Fontainebleau, thirty-three miles away, where Napoleon remained from 31 March to 20 April.[6] At first Napoleon be-lieved he might still be able to restore his fortunes by a swift march on the capital with Marshal Marmont's corps, which was holding the town of Essones halfway between Fontainebleau and Paris. But this proposal seemed to the remaining dignitaries of the Empire no more than a forlorn gamble and they persuaded Napoleon during the afternoon of Monday, 4 April, that there was no longer any reason to suppose that continuance of the war would improve his position. He accordingly chose three emissaries whom he sent to the Tsar with an offer to abdicate in favour of a Regency for his son. The original three envoys were Caulaincourt, Ney and

Macdonald although they were subsequently joined by Marmont, who had already been in touch with the Austrians on his own initiative.

They arrived in the Rue St Florentin about three o'clock on Tuesday morning, 5 April. Alexander was waiting for them and received them at once, 'expressing in warm and chivalrous terms his admiration for the French forces' says Macdonald.[7] It was a curious situation. Downstairs Talleyrand was discussing detailed plans for the return to Paris of Louis XVIII's brother, the Comte d'Artois, with the Bourbon representative, Baron Vitrolles. The two men knew that only a surprising development would have brought Caulaincourt and three Marshals to Alexander at such an hour of the morning. They could hear the clatter of the Marshals' spurs on the parquet blocks above their heads. 'This is an incident and we must see what happens', Talleyrand remarked. 'Tsar Alexander does unexpected things – after all he is the son of Paul I.'[8]

But Alexander, unlike his father, rarely took decisions in a hurry. He listened for two hours to Caulaincourt's arguments in favour of retaining the Bonaparte dynasty, noting in particular the stress which he (and the Marshals) put on the need for France to have a government 'that would have no bitter memories to recall, and no reason for delving into an unhappy past'. The Tsar asked for a categorical assurance that Napoleon had consented to abdicate. '"In favour of his son" was our answer', writes Caulaincourt, 'which was well received.' At five in the morning Alexander closed the discussion and asked for the four envoys to return later in the day.[9]

They met again soon after midday. News had come through that Marmont's corps had, in his absence, gone over to the Allies, thus depriving Napoleon of his last effective body of troops. Alexander received confirmation of this report during his meeting with the envoys, and at once went downstairs to consult Talleyrand who pressed him on no account to accept a Regency since Napoleon's influence would dominate whoever was the nominal head of state. When Alexander returned to the first floor he had at last made up his mind. 'A Regency gives France no prospect of repose', he said. 'The Emperor must abdicate unconditionally. He will be furnished with a living; he will be given an independent state.' The Marshals left the conference but Alexander asked Caulaincourt to remain with him. Tentatively he enquired if Bernadotte would be more acceptable to the French than the Bourbons. Caulaincourt replied, 'He has lost everything by coming here with your bayonets'; and he even suggested that Alexander might like to consider one of 'the young Grand Dukes, your brothers' as a Regent. But this extraordinary proposal fell on deaf ears. All that remained was to decide where Napoleon could exercise his 'independent living'. Corsica? Sardinia? Corfu? In the end it seemed that the island of Elba was the least politically objectionable place of exile among those named.[10] That evening there was yet another meeting between Alexander and the four envoys. The Tsar was courteous but firm; bluntly he told Caulaincourt and the Marshals to return to Fontainebleau and secure from Napoleon a definitive pledge of abdication. Further prevarication and delay would not be in the interests of France or of the Bonapartes, Alexander declared; but he sympathized with Caulaincourt in his difficult mission.

The dynastic question was settled at last. Napoleon signed an act of abdication on Wednesday, 6 April, and Caulaincourt was back with the document in Paris at midnight.[11] Never before had Alexander stood out so dramatically as arbiter of Europe's destiny. It remained to decide on the terms of monetary compensation, the nature of Napoleon's establishment on Elba, and the position of Marie Louise and her son. Over all these matters Alexander was co-operative and even sympathetic towards the fallen dynasty. He was not, however, left to resolve these problems by direct negotiation. The other Allies were becoming alarmed at his power and independence. Frederick William was still perfectly content to do whatever Alexander wished. Metternich and Castlereagh, on the other hand, were profoundly disturbed by the Tsar's ascendancy. Both disliked the thought of sending Napoleon to Elba, believing it was far too near the mainland of Europe. Alexander was not prepared to change his decision on Elba to satisfy the Austrians or anyone else; but he did allow the Austrians a freer hand over settling the future of Marie Louise and her son than he had given Caulaincourt to understand.[12] It was, after all, Metternich who had tied the marriage-favours in the first place.

On 11 April the Allies agreed on Napoleon's fate. Their terms were embodied in a formal document subsequently known as the Treaty of Fontainebleau.[13] It was conveyed by Caulaincourt to Napoleon on the following day. After an abortive attempt to poison himself, Napoleon signed the Treaty on the morning of 13 April. Seven days later, with the Treaty duly ratified, he set out for Elba; and in Paris Alexander and his allies began to study the possibilities of drafting a peace treaty with France, as a first step towards the reconstruction of Europe as a whole.

Peacemaking in Paris

Castlereagh had hoped it would be possible to reach a preliminary agreement on outstanding diplomatic questions while the Allies were together in Paris that summer.[14] He was speedily disillusioned. The capital of France, he confessed in a note to his government, 'is a bad place for business'.[15] After weary months of campaigning across the continent it was tempting for the political and military leaders of the Allied states to enjoy the trivial whirl of festivity and entertainment before again immersing themselves in what Alexander described apologetically as 'the muddied waters of politics'.[16] It was also, from the Tsar's point of view, expedient to protract as long as possible the celebration of peace. Militarily he was in an unassailable position. His troops were masters of central and eastern Europe from the Vistula to the Rhine: they stood guard over Dresden and Leipzig; they garrisoned the cities and towns of Poland; they paraded in Basle and Magdeburg; and they completed construction of 'Fort Alexander' and 'Fort Constantine' on the Karthaus hill at Coblenz, above the vineyards of the Moselle. A string of fortified camps across France from Montmirail to Metz confirmed Russian military power: no other national contingent in Paris itself was so strong. Because of the slow response in the Tsar's vast Empire to any sense of urgency, Russia was in 1814 at last ready for war at a time when her Allies sought only peace. Time was as much on Alexander's side now as in the crisis months of the Napoleonic invasion. His prime task was to undermine the political influence of Austria, by wearing thin the friendship of Castlereagh and Metternich and by establishing a new Franco-Russian understanding, ensuring close collaboration between his own ministers and the representatives of Bourbon France. If he could also retain his undoubted popularity with the people of Paris and win the support of what Metternich termed 'the Polish French and Frenchified Poles' in the city, so much the better for Russia.[17] The hour called for elaborate exercises in charm and in tact. No other contemporary public figure could display these qualities to such advantage.

Alexander began well enough. He was generous, tolerant and courteous. When obsequious French dignitaries suggested a change in name for the Pont d'Austerlitz so as to spare their liberator pained memories, he declined the proposal: 'It is enough', he declared, 'for people to know that the Emperor of Russia and his army have crossed over the bridge.'[18] He found the right words for any occasion. Thus he was heard acknowledging to Lafayette the need to abolish serfdom in Russia and he went out of his way to assure Kosciuszko publicly at Countess Jablonowska's ball that he believed in the merits of a free Polish state.[19] It is true that when passing through the ground floor of the Louvre he asked, with gentle irony, whether Napoleon had found a use for the Salle de la Paix; but he was in no sense vindictive towards his fallen enemy or his dignitaries of state. The young English radical, John Cam Hobhouse, went to Sir Charles Stuart's ball in the Hotel de Montesquieu on 4 May and was surprised to find Tsar Alexander waltzing with the wife of Marshal Ney and the widow of Marshal Augereau, 'both nice-looking women';[20] and other visitors to Paris commented on the attentions Alexander lavished on Napoleon's stepdaughter, Hortense, and his stepson, Eugène Beauharnais, who had commanded the left wing of the Grand Army at Borodino. Years afterwards Hortense's second son, Louis (then aged six), remembered the tall curly-haired Russian visitor to whom he had tried furtively to present a small ring as a gesture of friendship and affection. Alexander, though retaining in the Hermitage many gifts from Napoleon I, politely declined this addition to the collection from the future Napoleon III.[21]

But the strangest and saddest of Alexander's friendships in Paris was the attachment he formed for young Louis's grandmother, the Empress Josephine. Robbed of her first husband by the Revolution and of her second by the empty necessity of dynastic ambition, Josephine had spent four years in seclusion at Malmaison, watching the shadows lengthen around her as the Imperial sun sank lower in Europe's skies. Although only fifty, she was a tired woman overtaxed by the buffeting of life but still regarded with sympathy and respect by the people of Paris whose changing fortunes she had shared for over thirty years. It therefore seemed natural to the Tsar to pay a courtesy call on her at Malmaison.[22] Each was charmed by the other. When Alexander returned to the Rue St Florentin he wrote at once to Josephine urging her not to be anxious for the future: 'Though I have no wish to exploit the permission you have been kind enough to accord me, Madame', he wrote, 'I look forward to presenting my respects to you on Friday at your dinner hour.'[23] He came again and again; and Josephine ordered new clothes and began planning elegant dinners, recapturing for Malmaison some of the glory the house and gardens had known during the Consulate. Other foreign royalties came, and in mid-May there was a party and picnic at Hortense's estate of Saint-Leu, near the forest of Montmorency, where Josephine was delighted by Alexander's company although, she confessed privately, saddened by the thought of Napoleon caged on Elba. That day she wore too flimsy a dress and contracted bronchial trouble from which she never fully recovered.[24]

Neither Alexander nor Josephine herself realized she was a sick woman, and she persisted in keeping up her self-imposed duty as First Lady of Paris. On Tuesday, 24 May, she gave a magnificent dinner for Alexander, to which were also invited the Grand Duke Constantine, the young

Grand Dukes Nicholas and Michael (recently arrived from St Petersburg) and the cream of Russian military society. Josephine and Alexander were partners for the opening dance of the ball which followed the dinner. Then, as it was a fine evening, they walked together between the rhodo-dendrons to the uniquely designed hothouse which was Josephine's especial pride. The night air, and all the contrasts in temperature, were too much for Josephine. By Saturday morning she was feverish and next day at noon she died.[25] Alexander, deeply grieved, went in person to Saint-Leu to convey his regrets to her son and daughter. Since the change of allegiance in the French army made it difficult to provide an appropriate guard of honour for her funeral procession, Alexander ordered his own regiments, in full-dress uniform, to line the simple country road from Malmaison to he parish church at Rueil, where she was buried.[26] It was a strange trick of irony that this final military homage should be rendered by Guards of the sovereign whom Napoleon had first taken into his confidence over his plans for a divorce and re-marriage. But there were so many surprising contradictions in Paris in these summer days that nothing, in life or in death, seemed unusual any longer.

Despite his romantic enthusiasm for Josephine, Alexander tried in all honesty and good sense to accord the restored Bourbons the dignity and respect which they deserved as rulers of France. On Easter Day he arranged for seven priests, assisted once again by singers from his Imperial chapels, to offer solemn thanks to Almighty God for the downfall of tyranny at an improvised altar close to the spot where Louis XVI and Marie Antoinette had been guillotined.[27] And as soon as Louis XVIII returned to France from Buckinghamshire, Alexander journeyed north to Compiègne to welcome him. It must, however, be admitted that the two sovereigns did not take to one another. Louis resented Alexander's advice that he should show moderation towards the French people so that they might bask in 'the memory of twenty-five years of glory'; and Alexander, for his part, was intensely irritated by the words chosen by Louis to thank the Prince Regent for Britain's help in securing his restoration.* The Tsar was also surprised at Louis's personal manners: it was odd to be pushed to one side by a monarch who insisted on entering the dining room ahead of his

* As printed in The Times of 22 April 1814 the offending passage ran: 'It is to the counsels of Your Royal Highness, to this glorious country, and to the steadfastness of its inhabitants, that I attribute, after the will of Providence, the re-establishment of my House upon the throne of its ancestors.' The Tsar received a copy of the message within a week and was furious at the apparent disregard by Louis XVIII of Russia's military contribution to the overthrow of Napoleon. The King's words also incensed him against the Prince Regent personally.

guests; and it was embarrassing to sit at table with a host who petulantly called on his attendants to serve him first with every dish. 'We barbarians of the North are more polite in our homes', Alexander remarked to one of his aides afterwards. 'Anyone would think it was he who had come to place *me* on *my* throne.'[28]

Such personal antipathies should not, of course, be exaggerated. Outwardly Alexander maintained good relations with the restored Bourbons. He wanted a treaty of peace with France so as to secure western Europe before tackling outstanding problems of European reconstruction elsewhere. For once Metternich agreed with him, though for different reasons. To the Austrians it seemed desirable to get Alexander away from the Polish expatriates in Paris before beginning serious negotiations over the future of Germany and the Vistulan lands. Castlereagh, too, wanted an early treaty with France so as to set it before Parliament while the country was still in such a haze of happy relief at the end of the war that it would not dispute too closely the actual terms of peace. The only statesman who believed that the treaty with France should form part of the general European settlement and not be drawn up on its own was the Prussian Chancellor, Hardenberg. On 29 April and again on 21 May Hardenberg proposed settlements of the German and Polish Questions; but each time the relative importance of differing regions in Europe produced such tension between the Great Powers that Alexander had no difficulty in convincing his colleagues that the time was not yet ripe to discuss such matters.[29] Good progress was made on the draft French treaty throughout May, the Russians showing greater generosity over the frontiers in the north than either the British or the Austrians. No reparations were claimed, no limitations imposed on the size of the French army, no troops of occupation were forced on the defeated country, no insistence was made on returning the art treasures brought to the Louvre by Napoleon as trophies of victory. The boundaries of France corresponded closely to the frontier line of 1792, with the addition of Chambery, Annecy and the Papal enclave of Avignon. All the peacemakers congratulated themselves on their moderation and the treaty was duly signed on 30 May.[30] It was subsequently known as the First Peace of Paris. Later settlements would prove far harder to achieve, as everyone suspected at the time.

Technically, with the state of war legally ended and with an international congress pending in the autumn at Vienna, there was no reason why the sovereigns and statesmen should not have left Paris and returned home as soon as the French treaty was signed. Emperor Francis, ill-at-ease in the French capital, did indeed go back to Vienna, leaving Metternich and

Schwarzenberg as his representatives with the other Allies. But for several months there had been talk of a visit by the Tsar to London, a proposal extended during the closing days of April into a general invitation for all the Allied leaders to participate in the peace celebrations of Napoleon's most persistent enemy. It was hoped, by both Castlereagh and Metternich, that the traditional calm of London would provide a more agreeable setting for discussions on Polish and German affairs than the crowded and excitable salons of Paris.[31] Alexander, too, expected diplomatic negotiations during the Allied State Visit and he accordingly insisted on taking with him to London, not only the surviving Russian military heroes whom the crowds wished to cheer, but Nesselrode and even Czartoryski (whose knowledge of Polish matters had brought him back into Alexander's favour once Napoleon was overthrown). The Tsar and his attendants left Paris on 3 June for the two-day carriage journey to Boulogne where the Duke of Clarence (the future King William IV) was waiting in H.M.S. *Impregnable* to sail the foreign dignitaries across to Dover.[32]

Catherine Blazes an English Trail

No Russian Tsar or Grand Duke had come to England since Peter the Great's sensational four months at Deptford in 1698. News of Alexander's forthcoming visit accordingly created widespread excitement in the daily press and there was a brisk and profitable trade in semi-biographical pamphlets lauding his virtues. He was hailed by one writer as 'the spotless hero' on one page and 'the magnanimous hero' on the next, while another author greeted him as 'the Christian Conqueror who Saved Paris', and the anonymous compiler of what purported to be his *impartial and authentic Life* described him as 'the agent appointed by Providence to restore Peace to the World'.[33] Some of these impressions coincided remarkably closely with Alexander's own estimate of his qualities, but ultimately they were an embarrassment. They necessitated a standard of behaviour and moral leadership which only a warrior saint or an accomplished actor could attain: Alexander had never been the one and was by now too exhausted to be the other.

For several weeks before leaving Paris Alexander received first-hand reports of life in England from his sister Catherine. She had arrived at Sheerness as a self-invited guest two months previously, disembarking from the Duke of Clarence's frigate on the very day the Tsar entered Paris.[34] Since there was a wealth of no-talent bachelors among the Prince Regent's brothers and cousins, everyone in London Society assumed Catherine had come in search of a husband. This was unfair. She was not out on a consort-safari as she already had high hopes of a Habsburg Archduke and, though she received proposals of marriage from the Dukes of Clarence and Sussex, she resolutely rejected all English suitors. The prime purpose of her visit was curiosity and the need for intellectual gratification. 'She speaks English fluently and readily', noted the Speaker of the House of Commons when he met her at dinner with the Prime Minister, Liverpool, on 5 April;[35] and there is no doubt she believed she could dazzle the cultivated society of London by exercising her extremely able mind. So indeed she might have done had she been able to infiltrate gracefully into Devonshire House, or one of the other accepted centres of feminine Whiggism. But Catherine made three mistakes: she behaved as the Grandest Duchess of Russia rather than as the widowed Duchess of Oldenburg, the title by which the English invariably called her; she made plain her detestation of music ('It makes me ill'); and she quarrelled early in her visit with the Russian ambassador who, had she been prepared to talk and listen to him, could have saved her from a crop of unfortunate solecisms.[36] As it was, she decided that she liked the City of London but not the world of fashion: 'People need different tastes from mine to find pleasure in Society here', she wrote to her brother four weeks after her arrival. She added, however, 'Some aspects of life command respect and admiration. By an unexpected favour I was able to visit Parliament and were I an Englishman I should never leave there.'[37]

This last sentence should have put Alexander on his guard. Already she was irritated beyond measure at the Regent and his Court: 'You know I am far from being puritanical or prudish', she declared, 'but with him and his brothers I have not only frequently to stand on my dignity but I do not even know what to do with my eyes and my ears. They have a brazen way of looking where eyes should never go. Our sister Marie would certainly *die* here.'[38] If life in London was too licentiously frivolous for the grand-daughter of Catherine the Great, she had every intention of amusing herself in her customary way by allowing free flow to her love of mischief and political intrigue. Henceforth she delighted in fanning her brother's jealousies, pitting his vanity and exhibitionism against the even more escapist vanity and exhibitionism of the Regent. Dorothea Lieven, the wife of the Russian ambassador, was too similar in temperament to the Grand Duchess to be a reliable chronicler of her visit and yet she was correct in suggesting that Catherine with her 'resolute and imperious character ... startled and astonished the English more than she pleased them'.[39] There is no doubt Alexander would have been better served in London by the presence of his wife than his sister. But there was never any question of Elizabeth's coming. She had seized the opportunity of returning peace to visit her mother in Baden, the first occasion she had gone home to her birthplace in twenty-two years. Catherine's flamboyant egotism was no substitute for her sister-in-law's patience and understanding.

It was Catherine who insisted that Alexander would be better advised to stay with her in the Pulteney Hotel, off Piccadilly, than accept a suite of rooms in one of the royal palaces – a gesture hardly pleasing to the Regent. And it was again Catherine who made a point of cultivating the Opposition leaders and who wrote enthusiastically to her brother about the young Princess Charlotte who was, at that moment, on bad terms with her father, the Regent.[40] The picture which Alexander gained of London's intrigues from his sister was mightily prejudiced before ever he set foot on the *Impregnable*'s decks. On the other hand, Catherine correctly recounted the way in which 'everyone smiles and claps hands at the mention of your name'. She went on a six-day tour of Oxfordshire, Warwickshire and Worcestershire: 'All classes bless you and pay homage to your private character', she wrote to Alexander on her return to London. 'At the little town of Banbury the inhabitants came to meet me and insisted on leading in my carriage unharnessed of horses simply because I was sister to the great Emperor of Russia.'[41] The visit to England held promise for Alexander of a triumphal progress: reality, alas, fell far short of expectations.

Alexander in England (June 1814)

The *Impregnable*, with Alexander and Frederick William and their suites aboard, made the crossing to Dover on 6 June in unseasonably gusty weather, and the Tsar had the mortification of discovering he was a bad sailor. The imperial and royal visitors were greeted with a twenty-one-gun salute from a naval squadron and a hundred rounds of ceremonial cannon from Dover Castle, which brought excited townsfolk rushing to the harbour. Alexander, coming ashore in the early evening, abandoned his original plan of driving immediately to London and thankfully accepted hospitality for the night from a local resident, a Mr Fector.[42] Among the crowd on the quay was the young daughter of a British diplomat, Maria Capel, who was far from impressed by the Tsar's bearing: 'I was near enough to touch them and think the Emperor not the least handsome', she wrote with the ruthless candour of a seventeen-year-old to her grandmother, '*horribly* Pink and Pudding-like.' He left Dover at seven the following morning, with the minimum of fuss. Maria Capel remained critical of him: 'I am afraid', she wrote, 'Alexander will cause great discontent by going Incog. this morning for the whole road has for 10 days been covered with triumphal arches and the inns full of flowers. Alexander did not pull off his hat or even bow to the people, which I think is rather odd.'[43]

She was not the only one to be surprised by his behaviour that day. His landau sped rapidly past the hedgerows and hop-fields of Kent, covering the sixty-five miles to the outskirts of London in little more than five hours. At Blackheath he was met by his ambassador with the news of great crowds awaiting him south of London Bridge, apparently eager to unhorse his carriage and receive him as warmly as the people of Banbury had his sister. Apprehension, or the peculiar shyness which at times swept unexpectedly over him, made him order a change of route. The landau swung to the south, and, passing through the Surrey villages of Camberwell and Clapham, crossed the Thames at Battersea and turned down Knightsbridge and into Piccadilly. There young Thomas de Quincey, strolling in the afternoon sunshine, was surprised to see a commotion at the corner of Albemarle Street. A tall and smiling man in a dark green uniform stepped down smartly from his carriage, blew a brotherly kiss to a woman at a window on the first floor and hurried up the steps of the Pulteney Hotel.[44] 'The countless crowds that awaited him . . . in amphitheatres . . . let at exorbitant prices', wrote Dorothea Lieven later, were 'a trifle angry at this smuggling in; the English people loves royalty to show itself in state.'[45]

But, if so, they soon forgave him. Within an hour Piccadilly was blocked by onlookers cheering for Alexander to appear on the balcony. The Prince Regent had announced his intention of paying his guest a courtesy call; and the Tsar and his sister waited for him to arrive in their suite on the first floor, occasionally stepping out on to the balcony to acknowledge the cheers, the Lievens accompanying them each time. Alexander grew impatient; Catherine made it clear this was the treatment she expected from the Regent, and Count Lieven was flustered with embarrassment. 'At last at four o'clock', writes Dorothea Lieven, 'came a note from Bloomfield (the Regent's secretary) to my husband to this effect: "His Royal Highness has been threatened with annoyance in the streets if he shows himself: it is therefore impossible for him to come and see the Emperor".' Alexander was forced to make his way in Lieven's carriage through the crowds to Carlton House for his first meeting with the Prince Regent.[46]

It was as frigid an encounter as Alexander's unfortunate visit to Louis XVIII at Compiègne. Quite apart from the frustrations of the day, the Regent was intensely jealous of the Tsar. Like Alexander he loved the trappings of soldiery but he had never been permitted to command troops in the field. From private letters written by the Regent to his mother during the campaigns of 1812–14 it is clear he identified himself with the fortunes of Allied arms on the continent as a whole and not merely in the Peninsula; he considered himself present in spirit at each great encounter, from the Berezina to Leipzig.[47] The arrival of the Tsar in person deflated these illusions. As if that were not in itself galling enough, Alexander had now spurned his invitation to go into residence at St James's Palace, choosing to stay at the Pulteney Hotel with that insufferable Duchess of Oldenburg who presumed to lecture him on the way he should bring up his own daughter. What each man said to the other in the half hour they were together remains unknown. It cannot have been a happy exchange of words. Afterwards Alexander commented dryly to his ambassador, 'A poor Prince', and it is not unlikely that the Regent may have spoken extravagantly of the part he had played in the defeat of Napoleon. At all events the two men remained coldly disposed towards each other for the remainder of Alexander's stay in England.[48] In all fairness the blame was not entirely the Regent's: the Tsar, as he had indicated to Napoleon at Tilsit, was not well-disposed towards the British, and the elaborate exchange of compliments between the Prince and Louis XVIII had irritated him even before he left Paris. Moreover he had just spent a couple of hours listening to the venomous barbs of his favourite sister's conversation. Only the most determined and well-disposed of charmers could overcome such prejudice, and this was a role which, in his present mood, the Prince Regent was incapable of fulfilling.

Yet, whatever the feeling at Court, popular adulation of the Russian visitors continued so long as the Tsar was in London. He was cheered to the King's Theatre in the Haymarket and the Theatre Royal, Covent Garden, and even when he drove out to breakfast at the 'Star and Garter' in Richmond he was nearly mobbed.[49] In a letter written a few days after the Tsar's departure, Mary Russell Mitford – soon to become famous for her essays on rural life, *Our Village* – described the excitement in polite Society over Alexander's charm and grace: 'Over him the ladies were as mad as maniacs at the full moon', she said. 'To obtain a kiss of the same magnanimous hand, they threw themselves *toutes éplorées* with nosegays at his feet.'[50] People up early could see this God-creature walking like a mere mortal beside his sister in the Park or riding out through the fields of Marylebone to the nothern slopes of Hampstead and Highgate, where the City families had their *dachas* as on the hills west of Moscow. Later in the day it was difficult for either Alexander or Catherine to move so freely. Returning to the Pulteney Hotel from the customary tourist's visit to Westminster Abbey and the British Museum, they found frenzied women trying to grasp them by the hand as they stepped down from their carriage. But Alexander, who had known this rapturous treatment in Moscow, was not especially troubled. 'On ascending the steps of his hotel', *The Times* reported with reverential awe, 'His Imperial Majesty turned round to the people and most condescendingly took off his hat.'[51]

For most of his three weeks in London Alexander's time was occupied with State occasions or formal functions. The public saw the Tsar in scarlet and gold dress uniform driving through the streets to banquets and gala performances, his sister invariably accompanying him and wearing, whenever possible, a hat with a pendant feather so as to give her the appearance of a stature she did not possess. Society, of course, amused itself by commenting on the women to whom Alexander seemed attentive. It was noted that his most frequent partner for waltzes was the Countess of Jersey, once the Prince of Wales's mistress but long since fallen from favour. The Tsar's preference for the Countess irritated the Regent, much to the amusement of the gossips.[52] On the first Sunday he was in London (12 June) they had another morsel to chew on. That afternoon the Tsar (and most of the other 'visiting heroes') went riding in Hyde Park, watched inevitably by a cheering crowd of Londoners. Princess Charlotte happened to decide to take a drive through the Park in her carriage while the excitement was at its peak. To everyone's satisfaction, Alexander 'gallantly rode up to speak to her twice'. Cam Hobhouse, good Whig that he was, thought the incident worthy of entry in his journal;[53] so no doubt did Charlotte.

Two days later the whole cavalcade of sovereigns and dignitaries made its way to Oxford, where the University had resolved to confer honorary doctorates on Europe's liberators. Alexander, wearing 'a plain blue coat', and Catherine in 'a plain travelling dress with a large straw bonnet shaded by a broad feather', arrived in an open barouche and four at the gate of Merton College, where the Russian visitors were to spend the night. They were received by Dr Vaughan, the Warden, and almost immediately taken on a tour of the University, which Catherine had already visited the previous month. The Tsar admired the Hall of Christ Church and the chapel of New College. At that point the Imperial progress was delayed by Catherine, who insisted on her brother being taken to see the rooms of Mr Walls, one of the Junior Fellows, who had entertained her in May. There was just time for a hurried visit to the Bodleian Library before preparing for the formal banquet under the dome of the Radcliffe Camera. Next morning the Prince Regent, the Tsar, the King of Prussia, Prince Metternich, Marshal Blücher and a long procession of generals and diplomats made their way from Christ Church to the Sheldonian Theatre where Alexander was made a Doctor of Civil Law. No less than seven Odes, written especially for the occasion, were then recited: two in Greek, one in Latin and five in English. They were, reported an anonymous member of the University, 'gracefully acknowledged and appreciated but by no one more than by the Duchess of Oldenburg, who seemed to live upon the applause and the merits of her Imperial Brother'.[54] This is hardly surprising for, though the metre and rhyming patterns were at times strange, the sentiments were gratifyingly generous. Thus Mr John Hughes B.A. of Oriel College declaimed:

> Reviving Europe breathes at last
> And hails in him th'Immortal Czar,
> The pure and steadfast ray of Freedom's morning star.[55]

No doubt it sounded good on a warm summer's day in the Sheldonian.

There followed a ceremony in Oxford Town Hall, where Alexander was made a Freeman of the City. At last, around two o'clock, lunch was served in All Souls' College before the Tsar and Frederick William were hurried off to Woodstock to be entertained at Blenheim Palace by the Duke of Marlborough. When he was about to leave Blenheim it was noticed that Alexander, unlike Frederick William, showed no interest in 'the magnificent prospect of the Park and the woods'.[56] This, however, was no sign of flagging energy or of sudden insensitivity to landscape, as at least one onlooker suspected. Alexander was becoming impatient. That night Lady Jersey was giving a ball, and he was determined to be back in London before it ended.[57] He arrived soon after 3 a.m. and was still dancing reels a couple of hours later. Was he not, after all, 'Freedom's morning star'?

The most impressive and ornate banquet of the State visit was offered by the City of London at the Guildhall on the following Saturday, 18 June. It was, the *Annual Register* declares, 'a dinner as sumptuous as expense or skill could make it'.[58] But it was marred by niggling friction between

the Regent and the Tsar and his sister. The trouble had begun that morning when the Prince Regent invited Alexander to accompany him in the
State Coach to the Guildhall. The Tsar declined to go unless Catherine
could also travel with him. The Regent sent a messenger back with the
curt rejoinder that this was impossible 'as no woman ever went in the same
coach with the sovereign when he appeared in public as such'.[59] Eventually
the State coach bore the Prince Regent and the King of Prussia to the
Guildhall at half-past five and returned to Piccadilly for the Tsar and his
sister, who did not arrive until an hour later. Alexander then distinguished
himself by stopping to talk to the leaders of the Whig Opposition as the
solemn procession made its way between seven hundred guests to the
dais of honour; and Catherine, faced by the prospect of operatic artists
with patriotic songs, dampened the festivities by reminding her neighbours that music always made her ill. The Prince Regent throughout the
evening treated the Tsar and his sister to 'a haughty silence'.[60]

Such episodes rapidly lost Alexander favour in Society. Even Lord
Grey, a member of the Whig Opposition especially befriended by the
Tsar, was annoyed and embarrassed by his behaviour, describing Alexander
to Creevey as 'a vain silly fellow'.[61] It is difficult to understand why a
sovereign who was, in St Petersburg, so full of charm and grace should
have deliberately persisted in this adolescent mood of social revolt. Was it
a reaction from the tensions of the war years? Was it an irrational and
largely subconscious resentment of England's urbane prosperity? Or was
it, perhaps, a political miscalculation, a belief that the Regent was so unpopular with the London masses that the best way to retain public
sympathy was to snub him on every occasion?

There is another possibility. Alexander's boorishness may well have
reflected an inner struggle of conscience; he might thus, in a clumsy
fashion, have been protesting against the complacent frivolity of life in
London at such a time of European crisis. Certainly, in the closing days of
his visit to England, the serious side of his character suddenly asserted itself.
The Tsar had long known of the existence of the 'Quakers', the Society of
Friends. As a child he had been inoculated by Thomas Dimsdale, who was
widely known as 'the Quaker Doctor', and Mrs Dimsdale had briefly
nursed Alexander in an illness.[62] The concept of the Friends was therefore
by no means strange to the Tsar, and when the London Quakers presented
him with a petition seeking protection for 'the many pious persons' in
Russia 'searching for themselves into the things pertaining to salvation',
the Tsar was at once interested. This language corresponded so closely
with the habit of religious contemplation which had come to mean so

much to him in the previous two years that he asked his ambassador, Lieven, to keep in touch with the Quakers who had brought the petition to the Pulteney Hotel.[63]

On the Sunday morning following the Guildhall Banquet the Tsar suddenly asked Lieven to arrange for him to attend a Quaker meeting that day. By good chance the ambassador was able to contact the prominent Quaker, William Allen, who conducted Alexander and Catherine to the Friends' Meeting House off St Martin's Lane, where they heard two brief addresses and an inspired prayer.[64] Alexander was so impressed that he invited William Allen and two other Friends to visit him at the Pulteney on the following Tuesday morning, the day before his departure from London.

It is difficult to recognize in the sober prose of William Allen's journal the same man who had caused such offence at the Guildhall:

The Emperor having been engaged till six o'clock that morning, was not up when we arrived, and we had to wait about two hours and a half. At last a message came for us, and Stephen Grellet, John Wilkinson and I were shown upstairs ... The Emperor stood to receive us; he was quite alone and dressed in a plain suit of clothes and, with a look of benignity, seemed to meet us as friends, rather than as strangers ... The conversation was carried on partly in English, which he spoke and even pronounced very well, and partly in French ... On the subject of worship he said he agreed entirely with Friends, that it was an internal and spiritual thing. He said that he was himself in the habit of daily prayer, that at first he employed a form of words but at length grew uneasy with them as not always applicable to the present state of his mind, and that now the subject of his prayer was according to the impression he felt of his wants at the time, and in this exercise he felt sweet peace ... He remarked that divine worship consisted not in outward ceremonies or repetition of words, which the wicked and the hypocrite might easily adopt, but in having the mind prostrate before the Lord ... He expressed how much he was disgusted with the practice which prevailed in this country, of sitting several hours after dinner, saying it was a waste of time which might be employed for the good of our fellow creatures.[65]

The conversation, which included many questions about the domestic way of life of Quaker families, lasted for 'about an hour'. At the end of it the Tsar asked that if any Friends visited St Petersburg they should at once come and see him. William Allen and his two friends were convinced of Alexander's sincerity of faith; and there is no reason for doubting that, at the time, the Tsar meant every word that he said.

Alexander set out for Portsmouth on Wednesday, 22 June. The Prince

Regent entertained the Tsar and his sister, for the last time, on the royal yacht and they witnessed the magnificent spectacle of a naval review at Spithead. They bade farewell to the Regent at Petworth and followed the coastal road through Sussex and into Kent. On the Downs behind Hastings, Alexander noticed two people in Quaker dress and immediately ordered his coachman to stop. Nathaniel Rickman and his wife, Mary, were a little surprised to be accosted in this way, but they too were deeply impressed by Alexander's searching questions and willingly showed their royal visitors around the farmhouse and their small dairy.[66] After taking refreshment, Alexander and his sister climbed back into the barouche and disappeared towards Dover in a cloud of summer dust.

The Tsar sailed for Ostend on Monday, 27 June. This time it was a calm crossing. He parted from his sister in Ghent, paid a brief courtesy visit to the Netherlands and then travelled on through the Rhineland, which was swept that midsummer by torrential thunderstorms.[67] On 5 July he reached Bruchsal, the summer residence of the Badenese royal family twenty miles north of Karlsruhe, and there at last he was reunited with the Empress Elizabeth. He spent five days at Bruchsal recovering from the rigours of the English visit and the strain of an exhausting journey.[68] Now that there was a lull in the excitement of Peace he needed some moments of rest and reflection before continuing the long drive to St Petersburg.

There was much with which he could occupy his mind. Socially and politically the three weeks which Alexander spent in London had proved to be a disaster. No major decisions were taken over the future of Europe, although Czartoryski had useful conversations on Poland with eminent members of both the Tory and the Whig establishments. Alexander himself did not realize the devastating effect of his apparent boorishness. Naturally he knew he had offended the Regent, and Castlereagh's cold manner left him in no doubt of the attitude taken by the Government but he was convinced that the attentions he had paid to the Whig leaders would win him support from the Opposition, particularly for his Polish policy. This was a double error of judgement. The Whigs, especially Brougham, did subsequently champion the liberties of Poland in their writings and speeches; but they wanted a more genuinely independent Polish State than Alexander contemplated. Moreover it was foolish for any foreign visitor to court the Opposition at a time of intensive feuding between the political parties: radical backing in the Commons for Polish nationalism confirmed Castlereagh's belief he was right to resist official Russian policy. None of the Whigs publicly lauded Alexander. They resented what they felt to be an arrogantly patronizing manner and they mistrusted his immediate intentions. Even the British people were disillusioned with their earlier idol. Significantly the popular cartoonist Cruickshank began to ridicule the Tsar, making great play with his surprise descent on the Rickman family at their farmhouse in Sussex. Only the English Quakers were pleased with the outcome of the Tsar's journey across the Channel, and politically they were of no account whatsoever.

It could, of couse, be argued that had Alexander roared London as gently as any sucking dove, British distrust of Russian expansion would still have thrown the government into opposition to his policy. There is truth in this: the Foreign Office had been suspicious of Russian intentions ever since the closing years of Catherine's reign; and Castlereagh was acutely conscious of the long shadow of Russia's armed strength across Europe that summer. But Alexander's behaviour – and his sister's indiscretions – hardened old prejudices which it should have been his intention to allay. Inevitably the Regent and Castlereagh drew close in sympathy to the Austrians, not least because of Metternich's skill in finding appropriate words of flattery for every occasion. So marked was the distrust between the Allies that when Alexander asked for the Vienna Congress to be postponed from mid-August until late September so that he could return to Russia and settle outstanding domestic problems, the British and Austrians suspected he was planning a unilateral declaration on Polish affairs which would pre-judge much of the Congress's work.[69] They accordingly induced the Russians to undertake that nothing would be irrevocably decided before the opening of the Congress and that no armies would be set on the march without prior agreement of all the Allied Powers. It was an ominous prospect for the making of peace that the master of the largest army in Europe should be asked to give such a pledge.

17

The Panorama of Europe

Preparing for the Vienna Congress in St Petersburg and at Puławy

Alexander returned home to Russia in a sombre mood. He had entered Berlin, Dresden, Frankfurt and Paris in grand style and celebrated with the English all the revelry of Peace: now, on his personal instructions, there was no ceremonial welcome for him in St Petersburg. While still at Bruchsal he had received a deputation of high dignitaries from the Church and members of the Council of State who asked him to sanction the erection of a victory column in the centre of his capital and begged him to accept the agnomen of 'Blessed' in acknowledgement of his leadership of the nation in the struggle against the invader.[1] But he was reluctant to be accorded any form of triumph; he refused to allow the monument to be constructed during his lifetime and, though he made no effort to prevent his subjects using the courtesy title which they sought to bestow on him, he let it be seen that he regarded himself as unworthy of such an honour. He slipped back into St Petersburg unheralded on 24 July. Although Marie Feodorovna insisted on giving a magnificent banquet at Pavlovsk, he forbade all other celebrations of his return. A *Te Deum* was sung in the Kazan Cathedral: the victory, he contended, came from the Grace of God, not from his own efforts. It seemed to him wrong to rejoice at the ending of the war while there was so much suffering and devastation in the Empire. Moreover he wished to remind his subjects of the need to attain victory in peace. Only when the final settlement was agreed and accepted by all the Allies would Russia's tribulations be finally at an end. If foreign observers commented on the contrast between his quiet homecoming and the celebrations in London and Vienna, so much the better.

As if to emphasize the temporary character of his return to St Petersburg, he had already insisted that Elizabeth should remain at Bruchsal and come to join him in Vienna for the opening of the Congress rather than accompany him back to Russia.[2] For most of the seven weeks which he spent in the capital he was busy with preparations for the Congress. There were two immediate tasks facing him: selection of a team of ministers and advisers who would participate in the negotiations at Vienna; and the establishment of a provisional administration for the Polish lands, which would show to the Allies his intention of consolidating Russia's gains in the Vistulan basin without frightening them into taking drastic counter-measures. He had also to resolve at least one, and possibly more than one, family problem. His sister, Catherine, could only remarry with her mother's consent, and Marie Feodorovna did not approve of her daughter's preference for the Austrian Archduke Charles as a second husband. Alexander had therefore to discover whether the Dowager Empress was adamant in her opposition and, if so, how she would regard a marriage between Catherine and her nephew, William of Württemberg, whom the Grand Duchess had met during her visit to England. Moreover, the Tsar's youngest sister, Anna Pavlovna, was still without a husband; and Alexander was anxious to sound out his mother on the possibilities of a marriage between her and the Prince of Orange, with whom Princess Charlotte had dramatically broken off her engagement in June.[3] These domestic matters were of trivial importance compared to the political questions uppermost in Alexander's mind; but it would appear as if they alone were responsible for the Tsar's unexpected decision to go back to Russia before the opening of the Congress. He could have chosen his team for Vienna and arranged affairs in Poland without setting foot inside his Empire: marriage projects, however, needed discussion with the matriarch at Pavlovsk. Since every eligible princely bachelor in Europe outside the House of Hanover would be present in Vienna for the Congress, it was essential to run through the list of starters with Marie Feodorovna in person. The fact that she failed to give Alexander a clear decision over the prospects for either of her daughters did not make his subsequent task any easier.

Selecting a delegation for Vienna was, on the other hand, relatively straightforward. Technically foreign affairs were still the responsibility of Chancellor Rumiantsev, but he had been handling only minor chancellery matters for the past two years and, as his health was poor, he welcomed Alexander's return as an opportunity to retire from all governmental posts. The Tsar thereupon named Nesselrode 'State Secretary for Foreign Affairs', although observers considered that by denying him full ministerial rank Alexander 'was disclosing that he himself could control this department'.[4] Of almost equal standing in the Russian delegation was Count Andrei Razumovsky, for many years ambassador in Vienna, and Alexander also ordered Adam Czartoryski to accompany him to the Congress as the chief spokesman of the Russian Poles. General Pozzo di Borgo, a Corsican who had been in Russian service since 1805, was invited to assist the Tsar as specialist on the affairs of France and the western Mediterranean lands in general.[5] The surprise selection was the thirty-eight-year-old Corfiote aristocrat, John Capodistrias, who first threw in his lot with the Russians when Admiral Senyavin's squadron occupied the Ionian Islands and who had recently been entrusted by Alexander with a delicate diplomatic mission in Switzerland. The Tsar himself described Capodistrias in a private letter to La Harpe as 'a very commendable man by virtue of his enlightened and liberal views'; but his rapid advancement caused alarm in Britain and Austria, where it was assumed that the favours shown towards him were a sign of renewed Russian interest in the Eastern Question and in the fate of the Greeks within the Turkish Empire.[6] Foreign chancelleries were also displeased at the extent to which the Tsar continued to depend for advice over German questions on Stein, although the delegation contained two other German specialists, Count Anstedt and Count Stackelberg. In the whole of Alexander's suite there was only one major adviser of Russian parentage, Count Razumovsky, and even he prided himself on his cosmopolitan outlook to such an extent that he disdained ever to write a letter or an official document in his native language. Small wonder Metternich's intelligence service reported that the old Russian families were incensed by the hold which foreigners were securing on their sovereign's way of thought.[7] What had once been condemned by simple patriots in the army now held good in the diplomatic service. There was not a single spokesman for the Tsar at the Congress who regarded himself as a representative of the Muscovite traditions of Holy Russia.

Nor was this the only aspect of peacemaking which disturbed the conservative landowners. They were alarmed at the implications of Alexander's policy towards Poland, fearing in particular the social effects on their estates in Lithuania and Byelo-Russia of incorporating into the Empire territories which had benefited from Napoleon's reforms. It seemed clear to them that serfdom would have to go, for a start; and what would follow serf emancipation? They viewed Alexander's provisional arrangements for the Polish lands with as much suspicion as did the statesmen abroad.[8]

Alexander knew well enough how he wished to solve the Polish Question: all the former territories of the Grand-Duchy of Warsaw would be annexed to Russia; to them would be added the province of Galicia, acquired, he hoped, by negotiation with Metternich and Emperor Francis; the Prussians would be compensated for the loss of Polish lands by the incorporation of Saxony in Frederick William's kingdom, and the Austrians placated by Russian support for Metternich's ambitions in Italy. Alexander would then proclaim the establishment of a Kingdom of Poland which would be technically independent of the other provinces of his Empire but united to them indissolubly through bonds of common allegiance to a joint sovereign. This was the future of Poland which he outlined to Czartoryski and other representatives of the great Polish families when he stopped at Pulawy once more on his way from St Petersburg to Vienna.[9] He assured the Poles he envisaged a kingdom with some ten or eleven million inhabitants and he approved a draft set of constitutional principles, drawn up and read out by Czartoryski and designed to establish a bicameral parliamentary system. On paper these concessions looked far more generous than the Poles had anticipated: many of them had fought for Napoleon – Czartoryski's brother, who was present at the Pulawy conferences, was actually decorated by the French for his bravery in the storming of Smolensk – and it seemed unbelievable that the Tsar would show such magnanimity. Was he, they wondered, promising more than he could give them?

Alexander was confident of success that autumn. He knew already he could count on Frederick William's support, even if the Prussian politicians were uneasy at the loss of so much territory in the east; he thought he could win over Metternich, and he discounted the significance of opposition from Castlereagh or Talleyrand. His greatest worry was the reluctance of the old Senatorial party at home to back his efforts and he sought to counter their hostility by appointing his brother Constantine, whom no one could suspect of liberal sentiments, as commander of the Polish Military Commission in Warsaw. Czartoryski was uneasy at finding the Grand Duke permanently settled in the Citadel but realized it was a sound political move on the part of the Tsar. He was also disturbed to find civil executive responsibilities entrusted to a provisional Supreme Council of which the chairman was the Russian Senator, Count Vasilli Lanskoy, but he consoled himself with the thought that Lanskoy's deputy was his friend and colleague from the old Secret Committee, Novosiltsov. None of the Poles doubted, then or later, that Alexander was perfectly sincere in the programme he outlined at Pulawy. He left them on 20 September full of hope for the immediate future.[10]

Alexander in Residence at the Hofburg

Five days later he made a grand ceremonial entry into the Austrian capital, the King of Prussia once more riding at his side. Emperor Francis placed at Alexander's disposal a whole wing of the Hofburg, his palace in the centre of the city. Also accommodated in the Hofburg were Frederick William and the heads of three other reigning dynasties, together with their wives. Everything was done to make the sovereigns happy and comfortable, and indeed to please the members of all the royal and princely families who flocked to Vienna that autumn. By modern reckoning Francis spent the equivalent of more than £5 million sterling on entertaining his guests. So that they might ride in the chestnut avenues of the Prater or hunt in the wooded hills to the south and west of the city, he saw to it that the Imperial stables were expanded in order to house fourteen hundred horses, from which the sovereigns and the princes might take their choice any morning or afternoon. A 'Festivals Committee' of Court dignitaries ensured that there were endless diversions and entertainments, quite apart from the numerous balls, banquets and concerts given by the great families of central Europe. Even in small matters, Francis was an attentive host; for when Alexander was suffering from a recurrence of erysipelas of the leg, it was arranged that every morning a block of fresh ice should be brought to him in the Hofburg, since immersion of the leg in melting ice was held (rather oddly) to be a cure for inflammation of the skin.[11]

Such generous hospitality at the very summit of Society set the fashion for Vienna that winter. More than a hundred thousand foreign visitors came to the city during the Congress, all but the most primly austere among them entranced by its dazzling social life. Perhaps one in twenty of these visitors actually participated in the business of peacemaking at some moment of their stay in Vienna. The remainder were extravagant extras in what one of the numerous police spies aptly described as 'the panorama of Europe'.[12] Never before had the cosmopolitan aristocracy of the whole continent staged so flamboyant a gala occasion; nor was the opportunity for them to lose themselves in such luxuriant excess to recur again. There was something magnificently baroque in the whole style of the Congress, from its concern with prescribing formal conventions of diplomatic behaviour down to its meticulous planning of social evenings and drawing-room receptions. At times the entertainments had a frenetic artificiality intolerable to sensitive spirits but, given the place and the occasion, they were undoubtedly in a minority.

To someone like Alexander the peculiar character of the Congress was perplexing in the extreme.[13] He always preferred to work his way painstakingly through memoranda and take his decision, or evade commitment, at leisure. This was impossible in Vienna. Although written documents were drawn up and presented, they tended to be mere statements of a position as often as not already invalidated by private conversation before the memoranda were circulated. He had assumed the actual task of peacemaking would be settled within six weeks and he would be back in St Petersburg – or, possibly, Warsaw – by the end of the year. To his dismay he found the representatives of the other Powers unaccommodating over his plans for Poland and distrustful of his intentions elsewhere in Europe. It was impossible for him to return home, leaving Nesselrode and Czartoryski to achieve the best settlement they could, for the delegation he had selected shared few principles in common and had no leader except himself. The Tsar was therefore forced to play an active political role in diplomatic gatherings which, because of their unusual form, he could never dominate. At the same time he had to appear, night after night, at ceremonial functions as sovereign of the most powerful State on the Eurasian land-mass. It was difficult for someone suffering from deafness and prone to erysipelas to preserve dignity and equanimity under such circumstances.

From the day of his arrival in Vienna Alexander was conscious of a particular cause of vexation. He knew he was surrounded by spies and informers who sent detailed reports to the Austrian Chief of Police, Baron Hager. At times the Tsar played an elaborate game of double bluff with them, carefully dropping astringent asides in private conversation which he dared not make publicly; but, he had no idea of the extent and efficiency of the Austrian intelligence service, nor of its skill in intercepting and copying other people's private letters.[14] As it was, he rapidly acquired a not undeserved reputation for amatory philandering on the grand scale, which was in striking contrast to the anguish and exultation of his spiritual life over the previous two years. Since there was such a close link in Vienna between the pattern of social behaviour and the serious tasks of the Congress, the revelations of Hager's spies were of considerable value. They emphasized, and probably intensified, the differences between Alexander and that arch-manipulator of feminine intrigue, Prince Metternich. It was hard to decide if the frequent eruptions of Austro-Russian friction were a consequence of genuine political doubts or ill-humour caused by the personal pique of rivals in the bed-chamber. Neither the Tsar nor Metternich wasted time during the Congress analysing the motives for their mutual antipathy: they accepted it as inevitable, and sought to counter each other's influence in public and private affairs, not always seeing a distinction between the two.

It was indeed difficult for Alexander to escape the vigilance of Hager's agents. Much of their work was fruitless. For example, at a display of horsemanship on the second Sunday of his visit to Vienna, Alexander was observed taking an interest in a young Viennese girl, the daughter of a petty official. By the following Wednesday morning Hager had the girl's name and address on his files and assigned an agent to keep her under regular surveillance: there is no evidence that she had further contact with the Tsar or any other visitor to the Congress.[15] It is less surprising to find Hager assigning a spy to watch No. 60 Paniglgasse, when Maria Naryshkin followed the Tsar to Vienna and took a lease of the house; the Austrians believed that, being Polish by birth, she was influencing Alexander's policy towards her native land; and the spy was able to discover that the Tsar had called on her twice in the same week and sent one of his aides-de-camp to her with confidential notes.[16] But the most rewarding place to report on his movements was the Schenkenstrasse, a small road only a few hundred yards from the Hofburg. For, by accident, two of the leading political courtesans of the day, the Duchess Wilhelmine of Sagan and Princess Katharina Bagration, had leased opposite wings of the same building in the Schenkenstrasse, the Palais Palm.[17] So much information reached Hager from the Schenkenstrasse that at times one feels everyone else in the road must have been a police spy: the only doubt remaining is in whose interest the two ladies themselves were working.

Alexander had known both of them for several years. Princess Bagration, widow of the army's heroic idol, was on her mother's side a great-niece of Catherine II and therefore a second cousin of the Tsar. She had left her husband soon after their marriage and spent most of her adult life in Dresden or Vienna and was intermittently one of the mistresses of Metternich, by whom she had conceived a daughter in 1802. Wilhelmine of Sagan was also technically a subject of Alexander as she was the eldest of the four daughters of the last Duke of Courland and still possessed considerable properties in the Baltic provinces. She was, however, essentially a member of the cosmopolitan aristocracy since, in addition to her Russian lands and the vast estate of Sagan in Prussia, she had a palace in Prague and a château at Ratiborzitz in Bohemia, where she had entertained Alexander (and, on the following day, Metternich) during the Armistice of Plaeswitz in 1813.[18] Her loyalties in Vienna were slightly strained: she was still excessively flattered by Metternich, to whom she had been a somewhat stormy mistress for the past eighteen months; she was visited and petted by Talleyrand, whose niece by marriage and official hostess at the Congress was her own youngest sister, Countess Dorothea de Périgord, later Duchess of Dino;* but she was also acutely conscious of the danger of losing her Russian and Prussian lands should there be a breach between Austria and the two other despoilers of Poland. The Tsar preferred the company of Princess Bagration who, at the age of thirty-two, retained the natural porcelain beauty of her youth, to which the years had added wit, intelligence and a mastery of the art of pleasing men. Wilhelmine, her rival, was more passionate but also more flagrantly libertine. Talleyrand, anxious to reassert the influence he had possessed over Alexander in Paris, encouraged Wilhelmine to fling herself wildly at the Tsar's head. As both Alexander himself and the Austrian police agents testify, there was one occasion when (in Alexander's words) 'they even shut us up *tête-à-tête* in the same carriage'.[19] But he considered himself too astute to fall for such clumsy wiles: he continued to visit the left wing of the Palais Palm, leaving Metternich, Talleyrand and others less discriminating to turn to the right and pay court to the Sagan.

At times the whole business sank to the level of a cheap farce. Thus on 30 September Princess Bagration had retired early to bed with a headache, having sent her servants out of the house for the evening, when she was disturbed by the porter ringing her bell four times. The Princess, dressed only in her negligée, came down the staircase, admitted Alexander with a proper show of pleased surprise and modest confusion, and ushered him upstairs to her room. There he at once noticed a man's hat, which had been left in a conspicuous position. 'It belongs to my decorator, Moreau', explained the Princess, 'he has come to get the house ready for my ball tomorrow.' Such an unlikely tale evidently satisfied the Tsar, for we are told they laughed heartily at his unfounded assumptions and he remained with her for two and a half hours; even the police agent who reported all this to Hager next day could not resist adding, at the end of

---

* Not least among the ironies of this complicated situation was the fact that Alexander himself had, in 1808, been largely responsible for arranging the marriage between Dorothea and Talleyrand's nephew, Edmond de Périgord (who subsequently appreciated his wife's gifts less than did his uncle). See Philip Ziegler's delightful biography, *The Duchess of Dino*.

his message, the injunction *Honi soit qui mal y pense*.[20]* And there were other episodes, hardly less ridiculous. Five evenings after the hat incident the Princess was disappointed to see, from her window, that Alexander's carriage turned into her courtyard and then drove away again. The Tsar had noticed so many vehicles drawn up outside the Palais Palm that he assumed the Princess was surrounded by numerous visitors and he did not wish to be counted among them. It appears, however, that the Duchess of Sagan was hostess that night. 'The poor Princess', wrote the sympathetic police informant in due course, 'was waiting for him quite alone, and she is waiting for him still.'[21]

Congress Diplomacy (October 1814–February 1815)

Meanwhile slowly, cautiously and reluctantly the statesmen were beginning their task of seeking a lasting settlement for Europe. The first talks had been held between Nesselrode, Castlereagh, Hardenberg of Prussia and Metternich before the Tsar arrived in Vienna. The ministers agreed on a method of work, if nothing more: decisions would be taken by the Big Four (Austria, Britain, Prussia and Russia) and then submitted to the French and Spanish for comment and approval, before being sent to the Congress as a whole for ratification; an inner council of the Four, together with France and Spain, would determine future work for the Congress and would pass all protocols for drafting to a nominated Secretary, Friedrich von Gentz; and it was finally agreed that the five leading German States would form a special committee to prepare a constitution for a German Confederation. These decisions were at once challenged by Talleyrand who, reaching Vienna only a week before the Congress was due to open, objected to his colleagues' refusal to give France equal status with the Big Four. The resultant procedural wrangles afforded Metternich an excuse for having the official opening of the Congress postponed until 1 November. In reality, as everyone knew, this delay was caused not so much by Talleyrand's tactics, inconvenient though they were, as by the desire of the other Allies to wear down Alexander's insistence on gaining for the Poles the settlement he had outlined at Pulawy. At Metternich's request Castlereagh, as spokesman for a Power not directly concerned in Polish matters, undertook to sound out the Tsar and seek to reason with him.[22]

---

* One naturally wonders who was Hager's informant. Since all the reports on Princess Bagration are written in French and show some style, it is probable that they originated with someone highly placed in her suite and enjoying her confidence to the full.

There were two aspects of Alexander's policy to which the Austrians and, for different reasons, the British objected: the incorporation of all the Polish lands in the Russian Empire, thereby assuring the Tsar of mastery in east-central Europe; and the prospect of handing over Saxony (which was, at that time, being administered by a Russian General) to Prussia as compensation for a renunciation of her former Polish possessions. Castlereagh failed to make any impression on Alexander, who said he would cede a small area in the north-west to Prussia but refused even to consider the return of the Tarnopol district to Austria. 'I have conquered the Duchy and I have half a million men to keep it', he declared bluntly to Castlereagh. 'I will give Prussia what is due to her but not a single village to Austria.'[23] In fact, though Castlereagh did not perceive it, Alexander was bitterly incensed with Metternich. He had expected to negotiate with the Austrians over the cession by them to his new Polish kingdom of the province of Galicia: he found instead a demand for the recovery of Tarnopol. He certainly had no intention of making concessions over Saxony, whose unfortunate King had come over to the Allied cause in the spring of 1813 and then returned to his old connection with Napoleon once the campaign opened in earnest. Although Alexander and Castlereagh exchanged elaborate verbal compliments and assured each other of their lasting friendship, the British Foreign Secretary was left in no doubt of Russian intentions. He continued to ply Alexander with arguments and memoranda throughout October, but he also made an effort to win over Hardenberg and thereby complete Alexander's isolation.[24]

In reality, the Tsar was in a far weaker position than Castlereagh appreciated. Though Nesselrode publicly backed up his sovereign's policy, privately he was appalled at what he termed the Tsar's 'unfortunate ideas on this fatal Polish Question'.[25] His doubts were shared by Pozzo di Borgo, who lost Alexander's favour temporarily by writing a memorandum on the subject in October, and even by the Tsar's old tutor La Harpe who had arrived in Vienna at the end of September, ostensibly to safeguard the interests of the Swiss cantons.[26] Criticisms and difficulties, together with what Castlereagh happily described as 'the impediments . . . of fêtes and private balls', threw Alexander into petulant ill-humour while, at the same time, increasing his obstinacy. 'There is always too much diplomacy around, and I don't like hypocrisy', he remarked loudly at a ball on the anniversary of the battle of Leipzig. 'I see too many diplomats here, and these people bore me.' And a week later he was grumbling testily in the salons, 'I'm only a simple soldier and understand nothing about politics.'[27] He convinced no one but himself.

Inwardly, however, he was beginning to see it was impossible to fulfil the whole of the Pulawy programme. By now he had discovered that Hardenberg was wavering under Castlereagh's pressure. But Alexander retained one trump. At the end of October he would accompany Frederick William and Francis to Hungary for peace celebrations in Buda. The sovereigns would not have their ministers in attendance. If he could delay any decision over the Polish Question, here would be an opportunity for the three autocrats themselves to settle matters without the tiresome diplomats fussing around them. Once they were agreed, they could come back to Vienna and send Metternich and his crew about their business. This would be a decisive gesture in the spirit of Tilsit: for had not Castlereagh hinted to Nesselrode only a few days previously that Russia was now the military legatee of Napoleon's imperium?[28]

First, however, Alexander was faced with difficult interviews with both Talleyrand and Metternich. The principal objection of the French to Alexander's plan for Poland was that it necessitated compensation for Prussia in Saxony or, worse still, on the Rhine. Talleyrand was therefore authorized by Louis XVIII to make it clear to Alexander that France would not accept his solution of the Polish Question. The Tsar accorded Talleyrand an audience on 23 October (having caused a sensation earlier that day by driving to the Palais Palm and turning to the right for a private lunch with the Duchess of Sagan rather than visiting Katharina Bagration, on his left). Alexander does not appear to have been at his best during his talk with Talleyrand. The Frenchman sought to defend King Frederick Augustus of Saxony's claims to the throne, on the ground that it would be dangerous for any sovereign to deprive a legitimate king of his rightful inheritance. 'But', maintained Alexander, 'Frederick Augustus was a traitor to the common cause.' 'That, Sire', replied Talleyrand blandly, 'is a question of dates.'[29] Alexander had found him far more reasonable six months ago in Paris.

The meeting with Metternich on the following afternoon was even stormier. The Prince had been asked to present to the Tsar, on behalf of the other Allies, a choice between three possible solutions of the Polish problem: a genuinely independent State, a truncated Polish kingdom as in 1791, or a return to the partitioned boundaries of 1795. Alexander rejected all three suggestions: he would, he explained yet again, proclaim an independent Poland linked indissolubly to the Russian Crown. But, replied Metternich, Austria could just as well create an independent Poland under the Habsburgs rather than accept this solution. The remark irritated the Tsar and he lost his temper. In language which Metternich likened to Napoleon's he made it clear that he did not consider the Austrian Foreign Minister a fit person to negotiate with him over Poland. 'You are the only man in Austria who would dare to oppose me in such rebellious terms', he declared; and for two hours he listed his grievances against Metternich and his way of work. It was impossible to transact any business that day. Soon rumour was embellishing the whole incident until it was said in the salons that the two men would have fought a duel but for the intervention of Emperor Francis.[30] Matters were not that bad but they might well have been, for personal antagonism over the ladies of the Palais Palm added salt to what were essentially political injuries. For nearly five months Alexander and Metternich did not address a word directly to each other.

The three sovereigns paid their brief State visit to Hungary in the closing days of October. It was a richly colourful pageant, dominated by the Magyar aristocrats and by Alexander's brother-in-law, the Palatine Archduke Joseph. During the return journey up the Danube the Tsar at last had an opportunity to let his companions know his views on diplomacy in general and the conduct of individual ministers in particular. Yet if he hoped to gain a moral ascendancy over the Emperor Francis he was disappointed. By now Francis knew him too well to be impressed by his contention that a monarch should be served by a minister who would always reflect his master's views. Alexander did not allow for the natural conservatism of Francis's temperament: he had no wish to dismiss a Foreign Minister whose ways and objectives he knew and almost understood; better every time the familiar than the unknown. Amiably but firmly, the Tsar was told that Francis had found from experience it was wiser to allow a minister to conduct business with someone else's minister or with an ambassador rather than with a king or emperor. Privately Francis appears to have been amused at Alexander's difficulties with Metternich, about which Hager's agents had, of course, kept him well informed.[31] With Frederick William, on the other hand, the Tsar had more success. He was still sufficiently under Alexander's influence to send for Hardenberg and instruct him, in the Tsar's presence, not to hold any more confidential negotiations with Metternich or Castlereagh over the problems of Poland and Saxony. At the same time the Tsar agreed to order the transference of administration in occupied Saxony from his own Generals to the Prussian army. This gesture was interpreted in Vienna as a sign of Alexander's growing impatience.[32] Rather than tolerate Metternich's delaying tactics any longer, the Tsar would impose his own solution of the Saxon-Polish Question and confront the Congress with a *fait accompli.* Even Princess Bagration was heard to complain that whenever she tried talking to Alexander about Poland and Saxony she found he would 'not listen to reason'.[33]

In reality, as Metternich and Gentz had foreseen, the Tsar could not impose his settlement of the Polish problem without sacrificing his older ambitions of reconstructing Europe as a whole according to generous principles of communal interest. As Stein made clear to him in a memorandum, the proposed bargain which would give Saxony to Prussia while leaving most of Poland under a Russian ruler was extremely unpopular with all the German States, including those with whom Alexander had traditional dynastic links.[34] Pozzo di Borgo supported Stein's arguments and, by the second week of November, it was clear to observers in Vienna that Nesselrode too was out of sympathy with his master's Polish policy.[35] Metternich, after the great quarrel at the end of October, refused to intervene but both Talleyrand and Castlereagh worried Alexander over the matter on which he was most sensitive, his image as a beneficent European statesman. The British Foreign Secretary wished to put the Polish Question before the Congress as a whole so that all the governments of Europe might see for themselves 'His Imperial Majesty's pretensions to an aggrandizement of Poland', while Talleyrand more succinctly warned Alexander that if he persisted in his attitude on the Polish and Saxon Questions he 'might sacrifice his fame as the pacificator of Europe'.[36]

At the end of the second week in December Alexander's mood changed with disconcerting rapidity. On 10 December he was so ill-disposed towards the Austrians that he could hardly bring himself to address any words to his host in the Hofburg: five days later he seemed full of benevolent goodwill, inviting Francis to meet him for two long discussions and showing for the first time a willingness to retrocede to Austria the Tarnopol region of eastern Galicia acquired, by grace of Napoleon, in 1809. Four days later still it was widely accepted in Vienna that the Tsar was ready to compromise over Poland and, a sone of Hager's agents put it, 'he was no longer warmly disposed towards Prussia'.[37] There followed, at the beginning of the New Year, a highly artificial crisis when, for a couple of days, it seemed as if Prussia and Russia might risk war rather than give way over Poland and Saxony; but the scare was totally without foundation in fact. Sensing that the Tsar's attitude towards them was indeed changing, the Prussians indulged in indiscreet sabre-rattling and their panic gestures were magnified by Talleyrand so as to improve the diplomatic status of France. A secret defensive alliance between Austria, Britain and France was actually concluded on 3 January 1815, theoretically to curb the pretensions of Alexander and the Prussians; but there was never any real prospect that the three signatories would be called upon to fight.[38] If Talleyrand's treaty had any significance at all it was as a bluff to call a bluff: Prussia lacked the resources to go to war for Saxony, and Alexander certainly had no intention of waging yet another campaign in Poland. The worst disputes were over before the alliance was concluded.

By the end of January it was clear the Powers were at last making progress towards a settlement. The Russians gave no trouble over the territorial boundaries in Italy and made clear their willingness to accept Castlereagh's design for a united Kingdom of the Netherlands provided the British assumed responsibility for settling debts incurred by the Dutch to the Russians.[39] More surprisingly, Alexander acquiesced in Castlereagh's proposal that Corfu and the Ionian Islands should become a British protectorate, despite the active Russian interest in the southern Adriatic and the assurances which the Tsar had given to his Corfiote adviser, Capodistrias, that he would 'never abandon the Ionian Islands'.[40] There remained, in these opening weeks of 1815, a suspicion that Alexander was intriguing with Bernadotte to secure joint Russo-Swedish rights on the Baltic coast of Pomerania, but the fear was groundless: the Tsar stood by the pledge he had given in 1812 that Sweden should acquire Norway from Napoleon's Danish ally as compensation for the loss of Finland, and although the British were uneasy at this particular territorial bargain, nobody at the Congress challenged it.[41] By the middle of February the principal spokesmen at Vienna, having scared each other with war talk over Poland, were eager to compromise in all other matters; and even the Polish-Saxon problems no longer seemed intractable.

Serious negotiations over Poland continued throughout the first six weeks of the New Year. It rapidly became clear Hager's spies were correct: Alexander's attitude had, indeed, mellowed during the Christmas period. He was now reluctant to support Prussian claims to the whole of Saxony and he abandoned the full Polish territorial demands which he had put forward in the autumn. In the third week of February he accepted a new partition of the Polish lands: Austria retained Galicia and received back Tarnopol and Czartow; Prussia recovered Poznania, including the towns of Posen (Poznan) and Thorn; Cracow, the ancient cultural and religious capital of the Polish nation, became a Free City; and the rest of Napoleon's Grand-Duchy, including Warsaw itself, was created a kingdom to be ruled in perpetuity by the sovereign of Russia.[42] This arrangement fell short of the generous scheme Alexander had outlined at Pulawy in September but the Polish aristocrats, hardened realists to the core by now, welcomed it as at least a partial restoration of their national State. They were fully prepared to co-operate with Czartoryski in preparing a constitution for the 'Congress Kingdom'; and they were deeply conscious of the need to retain Alexander's goodwill and his interest in their country's future. Ultimately everything depended on the Tsar's willingness to distinguish between his obligations as Autocrat of All the Russias and the new responsibilities he was assuming as a specifically Polish sovereign. Not everyone shared Czartoryski's sanguine optimism.[43]

The Saxon settlement took longer to determine. Rather belatedly, the legitimate ruler of Saxony, Frederick Augustus, was brought to Pressburg (Bratislava) for consultation. After more than a year of virtual internment he proved less accommodating than the representatives of the Great Powers anticipated. By the end of February it was agreed by everyone except the King himself that he would receive back three-fifths of his territories (including the cities of Dresden and Leipzig) while the remaining two-fifths would be incorporated in Prussia. Diplomatic wrangling between the King and the Allies continued until the first week of April when Frederick Augustus, perceiving that none of the Great Powers was impressed by his protests, gave way and returned chastened to his capital. Alexander, for his part, had long since lost all interest in Saxony and refused to send a minister to Pressburg for talks with the King.[44]

Alexander's Change of Heart

Participants in the Congress, and casual observers as well, were intrigued by the evident change of heart in Alexander during the second part of December and the first weeks of January. There was much speculation over what had caused him to modify his views. Metternich at first feared he had merely abandoned the struggle over Poland because of the growing influence of Capodistrias and the anti-Turks, who wished him to champion the Greek Christians and raise the problems of the Eastern Question at the Congress.[45] Others said Alexander had lost his enthusiasm for the Poles because Czartoryski and the Empress Elizabeth had re-kindled the mutual enchantment which had drawn them to each other in the reign of Paul; but, although there is no doubt they experienced in Vienna a passionate resurrection of their old love, Alexander certainly did not lessen his political reliance upon the Polish Prince; nor does he appear to have resented his liaison with Elizabeth any more intensely than fifteen years previously.[46] It is unlikely to have influenced Alexander's policy in any respect.

The Austrian intelligence service tended to attribute his change of attitude to the influence of the Grand Duchess Catherine.[47] This was a reasonable assumption. Catherine had made her presence felt in Vienna ever since her arrival in the city. Her command of languages, her knowledge of scientific matters, her determined views on war and soldiering, won respect among the great European aristocrats, who treated her in a very different manner from the Tories and Whigs of London. Who, the gossips wondered, would be her second husband? Until the beginning of December Catherine seemed still to favour the Archduke Charles, who was, after all, one of the most respected military commanders of his generation. It is, however, impossible to believe that two such masterful egotists would have lived happily together for more than a few weeks, and it would seem that one of them – probably the Archduke – was sensible enough to realize the absurdity of such a marriage. At all events by the middle of December one of Hager's spies confidently reported that 'the projected marriage between the Prince Royal of Württemberg and the Grand Duchess Catherine has been finally arranged'.[48] There was a dramatic morning in which Catherine, between two fainting fits, managed to renounce Charles and declare herself for William; then all that remained was to determine the form of settlement and the date of marriage. Since the King of Württemberg was, at sixty, prematurely old and said to be ailing, there was a good prospect Catherine would find herself a Queen-Consort before many months had passed. In that case she had every reason for wishing Alexander to retain influence over the new German Confederation, which would be impossible if he continued to encourage the Prussians to annex Saxony. Once Catherine began to see herself as a good Württemberger she naturally sided with the anti-Prussian camp. Alexander, as ever, listened to her readily and with respect.

It would, however, be a mistake to credit Catherine exclusively with the conversion of Alexander. He experienced this December a deeper change of mood and behaviour. During the first ten or eleven weeks he spent in Vienna he continued to scandalize the prurient by a casual display of sensual indulgence on the grand scale. He amused himself, not only with the ladies of the Palais Palm, but with two Hungarian Countesses, three members of the German-Austrian aristocracy and a number of pretty Viennese girls of considerably lower social standing.[49] But in the second week of December he suddenly began to discipline his habits.

Significantly the printed police reports on his movements do not mention any private visits to ladies of fashion after 5 December, when he was said to have been taken ill while alone with Princess Bagration.[50] In January a Madame Schwarz arrived in Vienna from St Petersburg with her husband, a banker. She was reputedly a former mistress of the Tsar but, though he visited her at the first opportunity, he saw to it that she was speedily encouraged to travel northwards to Berlin.[51] Throughout the Christmas period and well into the New Year the Tsar took care to accept invitations to dine with the principal hostesses of Viennese Society only when he knew other men of rank would be among his fellow guests. Occasionally Elizabeth would accompany him, so that we catch a glimpse of them helping Marie Louise celebrate her first birthday since ceasing to be Empress of the French.[52] It is as if Alexander had suddenly reverted to respectable domesticity after his wild burst of dissipation.

Hager's agents had a simple explanation. The Tsar, they said, was suffering from venereal disease.[53] They may well have been correct. But if so, it appears to have borne heavily upon his conscience. For, as Metternich noted later, during these crisis weeks of the Congress, Alexander underwent what the Prince termed 'one of the periodic evolutions of the mind' to which his psychology naturally inclined him.[54] Suddenly his spirit became so mystically exalted that he despised the haggling and bargaining of peacemaking as an unworthy exercise for a sovereign blessed by Divine revelation. For the following two years, perhaps longer, he was inspired by that curious religious ecstasy which had uplifted him during the halcyon days of the campaign against Napoleon.

This re-discovery of religious faith was assisted by the presence among Elizabeth's attendant ladies of a young and devout Greek, Roxane Stourdza, whose brother acted as the Tsar's private secretary. Roxane was a follower of a much-revered evangelical prophetess, Baroness Julie von Krüdener, a Latvian by birth.* The Baroness's writings, and in particular her semi-autobiographical romance *Valerie*, had interested the Empress

---

* The Stourdzas came from Moravia (part of modern Roumania). They were Phanariot Greeks, that is to say, members of a Greek family which had served as agents or officials of the Turkish authorities within the Ottoman Empire. By St Petersburg society the Stourdzas were recognized as virtual leaders of the Greek colony in the capital.

Julie von Krüdener was born at Riga in 1764. She was the daughter of a Baltic German landowner, Baron Otto von Vietinghof, and on her mother's side a great-granddaughter of the redoubtable Marshal Munnich who had distinguished himself in Russian service against the Turks in the 1730s. Julie married a Russian diplomat, Alexis von Krüdener, in 1782 and accompanied him on embassies in Venice and Copenhagen. They had two children, Paul (born in January 1784) and Juliette (born July 1787). Alexis and Julie separated in 1792 and he died ten years later.

Elizabeth for some six or seven years, but not it would appear her husband.[55] He began to take Baroness Julie seriously only because of the influence of Roxane Stourdza and her brother. While Roxane was in Vienna she received some remarkable letters from her friend which were so full of apocalyptic revelation that their content was passed on to Alexander, probably in the first instance by his secretary. It was comforting for the Tsar to learn, during the worst period of tension with the Austrians, that Madame von Krüdener knew him to be 'one upon whom the Lord has conferred a much greater power than the World recognizes'. And if Alexander was indeed suffering from a socially humiliating disease, it was especially gratifying to be told that this strange and holy woman, technically one of his own subjects, was 'quite familiar' with 'all the deep and striking beauties in the soul of the Emperor'.[56]

During the second half of December, the time in which foreign observers were amazed at the 'serene cheerfulness' of the Tsar's disposition, he spent many free evenings visiting Roxane in the small room which she occupied on the fourth floor of the Hofburg.[57] She was an attractive girl with a charmingly gentle smile and a pleasant voice, but there was never any suggestion that Alexander wished her to become his mistress. He looked upon Roxane as a religious, someone with whom he could discuss the simple problems of theology which troubled his mind. Neither Roxane nor the Tsar were, in any sense, profound thinkers; nor indeed were Roxane's brother and her friend, Catherine Valouiev, who joined in their discussions from time to time. All four shared the characteristic Orthodox desire for religious contemplation without the spiritual training which would have assisted them to benefit from what Roxane herself later described as 'the consolation of solitude'. Psychologically Alexander was experiencing a similar need to the inner calling which, in London, had awakened his interest in the Quakers. But the knowledge that in Germany there was a strange prophet, who had kept faith in his mission when he had forgotten it, gave to those meetings in the Hofburg an extraordinary sense of the mysterious, an exciting cerebral pleasure made doubly satisfying because of its secrecy. Not once did Hager's spies pick up reports of Alexander's visits to Roxane, nor, strangely enough, do they appear to have intercepted any of Julie von Krüdener's Sibylline messages.

Napoleon's Return from Elba and the Close of the Vienna Congress

One at least of the Krüdener letters would have interested any intelligence service. In the second week of November Roxane Stourdza received a letter which the Baroness had written in Strasbourg at the end of the previous month. It was, as usual, a medley of biblical prophecy and cryptic imprecision. 'A storm is approaching', it declared, which will mean that the Bourbon lilies of France 'have appeared only to disappear'.[58] Since everyone visiting Louis XVIII's kingdom could see that his subjects remained unreconciled to the Bourbon restoration this prediction was not in itself especially significant; but the Baroness wrapped her warning in tempting mystery. She told Roxane that she had 'tremendous things' to say to Alexander, 'him whom we are ordered by God Himself to love and respect'. There were at that moment in Vienna quite enough well-wishers eager to inform the Tsar of matters which interested them and, although Alexander was glad to have Madame von Krüdener's messages conveyed to him by Roxane, he was disinclined to propose she might join the foreign visitors to the Congress. In February 1815 she tried again. Once more she declared to Roxane that she had 'most important things to say to him'. Alexander politely instructed Roxane to let her know he would be pleased to make her acquaintance at a suitable moment, but he still showed no desire for her to come to Vienna.[59] This is hardly surprising, for her presence would at once have excited comment and destroyed the privacy of his cherished hours of contemplative retreat.

On 7 March, however, news reached Vienna so staggering that for the moment it ruled out all prospect of further quiet evenings wrapt in spiritual introspection. At half-past seven that morning Metternich opened a despatch from his consul in Genoa and discovered that Napoleon had disappeared from Elba. Three-quarters of an hour later the Austrian minister was received in Alexander's wing of the Hofburg for the first time in four months.[60] The news placed Alexander in an embarrassing position; he was acutely conscious that it was on his initiative that Napoleon had been assigned the island of Elba during the negotiations at Paris. He agreed at once to order the Russian armies to be placed on a war footing: he went further, and offered to assume supreme command himself so as to scourge France once more of the Corsican. Tactfully this proposal was ignored, for no one outside Alexander's immediate circle ever rated highly his abilities in the field, but it was gratifying to know that the Russians were prepared to assume their treaty responsibilities and help maintain the settlement in western Europe.

By ten o'clock that same morning all the leading Allied statesmen were gathered in Metternich's study. There was some doubt as to whether Napoleon would make for France or for Italy in the first instance. But as a precaution couriers were sent out from Vienna to the commanders of every

Allied corps on the continent to make certain they placed their men on the alert. If Napoleon hoped to exploit the discord between his former enemies he was disappointed. 'No peace with Bonaparte!' Alexander declared as of old. 'The first task must be to overthrow him.'[61] A solemn proclamation branded 'Napoleon Bonaparte' an outlaw for having 'again appeared in France with projects of confusion and disorder'. At the end of March a renewed grand alliance bound the Austrians, British, Prussians and Russians to supply 150,000 men each to defend the contested frontiers of Europe against the menace which had broken out of Elba. By midsummer it was hoped that a million men would be on the march towards Paris once more, and this time the military commanders would give the disturber of world peace no quarter.[62]

The news of Napoleon's return to France sobered the peacemakers in Vienna. They began to settle their business with as little delay as possible. The Russian ministers co-operated readily enough with the Austrians and the British, whose delegation had been led by the Duke of Wellington since Castlereagh's return to London in February. The frontiers of the Netherlands and Poland were formally delineated; agreement was reached on the character of the new Swiss Confederation and on a proclamation calling for abolition of the slave trade (a question on which Alexander, like Wellington, felt deeply); measures were proposed for improving the position of the Jewish communities in Germany and for determining the precise status of diplomats in the capitals to which they were accredited; and a guarantee was prepared ensuring free navigation of the rivers Rhine and Meuse.[63] From the middle of March onwards a special committee of thirty-three delegates and secretaries began drafting a Final Act, which would embody the decisions of the statesmen in a single document. It was harder to settle the form of confederation for Germany or the precise relationship of the states in the Italian peninsula to each other, and neither of these questions was satisfactorily resolved before the Tsar left Vienna. The difficulties, however, were caused either by internal confusion or by the suspicions of the smaller states rather than the Great Powers. Significantly after Napoleon's recovery of his authority in France, Alexander did not once clash with Metternich over the political form of the new Germany. To Stein's disgust the Tsar remained totally uninterested in the movement for German unity and declined to antagonize his allies by defending the champions of enlightened reform in their debates in the German Committee of the Congress. 'I had influence over very imperfect human beings', Stein complained bitterly in his diary at the end of March.[64]

There was, however, at least one moment that spring when it seemed as if the thin bonds of Austro-Russian friendship might snap. Napoleon, who had been amused to hear on Elba of the friction between Alexander and Metternich over Poland, sent a conciliatory message to the Tsar soon after his return to Paris and accompanied it with a copy of the secret alliance made by Talleyrand with the Austrians and British on 3 January, which had been found in the archives of the French Foreign Office. As Napoleon anticipated this revelation made Alexander angry, but it did not dispose him to respond to French blandishments. Since he had for several weeks suspected the existence of such a treaty, he was able to treat the whole affair magnani-mously. Indeed, he seemed more irritated that such a mischievous docu-ment should have fallen into the restored Emperor's hands than that the alliance was concluded in the first place. He sent for Metternich, who came at once to his apartments in the Hofburg, where Alexander presented him with the papers forwarded from Paris. The Tsar, savouring the advantage which Napoleon's action had given him, enjoyed acting out an affecting scene of forgiveness and reconciliation in which Metternich, anxious to avoid diplomatic embarrassment, willingly participated. The two men embraced, assured each other that all would be forgotten, and pledged themselves to 'attend to more serious matters'.[65] What had seemed a document of top-secret importance in January was twelve weeks later yet another historic relic.

The main Russian army, with Barclay de Tolly still in command, was concentrated in Poland, with a few advanced garrisons in Silesia. It was therefore clear the Russians would not be in a position to chasten Napoleon for several months to come. Since the Austrians were engaged with pacifying Italy, it was agreed that the prime task of defending the threatened frontiers of the Netherlands should be left to the British and the Prussians. Meanwhile Schwarzenberg, as supreme Allied generalissimo, would con-centrate an army on the right bank of the Rhine ready to invade France, in conjunction with Barclay de Tolly, at the height of the summer if Napoleon had not already been defeated. The British offered Wellington command of the Anglo-Dutch force gathering in Belgium and he was able to hold military talks with both Schwarzenberg and the Tsar before setting out from Vienna on 29 March. Alexander liked Wellington personally, far more than he did most Englishmen, and he had always respected him as a soldier for his triumphs in Portugal and Spain. He had no doubt the Duke would be able to contain the new threat from France, perhaps even to destroy it with the help of Blücher's Prussians. When Alexander bade Wellington farewell at the end of March he therefore placed his hand on the Duke's shoulder and declared, 'It is for you to save the World again.'[66]

The Tsar was too loyal a European to stop and think whether at that moment a decisive Anglo-Prussian victory, with no Russian regiments on the field of battle, would be in the best interests of his own Empire. By now, too, he was sufficiently experienced in war to hope that it would not be necessary for Russian blood to be shed once more.

Alexander was himself tempted to leave Vienna. He considered joining his brother Constantine in Poland and travelling westwards with the army once it was fully mobilized. On reflection, he decided it would be a mistake to cut himself off from the centre of political affairs until it was certain the Final Act of the Congress would be successfully drafted. He therefore stayed on in the Hofburg throughout April and most of May. Elizabeth, however, left Vienna and travelled to Munich in order to spend the spring months with her sister, the Queen of Bavaria. For companionship the Tsar still had his sisters Marie (who had come to Vienna with the representatives of Weimar) and Catherine, who was impatiently waiting for an invitation to Württemberg and planning a short visit to Buda from mild pique and genuine curiosity.[67] In general, however, Vienna was emptying fast as the soldiers prepared for war and the social adventurers realized the festivities were at an end.

Life in the Austrian capital became almost normal during April. Nobody tried to mount preposterous entertainments any more. Alexander attended military conferences, rode in the Prater or on the hills, discussed the slow deliberations of a committee with his ministers, and dined in almost celibate austerity. The police spies noted that he made occasional flirtatious remarks to one of the Bohemian aristocrats and once his carriage took him to the Palais Palm and he spent a short time with Katharina Bagration.[68] But on many evenings he was left on his own to resume that spiritual quest for understanding of the Scriptures which was absorbing his mind more and more. Since Roxane Stourdza had accompanied Elizabeth to Bavaria, he was no longer in a position to receive reports of prophecies by Julie von Krüdener but, as he admitted later that summer, her revelations were much in his thoughts during those weeks of military and political uncertainty. The Baroness herself did not hesitate to claim she had foreseen Napoleon's return and had warned Roxane cryptically from Strasbourg in October, and she was now predicting that the Tsar's soul was about to achieve 'a glorious destiny which will astonish the World'.[69] There is no evidence that any of these feverish outpourings reached the Tsar's ears while he was still in Vienna; but they corresponded remarkably closely with his own growing certainty he had a divine mission to fulfil. All that was needed to convince Alexander was a miraculous encounter with his prophet. Since a sound instinct had induced Julie von Krüdener to settle in the village of Schluctern, full in the path of the Allied armies as they moved westwards to mass in Baden, there was a reasonable likelihood that the miracle would indeed take place.

Alexander remained in Vienna until the last week of May. It then became clear that, though there would still be tedious disputes in committee on the German Confederation, the basic work of the Congress was over and there would be no serious obstacles to delay signing of the Final Act sometime in June. Emperor Francis announced his intention of leaving Vienna for Schwarzenberg's headquarters on 27 May, and the Tsar and Frederick William accordingly determined from courtesy to set out, independently, a day ahead of him. Once again Alexander set his horses a cracking pace, reaching Lambach for dinner on that first evening and continuing through the night to Munich.[70] He spent a few days with Elizabeth and his sister-in-law in Bavaria and then journeyed on into Württemberg and Baden. Late in the afternoon of 4 June he arrived in the town of Heilbronn and established headquarters in one of its finest buildings, the Rauch'sche Palais. It was a Sunday and, having spent most of the day in his carriage, Alexander retired to his room and began to read his Bible.[71] From a village eight miles to the west of Heilbronn a woman in her early fifties, clad in simple clothes and unlikely to attract anyone's notice, was travelling into town: the Baroness von Krüdener was on her way to meet the Emperor to whom she had known for a long time that the Lord would at last summon her.

⚜18⚜

Holy Alliance

The Heilbronn Prophetess

The first meeting of Alexander and Julie von Krüdener, though attested in essentials by both participants, was sufficiently improbable and dramatic to please any hagiographer looking for signs of the workings of a special providence. It was already late at night when the Baroness, accompanied by her twenty-seven-year-old daughter Juliette, reached Heilbronn. The guards outside the Rauch'sche Palais at first paid little attention to the poorly dressed woman who was asking, at this unconventional hour, for an immediate audience with the Tsar. Understandably they did their best to send her about her business. She insisted, however, that this *was* her business: only let someone inform His Imperial Majesty of her name and he would command her to be brought to his presence. Eventually her obstinate persistence attracted the attention of Prince Volkonsky, the Tsar's aide-de-camp. He agreed reluctantly to go to Alexander's room and find if he was still awake. According to the account which Alexander himself gave to Roxane Stourdza, he had been studying the Scriptures and thinking of the prophetess on that same evening. 'Where is she now, I wondered, and how will I be able to meet her?' he told Roxane. 'At that moment I heard a knock on the door and Prince Volkonsky came in, looking rather embarrassed. He apologized for disturbing me but he did not know how to get rid of a woman who was insisting on seeing me. To my amazement he gave her name as Madame de Krüdener. I received her at once. She spoke to me with words of hope and consolation, as though able to read my very soul.' Only in humility and contrition 'at the foot of the cross of Christ'

325

could he free himself from the burden of accumulated sin, she told him, speaking as 'one who has been a great sinner, but who has found pardon'. This was not a new message but its simplicity was enough to calm the conflict of spiritual emotions surging within him.[1] She stayed that night for several hours and he invited her to visit him again and again, attaching herself to headquarters as they moved westwards, the holiest of camp-followers, protected for several hundred miles by a single Cossack horseman with a broken lance.[2]

Julie von Krüdener's behaviour at Heilbronn scandalized and dismayed some of Alexander's suite. Others, one suspects, were amused by her presumption and self-confidence. It seemed extraordinary for a woman to burst into the apartments of the most powerful ruler in Europe and unctu-ously seduce him into baring his soul. She had, of course, certain advantages, among them familiarity with the Russian social and political background; for, not only was she born in Riga, but once as young wife to an ambitious diplomat she had even entertained Tsar Paul when he was still a Grand Duke and uncertain if he would ever inherit the throne. Moreover Julie's spiritual talents had subsequently brought her into the company of people whom Alexander deeply respected, including poor Louise of Prussia. Nevertheless Julie's powers of self-advancement and her unabashed confidence were remarkable; they were enough in themselves to provoke comment. Was she a handmaid of the Lord, a latter-day Joan of Arc vouchsafed a vision of a new and holier Europe? Or was she a bogus seeker after notoriety, a would-be literary lioness of the salons, frustrated in her ambitions by the seemingly perpetual eminence of Germaine de Staël? Many who listened to Julie von Krüdener in 1815 were contemptuously critical of what she said and did; some even maintained privately that Alexander's mind could not be 'completely sound' if he accepted his prophetess at her face value. To others, however, it was as though she dissipated the mists which shrouded his spirit and gave to him tranquillity in place of gloom.[3]

The passage of time has not made it easier to assess the sincerity of their spiritual experience. No task taxes the historical imagination so deeply as an understanding of past religiosity: Faith and Worship are subjective and may never be verified, and the borderline between a mystical happening and mere charlatanry is as tenuous as that which separates the man of grace from the hypocrite. Nor is this the only problem. The unfamiliar emotional ecstasy of early-nineteenth-century pietism necessarily raises in modern minds a doubt over the honesty of its impulse and form of witness. Yet given all these grounds for scepticism, there remains in Julie's exultations and Alexander's agonies of the soul a passionately compulsive power of conviction, so that one feels even in their most incongruously absurd modes of expression a genuine attempt to rend the veil of mortality and achieve a state of mind whence would emerge the new heaven and new earth of Revelation. 'Be filled with divine creation! Let the life of Christ permeate morally your spiritual body'! she told Alexander as he made ready once more to impose his will on the Allied peacemakers.[4] To Generals and ministers concerned with the day-to-day task of defeating Napoleon and making certain there would be no future resurgence of Bonapartism it seemed that she spoke a strange language, visionary and tiresomely imprecise; but after those first disillusioning months in Vienna, these were the very words of comfort and inspiration for which Alexander was seeking. As far as he was concerned that summer, had Julie not existed it would have been necessary to invent her.

Peacemaking in Paris Once More

Alexander stayed only a few days at Heilbronn after his meeting with the Baroness. He then moved on to new headquarters at Heidelberg, some sixty miles down the river Neckar, where Francis and Frederick William were already established with Prince Schwarzenberg and the Rhine army. It was there, on 21 June, that the Tsar heard the news which changed his own status in the Allied counsels almost overnight.[5] For on that Wednesday arrived the first reports of the battle which had taken place the previous Sunday at Waterloo. From the confused picture of the fighting two matters stood out beyond dispute: Napoleon was decisively defeated; and honours for the victory were shared by the Anglo-Dutch forces of Wellington and the Prussians under Blücher and Bülow. There was now no possibility that Alexander would be able to enter Paris at the head of a liberating army, as in the spring of 1814, for he had with him at Heidelberg only one army corps already exhausted from a march across Poland and Germany in full kit at midsummer. The laurels of liberation, together with the political influence which went with them, would this time rest on Wellington's brow. That, as Alexander saw it, was hardly surprising though he had not expected a decision so soon. What mattered far more to the Russians was the improved position of Prussia, so long the poor relation among the Great Powers. The Tsar was determined to reach the French capital as rapidly as possible rather than permit Blücher to rule the roost in Paris. On 25 June, escorted by a mere hundred Cossacks, Alexander left Heidelberg for Mannheim and the long march across Lorraine and Champagne to the Seine.[6]

There followed a fortnight of frustration. Because of the risk of attack by

French irregulars the small Russian force moved slowly. Alexander did not arrive in Paris until the evening of 10 July. Louis XVIII was some forty-eight hours ahead of him. The King of France returned to the Tuileries confident of protection from Wellington and knowing full well that neither the British nor the Prussians would accept any alternative to a Bourbon restoration, as Alexander might well have done: the King's only immediate problem was the alarming manner in which the Prussians were exploiting their victory at the expense of his subjects' security of person and property. Alexander was therefore too late to challenge the assumption of his allies that a second Bourbon restoration was the most appropriate form of government for the French nation; but at least he had the comfort of arriving in Paris before the latest of peace conferences opened.[7] Theoretically there was nothing to prevent him from lifting its discussions to a nobler level, away from the shifts and expediencies of frontier drafting to that apocalyptic vision of which he was the Messiah and Julie von Krüdener the Prophet.

Alexander did not wish to humiliate or punish the French for their rejection of the government which he and Talleyrand had set up a year before. But he was determined that this time he would stand above the feuds of French politics, no longer courting favour as friend and protector of the city of Paris. He would reside in state at the Elysée Palace rather than in apartments assigned by grace and favour of Talleyrand. The Elysée, recently the town residence of the Empress Josephine, had to much recommend it, above all elegance and isolation, with pleasant gardens where he might meditate in peace and solitude. But this was a different Alexander from the man who had walked with Josephine between the rhododendrons of Malmaison fourteen months ago. Then he had looked with benign gallantry on the unfortunate Hortense: now he shunned her, for she had secretly sought to enlist his support for her stepfather soon after Napoleon's return in March. When, at the end of the Tsar's first week in Paris, the Prussian military command resolved to expel Hortense from France as a dangerous Bonapartist firebrand, he made no effort on her behalf. Those who had presumed on Alexander's magnanimity should learn respect for the majesty of God's elect.[8]

There was another change, too, in his outlook which surprised his own ministers as much as it did his allies. Half an hour after his arrival at the Elysée the Tsar received a courtesy call from Louis XVIII. Alexander had never forgiven the King of France for the arrogant bad manners he displayed at Compiègne on the eve of his first return to Paris. But now Louis was graciously charming, praising Alexander for his depth of understanding and for the moderation he was showing towards the French, in contrast to the greed of the Prussians. The Tsar was sufficiently experienced in such matters to suspect Louis's honesty of purpose, and he responded at first with polite evasion.[9] But, on reflection, it seemed there was something to be said for friendship with the rulers of France, if not with the French people. Alexander's old cordiality towards Frederick William was strained by the latest military successes of Blücher: Prussia no longer needed Russian patronage. On the other hand, there were still too many potential causes of friction with Austria in central Europe and the Balkans for the Tsar to share Nesselrode's willingness to work with Metternich. It was clear that politically Louis XVIII did not wish to appear indebted to Wellington and the British; nor, for that matter, did Alexander even if he presented the Duke with a diamond-hilted sword as 'Conqueror of Waterloo'.[10] All in all there was enough mutual interest between Russia and France to justify an effort at reconciliation; and within a few days of the King's visit to the Tsar foreign diplomats in Paris were commenting on the rare regard in which Alexander now held the Bourbons whom he had for so long despised. 'New needs always create new forms', commented Metternich dryly a few weeks later.[11]

Alexander's diplomatic advisers were quick to respond to their sovereign's latest shift of policy. Two men in particular favoured Franco-Russian collaboration, Capodistrias and Pozzo di Borgo, and they tended to replace Nesselrode in the Tsar's confidence during the Paris negotiations. They argued that French interests in the Mediterranean coincided more closely with those of Russia than any other Power, and they were able to convince Alexander that his dynastic links with Bavaria and Baden – to say nothing of his forthcoming marriage connection with Württemberg – necessarily required Russia to seek a balance of interests along the Rhine, instead of permitting Prussia to achieve mastery in the German lands as custodian of the frontier with France.[12] Capodistrias, wrote the French diplomat Barante later, 'contributed more than any man to render the [peace] treaties less burdensome for France and to inspire comparative moderation among the Allies'.[13] It was the Russians who took the lead in countering Prussian efforts to rob France of Alsace and Lorraine and much of Burgundy and Franche-Comté, too, although it is true that neither the British nor the Austrians wished to see a vindictive peace imposed upon the restored Bourbons. Louis's tenure of the throne was not so secure that it could survive national humiliation.

From the Russian point of view the strangest feature of this peacemaking in 1815 was Alexander's willingness to leave all details of negotiation to his ministers and ambassadors. This sublime and self-imposed isolation was in striking contrast to his attitude in the previous year, both in Vienna and in Paris itself. Never before had he seemed to possess such confidence in a team of negotiators. They talked and argued round the conference table while he meditated at the Elysée or attended the Krüdener prayer meetings, re-membering from time to time to exchange courtesies with his restored Majesty in the Tuileries.

In the autumn this manifest sympathy for the Bourbon cause brought the Tsar an unexpected success. Louis XVIII, to his regret, had been forced in July to accept a ministry headed by Talleyrand and supported by Fouché. Elections in August returned a Chamber royalist in sympathy and the King felt inclined to dismiss the ministry and purge his kingdom of names so stained with liberal disrepute. Both men, however, were working in harness with Wellington, and Talleyrand still retained his old skill as a negotiator; if they went, who would take their place? It was the newly appointed Russian ambassador, Pozzo di Borgo, who provided Louis with an answer, and incidentally afforded Alexander revenge for the secret treaty of January 1815. Let the King force Talleyrand to resign, suggested Pozzo, and appoint as his successor the Duke of Richelieu; here was a man who bore one of the most illustrious titles in French history but who, like Pozzo himself, had emigrated to Russia and entered the Tsar's service. Richelieu was largely responsible for the rapid commercial development of the port of Odessa and for other enterprises in southern Russia. Alexander respected him and was grateful for his services. In the last week of September Richelieu became prime minister. 'An excellent choice, indeed', commented the fallen Talleyrand wryly, 'M de Richelieu cer-tainly knows the Crimea better than any man in France.'[14] This was, no doubt, the truth; but he also knew Alexander better than any Frenchman save Caulaincourt (whose loyalty to Napoleon ruled out offers of service from the Bourbons). From September 1815 until December 1818 the French government was headed by a returned émigré who could look back on nearly a quarter of a century in the Russian administration, a fact of some significance in the international relations of the period.

Julie von Krüdener at her Prime

While the diplomats poured over maps and ministers intrigued for position and influence, the social life of Paris in that late summer and autumn of 1815 remained spectacularly brittle. People who, like Metternich and Nesselrode, had known the city in other times found it 'curious to observe', perhaps even slightly sinister. Strange episodes revealed uneasy tempers: Prussian Guardsmen impeded by a traffic block set about the coachmen with the butts of their muskets; an angry crowd brimmed over with resentment when British soldiers arrived at the Louvre to remove art treasures filched by Napoleon from the countries he had occupied; and everywhere there was uncertainty over the extent of the 'White Terror', seeking vengeance on Bonapartists of all classes in society. Yet, on the surface, life was as frivolous as ever: plenty of light entertainment in stifling and grubby theatres; a prospect of unlimited gambling; good singers at the Opéra; puppet shows in booths along the boulevards; and a hurriedly mounted ballet which claimed to represent the Waterloo campaign in such a way that neither Frenchman nor foreigner would take offence. Once more everyone of eminence in Europe seemed present in the city: not merely soldiers and statesmen and rulers, but great literary figures, doyens of salons, and women of beauty and distinction. Some diplomats, having negotiated in Paris during the previous summer and then in Vienna and now in Paris again, found it all rather tedious. Yet it is hard to believe in the dullness of a social scene enriched by four such contrasting luminaries as Madame Récamier, Princess Bagration, the Duchess of Sagan and Lady Caroline Lamb.[15] And this year, too, there was at least one novelty. For Julie von Krüdener, having at first committed the disastrous error of moving into a hotel on the wrong bank of the Seine, established herself at the end of July in the Rue Saint-Honoré, whence religious exhortation fell upon a slightly astonished world of fashion each evening with the carefully modulated fluency of soirée conversation.

Some people were impressed by Julie's talents, but not everyone. Castlereagh, himself a sound Matins worshipper each Sunday, thought her influence sufficiently important to merit explanation in a despatch to London; but he described her, a shade uncharitably, as 'an old fanatic who has a considerable reputation amongst the few highflyers in religion that are to be found in Paris'.[16] Others, though willing enough to listen to her message, were disturbed by her apparent trances and visions. Yet, as summer passed into an unusually early autumn, it became clear that Julie von Krüdener possessed one supreme advantage over less spiritual hostesses elsewhere in the city. For this year it was her extraordinary salon Alexander frequented and no other. Not that he was often seen there: it was enough for Society to know that he was expected at some time that night. The notion of conspiratorial confessions, with the suppliant slipping furtively through a hidden gateway in the wall of the Elysée garden, brought to religious observance the thrill of a romantic assignation. Soon these nocturnal visits were providing the tattlers with all the gossip they needed.[17] At fifty-one Madame de Krüdener was pale and hollow-eyed, with grey hair parted severely down the middle: did she, they wondered, possess a hidden magnetism to which only the most complex of characters could respond? Her relationship with Alexander was a topic of fascinating but fruitless speculation.

The Tsar's mind, observed Castlereagh with sage detachment, 'has of late taken on a deeply religious tinge'.[18] Socially he was almost a recluse that year. He was prepared to take the salute at parades of his own troops or to stand beside Wellington in the Place Louis xv as the Highlanders and Grenadiers and Lifeguards marched by in review. At the Elysée he received Walter Scott and other foreigners of distinction, asking them polite questions free from controversy as he would have done at home in St Petersburg.[19] But he cut down public appearances to a minimum, limiting them in effect to obligations of duty. Not one light-hearted story of Alexander's second visit to Paris ran the rounds of the capital, not even a single gallant remark. These people who had known or observed him a year before found now that he possessed an abstracted and preoccupied air, intensified by his increasing deafness and by myopia which he did his best to conceal. Now and again he surprised visitors to his receptions by the drift of his conversation. According to Lady Frances Shelley, who trailed at Wellington's heels like a devoted spaniel, the Tsar now regretted his behaviour in London and was willing to attribute it to the bad advice of his sister.[20] Unfortunately Lady Frances, as a reporter of conversations, could never quite distinguish between statements of fact and her own inspired guesswork and it is possible she completely misunderstood her host. On the other hand, there was a moment in August when it appeared even to Castlereagh as if the Tsar's sense of remorse might brave him to face another Channel crossing rather than allow his quarrel with the Prince Regent to linger on into the new age of peace.[21] But such an undertaking could well have strained anew Alexander's Christian benevolence. It was wiser to be content with an outwardly cordial exchange of letters, and the offering of joint prayers with his pocket prophetess in the Rue Saint Honoré. Over the years there was an accumulation of trespasses for which he needed forgiveness, and of these his social sins in London seemed by no means the most grievous when thrust under the moral microscope of conscience.

The highest point in Julie von Krüdener's ascendancy over the Tsar was reached on the Feast of St Alexander Nevsky, his patron and protector. On that day, 11 September, there was an impressive ceremony which took place, not in Paris, but on the Plain of Vertus, between Montmirail and

Chalons in the natural amphitheatre separating the upper Marne from Champagne, some eighty miles east of the capital.[22] For there Alexander reviewed more than one hundred and fifty squadrons of cavalry and well over a hundred battalions of infantry, together with some six hundred pieces of artillery. Francis of Austria, Frederick William of Prussia, Prince Schwarzenberg, Marshal Blücher and the Duke of Wellington were all present. With them was the Baroness von Krüdener, a plain figure in a blue serge dress and a straw hat. After the march-past the troops assembled around seven altars – the mystic number of the Apocalypse – while bishops and priests celebrated Mass according to the Russian Liturgy. Alexander, with the Baroness beside him, moved in procession at the end of the Mass from altar to altar. It was a curious addition to the traditional rites, not least because Julie was an evangelical Protestant and had never belonged to the Orthodox congregation.

Yet so powerful was the ecstasy of the occasion that such doctrinal niceties mattered little. Julie was deeply moved. 'Here Jesus Christ was adored by the hero and by his beloved army', she wrote soon afterwards. 'Here the nations of the North prayed for the happiness of France . . . The Almighty had summoned Alexander and Alexander harkened to the voice of the Lord.'[23] And that evening, after he had once more read through the litanies of the Mass, the Tsar tried to commit to paper his awareness of the exalted atmosphere in which his mind was moving. 'This day has been the most beautiful in all my life', he wrote to Julie. 'My heart was filled with love for my enemies. In tears at the foot of the Cross, I prayed with fervour that France might be saved.'[24] In Alexander's agonies of belief the fire of faith seems to burn more spontaneously than in her exultant prose: within a fortnight it was to blaze forth so unexpectedly as to throw into shadow the carefully balanced protocols of conventional diplomacy.

The Treaty of the Holy Alliance, 26 September 1815

Shortly after returning to Paris from the Plain of Vertus Alexander presented his brother sovereigns, Frederick William and Francis, with a sacred treaty which he urged them to sign and publish in Europe. This strange document was designed to bind the rulers of the continent in a union of virtue, for it required them 'to take as their sole guide the precepts of the Christian religion'.[25] The King of Prussia, whose dreams at times soared similarly to the sublime, welcomed the project, though he barely disguised the fact he did not understand it. The Emperor of Austria, on the other hand, was frankly perplexed and embarrassed. There had long been a feeling among the peacemakers that their settlement needed, for the inner security of Europe, to be based upon a general code of principles. But, as Pitt had sought to warn Alexander in 1804, there was a considerable difference between a pledge to uphold precisely defined aspects of the public law and an idealistic notice of intent to rest the behaviour of governments on 'the sacred rights of humanity'.[26] Francis, who had raised a doubting eyebrow at the holy gyrations on Alexander Nevsky's Day, read through the text of the treaty and decided that the Tsar of Russia was, as he had long suspected, mad. Metternich privately agreed with his sovereign.[27] Wellington, who was with Castlereagh when Alexander came to explain his brain-child to the British, confessed that he found it difficult to keep an appropriately solemn and serious expression on his face. Once the Tsar had returned to the Elysée both men treated the proposed Alliance with the irreverence they thought to be its due.[28]

Neither man was a cynic; but they had been trained to assume that in public affairs sentiment was invariably disciplined with common sense. By contrast, Alexander's education was incomplete and throughout his reign he tended to reject systematic thought in favour of instinct and emotion. Yet, as Castlereagh explained to his colleagues in London, the ministers felt they could hardly thwart the Tsar: better to humour him, modify the more flamboyant flights of Apocalypse in the text, reconcile Alexander's nebulous notions with their own aspirations, and extricate themselves from 'what may be called a scrape' with dignity.[29] Discreetly Metternich set about changing the form of the 'Holy Alliance', ridding the draft of those phrases which implied penitence for past imperfections; contrition smacked too strongly of revolutionary presumption to satisfy those who identified the truths of religion with orderly and conservative government. Their only doubt was whether the Tsar would accept major modifications in a document which he seemed to treat as a new dispensation of Holy Writ.[30]

Much depended on the extent to which Alexander identified himself personally with the elevated sentiments of the Holy Alliance. Were they a written draft of his own meditations, or an echo of Julie von Krüdener's fluent prophecies? If they were the product of long months of mental anguish, then it would be possible to change the text of the Alliance only if the Tsar could be convinced that, in seeking to express undoubted truths, he had selected phrases of ambiguous intent. If, on the other hand, the Alliance was written under the spell of the Prophet Julie, then it was high time she was exposed and sent to seek honour in her own country.

Most contemporary observers gave Julie von Krüdener credit for having inspired the Holy Alliance, a claim made by the Baroness herself in conversation with Roxane Stourdza a couple of years later.[31] Yet those who knew Alexander well (including Roxane) indignantly refuted this suggestion, denying that the Alliance was in any sense a spiritual whim of the moment. Long before the Tsar heard of the Baroness he had shown an inclination to envelop statements of political convenience with high-sounding phrases: thus both the Potsdam Oath and the Bartenstein Convention hid their intrinsic poverty of objective under a sanctimonious wreath of mystic allusion. Moreover for the past three years he had been an eclectic in religious thought: from the Badenese fanatic, Jung-Stilling (whom he had met at Bruchsal), he acquired a notion of leading Europe back to ideals of Christian charity; from the German Catholic theologian, Franz von Baader, he received pamphlets maintaining the virtues of striving to establish a universalist theocratic community; from Golitsyn and Koshelev in Russia he gained a passing acquaintance with native mystic traditions and some of the patristic teachings of the mediaeval Schoolmen in the West; and from the Society of Friends in England he learnt virtues of pietistic Protestantism some months before Roxane Stourdza showed him the first letters from the Baroness.[32] Add to all these influences the consequence of his own constant reading of the Scriptures – and in particular of his favourite Book of Daniel – and it becomes clear that Alexander's brand of religious thought was a confused medley of ideas, all-embracing in its incomprehensibility. Although Julie von Krüdener conditioned the hothouse atmosphere in which the Holy Alliance burst upon the world, it was not she who had sown the seed.

Yet, when all reservations are made, it remains true that the timing was unquestionably Julie's. She had used the phrase 'Holy Alliance' in one of her exhortations (though she may well have borrowed it from the Book of Daniel rather than coined it herself) and there is a direct echo of her sentiments in Alexander's curious insistence on the virtues of proclaiming a treaty dedicated to 'the Holy and Indivisible Trinity' in Paris because it was the most irreligious of all Europe's capital cities.[33] Possibly, too, the Baroness amended the original draft, adding a flourish to the Tsar's own handiwork. But, if so, it was almost the last occasion upon which she had any influence on his activities; for, at the very time when Metternich was modifying the character of the Holy Alliance, the close accord between Alexander and his spiritual counsellor was broken. By 26 September when the revised version of the Alliance was signed by the Tsar, the King of Prussia and the Emperor of Austria, Alexander had already emerged from the religious ecstasy in which the original declaration was drafted. Hence, no doubt, the willingness with which he accepted the verbal alterations in the text.* It is not clear precisely when or why Alexander ceased to find the revelations of the Baroness significant. As late as 23 September her influence was sufficiently strong to secure for the East Anglian Quaker, Thomas Clarkson, a private audience with the Tsar. In his account of his conversation with Alexander, Clarkson takes some pains to explain that Baroness Krüdener 'is a Lady of the most exemplary Life' on whom the Tsar called 'every evening at seven in order to converse upon spiritual subjects'.[34] Yet, in reality the path of spiritual love had not run smoothly ever since Julie's arrival in Paris. There are fragments of her correspondence with the Tsar which show a shrewish impatience towards him for not visiting her at an agreed hour: 'If you can go forward without me, I will absent myself from you' she wrote. 'But where else will you find anyone able to render for you the services I can? Where will you find a spirit created entirely to understand you?' Even before the great day on the Plain of Vertus there had been an awkward scene when two of her closest followers attempted, by means of a spurious trance, to induce Alexander to make them a monetary grant in order to establish a religious cell in Baden.[35] And one evening there was an episode which was strangely parallel to the incident of the hat at the Palais Palm; for Alexander, having apparently heard Julie von Krüdener in conversation, entered her drawing-room and found nobody else present. Her subsequent explanation that she had just been asking the great naturalist and writer, Bernardin de Saint-Pierre (who had died in the previous year), how many Jews he had found in Paradise was not entirely reassuring.[36] It had been easy enough to laugh off the tale of M. Moreau's hat in Vienna; but it was another matter here in impious Paris, especially if the deception was practised by a person whose claims for attention rested solely on devotional affinity. Other visitors to the Baroness's prayer-meetings thought her a fraud.[37] Alexander never went so far as that: he accepted the sincerity of her piety, but his old lack of confidence in himself prevented him from trusting her as prophet or mentor. Once his faith in her messages declined, her influence on his thoughts and actions was at an end.

There was no dramatic finale to their relationship. She was ready, she

---

* The Holy Alliance, in its revised form, was a statement by the rulers of Austria, Prussia and Russia asserting their conviction of the need for 'the Councils of Princes' to be influenced by 'the precepts of Justice, Christian Charity and Peace'. Other European sovereigns were invited to subscribe to the Alliance. Most of them did so; but not the Pope (who would not be associated with heretics and schismatics) nor the King of England (for constitutional reasons). As originally drafted the Alliance implied a promise of universal brotherhood between subjects as well as between rulers. Metternich left out such dangerous phrases; but significantly, when the terms of the Holy Alliance were announced in Russia, Alexander published the original text rather than the Treaty actually signed on 26 September.

told him in Paris, to follow her sovereign back to Russia when his business in the French capital was completed; firmly and kindly, with promises of future hours spent together in prayer and exegesis, Alexander declined her offer. He left Paris abruptly as soon as the Holy Alliance Treaty was signed. They met again on only two occasions, once near Pskov in the autumn of 1819 and a brief encounter a couple of years later in a small cottage outside St Petersburg.[38]

Disillusionment?

From Brussels on 1 October Alexander sent his sister Catherine a letter of relief: 'Here I am, away from that accursed Paris' he began, and added the information that he had arrived 'the evening before last'.[39] His sudden departure surprised the ministers still concerned in the task of peacemaking. It took another six weeks before they completed the Second Treaty of Paris, with its provisions for a French indemnity and its arrangements for an Allied army of occupation.* There was, strictly speaking, no need for Alexander to be at hand while his ministers thrashed out the terms of the settlement, for Nesselrode, Capodistrias and Pozzo di Borgo knew clearly enough what he wanted. More surprisingly, however, he was prepared to leave his ministers to discuss with Castlereagh the final form of the political alliance among the Great Powers, which Alexander had himself originally drafted. In consequence, on Castlereagh's initiative, Bourbon France was excluded from the arrangement by which the foreign ministers of Austria, Britain, Prussia and Russia pledged themselves to meet in conference from time to time to discuss matters of general concern.[40] Had Alexander insisted on his original project, not only would France have been a contracting member of what would then have been a Quintuple Alliance, but the resultant Congress System would have been based on a regular pattern

---

* The Second Treaty of Paris (20 November 1815) deprived France of two fortresses ceded to the Netherlands, the Saar valley to Prussia, and small areas along the frontiers with Switzerland, Bavaria and Sardinia-Piedmont. The French had to accept and maintain an Allied army of occupation which would garrison seventeen fortresses in northern and eastern France for at least three years and possibly five. They were also required to pay a war indemnity of seven hundred million francs and to return the art treasures originally brought to Paris by Napoleon as trophies of war.

On the same day the British, Austrian, Russian and Prussian representatives signed a Quadruple Alliance, renewing the Treaty of Chaumont of 1814, and pledging themselves to joint action to uphold the peace settlement if it were again menaced by France. Article VI of the Quadruple Alliance provided for occasional meetings of the spokesmen of the Four Great Powers to discuss the general problems of Europe. It was from this Article that the so-called 'Congress System' of the period 1818–25 emerged.

of meetings held at fixed intervals and limited to matters arising from the nature of the Alliance itself. That the Tsar should suddenly have lost interest in a project which he had supported in various forms ever since his first exchanges with Pitt in 1804 suggests that once again, at the end of September 1815, he was racked by doubt and indecision. After the emotional excitement of Vertus, a cloud of depression enveloped his soul and challenged his reason. 'I have found no easing of my troubles', he confessed to Catherine, 'save in the sublime consolation which flows from the grace of the Most High.'[41]

In Paris it was said Alexander had left the city because urgent business called him back to Warsaw and St Petersburg. But his itinerary for the following five weeks gives the lie to that story. After two days in Brussels he turned south and travelled nearly two hundred and fifty miles as fast as his carriage would carry him to Dijon, then after attending a review of Austrian troops he crossed the Rhine and made for Wiesbaden and Frankfurt. Subsequently he travelled to Switzerland, visiting Konstanz, Zurich and Basle 'journeying a great deal on foot, admiring the natural wealth of the countryside, often entering the homes of the peasants', wrote one of his aides.[42] Then northwards to Nuremberg and ultimately Berlin, before at last turning eastwards on 8 November and heading for Warsaw, and the responsibilities he was assuming as King of Poland. He had wandered across Europe as though in flight from himself, or from others. It was a strange epilogue to his years of mission.

19

Contrasts

Alexander in Congress Poland (November 1815)

Warsaw welcomed Poland's new king on 7 November 1815 with guarded optimism and a display of officially stimulated enthusiasm. Alexander, wearing Polish uniform and the cordon of the White Eagle, made a fine entry into the city. He graciously declined the keys offered to him at the western gate by the civic dignitaries: 'I come here not as a conqueror but as a protector and friend', he declared. As he rode on to the Citadel acknowledging cheers from pretty Polish girls at open windows in the old town, it seemed as if the Poles had indeed, as one of them remarked, 'finally found a King and a father'. At one moment he saw the mother of Adam Czartoryski curtseying to him from a balcony and raised his sword to her in a deeply respectful salute.[1] Observers found the gesture comforting for as commander-in-chief of the Polish army the Grand Duke Constantine was already arousing opposition by his harsh discipline and bursts of ungovernable rage; the Polish nobility were counting on Alexander's good sense to restrain his brother and they hoped he would turn for advice to his old friend, Prince Adam. Provided the Tsar-King respected the wishes of the patriots, there was some prospect of genuine Russo-Polish collaboration. It was gratifying to see he had not forgotten the ageing Princess Isabella Czartoryska, and most people assumed that, before leaving his Polish capital, he would nominate her eldest son as his Viceroy.

For three weeks the aristocracy entertained Alexander liberally and he responded with appropriate pleasantries. There were brilliant receptions in the great houses night after night. On 17 November Alexander attended a ball given by Adam Czartoryski's sister with whom he danced a vigorous Polonaise. Once again he was dressed as a Polish officer, wearing the distinctive cavalry uniform of his new subjects, the dress of men who had led charges against the Russians at Borodino and Dresden and Leipzig. He was amiably disposed to the Radziwills and other families whose members had fought against Russia in the recent campaigns. Tactfully he explained that he wished to 'forget' the past: he wisely refrained from using the words 'pardon' or 'forgive'. Privately he even admitted he was disappointed at not having been able to achieve more for Poland at the Congress of Vienna: 'The other sovereigns were strongly opposed to all my Polish projects', he declared; and he added encouragingly, 'But at least we have made the first step forward.'[2] If this was the mood of their new King then there seemed to the Poles no reason why in time they should not receive 'the western lands' of Russia, the Polish-Lithuanian territories annexed by Catherine in 1793 and 1795. To any patriotic Pole this would be 'the second step' of a truly enlightened ruler.

The Poles had no cause for complaint over the constitutional structure of the 'Congress Kingdom'. At the end of his third week in Warsaw Alexander duly signed the Constitutional Charter drawn up by Czartoryski. On paper it was a liberal instrument of government.[3] The Polish nation was promised 'for all time to come' a bi-cameral Diet (Sejm), which would share legislative power with the Tsar-King, and a separate executive State Council of five ministers and a number of royal nominees. The Charter guaranteed to the Poles freedom of worship for the 'Christian faiths', freedom of the press, and freedom from arbitrary arrest; and it also provided for an independent judiciary. There would be a Polish Secretary in St Petersburg and an Imperial Commissioner in Warsaw. In practice, of course, all these institutions were oligarchic rather than democratic and there was an almost inevitable risk of encroachments on civil liberties from the Russian element in the administration. The Upper House, the Senate, was a nominated body, with preference given to the older aristocracy and the Catholic episcopate; and the right to elect to the Lower House (in which there were nominated representatives as well as deputies) was limited to the gentry in the countryside and to property-owners in the towns. Moreover the Diet met for only one month in every two years and possessed no right to initiate legislation, being permitted only to discuss laws laid before it. Nevertheless these provisions did at least give the Poles the opportunity of internal self-government with a system of tariffs and taxation of their own, and the terms of the Charter were accepted by Alexander with perfect sincerity. Whatever others at St Petersburg might feel, the Tsar himself consciously separated in his mind the 'Kingdom of Poland' from the Empire as a whole. On more than one occasion in the following seven years he gave his advisers the impression that he was using Poland as a field for constitutional experiments which might be implemented on a larger scale in Russia proper.[4]

Yet when he travelled on eastwards from Warsaw to Vilna in the closing days of November, Alexander left behind him a disappointed city. On the eve of his departure he had, as expected, nominated a Viceroy; but he chose, not Adam Czartoryski nor any other representative of the traditional Polish dynasties, but a relatively obscure member of the lesser nobility, General Joseph Zaionczek, who had previously served Napoleon. The General was an old man, incapacitated from a war wound. If the sovereign was to be represented by a figurehead then he was an admirable man for the post. But real authority rested with Constantine, as commander-in-chief of the army, and Novosiltsov, the Imperial Commissioner. Czartoryski was indeed made a member of the State Council and a Senator, nominally President of the Senate; but he saw the elevation of Zaionczek as a warning that Alexander was under pressure from Russian nationalists who resented the reconstitution in any form of a Polish kingdom. And as Constantine and Novosiltsov became increasingly powerful in Warsaw, there were many others in the city who shared Czartoryski's misgivings.[5]

There is no doubt Alexander's Polish policy aroused resentment among many Russian landowners and veteran officers. Count Lanskoi, the Tsar's first administrator of the liberated Grand-Duchy, had voiced the feelings of a considerable number of his compatriots when, in the previous May, he protested to the Tsar at the proposal to give the Poles an army of their own: it would be, he said, 'a snake spouting its venom at us'.[6] Alexander knew that many of his Russian subjects regarded the Poles as hereditary enemies, hardly less of a menace than the Turks, and it was intolerable that a nation which had collaborated so flagrantly with Napoleon in 1812 should be the chief beneficiary of Russia's final victory. Hence Alexander could not identify himself too closely with specifically Polish causes and ambitions, and he certainly could not risk returning to Russia dependent for what happened in Warsaw on so able and unpopular a figure as Czartoryski. It would, of course, have been far wiser not to have patronized the Polish nobility in the first place. As it was, the Tsar's inconsistencies alienated the sympathies of his new subjects in the Congress Kingdom while failing to allay the suspicion of his old subjects that the Poles had in some way stolen a march on them. The contradictions of his half-solution of the Polish

Question were to confound politics for the remainder of his reign and beyond it.[7]

St Petersburg Once More

It took Alexander more than a fortnight to travel back from Warsaw to St Petersburg, far longer than he had anticipated. The roads were deep in snow and passage of the rivers was treacherous. Moreover there were frequent delays caused by broken bridges, only partially repaired after the ravages of the 1812 Campaign. Alexander was well able to see for himself the huge tasks of reconstruction. He stopped briefly at Vilna, where once again the aristocrats in Society fluttered around him[8] and then he journeyed on through Riga and Pskov until he eventually reached the Winter Palace in the small hours of 14 December. Elizabeth, who had lingered in Germany while he was in Poland, was already back in the capital, having arrived a day and a half ahead of her husband.[9] For the first time in three years sovereign and consort were in residence at St Petersburg.

'The great soul has now once more entered its great body', reported Joseph de Maistre to his master,[10] and the metaphor was well chosen. For the Tsar returned home still uplifted by the spiritual introspection of the past year. Peace was celebrated not with public festivities but with a long and solemn act of thanksgiving in the Kazan Cathedral. The clergy, in all the cities of the Empire, read out the original draft of the Holy Alliance, and the manifesto which the Tsar promulgated on the Russian New Year's Day reflected his preoccupation with mystical experiences. His subjects were told that their deeds had been accomplished through the strength of God and that, for the betterment of their souls, they should choose to humble themselves before the Almighty rather than take pride in what had been achieved. When he was hailed as 'conqueror of the invincible' he modestly deprecated the honour: he thanked army and people for their courage and fortitude during the long struggle with that 'impious criminal of common law', Bonaparte, but in general he called upon those who wished to serve him to continue 'the fight against the spirit of evil which is threatening to overcome the good'.[11] Whatever might happen elsewhere in Europe, the public morality of Russia would be based upon the tenets of the Holy Alliance. For the next five years his statements of policy, both in home affairs and diplomacy, were befogged with apocalyptic obscurity.

Those of his subjects who understood the problems of government were puzzled. During the Tsar's absence abroad, administration had depended on the decisions of a Committee of Ministers headed by old General Saltykov. The Committee had been able to handle day-to-day problems but refused to accept responsibility for any major changes in finance or home affairs. Alexander himself was aware that good government had virtually broken down; shortly before leaving Warsaw he sent a stern message to Saltykov complaining of the way in which the Committee was shirking its duty.[12] But by then the damage was already done. 'A quarter of a million unsettled matters await the supreme decision', a French diplomat reported to Paris shortly after Alexander's return.[13] Some, at least, of the public acclamation welcoming the Tsar sprang from a belief he would set things right again. Alexander was pleased to receive a verse epistle written 'in love and gratitude to our great monarch' by the star pupil of the new Lyceum at Tsarskoe Selo, Alexander Pushkin.[14] But sixteen-year-old romantics, with an age of peace ahead of them, are not likely to be satisfied with vague assurances of religious exaltation and, like others of his generation, young Pushkin was soon to be disillusioned. For veterans, who had seen for themselves 'how good it is in foreign lands', it was even harder to be expected to find consolation for the incompetence and iniquities around them in words of Holy Writ.[15] The contrast between the Tsar's status as Europe's liberator and arbiter and his failure to provide the 'great body' of his Empire with a wise administration was an intolerable affront to officers and men who had fought their way 'to the banks of the Rhine and the Seine' and wished to see a policy of benevolent reform in their own land. As one of the returning Guards officers later explained, 'It became unbearable to watch the empty life in St Petersburg, listening to the grey beards who lauded everything that was old and poured scorn on every progressive thought. We had left them a hundred years behind.'[16]

Had Alexander been an unimaginative reactionary ruler, insensitive to foreign impressions himself, like his brothers Constantine and Nicholas, he might well have met this mood of frustration by rigid repression, establishing a régime at least as tyrannical as in his father's day. But, in a muddled way, he understood and sympathized with the soldiers who had served him abroad. Despite his love of military showmanship, he always hated the all-pervading grief and social disruption of war and he felt a responsibility for those who had suffered. He believed, rightly, that the best way of combating Russia's ills was by efficient administration. Less justifiably, he thought this objective could be attained only through a disciplined and fundamentally militaristic system, for he was after all his father's son. Almost as soon as he returned to St Petersburg he selected the man who was to have his confidence for the remainder of his reign, and who indeed in a sense had never lost it. On 5 January 1816 General Arak-cheev was appointed Saltykov's deputy on the Committee of Ministers, with responsibility for supervising the Committee's activities and reporting on them to the Tsar. Although Arakcheev was not given the titles which Speransky enjoyed six years previously, he was now as much the Tsar's grand vizier as the State Secretary had ever been, the sole intermediary between the sovereign and his ministers.[17] Speransky's elaborate Council of State was a thing of the past.

The Arakcheev System and the Military Colonies

Arakcheev had never been a popular figure in St Petersburg. The passage of time had not brought out any redeeming features in his character. In Alexander's eyes he had two supreme virtues: absolute loyalty and a capacity for hard work. To everyone else, however, he seemed an un-cultured bully, terrifying and unlovable, 'a man', wrote one of his lieu-tenants, 'with ... cold colourless eyes, a thick and very inelegant nose shaped like a shoe, a rather long chin, and tightly compressed lips on which no one could remember having seen a smile or a laugh'.[18] He carried out orders without questioning them and had something of the brutal admin-istrative energy which had marked out Peter the Great, but he also possessed greater mental powers than his enemies cared to admit; he was, for example, perfectly able to prepare digests of the Committee's sessions, summarizing for Alexander details of financial questions with the skill he had once shown in explaining army regulations and all the ritual of a military parade. Since Arakcheev sought neither monetary rewards nor honours, he regarded the sheer exercise of authority as sufficient recompense for the services he was rendering to the State; but he was determined to let people discover how powerful he was, and he therefore took delight in making petitioners to the Tsar deliver their appeal in the first instance to his own office in Liteiny Prospect.[19] He alone – and not the Minister of the Interior or the Minister of Police or one of the chamberlains of the Palace – would decide who was to see the Tsar, when, and about what topics. The fact that unlike so many of his petitioners Arakcheev had remained in St Petersburg during the dramatic months of the campaign against Napoleon did not increase the general respect for him or for his office. It was bad enough to return from 'free-thinking Europe' and endeavour to settle down again in 'feudal Russia'; but then to find every prospect of improved con-ditions blocked by the obdurate taskmaster in Liteiny Prospect was galling in the extreme. Arakcheev, long despised by St Petersburg Society and feared throughout the lower ranks of the army, swiftly became the hated symbol of frustrated hopes and repression, the most evil of the good Tsar's counsellors.

This round condemnation of Arakcheev was a distortion of the truth. Had the General been a cruel and capricious taskmaster and nothing else, Alexander would never have given him such authority. Arakcheev did more to remedy abuses in the administration of the Empire than any other of Alexander's public servants. He visited every region through which the invaders and liberators had fought their way. If the local provincial Governors were incompetent or corrupt, Arakcheev himself took charge of the tasks of reconstruction, intimidating fumbling bureaucrats and serf labourers alike. It was his will-power which enabled Smolensk to be speedily re-built and his systematic attention to detail that instituted a comprehensive survey of all the devastation caused by the war.[20] Local officials were never certain when 'the Tsar's representative' was going to descend on them, and he had an unfailing instinct for discovering graft and corruption. If told by one of the ministries there was no need to inspect a particular area since it had already been visited by a high-ranking civil servant, he made a point of going there at the first opportunity, suspecting that someone was covering up major irregularities. Alexander invariably supported Arakcheev:[21] to stamp out fraud, embezzlement and bureau-cratic knavery was essential as a first stage towards the modernization of the Empire. Unfortunately Arakcheev was not good at picking subordinates nor at showing others what should be done: one of his most loyal assistants, General Maevsky, once grumbled that Arakcheev 'always thought that by being rude to someone he was in fact teaching them'.[22] When Arakcheev was present in a town or province things got done. In his absence all the old abuses flourished – and continued to do so well into the eighteen-thirties when Gogol satirized the whole bureaucratic maladministration in his classic comedy *The Government Inspector*.

In July 1816 Alexander showed his confidence in Arakcheev by travelling to Gruzino with Prince Volkonsky and spending two nights as the General's guest. So devoted was Arakcheev to his sovereign that he kept a record of everything done by the Tsar in his thirty-six-hour visit and deposited it in the church. We can thus read how Alexander took breakfast in a tent beside the Volkhov river, how he inspected by *droshky* all the recent buildings constructed on the estate, and how he lunched at two o'clock while an orchestra played in the shaded avenues of Arakcheev's private garden.[23] But Alexander's visit was more than a social courtesy. After seeing Gruzino for the first time in 1810 the Tsar had encouraged its master to draw up the plans of an experimental military colony in the province of Moghilev:* it had failed, partly through the conflict of settlers and peasants and partly because the worsening situation abroad made it an inappropriate time to beat swords into plough-shares. But now that the wars were over, Alexander was increasingly attracted by the possibilities of combining soldiery with farming. With Arakcheev's collaboration, he planned another pilot military colony, to be sited this time on the Volkhov river itself, between Gruzino and the city of Novgorod, where the General could in person make frequent inspections and keep Alexander informed month by month of how the experiment was progressing.

Less than eight weeks after Alexander's visit to Gruzino the first troops, a battalion of the Count Arakcheev Regiment, arrived at Vysotsk on the Volkhov.[24] The General gave them little time to settle in. He was determined the Tsar should find the colony a flourishing enterprise by the following summer. Before the end of autumn they had constructed a nucleus of stone buildings and delimited the fields and boundaries of the settlement. Arakcheev drove his officers relentlessly, threatening backsliders with severe disciplinary action, and the officers duly gave their men no peace. Within a mere nine months Arakcheev was able to report success to the Tsar, who was delighted. Despite strong opposition from Barclay de Tolly and the whole military establishment in St Petersburg the Tsar gave orders for new military settlements to be set up near Novgorod and Pskov and also in the Ukraine.[25] Within five years over a hundred infantry battalions and some two hundred squadrons of cavalry were stationed in these so-called colonies, which collectively housed as many as three-quarters of a million people. No enterprise of comparable scale, involving the regimentation of so many human beings, had been attempted by any Tsar since Peter the Great's construction of his new capital: nor was Russia to witness a similar social revolution until the enforced collectivization of Stalin's first Five Year Plan.

The military colonies, more than any other institution, reflected Alexander's own ideas of enlightened reform. He believed the system would be beneficial for the soldiery and valuable to the State. Peasants and soldiers would live together, under the patriarchal protection of a regiment but quartered with their families rather than in some remote garrison town. The military settlements, so the Tsar himself declared, were intended 'to make the obligation of those entering military service less burdensome' by ensuring that 'in peacetime a soldier serving the Fatherland is not separated

* See above, Chapter 12, p. 194.

from his home area'.[26] Eventually, he believed, the whole organization of the Russian army, in time of peace, would be based upon this system: 'When, with God's help, these settlements take their final form', he wrote in August 1818, 'there will be no need for general recruitment anywhere in the entire Empire.'[27] The combination of soldiering and farming would make it possible for veterans who had served more than twenty years with a regiment to spend the remainder of their days gainfully employed on the land. Organization and experience should raise the agricultural yield of the Russian countryside. There was even a possibility that the new system would, by contrast, show up the deficiencies of the serf economy and thereby speed a process of serf emancipation by progessively-minded landowners, a development Alexander had always favoured (and one in which he sought to interest Arakcheev).[28] The scheme promised to reduce the expenses of supporting a large army while, at the same time, making it certain that difficult tracts of land were beneficially farmed. It was a typical product of muddled sentiment in an eighteenth-century mind: the soldier became, in Alexander's dream, almost a 'Noble Savage', practising domestic virtues in Arcadian delights and uncorrupted by the thoughts and habits of town life. Unfortunately those who sought to put Alexander's ideal into practice were not themselves products of the Age of Reason; they did not share their sovereign's good intentions, if only because they could not understand them.

Foreign visitors to the military colonies were favourably impressed.[29] The settlers were well-housed, cared for with hospitals and improved sanitation, and their children received a good schooling, in many cases even learning a language other than their own. But the colonies were regarded by soldiers and peasants as a new form of servitude, rural stamping-grounds of despotism in which harsh discipline was imposed alike on men, women and children. 'Nothing at the end of the war provoked as much public indignation against Alexander . . . as the compulsory establishment of military settlements', wrote a young Guards officer, looking back on these years more than a decade later.[30] 'All was organized in the German, Prussian manner', another contemporary wrote: 'Everything was counted, weighed and measured. Exhausted by the day's labour in the fields, the military settler had to stand at attention and march. When he came home, he found no peace; he was compelled to scrub and clean his house and sweep the street. He had to report every egg laid by his hens.'[31] The settlements were universally unpopular: soldiers disliked the imposition of farming duties; peasants disliked the imposition of military discipline; independent landowners disliked economic competition from what were (in material terms) pampered collectives; and the military establishment disliked the creation of a private Arakcheevan empire. But no one could convince Alexander that the military colonies were as grimly repressive as penal settlements. His faith in their beneficent qualities remained unshaken – despite petitions, revolts and mutinies – until the end of his reign.

Technically the colonies were a success, with a record yield of cereals to their credit. They were, however, too closely associated with the Alexander-Arakcheev partnership to become a permanent feature of Russian life. Effectively they were already a thing of the past when Arakcheev died in 1834.[32]* Liberal intellectuals, disillusioned by the Tsar's failure to do more for the veterans returning from the wars, remembered the military settlements as 'the most despotic and hateful' institutions created in Alexander's reign. It would have been happier for Russia had he concentrated on constitutional reform and on securing the emancipation of the serfs; it would have been better for his reputation had he summoned back Speransky rather than looked to Arakcheev as his principal lieutenant. But Speransky, quite apart from the unpopularity he had aroused among the landowners, was too closely identified in Alexander's mind with specifically Napoleonic-style reforms. Ironically, it was through Arakcheev's intervention that Speransky was reinstated as a government official for, at the end of 1816, Alexander at last appointed the disgraced State Secretary to a post: he was made Governor of the town of Penza, more than three hundred miles east of Moscow and over seven hundred miles from the centre of affairs in St Petersburg.[33] The Tsar's choice of advisers on home affairs was limited by the embarrassment with which past enthusiasms assailed him. No far-sighted and dispassionate judge of men, faced with the problems of modifying autocratic government after a foreign war, would have retained Arakcheev and his private Chancery in Liteiny Prospect while allowing Speransky to waste his talents in running a small town on the Mordovian steppes.

Imperial Weddings

One at least of Alexander's closest associates from earlier years was soon removed from further interference in Russian affairs. On 9 January 1816

* The colonies were changed out of all recognition in 1831 after being weakened by the cholera epidemic of that year and subsequent rioting. Nicholas I and the orthodox generals who formed his chief advisers had always disliked them, fearing that they constituted an armed state within an army state, as it were. Legally the colonies were not abolished until after the Crimean War, in the reforming era of Alexander II, when preparations were being made for the final emancipation of the serfs.

Grand Duchess Catherine was at last betrothed to William of Württemberg. There was a religious ceremony at midday and a grand dinner and grand ball in the evening, to which all the ladies of the Imperial Household, headed of course by the indefatigable Marie Feodorovna, wore traditional Russian robes. The marriage itself was celebrated a fortnight later: 'I do not know why there is, in this marriage, something that makes me shudder', wrote the Empress Elizabeth in a note to her mother.[34] And soon afterwards Catherine left Russia for the Neckar and the Black Forest. She had not been able to visit Oldenburg in the lifetime of her first husband but conditions had changed in Europe with the creation of the German Confederation, and William, as heir to the throne, was needed in Stuttgart. Within ten months Catherine was a Queen and the mother of a daughter. She never saw Russia again and, though she continued to seek from Alexander favours for the Württemberg family,[35] there is no evidence that she offered him advice any longer on political questions. He remained deeply devoted to her and had every intention of visiting her in Germany as often as his travels permitted; but, perhaps fortunately, there was never again that close affinity between brother and sister which had proved so disastrous during the English visit of 1814.

Little more than a fortnight after Catherine's second marriage the youngest of Alexander's sisters, Anna, was betrothed to Prince William of Orange, the twenty-three-year-old heir to the throne of the Netherlands. He was popular with all the members of the Russian Imperial family (which says much for his tact and charm) and had fought under Wellington both in the Peninsular Campaign and at Waterloo. Since there was a difference of seventeen years between Alexander and Anna, he never became so closely attached to her as to his older sisters. Anna, for her part, had spent her childhood with Nicholas and Michael at Pavlovsk and Gatchina and looked on her elder brother as a distant and awe-inspiring person. Yet the prospect of her departure for the Netherlands drew all the family closer together. The Orange wedding took place before the coming of Lent but the young couple remained in Russia until the end of June and that spring and summer there were long evenings of nostalgia and sentiment in the gardens of Tsarskoe Selo and beside the fountains of Peterhof.[36] When at last Anna and her husband set out westwards Alexander himself accompanied them on the first stages of the slow journey to The Hague. It was the first time for many decades that a Romanov bride had left Russia for a non-Germanic kingdom.*

* Anna and the Prince of Orange settled at first in Brussels, then second city in the United Kingdom of the Netherlands. There, early in 1817, she gave birth to a son, the future

A year later Alexander's emotions were subjected to a different stress. In July 1817 Grand Duke Nicholas married the eldest daughter of Louise of Prussia, who was originally baptized Charlotte but took the names Alexandra Feodorovna on her reception into the Orthodox Church. The Tsar had known the newest Grand Duchess since his first visit to Berlin at the end of October 1805, when she was a girl of seven, and it was Alexander who acted as matchmaker for Nicholas, although as soon as the two young people met (in the early summer of 1814) they did indeed fall deeply in love.[37] Nicholas was considered in Berlin, not without justice, to be 'the most handsome prince in Europe' while his bride had enough of her mother's beauty and vivacity to trouble the mind with ghostly memories. Alexander was pleased at the union of the two dynasties and his admiration for Alexandra's intelligence and light-hearted spirits led him to pay more attention to Nicholas than in the past. Here was a man who seemed to possess the qualities for which Alexander looked in a sovereign – and who knew it. Although everyone assumed that Constantine was heir-apparent, the Tsar began in the first year of Nicholas's married life to treat him increasingly as the most fitting successor. With Constantine long separated from his wife and permanently resident in Warsaw, it was natural that Nicholas and Alexandra should be welcomed in the whirling centre of Petersburg Society. There were some doubts about him – a prudish temperament ill-fitted his cavalry-officer mentality – but hardly about her. No one waltzed so lightly or danced so graceful a mazurka as the Grand Duchess Alexandra.[38]

The Empress Elizabeth, long since weary of solemn festivities, was pleased to welcome the Prussian Princess to St Petersburg. It was good to have a young sister-in-law with whom to exchange confidences. When Elizabeth arrived back in Russia after her long absence in Germany she had been deeply moved by the sight and smell of a country she loved so deeply; but, so she wrote, 'my heart stopped short as the Winter Palace loomed up ahead of us', and the prospect of Court life in full tedium nearly overwhelmed her.[39] Within weeks she was complaining in her letters of intrigues, of the presumption of the Naryshkin family, of the cold hostility shown by the Dowager Empress; nothing had changed at St Petersburg or Pavlovsk.[40] But in the autumn of 1817 there was an innovation in Court routine. Alexander and Elizabeth travelled to Moscow, where they remained in residence throughout the winter, the Empress staying even

William III of the Netherlands (reigned 1849–90), grandfather of Queen Juliana (who is thus today the reigning sovereign closest in descent from Catherine the Great, Paul and Marie Feodorovna).

longer as her husband set out to tour the central provinces, the heart of old Muscovy. In earlier years Elizabeth had found the old capital a greater strain than the new but on this occasion she was spiritually uplifted by the phoenix-like quality of life in Moscow after the tragedies of occupation and fire. Now at last Elizabeth sensed the historical continuity which gave to the city its will to endure, its extraordinary atmosphere of resilient piety.[41] If Elizabeth could be so moved by the experience of wintering in the Kremlin, the effect of Moscow on Alexander was greater still. He always identified himself with its tremendous sense of a holy past.

Alexander continues his Spiritual Quest

When Alexander returned from western Europe and Poland, he freed himself from the compelling mysticism of Julie von Krüdener. His personal religious devotions continued to play a prominent role in his life, but he now turned for guidance to those whom he had long known and trusted rather than to the prophetess who had descended on him so opportunely at Heilbronn. She continued to write him long letters, rambling on through pages of incoherent ecstasy. He did not answer them himself but tended increasingly to leave all such matters to Prince Golitsyn, the friend who had first taught him how to find in the Scriptures the inspiration to bear the burdens of 1812.[42] From 1816 to the spring of 1824 Golitsyn served Alexander as a kind of devotional secretary, not so much a conventional confessor as a courier escorting him on a quest for spiritual satisfaction.[43] During these years the Tsar's religious emotions were more highly developed than the commoner emotions of private life; and Golitsyn was closer to him than Arakcheev or any other minister of the State.

Prince Alexei Golitsyn had been Procurator of the Holy Synod, the chief lay official in the Russian Church, since the year 1802. He was also Director of the Spiritual Affairs of Foreign Confessions, an office which the Tsar had created in 1810 in order to integrate non-Orthodox religious bodies within the general structure of his Empire. In addition to these posts, Golitsyn became in 1816 Minister of Education and in the following October all his responsibilities were amalgamated in a special government department, the Ministry of Spiritual Affairs and Education. Quite apart from his personal friendship with the Tsar, he was thus a person of outstanding influence in Russia.[44]

Golitsyn, whose responsibilities for education included the censorship of dangerous publications, was far from being a liberal in social thought or in politics; but he was a remarkably tolerant religious believer, intellectually curious over the teachings and practices of other faiths and convinced that it was natural to gratify the longings of the soul by self-absorption in a mystical emotionalism. In this respect there was little difference in the attitude of Golitsyn and Alexander. It was under the Prince's guidance that the first Russian Bible Society was set up but it was the Tsar himself who persuaded the Holy Synod to have the Scriptures translated into the vernacular. At times Golitsyn was, perhaps, unduly generous in his comprehensive tolerance and some odd religious practices crept into the capital. There was, for example, a sect of ecstatic dancers, moved on occasions to utter prophecies in a language no one could understand, some of whose gatherings were attended by Golitsyn himself. Although Alexander knew of their existence, it is unlikely he had any direct contact with the sect for its leader was an officer's widow granted a grace-and-favour apartment in the Mikhailovsky Palace; and Alexander would never have sought mystic joy within the Mikhailovsky's grim walls.[45]

But over most spiritual matters there remained a close affinity between the two men. In 1817 Alexander, remembering the orderliness of the Quaker settlement he had visited in England, instructed his ambassador in London to see if the Friends could provide him with a specialist in husbandry who would supervise reclamation of the marshland between St Petersburg and Tsarskoe Selo.[46] A Quaker from Yorkshire, Daniel Wheeler, duly arrived in the Russian capital and it was Golitsyn who became his principal patron, guide and protector. A year later the Prince made himself responsible for the welfare of William Allen and Stephen Grellet, two of the Friends whom Alexander had met in London, and who now came to St Petersburg from a sense of mission and of service to a sovereign whose Christian virtues they continued to admire.[47] It is, of course, true that Golitsyn's duties necessitated the protection of foreign religious communities within the Empire, but it is clear from the narratives of the Quaker visitors that he shared Alexander's interest in the Society of Friends and its religious ideals. The quietistic contemplation of the Quakers came closer to the spiritual needs of Golitsyn and Alexander than any orgiastic exhibitionism in the Mikhailovsky or the over-dramatized prophesying of Baroness Julie. On the other hand it was difficult for any Russian in Society, from Alexander downwards, to accept the sober dress and habits of the Friends, however much they might respect their sense of Christian witness. The tradition of the Russian Church expressed itself, not only through words of inspiration, but in the colour and symbolism of ceremonial. Ultimately, for Alexander and for his subjects, there could never be a more intensive climax of religious ecstasy than the surging chant of a choir, the battalion of acolytes with candles and banners, and the crescendo of discordant bells in Holy Moscow.

In one of her letters to Elizabeth, the Margravine of Baden declared emphatically that if Alexander was moved 'by genuine religion' it was 'impossible for him not to return' to her,[48] treating his wife as the natural companion of body and soul. The problem of his own domestic situation bore heavily on Alexander's conscience, but nowhere so markedly as in Moscow, where he had first been enticed by the seductive allure of the young Maria Naryshkin, during the Coronation festivities. Golitsyn never disguised from Alexander his conviction that God would punish him for the sins he committed in his adulterous love for Maria,[49] and indeed was already punishing him with every misfortune that troubled his domestic life. The Tsar respected Golitsyn's judgement but he was fond of Maria and of the surviving daughter of this liaison, Sophia. He did not feel able to end a relationship which had continued, intermittently, for some sixteen years. But at last, on returning from Moscow in the summer of 1818, Alexander finally broke off his connection with Maria, though seeking as much as possible to lessen the wretchedness of parting from those whom, to his sister Catherine, he had sometimes referred to as 'my family'.[50] Some months later he gave an account of his separation from Maria Naryshkin in a letter written, not to the stern Golitsyn, but to a more sympathetic spiritual mentor, Roxane Stourdza (or, as she had now become, the Countess Edling):

I am guilty but not so guilty as some people think. It is true that when certain unfortunate events ruined my domestic happiness I sought the society of another woman. I imagined, no doubt wrongly as I now clearly perceive, that since convention had united my wife and myself without our own doing, we were free in the eyes of God though bound to each other in the eyes of Man. My rank obliged me to respect convention; but I believed I was free to give my heart where I wished, and for years it remained faithful to Madame Naryshkin. She also, finding herself in a similar position, fell into the same error. We assumed there was nothing for which we should reproach ourselves. Despite the revelation I have lately been given into my obligations, I would never have possessed the courage to break a tie so dear to me had she not herself asked me to do so. My sorrow was beyond words; but the reasons she gave me were so noble, and so creditable to her in the eyes of the world and in my own eyes, that I could not oppose them. Accordingly I bowed to a sacrifice which broke my heart, one for which it continues to bleed even at this moment.[51]

As an apologia, the letter is a shade disingenuous, and it is probable that Alexander was not being entirely honest with himself, with Maria

Naryshkin, or with Roxane. But at least the decisive break had been made. Diplomats, meeting Alexander that autumn for the first time in three years, were surprised by the lightness of his spirits.[52] Whatever he might tell Roxane Stourdza, there is no doubt a burden was lifted from his troubled conscience. He was not yet prepared for a full reconciliation with Elizabeth (to her disappointment)[53] but one cause of remorse and repentance was at an end. The moral victory made his spiritual quest that much easier.

Disarmament and Foreign Affairs (1816–18)

Alexander's religious beliefs continued to find their deepest outlet in international affairs. Although he had left Paris so abruptly in 1815 he believed, as much as Metternich and Castlereagh, in the absolute necessity of occasional meetings between sovereigns and statesmen in order to preserve the peace of Europe. As he later explained to his Quaker visitors, William Allen and Stephen Grellet, the notion of a Holy Alliance was intended by him as a gesture of love towards God and towards mankind and, though he knew his motives were misunderstood, he was determined to persevere in the hope he would eventually awaken his fellow Princes to an awareness of the 'sacred precepts' of the Christian faith: the scenes of bloodshed and suffering he had witnessed in the advance across Europe had borne heavily on his mind, and he assured his Quaker guests that he shared their abhorrence of war.[54]

There is no doubt Alexander was perfectly sincere in putting forward such pacific sentiments. Unfortunately, however, the huge size of the Russian army and his own obvious love of military parades made contemporaries doubt his words. There was, as in so many aspects of Russian life at this time, a striking contrast between what was said and what was done. This uncertainty over the Tsar's motives led to the failure of one of Alexander's most far-reaching, and least publicized, proposals – a project for general disarmament, first put forward in a private letter to Castlereagh in April 1816.[55]

It is probable that Alexander's plan, like many of his later ideas, was a spontaneous gesture of the moment rather than the product of long discussion. The Tsar began his letter by thanking the British Foreign Secretary for having defended in the Commons his honesty of purpose in drawing up the Holy Alliance Treaty. He then went on to suggest that the time had come for 'a simultaneous reduction of the armed forces of all kinds' raised during the wars against Napoleon; he argued that the maintenance of troops on a war footing weakened the validity of existing treaties by bringing their good faith into question and he emphasized that large armies inevitably placed a heavy financial burden on the various governments. Accordingly he proposed a joint Anglo-Russian initiative to bring about general disarmament 'by methods best suited to the present situation and the relations between the various Powers'.[56]

The British government was interested but suspicious. Castlereagh could not understand why Russia favoured a general and agreed scheme instead of taking unilateral action, and in his reply to Alexander he pointed out there had already been reductions in the size of the British, Austrian and Prussian armies but not in the numbers of Russian troops on active service.[57] Although he did not confide all his doubts to the Tsar, he privately informed the British ambassador of the Russian approach and explained that he was worried over the contradiction between Alexander's assurances and the fact that, despite 'the magnitude . . . and invulnerability' of Russia, Alexander clearly 'likes an army, as he likes an influence in Europe'.[58]

The cool response of the British put an end to Alexander's project. The peculiar nature of the Russian system of recruitment and mobilization meant that the Tsar could not risk ordering extensive cuts without some guarantee that neighbouring Powers would not suddenly increase the size of their own armies; for each of the successive emergencies of the Napoleonic Wars had shown that Russia needed a far longer period of time to bring men to the colours than any other state. Her 'magnitude', which Castlereagh regarded as an advantage, was seen by Alexander as an obstacle to modernization. Since anything he attempted within his Empire was slower to take effect than in foreign lands, it was essential for Russia to act in partnership with her former allies over all changes in the general balance of power. But it was difficult to convince other countries of this strategic dilemma, and much of Alexander's diplomacy in the three years following the Holy Alliance Treaty sought, quite simply, to prove the honesty of his own ideals. When, in May 1817, an officially inspired article in a Petersburg journal declared the Holy Alliance to be 'the surest guarantee of a well-ordered liberty, the true safeguard of law, and the most implacable enemy of arbitrary power' the European chancelleries remained politely sceptical.[59]

The task of interpreting Alexander's idealism to a doubting world devolved, in the first instance, on his Corfiote adviser, John Capodistrias. Technically, for the first seven years of peace, Capodistrias shared control of the Russian Foreign Ministry with the more orthodox and phlegmatic Nesselrode;[60] but Alexander found the Corfiote's general ideas so close to his own that he tended to rely primarily on his advice in foreign affairs, though maintaining considerable respect for his ambassador in Paris,

Pozzo di Borgo. Probably Capodistrias came nearer than any other states-man to understanding the religious fervour which inspired Alexander in later years. Although not himself inclined to introspective soul-searching he was a close personal friend of both the Stourdzas, at one time even hoping to marry Roxane. He had accompanied Alexander to some of Julie von Krüdener's meetings in 1815 and, like his sovereign, he was interested in the theocratic universalism of the Bavarian Catholic publicist, Franz von Baader. Capodistrias combined service to the Russian Tsar with a deep feeling of patriotism towards his homeland. He never became so intimate a friend as Czartoryski in Alexander's first years on the throne, nor did his attachment to the Greek cause provoke such resentment within the Russian governing circle as the Pole's dual loyalty had done; philhellenism was not the menace to Russia's own traditions that Polish nationalism inevitably seemed to be. Hence although Capodistrias had many critics in St Petersburg he was not, like Czartoryski, assailed bitterly as a foreign favourite of the sovereign.

In London and Vienna, on the other hand, Capodistrias was regarded with considerable suspicion.[61] No one in authority in either capital wished to see the Russians re-open the Eastern Question and Metternich distrusted Capodistrias's alleged sympathy with liberal causes. He convinced himself that Capodistrias, this 'pseudo-Saint John of the Apocalypse' as he dubbed him, was Alexander's evil genius.[62] Anxiously the Austrians and British watched for signs of renewed Russian interest in Serbia and the Danubian Principalities and Greece. It was assumed the ascendancy of Capodistrias in St Petersburg foreshadowed a resumption by Alexander of Russia's historic mission to free Orthodox Europe from the Turks.

But Alexander was resolutely set against any expansionist policy so long as the Empire was still faced by problems left over from the wars. In 1816 Capodistrias drew up a comprehensive memorandum in which he proposed Russia should assume control of the Danubian Principalities and make use of religious protective rights to strengthen political influence in the whole of the Balkan peninsula. To support Christians persecuted by the Turks in the Serbian lands and in Greece would, he argued, prove to all the European chancelleries 'the justice and generosity of Russian policy'. Although the Tsar received Capodistrias's memorandum amiably, he refused to be tempted: 'To carry it out, we would need to set the cannons moving and that I have no wish to do', Alexander firmly declared.[63] He had seen too much of war to support a project so dangerous to the peace of the continent.

Yet although Alexander had checked Capodistrias's Balkan ambitions, the mutual esteem of the Corfiote and his sovereign remained undiminished. Alexander began to consult him over questions which were not, strictly speaking, the responsibility of the Foreign Ministry. During the Vienna Congress Capodistrias looked askance at many aspects of the Tsar's Polish policy but once a constitutional kingdom was established in Warsaw he recognized that the Polish experiment was a matter of importance to European liberalism as a whole and not only to the future of Russia. At the beginning of March 1818 he assisted Alexander to draft a remarkable speech which the Tsar-King read to the Diet in Warsaw. The words were wrapped in that ambiguously subjunctive mood so essential to any Tsarist statement of intent but they created a sensation, both in Russia and in the foreign capitals. 'The salutary influence ... of these liberal institutions [*ces institutions libérales**] I hope to spread with the help of the Almighty, over every region entrusted by Providence to my care', Alexander declared, 'Thus you are giving me the opportunity of presenting before my country something I have long been preparing for her and which she will possess when this great undertaking now beginning shall reach its proper maturity.'[64] To most observers it seemed as if the Tsar of Russia had at last aligned himself firmly with the cause of constitutionalism despite the tradition of autocracy within his own Empire.

The effect of Alexander's address on the Russians was not felt for several months to come, for it took time for the intelligentsia to perceive its full significance. But in Vienna Metternich was seriously alarmed.[65] Already Alexander had shown he sympathized with the smaller German States in their efforts to secure constitutional rights within the new German Confederation, a political campaign which ran counter to Austrian policy. How far was he prepared to carry his concept of Providential protection? And what would be the consequence of his remarks on Prussia, whose links with the Russian Empire had been strengthened by Nicholas's marriage? The diplomatic game, as seen from Metternich's study in the Ballhausplatz, appeared to be swinging to Russia's advantage. With Pozzo di Borgo and Richelieu already co-operating closely in Paris, and with Alexander in Poland now setting a bad example in constitutionalism for his relatives on the thrones of Württemberg and Weimar, the prospect of orderly government in Europe seemed bleak to Metternich. There were only two crumbs of comfort to him: the cordial co-operation of Lebzeltern, the Austrian

* Alexander spoke in French and it is a matter of doubt precisely what he meant by this particular phrase. It is unlikely that he intended it to signify 'liberal' in the classical political sense. A recent translation of the Russian text (Vernadsky's *Source Book of Russian History*, Vol. 2, p. 503) renders the phrase as 'these legally free institutions' and this may well have been what Alexander had in mind. One wonders if this phrase, with its remarkable ambiguity, was suggested by Capodistrias.

ambassador in St Petersburg, with Capodistrias's rival, Nesselrode; and the continued strength of the Anglo-Austrian entente, resting on the friendship he had personally reached with Castlereagh in those early weeks of 1814 when Alexander had been so obdurate.[66]

It was in fact Castlereagh who provided both Alexander and Metternich with an opportunity to check the polarization of Europe into 'Austrian' and 'Russian' camps. For at the end of March 1818 the British Foreign Secretary proposed that the first of the periodic conferences envisaged in the Quadruple Alliance Treaty of 1815 should be held in the near future: the principal task of the meeting would be to discuss relations between the old wartime allies and France, but it would also consider 'the several other political questions which are in progress of discussion'.[67] Alexander welcomed the resumption of round-table diplomacy and had, indeed, been pressing for a congress for several months. Metternich, for his part, was also pleased at the prospect of an international gathering, believing that confidential exchanges between the leading statesmen always provided an interesting diversion from routine, if nothing more. The only problem was where the Congress should be held and what governments should attend.

The Congress of Aix (1818)

After considering Dusseldorf, Mannheim and Basle, the old allies settled for Aix-la-Chapelle (Aachen), a city rich in historical associations and militarily easy to secure against neo-Jacobin interlopers.[68] It was harder to decide on the composition of the Congress. Alexander, wishing to appear as a protector of small States and not merely as master of the largest Empire on the continent, was eager to invite representatives from the lesser German States and from Spain. The Austrians and British maintained that, since there had never been a conference of this character under normal conditions of peace, success depended on keeping attendance down to a manageable size. Neither Capodistrias nor Pozzo di Borgo were impressed by this argument but Alexander himself, who had always deplored the cumbersome form of the gathering in Vienna, accepted its validity and called his minister and his ambassador to heel.[69] It was settled that the Congress should consist of representatives from the four allies, to whom it was eventually agreed, on Russian insistence, that plenipotentiaries from France should be added. This decision, at least, was a concession to the Tsar who firmly believed that peace could only be maintained if spokesmen for Bourbon France joined the victors of Leipzig and Waterloo at the conference table.[70]

But, though anxious to strengthen the links he already held with the Duke of Richelieu, Alexander was also determined to emphasize the close bonds between the Hohenzollern and Romanov dynasties. In June 1818, four months before the opening of the Aix Congress, Alexander welcomed Frederick William III and his eldest son on a State visit to Moscow, subsequently travelling with them to St Petersburg for a fortnight of parades and festivities in the capital and the surrounding ring of Imperial palaces.[71] On his last visit to Russia, at the beginning of 1810, the King of Prussia was given lavish hospitality but treated as a poor non-relation. Now the hospitality was even more ostentatious and the respect shown by Alexander to his brother's father-in-law would have gratified any royal visitor, let alone the soulful widower from Berlin. Politically the Tsar wished to prevent Prussia from meekly following the Austrian lead in German affairs. Sentimentally he still felt bound to the pledges he had given to Louise. Both monarchs enjoyed revelling in an idealized past. In the autumn Alexander broke his journey to Aix at Berlin, so that he and Frederick William could once more cross Germany together as in the historic months of 1813.

Throughout the summer of 1818 Alexander stood out as the champion of German state rights and of restoring France as a Great Power. Yet as soon as he reached Aix his political strategy seemed to change. He allowed Capodistrias to put forward proposals on France and on Europe in general, matters already agreed between the Russian delegates,[72] but he made little effort to press them. There was a project for linking all governments together in a protective union against revolution, a proposal for a European army, with Wellington as commander and Brussels as his headquarters, and once again the Russians entered a pious plea for disarmament. Yet when the Allies rejected Alexander's ambitious schemes, he meekly gave way. After a few days Metternich noticed he was not in the least interested in any suggestions from Pozzo di Borgo and he showed a greater willingness to listen to Wellington than to Capodistrias.[73] It is true that the Duke and the Tsar were agreed on the early need for the armies of occupation to be withdrawn from France and that there was a precision in Wellington's advice lacking in the Corfiote's subtle phrases. But it remained a matter of comment that Alexander was so unusually amenable. He was even charming to Metternich. 'It struck me as wholly amusing to see Papa one evening arm in arm with the Tsar', wrote Metternich's twenty-one-year-old daughter, Marie Esterhazy, back to her mother in Vienna;[74] and there were many others who shared her gratified surprise at Alexander's obvious desire for reconciliation.

Yet there is no reason for supposing that Alexander had suddenly experienced one of those disconcerting 'periodic evolutions of the mind' which Metternich later maintained were a feature of his psychology.[75] The truth is far simpler. At Aix, as in Paris and London in 1814, he was once again the centre of public attention, dominating the diplomatic stage as he had rarely been able to do in Vienna and only at Vertus during his second visit to France. In his own Empire Alexander seldom responded to public acclaim: he expected it, as of right. But abroad he enjoyed the sensation of having all eyes focused upon him, of knowing that the Prime Minister of France and the Foreign Ministers of Britain and Austria were watching anxiously the changing expressions of his face. Nor were the statesmen the only observers at Aix waiting on his nod of approval: there were petitioners to end the slave trade, spokesmen for other humanitarian projects, and special correspondents from newspapers in the German cities, France and England.[76] Friedrich Gentz, Metternich's principal public relations man, recorded his impressions of Alexander at Aix:

The Emperor of Russia is the only sovereign who is in a position to achieve a great enterprise . . . Obstacles, such as constitutional forms or concern for public opinion, may shackle other rulers, but they do not exist for him. Anything he decides today can be carried out tomorrow. Though said to be impenetrable, all the world amuses itself discussing his designs. He attaches extraordinary importance to what others think of him and it is probable that he is more eager to acquire a reputation for goodness than merely to win glory. He values terms such as peacemaker, protector of the weak, saviour of his empire rather than the title of conqueror. A natural religious sentiment almost fills his heart and dominates his emotions.[77]

If so astute and caustic an observer as Gentz could write in such terms, it is small wonder Alexander found the Congress such an enjoyable experience. Moreover, though his most detailed proposals came to nothing, he was gratified to find Castlereagh and Metternich still talking of the 'moral solidarity' of the alliance, while the final declaration of the Congress, with its insistence on the virtues of 'justice, moderation and concord' in the politics of nations, was happily reminiscent of the Holy Alliance.[78]* Everyone was pleased with Aix, except perhaps Capodistrias.

* The Congress at Aix-la-Chapelle ended the military occupation of France and settled all questions of reparations. The validity of the Quadruple Alliance of 1815 was re-affirmed by a secret protocol of the original signatories while, at the same time, Louis XVIII was invited to associate France with all efforts to maintain peace and the *status quo* in Europe. The Congress agreed on measures to strengthen security on St Helena, in case Napoleon sought to escape to America, and confirmed a decision already taken at the Vienna Congress ensuring that German Jews enjoyed their civil rights.

Still delighted at finding himself once more the cynosure of the European galaxy, Alexander lingered in western and central Europe. He crossed over into France, reviewed the last units of the Russian army of occupation at Sedan and Valenciennes and even made a hurried trip to Paris, where Louis XVIII thanked him profusely for supporting France's admission to the Great Power league. And then there were his sisters to visit, Anna at Brussels, Marie at Weimar, and the dearest of them all at Stuttgart; and he managed a few nights at Karlsruhe, where Elizabeth was once again spending part of the winter with her mother and brother. Finally, in the last week of the old year, Alexander surprised the Austrians by going to Vienna, where he was entertained to lunch by Metternich in the house he had shunned during the tension of the great Congress. The spirit of peace and goodwill was, indeed, mightily active that Christmas. At last he set out for his own Empire, determined to reach St Petersburg before the Russians celebrated the Epiphany. Slowly, escort and carriage headed north-eastwards from Vienna towards southern Poland.[79] At some moment, as he was travelling between Brno and Olmütz, the familiar contours of the Pratzen Plateau lay to the right of his carriage window, silent and empty in the winter snow; but there is no record of what he said or thought as he journeyed back this second time from Austerlitz. His star had not always shone so brightly in the ascendant as at Aix.

20

The Absentee Tsar

Sad News from Stuttgart (January 1819)

Alexander was back in St Petersburg in time to celebrate the Russian New Year. People noticed he was still in good spirits and apparently tireless. So, for that matter, was his mother. At fifty-nine Marie Feodorovna had just completed a winter journey in which she visited her three married daughters in Germany and the Netherlands, and yet a week later she was fresh enough to walk immediately behind the Tsar in procession to the Jordan Steps where the annual ceremony of blessing the waters of the frozen Neva took place in a crisp frost and bright sunshine. With the Empress Elizabeth not expected to return from Karlsruhe until the end of the month, Marie Feodorovna was once again at the centre of affairs, planning a lively winter season of entertainments before the coming of Lent. Since the Court had wintered the year before in Moscow, the young Grand Duchess Alexandra had not as yet been in St Petersburg during the carnival weeks. Once the Dowager Empress felt inclined to enjoy herself she always wished to celebrate in grand style, and if her eldest son had shaken off his despondency there was good reason for a round of dinners and theatricals and dancing. 'I was delighted', wrote Alexandra looking back on these months in a brief memoir. 'It was all new to me and I was only twenty.'[1]

This nursery freshness of the year was suddenly dissolved by news which threw the family into grief and mourning. Soon after Alexander returned from the ceremony at the Jordan Steps a courier arrived from Stuttgart and the Tsar learnt that Catherine Pavlovna was dead. Marie Feodorovna refused at first to believe it: had she not herself been Catherine's guest in the previous month? She seemed well enough then and no word of any illness reached St Petersburg. So unexpected was Catherine's death that Elizabeth was actually on the way from Karlsruhe to Stuttgart to pay her respects to her sister-in-law when she was intercepted by a messenger who told her what had happened and advised her not to proceed with her journey but to return to Russia.[2] Inevitably there remained some mystery over Catherine's death. Everyone knew that she, of all Alexander's brothers and sisters, was the one most capable of provoking a personal enemy to murder and, as the young Grand Duchess wrote, 'the name of Prince Paul of Württemberg was whispered'. But, though there had indeed been tension between Catherine and her husband's younger brother, it appears certain she died from natural causes. Officially Catherine succumbed to 'an attack of erysipelas in the head' but it seems more likely that her constitution, weakened by the birth of two daughters within twenty months, was unable to throw off a bout of influenza.[3] She was only thirty years old.

Catherine had been Marie Feodorovna's favourite child and the sad news from Stuttgart almost unhinged her. Alexander was so concerned over his mother's health that the full sense of loss only came upon him gradually, reaching a climax when Elizabeth arrived home from Germany on 7 February. He could not mention the sister for whom he had felt so deep an affection without tears in his eyes. It was, for all the Imperial family, a 'slow and heavy winter'. Alexander was often deep in melancholy reverie. Religion alone raised in him the spark of hope, though all too frequently his reading of the Old Testament intensified the fire of agony in his conscience. Later that year it seemed to some of his suite as if he were being deliberately careless of his own welfare, riding recklessly on horseback or in his smaller and lighter carriages. To those sufficiently intimate with their sovereign to suggest he should not run such risks he replied, 'Why should I be cautious? I have two saints praying for me, Queen Louise of Prussia and my dear sister Catherine.'[4] It is hardly surprising that he began to discuss with Golitsyn the possibility of a private meeting with Julie von Krüdener.[5] But not yet.

Government by Post Chaise

That spring another sudden death, though less personal, also disturbed him. On 23 March, August Kotzebue, the German dramatist who had for some years served as a Russian intelligence agent, was assassinated in Mannheim by a fanatical theological student from the University of Jena. Alexander had admired Kotzebue's work ever since his youth and had known

Kotzebue during Paul's reign when he was director of the German Theatre in St Petersburg. But what troubled Alexander now was not so much the loss to the dramatic arts nor even to the Russian spy service, but the evidence that the German students were turning against the established order and that they were identifying the Russian State with counter-revolution. Metternich had argued in Aix that the autocracies should stand together against radical Jacobinism but did not succeed in converting Alexander, and at the time of Kotzebue's assassination each of the dynasties in Germany which had marriage links with the Tsar was committed, in varying degree, to some project of constitutionalism. The crime at Mannheim played directly into Metternich's hands, making it possible for him later that summer to induce the German States to adopt a series of repressive measures: the so-called 'Carlsbad Decrees' restricted rights of political assembly, established general surveillance of the German universities, and tightened up censorship of the Press.[6] Inevitably the knowledge that Germany was being subjected to such a rigorous system of repression raised doubts in Russia over the Tsar's intentions for his own lands. Would he now follow Metternich's lead, abandoning the last vestiges of liberalism, as Frederick William was doing in Prussia? What then would happen to the promised Russian constitution? On his visit to Warsaw in March 1818 he had told the Polish Diet he wished to introduce 'free institutions' in 'all the regions entrusted by Providence' to his care:* would he stand by this declaration? There were many in St Petersburg and Moscow who hoped they would hear nothing more of such nonsense.

Alexander was not ready to answer these questions. Outwardly he made no response to Kotzebue's murder. He continued to approve a more relaxed policy of censorship than during the five years following the Napoleonic invasion. It seemed as if he was still looking to some of his old friends for enlightened reform. Kochubey, as Minister of the Interior, complained that, 'Police agents have not been confining themselves to gathering information, they have been seeking to incite crimes and suspicions';[7] and Alexander agreed that the Ministry of Police should accordingly be abolished, its responsibilities passing to the Interior, with Kochubey to keep watch on its activities. Nor was he the only veteran of the Secret Committee to be employed on measures of liberalization. Throughout the months when Germany was groaning in resentment at the Carlsbad Decrees, Novosiltsov was working on a draft constitution for Russia, which would have endowed the Empire with a federal structure and bicameral assemblies (though consultative rather than legislative in scope).[8] The preparatory

* See above, p. 357.

draft at least proved that Alexander's ambiguous pledge to the Polish Diet still had some substance. As late as midsummer 1819 the Tsar confirmed, in private conversation, that he had every intention of giving Russia a constitution once he had seen that the Polish experiment was working effectively. But he had not made up his mind on the project: Russia was short of the funds necessary to establish genuinely decentralized institutions, he told Prince Viazemsky; and he complained of the marked anti-liberal prejudice of the governing class in the two capitals.[9]

His enthusiasm for administrative reform was easily muted. He was prepared, for example, to reinstate Speransky and appointed him as Governor-General of Siberia. The most primitive province of the Empire certainly needed a person of Speransky's gifts to organize its administration and he was able to draft a remarkable statute which reconciled the rights of nomadic natives with the traditional forms of government; but although Alexander appreciated Speransky's services in Siberia, he was uneasy in case he might seek once more to change policy at the centre of affairs. 'I advise you to become as friendly as you can with Count Alexei Andreevich', Alexander told Speransky at their first meeting after his return to St Petersburg.[10] It was a pointed message; for Alexei Andreevich Arakcheev could be relied on to check any excessive sympathy with constitutional liberalism.

Arakcheev's own position remained unchanged and unchallenged. For those outside the Court, access to the Tsar was possible only through Arakcheev's private chancery in Liteiny Prospect. His powers as overlord of the military colonies were not affected by the reorganization of Kochubey's department. When Alexander was in St Petersburg, Arakcheev 'was indispensable to him and worked with him every day', as the Grand Duchess Alexandra wrote. 'He was liked by no one', she added. 'I have never been able to understand how he remained in favour.'[11] She was not the only person to be puzzled.

In June 1819 soldiers and peasants on a military colony at Chuguev, near Kharkov in the eastern Ukraine, rose in protest at the harsh discipline of the local commanders and at the requisition by military authorities of cereals they had cultivated. There had been serf risings earlier in Alexander's reign, notably during his absence abroad in 1813–14,[12] but the Chuguev troubles were more serious, because they involved a military mutiny. Arakcheev at once travelled down to the Ukraine and punished the rebels by brutal floggings which caused many deaths. There is some evidence he was worried in case he had over-reached himself, for he wrote to Alexander confessing that he had been forced to think 'about this business day and night' lest 'my human imperfections might make me harsh or vindictive'. But the Tsar expressed sympathy for his loyal servant's 'sensitive soul' and gave him 'sincere and warm approval' for his 'good and Christian feelings'.[13] However generous Alexander might feel when talking to his Quaker visitors, he could not tolerate the threat of mutiny. Yet he refused to see the terrible incident at Chuguev as a warning of impending revolution. Though Arakcheev's reign of terror coincided with the implementation of the Carlsbad Decrees in Germany there was no parallel between the two systems of repression, nor between the events which had given rise to them. In Alexander's eyes what happened at Chuguev was endemic to Russia, not part of the Jacobin contagion which Metternich insisted was already spreading across the continent.

In this instance Alexander was perfectly correct. But the generation which had attained manhood in this second decade of the century saw things differently. They were eager and willing to receive ideas from abroad and to identify specifically Russian problems with the general discontent. Hence to young officers and to students in the new universities there was confirmation in the reports from Chuguev of the need for organized resistance to the old order. Secret societies, many of them masonic in organization and symbolism, proliferated; and at least one group of young aristocratic intellectuals began to prepare a more radical constitution than anything which Novosiltsov had in mind.[14] To the surprise of foreign observers, the authorities did little to hamper them. There was a time-lag of more than a year between the restrictions imposed on the German universities by the Carlsbad Decrees and the tightening of academic discipline within the Russian Empire. It was, in fact, during these very months of uncertainty that the Pedagogical Institute in St Petersburg was raised to the status of a university. New and stricter regulations on censorship were not enforced until June 1820, coinciding with the first systematic purge of academic teachers.[15] Much of this delay was a direct consequence of Alexander's own reluctance to proscribe liberal beliefs. Whatever might happen beyond the frontiers of his Empire, he could never entirely forget he was himself a child of Catherine II's 'enlightenment' and a pupil of La Harpe. When in the early summer of 1821 the Governor-General of St Petersburg urged the Tsar to strike at the secret societies in the capital, Alexander replied sadly, 'You know that I have shared and encouraged these illusions and errors. It is not for me to deal severely with them.'[16] Harassed officials, far more aware than their sovereign of the mounting intellectual discontent, found Alexander's moderation perplexing and exasperating, and not without reason.

There was indeed much in Alexander's behaviour during the three years following his sister's death to tax the patience of even the most loyal among his civil servants. For months at a time he was absent from the capital, sometimes travelling in the provinces of the Empire or in his Polish Kingdom but on other occasions crossing the frontier and attending the international Congresses which were a feature of the diplomatic system in this period. Elizabeth once explained to her mother that he found all this travelling inside Russia tedious but essential if he were to keep in touch with the mood of his people.[17] Certainly in the first part of his reign he had tended to identify St Petersburg with Russia as a whole and it was therefore sensible for him to see what was happening in distant regions of the Empire. In June 1819, for example, he travelled north to Archangel and then returned by way of Finland, seeing a country where conditions were totally different from the plains and steppes with which he was familiar. He felt, too, that it was necessary for him to attend in person the annual sessions of the Polish Diet in Warsaw, not least because of the growing unpopularity of Constantine. Yet it is questionable whether he gained much from these long journeys. Too often he travelled at the madcap pace which he had always affected in moments of worry and tension. What could the racing wheels of a carriage teach him of the real problems of his peoples? Moreover it was as difficult to govern an autocracy with a peripatetic sovereign in time of peace as it had been when he was leading his armies across Europe. There were delays in tackling the problems of other parts of the Empire, and in answering despatches from ambassadors abroad. 'At present', Prince Viazemsky complained, 'Russia is governed from the seat of a post chaise.'[18]

The Tsar's restlessness, his utter inability to stay for any length of time in one place, could not be rationalized, however much Elizabeth might try to make it sound as if he were travelling in search of knowledge. He was tired and bored, interested in religion but in little else. During the summer of 1819 (apparently before setting out for Archangel) he visited Krasnoe Selo, where his brother Nicholas's brigade was in camp. After inspecting the Ismailovsky Regiment the Tsar dined with Nicholas and the Grand Duchess Alexandra and suddenly informed them 'that he was doubly pleased to see Nicholas carry out his duties well because on him would fall one day a heavy weight of responsibility'. Alexandra has left a record of the Tsar's further remarks that evening:

He looked on him [Nicholas] as the person who would replace him; and this would happen much sooner than anyone imagined, since it would occur while he himself was still alive. We sat there like two statues, open-eyed and dumb. The Emperor went on: 'You seem astonished, but let me tell you that my brother, Constantine, who has never bothered about the throne, is more than ever determined to renounce it formally and to pass on his rights to his brother Nicholas and his descendants. As for myself I have decided to free myself of my functions and to retire from the world . . . I am no longer the man I was, and I think it is my duty to retire in good time' . . . Seeing us on the verge of tears he tried to comfort us and reassure us by saying that this was not going to happen at once, that some years must pass before he carried out his plan, then he left us alone, and it can be imagined in what sort of state of mind we were.[19]

Some of these phrases are familiar; they echo words from his youth, a longing to escape from responsibility both during the last years of Catherine and after his father's accession. Although there is no other account of Alexander's table-talk, the whole tone of his sister-in-law's narrative corresponds so closely with this earlier desire to renounce his rights and withdraw from the public eye that there is no reason to doubt the authenticity of her story.

There were other occasions when the Tsar suggested, obliquely in conversation, that he might abdicate.[20] He refused, however, to make any public pronouncement over the succession, nor did he give any indication when he was thinking of handing over the crown or where he would reside during his successor's reign. This is hardly surprising. There was no precedent for a voluntary renunciation of the Imperial prerogatives in Russian history, although sovereigns in other lands had abdicated in this way, especially when moved by a desire for spiritual meditation in monastic seclusion. The Emperor Charles V, for example, divested himself of his crowns and retired to the cloisters of Yuste at the age of fifty-five, rendered prematurely old by the strain of war and the sin of gluttony; but, at the time of his conversation with Nicholas and Alexandra, Tsar Alexander was a mere forty-one years old. He was rapidly becoming so deaf and so short-sighted that he believed people were mocking him behind his back,[21] and he limped at times when tiredness tensed the muscles of his injured leg. Some people said that he looked far older than his years but, as his ministers complained, he was still extraordinarily active; not one, it would seem, who wished as yet to seek monastic sanctuary from temporal affairs. Were the remarks he made at Nicholas's private dinner-party as earnest as the Grand Duchess maintained? Was he, as at other moments of boredom, speaking his thoughts aloud, vaguely giving substance to a dream of escape which comforted him when his day-to-day existence seemed tedious? He undoubtedly believed that Nicholas, rather than Constantine, should be his successor, but it is unlikely he was as yet so resolved on abdicating as the young Grand Duchess assumed.

Some three months after Alexander's visit to Krasnoe Selo he met Baroness von Krüdener for the first time since those heady religious sessions in the Rue du Faubourg Saint-Honoré. The Baroness had long been seeking an opportunity to talk once more to 'the young hero' (as she still called Alexander in correspondence with her daughter)[22] and he had himself mentioned her, on several occasions, to Prince Golitsyn. It was arranged the meeting should take place on the morning of 21 September at Petchory, a small town between the ancient city of Pskov and the marshes of Estonia, a convenient staging-post for Alexander on his way to Warsaw. There, beneath the golden cupolas of a conventual church, he listened while Julie von Krüdener poured out to him the latest revelations vouchsafed to her by the Almighty; the King of Prussia's life was in danger, she insisted, and it was essential for Alexander to urge him to give himself without reserve to God and entrust the Prussian Kingdom to His protection; the Holy Alliance must be built up, integrated more closely against those who were seeking to overturn the kingdoms of this world.[23] How much of Julie's ravings Alexander accepted as genuine inspiration is open to doubt. He spoke encouragingly to her but when next day she sought a second meeting with him she was told he had already left for Warsaw. As at other times in their strange relationship, Julie's words were a mixture of Sibylline warnings and nonsense. Although Alexander took no apparent notice of her messages, he did not break off contact with her. She remained in touch with both Golitsyn and Koshelev, the two unofficial custodians of Alexander's spiritual conscience. On his return from Warsaw he seems, momentarily, to have favoured a pocket prophetess from Marseilles, a Madame Bouche, who had been inspired to travel to the Russian capital. Her influence was, however, short-lived for it was in the interests of both Julie von Krüdener and Prince Golitsyn to expose her as a charlatan: could a Marseillaise arise as a true prophet in such times?[24]

The Tsar Goes to Troppau

The year 1820 seemed, in one respect, to confirm Baroness von Krüdener's warnings. Half the continent wrapped itself in conspiracy against the conservative doctrines of the Holy Alliance. In the Italian peninsula the *Carbonari* put forward holy principles of their own, binding themselves with fearsome oaths and dramatic symbolism to drive out foreign rulers and establish governments based on written constitutions. The unrest spread to Spain, where in March insurgents forced King Ferdinand VII to restore the liberal constitution of 1812, setting an example which the people of Naples sought to emulate in July. By the end of the summer there was a splutter of revolt across Europe from Portugal to Sicily. Nor was unrest confined to the southern extremities of the continent. In February Thistlewood's conspirators in London's Cato Street planned to liquidate the British cabinet, and failed; while in Paris the radical fanatic Louvel plotted to murder Louis XVIII's nephew, the Duc de Berri, and succeeded. Alexander was alarmed at the succession of bad news. It was impossible for any champion of order to stand aside and watch governments overthrown by men whose ideas 'were formed in the school of popular despotism during the French Revolution'.[25]

The Spanish emergency stirred him to action. For the past four years the Russian ambassador in Madrid, Dmitri Tatischev, had enjoyed a privileged position at Ferdinand's Court, giving him something of the influence and patronage Caulaincourt had exercised in Petersburg after Tilsit. Tatischev represented the Spanish liberals to the Tsar as dangerous neo-Jacobins and his warnings were reiterated from Paris by Pozzo di Borgo. Accordingly when he heard the insurgents had secured a constitution from the King, Alexander insisted it was the duty of the five allies of Aix to intervene, so as to stamp out the flames of revolution before they menaced the whole of Europe. At the end of April he instructed Capodistrias to propose collective measures aimed at freeing Ferdinand from all restraint.[26] As yet Alexander was thinking of a joint remonstrance rather than of military intervention, but it was clear he did not rule out the possibility of sending troops to coerce the Spanish liberals if they continued to defy the will of the Great Powers.

The Russian response to events so far distant from their frontiers aroused suspicion in London and embarrassed Metternich. Nobody wished to see Alexander send a punitive expedition across the continent, nor indeed to assemble troops for a new Peninsular Campaign themselves. The British were already alarmed at Tatischev's activities in Madrid and suspected a Russian design to establish naval bases in Spain in order to maintain a Mediterranean fleet. Metternich disliked the way in which the Russians were seeking to take the diplomatic initiative although he was gratified that Alexander was now associating himself with the anti-liberal cause rather than with the constitutionalists. The British were so resolutely opposed to intervention in Spanish affairs that Castlereagh had little difficulty in convincing the Allies of the folly of the Tsar's proposals.[27] As a compromise, however, Metternich suggested a meeting between Alexander and the

Emperor Francis at which the Russians and Austrians could discuss ways of countering revolutionary conspiracy on a grand scale. It was agreed that Alexander and Francis should meet in the autumn in Troppau (Opava), the capital of Austrian Silesia.[28]

In mid-July a liberal revolution, similar in character to the rising in Spain, broke out in Naples. The Austrians were far more alarmed at finding the spirit of revolt active in Italy than they had been over the troubles of Spain. Metternich did not want to tie up Austrian forces in police operations throughout Italy while leaving Russia and Prussia a free hand in central Europe and the German States. He therefore proposed a conference of ambassadors which he hoped would result in agreement on a common policy over European affairs in general while leaving punitive measures to the Austrians alone. Alexander, however, wanted to keep the strings of policy in his own hands, and in September he suggested that the Troppau meeting should be transformed into a full Congress, attended by Frederick William of Prussia and representatives of France and Britain. But so strong was the feeling in London against involvement in continental affairs that Castlereagh would send only an observer to Troppau, and the French (who wished to pursue an independent policy over Naples) followed the British example.[29] By the beginning of October it was clear the forthcoming conference would be primarily a gathering of the three east European autocrats and their advisers rather than a full Congress, another Teplitz and not another Aix-la-Chapelle. Metternich intended to use the opportunity to convince Alexander of the need for close Austro-Russian collaboration, his first objective being the dismissal of Capodistrias, whom the Austrians profoundly distrusted. Alexander's aims were more confused: he still believed that if you growled fiercely enough, rebel governments would quail; but he was prepared to despatch troops to restore erring states 'to the bosom of the Alliance' if other methods failed. Though conscious of the strain on Russia's resources, he was willing to offer Emperor Francis 100,000 men to help keep order in southern Italy.[30] Nobody bothered any longer about distant Spain.

Alexander left St Petersburg on 21 July 1820, expecting he would be away for three or four months. He intended to spend the early autumn in Warsaw, so as to dispose of the problems of the Diet, and then continue southwards to Troppau for the Congress.[31] But the diplomatic situation deteriorated so rapidly in the late summer and autumn that it was impossible to complete the work of the Congress as swiftly as at Aix, and Alexander did not return to his capital for a whole year. This prolonged absence imposed a considerable strain on the Russian administration. Elizabeth herself complained, in a letter to her mother, that uncertainty over Alexander's movements was a serious blow to the government, not least because, once winter had come to central Europe, it took a month for despatches and documents to be sent from St Petersburg to Troppau and back with the sovereign's comments.[32] Moreover for much of the winter Alexander insisted on having the Grand Duke Nicholas with him in Troppau, introducing him to the problems of diplomacy by congress. With Constantine in Warsaw and Nicholas with the Tsar in Silesia, the ceremonies of state devolved upon Marie Feodorovna and Elizabeth. Inevitably effective control of internal policy was left to Arakcheev. The disillusionment of the younger generation was complete.

Mutiny in the Semeonovsky Regiment (October 1820)

The Tsar reached Troppau on 20 October. Within hours of his arrival, he was closeted with Metternich. If the Austrian's account of the conversation is correct, Alexander was already in a mood of abject apology for his earlier sympathy with constitutionalism, while Capodistrias too was prepared to agree with everything Metternich said to him.[33] Neither wished to prolong the Troppau Congress. By flattering the Austrian Foreign Minister there was a good prospect of securing that general statement condemning revolution, on which the Tsar appeared to lay such stress. Once that business was settled, it only remained to agree over the movement of troops from Poland to Italy and the appointment of a joint commander. These were tiresome but familiar topics; they need not long detain the sovereigns. Unlike Vienna or Aix, Troppau was a town in which there was no good reason for lingering, especially in the depths of winter.

To Alexander's surprise, however, Metternich was reluctant to approve a general statement on the rights of a Great Power to intervene in the affairs of another state. The Austrian attitude was more sophisticated than the Russians had anticipated. Metternich argued that only a Power whose security was threatened by a foreign rebellion had a right to intervene in the internal affairs of another state. He implied that Austria had an obligation to cleanse Italy of the revolutionary contagion before the disease spread to the provinces of the Empire itself, but Prussia and Russia were too distant to be menaced by what went on in the peninsula and therefore possessed no right to intervene. This was a difficult argument to refute, especially as Frederick William and Hardenberg publicly associated themselves with the Austrians.[34] But in the first days of November Capodistrias, with Alexander's warm support, put forward a different set of general principles.

He did his best to reconcile a belief in repression with support for con-stitutionalism: the Great Powers, he argued, had accepted responsibility for upholding the 1815 Treaties and therefore collectively they had a duty to intervene once that settlement was in danger; but it would be wrong for them to impose alien rule or methods of government on a people and therefore intervention should be preceded by a joint declaration that, once the revolutionary movement was suppressed, it would be succeeded by a government based upon the 'dual freedoms': national independence and political liberty.[35] This was an ingenious exercise in political theory which left Metternich momentarily 'out of spirits', and the Austrians were forced to fall back on the old game of playing off Nesselrode against Capodistrias.

By the end of the second week in November it became possible for Metternich to excite Alexander's fear of unrest sufficiently for him to disown the Corfiote's basic principles. For on 9 November the Tsar received news which disturbed him more than any event since Napoleon's escape from Elba: an officer arrived with messages from Arakcheev and the military commandant of St Petersburg informing him that, on the night of 28 October, soldiers in the Semeonovsky Regiment had mutinied, demanding the dismissal of their commanding officer, Colonel Schwarz. Alexander was overwhelmed by the news: he regarded the Semeonovsky as his personal Guard Regiment, and he saw the incident as far more serious than the troubles at Chuguev, a sign that evil doctrines were eating away the loyalty of his most trusted troops. In reality, the mutiny was an isolated episode, sparked off by resentment at the cruelty of a non-Russian officer who had ordered veteran war heroes to be flogged for trifling offences.[36] The Empress Elizabeth played down the episode, even admitting to her mother privately that the men had a just grievance;[37] but Alexander insisted on severe punishment, although he agreed that Colonel Schwarz should be dismissed from the service for allowing the situation to get out of hand. To Metternich's surprise, the news of the mutiny convinced Alexander that there was an international radical conspiracy eager to frustrate the efforts of the 'Holy Allies' at Troppau.[38] It was this theory which Alexander developed in an extraordinary letter to Arakcheev on 17 November:

It is easy for you to imagine the sorrow this has caused me. Such an incident is, I think you will agree, unheard of in our army. It is even sadder that it should have taken place in the Guards and, bitterest blow for me personally, in the Semeonovsky Regiment. Since I am accustomed to speaking to you con-fidentially, I can say that nothing will convince me, whatever people may say, that this action was planned by the soldiers or arose solely from their harsh treatment by Colonel Schwarz . . . I do not think the origin was military because the training of soldiers would naturally induce them to take up weapons, which none of them did . . . I think the incitement came from outside the army. The question, of course, arises from where? It is hard to say. I admit that I blame the secret societies which, according to the evidence both you and I possess, are much displeased with our alliance and our work at Troppau. It would appear as if the object of the insurrection was to intimidate us . . . to force me to abandon my work at Troppau and make me return speedily to St Petersburg. But through the will of God we have avoided this and snuffed out the evil at birth.[39]

The mutiny made Alexander resolved to reach agreement with the Austrians and Prussians and to remain in conference as long as was necessary for the security of Europe. He at once instructed Capodistrias to seek a diplomatic compromise with Metternich over the problem of intervention in Italy and to abandon all reference to the 'dual freedoms' or any other principle of enlightenment.[40]

Metternich was prepared to make token concessions to the Russians provided he was left to settle Italy in his own way. He agreed that Capodistrias should draft the 'Preliminary Protocol' of Troppau, a document summarizing the views of the delegates to the Congress which was made public at the end of the third week in November. It asserted a right of intervention to bring back to the Alliance states which had suffered an 'illegal' change in government. At the same time it was proposed that an Austrian army of occupation should be sent to southern Italy, accompanied by representatives of the Allied Powers, and that the King of Naples should be invited to a further meeting of the sovereigns in Laibach (Ljubljana) where the future of his kingdom would be discussed.[41] Both Metternich and Alexander were well satisfied by the Protocol, although it aroused protests from the British who insisted there was no natural right by which any Power was entitled to interfere in the internal affairs of another state, large or small. The British attitude did not especially worry Alexander, who had by now come to assume London would almost automatically disapprove of any measure he proposed.[42]

Technically the Protocol should have ended the Troppau Congress. Nothing could be done until a reply was received from the King of Naples. But Alexander had no wish to return home, especially after the Semeonovsky mutiny. Throughout a wet November and December the rulers of Austria, Prussia and Russia, together with their foreign ministers, remained immured in the mud and slush of Silesia. At times they were very, very bored. Only Metternich seems to have been in relatively high spirits. He amused himself by writing a light-hearted description of the difficulties in etiquette caused by the Tsar meeting a lady coming in the opposite direction while both were walking over duckboards spread across the 'chocolate ice' mud of the Troppau streets.[43] In the evening there was little to do except play whist, talk and drink tea. Never before had Alexander and Metternich exchanged views so freely and in such detail. The Austrian saw more of the Tsar than did either Capodistrias or Nesselrode and he used these meetings to convert Alexander to his own beliefs in a just, orderly and strong system of government. In mid-December he presented Alexander with an eight-thousand-word document which he entitled a 'Profession of Political Faith', emphasizing the need of governments to be on guard against the presumption of a middle class jealously and ruthlessly striving for political power.[44] It was not a profound or original work of philosophical specula-tion but it was subtly worded so as to appeal to Alexander's latent religious fervour. It was, Metternich warned, the duty of the good European sovereign to 'maintain religious principles in all their purity' without permitting 'the faith to be attacked or morality interpreted according to the vision . . . of foolish sectarians'.[45] This was a deft blow at Julie von Krüdener (and, indeed, Prince Golitsyn) just as Metternich's criticism of presump-tuous liberals was an attempt to discredit Capodistrias. Alexander was impressed by the sententious moralizing of this dreary manifesto, and a few weeks later echoed some of its sentiments in a letter to Golitsyn.[46] He was not, however, prepared to change either his attitude to political questions or his policy in any decisive way: he still listened to Capodistrias, even if he took little notice of his advice; he still consulted Nesselrode and Pozzo di Borgo; and, for that matter, he still wrote to Golitsyn asking him to give Baroness von Krüdener (who had come to St Petersburg because her son-in-law had been taken ill there) his fondest wishes (*mille choses affec-tueuses de ma part*).[47] At times it seems almost as if he were so disappointed at his failure to provide Europe with a new and nobler concept of inter-national morality in politics; that his willpower was paralysed and he was content to drift aimlessly in Metternich's wake.

Laibach and the Re-opening of the Eastern Question

Alexander left Troppau in the fourth week of December, spent a few days in Vienna, and arrived in Laibach on 8 January 1821. The weather was much milder than in Silesia, three hundred miles to the north, and the city itself was livelier. Two days after reaching Slovenia he was once more locked in conference with the Austrians and a Prussian representative (for Frederick

William himself had shown good sense and gone home rather than watch another diplomatic production stage-managed by Metternich). The Congress formally lasted until 28 February, its sessions dominated throughout by the Austrian Foreign Minister.[48] Alexander gave his approval for Austrian troops to be sent southwards into Naples and dutifully praised each of Metternich's actions. Once and once only the Tsar attempted to take the initiative, suggesting that if Austria was quelling radicalism in Naples then the French should be invited to cross the Pyrenees and free Ferdinand of Spain from liberal restraints. But Metternich did not wish to see France accepted as the agency of good order in Europe. He explained to the Tsar that the French could not be trusted since Paris was the headquarters for a massive international conspiracy, dominated by a secret committee of revolutionaries; and Alexander accepted Metternich's suggestion that Spanish affairs should be left for a later Congress.[49] He was quite happy to wait upon events.

It seemed, indeed, as if he would even be prepared to wait for them in the city of Laibach itself. For though the Congress was formally dissolved at the end of February, Alexander agreed to remain in Slovenia (or rather, as it was then called, Carniola) until the Italian crisis was over. Within a fortnight the situation had become worse rather than better. Garrisons of the Piedmontese army in Turin and Alessandria mutinied, calling for a war against Austria on behalf of the Neapolitans. The Tsar, still shocked by what had happened to his own Semeonovsky Guards, was deeply affected, wanting to order his army from Poland to march to the assistance of the Austrians at once: 'Now I understand why the Lord has kept me here until this moment', he exclaimed. 'How much gratitude do I owe Him for so arranging things that I was still together with my Allies ... If we save Europe it is because He has desired it.'[50] While the Austrians prepared to send an army across the north Italian plain, the Tsar sent a courier to St Petersburg with instructions for 90,000 men to be concentrated along the Russo-Austrian frontier ready to march westwards if they were needed. In reality, as so often with Russian military deployment, the emergency in Piedmont was over before the troops reached their destination, but Metternich and his publicists made much of Alexander's action. All Europe should learn of the complete accord between the Austrian and Russian Courts, the two greatest powers on the continent acting in concert against Revolution.

Yet, only five days after hearing of the risings in Turin and Alessandria, more serious news still brought alarm to the sovereigns and ministers in Laibach. At the beginning of March one of the Tsar's aides-de-camp,

Prince Alexander Ypsilanti, gathered a force of Greek patriots in Odessa, crossed the river Pruth into Moldavia and raised a revolt against the Turkish authorities in the Danubian Principalities. Within a month the Greek Christians of the Peloponnese were in full-scale rebellion against the Sultan's government and their acts of defiance had received official sanction from the Orthodox Archbishop of Patras. Thus, at the very moment when the Russians were mobilizing in defence of the established order in Italy, their co-religionists in the Balkans re-opened the Eastern Question with a dramatic flourish that no Tsar of Russia could ignore, least of all one whose joint Foreign Minister was himself a Greek.

Ypsilanti was not an obscure agitator, he was a Russian General, a friend of the Stourdzas and a prominent figure in Viennese Society during the Congress. He had met Capodistrias on several occasions and had made no secret of his ambition to kindle a patriotic insurrection of the Greek peoples. It is probable that he believed he could force Alexander's hand by his raid across the Pruth. At the very outset of his enterprise he sent an appeal to Alexander, 'Save us, Your Majesty, save our religion from those who would persecute it, return to us our temples and our altars whence the divine light once spread its beams to the great nation you govern.'[51] It was difficult for Alexander to reject such a plea, based as it was on the deepest of religious sentiments. But the Tsar was in an impossible position. Ypsilanti's action was ill-timed. So long as Alexander was at Laibach with Metternich and the Emperor Francis, he had to condemn revolution wherever it might break out. There was, as Metternich speedily saw, a case for arguing that if Austria sent troops to restore order in Italy then Russia should intervene in Turkey. But Metternich drafted an early note denying that there was any parallel in the situation and arguing that the Balkan insurrections had been planned so as to weaken Austro-Russian collaboration and destroy the Concert of Europe.[52] The Tsar accordingly instructed Capodistrias to let Ypsilanti know that he could never approve of his actions, that national liberty for the Greek peoples could not be won by armed rebellion and that it was his duty, as an officer in the Russian service, to repent and lay down his arms.[53] At the same time Alexander gave Metternich a pledge that Russia would not resort to independent action in the Balkans. Ypsilanti's raid was doomed to disavowal from the start. Without official patronage it had no chance of success,* and once Alexander had become alarmed by

---

* Ypsilanti's invasion failed to win peasant support and aroused the resentment of the Roumanians. A Turkish force defeated him to the west of Bucharest in the first week in June and he fled to Transylvania, where he was imprisoned by the Austrians for the remaining seven years of his life.

the threat of mutiny and the bogey of secret societies, he was unlikely to respond to the call for an Orthodox Crusade against the Turks. The chief immediate effect of the Greek insurrection on the Tsar was to prompt his return to St Petersburg. With the emotions of his subjects stirred by what was happening in the Balkans, he could remain abroad no longer. At the end of the first week in June he reached Tsarskoe Selo.

Alexander's Dilemma over the Greek Insurrection

He arrived back in his capital worried and depressed. As he travelled east-wards so the news which reached him grew worse and worse. For what had begun as a piratical raid by irregular forces on the northern frontier of the Ottoman Empire fast became a major insurrection setting all south-eastern Europe aflame. Sultan Mahmud II called on the faithful to resist the Greek Christians and, at the end of April, ordered the public execution of the Patriarch Gregorius outside his palace in Constantinople. There were ferocious massacres of Greeks by Turks in Asia Minor and no less terrible deeds committed by the Greek patriots in the Peloponnese and on the islands. The Russian ambassador in Constantinople was insulted and the Turkish authorities interfered with vessels exporting grain from Odessa through the Straits to the Mediterranean; a number of Russian sailors were killed. All these provocative acts, and especially the hanging of the Patriarch on Easter Day, aroused indignation in Moscow and St Petersburg. There had long been friction between Russian and Turkish authorities in the Caucasus, with frequent disputes over the ill-defined frontier; and almost every political, religious or commercial interest in the capital could make out a case for war against Turkey.[54] As soon as he returned from Laibach Alexander protested to the Turkish authorities at the callous treatment of Christians and at interference with the Odessa grain trade. He also wrote to the Emperor Francis and to Castlereagh seeking their support in condemn-ing 'the deplorable affairs in Turkey'; but he would not be stampeded into a declaration of war. 'Heaven is my witness', he declared. 'My only wish, my sole ambition, is to conserve that peace which cost the world so much to attain.'[55]

Yet throughout the summer of 1821 the temptation to declare war and resume Russia's thrust to the south was considerable. Capodistrias spared no effort to secure Alexander's active support for his compatriots; he let him learn of every movement of Turkish troops along the frontier; he saw to it that no insult to the Russian flag went unrecorded; he informed him of every tale of atrocity against Christian communities, trusting that his conscience would induce him to intervene. Foreign diplomats were puzzled at the Tsar's apparent passivity, especially as he was heard to admit that there was 'a very strong public feeling in favour of war' in the capital.[56] The French *chargé d'affaires* saw to it that Paris had a full account of Baroness von Krüdener's activities: once again she was favoured by people of influence, to whom she predicted the imminent fall of the Turkish Empire. 'Alexander', she declared, 'will be in Constantinople during the year 1823 but it will be later, in Jerusalem itself, by the tomb of the Saviour that the Glory of God will be made manifest to him.' He had, it appears, a second mission to fulfil: having liberated Paris from the ungodly, he must now liberate the Holy Places from Islam and proclaim the unity of Christendom in the city where there could be 'only one sheepfold and one pastor'.[57]

This vision went much farther than any design of Capodistrias for his compatriots or the traditional Russian dream of restoring the Cross of Orthodoxy to the dome of Saint Sophia. If these were the revelations with which the Baroness was exciting his capital, it is hardly surprising that Alexander told Golitsyn he wished to have a secret meeting with Julie. It was accordingly arranged that on 19 September he would receive tea and prophecy from her in a peasant's house off the road to Tsarskoe Selo, on the outskirts of Petersburg. Although both Golitsyn and the Baroness's secretary were present in the house there is no clear record of what was said. Alexander was once again showing that inscrutable blandness he had perfected in his youth: he listened attentively and said nothing of significance. When he left he told Julie, 'I am setting out for Warsaw but in six weeks I will see you once more.' To Golitsyn he remarked enigmatically that he had found the Baroness 'as she had been in Paris'.[58] They never met again, for by the time Alexander returned from Poland his mood had changed and she was no longer in favour. In the following spring the Tsar recommended her to leave the capital. After writing a last appeal (some two thousand words long) in which she urged him to lead a crusade to free the Christians of the East, she withdrew to exile in Latvia.[59]

There is no doubt the Tsar's religious conscience was racked with uncertainty over the Greek Question. In August 1821 Alexander told Capodistrias he could not go to war against Turkey because this was the very action which 'the Paris directing committee' of revolutionaries most desired in order to disrupt the growing understanding between the Great Powers.[60] These were the sentiments which Metternich, the Emperor Francis and even Castlereagh were feeding to him in letters and despatches. In private, the Austrian Chancellor went so far as to declare, with characteristic lack of modesty, that there were two parties in Russia, the Metternichers and the Capodistrians and that Alexander was a Metternicher.[61] But all these judgements over-simplified the Tsar's dilemma. Basically there was a conflict in his mind between the old traditions of Orthodoxy and his conviction that Europe needed peace in order to purge its soul of the subversive doctrines of revolution. It may even be that the pietism he had shown in his talks with the Quakers made him question the natural assumption of the Orthodox hierarchy that a campaign on behalf of the Greeks would possess the merits of a Holy War. There was no easy solution for an autocratic ruler pulled in opposing directions by the dictates of a Christian Providence which offered him a choice he could not understand. Brooding in melancholy day after day, he searched the Scriptures for revelation as he had done in the sombre hours of the struggle against the invader, but this time no apocalyptic vision leapt to the eye.[62]

His silence alarmed the other European Powers. Throughout the closing months of 1821 and on into the New Year he allowed Capodistrias to draft all important despatches to Vienna. Hence there were moments when Metternich felt uneasy, suspecting that once the snows began to melt the Tsar would be unable and unwilling to resist the call of the war party in the capital for a march into the Balkans.[63] But in the third week of February 1822 he finally decided in favour of a peaceful solution of the Greek Question. He wished the British and Austrian governments to sign a secret understanding with Russia, requiring the Sultan to observe existing treaty obligations and providing for the protection of the Greeks under Allied guarantee. Although Capodistrias remained in Russian service until midsummer, his influence was gone. Alexander relied primarily on Nesselrode (who had no interest in Greek affairs) and in Tatischev, whom he sent to Vienna in the spring of 1822 in order to collaborate as closely as possible with Metternich over the Eastern Question.[64] Tatischev could not get the Tsar the pledges which he sought from Austria, and had he done so the British would have remained obdurate; but at least he was able to secure some assurance of diplomatic support. If Turkey rejected Russian demands for fulfilment of her treaty obligations, Metternich undertook to break off diplomatic relations with the Sultan provided that Britain, France and Prussia would follow suit. This was an empty concession, for the Allies would never have acted in concert with Russia and Austria over such a question (as Metternich well knew); but Alexander was impressed. He agreed to ministerial conferences in Vienna in the summer and made ready to set out on his travels again, for in the autumn there would be another Congress, this time in northern Italy.[65]

Vienna and Verona (1822)

Alexander planned to leave St Petersburg, on what was to be the last of his long journeys abroad, during the first week of August. On this occasion, however, his departure stirred Elizabeth to bitterness. Although there had been no close love between husband and wife for several years, she did not wish him to set out for Austria and Italy with no idea of when he would return. When he had been on his travels in the early years of the Congress System she had explained to her mother that his absence, though sad for her, was necessary for Russia: she had contented herself with reading Russian history and novels (including a French translation of Lady Caroline Lamb's *Glenarvon*, which had shocked her sensitivities). But now she could see no good reason for his journey. She was afraid of trouble within Russia once he left the Empire. Moreover she confessed to her mother that she would be wretchedly lonely: Marie Feodorovna was only interested in 'the young Court, her children' (as she called them), who were allowed 'to follow a way of life she would have been the first to condemn fifteen years ago'. Elizabeth would have liked, she said, to take a holiday at Odessa or in the Crimea, 'but the Tsar would never let me go there in present circumstances as that area is full of Greeks', and she added, parenthetically, 'My poor Greeks! that is a reason for making me wish to go there even more!' Although her letter shows confusion between her own sorrow and her concern for Russia as a whole, there is no doubt that she sensed Alexander's constant travelling weakened government within the Empire and lost him credit with many of his subjects.[66] She was not alone in her observations.

But nothing would deter him. By now he had another interest in general policy. In the spring he had let his brother sovereigns know that he wished the Alliance to do something about Spain, and he insisted that the Spanish Question, dormant for two years, should be placed high on the agenda of the conference in Vienna and the subsequent Congress at Verona.[67] Russia had no direct interest in the affairs of the Iberian Peninsula, and Castlereagh was probably correct in assuming that Alexander had raised the Spanish Question so as to cover a diplomatic retreat over Greece and re-affirm the validity of the Holy Alliance by intervention in a region where there was less conflict in policy between the Eastern autocrats. Metternich personally was uneasy at this development and unresponsive to Alexander's offer to send an expeditionary force at once to the foothills of the Pyrenees. But he, too, welcomed the prospect of a Congress where it would be 'a matter of courtesy not to mention difficulties in Turkey'.[68] All the Austrian Chancellor sought was the collaboration of Castlereagh, ready as he was to restrain the Russians from too adventurous a policy.

In this, however, Metternich was disappointed. Castlereagh committed suicide on 12 August and British interests at the Congress were in the hands of Wellington, a man for whom Alexander had the deepest personal admiration. The conference and the Congress made a mockery of round-table diplomacy. As a social occasion Verona was superior to Laibach and Troppau and far grander than Aix-la-Chapelle. Alexander enjoyed a banquet in the Roman amphitheatre and Rossini operas conducted by the composer himself. It was amusing to flirt with the new Lady Londonderry (poor Castlereagh's sister-in-law) and to ride in the mornings in the Italian countryside, with November sunshine delaying the coming of winter. But little was achieved. 'When the civilized world is in danger', Alexander declared, 'there can be no English, Prussian or Austrian policy, there can only be a general policy that ought for the salvation of all to be accepted by peoples and Kings alike.'[69] The sentiment was splendid; but nobody took it to heart. Wellington refused to approve any plans for restoring order in Spain, a subject on which he was an authority, and made it plain that Britain would never consent to any method of 'salvation' which involved interference with the internal affairs of other lands. The true victors of Verona were the French, who (though the British dissented) were authorized to take military action against the Spanish liberals if the situation in Madrid deteriorated to a point where intervention was felt in Paris to be necessary for the well-being of Europe.[70] It was hardly worth travelling from St Petersburg to Verona to sign a blank cheque for Louis XVIII. A deputation of Greek patriots, eager to put their case before the statesmen of Europe, was intercepted by the Austrian police and turned back at Ancona: the Tsar was not to be distracted by such matters.

Diplomats who had known Alexander at Paris, and even at Aix, found him much older and low in spirits. Chateaubriand thought his face was now lined with melancholy, and at one moment he told the Emperor Francis he had 'a presentiment of early death', a fate which did not especially disturb him as he was 'becoming tired of life'.[71] At Verona, too, he gave an audience to his old Quaker friend, William Allen (who had made the journey under Wellington's patronage, since no one was admitted to the city who was not a member of an official delegation). Allen found Alexander as distressed as had Chateaubriand. 'He opened his heart to me', Allen wrote, 'told me of his trials and temptations, comparing them to the thorn in the flesh which the Apostle describes.' And he added, significantly, 'He felt himself so weak he dared not look far ahead.'[72]

Unfortunately he seems to have 'opened his heart' to nobody else and William Allen himself was too reticent to indicate the form of the 'trials and temptations' with which Alexander believed himself afflicted at this time. His weariness may have had physical origins, for he had not relaxed for a length of days in five years; possibly, though there is no evidence for it, he was troubled again by the venereal disease from which he is said to have been suffering during the Vienna Congress; certainly he was gripped by deep melancholia. Now and again a bright remark from Lady Londonderry or an ornate and flattering reception (such as he received at Venice after the Congress was over) would dispel the mist of gloom in his mind, enabling him to radiate some of the gaiety and charm which had made his reputation in happier times. But these occasions were rare indeed. Rather surprisingly, Metternich insisted on accompanying Alexander back through the Austrian lands, acting as host in Venice and in Innsbruck as though anxious to see him safely across the frontier into Bavaria.[73] The Tsar's movements were not predictable, even by those closest to him. At times it seems as if he did not himself know what he wished to do. Although in mid-November he had written to his sister Anna from Verona and told her he could not prolong his stay abroad, 'as I urgently need to be back in St Petersburg by January at least', he showed no sign of hurrying home.[74] He lingered in both Bavaria and Württemberg, drove slowly to Warsaw (where he stayed for another three weeks), and did not reach St Petersburg until the second week of February. Even then he chose to escape as soon as possible to Tsarskoe Selo rather than participate in the revels and frivolity of the pre-Lenten carnival.[75] There is no doubt that, as it came round once more to the anniversary of his accession, his health was nearer to breaking point than at any moment in his twenty-two years on the throne.

❦21❦

'An Island Battered by the Waves'

Procrastination

Fortunately for Alexander the pace of public affairs slackened in the spring and summer of 1823. He was able to rest and recover some of his lost strength. For six months he remained either in the capital or its immediate vicinity, studying reports from Nesselrode and Pozzo di Borgo on the intractable Eastern Question and going over the problems of the military colonies once again with the indefatigable Arakcheev. Outwardly Alexander was extremely busy. But, as so often in the early years of his reign, he was reluctant to make up his mind over any matter: 'One scarcely ever repents of having waited', he would say. Procrastination was second nature to him, unless he could sense clear purpose in what he was doing.

By the beginning of September he was sufficiently well to set out once more on his restless tours through the Empire. He travelled down to Moscow and then turned south-westwards across the Central Russian Uplands and through the Ukraine to the Austrian frontier on the upper Pruth. He then crossed some ten miles into Austria for a meeting with the Emperor Francis and his Chancellor at Czernowitz (Chernovtsy). But by now the strain of congress diplomacy was proving too much even for Metternich, who fell sick on his way to the conference, and Alexander was left to discuss the great questions of the hour with Francis and the Chancellor's understudies. Not surprisingly, the meeting resolved nothing.[1] But Alexander took the opportunity to reaffirm his faith in round-table diplomacy and suggested that the next congress might meet in St Petersburg and concern itself solely with the affairs of Turkey and Greece. The idea was hardly likely to speed Metternich's convalescence; for he had no wish to see Alexander or one of his ministers dominating a congress. There was accordingly a whole year in which Metternich was as eager to avoid decisive action in foreign affairs as the Tsar himself. But the Czernowitz meeting was at least a reminder to Europe that, though at Verona Alexander had been little more than a sad spectator of events, over international issues he possessed remarkable powers of resilience. His name and reputation continued to count for something in foreign capitals.

The domestic scene in Russia remained, none the less, drab and disillusioning. Nothing more was heard of Novosiltsov's project for a constitution, nor of Alexander's resolve to end serfdom. Almost imperceptibly the hand of authority tightened its grip on freedom of expression: obscurantist inspectors searched for atheism and heresy in the teaching curricula of the universities; Masonic lodges and other secret societies were placed formally under a ban of the law; and the censorship was active, although casual and arbitrary in methods and totally ineffectual. Young Pushkin, for example, was banished to his mother's estate in northern Russia for expressing religious scepticism (though it is significant that the authorities only took action after he had started an affair with the wife of an important government official).[2] Others of Pushkin's generation were forbidden to go to German universities, lest the purity of their thoughts be contaminated by false ideals; and a professor of Euclidean geometry was reprimanded for not having emphasized to his students the parallel symbolism between the mathematical concept of a triangle and the doctrine of the Holy and Blessed Trinity.[3] Alexander himself had nothing to do with such capricious methods of repression, but he was blamed for what was done in his name, and even more for what was left undone. Despite the hounding of the secret societies, groups of young officers – many of them members of aristocratic families – began to form revolutionary cells: there was talk of kidnapping the Tsar at Bobruisk, on his way back from Czernowitz; vague plans were even drawn up for assassinating Alexander and his brothers as a first step towards the proclamation of a Russian Republic.[4] Whatever might be thought of him in Vienna, Paris and London, at home 'Alexander the Blessed' – the God-gifted sovereign who had saved Russia and whose nobility of purpose once guaranteed hope for the future – was by now a mythical figure from a past in which it was becoming increasingly difficult to believe. He was a holy ikon refusing to work its miracle.

Sadly Alexander recognized this failure to live up to his reputation.

Once again he began to speak of the possibility of abdication, leaving the problems of government at home and abroad to Nicholas. Although Constantine was still officially termed 'Tsarevich', it was clear he would never come to the throne. Privately the two eldest brothers had decided on this before Alexander's visit to Nicholas at Krasnoe Selo in 1819. A year later Constantine weakened his standing in the eyes of the Orthodox by securing an annulment of his marriage to the Grand Duchess Anna Feodorovna (from whom he had been separated for over twenty years) and then morganatically taking as his second wife a Polish Countess, Joanna Grudzinska, who was a Roman Catholic. Technically there was no reason why Constantine should have forfeited his right of succession, but he was genuinely reluctant to rule the Empire and in January 1822 he wrote a brief letter to Alexander in which he formally renounced 'that eminence to which, by birth, I may have the right'.[5] This should, of course, have settled the matter: but there was an ambiguity in Constantine's wording which worried Prince Golitsyn, who began to press Alexander for a clear statement of the rules for the Succession. Like so many other rulers, the Tsar was reluctant to be precise in such matters. But eventually, in the summer of 1823, he responded to Golitsyn's tactful pressure and drew up a decree which recorded the voluntary renunciation by Constantine and at the same time declared Nicholas to be the rightful heir. The decree was, however, prepared in the utmost secrecy, neither of the brothers knowing of its existence until after Alexander's death. The original document was handed over by Alexander to the Metropolitan of Moscow for safekeeping alongside Paul's coronation decree on the Succession in the Uspensky Cathedral within the Kremlin.[6] Presumably Alexander insisted on this high level of secrecy in order to prevent the growth of a reversionary interest around Nicholas's miniature Court, a development which might have weakened his own position as well as that of Constantine. But in this instance the Tsar's fondness for devious ways intensified the confusion in which his reign was to end.

It must be admitted that throughout the years 1823 and 1824 the behaviour of all three of his brothers troubled him. Constantine, who spent most of his days at the Belvedere outside Warsaw, was personally happier than at any previous time in his adult life: he was also more popular inside Russia than ever before, largely because he was acquiring, among the Russian liberals, an undeserved reputation as someone who knew how to deal justly with a political assembly. In Warsaw, on the other hand, his partiality for certain families alienated many of the great names in Poland, while his hot temper and liking for parade-ground discipline reminded the

older generation of his father's unstable temperament. It is significant that
Alexander made a point of travelling to Warsaw whenever possible for
the opening and closing of the Diet: he had no confidence in his brother's
tact or his sense of discretion.

By now, too, Alexander was less pleased than in earlier years with
Nicholas. He faithfully reflected the views of the military establishment in
the capital and made little effort to hide his hopes of seeing active service in
a campaign against the Turks.[7] But it was the youngest of his brothers,
Michael – twenty-one years Alexander's junior – who remained the perpetual problem for all the family. As Constantine remarked in a private
letter, 'The two things he cares about are giving [military] service and
sleeping.'[8] He showed no desire whatever to take a wife, but in the closing
months of 1823 he was betrothed to a Württemberg princess, who took
the name Elena on being received into the Orthodox Church, and it was
arranged that their marriage should take place early in the following year.
There was, however, never any prospect of the marriage being a success.
Again to quote Constantine, 'the married state is an accessory which he
[Michael] might well have been able to do without'. Elena was much too
intelligent for him.* Both Alexander and Elizabeth admired her wit and
strength of character; but these qualities did not make her popular with her
mother-in-law, nor indeed with the soldier-courtiers around Nicholas and
Michael. The Romanovs were not a closely knit and happy family, and
Elena fitted uneasily into the group.

Alexander's Illness; His Reconciliation with Elizabeth; and the Ascendancy of Photius

The arrival of Elena at the Russian Court was in part responsible for a happy
change in Alexander's private life. Although her own existence at St
Petersburg was, all too often, wretchedly depressing, she was fond both of
her eldest brother-in-law and his Empress. Since she was a kind-hearted
girl, with courage and initiative, she went out of her way to see that
Alexander and Elizabeth, though nearly thirty years her senior in age,
re-kindled the mutual warmth and affection they had once known and
which was so sadly lacking in her own marriage. It would be incorrect to

* The Grand Duchess Elena Pavlovna became a revered figure in Russian social history.
After Michael's death (in 1848) she helped organize the first service of nursing sisters in
Russia, caring for the wounded in the Crimean War much as Florence Nightingale was doing
on the British side. She was also a forthright champion of the Russian peasant and his rights.
She encouraged her nephew, Alexander II, to emancipate the serfs in 1861, having already
set an example of generous treatment on her own estates.

regard Elena as a second match-maker, for there were already other sentiments drawing the Imperial couple closer to each other, but (as Elizabeth herself admitted) it was the seventeen-year-old Grand Duchess who prevented new misunderstandings from cooling their relationship, enabling them to enjoy an Indian summer of happiness for the last two years of their married life.[9]

There had, of course, never been a complete breach between Alexander and the child-bride his grandmother had chosen for him back in 1793. Elizabeth accepted his infidelity over the years just as he had resigned himself to the attachment she felt, on more than one occasion, for Adam Czartoryski. Yet their marriage remained essentially a convenience of State: he looked on her as a companion to whom he turned for support when his domestic sensitivity was strained, just as he would look to Golitsyn for guidance in the troubles of a spiritual life. Each was in the habit of taking the other for granted: they exchanged confidences as friends; they even regretted the increasing number of occasions upon which State affairs separated Alexander from his home; but the intimacy of a husband and wife relationship continued to be strange for them. Then suddenly, at the start of the year 1824, Alexander's emotions were stirred by the patient care which Elizabeth was lavishing on him, and they recovered some of the lost raptures of love.[10]

The reconciliation, if such it may be called, began when Alexander at last succumbed to the physical collapse which had threatened him for so long. At the Epiphany he again attended the blessing of the Neva: for hours at a time he stood bareheaded on the Jordan Steps above the frozen river, while a hole was bored through the ice and, with great solemnity, the Metropolitan sprinkled consecrated water over all who were present, and over the standards of the regiments in the capital as well. The Tsar returned to the Palace shivering with the cold. That night there was, as usual, a round of festivity in the Winter Palace from which Alexander could not escape. He remained unwell throughout the following week although he insisted on going to Tsarskoe Selo, travelling along roads on which a recent blizzard had piled the snow high, making the journey abnormally difficult. On Saturday, 24 January, he found himself so feverish he could hardly stand, and he ordered his carriage to take him back at once to the Winter Palace. He looked so ill that Elizabeth was alarmed, though she was reassured to hear from Wylie* that he believed it was a recurrence of the erysipelas in

* Sir James Wylie had been principal court physician in St Petersburg since 1798. He accompanied the Tsar to England in 1814 and, at Alexander's request, was knighted by the Prince Regent on board a warship at Portsmouth during the State Visit to the fleet. He was

the leg from which the Tsar had already suffered on two occasions. But this time his health seemed completely broken, and he lay for several days in a torpor, barely conscious of what was going on around him.[11]

For nearly a fortnight he was slow to respond to treatment, momentary improvements giving way to relapses. Elizabeth was worried both by the feebleness of his responses and by the resignation with which he accepted the illness: 'Never have I seen the Emperor as patient in an illness as this time', she wrote to her mother on 27 January, 'and this both puzzles me and torments me.'[12] Yet by the end of the month she was finding some comfort in nursing him. On 31 January she sent a deeply touching note to the Margravine:

The day before yesterday he said something to me so dear to my heart that I wish to share it with you alone, Mamma. He said, 'You will see that I shall owe my recovery to you', for he thought he owed the first good night's sleep he had enjoyed to a bolster I had given him for his head, from which he has been suffering severe pains these first days . . . When he tried my bolster, it suited him splendidly. Moreover I was responsible for finding the one stool which is convenient for his footing and allows him to be helped to sit in an armchair. You can imagine, dearest Mamma, how sweet all this is to me, but you can also imagine how I keep all this sense of delight secretly in my heart.[13]

For six weeks Alexander remained confined to his room in the Winter Palace; and, indeed, it was there that Michael and Elena were married, in an antechamber converted into a chapel for the Tsar's private devotions. Throughout Alexander's battle against the infection in his leg Elizabeth was at his bedside, hours at a time. Sometimes she read to him, but often they were content simply to talk, re-discovering lost delights in timeless conversation, words and thoughts wandering on unhurried by imminence of public duty. With so few leisure hours spent together in recent years, the novelty of allowing their minds to meet again, pensively or playfully as the mood of the moment suggested, was in itself pleasantly recuperative. Elizabeth's letters to the Margravine acquired a fresh serenity, although perhaps she was reluctant to admit he was recovering his strength, as winter gave way to spring. 'Long and noisy visits from the Grand Dukes Nicholas and Michael brought on his fever again and left him in need of rest', she complained as late as 1 March, and she added, 'I begged the Empress [Marie

---

virtually the founder of the Russian Imperial Academy of Medicine, of which he was for many years the President. At Marie Feodorovna's insistence he travelled with the Tsar on all his journeys, whether within Russia or abroad, and was held in awe as a figure whose diagnoses one did not challenge. But can erysipelas have been quite such a common complaint?

Feodorovna] not to trouble him with matters that were not really urgent.'[14] The truth was that she resented any draught of public business from the outer world, fearing it might dissipate the atmosphere of rapture which had glowed so warmly in the sick-room these past five weeks.

It was only to the Margravine that Elizabeth confided this curious idyllic romance of wife and husband:

Never had I seen him so ill, and never have I seen him, being ill, so patient and good. You must realize, Mamma, that this circumstance intensified the pain it caused me to see him suffering and aroused in me involuntary fears, especially when he said to me, 'I don't know whether it is the effect of illness or the effect of age but I feel less able now than ever before to fight against suffering'. . . One day in particular he appeared so weak and so exhausted that I could not look at him without a feeling of deep tenderness . . . You can imagine, dearest Mamma, what a time of trial and tribulation this has been for me. Yet it has been made to seem shorter by the real affection the Emperor has shown for me, as well as having me near him; he willingly accepted the little things I did for him, letting me watch beside his bedside when he slept and feed him his light meals . . . I could not say this to anyone but you. To some people it would all seem so natural and simple as not worth recording and to others it would seem like boasting, and of what? Of something ordained by all law, human and divine, the most simple thing in the world in other families; and yet, as I once wrote to you, the passions and rivalries in the family around the Emperor make me some-times look upon myself as his mistress or as if we were secretly married.[15]

The unconscious irony in the letter, the dutiful daughter at last happy to imagine herself mistress to her own husband, cannot have been lost on Elizabeth's mother. But it seemed hardly likely that such a reconciliation could survive the buffeting of public affairs when the Tsar wished his subjects to see him once more as true Autocrat of All the Russias. Even Elizabeth had few illusions on this score.

Her doubts were resolved by a strange and tragic episode, its origins rooted deep in their mutual experience. Although Alexander was well enough to travel to Tsarskoe Selo for a few days in April, it was not until the last week in June that he felt able to resume his full military duties. On 29 June he went to Krasnoe Selo for the annual manoeuvres. Elizabeth, who detested regimental occasions, remained in the capital; but the Grand Duchess Elena was at Krasnoe, as Michael's brigade was engaged in the exercises.[16]

No sooner had Alexander lifted himself into the saddle on the first morning of the manoeuvres than he became aware that his aides-de-camp were trying to keep something from him. Wylie, who though a brilliant physician was not always attuned to his patients' psychological problems, bluntly informed him that they had just learnt from St Petersburg that his only surviving daughter by Maria Naryshkin, Sophia, had died at the age of eighteen from consumption. The Tsar had known she was terribly weak before he left the capital, but the shock of the sad news unnerved him. Momentarily it seemed to the officers around him as if he had once more been taken ill for, as Elizabeth wrote afterwards, 'he could not hide his anguish'. But years of steeling himself to disasters and frustrations enabled him to recover. For the rest of the morning he sat impassive and virtually silent on his horse.

That night, however, he collapsed. He was convinced yet again that his daughter's death was a punishment for his sins. Elena, who knew nothing of the background to the affair, was shocked by his wretchedness, his certainty that his soul was cast already on the dust-heap. Yet through his despair there was one person to whom he looked constantly as an angel of salvation: and she was not with him, but at Tsarskoe Selo. Poor Elena, at seventeen, was lost in a world she could hardly begin to understand. She at once wrote to Elizabeth, guarded words sent off by a courier travelling through the night, not daring to tell the unfortunate Empress what had prompted her alarm; and she received a polite but slightly angry reply. Next night she wrote again, begging Elizabeth to comfort and protect Alexander in his misery.[17] For Elizabeth it was, of course, a familiar role; but the knowledge that Alexander had spoken so affectionately of her to Elena made her willingly accept the task. She saw that the child's death and the torment of conscience it provoked proved to Alexander he was still dependent on his wife, if he were to retain his sanity. Now she knew that, no matter how much duties of State might keep them apart, the understanding kindled during his illness would continue to link him to her spiritually in the months ahead.[18]

There was another reason why Alexander began to turn more and more towards Elizabeth: that spring he was deprived of a valuable confidant. For twelve years he had looked for religious guidance, in the first instance, to Prince Golitsyn. But Golitsyn's wide responsibilities inevitably made him many enemies: ecclesiastics, such as the Metropolitan Seraphim, suspicious of his powers of patronage and distrusting his sympathy for the Bible Societies and other protestant sects; cultural xenophobes, like the educational publicist Magnitsky, who believed Golitsyn was too tolerant of Western ideas in the universities; and, above all, Arakcheev, intensely jealous of the only man more closely in his master's confidence than himself.[19] In May 1824 the combination of these three, very different, enemies succeeded in ousting Golitsyn from his privileged position at Court.

Not, however, on their own. Two years earlier, shortly before the Tsar's departure for Verona, Golitsyn had been introduced to a young monk, Photius, whose extraordinary powers of mental divination and protracted fasting were rapidly making him the spiritual darling of the Petersburg salons. This is not surprising; he was someone to whom interesting visions and exciting temptations were granted, experiences he showed little reticence in describing.[20] When invited by Satan to walk across the waters of the Neva to the Winter Palace, he summoned the necessary willpower to cast the Evil One aside and took the bridge instead. However not every worldly proposal was so easily resisted, especially when demons assailed him in the form of young women, and soon Photius began to enjoy the type of fame which was to spur Gregory Rasputin into the histories of a later reign. Photius, like Rasputin, possessed dramatic talent and gifts of hypnosis; he also acquired a wealthy patron, the Countess Anna Orlova-Chemenskaya; and, in the summer of 1822 it looked as if he would soon have an Imperial protector as well, for Golitsyn was so impressed by the monk that he arranged for Alexander to receive him in a private audience.[21]

Alexander was more accustomed to holy women than to visits from men of God. It was puzzling to receive a priest who knelt in long adoration before the ikon on the wall before acknowledging that he was in the Imperial presence. The Tsar kept Photius with him for three hours, asked for his blessing and received it, and subsequently gave him a cross of diamonds. But was he convinced? He took no notice of Photius's efforts at proving to him that the Bible Societies were responsible for all the unrest in the young generation; but he nevertheless induced Golitsyn to have Photius elected Archimandrite of the monastery at Yurev, a post of some significance in the Church hierarchy. He had not, however, heard the last of Photius. Yurev was close to Arakcheev's estate at Gruzino; and for the next eighteen months Arakcheev willingly acted as the mouthpiece of the Archimandrite at Court, occasionally seeing that messages of inspired revelation reached the Tsar personally. 'Know, great Tsar, that the Lord has always shown me everything, and always will', ran one. 'There will be no misfortune if you heed the Lord, who speaks to you through me.'[22] Just as the Stourdzas had encouraged Baroness von Krüdener, so now Arakcheev put Photius forward as the true voice of Russia's religious conscience. It is a sad commentary on Alexander's failing perception that he did not scent a conspiracy in so strange a partnership.

The Tsar's illness brought to a climax the latent conflict between the Procurator and his enemies. Ecclesiastics throughout the Empire prayed for Alexander's recovery; so, in her Latvian place of exile, did Julie von Krüdener. The Baroness went further than prayer: she wrote to Golitsyn in February asking that Alexander should receive her in the Palace; and she received a reply, indicating that the Tsar would welcome a secret meeting. But the hostility shown towards Golitsyn and the sects made Alexander change his mind dramatically. Within ten days Golitsyn had to inform the Baroness's daughter, Juliette, that a meeting was impossible and that it seemed to the Tsar advisable for the Baroness and the whole of her spiritual family to leave northern Russia as soon as conditions made travel possible and settle in the Crimea.[23] At the same time Arakcheev sent a courier to Yurev urging the Archimandrite to set out at once for the capital.[24]

Through Arakcheev's offices, Photius was permitted the private audience with the Tsar for which Julie von Krüdener had asked in vain. It took place as soon as Alexander was sufficiently convalescent to attend to public business. This time the Archimandrite came directly to the point: the illness, he insisted, was a warning from God against the heresies permitted within Russia by the Procurator of the Synod; and it was therefore the will of God and His Church that Golitsyn should be dismissed from office. Alexander was impressed by Photius's vehemence but he was not inclined to take a decision for or against Golitsyn without long thought and prayer; and he sent Photius back to Countess Orlova's palace, where he was lodging in the city. There, however, Photius took affairs into his own hand. Golitsyn was invited to call on the Countess. When he arrived, he was received by the Archimandrite who demanded that he should confess his sins against the Church and make a fitting repentance. Naturally Golitsyn refused, and prepared to leave for his official residence in Senate Square. But, to the Prince's amazement, Photius then pronounced a solemn curse upon him, dramatically hastening to the doorway of the Orlova palace and publicly declaring him to be anathema. Nor was Photius alone in showing hostility to the Prince. Magnitsky stirred up the officials in the Ministry of Education and by the end of the day the Metropolitan Seraphim had personally confirmed the validity of the Archimandrite's act. Thus the Minister of Spiritual Affairs, senior lay official of the Russian Orthodox Church for the past two decades, was virtually excommunicated by a thirty-two-year-old monk who had climbed to social eminence on tall stories and fashionable shoulders; and there was nothing Alexander could do to save his friend.[25] In the last week of May

1824 Golitsyn formally resigned as minister responsible for religious matters and education: he was permitted to remain Minister of Posts.

Alexander was angry. He sent for Photius and did not spare his words. When the Archimandrite emerged from the audience it was noticed he was 'soaked in sweat from head to foot'.[26] Yet Photius possessed some strange persuasive power; for though the Tsar bitterly resented the way in which Golitsyn had been treated, he seems readily to have forgiven the Archimandrite and the Metropolitan and there is no evidence that he knew Arakcheev was involved in the conspiracy against Golitsyn. Twice in the following year Alexander invited Photius to the Winter Palace, treating him with respect and awe as a man favoured of God.[27] With Golitsyn's fall, and the disappearance of the Krüdener pietists to the Crimea, Alexander was left under the religious influence only of the established Orthodox hierarchy and the bigoted reactionary ideas of its favoured Archimandrite. Moreover his circle of personal friends was growing smaller; he was thankful for Elizabeth's loyalty.[28]

The Flood of 1824

Late in August Alexander set out on one more journey into the interior of his Empire. This time he travelled to the western fringe of Siberia, seeing for himself the settlements in Perm (later renamed Molotov), Ekaterinburg (now Sverdlovsk) and Orenburg (Chkalov). It was a tour of inspection he had long wished to make, but there was little chance that he would be able to cover so great a distance in less than eight or nine weeks and he did not expect to return until the end of October. Once again Elizabeth was sad at his departure, although on this occasion the Tsar's absence from the capital was less serious for the smooth running of government than in other years, if only because home and foreign affairs were, for once, totally becalmed. In January, on the eve of his illness, Alexander had proposed a solution of the Greek Question which envisaged the establishment of three autonomous principalities in Greece; he had also suggested holding an ambassadorial conference in St Petersburg to discuss a Near Eastern settlement in general.[29] But nothing had come of his initiative for three reasons: the British and the Austrians were determined to obstruct any move which might extend Russian influence in the Balkans; the Greeks, and their sympathizers inside and outside Russia, were disappointed in a proposed solution which fell short of independence; and the Tsar's own physical collapse meant that foreign affairs were left in the hands of Nesselrode, who strongly favoured a passive policy in Europe as a whole and the

Balkans in particular.[30] The intermittent discussions in St Petersburg on the Eastern Question during 1824 showed the Powers to be more concerned with manoeuvring for later diplomatic advantages than with securing any immediate solution; and by the autumn it was clear there was no chance of summoning Alexander's full Congress until the following spring, if then. The Tsar was able to spend eight weeks away from the capital without any pressing problems. The weather was unusually fine and he returned home on 5 November 'delighted with his expedition'.[31]

Almost immediately the weather broke, and for a fortnight the whole of Europe from the Channel to the Urals was soaked with ceaseless rain, lashed for days on end by south-westerly gales. There was serious flooding of the Rhine, the Danube and the Vistula, but it was on St Petersburg that the full force of the tempest fell, the winds sweeping up the Gulf of Finland with such intensity that on the night of 18–19 November they seemed to reach hurricane force.[32] By eleven o'clock in the morning the water in the Fontanka Canal was so high that it was lapping the surrounding streets while the river Neva itself was rapidly climbing the protective embankment in front of the Senate Square and the Winter Palace, where the Imperial family were in residence. The Grand Duchess Anna, paying her first visit home in seven years, described the scene in a letter to Holland:

A violent sea wind . . . caused the Gulf of Finland to overflow, and the Neva River was driven back contrary to its natural direction . . . In the space of one hour the square in front of the Winter Palace, the boulevard and the streets which lead to the Palace showed a terrible sight of a raging sea with waves and eddying water. The Winter Palace appeared to be an island battered by the waves.[33]

For much of that Friday Alexander himself remained on the balcony of the Palace, overlooking the Neva. He was appalled at the magnitude of the disaster, sending out a huge long-boat from the palace steps in the hope of rescuing people marooned on Vassilevsky Island. Elizabeth, who oddly enough had received on the previous day a letter from her mother describing the flood devastation in Germany, remained with her husband. At half-past two in the afternoon she wrote a note to the Margravine:

We are in the Winter Palace as though in a vessel at sea . . . Our generation has seen nothing like it . . . The bridge of boats has been smashed to pieces; barges of hay, overturned at the mouth of the river, are being swept past the Palace . . . The sight is terrifying because of the destruction which it represents; it is worse than a fire because one can do nothing to check it.[34]

By nightfall half the city was under water but the wind had begun to subside, and by Saturday morning the flood level, which in places was eighteen feet above normal, was receding. Alexander insisted on visiting the devastated areas, supervising relief work. It was estimated that between twelve and fifteen hundred people had perished in the capital itself, with five hundred workers drowned in the dockyard at Kronstadt (which had never before suffered from flooding) and two hundred more in Peterhof.[35]

The superstitious and the devout regarded the flood as divine retribution on a city which had given itself too much to gaiety. Even the officially 'atheistic' Pushkin, who was later to base his poem *The Bronze Horseman* on the terrible disaster, wrote at first from exile that 'it serves accursed Petersburg right'.[36] Less sophisticated souls were filled with repentance. As Alexander moved through the wretched mud-caked streets of the poorer quarters on the day after the waters receded, he heard a voice call out, 'It is a punishment from God the Almighty for our sins.' At once he answered, bitterly, 'No, it is a punishment for my sins.' The obsessive sense of guilt, which had troubled him over every personal tragedy in past years, now dominated his mind as he saw the way in which Nature had chastened the capital of his Empire. The last occasion on which there had been severe flooding in St Petersburg was in 1777, a few months before Alexander's birth; and he tended to see this fresh inundation of the angry waters as a portent, which he could not understand.[37]

The immediate effect of the flood was to make life in St Petersburg, never a healthy city, even more uncertain in the months ahead. 'Owing to the damp and unwholesome state of the lower parts of the houses and cellars, the mortality during the subsequent winter was nearly doubled, from typhus chiefly, as also from affections of the lungs', wrote one of the city's principal physicians subsequently, 'and many dated their rheumatic pains and various other maladies to the sufferings they then underwent.'[38] St Petersburg continued to show the marks of the flood long afterwards. Yet, in a strange way, the tragedy won back for Alexander some of his lost popularity in the capital. Too long he had been isolated from his people. Now he emerged from the Palace and they could see him, deeply affected by their tribulation. They remembered his benevolence in those closing weeks of 1824, just as they remembered his fortitude amid the uncertainties of 1812: it was as well to forget the years of hesitation, frustration and withdrawal that had come between these peaks of drama in the life of the capital.[39]

The Decision to go to Taganrog

It was not only the poorer townsfolk whose health suffered from the disaster. Less than a week later Elizabeth took to her bed with a fever which puzzled the doctors. She herself blamed it, at first, on the cold and damp of that terrible Friday, 'since we could not risk fires in the chimney that day because of the violence of the wind'.[40] But the illness was far more serious than she suspected. For a month she was confined to her bedroom, and it was not until the first week of February that she was allowed briefly out of the Winter Palace. Her four doctors do not appear to have agreed on the nature of her illness. She was never physically strong, and for several years had been longing to take a holiday again somewhere warm, where she could enjoy once more the delights of sea-bathing. But there is no doubt her collapse in the winter of 1824-5 was caused by a particular infection rather than by a general deterioration of her health. Almost certainly, she was suffering from rheumatic fever, which considerably weakened her heart. She never entirely recovered.[41]

Alexander remained with Elizabeth during the crisis weeks of her illness. He was himself in low spirits. The exertions of his journey to the interior and his efforts after the flood irritated his leg. Moreover, quite apart from his fears for his wife, there seemed that winter nothing but a succession of bad news. Early in the New Year he learnt that Julie von Krüdener had died suddenly on Christmas Day at Karasubazar (Belogorsk) in the Crimean mountains;[42] and within a few days Alexander was also mourning the death of General Uvarov, a friend and companion since the days when they were regimental officers together.[43] Nor was there any comfort for the Tsar in the political scene; police reports indicated unrest in some of the garrisons of western Russia; and messages from Constantinople predicted a strengthening of Turkish resistance to the Greek patriots with the arrival of reinforcements from Egypt in the Peloponnese, commanded by the redoubtable Ibrahim Pasha.[44] It was a bad beginning for the year.

The spring brought Alexander small solace. Elizabeth's health continued to worry Wylie, who was particularly concerned over the irregularity of her heart-beats, and she was again confined to her room for days at a time. But in the first week of April it was agreed, in conversation between Alexander and Elizabeth, that they would leave St Petersburg before the coming of the autumn rain and mists; they planned to go to Moscow, and then travel further south.[45] The details of the journey were not worked out for another four months: Alexander had first to go to Warsaw for the Diet and then to Gruzino to discuss, with Arakcheev, the future of the military colonies. Moreover, the summer months of 1825 witnessed the beginnings of a diplomatic revolution in Russian policy: Metternich's lack of support over Greece, and some ill-considered boasts he had made during a visit to Paris, aroused in Alexander grave doubts over the value of his partnership with Austria.[46] At the same time, a visit home by Dorothea Lieven (whose husband was still Russian ambassador in London) afforded Alexander a new insight into the policy of Canning, whom he had hitherto regarded as a neo-Jacobin.[47] By the beginning of August it seemed likely that the Russo-Austrian understanding would be replaced by an Anglo-Russian agreement over the Eastern Question.[48] With such a major re-adjustment of policy under consideration, it is small wonder that Alexander had little opportunity to settle his movements for the autumn and winter until August.

Elizabeth herself would have liked to go to Germany, but her physicians did not think a winter in Baden would benefit her. There was talk of Italy, but she did not want to spend several months in a totally foreign land. Moreover she hoped Alexander would accompany her, and the political situation made it impossible for him to contemplate a long absence from Russia. Finally Wylie suggested that she should winter 'at Taganrog, a port on the sea of Azov'.[49] Elizabeth was not at first enthusiastic at the proposal, but she was willing to accept any place recommended by Alexander and Wylie. They had visited Taganrog briefly in the spring of 1818, when the Court had wintered in Moscow: they thought the port had an agreeable climate, and they believed it would be possible to maintain links between the town and the greater centres of the Empire. Elizabeth accordingly agreed with them: for, after all, the choice of Taganrog was, in a sense, an extension of the vague project for going somewhere south of Moscow which she had discussed with Alexander in April. The Tsar himself warmed to the idea: he hoped he would spend some months with her in the Governor's residence and then journey eastwards to Astrakhan and the Volga delta, a region no Tsar had visited since the conquests of Ivan the Terrible in the middle of the sixteenth century. And from Taganrog it was not difficult to cross to the Crimea. All in all, a winter by the Sea of Azov began to seem an interesting prospect.[50]

At first some attempt was made to keep these plans secret. But it was necessary to send an architect, and a small labour force, southwards in order to ensure that the Governor's house was in a fit state for the Imperial couple. Moreover, doctors and aides-de-camp had to be chosen for Alexander and for Elizabeth, since it had been decided they would travel separately – Elizabeth's health would never stand the strain of a journey at Alexander's reckless pace. By the middle of August the diplomatic corps in the capital had picked up rumours of the proposed trip. Lebzeltern, the Austrian ambassador, was frankly puzzled: writing to Metternich on 17 August, he informed him that the decision 'to move the Court to Taganrog' had been taken for the sake of the Empress's health, but he did not hide his surprise that the Sea of Azov, of all places, had been chosen.[51] In April 1812, when Alexander left for his army in the field, it had been officially declared that he was going to inspect his provinces; was this sudden announcement of a visit to the southern shores a prelude to war against Turkey? For a month Lebzeltern's despatches to Vienna, which throughout the summer had concentrated on Greek affairs, showed a rare concern with the Empress's well-being.[52] The British, like the Austrians, also suspected that Alexander was planning eventually to go to war 'as the only means of compelling Turkey to enter into an arrangement respecting Greece', as the ambassador later reported to London.[53] It was all rather disturbing.

And yet, as the plans were completed, the fears of the diplomats seemed groundless. Gradually they came to accept that the reason given for the journey was genuine. Everyone could see that a new affection had developed between husband and wife. It was natural that they should seek a period of rest and recuperation together. Moreover Alexander was taking with him only two aides-de-camp and a small personal staff. The cautious Nesselrode was left in charge of foreign affairs; while the Grand Duke Nicholas was, for the first time, appointed head of the Council of Regency. Had Alexander been planning a dramatic move, then he would have gone into residence at Odessa or Sebastopol and he would certainly have been accompanied by a representative of the Foreign Ministry. A winter of isolation from the politics of the capital seemed, on reflection, a guarantee of calm and continuity. But why, people continued to ask, choose Taganrog? There was no satisfactory answer. Soon other questions were to weave a mystery around these closing months of 1825 until it became impossible to separate fact from fable.

22

Taganrog

To the Sea of Azov

There was nothing extraordinary about Alexander's last days in his capital. He attended, as usual, the protracted services in honour of his patron saint, Alexander Nevsky, on Sunday, 11 September, and that night was principal guest at a dinner given by his brother Michael to celebrate the completion of work on his new official residence. After this combined palace-warming and farewell party, Alexander crossed to the villa on Kammionyi Island and completed arrangements for his departure early on the Tuesday morning.[1]

He set out, unobtrusively, long before dawn on 13 September, riding in a calèche drawn by three horses and with the smallest of escorts. They drove at first across the city to the monastery of St Alexander Nevsky, one of the three holiest shrines in Orthodox Russia and the seat of the Metropolitan Seraphim. It was Alexander's practice to attend Mass at a cathedral in the capital before beginning any long journey, either in war or peace, and he was expected by the Metropolitan and Archimandrites who met him at the principal entrance to the cloisters wearing their full vestments. He stepped down from his carriage, knelt to kiss a crucifix held before him, was asperged with holy water, and walked in a candle-lit procession to the shrine of the warrior saint, while choristers chanted the *Trisagion*, seeking the mercy of God on His sinners.[2] It is said that Alexander participated in a *Pannykhida*, or Mass for the Departed; that after the Liturgy he handed the Metropolitan a sealed package; and that he was deeply moved by the private exhortations of a hermit.[3] There is no reason to doubt the authenticity of these tales; but they do not, in themselves, necessarily prove that Alexander had intimations of mortality or anticipated any diminution in his status as Tsar and Autocrat. It was natural for a man of his spiritual intensity to prostrate himself at the shrine of his patron in renewed dedication before the start of so exhausting an undertaking. The only unusual feature of the ceremonies was the early hour, and this was made necessary by his resolve to travel as speedily as possible to the staging-posts he had assigned for Elizabeth's journey in order to ensure that every arrangement had been made for her rest and comfort. One version of his visit to the monastery even records him as having tried politely to cut short the Metropolitan's farewell with the characteristic explanation, 'I am already half an hour behind my programme.'[4] This is not the comment of a ruler filled with premonitions of disaster.

Alexander and Elizabeth had given up the original plan of travelling by way of Moscow. The route he mapped out avoided all cities where there might be long and fatiguing ceremonies: it went due south from St Petersburg to Velizh, in Vitebsk Province, then turned south-eastwards by way of Dorogobuzh, Roslavl and Novgorod-Severskiy to Belgorod, a town on the road from Kursk to Kharkov; and finally it went on through the Don Cossack country to Bakhmut (now Artemovsk) and so down to the headwaters of the Sea of Azov. It was, all in all, a journey of rather more than twelve hundred miles. Given good weather, Alexander hoped to cover the distance in less than a fortnight.[5]

He did; and with time to spare. The calèche reached Taganrog on the evening of 25 September, having therefore taken thirteen days on the road from northern to southern sea. At almost every halting-stage, Alexander wrote a note to Elizabeth, giving her details of the route, with advice on where she should stop, although he left supervision of her journey to his old friend, Volkonsky, whom he had appointed principal aide-de-camp to the Empress. Elizabeth, too, made good progress in the fine weather. She had set out three days after her husband, and Volkonsky took care not to tire her. Even so, she reached Taganrog in the afternoon of 5 October and Alexander rode out to accompany her over the last stage of the long journey. They went first to give thanks to God for their safe reunion, Alexander insisting that they should go to the church of the Greek monastery rather than to the cathedral 'which seemed too cold to him'. He was full of kind attention to his wife, and she was delighted.[6]

'My apartments', she wrote to her mother, 'are pretty and homely, the Tsar having gone into every detail with great solicitude.'[7] It was not the most exciting of houses, merely a long and low building on the outskirts of the town. On one side there was a view of the sea and, on the other, a view of the six spires and two domes which relieved the monotony of the Taganrog skyline. There was a garden, well-protected from the wind, with natural sun-traps which delighted the Empress as she remembered how winter was creeping down on St Petersburg.[8] Accommodation was cramped, although there were plans for making use of more rooms once the Imperial couple had settled their routine of life. Elizabeth had a bedroom, a dressing-room and a small sitting-room, while Alexander managed with a combined study and bedroom and a dressing-room opening out of it. The principal reception room ran along the whole front of the house; it was used for dinners and the small gatherings of local worthies over which Alexander and Elizabeth presided in their first weeks of residence. 'There is a club here', Elizabeth wrote, 'where they have balls once a week, which I understand are not very showy but where we must go once at least.'[9] Taganrog was indeed a long way from St Petersburg. Yet it is clear from her letters to the Margravine that Elizabeth was happy. Never before in their married life had husband and wife enjoyed such quiet domesticity. Alexander told her on 20 October that he certainly had no intention of retu ning to St Petersburg before the New Year, and the later the better.[10]

But he soon became restless. After four weeks of Taganrog he began to take drives deeper and deeper into the surrounding countryside. In the last week of October he went on a four-day journey eastwards to Cherkask. His uite, too, were becoming bored with the gentle delights of Taganrog. General Diebitsch, his principal military aide, encouraged Alexander to make a journey to the Crimea before the roads became impassable. The Tsar, who had spent a few days in the peninsula in May 1818, was inclined to postpone the visit to the following spring, when he hoped Elizabeth might accompany him. He was interested in seeing Bakhchisarai, where Potemkin had once solemnly enthroned his grandmother in the Khan's former palace, and he wanted to inspect Sebastopol and the growing Black Sea Fleet; but he was in no hurry to undertake so extensive a journey. The prospect of a round tour of seven hundred miles by carriage, boat and horse did not excite him, and he was only persuaded to agree on crossing to the Crimea by Count Michael Vorontsov, the Governor of 'New Russia', who had come to visit him in Taganrog and who told the Imperial couple of the delights to be found along the southern coast of the peninsula.[11] 'The Tsar, who returned on Thursday from his trip to Cherkask, leaves tomorrow for the Crimea', Elizabeth wrote on Monday, 31 October. 'He would rather stay here but it is necessary and then he wishes to see for himself if it would be possible to go and spend the winter in the Crimea. Everyone has invited us there and insists that the climate is even better there than here . . . He will not be back for seventeen days.'[12] Diebitsch had, in fact, already had two proposed itineraries rejected on the grounds that three weeks away from the Empress was far too long.[13]

Alexander in the Crimea

The Tsar drove rapidly along the shore of the Sea of Azov through Mariupol and Berdyansk, reaching the Perekop Isthmus on 4 November. He remained in his carriage as far as Simferopol, where he arrived late the next evening. There followed an exciting, exhausting and ultimately fatal week. On Sunday, 6 November, he attended an early service in the cathedral and then set out to cross the main pass (which was still being constructed) linking Simferopol with the coast at Gurzuf. Although he covered twenty-five miles in the saddle that day, he reached Gurzuf at four in the afternoon. The weather was still mild, with some of the trees as green as in early autumn.[14] He was delighted by the grandeur of the mountain back-cloth to the largely Tartar village. 'Was there ever such magnificent scenery?' he exlaimed as he looked out on the hazy sunlight reflected off a calm sea. Count Michael Vorontsov, as provincial Governor, had been at pains to clean up Gurzuf for some days. He had also seen to it that his personal physician, Dr Robert Lee, administered the new cure of 'calomel and sulphate of quinine' to the principal Tartar of the village, 'who had been suffering severely from intermittent fever for several weeks'.[15] It might have been wiser for the Tsar to have gone elsewhere that night than a 'common Tartar cottage', newly whitewashed and with its walls hung 'with a coarse white linen cloth'.

But on the Monday morning Alexander awoke refreshed and in good spirits. He rode slowly along the sub-tropical littoral, dismounting to walk in the botanical gardens at Nikita, which had been founded a dozen years previously. So pleasant did he find this stretch of coast that he immediately arranged to purchase an estate at Oreanda, a few miles south-west of Yalta. Later that Monday he visited Princess Anna Golitsyn, who was living three miles from Oreanda at Kureis, with Julie von Krüdener's daughter and son-in-law and some of the Baroness's religious disciples (who, General Diebitsch roundly declared, were all 'suffering from the ague').[16] It was clear to the small community at Kureis that Alexander was pleased at the prospect of setting up a new palace on the Crimean coast: he told his hostess he hoped it would be possible to bring Elizabeth by sea from Taganrog to Yalta or Gurzuf so that they could spend the winter together in Oreanda.[17] That night he stayed on the Vorontsov estate at Alupka. He took little food at dinner, having stopped to eat fruit along the road: there was a worm adhering to the shell of one of the oysters served to the Tsar that evening, but Sir James Wylie assured him it was 'quite common and harmless'. Alexander was in a happy and contented mood: he began to tell his fellow guests of his plans for having 'a palace built as expeditiously as possible', and he made it clear he was looking forward to a future when he would retire from his responsibilities as sovereign, and find rest and contentment with Elizabeth on the Crimean coast.[18] It was a remote dream which he had first held more than a quarter of a century previously, although then the banks of the Rhine bounded his imagination. Now at last the possibility of escape to Oreanda made the dream close to fulfilment.

On Tuesday Alexander walked in the grounds at Alupka in the morning, mounted his horse about noon, and rode off westwards towards Balaklava, remaining in the saddle for thirty miles. The weather was less hot than on the previous days, low clouds covered the peaks of the mountains and there was some rain. He took the high road through beechwoods into the exceptionally beautiful Baidar valley, but he found the going difficult and reached Baidar tired and hot, only to find there was no opportunity for him to eat there. One of his suite wrote subsequently, 'He was rather irritable during the whole of the day and complained very much of the horse.' From Baidar he drove in his open carriage towards Sebastopol, but two miles from Balaklava he again mounted his horse and rode with General Diebitsch to inspect a battalion raised from Greek families in the Crimea. There at last he was able to take some food 'and eat a good deal of fish'. Before going to the fortress he rode, once more in the saddle, for six miles to the monastery at St George. 'He had neither great coat nor cloak, though the sun had set and the air was very cool;' and he remained for two hours there. Between eight and nine at night he drove into Sebastopol in his calèche, visited the church by torchlight, inspected troops lining the street; and when at last he was served with an evening meal, he felt unable to eat anything.[19]

Next morning, at what must have been a cracking pace, he inspected two forts, the ramparts, a military hospital, the dockyard, an arsenal, and an unspecified number of ships in the eleven-vessel Black Sea Fleet. He was then driven to Bakhchisarai, sleeping in his carriage most of the afternoon in utter exhaustion, He remained at Bakhchisarai for two nights, riding out on the Friday to the historic Karaite Jewish walled city of Chufut Kale, four miles away. The Karaites, with their emphasis on a narrowly scriptural source for religious observance and the moral law, interested Alexander; he talked to the Elders of the community and visited the principal synagogue. But he was ruler of peoples of many faiths, and from Chufut Kale he went on to a Greek Orthodox monastery, perched high on a cliff: there, 'whilst ascending the staircase he felt himself so weak he was obliged to rest'. That afternoon, back in Bakhchisarai, he entertained Moslem dignitaries and visited several mosques.[20] At some point during his stay at Bakhchisarai, Alexander sent for Wylie, nominally to tell him how worried he was about the health of the Empress Elizabeth (to whom he did, indeed, write an agitated letter on the Friday evening)[21]; but Alexander took the opportunity of letting Wylie know he felt unwell and had slept little for several nights. It is not clear why he thus confided in Sir James, because he promptly told him that he needed neither medicine nor advice: 'I know how to doctor myself', he said defiantly.[22]

There still remained another six days of the Crimean tour. Although Alexander was obviously tired and disinclined to eat, he continued to carry out all his engagements both in Eupatoria and Perekop. The roads were less difficult in this north-western corner of the peninsula, much of which consisted of steppe-land and occasional marshes, some of them evil-smelling. While riding in his carriage with Diebitsch on Wednesday, 16 November, Alexander was seized with violent shivering and his teeth began to chatter. That night he took some hot punch, but no food, and there was talk of resting at Mariupol. The accommodation, however, was poor; he was anxious to keep to the itinerary; and, since it was only another sixty miles to Taganrog, he insisted on completing the journey.[23] He left Mariupol at ten o'clock on the Thursday morning in a closed carriage, his feet covered by a bear skin and his whole frame wrapped in a massive winter greatcoat. Nine hours later Elizabeth caught sight of her husband under the glow of the lanterns at the gate of their residence: she had a presentiment of disaster.[24]

The Last Fourteen Days

At first no one in the household was especially alarmed. The Tsar's complexion was yellow, he had an almost insatiable thirst, and he was drowsy; but he spent little time in bed, was dressed by eight o'clock each morning and talked cheerfully to Elizabeth, Volkonsky and Wylie. When Elizabeth wrote to her mother on Sunday evening, she was optimistic: he had been suffering from intermittent bouts of fever, but she thought he had begun to recover; and she added a cheering postscript the following afternoon. No one as yet bothered to alert St Petersburg about the sovereign's indisposition.[25]

Alexander, rather strangely, said he knew he had a fever because he could not hear very well, a condition he had noticed during the first days of his erysipelas eighteen months before: 'I am as deaf as a post', he remarked to Wylie, in English.[26] To Prince Volkonsky Alexander explained that he thought he was suffering from 'a slight attack of ague . . . caught in the Crimea in spite of its fine climate, which is so highly extolled', and he added, 'I am now more than ever convinced it was best to have the Empress at Taganrog.'[27] Volkonsky, who preferred the southern shores of the Crimea to the Sea of Azov, told Alexander that he did not take enough care of himself: he was, the Prince said bluntly, too old to attempt things he might have done easily at the age of twenty.

There was truth in this observation. On several days Alexander had ridden too far for a man of forty-seven, and he made little allowance for the changes of temperature between noon and nightfall. It was foolish of him to overtax a constitution already weakened by a debilitating illness in the preceding year. On the other hand, there seems also to have been surprising carelessness by some of the Tsar's advisers. It is extraordinary, for example, that the provincial Governor, Count Michael Vorontsov, should have urged him to come to Alupka at this time of the year. For, only a few weeks previously, Vorontsov was staying in the Crimea and had seen for himself the chronic sickness of 'this terrestrial paradise'. His personal physician, Robert Lee, wrote, 'in the villages along the coast between Gurzuf and Simeis, I saw and treated more than a hundred cases of intermittent and remittent fever'.[28] Two members of Vorontsov's suite, Lee adds in his narrative, 'were seized with severe shivering, headache and the other characteristic symptoms of bilious remittent fever', one of them dying on his return to Odessa. Lee blamed the high incidence of sickness at this time in the Crimea to 'noxious exhalations from the earth'.

As Alexander's condition worsened so the symptoms corresponded more and more with this 'Crimean Fever': there were days of apparent recovery, followed by a drastic relapse; burning sensations in the head began on 20 November; and there were fainting fits, bouts of feverish perspiration, mental exhaustion and nausea.[29] It was not until the Tuesday evening (22 November) that Elizabeth became seriously alarmed by his condition: he seemed weak, and yet he was obstinately refusing to take the medicine prescribed by Wylie or to allow his doctors to bleed him with leeches. For the first time it was decided to inform Marie Feodorovna in the capital and Constantine in Warsaw of the Tsar's illness, but not in such a way as to cause undue concern.[30] Since it took couriers over a week to travel from Taganrog to St Petersburg, this decision could not well be delayed any longer.

Alexander had a good night's sleep and seemed much improved on Wednesday morning. Elizabeth went to see him shortly after eleven and found him in good spirits. They chatted inconsequentially until about two o'clock in the afternoon. He wanted to hear about some Kalmuck horsemen who had come to town, and he discussed where she would take her walk that afternoon. Elizabeth told him of the progress being made by an English gardener, Gray, whom he had brought from St Petersburg and was encouraging to lay out a park two miles from the centre of the town. The special cordial drink prepared for him seemed, he said, to leave an unpleasant after-taste: one of his valets had tried it and agreed with his master's opinion; and so did Elizabeth when she took a sip. Wylie, however, came in, tasted the drink, and found nothing wrong with it. About two in the afternoon Alexander told Elizabeth to leave him and take the main meal of the day. It had been, in fact, a perfectly normal morning for a wife attending her husband's sick bed.[31]

The point is important; for a number of writers have seen in the events of Wednesday, 23 November, a vital clue to the 'enigma' of Taganrog. To Maurice Paléologue, for example, 'it is the crucial day'; to Prince Bariatinsky 'the day of exceptional mystery'; and to Leonid Strakhovsky the date 'which decidedly marks the turning point in Alexander's last days as ruler of the Russian empire'.[32] According to these writers, the Tsar held an important conversation on this Wednesday in which he told Elizabeth of his immediate plans for the future, a mysterious disappearance from the public eye of which no written record was to exist. They claim she was so upset by this exchange of confidences ('six hours' according to Paléologue, 'the whole evening' according to Strakhovsky) that she then poured out her sorrow and frustration in a despondent but guarded note to her mother. They also point out, correctly, that there are no extant passages in Elizabeth's daily journal for any subsequent date during Alexander's illness. If she continued to keep a diary, the pages were subsequently lost or destroyed, presumably on instructions from Tsar Nicholas I.[33]

These hypotheses do not stand up to examination. The absence of journal entries is hardly surprising: Elizabeth was only an intermittent diarist and may well, in the following days, have been too emotionally moved by what was happening in the other room of the small house to commit her feelings to paper. Moreover for the last week of his life she was constantly at Alexander's bedside. The tale of the imparted confidence is not convincing, for there was no moment on that Wednesday when husband

and wife could have held a long discussion of this character. The events of the morning have already been described. After dining, as usual, in mid-afternoon Elizabeth appears to have rested and taken the projected walk until five o'clock when she sent for Wylie, who gave her an encouraging report on Alexander's condition; he told her that the Tsar was still very hot but he was awake, and she should go to his room and see him before he fell asleep.[34]

Elizabeth cannot, however, have talked to Alexander for long. Half an hour after her conversation with Wylie she began a letter to her mother which she headed, 'Taganrog, 11/23 November 1825, Wednesday at half past five'. It is this letter which, it is maintained, shows the Empress's despair.* She writes:

The Emperor is still not free from his fever. How sad it is that he is kept from benefiting from this finest weather in the world and that I also am deprived of the privilege of enjoying it, although I go out every day! Where can one find peace in this life? When you think you have arranged everything for the best and can enjoy it, there comes an unexpected trial which robs you of the ability to revel in the blessings around you . . .[35]

There is no evidence that Elizabeth returned to converse at length with Alexander later that evening; and clearly she cannot have had the alleged discussion before writing the letter. Nor, indeed, does it show her to have been disturbed by any sudden revelation: she is sorry for Alexander, and for herself, because a holiday in splendid weather during the first month of winter has been ruined by an unforeseen illness. As she subsequently admitted, she still did not appreciate the gravity of the mysterious fever, which seemed from time to time to leave him, only to return suddenly a few hours later.[36] Her letters for the first nine days after his return to Taganrog show less anguish than in the weeks when he was suffering from erysipelas.

But by the weekend she began to realize the full tragedy facing her. 'Oh, Mamma', she wrote on Sunday, 27 November, 'if God does not come to our aid, I foresee the greatest of misfortunes.' That morning a Greek priest came to administer the sacraments to Alexander, urging him

---

* As the importance of this letter from Elizabeth to her mother has sometimes been exaggerated, particularly in translation, it is perhaps advisable to quote the relevant passages in the original French:

'*L'Empereur n'est toujours pas quitté encore de sa fièvre. C'est triste! Cela l'empeche de profiter du plus beau temps du monde et m'ôte la faculté aussi d'en jouir, quoique je sorte tous les jours. Où est le repos dans cette vie! Lorsqu'on croit avoir tout arrangée pour le mieux et pouvoir le goûter, il survient une épreuve inattendue qui ôte la faculté de jouir du bien dont on est entouré . . .*'

as a Christian duty to take the medicine and cures prescribed by his doctors.[37] By now the Tsar, too, knew he was gravely ill and placed himself fully in the hands of his physicians. But it was too late. Hour by hour he became increasingly weak, the periods of unconsciousness growing longer until he was virtually in a coma. At ten minutes to eleven on the morning of Thursday, 1 December 1825, he died, with Elizabeth, his aides-de-camp and his physician around his bed.[38] He was just twenty-three days short of completing his forty-eighth year.

The Aftermath

There followed six weeks of misery and confusion for the little group at Taganrog and, in a different sense, for Russia as a whole. Elizabeth spent days of self-mortification, praying beside his bier and later beside the catafalque in the Greek church where his body rested: she hoped, she said in more than one letter, she would soon be re-united to him in another world; and so weak was her heart that those around her believed this to be likely.[39] In her wretchedness, the day-to-day responsibilities for the bereaved Court fell on Prince Volkonsky and General Diebitsch, although arrangements for the autopsy and embalming were left to Sir James Wylie. The body was examined by ten doctors, physicians from the local garrison as well as from the Imperial household, thirty-two hours after Alexander's death. The post-mortem showed that the liver was much enlarged, swollen with blood and dark in colour; the bile duct and colon were 'unusually large'; and there appeared to have been a rush of blood to the head.* It was formally recorded that 'our August Sovereign was suffering at first from a disease of the liver and other organs secreting the bile. This disease, little by little, degenerated into a high fever, with frequent fits of delirium, the secretion and accumulation of serum on the brain being the cause of His Imperial Majesty's decease.'[40]

It was not until 23 December that Alexander's body was moved from the room in which he died to the church where he had gone to pray beside Elizabeth on her arrival in Taganrog eleven weeks before. Even before the corpse was removed to the church putrefaction set in, for the morticians' skills in a small town in southern Russia were not suited to long embalming, and Elizabeth, alarmed at the speed of decomposition, had the face

---

* The printed version of the autopsy says the spleen was normal, but Robert Lee gathered from Wylie a week later that 'the spleen was enlarged, and softened in texture' (Lee, *The Last Days of the Emperor Alexander*, p. 48). This is an odd variation: Lee's version might well suggest malaria.

covered from 11 December onwards.[41] The head of the coffin was, however, left open during the solemn procession from the Governor's residence,
and for a time it was also exposed in the church, but its features were barely
recognizable and some who went to pay their respects to the body lying in
state found it a macabre experience.[42] The funeral procession did not set
out for St Petersburg until 10 January 1826, nearly six weeks after the Tsar's
death, and the coffin was not finally lowered into a tomb in St Petersburg
until 25 March.

The delay in leaving Taganrog was, in part, a consequence of the
extraordinary confusion over the Succession. Volkonsky could not order
the removal of the body until he had received instructions from the new
Tsar. But who was the new Tsar? Alexander may have made it clear to his
mother, his brothers, Golitsyn and the Metropolitans that he regarded
Nicholas rather than Constantine as his successor; but nobody at Taganrog
was in the secret, not even Elizabeth.[43] As soon as Alexander died, couriers
were sent directly to St Petersburg and to Warsaw. The news reached the
Russian capital about midday on 9 December;[44] and Nicholas, despite the
disapproval of Golitsyn, at once insisted on renouncing any rights bestowed
on him in secret by Alexander. He had the palace guards take an oath of
allegiance to Tsar Constantine, formally swore the oath himself, and gave
instructions for all government departments and military units to pledge
their allegiance to Constantine without delay. But the courier to Warsaw
had arrived two days earlier, on 7 December: Constantine, keeping to the
arrangement with Alexander, duly swore an oath of allegiance to Nicholas
and sent the Grand Duke Michael, who was with him in Poland, back to
St Petersburg to assure their brother of his loyalty. At the same time he
proclaimed Nicholas Tsar and King of Poland in a document which he
ordered to be read publicly in Warsaw.[45]

At Taganrog Elizabeth received a letter of sympathy from Constantine,
written to her 'as a brother and not a sovereign', while an official decree
from St Petersburg gave orders to the public authorities and troops in the
town to swear allegiance to the new Emperor and Autocrat of All the
Russias, Constantine I. There was accordingly a solemn ceremony of
oath-taking on the morning of 22 December.[46] But no message came from
the new Tsar about arrangements for his brother's burial: a letter from
Marie Feodorovna to Volkonsky at last left him with sole responsibility
for the translation of 'the mortal remains of the best of sons'.[47]

Meanwhile, some twelve hundred miles away, the confusion in the
capital grew worse with every day. Nicholas and the Senate awaited the
arrival of Constantine from Warsaw and they were surprised when

Michael came instead of his elder brother. Marie Feodorovna, learning of Constantine's proclamation of his brother in Warsaw, urged Nicholas at once to accept the throne everyone was thrusting on him. This was sensible advice: no autocracy could function under such conditions. But Nicholas still hesitated, sending messages back to Warsaw in the hope Constantine would change his mind. It was impossible to keep this glorious Imperial muddle secret and there was a certain amusement among foreign visitors to the capital. The absurd situation was aptly summarized by a correspondent for the London *Times*, who reported, 'The Empire is in the strange position of having two self-denying Emperors and no active ruler'.[48]

But this absence of leadership had serious repercussions. Earlier in the year Alexander had been informed of plots among the garrisons of the Ukraine; and agents were sent to discover more about the conspiracy. Alarming reports reached the Tsar, either while he was in the Crimea or soon after his return to Taganrog: it was clear there would be a risk of mutiny or revolt in the spring, but Alexander's illness prevented him from taking decisive action. Similar information also reached Arakcheev, but he too remained inactive, largely because of his grief at the murder of his mistress by young serfs she had ill-treated at Gruzino.[49] On 16 December, however, General Diebitsch came across the reports of the agents while he was sorting through papers which had accumulated during Alexander's illness. He saw to it that measures were taken against the dissident officers in the Ukraine and, at the same time, sent an express courier to St Petersburg to alert the Grand Duke Nicholas, who had already received police reports of unrest among the officers of two regiments in the capital. It was this fear of revolt which finally reconciled Nicholas to his own proclamation.[50]

Hence on the morning of 26 December, after two and a half weeks of tergiversation, Nicholas consented to have the troops of the Petersburg garrison paraded in order to swear allegiance to him. A battalion of the Moscow Regiment and some companies of the Izmailovsky refused to take the oath. They assembled defiantly on the Senate Square, calling for 'Constantine and a Constitution';* they were joined by marine Guards

---

* Popular legend maintains that the troops cheered for 'Constantine and *Konstitutsia*' in the belief that this was the name of the Grand Duke's Polish wife. The story first appears in a letter from the wife of the acting British ambassador dated 2 January 1826 (recently re-printed in Anthony Cross, *Russia under Western Eyes*, p. 379) but she was not herself present on the Senate Square at the time. Tsar Nicholas's own account of events has the troops declaring merely, 'We're for Constantine.' There is no doubt some of them believed Nicholas and the Generals in St Petersburg were attempting to seize power in order to keep out the allegedly liberal Constantine, a man strangely idealized during his absence in Poland. In a private letter Pushkin, for example, though not a Decembrist, welcomed 'the accession

and a regiment of Guards Grenadiers, and supported by labourers building the new cathedral of St Isaac. When General Miloradovich urged the troops to lay down their arms, he was shot and mortally wounded. An appeal by the Metropolitan Seraphim, rich in full canonicals, was accorded more respect but he was urged to retire to the cathedral and pray for their souls. At last, reluctantly, Nicholas ordered three cannons to be loaded with grape-shot: 'I sent Major General Sukhozanet', he wrote, 'to announce to them that, unless they put down their arms at once, I would give the order to fire. They replied with shouts of "Hurrah" and the same exclamations as before, and after that with a volley. At that point, seeing no other alternative, I ordered: "Fire" !'[51] The insurgents scattered in disorder, pools of blood in the snow around Falconet's statue to the founder of the city. It was a terrible prologue to Nicholas's reign.

Or was it, rather, an epilogue to the reign of Alexander, a consequence of the frustration and disappointments of his later years? For the leaders of this 'Decembrist Rising' were, for the most part, members of the aristocratic intelligentsia, distinguished and brave veterans of the campaigns, the very groups who had come together in the secret societies rather than accept as final the system of Arakcheev. Politically the conspiracy was a mistake, confused in immediate objectives and premature in execution. It was all too easy for the authorities to restore order in the capital and round up dissidents in Kiev and Odessa. Only a far larger conspiracy, involving every great city and the principal regiments throughout the army, could have succeeded in changing the structure of Russian government towards the liberal constitution system which the Decembrists desired. Their failure led to the consolidation of reactionary rule in Russia for another thirty years. Yet it must be admitted that if such a rising had taken place while Alexander was still on the throne, it would almost certainly have had similar consequences. No son of Paul was likely to give way to the dictation of mutineers.

Legends

The Decembrist unrest, and the confusion over the Succession, made it important that Alexander's burial should follow protocol and tradition so far as was possible. Already, among a people accustomed to look for

---

of Constantine I' because 'there is much romanticism in him; his stormy youth, his campaigns together with Suvorov . . . all call to mind Henry v'. (Thomas Shaw, *Letters of Alexander Pushkin*, p. 265.)

mystery in the sudden death of sovereigns, there were disturbing rumours. Why had there been so much uncertainty in St Petersburg? Was Alexander, isolated in a remote town on the fringe of Asia, the first victim of a conspiracy? Had he been poisoned, or done to death like Peter III? As the long funeral procession wound its way slowly northwards through the snow to Kharkov, Kursk, Orel and Tula silent crowds watched the great funeral coach go by, sad and apprehensive. On 15 February the procession reached Moscow; eight greys, draped in black with the Imperial insignia on their covering, hauled the cumbersome carriage along the route Alexander had followed for his Coronation. For two days the coffin rested within the Kremlin, at the Cathedral of the Assumption where the earliest Romanovs are buried. The people of the city wished the body to be exposed so that they could honour the sovereign who had refused to make peace with Napoleon in the epic days of 1812. The authorities would not open the coffin, and there was nearly a riot. It was, by now, two and a half months since the unskilled morticians of Taganrog had sought to embalm the corpse; and there was good sense in the decision not to permit the corpse to be exposed. But the episode intensified the general air of mystification: another thread of doubt was added to the loom of legend.[52]

As the procession neared Tsarskoe Selo, Marie Feodorovna came to meet the escorting troops and the coffin was received in the palace chapel with fitting ceremony. She insisted on seeing for herself the body of her son: 'Yes, that is my dear Alexander', she was heard to say. 'Oh, how he has wasted away' (*Ah, comme il a maigri!*).[53] As a form of identification, it did not entirely carry conviction. There followed then another puzzling episode: the coffin was left for a week in the military hospital at Chesme, while arrangements were completed for the final interment. Only after this last delay were the funeral rites observed in what the Duke of Wellington (who was present as representative of George IV) described as 'a terrible ceremony'.[54] The coffin was placed beside the tomb of Paul on the north side of the small cathedral in the fortress of St Peter and St Paul. To encourage belief that this was indeed the body of Alexander, the wedding ring which he had worn for thirty-two years was fixed to the ikon facing the sarcophagus.

His widow never saw the tomb. Originally Elizabeth had intended to accompany the funeral procession northwards. The shock of Alexander's death weakened her own condition and it was clear by the beginning of January she could not journey across the Russian steppes in the depth of winter. She therefore paid her last homage to Alexander on the day the cortège set out from Taganrog. With a doctor in attendance and Roxane

Stourdza (Countess Edling) assisting her ladies-in-waiting, she remained in Taganrog until the snows melted and the warmth of spring came to southern Russia. Then, at last, she prepared to go back to the heart of the Empire, planning to settle near Kaluga, and perhaps later go to Germany if she recovered her strength.[55] She had no wish to return to St Petersburg.

At nine in the morning of 4 May she prayed alone in the Greek church which held so many memories for her, and set out slowly towards Kharkov, travelling no more than fifty miles a day. On the evening of 15 May she reached the small town of Belev, eighty miles north of Orel. She went to bed, anticipating a visit next day from Marie Feodorovna, the first meeting with a member of the Imperial family since Alexander's death. Possibly the anticipated strain of the encounter was too much for her. At five o'clock in the morning of 16 May Elizabeth's heart stopped beating: and her soul was free to follow 'the angel' she had lost twenty-four weeks before.[56]

Elizabeth's death did not surprise those who knew her personally. To others, however, this sudden disappearance of Alexander's consort intensified the mystery of his own fate. Gradually doubts over what had happened at Taganrog changed their form. People became less interested in whether Alexander had, or had not, been poisoned. The stern repressive policies of Nicholas I created a nostalgia for the magnificent era of 1812-14, when Russia was ruled by a sovereign for whom the world was bright with promise. Now, as official policy caused monuments to proliferate to the dead Tsar, so among simple people of all classes one of the most primitive instincts of folk fable began to assert itself: Alexander, it was said, had not died but was living out a life of prayer in some distant monastery. Neither for the first time nor the last, the credulous and superstitious refused to accept the fact of mortality in the Russian Imperial dynasty.

There were, of course, good reasons why Alexander of all Russia's rulers should have his last days embellished in this way. He had, for much of his reign, seemed to many of his subjects a romantic hero; his own psychology constantly favoured the devious rather than the direct; and there was, anyhow, sufficient confusion over events at Taganrog and along the whole funeral trail to raise unanswerable questions in the mind. But some of the hypotheses put forward by the champions of Alexander's survival stretch credulity to the utmost extent. It has been maintained, for example, that a substitute corpse was brought into the sick room at Taganrog while the real Alexander was smuggled out and put aboard an English yacht, which then conveyed him through the Bosphorus and Dardanelles to the Holy Land.[57] The gravest objection to this particular sleight of hand is that it would have necessitated from the Empress Elizabeth a degree of religious dissimulation totally against her character and her conscience. She could not have acted out the role while showing the spiritual feeling and sincerity of grief revealed in her letters. Nor is there any reason why a husband who was so interested in purchasing an estate at Oreanda where he could find rest with a wife for whom he felt the deepest concern should, a fortnight later, have lent himself to a conjuring trick of this nature. No life of repentance could be based upon deceit, least of all upon an act which required the Church to fulfil sacred rites knowing them to rest upon a falsehood.

The belief that Alexander had, in some way, survived was however strengthened by tales of a Siberian *starets*, or holy man, who began to excite attention in the early 1840s. This *starets* – tall, with a stoop, middle-aged, and possessing an impressive presence – was not a dabbler in miracles, like Photius or the later Rasputin; he was an austere practitioner of a life of prayer and meditation, and he was known as Fyodor Kusmich. Nobody was certain of his true age or his background; but he was someone with connections at Court, he enjoyed recalling the reign of Catherine II, and it was believed by those who met him that he occasionally received visits from eminent figures in the Empire. By the late 1850s, when Kusmich settled in a village near Tomsk, there were many people convinced he was in reality Tsar Alexander, expiating his sins by prayer, as a voluntary exile in the wastes of Siberia.[58]

There is no doubt Kusmich was a remarkable personality, possibly an unfortunate offspring of the Imperial family. But he cannot have been Alexander. Fyodor Kusmich did not die until February 1864; and it is impossible to believe a man of Alexander's constitution could have lived until the age of eighty-six. Moreover the records of Fyodor Kusmich's table talk about public affairs show him to have had a totally different attitude from the Tsar to the great campaign of 1812–14: in particular, Kusmich delighted in praising Kutuzov; and he made the odd slip of describing once how the Tsar of Russia had ridden in triumph into Paris in 1814, with Metternich at his side.[59] His identity, like that of other holy men in Russia, remains unknown: he died, as he had lived, a man of mystery in a house of sanctity. It is later writers who made him famous.

Yet while it seems certain that the legends of Alexander's survival are false and that he died at Taganrog on 1 December 1825, as the records maintain, there is still one peculiar circumstance for which there is no ready explanation. On at least two occasions, and possibly more, the tomb in the fortress of St Peter and St Paul has been opened and found empty.[60] Either no corpse was ever buried in it or the body that was laid in the sarcophagus was subsequently removed; and there is indeed a story which claims that a body was taken from the tomb in 1866, under the orders of Alexander II, and secretly buried in the principal cemetery of the city, the graveyard of the Nevsky Monastery.[61] If the Alexander tomb is, as seems likely, a cenotaph then this macabre tale would appear to support the champions of Kusmich.

There may, however, be a less sensational explanation of the empty tomb, though one based purely on conjecture. Alexander I disliked the traditional burial place of the Tsars, associated as it was in his mind with the interment of his father. He had, on the other hand, a strong personal attachment to the memory of the only previous ruler in Russia to bear his name, St Alexander Nevsky, a warrior prince as he had once thought himself to be. What therefore would be more natural than that he should wish to be buried in the confines of the Alexander Nevsky Monastery, where he had prayed as he set out on so many journeys, including the final expedition to Taganrog? Did he, one wonders, leave with the Metropolitan Seraphim a written request that, should he die, his remains were to be buried at the monastery rather than at the fortress? A secret testament of this kind was in character, a similar commitment to his secret decree on the Succession.

Yet such an arrangement would have been highly inconvenient for Nicholas and politically inexpedient. The only sovereign ever buried in the cathedral of Alexander Nevsky was the murdered Peter III (whose body Paul insisted on translating to the fortress cathedral at the time of his mother's State funeral). To bury Alexander in the Nevsky cloisters in 1826, after all the uncertainties of December, would incite startling rumours over what had happened at Taganrog. If Nicholas fulfilled any such wish of his brother, then he can only have done so by a secret burial preceding the long and involved funeral ceremonies and the lowering of an empty coffin in the cathedral of St Peter and St Paul. Alternatively it is possible – though highly speculative – that the remains allegedly moved from the fortress under the direction of Alexander II were in fact those of Alexander I, the young Tsar thereby at last fulfilling the secret wishes of his uncle and namesake. In either case, the true burial place of Alexander I would therefore be within the monastery at the end of the Nevsky Prospect rather than in the grim fortress across the river.

All this, of course, is a more appropriate subject for detective fiction than historical narrative. The most impressive memorial to Alexander I is not in any fortress or any monastic cloister but in the centre of modern Leningrad, outside the Winter Palace. In 1832 the Frenchman Monferrand, whom Alexander himself had encouraged to settle in Russia so as to re-build St

Isaac's Cathedral, was instructed to erect a column in the dead Tsar's honour that would dominate the massive Palace Square. The monument, completed two years later, is 158 feet high, slightly lower than Nelson's Column in London. It consists of a monolith resting on a granite plinth which is ornamented with bas-reliefs and inscribed, quite simply, 'To Alexander I, Grateful Russia'. In a sense the column complements Falconet's equestrian statue half a mile away in Senate Square, which Alexander as a child had watched his grandmother unveil. Yet one feature of Montferrand's tribute to Alexander distinguishes it from other commemorative columns; for, though honouring the Tsar whose armies marched across Europe, it is crowned at the summit not by the figure of a human conqueror, but by a winged angel looking out towards Peter the Great on his prancing horse. In the left hand the angel holds a cross while the right is raised in perpetual blessing of a city once dedicated to St Peter and now to Lenin. It is an appropriate symbol, a parable in stone commemorating the Tsar whose sense of Divine Mission elevated him, until he lost touch with the people his fortitude had saved.

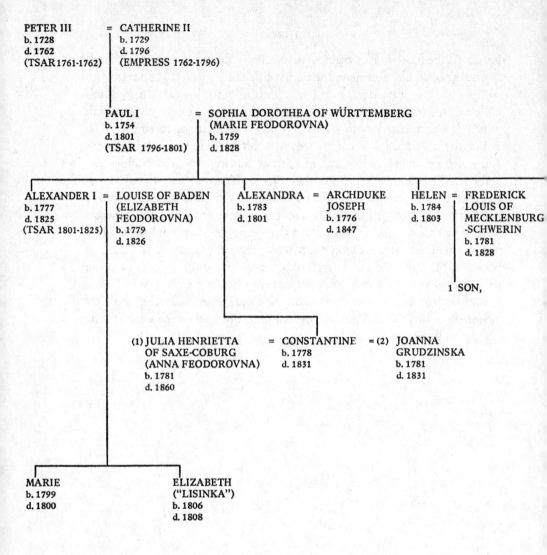

PETER III = CATHERINE II
b. 1728   b. 1729
d. 1762   d. 1796
(TSAR 1761-1762)   (EMPRESS 1762-1796)

PAUL I = SOPHIA DOROTHEA OF WÜRTTEMBERG
b. 1754   (MARIE FEODOROVNA)
d. 1801   b. 1759
(TSAR 1796-1801)   d. 1828

ALEXANDER I = LOUISE OF BADEN   ALEXANDRA = ARCHDUKE   HELEN = FREDERICK
b. 1777   (ELIZABETH   b. 1783   JOSEPH   b. 1784   LOUIS OF
d. 1825   FEODOROVNA)   d. 1801   b. 1776   d. 1803   MECKLENBURG
(TSAR 1801-1825)   b. 1779   d. 1847   -SCHWERIN
                     d. 1826   b. 1781
                                                                                         d. 1828

                                                                        1 SON,

(1) JULIA HENRIETTA = CONSTANTINE = (2) JOANNA
OF SAXE-COBURG   b. 1778   GRUDZINSKA
(ANNA FEODOROVNA)   d. 1831   b. 1781
b. 1781   d. 1831
d. 1860

MARIE   ELIZABETH
b. 1799   ("LISINKA")
d. 1800   b. 1806
                        d. 1808

SIMPLIFIED GENEALOGY OF
THE ROMANOV DYNASTY

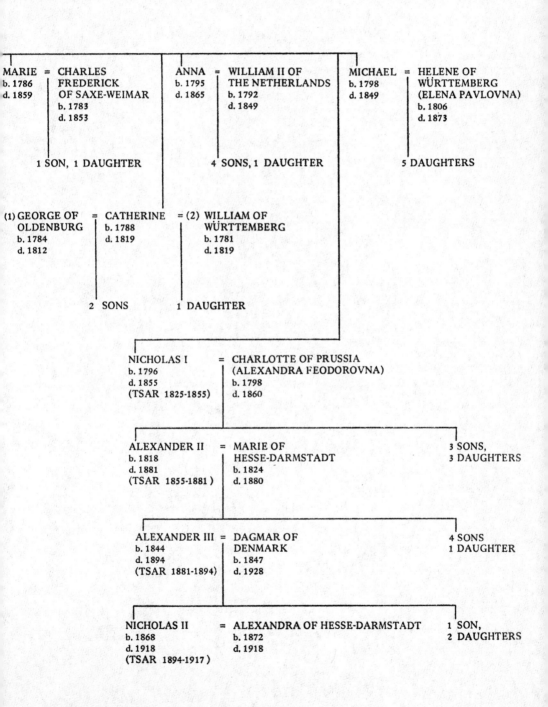

MARIE = CHARLES
b. 1786   FREDERICK
d. 1859   OF SAXE-WEIMAR
          b. 1783
          d. 1853

ANNA = WILLIAM II OF
b. 1795   THE NETHERLANDS
d. 1865   b. 1792
          d. 1849

MICHAEL = HELENE OF
b. 1798   WÜRTTEMBERG
d. 1849   (ELENA PAVLOVNA)
          b. 1806
          d. 1873

1 SON, 1 DAUGHTER

4 SONS, 1 DAUGHTER

5 DAUGHTERS

(1) GEORGE OF   = CATHERINE   = (2) WILLIAM OF
OLDENBURG   b. 1788   WÜRTTEMBERG
b. 1784   d. 1819   b. 1781
d. 1812   d. 1819

2 SONS

1 DAUGHTER

NICHOLAS I   = CHARLOTTE OF PRUSSIA
b. 1796   (ALEXANDRA FEODOROVNA)
d. 1855   b. 1798
(TSAR 1825-1855) d. 1860

ALEXANDER II   = MARIE OF   3 SONS,
b. 1818   HESSE-DARMSTADT   3 DAUGHTERS
d. 1881   b. 1824
(TSAR 1855-1881) d. 1880

ALEXANDER III = DAGMAR OF   4 SONS
b. 1844   DENMARK   1 DAUGHTER
d. 1894   b. 1847
(TSAR 1881-1894) d. 1928

NICHOLAS II   = ALEXANDRA OF HESSE-DARMSTADT   1 SON,
b. 1868   b. 1872   2 DAUGHTERS
d. 1918   d. 1918
(TSAR 1894-1917)

Reference Notes

Full details of the books and articles cited in this reference section will be found in the Select Bibliography. I have used the following abbreviations:

Adams, *Memoirs of J.Q. Adams, comprising parts of his Diary*, Vol. 2.

Corr. Alex., Nicholas Mikhailovich, *Correspondance de l'Empereur Alexandre I avec sa Soeur la Grande-Duchesse Catherine.*

F.O., Foreign Office papers in the Public Record Office, London.

HHSA, Documents in the *Haus-, Hof- und Staatsarchiv*, Vienna.

JMH, *Journal of Modern History.*

LPN, Nesselrode, *Lettres et Papiers du Chancelier Comte de Nesselrode.*

Nap. Corr., *Correspondance de Napoleon I.*

N.M., Alex. 1, Nicholas Mikhailovich, *L'Empereur Alexandre I.*

N.M., Elis, Nicholas Mikhailovich, *L'Impératrice Elisabeth.*

Seer, *Slavonic and East European Review.*

Shilder, Alek. I., N.K. Shilder, *Imperator Aleksandr I.*

Shilder, Pavel, N.K. Shilder, *Imperator Pavel I.*

Sirio, *Sbornik Imperatorskogo Russkogo Istoricheskogo Obshchestva.*

Vandal, A. Vandal, *Napoléon et Alexandre.*

VPR, Ministry of Foreign Affairs U.S.S.R., *Vneshniaia Politika Rossi XIX i nachala XX veka.*

Waliszewski, K. Waliszewski, *La Russie il y a Cent Ans, Le Règne d'Alexandre.*

Webster, *Castlereagh*, C.K. Webster, *The Foreign Policy of Castlereagh.*

Weil, M.H. Weil, *Les Dessous du Congrès de Vienne.*

Western MSS. bod., Western Manuscripts in the Bodleian Library, Oxford.

Alexander I

❧❦❧

Chapter 1: The Crow in Peacock Feathers

1. Castera, *Catherine II*, III, pp. 15–16; Shilder, *Pavel*, pp. 170–1 (quoting a letter from Catherine to Paul of 20 August 1782; Kochan, *Life in Russia under Catherine the Great*, p. 10 and p. 46.

2. Catherine II, *Memoirs*, p. 23; Castera, *op. cit.*, I, p. 74; Grey, *Catherine the Great*, pp. 98–110.

3. Masson, *Memoirs of Catherine II and the Court*, pp. 177–8.

4. Catherine II to Grimm, 25 December 1777, *SIRIO* XXIII, p. 71.

5. Harris, *Diaries and Correspondence*, I, p. 140.

6. Grey, *op. cit.*, p. 147.

7. *Ibid.* (cf. Klyuchevsky, *History of Russia*, V, p. 32).

8. Catherine II to Grimm, 13 February 1780, *SIRIO* XXIII, p. 174.

9. The same to the same, 11 October and 25 November 1782, *Ibid.*, pp. 250 and 252.

10. Shilder, *Alek I*, I, pp. 8–9.

11. Catherine II to Grimm, 4 June 1781, *SIRIO* XXIII, p. 205.

12. The same to the same, 12 June and 16 July 1782, *Ibid.*, pp. 236 and 246.

13. The same to the same, 12 April 1782, *Ibid.*, p. 233.

14. The same to the same, 19 May 1784, *Ibid.*, p. 307.

15. Shilder, *Alek I*, I, pp. 29–30 and 225–6; *SIRIO* XXVII, pp. 301–30.

16. Waliszewski, I, pp. 5–7; Shilder, *Alek. I*, pp. 46 and 229.

17. Shilder, *Pavel*, pp. 206–7 and Shilder, *Alek. I*, pp. 35–6 and 259–60.

18. Genet to Dumouriez, 8 June 1792, *Ibid.*, p. 269.

19. Alexander to Catherine II, 11 April 1785, *Ibid*, p. 261.

20. The same to the same, 19 January 1787, *Ibid.*, p. 262; Catherine II to Grimm, 12 December 1787, *SIRIO* XXIII, p. 431.

21. Shilder, *Pavel*, pp. 238–40 and 243; Jenkins, *Arakcheev*, pp. 39–40; Gielgud, *Memoirs of Czartoryski*, I, p. 108.
22. Shilder, *Pavel*, p. 203; Shilder, *Alek. I*, pp. 49–50.
23. Shilder, *Pavel*, pp. 209–11.
24. Catherine II to Grimm, 11 May 1791, *SIRIO* XXIII, p. 520.
25. The same to the same, 10 May 1791, *Ibid.*, pp. 517 and 519; Shilder, *Alek. I*, pp. 56–9.
26. Jenkins, *Arakcheev*, p. 40.
27. Catherine II to Grimm, 25 August, 10 November, 12 November 1792, *SIRIO* XXIII, pp. 573–4, 577 and 579.
28. N.M., *Elis.*, I, p. 20.
29. Shilder, *Alek. I.*, I, p. 233.
30. Catherine II to Grimm, 18 December 1792, *SIRIO* XXIII, pp. 579–80.
31. Shilder, *Alek. I*, p. 74.
32. Elizabeth to her mother, 7 May 1793, N.M., *Elis.*, I, p. 90.
33. Catherine II to Grimm, 25 May 1793, *SIRIO* XXIII, p. 583.
34. *Ibid.*, Shilder, *Alek. I*, I, p. 233.
35. Shilder, *Pavel*, pp. 257–9; Almedingen, *Emperor Alexander*, p. 31.
36. Shilder, *Alek. I*, I, p. 84; Protassov Journal quoted in N.M., *Elis.*, I, p. 25.
37. Catherine II to Grimm, 16 August 1793, *SIRIO* XXIII, p. 506.
38. Shilder, *Alek. I*, p. 86.
39. Shilder, *Pavel*, p. 259.
40. Elizabeth to her mother, 13 June 1794, N.M., *Elis.*, I, p. 156; Protassov Journal, *Ibid.*, pp. 30 and 31.
41. Almedingen, *op. cit.*, p. 34.
42. Letters of Elizabeth to Varvara Golovina in N.M., *Elis.*, I, pp. 406–26.
43. Shilder, *Alek. I*, I, pp. 108–9 and 238.
44. *Ibid.*, pp. 115–16; Gielgud, *op. cit.*, pp. 109–14; Schiemann, *Geschichtes Russland* I, p. 10; Kukiel, *Czartoryski and European Unity*, p. 5.
45. *Ibid.*, pp. 3–17.
46. Gielgud, *op. cit.*, p. 115.
47. Mazade, *Mémoires de Czartoryski*, I, p. 268.
48. Jenkins, *Arakcheev*, p. 50.
49. Shilder, *Pavel*, pp. 263–4.
50. *Ibid.*, pp. 269–70.
51. Alexander to Catherine II, 11 October 1796, *Ibid.*, pp. 270–1.
52. Jenkins, *Arakcheev*, p. 51.

Chapter 2: Empire on Parade

1. Shilder, *Pavel*, pp. 277–8.
2. *Ibid.*, p. 279.
3. Jenkins, *Arakcheev*, p. 54; Shilder, *Pavel*, p. 280.
4. Masson, *Memoirs of Catherine II and the Court*, pp. 145–8.
5. Shilder, *Pavel*, pp. 290–3 and 303; Shilder, *Alek. I*, pp. 355 and 359.
6. *Ibid.*, pp. 309–11.
7. Elizabeth to her mother, 10 February 1797, N.M., *Elis.*, I, pp. 239–40.
8. *Ibid.*, p. 246.
9. *Ibid.*, p. 245.
10. Shilder, *Pavel*, pp. 343, 565–72; Shilder, *Alek. I*, I, p. 363; N.M., *Elis.*, I, pp. 248–9; Mazade, *Mémoires de Czartoryski*, I, pp. 146–7.
11. An English translation of the decree is in Vernadsky, *Source Book for Russian History*, II, p. 473.
12. Seton-Watson, *Russian Empire*, pp. 74–5; Narkiewiecz article on 'Alexander I and the Senate Reform,' *SEER*, Vol. 49, pp. 117–19.
13. Shilder, *Alek. I*, I, p. 153; Elizabeth to her mother, 14 and 19 May 1797, N.M., *Elis.*, I, pp. 284–5.
14. Jenkins, *Arakcheev*, p. 64.
15. N.M., *Alex. I*, II, p. 111; Jenkins, *Arakcheev*, p. 62.
16. *Ibid.*, p. 67.
17. Alexander to La Harpe, 8 October 1797, full French text in Shilder, *Alek. I*, I, pp. 280–2 (Abridged English translation, Vernadsky, *op. cit.*, p. 477).
18. Shilder, *Pavel*, pp. 431–2.
19. Jenkins, *Arakcheev*, p. 66; Shilder, *Alek. I*, I, pp. 284–5.
20. Marie Feodorovna to Catherine Nelidov, 15, 16 August and 22 December 1797; Shilder, *Pavel*, pp. 573–5. See also the Dowager Empress's letters in *Corr. de Marie Feodorovna*, pp. 39–43.
21. Pares, *History of Russia*, pp. 291–2; Seton-Watson, *op. cit.*, pp. 65–6.
22. Andolenko, *Histoire de l'Armée Russe*, p. 68.
23. Kukiel, *Czartoryski and European Unity*, pp. 21–3; Grimsted, *Foreign Ministers of Alexander*, p. 109 (citing the correspondence of Czartoryski and his sister); Paléologue, *Enigmatic Czar*, p. 28.
24. Shilder, *Pavel*, pp. 461–2.
25. Temperley, *Unpublished Diary of Princess Lieven*, p. 247.
26. Shilder, *Pavel*, pp. 467 and 471–2.
27. The letters are printed in Shilder, *Pavel*, p. 416. For a recent assessment of Paul's changing attitudes to France see the article by Hugh Ragsdale

on 'The Origins of Bonaparte's Russian Policy' in *Slavic Review*, Vol. 27, pp. 85–90.

28. Strong, 'Russia's Plans for an Invasion of India,' *Canadian Slavonic Papers*, Vol. 7, pp. 114–26.

29. Shilder, *Pavel*, p. 463.

30. Almedingen, *Emperor Alexander*, p. 55; *Corr. de Marie Feodorovna*, p. 75,

31. There are extensive plans of the Mikhailovsky in Shilder's *Pavel*. pp. 417–81, *passim*.

32. Elizabeth to her mother, 7 March 1801, N.M., *Elis.*, I, p. 390.

33. Strakhovsky, *Alexander I*, p. 19.

34. Shilder, *Pavel*, p. 473; Loewenson article on 'Death of Paul,' *SEER*, Vol. 29, p. 224.

35. Jenkins, *Arakcheev*, pp. 79–80.

36. Strakhovsky, *op. cit.*, p. 22.

37. Shilder, *Pavel*, p. 489.

38. Loewenson article, *loc. cit.*, pp. 212–13; Almedingen, *op. cit.*, pp. 60–2; Strakhovsky, *op. cit.*, pp. 22–4.

39. Loewenson article, *loc. cit.*, pp. 225–7.

40. N.M., *Elis.*, I, p. 267; Temperley, *op. cit.*, p. 246.

41. *Ibid.*, p. 258.

42. *Ibid.*, p. 261.

43. Elizabeth to her mother, 25 March 1801, N.M., *Elis.*, I, p. 268.

Chapter 3: The Cracking of the Ice

1. Shilder, *Alek. I*, II, pp. 312–23.

2. *Ibid.*, pp. 309–11; cf. Grimsted, *Foreign Ministers*, pp. 52–3.

3. Shilder, *Alek. I*, II, p. 6.

4. *Ibid.*, p. 32.

5. *Ibid.*, pp. 32–6; Waliszewski, I, pp. 36–7.

6. See the article by Olga Narkiewicz, 'Alexander I and the Senate Reform,' *SEER*, Vol. 49, p. 120.

7. N.M., *Alek. I*, I, pp. 19–24; Shilder, *Alek. I*, I, p. 172.

8. Raeff, *Michael Speransky*, pp. 41–2.

9. Narkiewicz article, *loc. cit.*, p. 120; N.M., *Stroganov*, II, pp. 30–2; N.M., *Alek. I*, II, appendix 8, no. 101.

10. Narkiewicz article, *loc. cit.*, p. 122; Raeff, *op. cit.*, p. 43; N.M., *Stroganov* II, pp. 185–96.

11. N.M., *Stroganov*, I, p. 66.

12. *Ibid.*, II, pp. 55–6.

13. *Ibid.*, II, pp. 30–93.
14. Raeff, *op. cit.*, pp. 66–8; Shilder, *Alek. I*, II, p. 22.
15. Vernadsky, *Source Book for Russian History*, II, pp. 482–6; Narkiewicz article, *loc. cit.*, pp. 115–16.
16. N.M., *Stroganov*, II, pp. 103–4.
17. Almedingen, *Emperor Alexander*, p. 64, citing a note by Kochubey in Old Slavonic.
18. *Ibid.*, p. 66.
19. Edling, *Mémoires*, p. 38.
20. Panin to Vorontsov, 24 September 1801, quoted from the Vorontsov archives by Grimsted, *Foreign Ministers*, pp. 70–1.
21. N.M., *Elis.*, II, p. 11; Shilder, *Alek. I*, II, pp. 65 and 274.
22. Elizabeth to her mother, 18 September 1801, N.M., *Elis.*, II, p. 43.
23. See the statistical analysis of the population in Blackwell, *Beginnings of Russian Industrialization*, p. 430.
24. Shilder, *Alek. I*, II, pp. 66–7; Elizabeth to her mother, 21 September 1801, N.M., *Elis.*, II, p. 45.
25. Shilder, *Alek. I*, II, p. 69; Waliszewski, p. 57.
26. Elizabeth to her mother, 21 September 1801, N.M., *Elis.*, II, p. 45.
27. The same to the same, 26 September 1801, *Ibid.*, p. 46.
28. Mazade, *Mémoires de Czartoryski*, I, p. 291; but Marie Feodorovna gives a different point of view, *Corr. de Marie Feodorovna*, pp. 103–9.
29. Elizabeth to her mother, 28 September 1801, N.M., *Elis.*, II, p. 47.
30. Shilder, *Alek. I*, II, p. 68; Waliszewski, p. 58; Bogdanovich, *Aleksander*, I, pp. 59–61.
31. Shilder, *Alek. I*, II, p. 275.
32. Mazade, *op. cit.*, p. 292.
33. Elizabeth to her mother, 16 October 1801, N.M., *Elis.*, II, pp. 49–50.
34. Shilder, *Alek. I*, II, p. 53.
35. Elizabeth to her mother, 2 November 1801, N.M., *Elis.*, II, p. 51.

Chapter 4: The Emperor Wants It Thus

1. N.M., *Alek. I*, I, pp. 8, 27 and 29.
2. See the extremely perceptive analysis of Alexander's political character in Grimsted, *Foreign Ministers*, pp. 31–40.
3. St Helens to Hawkesbury, 24 May 1801, F.O. 65/48/Private.
4. N.M., *Stroganov*, II, pp. 44–54.
5. St Helens to Hawkesbury, 10 September 1801, F.O. 65/49/33.
6. *VPR*, I, 98–9.

7. Grimsted, *op. cit.*, pp. 81–3.
8. N.M., *Stroganov*, II, pp. 110–11 and 118–19.
9. Almedingen, *Emperor Alexander*, pp. 64–5.
10. Frederick William III to Alexander, 15 October 1801, Bailleu, *Brief-wechsel*, p. 11.
11. The same to the same, 13 January 1802, *Ibid.*, p. 14; Alexander to Frederick William, 8 February 1802, *Ibid.*, p. 15.
12. Kochubey to Simon Vorontsov, 19 May 1802, quoted by Grimsted, *op. cit.*, p. 88; N.M., *Stroganov*, II, pp. 138–9.
13. Wright, *Louise Queen of Prussia*, pp. 60–3.
14. Kochubey to Simon Vorontsov, 14 June 1802, quoted by Grimsted, *op. cit.*, p. 89.
15. Shilder, *Alek. I*, II, p. 70.
16. Almedingen, *op. cit.*, p. 77.
17. Mazade, *Mémoires de Czartoryski*, I, pp. 294–8.
18. Kochubey to Simon Vorontsov, 30 July 1802, quoted by Grimsted, *op. cit.*, p. 89.
19. Vernadsky, *Source Book for Russian History*, II, pp. 483–4.
20. Raeff, *Speransky*, p. 106.
21. Mazade, *op. cit.*, I, pp. 300–1.
22. Raeff, *Plans for Political Reform*, pp. 75–84.
23. Grimsted, *op. cit.*, pp. 91–3.
24. Lefebvre, *Napoléon*, I, pp. 164–78.
25. *VPR*, I, pp. 326–8.
26. *Ibid.*, pp. 342–3; and Alexander to Vorontsov, 13 July 1803, *Ibid.*, pp. 483–4.
27. *Ibid.*, pp. 468–9.
28. Jenkins, *Arakcheev*, p. 94.
29. Elizabeth to her mother, 26 February 1803, N.M., *Elis.*, II, p. 73.
30. The same to the same, 21 May and 1 June 1803, *Ibid,.* II, pp. 87 and 89.
31. The same to the same, 10 May 1803, *Ibid.*, II, p. 83.
32. The same to the same, 15 December 1801, *Ibid.*, II, p. 53.
33. Grunwald, *Alexandre I*, pp. 74–7; N.M., *Elis.*, II, pp. 23–4.
34. Almedingen, *op. cit.*, pp. 84–6.
35. Elizabeth to her mother, 26 February 1803, N.M., *Elis.*, II, p. 73.
36. *Ibid.*, II, p. 24; Elizabeth to her mother, 3 December 1804, *Ibid.*, II, p. 146.
37. Temperley, *Unpublished Diary*, p. 262; Elizabeth to her mother, 3 April 1801, N.M., *Elis.*, II, pp. 37–8; *Ibid.*, II, p. 2.

38. Elizabeth to her mother, 5 April 1803, *Ibid.*, II, p. 79.
39. Alexander to Catherine Pavlovna, 1 October 1805, *Corr. Alex.*, p. 4.
40. *Ibid.*
41. Martha Wilmot to her mother, 31 July 1803, Londonderry and Hyde, *Russian Journals*, p. 27.
42. Almedingen, *op. cit.*, p. 87.
43. Elizabeth to her mother, 13 September 1803, N.M., *Elis.*, II, p. 103.

Chapter 5: Shadow of War

1. Lefebvre, *Napoléon*, I, pp. 166–213.
2. Grimsted, *Foreign Ministers*, pp. 104–5; Warren to Hawkesbury, 4 June 1803, F.O. 65/52/Private.
3. Seton-Watson, *Russian Empire*, p. 85.
4. *Ibid.*; Mazade, *Mémoires de Czartoryski*, I, pp. 354–5.
5. Lefebvre, *op. cit.*, p. 202.
6. *Ibid.*; *VPR*, I, p. 520.
7. Mazade, *op. cit.*, I, pp. 355–9; Alexander to Morkov, 28 October 1803, *VPR*, I, p. 532.
8. A. Vorontsov to S. Vorontsov, 2 December 1803, *VPR*, I, pp. 557–8; cf. A. Vorontsov to Amstedt, 18 October 1803, *Ibid.*, pp. 522–5.
9. Mazade, *op. cit.*, I, pp. 354–5.
10. Anderson, *Eastern Question*, p. 34; Czartoryski to Alexander, 29 February 1804, *VPR*, I, pp. 620–4.
11. Anderson, *op. cit.*, pp. 34–5.
12. Grimsted, *op. cit.*, p. 99.
13. *Ibid.*, pp. 97–8; Mazade, *op. cit.*, I, p. 379; N.M., *Elis.*, II, p. 19.
14. Council Minutes, 17 April 1804, *VPR*, I, pp. 686–92.
15. Duff Cooper, *Talleyrand*, p. 143; Paléologue, *Enigmatic Czar*, p. 31.
16. Czartoryski to Alexander, 17 May 1804, *VPR*, I, pp. 57–9.
17. Grimsted, *op. cit.*, pp. 117–21.
18. Mazade, *op. cit.*, II, pp. 27–33; Webster, *Castlereagh*, I, pp. 55–7.
19. *Ibid.*, p. 55; Grimsted, *op. cit.*, p. 131.
20. Secret instructions to Novosiltsov, 23 September 1804, *VPR*, II, pp. 138–46 and 151–4.
21. Webster, *Castlereagh*, I, p. 57: Novosiltsov Memorandum of 25 December 1804, *VPR*, II, pp. 219–46; Novosiltsov to Alexander, 5 January 1805, *VPR*, II, pp. 257–60.
22. Webster, *Castlereagh*, I, p. 57.
23. Webster, *British Diplomacy*, Appendix I.

24. Grimsted, *op. cit.*, p. 131; Leveson-Gower to Harrowby, 17 February 1805, F.O. 65/57/4.
25. Webster, *British Diplomacy*, Appendix 1.
26. Kukiel, *op. cit.*, p. 56.
27. *Ibid.*, pp. 57–8.
28. Draft Treaty of 11 April 1805, *VPR*, II, pp. 355–68; Ratification document, 24 July 1805, *VPR*, II, p. 488.
29. Kukiel, *op. cit.*, p. 60; Seton-Watson, *op. cit.*, pp. 87–8.
30. Metternich, *Mémoires*, II, pp. 38–66; Palmer, *Metternich*, pp. 42–3; Kraehe, *Metternich's German Policy*, pp. 37–9.
31. Rose, *Despatches relating to the Third Coalition*, pp. 88–92.
32. Gielgud, *Memoirs of Czartoryski*, II, p. 125; Mazade, *op. cit.*, pp. 104–31.
33. Kukiel, *op. cit.*, p. 63.
34. Czartoryski to S. Vorontsov, 21 August 1805, quoted from the Vorontsov archives by Kukiel, *Ibid.*, p. 64.
35. Almedingen, *Emperor Alexander*, p. 81.
36. Alexander to Frederick William, 7 August 1805, Bailleu, *Briefwechsel*, pp. 68–70; Grimsted, *op. cit.*, p. 137.
37. Mazade, *op. cit.*, II, p. 243; Beer, *Zehn Jahre*, p. 460.
38. Elizabeth to her mother, 21 September 1805, N.M., *Elis.*, II, p. 168.
39. Kukiel, *op. cit.*, pp. 64–5; Bailleu, *op. cit.*, pp. 75–83.
40. Nicholas Mikhailovich, *Die Fürsten Dolgorukij*, pp. 12–13 and 84–6.
41. See the article by M. Lempitskii, 'Aleksandr I v Pulavakh,' *Russkaia Starina*, Vol. 55, pp. 172–3.
42. Kukiel, *op. cit.*, p. 65; Nicholas Mikhailovich, *Dolgorukij*, pp. 146–52.
43. Elizabeth to her mother, 19 October 1805, N.M., *Elis.*, II, p. 170.
44. Alexander to Catherine Pavlovna, October 1805, *Corr. Alex.*, pp. 3–6.
45. Kukiel, *op. cit.*, p. 65; Nicholas Mikhailovich, *Dolgorukij*, pp. 85–6; Frederick William to Alexander, 7 October 1805, Bailleu, *op. cit.*, pp. 82–3.
46. Czartoryski to Razumovsky, 10 October 1805, *VPR*, II, pp. 602–4.
47. Dolgoruky to Alexander, 15 October 1805, Nicholas Mikhailovich, *Dolgorukij*, pp. 87–8.
48. Kukiel, *op. cit.*, p. 66; Mazade, *op. cit.*, II, p. 82; Shilder, *Alek. I*, II, pp. 130 and 282; Waliszewski, I, pp. 166–7.
49. Wright, *Louise*, pp. 83–4.
50. Metternich, *Mémoires*, II, pp. 66–71.
51. *Ibid.*, pp. 73–4; Kraehe, *op. cit.*, pp. 40–2; *VPR*, II, pp. 613–16, 619–20 and 625–6.
52. Wright, *op. cit.*, p. 85; Shilder, *Alek. I*, II, p. 132.

Chapter 6: Austerlitz and After

1. Shilder, *Alek. I*, II, p. 132; Mazade, *Mémoires de Czartoryski*, I, p. 402.
2. Palmer, *Napoleon in Russia*, pp. 93–5; Duffy, *Borodino*, pp. 63–5.
3. Waliszewski, I, p. 171; Manceron, *Austerlitz*, p. 121.
4. Shilder, *Alek. I*, II, p. 283.
5. Memoirs of Langeron, quoted by Shilder, *loc. cit.*
6. Manceron, *op. cit.*, p. 155.
7. *Ibid.*, p. 183.
8. Andolenko, *Histoire de l'Armée Russe*, p. 149; Grunwald, *Alexandre I*, p. 107.
9. Manceron, *op. cit.*, pp. 152–6. For Alexander in Olmütz see also N.M., *Stroganov*, II, pp. 210–11.
10. Napoleon to Alexander, 25 November 1805, *Nap. Corr.*, XI, no. 9538, p. 440.
11. Shilder, *Alek. I*, II, pp. 135 and 283–4.
12. Manceron, *op. cit.*, p. 156.
13. *Nap. Corr.*, XI, p. 447; Manceron, *op. cit.*, pp. 158–9; Shilder, *Alek. I*, II, pp. 136 and 284.
14. Manceron, *op. cit.*, p. 27.
15. Chandler, *Campaigns of Napoleon*, pp. 417–20; Shilder, *Alek. I*, II, p. 138.
16. Memoirs of Langeron, quoted by Manceron, *op. cit.*, p. 183.
17. *Ibid.*
18. Garros, *Quel Roman que ma Vie!*, p. 252; Manceron, *op. cit.*, pp. 210–13.
19. Shilder, *Alek. I*, II, p. 284.
20. *Ibid.*, p. 140 (citing Mikhailovsky–Danilevsky, the source also used by Tolstoy for his account of the incident in *War and Peace*, Book 3, Chapter 13).
21. Mazade, *op. cit.*, I, p. 407; Chandler, *op. cit.*, p. 425.
22. Mazade, *op. cit.*, I, pp. 408–9.
23. Chandler, *op. cit.*, p. 426.
24. *Ibid.*, p. 431.
25. *Ibid.*, p. 432.
26. Manceron, *op. cit.*, p. 180.
27. Mazade, *op. cit.*, I, p. 410.
28. Manceron, *op. cit.*, pp. 299–300.
29. Elizabeth to her mother, 23 December 1805, N.M., *Elis.*, II, p. 175. The version by Czartoryski (Mazade, *op. cit.*, I, p. 410) is far less dramatic.

30. Chandler, *op. cit.*, p. 438.
31. Alexander to Frederick William, 6 December 1805, Shilder, *Alek. I*, II, pp. 349–50.
32. *Ibid.*
33. Lefebvre, *Napoleon*, I, p. 242.
34. Grunwald, *op. cit.*, pp. 109–10.
35. Elizabeth to her mother, 23 December 1805, N.M., ., *Elis*II, p. 174.
36. *Ibid.*
37. *Ibid.*, II, p. 176.
38. *Ibid.*
39. Novosiltsov to Stroganov, 18 January 1806, N.M., *Stroganov*, III, pp. 106–8.
40. Countess Stroganova to her husband, 24 December 1805, *Ibid.*, III, pp. 123–4.
41. *Ibid.*

Chapter 7: Anathema

1. Elizabeth to her mother, 22 January 1806, N.M., *Elis.*, II, p. 178.
2. Novosiltsov to Stroganov, 18 January 1806, N.M., *Stroganov*, III, pp. 106–8; Countess Stroganova to her husband, 31 January 1806 and 11 February 1806, *Ibid.*, III, pp. 125–6.
3. Jenkins, *Arakcheev*, pp. 102–3.
4. Novosiltsov to Stroganov, 18 January 1806, *loc. cit.*; Stroganov to his wife, 18 February 1806, N.M., *Stroganov*, III, pp. 127–8.
5. *Ibid.*, III, p. 107.
6. Mazade, *Mémoires de Czartoryski*, II, pp. 162–4.
7. Czartoryski to Stroganov, 18 February 1806, N.M., *Stroganov*, II, p. 226.
8. Stroganov to his wife, 18 February 1806, N.M., *Stroganov*, III, p. 127.
9. Czartoryski to Stroganov, 25 May 1806, *VPR*, III, pp. 168–73; Grimsted, *Foreign Ministers*, p. 143; Mazade, *op. cit.*, II, pp. 83–93.
10. Czartoryski to Stroganov, 15 May 1806, N.M., *Stroganov*, II, pp. 381–2.
11. Czartoryski to Alexander, 1 April 1806, Mazade, *op. cit.*, II, pp. 95–103.
12. Grimsted, *op. cit.*, p. 144.
13. Czartoryski to Oubril, 12 May 1806, *VPR*, III, pp. 134–7. (Cf. *Ibid.*, pp. 672–3.)
14. Kukiel, *Czartoryski and European Unity*, p. 76; Czartoryski to Stroganov, 25 May 1806, N.M., *Stroganov*, II, p. 384; Mazade, *op. cit.*, II, pp. 99–100.

15. Novosiltsov to Stroganov, 29 March 1806, N.M., *Stroganov*, III, p. 172.
16. Rostopchin, quoted by Almedingen, *Emperor Alexander*, p. 95.
17. Grimsted, *op. cit.*, p. 155.
18. Kukiel, *op. cit.*, pp. 78–9.
19. Elizabeth to her mother, 4 June 1806, N.M., *Elis.*, II, pp. 183–4; Bogdanovich, *Aleksandr. I*, II, pp. 105–6.
20. The Margravine of Baden to Elizabeth, 3 April 1806, N.M., *Elis.*, II, pp. 195–6.
21. Palmer, *Metternich*, pp. 31–2.
22. The Margravine of Baden to Elizabeth, 24 January and 3 April 1806, N.M., *Elis.*, II, pp. 195 and 196.
23. Elizabeth to her mother, November 1806, *Ibid.*, II, p. 187.
24. The same to the same, November 1806, *Ibid.*, II, p. 186.
25. The same to the same, November 1806, *Ibid.*, II, p. 187.
26. Napoleon to Talleyrand, 9 June 1806, *Nap. Corr.*, XII, no. 10339, pp. 146–7.
27. Anderson, *Eastern Question*, pp. 37–8.
28. Text of the treaty of 20 July 1806 in *VPR*, III, pp. 226–8.
29. Lefebvre, *op. cit.*, I, p. 254; Markham, *Napoleon*, pp. 125–6.
30. Seton-Watson, *Russian Empire*, p. 92; *VPR*, III, pp. 242, 263, 320, 361 and 412, partly summarizing the Alexander–Frederick William correspondence in Bailleu, *Briefwechsel*.
31. Declaration by Alexander, *VPR*, III, July 1806, pp. 231–3.
32. Almedingen, *op. cit.*, p. 97; Shilder, *Alek. I*, II, pp. 155, 158–9 and 287.
33. *Ibid.*, II, p. 155.
34. Markham, *op. cit.*, pp. 126–7.
35. Almedingen, *op. cit.*, pp. 97–8; N.M., *Alek. I*, I, pp. 46–7.
36. Paléologue, *Enigmatic Czar*, p. 57; Wright, *op. cit.*, pp. 134–8.
37. Shilder, *Alek. I*, II, p. 154.
38. Grimsted, *op. cit.*, p. 160.
39. Shilder, *Alek. I*, II, pp. 357–61; Paléologue, *op. cit.*, p. 56.
40. Shilder, *Alek. I*, II, p. 164.
41. Chandler, *Campaigns of Napoleon*, pp. 535–45 and 555.
42. Shilder, *Alek. I*, II, p. 165.
43. Elizabeth to her mother, 4 April 1807, N.M., *Elis.*, II, p. 241.
44. Convention of Bartenstein, April 1807, *VPR*, III, pp. 557–61.
45. Shilder, *Alek. I*, II, p. 168.
46. *Ibid.*, II, pp. 176 and 292.
47. Chandler, *op. cit.*, pp. 572–84.

Chapter 8: Tilsit

1. Almedingen, *Emperor Alexander*, pp. 99–101.
2. Alexander to Budberg, 16 June 1807, cited from the Budberg Papers by Grimsted, *Foreign Ministers*, p. 161. (Cf. letter of same date to Frederick William, Bailleu, *Briefwechsel*, p. 157.)
3. Vandal, I, pp. 50–1.
4. Napoleon to Talleyrand, 24 June 1807, *Nap. Corr.*, xv, no. 12813, p. 366.
5. Vandal, I, p. 53; Waliszewski, I, pp. 225–6.
6. Shilder, *Alek. I*, II, pp. 179 and 292.
7. Napoleon to Talleyrand, 24 June 1807, *loc. cit.*
8. Chandler, *Campaigns of Napoleon*, p. 586; Shilder, *Alek. I*, II, p. 181.
9. Vandal, I, p. 57; Garros, *Quel Roman . . . !*, p. 282.
10. Vandal, I, pp. 53–7; Waliszewski, I, pp. 225–7. (See also 86th Bulletin of the Grand Army, *Nap. Corr.*, xv, pp. 372–3.)
11. Shilder, *Alek. I*, II, p. 186.
12. Quoted by Almedingen, *op. cit.*, p. 101.
13. Napoleon to Josephine, 25 June 1807, *Nap. Corr.*, xv, no. 12825, p. 372.
14. Napoleon to Talleyrand, 25 June 1807, *Ibid.*, no 12826, p. 372.
15. Shilder, *Alek. I*, II, pp. 190–1.
16. *Ibid.*, II, p. 192.
17. Wright, *Louise*, pp. 166–7.
18. Grimsted, *op. cit.*, p. 162; Shilder, *Alek. I*, II, p. 294.
19. Alexander to Marie Feodorovna, June 1807, quoted in the original French in Almedingen, *op. cit.*, p. 101.
20. Shilder, *Alek. I*, II, p. 178.
21. Alexander to Catherine Pavlovna, 29 June 1807, *Corr. Alex.*, p. 18.
22. Catherine Pavlovna to Alexander, 7 July 1807, *Ibid.*, p. 19.
23. Vandal, I, pp. 73–81; Waliszewski, p. 224; Lefebvre, *Napoléon*, I, p. 272.
24. *Ibid.*, I, p. 273; Vandal, I, p. 82.
25. *Ibid.*, I, pp. 95–6; Paléologue, *Enigmatic Czar*, p. 69; Louise to Alexander, 25 June 1807, Bailleu, *Briefwechsel*, p. 190.
26. Paléologue, *op. cit.*, p. 66; cf. Alexander to Frederick William, 27 June 1807, Bailleu, *Briefwechsel*, p. 158.
27. Vandal, I, p. 89; Kukiel, *Czartoryski and European Unity*, p. 85.
28. Shilder, *Alek. I*, II, p. 295; Anderson, *Eastern Question*, pp. 40–1.
29. Vandal, I, pp. 107–9.

Chapter 9: As Destiny Demands

1. Napoleon to Cambacérès, 8 July 1807, *Nap. Corr.*, xv, no. 12876, 8 July 1807.

2. Metternich to Stadion, 19 August 1807, HHSA, Diplom. Korr. Frankreich, Karton 200, Fascicle B.

3. Anderson, *Britain's Discovery of Russia*, pp. 213–14. See also the anonymous pamphlet *Key to the Recent Conduct of the Emperor of Russia*, pp. 33–8, published in London in the autumn of 1807. The extent of the Tilsit obligations did not become clear until early December.

4. Rolo, *Canning*, p. 196; Alopeus to Alexander, 3 August 1807, *VPR*, IV, pp. 15–16; Seton-Watson, *Russian Empire*, p. 113.

5. Leveson-Gower to Canning, 2 September 1807, F.O. 65/70/19; see also Grimsted, *Foreign Ministers*, p. 164 (footnote).

6. Stroganov to Simon Vorontsov, 2 September 1807, *VPR*, IV, pp. 42–4, (cf. *Ibid.*, p. 568).

7. Shilder, *Alek. I*, II, pp. 298–9; Savary, *Mémoires*, II, p. 265.

8. Shilder, *Alek. I*, II, pp. 211 and 299; Tatischev, *Alexandre et Napoléon*, p. 192.

9. Grimsted, *op. cit.*, pp. 162–7.

10. *Ibid.*, pp. 167–9.

11. Almedingen, *Emperor Alexander I*, pp. 102–3; N.M., *Elis.*, II, p. 245; Londonderry and Hyde, *Russian Journals*, pp. 299–300; Jenkins, *Arakcheev*, p. 108.

12. Elizabeth to her mother, 10 September 1807, N.M., *Elis.*, II, pp. 250–4.

13. The same to the same, 11 October 1807, *Ibid.*, p. 258.

14. Shilder, *Alek. I*, II, pp. 210 and 298; Paléologue, *Enigmatic Czar*, p. 71.

15. Tatischev, *op. cit.*, p. 203.

16. Raeff, *Speransky*, p. 18; Elizabeth to her mother, 11 October 1807, N.M., *Elis.*, II, p. 258.

17. Declaration by Alexander, 7 November 1807, *VPR*, IV, pp. 98–101; Rumiantsev to Alopeus, 7 November 1807, *Ibid.*, IV, pp. 103–4.

18. Jenkins, *op. cit.*, pp. 108–11.

19. *Ibid.*, p. 111.

20. Paléologue, *op. cit.*, p. 71.

21. See Savary's notes on personalities at the Russian Court edited by Vandal in *Revue d'Histoire Diplomatique* for 1890, no. 3, especially pp. 402–7.

22. Caulaincourt, *Mémoires*, I, p. 245; Waliszewski, I, pp. 250–1.

23. Vandal, I, pp. 118–20.

24. Napoleon to Alexander, 2 February 1808, *Nap. Corr.*, XVI, Appendix, pp. 498–9. (English translation, Thompson, *Napoleon's Letters*, pp. 193–194.)
25. Tatischev, *op. cit.*, pp. 312–13.
26. Declaration by Alexander, 22 February 1808, *VPR*, IV, pp. 168–70.
27. On the Finnish War see Jenkins, *op. cit.*, pp. 115–24 and *VPR*, IV, pp. 192–6 and 203. For the subsequent parade in St Petersburg see N.M., *Elis.*, II, p. 206.
28. *Ibid.*, II, p. 207.
29. Vandal, I, pp. 284–304; Anderson, *Eastern Question*, pp. 41–3.
30. Vandal, I, pp. 378–9.
31. Garros, *Quel Roman . . . !*, p. 300; Napoleon to Alexander, 7 September 1807, *Nap. Corr.*, XVII, no. 14304, pp. 496–7.
32. Garros, *loc. cit.*
33. Vandal, I, pp. 379–82.
34. Marie Feodorovna to Alexander, 25 August 1808, Shilder, 'Nakanune Erfurtskogo svidaniia 1808 goda,' *Russkaya Starina*, XCVIII, pp. 4–17.
35. Alexander to Marie Feodorovna, 5 September 1808, *Ibid.*, pp. 17–24.
36. Waliszewski, I, p. 265.
37. Wright, *Louise*, pp. 200–4.
38. Schmitt, 'Stein, Alexander I and the Crusade against Napoleon,' *JMH*, Vol. 31, p. 326.
39. Shilder, *Alek. I*, II, p. 301.
40. Garros, *op. cit.*, p. 301; Vandal, I, pp. 411–13.
41. *Ibid.*, I, p. 417.
42. Napoleon to Josephine, 2 October 1808, *Lettres de Napoléon à Josèphine*, p. 144.
43. Vandal, I, p. 453.
44. Napoleon to Josephine, 9 October 1808, *Nap. Corr.*, XVII, no. 14366, p. 542.
45. Alexander to Catherine Pavlovna, 8 October 1808, *Corr. Alex.*, p. 20.
46. Palmer, *Metternich*, p. 63.
47. Caulaincourt, *Mémoires*, I, p. 273.
48. Vandal, I, p. 435.
49. Caulaincourt, *op. cit.*, I, pp. 108–14.
50. Metternich, *Mémoires*, II, p. 248; Shilder, *Alek. I*, II, p. 302.
51. Text of the agreement in *VPR*, IV, pp. 359–61.
52. Vandal, I, p. 464.
53. Caulaincourt, *op. cit.*, I, pp. 274–5.
54. Tatischev, *op. cit.*, pp. 458–9; Savary, *Mémoires*, IV, p. 6.

Chapter 10: The Primacy of Speransky

1. Raeff, *Speransky*, pp. 1–2.
2. Vandal, I, p. 408; Raeff, *op. cit.*, p. 55; Grimsted, *Foreign Ministers*, p. 185; Shilder, *Alek. I*, IV, p. 472.
3. Raeff, *op. cit.*, p. 76.
4. *Ibid.*, pp. 16–17.
5. *Ibid.*
6. Shilder, *Alek. I*, III, p. 366.
7. Raeff, *op. cit.*, p. 18.
8. Maistre, April 1812, *Correspondance*, pp. 101–2.
9. Raeff, *op. cit.*, pp. 170–3.
10. *Ibid.*, pp. 211–12.
11. *Ibid.*, pp. 19–22, 243 and 253.
12. *Ibid.*, pp. 90–2.
13. Vernadsky, *Source Book for Russian History*, II, pp. 490–3.
14. Raeff, *op. cit.*, pp. 67, 126–7.
15. *Ibid.*, p. 76.
16. Jenkins, *Arakcheev*, p. 149.
17. Kochubey to Speransky, 1808, Raeff, *op. cit.*, p. 60.
18. *Ibid.*, pp. 60–2.
19. *Ibid.*, pp. 57, 62 and 174–5; Seton-Watson, *Russian Empire*, p. 106.
20. Raeff, *op. cit.*, p. 64.
21. *Ibid.*, pp. 175–6; Seton-Watson, *op. cit.*, pp. 108–9; Waliszewski, I, p. 399.
22. Raeff, *op. cit.*, pp. 172–3.
23. Seton-Watson, *op. cit.*, p. 73.
24. Vernadsky, *op. cit.*, II, pp. 493–4.
25. Raeff, *op. cit.*, p. 115.
26. Jenkins, *op. cit.*, p. 124.
27. Shilder, *Alek. I*, II, p. 261; Jenkins, *op. cit.*, p. 134.
28. Arakcheev to Alexander, 5 January 1810, Shilder, *Alek. I*, II, pp. 261–2.
29. Alexander to Arakcheev, January 1810, *ibid.*, pp. 262–3. There are long extracts from this correspondence, in an English translation, in Jenkins, *op. cit.*, pp. 134–7.
30. Elizabeth to her mother, 2 January 1810, N.M., *Elis.*, II, p. 362, and 9 January 1810, *ibid.*, p. 364.
31. Vernadsky, *op. cit.*, II, pp. 494–5.
32. Raeff, *op. cit.*, p. 175.
33. *Ibid.*, p. 104.

34. *Ibid.*, pp. 153, 158–9.
35. *Ibid.*, pp. 183–4.

Chapter 11: The Viceroy

1. Caulaincourt, *Mémoires*, I, p. 95; Waliszewski, I, p. 251.
2. Caulaincourt, *op. cit.*, I, p. 247; Paléologue, *Enigmatic Czar*, p. 131.
3. Caulaincourt, *op. cit.*, I, pp. 98–9.
4. *Ibid.*, I, p. 99; Adams, p. 72.
5. *Ibid.*, pp. 96 and 98; Vandal, II, p. 28.
6. Paléologue, *op. cit.*, pp. 131–2.
7. Queen Louise kept a diary of the visit. It is printed in Bailleu, *Brief-wechsel*, pp. 542–3.
8. Waliszewski, I, p. 274, quoting from Joseph de Maistre.
9. Elizabeth to her mother, 1 February 1809, N.M., *Elis.*, II, p. 313.
10. Vandal, II, pp. 37–40; Paléologue, *op. cit.*, p. 100.
11. Elizabeth to her mother, 1 February 1809, N.M., *Elis.*, II, p. 313.
12. Louise to Alexander, 9 February 1809, Bailleu, *op. cit.*, p. 435.
13. See Louise's journal, *Ibid.*, p. 549.
14. Elizabeth to her mother, 6 May 1809, N.M., *Elis.*, II, p. 320.
15. The same to the same, 26 August 1809, *Ibid.*, II, p. 340.
16. Adams, p. 89.
17. Vandal, II, p. 38.
18. Alexander to Rumiantsev. 14 and 22 February 1809, *VPR*, IV, pp. 493–5 and 502–4; Rumiantsev to Anstedt, 23 March 1809, *Ibid.*, IV, pp. 543–4.
19. Elizabeth to her mother, 12 April 1809, N.M., *Elis.*, II, p. 319.
20. Vandal, II, pp. 75–7.
21. *Ibid.*, II, p. 82.
22. Elizabeth to her mother, 12 May 1809, N.M., *Elis.*, II, p. 322.
23. Vandal, II, p. 93.
24. Champagny to Caulaincourt, 2 June 1809, *Ibid.*, II, p. 95.
25. Lefebvre, *Napoléon*, II, p. 69.
26. Seton-Watson, *Russian Empire*, p. 120.
27. Vandal, II, p. 169.
28. Shilder, *Alek. I*, II, pp. 246–7 and 304–5.
29. Vandal, II, pp. 182–4.
30. *Ibid.*, II, pp. 224–32.
31. Adams, p. 93.
32. Alexander to Catherine Pavlovna, 4 January 1810, *Corr. Alex.*, p. 27.

33. Waliszewski, I, pp. 301–8; *VPR*, v, pp. 403 and 690.
34. Marie Feodorovna to Catherine Pavlovna, 4 January 1810, *Corr. Alex.*, pp. 251–7.
35. Catherine Pavlovna to Marie Feodorovna, 7 January 1810, *Ibid.*, pp. 259–60.
36. *Ibid.*, Vandal, II, pp. 271–80.
37. Palmer, *Metternich*, pp. 74–5.
38. Vandal, II, pp. 290–2.
39. *Ibid.*, II, p. 222; Kukiel, *Czartoryski and European Unity*, p. 92.
40. Vandal, II, p. 363, quoting *Nap. Corr.*, XXI, no 16180 of August 1810.
41. Kukiel, *op. cit.*, pp. 92–3; Mazade, *Mémoires de Czartoryski*, II, pp. 229–234.
42. Gielgud, *Mémoires of Prince Czartoryski*, II, pp. 200–12.
43. *LPN*, II, pp. 66–71.
44. Grimsted, *Foreign Ministers*, p. 185 (citing Tarlé's study of Talleyrand).
45. *LPN*, III, pp. 225–370.
46. *Ibid.*, III, p. 317.
47. Caulaincourt, *op. cit.*, I, pp. 117–18.
48. Adams, p. 130.
49. *Ibid.*
50. Paléologue, *op. cit.*, p. 130.
51. Adams, *loc. cit.*

Chapter 12: 'Blood Must Flow Again'

1. Adams, p. 244.
2. Alexander to Catherine Pavlovna, 19 January 1810, *Corr. Alex.*, p. 32.
3. *Ibid.*, pp. 32–3; Jenkins, *Arakcheev*, pp. 144–6.
4. Pipes, 'Russian Military Colonies,' *JMH*, Vol. 22, p. 206.
5. Adams, p. 135.
6. Alexander to Catherine Pavlovna, 9 July 1810, *Corr. Alex.*, p. 33.
7. Wrangel's account of his mission was printed by the German historian, Thimme, and is cited by Hans Schmitt in his article on Stein and Alexander, *JMH*, Vol. 31, pp. 326–7.
8. Adams, pp. 148–9.
9. N.M., *Elis.*, II, pp. 212 and 434–5.
10. *Ibid.*, II, pp. 213–14.
11. For Elizabeth's letters to her mother from Plöen see N.M., *Elis.*, II, pp. 381–6. Letters to others from Plöen appear earlier in the same volume (pp. 215–25).

12. Parrot to Alexander, 27 October 1810, *Ibid.*, II, pp. 228–33.

13. Lefebvre, *Napoléon*, II, pp. 133 ff.; Tarlé, *Nashestvie Napoleona*, p. 14.

14. Shilder, *Alek.I*, II, pp. 397–8.

15. Rumiantsev's report to the Senate, October 1811, *VPR*, V, pp. 558–66.

16. *Ibid.*, p. 641.

17. *Ibid.*, p. 644; Seton-Watson, *Russian Empire*, p. 123; Adams, p. 213; Raeff, *op. cit.*, p. 78.

18. Alexander to Catherine Pavlovna, 7 January 1810, *Corr. Alex.*, pp. 35–6.

19. Gielgud, *op. cit.*, II, pp. 218–22.

20. Alexander to Comte de Mocenigo, 2 February 1811, *VPR*, VI, pp. 21–4.

21. Kukiel, *Czartoryski and European Unity*, p. 95; Gielgud, *loc. cit.*

22. Seton-Watson, *op. cit.*, p. 122; *VPR*, VI, pp. 62–4, 71; N.M., *Alex. I*, I, pp. 393–4.

23. Palmer, *Napoleon in Russia*, p. 26; Adams, p. 230.

24. N.M., *Alex. I*, I, p. 351; Palmer, *Metternich*, pp. 82–3; Metternich, *Mémoires*, II, p. 418.

25. Napoleon to Alexander, 28 February 1811, *Nap. Corr.*, XXI, no 17395; Vandal, III, p. 89.

26. *Ibid.*, III, p. 115–17 and 127; *SIRIO*, XXI, pp. 49–67.

27. Lefebvre, *op. cit.*, II, pp. 149–50.

28. Adams, p. 245.

29. Rumiantsev to Kurakin, 21 March 1811, *VPR*, VI, pp. 136–8.

30. Adams, p. 247.

31. Vandal, III, p. 170–71.

32. Caulaincourt, *Mémoires*, I, pp. 117–18 and 279–80; N.M., *Alex. I*, I, p. 412; Adams, p. 262.

33. Caulaincourt, *op. cit.*, I, p. 280; Edling, *Mémoires*, p. 50; Tarlé, *op. cit.*, p. 21.

34. Palmer, *Napoleon in Russia*, p. 27; Caulaincourt, *op. cit.*, I, p. 285; Vandal, III, p. 185.

35. Alexander to Catherine Pavlovna, 17 July 1811, *Corr. Alex.*, p. 51.

36. Adams, p. 296.

37. Metternich, *Mémoires*, II, pp. 194–6; Botzenhart, *Metternichs Pariser Botschafterzeit*, pp. 239–41.

38. Vandal, III, pp. 211–17; *VPR*, VI, p. 146.

39. Caulaincourt, *op. cit.*, I, pp. 308–9.

40. Vandal, III, pp. 217–18.

41. *Ibid.;* Palmer, *Napoleon in Russia*, p. 28.

42. Adams, pp. 310–11.
43. Shilder, *Alex. I*, III, p. 364; Adams, p. 329.
44. Tolstoy, *War and Peace*, Book 8, Chapter 22.
45. Vandal, III, pp. 41–2, 127–34, 311–22.
46. Tarlé, *op. cit.*, pp. 21–2; Kurakin to Rumiantsev, 10 November 1811, *VPR*, VI, pp. 217–18.
47. Alexander to Catherine Pavlovna, 3 December 1811 and 5 January 1812, *Corr. Alex.*, pp. 59 and 61.
48. *VPR*, VI, pp. 191–7; Lefebvre, *op. cit.*, II, p. 151.
49. Palmer, *Metternich*, p. 84.
50. Anderson, *Eastern Question*, p. 46; *VPR*, VI, pp. 282–3, 306–7, 317.
51. *Ibid.*, VI, pp. 318–23.
52. Adams, p. 72; Waliszewski, I, pp. 22–6.
53. Clausewitz, *Campaign of 1812*, p. 5; Tarlé, *op. cit.*, pp. 51–2.
54. For a sound assessment of Barclay's qualities see Duffy, *Borodino*, pp. 38–41, and the fascinating analysis of the changing Soviet views on Barclay's military ability in the article by Barry Hollingsworth on 'The Napoleonic Invasion of Russia and recent Soviet historical writing,' *JMH*, Vol. 38, especially pp. 41–50.
55. Barclay de Tolly to Alexander, 3 February 1812, *VPR*, VI, pp. 267–8.
56. Palmer, *Napoleon in Russia*, p. 29.
57. Raeff, *Speransky*, p. 187.
58. *Ibid.*, p. 190.
59. *Ibid.*, pp. 190–1.
60. *Ibid.*, Jenkins, *Arakcheev*, p. 149; Shilder, *Alek. I*, III, p. 48.
61. *LPN*, II, pp. 75–6.
62. Raeff, *op. cit.*, pp. 174–8.
63. *Ibid.*, pp. 170–3 and 191–2.
64. Waliszewski, II, p. 62.
65. Alexander to Catherine Pavlovna, April 1812, *Corr. Alex.*, p. 51.
66. Adams, p. 353.
67. *Ibid.*, p. 352.
68. Vandal, III, p. 310.
69. See the article by Hans Schmitt on Stein and Alexander I, *JMH*, Vol. 31, p. 327.
70. Grimsted, *Foreign Ministers*, p. 174; Anderson, *op. cit.*, p. 47; Rumiantsev to Suchtelen, 24 April 1812, *VPR*, VI, pp. 370–2.
71. Vandal, III, pp. 373–4; Seton-Watson, *op. cit.*, p. 126.
72. Adams, p. 365.
73. Tarlé, *op. cit.*, p. 29.

74. Adams, pp. 364–5.
75. Elizabeth to her mother, 22 April 1812, N.M., *Elis.*, II, p. 525.

Chapter 13: Captain in the Field

1. Waliszewski, II, pp. 13–18.
2. Kukiel, *Czartoryski and European Unity*, p. 97.
3. Choiseul-Gouffier, *Historical Memories*, p. 67; Waliszewski, II, pp. 14–15 and 21–3.
4. Choiseul-Gouffier, *op. cit.*, pp. 66 and 84–7; Narichkine, *Rostopchine et son Temps*, p. 110.
5. Choiseul-Gouffier, *op. cit.*, pp. 72–4.
6. *Ibid.*, p. 82.
7. *Ibid.*, p. 90.
8. Lebzeltern to Metternich, 18 June 1812, quoted Grimsted, *Foreign Ministers*, p. 186.
9. Duffy, *Borodino*, p. 54.
10. Nesselrode memoirs, *LPN*, II, p. 75; Nesselrode to his wife, 25 May 1812, *LPN*, IV, p. 32.
11. Grimsted, *op. cit.*, pp. 190–1; Rumiantsev to Alexander, 5 July 1812, *VPR*, VI, pp. 452–3.
12. Nesselrode to his wife, 1 June 1812, *LPN*, IV, p. 43.
13. Tarlé, *op. cit.*, p. 24; Palmer, *Napoleon in Russia*, pp. 43–4.
14. Waliszewski, II, p. 15; Shilder, *Alex. I*, III, p. 75.
15. Catherine Pavlovna to Alexander, June 1812, *Corr. Alex.*, p. 76.
16. Alexander to Catherine Pavlovna, 9 June, 1812, *Ibid.*, p. 73.
17. Vandal, III, pp. 402–25; Palmer, *op. cit.*, pp. 17–23.
18. Rambuteau, *Mémoires*, pp. 67–8; Fain, *Manuscrit de 1812*, I, p. 77.
19. Rambuteau, *loc. cit.*, and Fain, *loc. cit.*; Vandal, III, pp. 429–31.
20. Fain, *op. cit.*, I, p. 77.
21. Tarlé, *op. cit.*, p. 24; Waliszewski, II, p. 26; Palmer, *op. cit.*, p. 44.
22. Waliszewski, II, p. 33.
23. Choiseul-Gouffier, *op. cit.*, pp. 91–3.
24. *Mémoires de Michel Oginski*, extract in translation, Brett-James, *1812, Napoleon's Defeat in Russia*, pp. 40–1.
25. Choiseul-Gouffier and Oginski, *loc. cit.*; Garros, *Quel Roman . . .!*, p. 380.
26. Castellane, *Journal*, I, pp. 108–9; Palmer, *op. cit.*, p. 48.
27. W. Löwenstern, *Mémoires*, I, p. 190; Tarlé, *op. cit.*, pp. 44–5.
28. *Ibid.*; N.M., *Alex. I*, I, p. 97; Shilder, *Alek. I*, III, p. 374.

29. *VPR*, VI, p. 443.

30. Adams, p. 382; Shilder, *Alek. I*, III, p. 375.

31. Rumiantsev to Alexander, 25 June 1812, *VPR*, VI, p. 441.

32. Tarlé, *op. cit.*, pp. 43–5; Vandal, III, pp. 515–28.

33. Tarlé, *op. cit.*, pp. 48–9.

34. Choisseul-Gouffier, *op. cit.*, p. 94.

35. W. Löwenstern, *op. cit.*, I, p. 190.

36. Oginski, *Mémoires, loc. cit.*

37. Choiseul-Gouffier, *op. cit.*, p. 95.

38. Tarlé, *op. cit.*, p. 53.

39. *Ibid.*, pp. 53–4; Palmer, *op. cit.*, pp. 56 and 58.

40. *Ibid.*, pp. 48–51.

41. Napoleon to Alexander, 1 July 1812, *Nap. Corr.*, XXIV, no 18878 (English translation in Thompson, *Napoleon's Letters*, pp. 268–70).

42. Caulaincourt, *Mémoires*, I, p. 360.

43. *VPR*, VI, pp. 46–68 *passim*.

44. W. Löwenstern, *op. cit.*, I, p. 377.

45. Jenkins, *Arakcheev*, p. 153.

46. Palmer, *op. cit.*, p. 57.

47. Alexander to Chichagov, 12 July 1812, *VPR*, VI, p. 461.

48. Clausewitz, *op. cit.*, pp. 41–2; Tarlé, *op. cit.*, p. 56; Wilson, *Narrative of Events*, pp. 44–8.

49. *VPR*, VI, pp. 468–82.

50. *Ibid.*, VI, p. 760; Webster, *Castlereagh*, I, p. 96.

51. Shilder, *Alek. I*, III, pp. 499–500 (cf. *VPR*, VI, pp. 463–4).

52. Duffy, *op. cit.*, pp. 55–6.

53. Tarlé, *op. cit.*, p. 57.

54. *Ibid.*; Jenkins, *op. cit.*, p. 153.

55. W. Löwenstern, *op. cit.*, I, p. 208.

56. Palmer, *op. cit.*, p. 58.

57. Jenkins, *op. cit.*, p. 153.

58. W. Löwenstern, *op. cit.*, I, p. 209; Brett-James, *op. cit.*, p. 78.

59. Tarlé, *op. cit.*, p. 58 (cf. Shilder, *Alek. I*, III, pp. 86–7).

Chapter 14: The Razor-Edge of Fate

1. Adams, p. 392.

2. Narichkine, *Comte Rostopchine*, pp. 126–7; Olivier, *L'Incendie de Moscou*, pp. 31–2.

3. Bakounina, 'Dvenadtsati God,' *Russkaya Starina*, Vol. 47, p. 401.

4. Alexander to Catherine Pavlovna, 24 July 1812, *Corr. Alex.*, p. 79.
5. Waliszewski, II, pp. 78–9; Tarlé, *Nashestvie Napoleona*, p. 110; Christian, *Tolstoy's War and Peace*, pp. 67–8 and 72.
6. Waliszewski, II, p. 73.
7. Aleshkin and Golovnikov article on the Moscow Militia in 1812, *Voprosy Istorii* (1962), no. 9, p. 27.
8. Stael, *Dix Années d'Exil*, p. 28.
9. Alexander to Catherine Pavlovna, 30 September 1812, *Corr. Alex*, p. 90.
10. Alexander to Catherine Pavlovna, 20 August 1812, *Corr. Alex.*, p. 82.
11. Adams, p. 395.
12. Alexander to Catherine Pavlovna, 20 August 1812, *loc. cit.*
13. Elizabeth to her mother, 10 August 1812, N.M., *Elis.*, II, p. 530.
14. *Ibid.*, II, p. 452.
15. Tarlé, *op. cit.*, p. 112. Although the factual material cited in Tarlé's book is reliable it is prejudiced against Barclay de Tolly. See the article by Barry Hollingsworth, *JMH*, Vol. 38, pp. 39–50 for a reassessment.
16. Alexander to Catherine Pavlovna, 20 August, 1812, *Corr. Alex.*, p. 82.
17. Duffy, *op. cit.*, pp. 65–6; Tarlé, *op. cit.*, p. 113.
18. Alexander to Catherine Pavlovna, 30 September 1812, *Corr. Alex.*, p. 87.
19. *Ibid.*
20. George of Oldenburg to Alexander, 17 August 1812, *Corr. Alex.*, p. 263.
21. Catherine Pavlovna to Alexander, same date, *Ibid.*, p. 81.
22. Clausewitz, *Campaign of 1812*, p. 115.
23. Shilder, *Alex. I*, III, p. 98.
24. Scott, *Bernadotte and the Fall of Napoleon*, p. 21; Waliszewski, II, pp. 95–6.
25. Cathcart to Castlereagh, 30 August 1812, F.O. 65/79; cf. Webster, *Castlereagh*, I, p. 98.
26. Palmer, *Napoleon in Russia*, pp. 96–7; Wilson, *Narrative*, pp. 114–20; Brett-James, *General Wilson's Journal*, pp. 36–7.
27. Wilson and Brett-James, *loc. cit.*
28. Wilson, *op. cit.*, p. 120.
29. Stael, *Dix Années d'Exil*, p. 169.
30. *Ibid.*, p. 168.
31. *Ibid.*, p. 167.
32. Elizabeth to her mother, 9 September 1812, N.M., *Elis.*, II, p. 534.

33. The same to the same, 7 September 1812, *Ibid.*, II, pp. 532–3.
34. Palmer, *op. cit.*, p. 105 (quoting from Altshuller and Bogdanov, *Borodino* p. 64).
35. Duffy, *op. cit.*, p. 11; Maistre, *Correspondance Diplomatique*, I, p. 177; Markham, *Napoleon*, p. 194.
36. Elizabeth to her mother, 13 September 1812, N.M., *Elis.*, II, p. 535.
37. Palmer, *op. cit.*, pp. 131–2.
38. Adams, p. 404.
39. Catherine Pavlovna to Alexander, 15 September 1812, *Corr. Alex.*, p. 83; Olivier, *op. cit.*, p. 131.
40. Adams, p. 405.
41. Edling, *Mémoires*, p. 79.
42. Adams, pp. 408 and 409–10.
43. Webster, *Castlereagh*, I, p. 99.
44. Napoleon to Alexander, 20 September 1812, *Nap. Corr.*, XXIV, no. 19213 (English version, Thompson, *Napoleon's Letters*, pp. 273–4).
45. Strakhovsky, *Alexander I*, pp. 136–8.
46. Elizabeth to her mother, 6 October 1812, N.M., *Elis.*, II, p. 539.
47. Catherine Pavlovna to Alexander, 18 September 1812, *Corr. Alex.*, pp. 83–4.
48. George of Oldenburg to Alexander, 18 September 1812, *Ibid.*, pp. 264–5.
49. Alexander to Catherine Pavlovna, 30 September 1812, *Ibid.*, pp. 86–93.
50. Catherine Pavlovna to Alexander, 5 October 1812, *Ibid.*, pp. 94–6.
51. Elizabeth to her mother, 1 January 1813 (quoting from Marie Feodorovna's earlier conversation), N.M., *Elis.*, II, p. 560.
52. Catherine Pavlovna to Alexander, 25 September 1812, *Corr. Alex.*, p. 85.
53. Alexander to Catherine Pavlovna, 6 October 1812, *Ibid.*, pp. 97–8.
54. Catherine Pavlovna to Alexander, 10 October 1812, *Ibid.*, p. 99.
55. Caulaincourt, *Mémoires*, II, pp. 30–45.
56. *Ibid*, II, pp. 46–7.
57. Ségur, *History of the Expedition to Russia*, II, p. 72; Caulaincourt, *op. cit.*, II, pp. 60–1.
58. Wilson, *op. cit.*, pp. 203–5; Tarlé, *op. cit.*, pp. 189 and 222.
59. Adams, p. 414.
60. *Ibid.*, pp. 416–17.
61. Elizabeth to her mother, 27 October 1812, N.M., *Elis.*, II, pp. 541–2.
62. Adams, p. 419.
63. Wilson, *op. cit.*, pp. 222–8; Ségur, *op. cit.*, II, pp. 110–13.

64. Shilder, *Alek. I*, III, pp. 116–17 and 378; N.M., *Alex. I*, I, pp. 160–4.
65. *Ibid.*, I, pp. 159–60.
66. Adams, p. 420.
67. Ségur, *op. cit.*, II, pp. 155–9.
68. Tarlé, *op. cit.*, pp. 246–7; Wilson, *op. cit.*, pp. 265–6.
69. Alexander to Catherine Pavlovna, 20 November 1812, *Corr. Alex.*, p. 103.
70. The same to the same, 22 November 1812, *Ibid.*, p. 105; Palmer, *op. cit.*, pp. 215–16.
71. Alexander to Catherine Pavlovna, 20 November 1812, *Corr. Alex.*, p. 103.
72. Adams, pp. 422–3.
73. Denniée, *Itinéraire*, pp. 166–7; Castellane, *Journal*, I, p. 201; Caulaincourt, *op. cit.*, II, pp. 205–7.
74. Arndt Memoirs, cited by Brett-James, *1812*, pp. 285–6.
75. Beskrovny, *Pokhod Russkoi Armii Protiv Napoleona*, 1813, pp. 1–4.
76. *Ibid.*, p. 5; Cathcart to Castlereagh, 30 August 1812, F.O., 65/79/9; Adams, p. 435.

Chapter 15: Tsar with a Mission

1. Choiseul-Gouffier, *Historical Memoirs*, p. 134.
2. *Ibid.*, pp. 131–44.
3. Rumiantsev to Alexander, 11 January 1813, *VPR*, VI, p. 475.
4. Wilson, *Narrative*, p. 352; Predtechensky article on 1812 casualties, *Istorichevsky Zhurnal*, 1941, combined nos. 7 and 8, p. 99.
5. Schmitt article on Stein and Alexander, *JMH*, Vol. 31, pp. 327–8.
6. Shilder, *Alek. I*, III, p. 137.
7. Ramm, *Germany*, p. 96; Wilson, *op. cit.*, pp. 360–3.
8. Beskrovny, *Pokhod Russkoi . . . 1813*, p. 10; Choiseul-Gouffier, *op. cit.*, pp. 155–6.
9. *Ibid.*, p. 157; Tarlé, *Nashestvie Napoleona*, p. 272.
10. Palmer, *Metternich*, p. 92.
11. N.M., *Alex. I*, I, p. 175; Strakhovsky, *Alexander I*, pp. 131–2.
12. Shilder, *Alek. I*, III, p. 142.
13. N.M., *Alek. I*, I, pp. 175–6.
14. Catherine Pavlovna to Alexander, 13 January 1813, *Corr. Alex.*, p. 116.
15. Alexander to Catherine Pavlovna, 7 March 1813, *Ibid.*, p. 132.

16. Anderson, *Britain's Discovery of Russia*, pp. 220–1, including quotation from Horatio Smith.
17. Lefebvre, *Napoléon*, II, p. 327.
18. Shilder, *Alek. I*, III, p. 142.
19. Alexander to Catherine Pavlovna, 28 April 1813, *Corr. Alex.*, pp. 141–2.
20. Tarlé, *op. cit.*, p. 273; Brett-James, *General Wilson's Journal*, p. 151.
21. Chandler, *Campaigns of Napoleon*, p. 881.
22. Shilder, *Alek. I*, III, p. 147, citing the memoirs of Count Donnersmarck.
23. *LPN*, V, p. 91; Catherine Pavlovna to Alexander, 10 May 1813, *Corr. Alex.*, pp. 142–3.
24. Shilder, *Alek. I*, III, pp. 147–8; Alexander to Catherine Pavlovna, 26 May 1813, *Corr. Alex.*, p. 150.
25. *Ibid.*, III, p. 154; Chandler, *op. cit.*, p. 892.
26. Palmer, *Metternich*, p. 95; Kissinger, *World Restored*, pp. 70–5.
27. Caulaincourt, *Mémoires*, II, p. 390; Lefebvre, *op. cit.*, II, p. 330.
28. Kissinger, *op. cit.*, p. 72.
29. Adams, p. 579.
30. Kukiel, *Czartoryski and European Unity*, p. 104.
31. Webster, *Castlereagh*, I, p. 125.
32. *Ibid.*, I, pp. 127–9, 143–5.
33. Palmer, *op. cit.*, pp. 95–6.
34. *Ibid.*, p. 97.
35. Alexander to Catherine Pavlovna, 14 June 1813, *Corr. Alex.*, p. 154.
36. Metternich, *Mémoires*, I, pp. 250–3.
37. *Ibid.*, I, pp. 147–54, 253–6 and II, pp. 461–3; Palmer, *op. cit.*, p. 99.
38. Gentz, quoted by Grimsted, *Foreign Ministers*, p. 217.
39. Alexander to Catherine Pavlovna, 1 August 1813, *Corr. Alex.*, p. 156.
40. Kissinger, *op. cit.*, pp. 81–2.
41. Metternich, *op. cit.*, I, pp. 165–6.
42. *Ibid.*; Palmer, *op. cit.*, p. 104; Shilder, *Alek. I*, III, pp. 166–7 and 383.
43. Chandler, *op. cit.*, pp. 903–10.
44. *Ibid.*, p. 912.
45. Waliszewski, II, pp. 201–3.
46. *Ibid.*, II, pp. 199–200.
47. Chandler, *op. cit.*, pp. 912–36.
48. Alexander to Golitsyn, 21 October 1813, N.M., *Alek. I*, I, p. 511.
49. Palmer, *op. cit.*, p. 109.
50. Kissinger, *op. cit.*, pp. 100–1.
51. Grimsted, *op. cit.*, pp. 207–8.

52. Cathcart to Castlereagh, 28 November 1813, Webster, *British Diplomacy*, p. 43.
53. Webster, *Castlereagh*, I, pp. 167–9.
54. Palmer, *op. cit.*, p. 111.
55. Alexander to La Harpe, 3 January 1814, *SIRIO*, V, pp. 42–5.
56. Metternich to Gentz, 13 January 1814, Wittichen and Salzer, *Briefe . . . Gentz*, III, pt. 1, p. 204.
57. Nesselrode to his wife, 16 January 1814, *LPN*, V, p. 152.
58. Shilder, *Alek. I*, III, p. 182.
59. Webster, *Castlereagh*, I, pp. 203 and 218; Metternich to Hudelist, 23 January 1814, *HHSA*, Inter. Korrespondenz, 77.
60. Webster, *Castlereagh*, I, pp. 204–10.
61. Fournier, *Congress von Chatillon*, pp. 93–4 and 317.
62. Webster, *Castlereagh*, I, p. 213.
63. Chandler, *op. cit.*, pp. 972–5.
64. Webster, *Castlereagh*, I, p. 215.
65. *Ibid.*, pp. 226–7.
66. Shilder, *Alek. I*, III, pp. 195 and 386.
67. *Ibid.*, III, p. 198.
68. *Ibid.*, III, pp. 200 and 387.
69. Caulaincourt, *Mémoires*, III, p. 69.
70. Shilder, *Alek. I*, III, pp. 203–4.
71. Caulaincourt, *op. cit.*, III, pp. 72–6.
72. *Ibid.*, III, pp. 87–9; Shilder, *Alek. I*, III, pp. 209–10.
73. *Ibid.*, III, pp. 210, 213; Cooper, *Talleyrand*, p. 224; N.M., *Alex. I*, I, p. 133.
74. Caulaincourt, *op. cit.*, III, p. 94.

Chapter 16: Paris and London

1. N.M., *Alex. I*, I, pp. 135–6; Alexander to Marie Feodorovna, 3 April 1814, printed in the article by Shumigorskii in *Russkaya Starina*, Vol. 157, pp. 486–8.
2. Shilder, *Alek. I*, III, pp. 213–15; Cooper, *Talleyrand*, pp. 225–8.
3. Nicolson, *Congress of Vienna*, pp. 85–6; Lefebvre, *Napoléon*, II, p. 351.
4. Webster, *British Documents*, pp. 147–8.
5. Caulaincourt, *Mémoires*, III, pp. 93–9.
6. *Ibid.*, III, pp. 141–338; Garros, *Quel Roman . . .!*, pp. 445–8.
7. Caulaincourt, *op. cit.*, III, p. 222.
8. Nicolson, *op. cit.*, p. 91.

9. Caulaincourt, *op. cit.*, III, p. 222.
10. *Ibid.*, III, pp. 226–30.
11. *Ibid.*, III, pp. 255–338.
12. Metternich, *Mémoires*, I, pp. 194–5.
13. Lefebvre, *op. cit.*, II, p. 252; Nicolson, *op. cit.*, pp. 94–6.
14. Webster, *Castlereagh*, I, pp. 263–4.
15. Bartlett, *Castlereagh*, p. 133.
16. See the letter of Alexander to Marie Feodorovna, from Paris, 15 April 1814, *Russkaya Starina* for 1914, p. 488.
17. Metternich to Hudelist, 24 May 1814, *HHSA*, Inter. Korrespondenz, 78.
18. For Alexander's magnanimity, see Almedingen, *Emperor Alexander*, pp. 151–3.
19. N.M., *Alex. I*, I, p. 137; Nicolson, *op. cit.*, p. 105.
20. Broughton, *Recollections*, I, p. 111.
21. Guedalla, *Second Empire*, pp. 43–4.
22. Knapton, *Empress Josephine*, p. 341.
23. Alexander to Josephine, 18 April 1814, quoted from Georges Maugin by Knapton, *loc. cit.*
24. *Ibid.*, p. 342.
25. *Ibid.*, p. 343.
26. *Ibid.*; Nicolson, *op. cit.*, p. 108.
27. Shilder, *Alek. I*, III, pp. 222–3.
28. Nicolson, *op. cit.*, p. 108.
29. Palmer, *Metternich*, p. 124; Webster, *Castlereagh*, I, pp. 280–1.
30. *Ibid.*, pp. 287–8; Kissinger, *World Restored*, pp. 142–4.
31. Palmer, *op. cit.*, p. 125.
32. Ziegler, *William IV*, p. 116.
33. Anderson, *Britain's Discovery of Russia*, pp. 221–2 and the anonymous pamphlets listed in the bibliography below.
34. Ziegler, *op. cit.*, pp. 114–15.
35. Colchester, *Diaries and Correspondence*, II, p. 500.
36. Dorothea Lieven Memoirs printed in *Corr. Alex.*, pp. 228–30. A translation of the same Memoirs was included in Temperley, *Unpublished Diary . . . Princess Lieven*, and is preferable to the complete translation of *Corr. Alex.* by Henry Havelock entitled *Scenes of Russian Court Life* (London, 1917).
37. Catherine Pavlovna to Alexander, 13 April 1814, *Corr. Alex.*, p. 187.
38. The same to the same, 4 April 1814, *Ibid.*, p. 180.
39. Lieven Memoirs, *Ibid.*, p. 228.

40. Catherine Pavlovna to Alexander, 4 April 1814, *Ibid.*, p. 180.
41. The same to the same, 9 May 1814, *Ibid.*, p. 189.
42. Nicolson, *op. cit.*, p. 111.
43. Anglesey, *Capel Letters*, pp. 36–7.
44. Masson, *Collected Writings of Thomas de Quincey*, III, p. 67; *Annual Register, 1814*, chronological section, p. 45; Broughton, *op. cit.*, I, p. 113.
45. Lieven Memoirs, *Corr. Alex.*, p. 234.
46. Lieven Memoirs, *Ibid.*, p. 235.
47. Webster, *Castlereagh*, I, p. 28.
48. Lieven Memoirs, *Corr. Alex.*, p. 235; Metternich to Hudelist, 13 June and 26 June 1814, *HHSA*, Int. Korrespondenz, 78.
49. Nicolson, *op. cit.*, pp. 113–14; Colchester, *op. cit.*, II, p. 501.
50. L'Estrange, *Mary Russell Mitford*, I, p. 287.
51. *The Times*, 9 June 1814; Grieg, *Farington Diary*, VII, p. 256.
52. Nicolson, *op. cit.*, p. 114.
53. Broughton, *op. cit.*, I, pp. 139–40.
54. Anonymous pamphlet, *Correct Account of the Visit . . . to . . . Oxford*, in the Bodleian Library, Oxford.
55. *Ibid.*
56. Grieg, *op. cit.*, VII, p. 258.
57. Lieven Memoirs, *Corr. Alex.*, p. 244.
58. *Annual Register, 1814*, pp. 552–67.
59. Colchester, *op. cit.*, II, p. 502.
60. Lieven Memoirs, *Corr. Alex.*, pp. 242–3.
61. Gore, *Creevey Papers*, p. 116.
62. Scott, *Quakers in Russia*, p. 43.
63. *Ibid.*, pp. 52–3.
64. W. Allen, *Life and Correspondence*, I, pp. 193–9.
65. *Ibid.*, pp. 52–3.
66. Scott, *op. cit.*, pp. 55–6.
67. Adams, p. 655; Alexander to Catherine Pavlovna, 29 June 1814, *Corr. Alex.*, pp. 191–2.
68. N.M., *Elis.*, II, p. 488.
69. Webster, *Castlereagh*, I, pp. 295–6.

Chapter 17: Panorama of Europe

1. Choisseul-Gouffier, *Historical Memoirs*, p. 188.
2. N.M., *Elis.*, II, p. 489; and Elizabeth to her mother, 20 September 1814, *Ibid.*, p. 582.

3. Shilder, *Alek. I*, III, p. 248; cf. Weil, I, no. 81, pp. 62–4.

4. Grimsted, *Foreign Ministers*, p. 210.

5. *Ibid.*, pp. 219–21.

6. N.M., *Alex. I*, I, p. 340; Edling, *Mémoires*, p. 146; *SIRIO*, III, p. 303; Grimsted, *op. cit.*, pp. 231 ff.

7. Weil, I, no. 10, pp. 8–9 (cf. *Ibid.*, no. 190, p. 153).

8. Talleyrand, *Mémoires*, II, p. 329; Seton-Watson, *Russian Empire*, pp. 149–51; Waliszewski, II, p. 270; Weil, I, p. 574.

9. Kukiel, *Czartoryski and European Unity*, pp. 119–20.

10. Waliszewski, II, p. 272; N.M., *Alex. I*, I, p. 143.

11. For contemporary accounts of the Congress, see Spiel, *Der Wiener Kongress*.

12. Weil, I, no. 108, p. 92.

13. Grimsted, *op. cit.*, p. 35; Metternich, *Mémoires*, II, p. 477.

14. See the introduction to Weil, I, and Nicolson, *op. cit.*, pp. 204–5.

15. Weil, I, no. 278, p. 224.

16. *Ibid.*, I, no. 277, p. 223.

17. *Ibid.*, I, no. 292, pp. 233–4.

18. Palmer, *Metternich*, p. 97.

19. Weil, I, no. 252, p. 205.

20. *Ibid.*, I, no. 233, p. 193.

21. *Ibid.*, I, no. 292, p. 234.

22. Webster, *Castlereagh*, I, pp. 342–47.

23. Nicolson, *op. cit.*, pp. 169–70; Palmer, *The Lands Between*, p. 24.

24. Webster, *Castlereagh*, I, pp. 347–8.

25. Grimsted, *op. cit.*, p. 211.

26. Shilder, *Alek. I*, III, pp. 534–47.

27. Weil, I, no. 457, p. 339 and no. 531, p. 384.

28. Castlereagh to Liverpool, 2 October 1814, Webster, *British Diplomacy*, p. 199.

29. Shilder, *Alek. I*, III, p. 279.

30. Palmer, *Metternich*, pp. 136–7 and sources cited, *Ibid*, pp. 357–8.

31. Weil, I, no. 598, pp. 422–3 and no. 608, pp. 427–8.

32. Webster, *Castlereagh*, I, pp. 349–50,; Kissinger, *World Restored*, pp. 161–2.

33. Weil, I, no. 661, p. 461.

34. Grimsted, *op. cit.*, p. 217.

35. Webster, *British Diplomacy*, p. 222.

36. Webster, *Castlereagh*, I, p. 347; Nicolson, *op. cit.*, p. 177.

37. Weil, I, no. 1036, p. 669; no. 1066, p. 687; and no. 1091, p. 699.

38. Webster, *Castlereagh*, I, pp. 362–75; Palmer, *Metternich*, pp. 141–2.
39. Webster, *Castlereagh*, I, p. 389.
40. Grimsted, *op. cit.*, p. 231.
41. Webster, *Castlereagh*, I, p. 495.
42. Nicolson, *op. cit.*, pp. 180–1; Palmer, *Metternich*, p. 142.
43. Maistre, *Correspondance Diplomatique*, II, pp. 40–1; Kukiel, *op. cit.*, p. 132.
44. Kissinger, *op. cit.*, pp. 167–70.
45. Grimsted, *op. cit.*, pp. 231–3; Palmer, *op. cit.*, p. 141.
46. Kukiel, *op. cit.*, p. 132; Weil, I, no. 1036, p. 669.
47. *Ibid.*, I, no. 1068, p. 687.
48. *Ibid.*, I, no. 1068, p. 687.
49. *Ibid.*, I, no. 416, pp. 317–18 and no. 417, p. 318.
50. *Ibid.*, I, no. 1006, p. 651.
51. *Ibid.*, II, no. 1319, and 1320, p. 45; no. 1380, p. 75 and no. 1409, p. 90.
52. *Ibid.*, I, no. 1104, p. 705.
53. *Ibid.*, I, no. 994, p. 647.
54. Metternich, *Mémoires*, I, pp. 315–16.
55. N.M., *Elis.*, II, p. 485.
56. Knapton, *Lady of the Holy Alliance*, pp. 140–1; Edling, *Mémoires*, pp. 217–18.
57. *Ibid.*; Ley, *Madame de Krudener et son Temps*, p. 434.
58. Knapton, *op. cit.*, p. 140.
59. *Ibid.*, p. 141.
60. Metternich, *op. cit.*, I, pp. 204–6.
61. Paléologue, *Enigmatic Czar*, p. 231.
62. Nicolson, *op. cit.*, p. 230.
63. Palmer, *op. cit.*, pp. 146–8.
64. Grimsted, *op. cit.*, p. 217, citing Stein, *Briefe*, V, p. 369.
65. Metternich, *op. cit.*, I, p. 328; Palmer, *op. cit.*, p. 145.
66. Longford, *Wellington, The Years of the Sword*, p. 389.
67. Weil, II, no. 2433, p. 585.
68. *Ibid.*, II, no. 2336, p. 539.
69. Knapton, *op. cit.*, p. 141.
70. Weil, II, no. 2460, pp. 595–6.
71. Edling, *op. cit.*, p. 231; N.M., *Alex. I*, p. 167.

Chapter 18: Holy Alliance

1. Knapton, *Lady of the Holy Alliance*, pp. 144–5; Edling, *Mémoires*, p. 232; Ley, *Madame de Krudener et son Temps*, pp. 449–51.

2. Knapton, *op. cit.*, p. 153.
3. Edling, *op. cit.*, p. 234; Knapton, *op. cit.*, pp. 154–6.
4. N.M., *Alex. I*, II, pp. 215–21.
5. Ley, *op. cit.*, p. 458.
6. Waliszewski, II, p. 358.
7. Shilder, *Alek. I*, III, p. 335.
8. Paléologue, *Enigmatic Czar*, pp. 239–40.
9. *LPN*, V, pp. 215–16; Waliszewski, II, p. 354.
10. Longford, *Wellington, Pillar of State*, p. 6.
11. Palmer, *Metternich*, p. 154.
12. Grimsted, *Foreign Ministers*, pp. 243–4.
13. Barantes, *Mémoires*, II, p. 225.
14. Shilder, *Alek. I*, III, p. 348; Cooper, *Talleyrand*, p. 286.
15. Broughton, *Recollections of a Long Life*, I, pp. 309–11, 316, 325; Metternich, *Mémoires*, II, pp. 523–5.
16. Webster, *Castlereagh*, I, p. 481; Knapton, *op. cit.*, pp. 155–6; Guedalla, *The Duke*, p. 286.
17. *Ibid.*, p. 157.
18. Webster, *Castlereagh*, I, pp. 481–2; Kissinger, *op. cit.*, p. 187.
19. Guedalla, *op. cit.*, pp. 282 and 285.
20. Shelley, *Diary*, I, p. 158.
21. Webster, *Castlereagh*, I, p. 464.
22. Knapton, *op. cit.*, p. 157.
23. *Ibid.*; Schwarz, *Die Heilige Allianz*, p. 55; Ley, *op. cit.*, pp. 491–6.
24. Empaytaz, *Notice sur Alexandre*, p. 40.
25. Schwarz, *Die Heilige Allianz*, pp. 50–2.
26. Webster, *Castlereagh*, I, pp. 55–7.
27. Webster, *British Diplomacy*, p. 381; Palmer, *op. cit.*, p. 153.
28. Longford, *Wellington, Pillar of State*, p. 31.
29. Webster, *Castlereagh*, I, p. 482.
30. Schwarz, *op. cit.*, pp. 52–7.
31. Knapton (*op. cit.*, p. 159) cites a letter from Roxane Stourdza to Capodistrias originally printed in *Russkii Arkhiv* no. 11 (1891), p. 421; but her brother, Alexander Stourdza, appears to have been more sympathetic towards the Baroness's claims (Ley, *op. cit.*, p. 498).
32. Knapton, *op. cit.*, pp. 160–5.
33. N.M., *Alex. I*, I, p. 524.
34. Clarkson, *Thomas Clarkson's Interview with the Emperor Alexander*, p. 5.
35. N.M., *Alex. I*, II, pp. 215–23; Knapton, *op. cit.*, p. 158; Ley, *op. cit.*, pp. 470 and 472.

36. Knapton, *op. cit.*, p. 158.
37. *Ibid.*, p. 155.
38. *Ibid.*, pp. 211–12 and 125; Ley, *op. cit.*, pp. 564–5 and 578–9.
39. Alexander to Catherine Pavlovna, 1 October 1815, *Corr. Alex.*, p. 202.
40. Webster, *Castlereagh*, I, pp. 483–4.
41. Alexander to Catherine Pavlovna, 1 October 1815, *Corr. Alex.*, p. 203.
42. Shilder, *Alek. I*, III, pp. 348–9.

Chapter 19: Contrasts

1. Choiseul-Gouffier, *Historical Memoirs*, pp. 206–7.
2. *Ibid.*, p. 209; N.M., *Alex. I*, I, pp. 188–90.
3. Extracts from the Polish Constitutional Charter are printed in Vernadsky, *Source Book for Russian History*, II, pp. 500–2.
4. Raeff, *Speransky*, p. 39.
5. Kukiel, *Czartoryski and European Unity*, pp. 134–5; Shilder, *Alek. I*, III, p. 356.
6. *Ibid.* III, pp. 551–2.
7. Schiemann, *Geschichte Russlands . . . Nikolaus, I*, I, pp. 112–78.
8. Choiseul-Gouffier, *op. cit.*, p. 211.
9. Elizabeth to her mother, 19 December 1815, N.M., *Elis.*, II, p. 600.
10. Shilder, *Alek. I*, III, p. 402.
11. *Ibid.*, IV, pp. 1–2 and 449.
12. *Ibid.*, IV, p. 10; Seton-Watson, *Russian Empire*, p. 154.
13. Waliszewski, II, p. 403.
14. Shaw, *Letters of Pushkin*, pp. 59 and 67.
15. See the memoirs of the Decembrist, Fonvizin, from which translated extracts are printed in Vernadsky, *Source Book*, II, pp. 522–5. See also Riha, *Readings*, p. 99.
16. Vernadsky, *loc. cit.*; Jenkins, *Arakcheev*, p. 205.
17. *Ibid.*, p. 172.
18. *Ibid.* p. 187.
19. *Ibid.*, p. 179.
20. *Ibid.*, p. 175.
21. Shilder, *Alek. I*, IV, pp. 30–2.
22. Jenkins, *op. cit.*, p. 188.
23. *Ibid.*, p. 182; Shilder, *Alek. I*, IV, p. 22.
24. Jenkins, *op. cit.*, p. 186; Pipes article, *JMH*, Vol. 22, pp. 208–9.
25. Jenkins, *op. cit.*, pp. 188–9; Vernadsky, *Source Book*, II, pp. 503–4.
26. *Ibid.*

27. *Ibid.*, II, p. 504 (quoting a decree signed by Alexander, 26 August, 1818).
28. Seton-Watson, *op. cit.*, pp. 160–1.
29. Pipes, *JMH*, Vol. 22, pp. 212–14; Lee, *Last Days of Alexander*, p. 85.
30. Fonvizin memoirs, quoted in Vernadsky, *Source Book*, II, p. 524.
31. Memoirs of F.F. Vigel, *Ibid.*, II, p. 512.
32. Pipes, *JMH*, Vol. 22, pp. 216–18; Jenkins, *op. cit.*, p. 273.
33. Raeff, *Speransky*, p. 201.
34. Elizabeth to her mother, 23 January 1816, N.M., *Elis.*, II, p. 608.
35. N.M., *Corr. Alex.*, Introduction, pp. xxv–xxvi.
36. Elizabeth to her mother, 14 June 1816, N.M., *Elis.*, II, p. 614.
37. Una Pope-Hennessey, *A Czarina's Story*, p. 11.
38. Memoir by Alexandra, *Ibid.*, p. 26.
39. Elizabeth to her mother, 30 December 1815, N.M., *Elis.*, II, p. 603.
40. The same to the same, letters of early 1816, *Ibid.*, II, pp. 606–12.
41. The same to the same, 13 October 1817, *Ibid.*, II, pp. 657–8.
42. N.M., *Alex. I*, pp. 159–84.
43. Strakhovsky, *Alexander I*, pp. 131 and 173.
44. Seton-Watson, *op. cit.*, pp. 164–71.
45. *Ibid.*, p. 166; N.M., *Alex. I*, I, pp. 178–9.
46. Scott, *Quakers in Russia*, pp. 59 and 60–1; Wheeler, *Memoirs*, p. 58.
47. Scott, *op. cit.*, p. 84.
48. The Margravine of Baden to Elizabeth, 4 May 1816, N.M., *Elis.*, II, p. 675.
49. N.M., *Alex. I* (Russian edition), I, p. 574, cited by Seton-Watson, *op. cit.*, p. 164.
50. N.M., *Corr. Alex.*, pp. 30, 39 and 59.
51. *Russkii Arkhiv*, XXVI, pp. 373–7; Paléologue, *Enigmatic Czar*, p. 267.
52. Metternich, *Mémoires*, I, p. 126; private letter of Castlereagh to Stewart, 29 November 1818, Webster, *Castlereagh*, II, p. 593.
53. N.M., *Elis.*, III, p. 10.
54. Allen, *Life*, II, pp. 13–16; Seebohm, *Memoirs of Stephen Grellet*, I, pp. 321–2.
55. Alexander to Castlereagh, 2 April 1816, F.O., 65/105/private. See on this question of disarmament, Webster, *Castlereagh*, II, pp. 97–9 and 103.
56. *Ibidem.*
57. *Ibid.*, II, p. 98.
58. *Ibid.*, II, p. 99.

59. Grimsted, *Foreign Ministers*, p. 60, and notes to p. 242.
60. *Ibid.*, pp. 226–50.
61. Webster, *Castlereagh*, II, p. 195; Palmer, *Metternich*, pp. 187 and 193.
62. Metternich, *Mémoires*, III, p. 373.
63. See the 'Aperçu' of Capodistrias in *SIRIO*, III, especially, p. 213.
64. Vernadsky, *Source Book*, II, p. 503; Grimsted, *op. cit.*, p. 243.
65. Hollingsworth article on Kunitsyn, *SEER*, Vol. 43, pp. 121–2; Palmer, *op. cit.*, p. 171.
66. Webster, *Castlereagh*, II, pp. 122–3.
67. *Ibid.*, II, p. 125.
68. *Ibid.*, II, p. 123.
69. *Ibid.*, II, p. 126.
70. Grimsted, *op. cit.*, pp. 244–5.
71. Una Pope-Hennessey, *A Czarina's Story*, p. 28; Shilder, *Alek. I*, IV, p. 108.
72. Webster, *Castlereagh*, II, pp. 148–9 and 162; Longford, *Wellington, Pillar of State*, pp. 50–1.
73. Palmer, *op. cit.*, p. 177.
74. *Ibid*, citing letter of Marie Esterhazy printed in Corti, *Metternich und die Frauen*, II, p. 82.
75. Metternich, *Mémoires*, I, p. 316.
76. See the pamphlet of Thomas Clarkson, *Interview with the Emperor Alexander*, and Webster, *Castlereagh*, II, pp. 167–72.
77. N.M., *Alex. I*, I, pp. 199–200.
78. Metternich, *op. cit.*, III, pp. 170–6.
79. N.M., *Alex. I*, I, p. 202.

Chapter 20: The Absentee Tsar

1. Alexandra Memoir in Una Pope-Hennessey, *A Czarina's Story*, p. 42.
2. *Ibid.*, p. 43; N.M., *Elis.*, III, pp. 12–13.
3. Una Pope-Hennessey, *op. cit.*, p. 43.
4. *Ibid.*, p. 44; N.M., *Elis.*, III, p. 7.
5. Ley, *Madame de Krudener*, p. 562.
6. Metternich, *Mémoires*, III, pp. 284–97.
7. Squire, 'Nicholas I . . . and Internal Security,' *SEER*, Vol. 38, p. 434.
8. Vernadsky, *Source Book for Russian History*, II, pp. 504–6, prints extracts from the constitutional project in English. A French text and

analysis is in Vernadsky's *Charte Constitutionelle* and a Russian text in Shilder, *Alek. I*, IV, pp. 499–526.

9. Seton-Watson, *Russian Empire*, p. 157.

10. Jenkins, *Arakcheev*, p. 215; see Vernadsky, *Source Book*, II, pp. 506–8 for Speransky's Siberian reforms.

11. Una Pope-Hennessey, *op. cit.*, p. 34.

12. Blum, *Lord and Peasant*, pp. 300–1; Tarlé, *Nashestvie Napoleona*, pp. 176–83.

13. Jenkins, *op. cit.*, pp. 194–5.

14. Seton-Watson, *op. cit.*, pp. 187–9.

15. Hollingsworth article on Kunitsyn, *SEER*, Vol. 43, p. 122; Seton-Watson, *op. cit.*, p. 170.

16. Shilder, *Alek. I*, IV, p. 204.

17. Elizabeth to her mother, 19 July 1820, N.M., *Elis.*, III, p. 140.

18. Paléologue, *Enigmatic Czar*, p. 262.

19. Alexandra Memoir, Una Pope-Hennessey, *op. cit.*, pp. 44–5.

20. Strakhovsky, *Emperor Alexander*, pp. 204–5.

21. Una Pope-Hennessey, *op. cit.*, p. 47.

22. Ley, *op. cit.*, p. 565.

23. *Ibid.*, pp. 563–5; N.M., *Alex. I*, II, pp. 227–8.

24. Ley, *op. cit.*, p. 568; Bertier de Sauvigny, *Une Marseillaise . . .*, p. 6.

25. Shilder, *Alek. I*, IV, pp. 176–80; Ley, *op. cit.*, p. 567.

26. Webster, *Castlereagh*, II, p. 203; Schroeder, *Metternich's Diplomacy*, p. 27.

27. Webster, *Castlereagh*, II, pp. 207–14.

28. Palmer, *op. cit.*, p. 192.

29. Schroeder, *op. cit.*, pp. 47–59; Webster, *Castlereagh*, II, pp. 278–9.

30. Schroeder, *loc. cit.*; Seton-Watson, *op. cit.*, p. 177.

31. Waliszewski, III, p. 53.

32. Elizabeth to her mother, 28 November 1820, N.M., *Elis.*, III, p. 157.

33. Metternich, *Mémoires*, III, pp. 373–4.

34. Schroeder, *op. cit.*, pp. 67–9.

35. *Ibid.*, p. 69; Webster, *Castlereagh*, II, p. 525.

36. Waliszewski, III, pp. 57–64; Jenkins, *Arakcheev*, pp. 211–13; N.M., *Alex. I*, I, pp. 233–8.

37. Elizabeth to her mother, 1 November 1820, N.M., *Elis.*, III, p. 152.

38. Waliszewski, III, p. 63; Jenkins, *op. cit.*, pp. 212–13.

39. Alexander to Arakcheev, 17 November 1820, Shilder, *Alek. I*, IV, p. 185.

40. Grimsted, *Foreign Ministers*, pp. 249–50.

41. Kissinger, *World Restored*, pp. 264–5; Webster, *Castlereagh*, II, p. 525.
42. *Ibid.*, II, p. 303.
43. Metternich, *Mémoires*, III, pp. 380 and 382–3.
44. *Ibid.*, III, pp. 425–55; Palmer, *op. cit.*, p. 197.
45. Metternich, *Mémoires*, III, p. 454.
46. Alexander to Golitsyn, letter 'commenced on 8 and finished on 15 February 1821' (? Old Style), N.M., *Alex. I*, I, pp. 521–9. Only the first two pages echo Metternich; the remaining six pages reflect deep study of the Scriptures.
47. *Ibid.*, I, p. 520; Ley, *op. cit.*, p. 572.
48. Schroeder, *op. cit.*, pp. 104–6.
49. Palmer, *op. cit.*, p. 200.
50. *Ibid.*; Kissinger, *op. cit.*, p. 278.
51. Grimsted, *op. cit.*, p. 259; Ley, *op. cit.*, p. 575.
52. Capodistrias, *Aperçu*, *SIRIO*, III, pp. 259–63.
53. Grimsted, *op. cit.*, pp. 260–1.
54. Anderson, *Eastern Question*, pp. 59–60; Kissinger, *op. cit.*, pp. 290–1.
55. Metternich, *Mémoires*, III, pp. 472 and 587; *SIRIO*, III, p. 276; Grimsted, *op. cit.*, p. 262.
56. *Ibid.*, p. 263; Paléologue, *op. cit.*, p. 281.
57. N.M., *Alex. I*, II, pp. 356–7.
58. Ley, *op. cit.*, p. 578.
59. *Ibid.*, pp. 579–83.
60. Capodistrias, *Aperçu*, *SIRIO*, III, p. 269.
61. Webster, *Castlereagh*, II, pp. 360–1.
62. Metternich, *Mémoires*, III, p. 483; Schroeder, *op. cit.*, p. 177.
63. Palmer, *op. cit.*, p. 210.
64. Metternich, *Mémoires*, III, p. 537.
65. Kissinger, *op. cit.*, pp. 303–4; Schroeder, *op. cit.*, p. 191.
66. Elizabeth to her mother, 24 July 1822, N.M., *Elis.*, III, pp. 210–13.
67. Schroeder, *op. cit.*, pp. 200–3.
68. The phrase is Gentz's; see Palmer, *op. cit.*, p. 215.
69. For the Verona Congress, see Schroeder, *op. cit.*, pp. 211–36.
70. Temperley, *Foreign Policy of Canning*, pp. 67–8.
71. Metternich, *Mémoires*, I, p. 320.
72. Scott, *Quakers in Russia*, pp. 96–7, quoting Allen, *Life*, II, p. 30.
73. Metternich, *Mémoires*, III, pp. 563–5.
74. Alexander to Anna Pavlovna, 16 November 1822, Jackman, *Romanov Relations*, p. 89.
75. Elizabeth to her mother, 11 March 1823, N.M., *Elis.*, III, p. 231.

Chapter 21: 'An Island Battered by the Waves'

1. Grimsted, *Foreign Ministers*, pp. 282–4; Palmer, *Metternich*, pp. 221–3.
2. Shaw, *Letters to Pushkin*, p. 50.
3. Almedingen, *Emperor Alexander*, p. 201; Seton-Watson, *Russian Empire*, pp. 168–9.
4. *Ibid.*, pp. 193–4.
5. Constantine to Alexander, 14 January 1822, Vernadsky, *Source Book*, II, p. 510.
6. Alexander's Secret Order concerning the Succession, 16 August 1823, *Ibid.*
7. For Nicholas's development, see Una Pope-Hennessey, *A Czarina's Story*, pp. 50–1.
8. Constantine to Anna Pavlovna, 11 March 1824, Jackman, *Romanov Relations*, p. 95.
9. N.M., *Elis.*, III, pp. 26–8.
10. Paléologue, *Enigmatic Czar*, p. 288.
11. Letters of Elizabeth to her mother, 27 January to 4 February 1824, N.M., *Elis.*, III, pp. 268–71.
12. The same to the same, 27 January 1824, *Ibid.*, III, p. 269.
13. The same to the same, 31 January 1824, *Ibid.*, III, p. 270.
14. The same to the same, 1 March 1824, *Ibid.*, III, p. 275.
15. The same letter, p. 276.
16. Elizabeth to her mother, 30 June 1824, *Ibid.*, III, p. 294.
17. The same to the same, 4 August 1824, *Ibid.*, III, pp. 300–1.
18. The same to the same, 30 August 1824, *Ibid.*, III, p. 302.
19. Jenkins, *Arakcheev*, pp. 224–6.
20. Almedingen, *op. cit.*, pp. 190–3; Seton-Watson, *op. cit.*, pp. 169–70; Shilder, *Alek. I*, IV, pp. 246–51.
21. *Ibid.*, IV, p. 248.
22. Jenkins, *op. cit.*, p. 229.
23. Ley, *Madame de Krudener*, pp. 578–9.
24. Jenkins, *op. cit.*, pp. 229–30.
25. Shilder, *Alek. I.*, IV, pp. 318–20.
26. Jenkins, *op. cit.*, p. 230.
27. Shilder, *Alek. I*, IV, pp. 320 and 336.
28. On the attitude of the Church, see Ley, *op. cit.*, p. 579.
29. Palmer, *op. cit.*, p. 223; Temperley, *Foreign Policy of Canning*, p. 330.
30. Grimsted, *op. cit.*, pp. 276–7.

31. Anna Pavlovna to Constantine, 9 November 1824, Jackman, *op. cit.*, p. 103.
32. Elizabeth to her mother, 19 November 1824, N.M., *Elis.*, III, pp. 312–14.
33. Anna Pavlovna to Mademoiselle de Sybourg, 22 November 1824, Jackman, *op. cit.*, pp. 103–4.
34. Elizabeth's letter of 19 November 1824, *loc. cit.*
35. Elizabeth to her mother, 23 November 1824, N.M., *Elis.*, III, p. 314; Lee, *Last Days of Alexander*, p. 8.
36. Shaw, *Letters of Pushkin*, p. 189.
37. Shilder, *Alek. I*, IV, p. 324.
38. Lee, *op. cit.*, p. 8.
39. *Ibid.*, p. 8. Some of Alexander's subjects are alleged to have regarded the flood as a sign of Divine anger, caused by the Tsar's refusal to help the Greek Christians; Waliszewski, III, p. 206.
40. Elizabeth to her mother, 24 November, 1824, N.M., *Elis.*, III, pp. 314–15.
41. *Ibid.*, III, pp. 29–30.
42. Ley, *op. cit.*, pp. 595–6.
43. Waliszewski, III, p. 207.
44. Anderson, *Eastern Question*, p. 63.
45. Elizabeth to her mother, 8 April, 1825, N.M., *Elis.*, III, p. 416.
46. Grimsted, *op. cit.*, p. 284; Schiemann, *Geschichte Russlands . . . Nik. I*, I, pp. 608–10.
47. Temperley, *Unpublished Diary*, pp. 85–100.
48. Temperley, *Foreign Policy of Canning*, pp. 347–8.
49. Shilder, *Alek. I*, IV, p. 349.
50. *Ibid.*, IV, p. 350; Elizabeth to her mother, 10 August 1825, N.M., *Elis.*, III, p. 432.
51. Lebzeltern to Metternich, 19 August 1825, *HHSA*, Dipl. Korrespondenz, Russland 1825 Karton 68.
52. Despatches of Lebzeltern to Metternich of 6 September, 13 September and 20 September 1825, also in HHSA, Karton 68.
53. Grimsted, *op. cit.*, pp. 284–5.

Chapter 22: Taganrog

1. Una Pope-Hennessey, *A Czarina's Story*, p. 53.
2. Shilder, *Alek. I*, IV, pp. 352–5 and 482.
3. Bariatinsky, *Le Mystère d'Alexandre I*, pp. 25–7.

4. Shilder, *Alek. I*, IV, p. 353.
5. Lebzeltern to Metternich, 6 September 1825, *HHSA*, Dipl. Korr. Russland, Karton 68.
6. Elizabeth to her mother, 5 October 1825, N.M., *Elis.*, III, p. 447; Shilder, *Alek. I*, IV, p. 358. Alexander's letters to Elizabeth during the journey southwards are printed in N.M., *Elis.*, III, pp. 534–8.
7. Elizabeth's letter to her mother of 5 October, *loc. cit.*
8. The same to the same, 8 October 1825, *Ibid.*, III, pp. 447–8.
9. The same to the same, 12 October 1825, *Ibid.*, III, p. 449.
10. The same to the same, 20 October 1825, *Ibid.*, III, p. 450.
11. 'Unpublished Details relative to the death of Emperor Alexander,' *Western Mss. Bod.*
12. Elizabeth to her mother, 21 October 1825, N.M., *Elis.*, III, p. 455.
13. 'Unpublished Details,' *Western Mss. Bod.*
14. *Ibid.*
15. Lee, *Last Days of Alexander*, pp. 25 and 27.
16. Ley, *Madame de Krudener*, p. 596; 'Unpublished Details,' *loc. cit.*
17. Ley, *op. cit.*, pp. 596–7.
18. Lee, *op. cit.*, p. 30; Shilder, *Alex. I*, IV, p. 376.
19. 'Unpublished Details,' *loc. cit.*; Lee, *op. cit.*, p. 43.
20. 'Unpublished Details,' *loc. cit.*
21. Alexander to Elizabeth, 10 November 1825, N.M., *Elis.*, III, pp. 538–9.
22. 'Unpublished Details,' *loc. cit.*
23. Bariatinsky, *op. cit.*, p. 39; Lee, *op. cit.*, p. 45.
24. Elizabeth's Journal, N.M., *Elis.*, III, p. 333.
25. Letters of Elizabeth to her mother, 20 and 21 November 1825, *Ibid.*, III, pp. 459–60.
26. Elizabeth's Journal, *Ibid.*, III, p. 335.
27. 'Unpublished Details,' *loc. cit.*
28. Lee, *op. cit.*, p. 21.
29. Elizabeth's Journal, N.M., *Elis.*, III, pp. 335–44.
30. Bariatinsky, *op. cit.*, p. 47.
31. Elizabeth's Journal, N.M., *Elis.*, III, pp. 342–4.
32. Paléologue, *Enigmatic Czar*, p. 304; Bariatinsky, *op. cit.*, p. 73; Strakhovsky, *Emperor Alexander I*, p. 226.
33. Paléologue, *op. cit.*, p. 305.
34. Elizabeth's Journal, N.M., *Elis.*, III, p. 344.
35. Elizabeth to her mother, 23 November 1825, *Ibid.*, III, p. 460.
36. The same to the same, 14 December 1825, *Ibid.*, III, pp. 466–7.
37. The same to the same, 27 November 1825, *Ibid.*, III, p. 460.

38. The same to the same, 1 December, 1825, *Ibid.*, III, p. 461; Shilder, *Alek. I*, IV, pp. 384–6 and 485.
39. See Elizabeth's letters to her mother, N.M., *Elis.*, III, pp. 461–76, and other correspondence in the same volume, pp. 630 and 641–2.
40. Shilder, *Alek. I*, IV, pp. 573–4; Bariatinsky, *op. cit.*, pp. 87–90.
41. *Ibid.*, pp. 90–1; Elizabeth to her mother, 11 December 1925, N.M., *Elis.*, III, p. 464.
42. Lee, *op. cit.*, p. 40.
43. See Elizabeth's letters to her mother of 17 and 19 December 1825, N.M., *Elis.*, III, pp. 468 and 469.
44. Lebzeltern to Metternich, 9 December 1825, *HHSA*, Dipl. Korr. Russland, 1825, Karton 68.
45. Una Pope-Hennessey, *op. cit.*, p. 55.
46. Lee, *op. cit.*, pp. 61–2.
47. Marie Feodorovna to Volkonsky, 15 December 1825, Shilder, *Alek. I*, IV, pp. 581–82.
48. *The Times*, 3 February 1826.
49. Jenkins, *Arakcheev*, pp. 252–4.
50. *Ibid.*, pp. 254–5.
51. Nicholas's account is printed in Vernadsky, *Source Book*, II, pp. 528–30.
52. Shilder, *Alek. I*, IV, pp. 436–7. A rumour that Alexander had been assassinated at Taganrog, possibly by poisoning, appeared in the London *Times* as early as 3 March 1826.
53. *Ibid.*, IV, p. 437; Bariatinsky, *op. cit.*, p. 108.
54. *Ibid.*, p. 166; Longford, *Wellington, Pillar of State*, p. 126.
55. Elizabeth to her mother, 12 March 1826, N.M., *Elis.*, III, p. 513.
56. Autopsy on Elizabeth, *Ibid.*, III, pp. 619–20.
57. Strakhovsky, *op. cit.*, pp. 237, 256 and 259; cf. Grimsted, *Foreign Ministers*, p. 333.
58. Bariatinsky, *op. cit.*, pp. 129–63; Strakhovsky, *op. cit.*, p. 258; Okun and Delianchikov article on Kusmich in *Voprosy Istorii* for 1967, no. 1, especially pp. 193–5; Krupensky, *Taina Imperatora*, pp. 41–60.
59. Bariatinsky, *op. cit.*, pp. 150 and 146–7.
60. *Ibid.*, p. 166; Strakhovsky, *op. cit.*, p. 258; Krupensky, *op. cit.*, pp. 88–9; *The Times*, 18 November 1965.
61. Strakhovsky, *op. cit.*, pp. 267, 270 and 273. For Alexander's dislike of the traditional burial place of the Tsars, see the article by Loewenson on the Bennigsen memoirs, *SEER*, Vol. 29, p. 229.

Select Bibliography

This book is based primarily on the printed material listed below. I have, however, used certain documents from the Foreign Office papers in the Public Record Office, London, and from the Metternich correspondence in the Haus-, Hof- und Staatsarchiv, Vienna. Details of this archival material will be found in the reference notes. I have also made use of back-numbers of *The Times* from 1814 onwards and of an anonymous sixteen-page manuscript in the Bodleian Library, Oxford, entitled 'Unpublished details relative to the death of Emperor Alexander' (MS, Eng. Hist. d. 263); this is, in fact, a selection of translated extracts from the private journal of 'a Russian nobleman' which originally came from the manuscript collection of Sir Robert Ker Porter, the distinguished traveller and painter of historical canvasses.

A.W.P.

Published Sources

Adams, C.F., *Memoirs of John Quincy Adams, comprising portions of his Diary*, Vol. 2 (Philadelphia, 1874).

Aleshkin, P.Y. and Golovnikov, V.K., 'Moskovskoye Narodnoye Opolchenie v Otechestvennoi Voine 1812 Goda', *Voprosy Istorii* (Moscow) no. 9, 1962, pp. 22–33.

Alexander I, Tsar, 'Pis'ma Imperatora Aleksandra I-go i drugikh osob tsarstvennogo doma k F. Ts. Lagarpu', *Sbornik Imperatorskogo Russkogo Isotricheskogo Obshchestva* (St Petersburg) Vol. 5 (1871), pp. 1–121.

Alexander I, Tsar, 'Pis'ma Imperatora Aleksandra Pavlovicha k R.S. Sturdze (Grafine Edling)', *Russkii Arkhiv* (St Petersburg) Vol. 26 (1888), pp. 373–7.

Allen, W., *Life and Correspondence*, Vols. 1 and 2 (London, 1846).

Almedingen, E.M., *Emperor Alexander I* (London, 1964).

Altshuller, R.E. and Tartakovsky, V., *Listovki Otechestvennoi Voini 1812 Goda* (Moscow, 1962).

Anderson, M.S., *Britain's Discovery of Russia, 1553–1815* (London, 1958).

—— *The Eastern Question 1774–1923* (London, 1966).

Anglesey, The Marquis of, *The Capel Letters, 1814–1817* (London, 1955).

Andolenko, S., *Histoire de l'Armée Russe* (Paris, 1967).

Annual Register for 1814 (London, 1815).

Anon., *A Key to the Recent Conduct of the Emperor of Russia* (London, 1807).

—— *The Christian Conqueror: or Moscow burnt and Paris saved* (London, 1814).

—— *The Christian Virtues of the Emperor of Russia and Others* (London, 1814).

—— *Correct Account of the Visit of HRH The Prince Regent and his Illustrious Guests to the University and City of Oxford in June 1814* (Oxford, 1814).

—— *An Important and Authentic Life of Alexander, Emperor of Russia* (London, 1814).

Bailleu, Paul (ed.), *Briefwechsel König Friedrich Wilhelm's III und der Konigin Luise mit Kaiser Alexander I* (Leipzig, 1900).

Bakounina, V., 'Dvenadtsati God', *Russkaya Starina* (St Petersburg), Vol. 47 (1885), pp. 391–410.

Bariatinsky, V., *Le Mystère d'Alexandre I^e* (Paris, 1929).

Bartlett, C.J., *Castlereagh* (London, 1966).

Beer, Adolf, *Zehn Jahre Österreichischer Politik, 1801–1810* (Leipzig, 1877).

Bertier de Sauvigny, G. de, *Metternich and His Times* (London, 1962).

—— 'L'extravagante equipée de la prophétesse Marseillaise à la cour du tsar Alexandre I', *Le Figaro Littéraire* (Paris, 10 December 1960), pp. 5–6.

Beskrovny, L.G. (ed.), *Pokhod Russkoi Armii Protiv Napoleona v 1813 Godu i Osvobozhdenie Germanii* (Moscow, 1964).

Blackwell, W.L., *The Beginnings of Russian Industrialization 1800–1860* (Princeton, 1968).

Blum, Jerome, *Lord and Peasant in Russia* (Princeton, 1961).

Bogdanovich, M.I., *Istoriya Tsarstvovanie Imperatora Alexandra I. 6 vols* (St Petersburg, 1869).

Bonnefons, André, *Un Allié de Napoléon, Frédéric Auguste, Premier Roi de Saxe, 1763–1827* (Paris, 1902).

Botzenhart, Manfred, *Metternichs Pariser Botschafterzeit* (Münster, 1967).

Brett-James, Anthony (ed.), *General Wilson's Journal, 1812–1814* (London, 1964).

Brett-James, Anthony (ed.), *1812: Eyewitness Accounts of Napoleon's Defeat in Russia* (London, 1966).

Broughton, Lord (John Cam Hobhouse), *Recollections of a Long Life.* 2 vols (London 1909–1911).

Bryant, Arthur, *The Age of Elegance 1812–1822* (London, 1950).

Capodistrias, John, 'Aperçu de ma carrière publique depuis 1798 jusqu'a 1822', *Sbornik Imperatorskogo Russkogo* Istoricheskogo Obshchestva (St Petersburg), Vol. 3 (1868), pp. 163–292.

Castellane, Boniface de., *Journal du Maréchal de Castellane*, Vol. I (Paris, 1895).

Castera, J.H., *History of Catherine II, Empress of Russia* (London, 1800).

Catherine II, Empress, *Memoirs* (London, 1955).

—— 'Pis'ma Imperatritsy Ekateriny II k Grimmu', *Sbornik Imperatorskogo Russkogo Istoricheskogo Obshchestva* (St Petersburg), Vol. 23 (1878), pp. 1–660.

Caulaincourt, Armand de, *Mémoires*, 3 vols (Paris, 1935).

Chambonas, Comte A. de la Garde, *Anecdotal Recollections of the Congress of Vienna* (London, 1902).

Chandler, D.G., *The Campaigns of Napoleon* (London, 1967).

Choiseul-Gouffier, Comtesse de, *Historical Memoirs of the Emperor Alexander I* (London, 1904).

Christian, R.F., *Tolstoy's War and Peace* (Oxford, 1962).

Clarkson, Thomas, *Thomas Clarkson's interview with the Emperor Alexander I of Russia at Aix-la-Chapelle as told by himself* (Wisbech, 1931).

Clausewitz, Karl von, *Campaign of 1812 in Russia* (London, 1843).

Colchester, Lord, *Diary and Correspondence of Charles Albert, Lord Colchester* (London, 1861).

Cooper, A. Duff, *Talleyrand* (London, 1932).

Crawley, C.W., *The Question of Greek Independence, 1821–1833* (Cambridge, 1930).

—— 'John Capodistrias and the Greeks before 1821', *Cambridge Historical Journal*, Vol. 13, No. 2 (1957), pp. 162–82.

Cross, Anthony, *Russia under Western Eyes, 1517–1825* (London, 1971).

Dashkova, Princess, *Memoirs*, 2 vols (London, 1840).

Denniée, P.P., *Itinéraire de l'Empereur Napoléon* (Paris, 1842).

Duffy, Christopher, *Borodino, Napoleon against Russia* (London, 1972).

Edling, Roxane, *Mémoires de la Comtesse Edling* (Moscow, 1888).

Empaytaz, H.L., *Notice sur Alexandre, empereur de Russie* (Geneva, 1840).

Esposito, V.F. and Elting, J.B., *Military History and Atlas of the Napoleonic Wars* (London, 1964).

Eynard, Charles, *Vie de Madame de Krudener*. 2 vols (Paris, 1849).

Fain, P., *Manuscrit de mil huit cent douze* (Paris, 1827).

Fournier, A., *Der Congress von Chatillon* (Vienna and Leipzig, 1900).

Garros, L.P., *Quel Roman que ma Vie! – Itinéraire de Napoléon Bonaparte* (Paris, 1947).

Gielgud, Adam (ed.), *Memoirs of Prince Adam Czartoryski*. 2 vols (London, 1888). [Contains material not in the French version of the *Memoirs*, edited by Mazade.]

Gleason, John H., *The Genesis of Russophobia in Great Britain* (Cambridge, Mass., 1950).

Gore, John (ed.), *The Creevey Papers* (rev. ed. London, 1963).

Grey, Ian, *Catherine the Great* (London, 1961).

Grieg, J. (ed.), *The Farington Diary*. Vol. 7 (London, 1926).

Grimsted, Patricia K., *The Foreign Ministers of Alexander I* (Berkeley, 1969).

—— 'Capodistrias and a New Order for Restoration Europe'. *Journal of Modern History* (Chicago), Vol. 40, No. 2 (1968), pp. 166–91.

Grunwald, C. de, *Alexandre I* (Paris, 1955).

—— *La Campagne de Russie*, 1812 (Paris, 1963).

Guedalla, Philip, *The Second Empire* (London, reprinted edition 1946, originally published 1922).

Gulick, Edward V., *Europe's Classical Balance of Power* (New York, 1955).

Hans, N., 'Tsar Alexander I and Jefferson: Unpublished Correspondence'. *Slavonic and East European Review* (London), Vol. 32 (December 1953), pp. 215–25.

Harris, James, Earl of Malmesbury, *Diaries and Correspondence*. Vol. 1 (London, 1844).

Herold, J. Christopher, *Mistress to an Age, Madame de Stael* (London, 1959).

—— *The Mind of Napoleon* (New York, 1961).

—— *The Age of Napoleon* (London, 1964).

Holbrand, Carsten, *The Concert of Europe* (London, 1970).

Hollingsworth, Barry, 'A.P. Kunitsyn and the Social Movement in Russia under Alexander I'. *Slavonic and East European Review* (London), Vol. 43 (January 1964), pp. 115–31.

—— 'The Napoleonic Invasion of Russia and Recent Soviet Historical Writing'. *Journal of Modern History* (Chicago), Vol. 38 (March 1966), pp. 38–52.

Jackman, S.W., *Romanov Relations* (London, 1969).

Jackson, W.F.G., *Seven Roads to Moscow* (London, 1957).

Jenkins, Michael, *Arakcheev: Grand-Vizier of the Russian Empire* (London, 1969).

Kissinger, H.A., *A World Restored* (London, 1957).

Klyuchevsky, V.O., *History of Russia*, Vol. V (New York, 1931).

Knapton, E.J., *The Lady of the Holy Alliance* (New York, 1939).

—— *Empress Josephine* (Cambridge, Mass., 1963).

Kochan, M., *Life in Russia under Catherine the Great* (London, 1969).

Kraehe, Enno E., *Metternich's German Policy, the Contest with Napoleon, 1799–1814* (Princeton, 1963).

Krupensky, P.N., *Taina Imperatora* (Paris, 1927).

Kukiel, Marion, *Czartoryski and European Unity, 1770–1861* (Princeton, 1955).

Lee, Robert, *The Last Days of Alexander and the First Days of Nicholas* (London, 1854).

Lefebvre, Georges, *Napoléon* (London, 1969).

Lempitskii, M., 'Aleksandr I v Pulavakh', *Russkaia Starina* (St Petersburg), Vol. 55 (July 1887), pp. 165–82.

L'Estrange, A.G., *Life of Mary Russel Mitford*, Vol. I (London, 1870).

Ley, Francis, *Madame de Krudener et son Temps* (Paris, 1961).

Lobanov-Rostovsky, A.A., *Russia and Europe 1789–1825* (North Carolina, 1947).

Loewenson, L., 'The Death of Paul I and the Memoirs of Count Bennigsen', *Slavonic and East European Review* (London), Vol. 29 (December 1950), pp. 212–32.

Londonderry, Lady and Hyde, H.M. (eds), *The Russian Journals of Martha and Catherine Wilmot* (London, 1934).

Longford, Elizabeth, *Wellington: The Years of the Sword* (London, 1969).

—— *Wellington, Pillar of State* (London, 1972).

Löwenstern, E. von, *Mit Graf Pahlens Reiterei gegen Napoleon* (Berlin, 1910).

Löwenstern, W. H. von, *Mémoires du General-Major Russe, Baron de Löwenstern*, 2 vols (Paris, 1903).

Lyall, R., *The Character of the Russians and a Detailed History of Moscow* (London, 1823).

Maistre, Joseph de, *Correspondance diplomatique*, 2 vols (Paris, 1860).

Manceron, Claude, *Austerlitz* (London, 1966).

Marie Feodorovna, Empress, *Correspondance de Marie Feodorovna à Md. de Nelidoff* (Paris, 1896).

Markham, Felix, *Napoleon* (London, 1963).

Masson, C.F.P., *Secret Memoirs of the Court of St Petersburg* (London, 1895).

Masson, D. (ed.), *The Collected Writings of Thomas de Quincey*, Vol. 3 (Edinburgh, 1889).

Mazade, Charles de (ed.), *Mémoires du prince Adam Czartoryski*, 2 vols

(Paris, 1887). [Contains material not in the English version of the Memoirs, edited by Gielgud.]

Mazour, Anatole, G., *The First Russian Revolution* (Berkeley, 1937).

Metternich, Richard (ed.), *Mémoires, Documents et Écrits laissés par le Prince de Metternich*, 8 vols (Paris, 1880–84).

Ministry of Foreign Affairs, USSR, *Vneshniaia Politika Rossi XIX i nachala XX veka*, Vols 1–6 (Moscow, 1960–1967).

Morley, Charles, 'Alexander I and Czartoryski, The Polish Question from 1801–1813', *Slavonic and East European Review* (London), Vol. 25 (April 1947), pp. 405–26.

Muehlenbeck, E., *Etude sur les Origines de la Sainte Alliance* (Paris, 1887).

Naeff, Werner, *Zur Geschichte der Heiligen Allianz* (Berne, 1928).

Napoleon, 1. Emperor, *Correspondance de Napoleon I*, Vols. XI–XXVII (Paris, 1863–8).

—— (ed. Cerf), *Lettres de Napoléon à Josephine* (Paris, 1928).

Narichkine, Natalie, *1812: Le Comte Rostopchine et son Temps* (St Petersburg, 1912).

Narkiewiecz, Olga A., 'Alexander I and the Senate Reform', *Slavonic and East European Review* (London), Vol. 49 (June 1969), pp. 115–36.

Nesselrode, A. de, *Lettres et Papiers du Chancelier Comte de Nesselrode*, Vols 1, 2, 3 (Paris, 1904–1907).

Nicholas Mikhailovich, Grand Duke, *Die Fürsten Dolgorukij* (Leipzig, 1902).

—— *Le Comte Paul Stroganov*, 3 vols (St Petersburg, 1905).

—— *L'Impératrice Elisabeth*, 3 vols (St Petersburg, 1908–9).

—— *Correspondance de l'Empereur Alexandre Ier avec sa Soeur la Grande Duchesse Catherine* (St Petersburg, 1910).

—— *L'Empereur Alexandre I*, 2 vols (St Petersburg, 1912).

Nichols, Irby C., Jr, 'The Eastern Question and the Vienna Conference, September 1822', *Journal of Central European Affairs* (Boulder, Colorado), Vol. 21, No. 1 (1961), pp. 53–66.

Nicolson, Harold, *The Congress of Vienna* (London, 1946).

Okun, S.B. and Delianchikov, N.N., 'Suschestvuet li "Taina Fedora Kuzmicha"?', *Voprosy Istorii* (Moscow), No. 1 (1967), pp. 191–201.

Olivier, Daria, *L'Incendie de Moscou* (Paris, 1964).

Paléologue, Maurice, *The Enigmatic Czar* (London, 1938).

Palmer, Alan, *Napoleon in Russia* (London, 1967).

—— *The Lands Between* (London, 1970).

—— *Metternich* (London, 1972).

Pares, Bernard, *A History of Russia* ('Definitive' edition, New York, 1953).

Phillips, W. Allison, 'An Imperial Idealist', *The Times* (London), 3 December 1925.

Pingaud, L., 'L'empereur Alexandre I et la grande-duchesse Catherine Pavlovna', *Revue d'histoire diplomatique* (Paris), Vol. XXV (1911), pp. 379–95

Pipes, Richard, 'The Russian Military Colonies, 1810–1831', *Journal of Modern History* (Chicago), Vol. 22 (1950), pp. 205–18.

Pope-Hennessey, Una, *A Czarina's Story* (London, 1948).

Porter, Robert Ker, *Travelling Sketches in Russia and Sweden* (London, 1809–13).

Predtechensky, A., 'Otechestvennaya Voinna 1812 Goda', *Istorichevsky Zhurnal* (Moscow), Nos. 7–8 (1941), pp. 81–101.

Putnam, P., *Seven Britons in Imperial Russia, 1698–1812* (Princeton, 1952).

Raeff, Marc, *Michael Speransky* (The Hague, 1961).

—— *Plans for Political Reform in Imperial Russia* (Englewood Cliffs, 1966).

Ragsdale, Hugh, 'The Origins of Bonaparte's Russian Policy', *Slavic Review*, Vol. 27 (March 1968), pp. 85–90.

Rambuteau, P., *Memoirs of the Count of Rambuteau* (London, 1908).

Ramm, Agatha, *Germany, 1789–1919* (London, 1967).

Remusat, Paul de, *Mémoires de la Comtesse de Rémusat* (Paris, 1893).

Richardson, William, *Anecdotes of the Russian Empire* (London, 1784).

Riha, Thomas, *Readings in Russian Civilization–The Decembrists* (Chicago, 1964).

Rolo, P.J.V., *George Canning* (London, 1965).

Rose, J. Holland, *Select Documents from the British Foreign Office Archives relating to the formation of the Third Coalition against France, 1804–1805* (London, 1904).

Savary, General, *Mémoires du duc de Rovigo*, 8 vols (Paris, 1828).

Schenk, H.G., *The Aftermath of the Napoleonic Wars* (London, 1947).

Schiemann, T., *Geschichte Russlands unter Kaiser Nikolaus I*, Vol. I (Berlin, 1904).

Schmitt, Hans A., '1812: Stein, Alexander I and the Crusade against Napoleon', *Journal of Modern History* (Chicago), Vol. 31 (December 1959), pp. 325–8.

Schroeder, P.W., *Metternich's Diplomacy at its Zenith, 1820–23* (Austin, Texas, 1962).

Schwarz, Wilhelm, *Die Heilige Allianz* (Stuttgart, 1935).

Scott, Franklin D., *Bernadotte and the Fall of Napoleon* (Cambridge, Mass., 1935).

Scott, Richenda C., *Quakers in Russia* (London, 1964).

Seebohm, B. (ed.), *Memoirs of Stephen Grellet*, 2 vols (London, 1861).

Ségur, Philip de, *History of the Expedition to Russia* (London, 1825).

Seton-Watson, Hugh, *The Russian Empire, 1807–1917* (Oxford, 1967).

Shaw, J. Thomas (ed.), *The Letters of Alexander Pushkin* (Madison, 1967).

Shilder, N.K., *Imperator Aleksandr I, ego zhizn' i Tsarstvovanie*, 4 vols (St Petersburg, 1897).

—— *Imperator Pavel I* (St Petersburg, 1901).

—— 'Nakanune Erfurtskogo nidaniia 1808 goda', *Russkaia Starina* (St Petersburg), Vol. 98 (April 1899), pp. 3–24.

Shumigorskii, E., 'Pismo imperatora Aleksandra I imperatritse Marii Feodorovne posle vziatia Parizha', *Russkiaia Starina* (St Petersburg), Vol. 157 (March 1914), pp. 483–90.

Sorel, Albert, *Lectures Historiques* (Paris, 1894).

Spiel, Hilde, *Der Wiener Kongress in Augenzeugenberichten* (Düsseldorf, 1965).

Squire, P.S., 'Nicholas I and the Problem of Internal Security in Russia in 1826', *The Slavonic and East European Review* (London), Vol. 38 (1960), pp. 431–58.

Staël, Germaine de, *Dix Années d'Exil* (Paris, 1904).

Strakhovsky, Leonid, I., *Alexander I of Russia* (London, 1949).

Strong, John W., 'Russia's Plans for an Invasion of India in 1801', *Canadian Slavonic Papers* (Toronto), Vol. 7 (1965), pp. 114–26.

Talleyrand, Périgord, C.M. de, *Correspondence Inédite du Prince de Talley-rand et du Roi Louis XVIII Pendant le Congrès de Vienne* (Paris, 1881).

Tarlé, E., *Nashestvie Napoleona na Rossiyu–1812 god* (Moscow, 1938).

Tatischev, Sergei, *Alexandre I et Napoléon d'après leur correspondance inédite, 1801–1812* (Paris, 1891).

Temperley, H.W.V., *The Foreign Policy of Canning, 1822–27* (London, 1925).

—— (ed.), *The Unpublished Diary and Political Sketches of Princess Lieven* (London, 1925).

Thompson, J.M., *Napoleon Bonaparte: His Rise and Fall* (Oxford, 1952).

—— *Napoleon's Letters* (London, 1964).

Vallotton, H., *Le Tsar Alexandre I* (Paris, 1966).

Vandal, A., *Napoléon et Alexandre I*, 3 vols (Paris, 1897).

—— (ed.), 'La Cour de Russie en 1807–1808, Notes . . . par le général Savary', *Revue d'histoire diplomatique* (Paris), Vol. 3 (March 1860), pp. 399–419.

Vernadsky, G., *La Charte Constitutionelle de l'Empire Russe de 1820* (Paris, 1833).

—— (ed.), *Source Book for Russian History*, Vol. 2 (New Haven, 1972).

Waliszewski, K., *La Russie il y a Cent Ans, Le Règne d'Alexandre*, 3 vols (Paris, 1923).

Webster, C.K., *The Congress of Vienna 1814–15* (London, 1919).

—— *British Diplomacy, 1813–15* (London, 1921).

—— *The Foreign Policy of Castlereagh*, Vol. I (London, 1931); Vol. 2 (London, 1925).

Wheeler, Daniel, *Memoirs of the Life and Gospel Labours of the Late Daniel Wheeler* (London, 1842).

Weil, M.H., *Les Dessous de Congrès de Vienne*, 2 vols (Paris, 1917).

Wilson, Sir Robert, *Narrative of Events during the Invasion of Russia* (London, 1860).

Wittichen, F.C. and Salzer, E., *Briefe von und an Friedrich von Gentz*, 3 vols (Munich, 1909–13).

Wright, Constance, *Louise, Queen of Prussia* (London, 1970).

Ullrichova, Maria, *Clemens Metternich, Wilhelmine von Sagan–Ein Briefwechsel, 1813–15* (Gräz and Cologne, 1966).

Zamoyska, P., *Arch Intriguer, a Biography of Dorothea de Lieven* (London, 1957).

Ziegler, Philip, *The Duchess of Dino* (London, 1962).

—— *King William II* (London, 1971).

Index

Abbreviation used: A for Alexander I

Äbo, A meets Bernadotte at (1812), 240–1, 248

Adams, John Quincy, American Minister in St Petersburg, 169n; diary of: on Caulaincourt, 178, 192, on A, 191, 207, 237, on confusion at Court, 196, on Pfuehl, 209, on preparations for war, 213, on 1812 campaign, 234, 246–7, 251, 252, 254

Adriatic: Russian navy in, 117, 123–4; cessions to France in, by Russia (1807), 142, and by Austria (1809), 184; ideas for action against France in, 214, 223

Aix, Congress of (1818), 358–61

Alexander, Grand Duke, and then Tsar Alexander I

childhood and youth: grandson of Empress Catherine the Great, 2, and son of Grand Duke Paul and Marie Feodorovna, 5; childhood of, 5, 7; suffers from deafness, 5, 24, 159, 218, 368; and short sight, 24, 368; his education, 8–11; learns English, 9, 16, and French, 10; his appearance, 11, 77, 218; Potemkin on, 12–13; his betrothal and marriage to Elizabeth Alexievna (Louise of Baden), 13–20; and the succession 19–21, 25–6; his friendships, 21–4, 33; his character, 24, 26, 43, 117, 178–9, 195, 210; at death of Empress Catherine, 28; recognized as Tsarevich, 32; tours western Russia, 33; suffers from his father's mental vagaries, 40; at Mikhailovsky Palace, 42; suggestion of Regency made to, 42, 44; shocked by murder of Tsar Paul, 45–6, 56; his coronation, 56–61;

and the army: with his father's military forces, 11, 21, 23, 30–1; Arakcheev as military instructor of, 23–4, 33–4, 35; appoints Arakcheev to reform army, 67–9; sets off to join army (allied with Austria against Napoleon, 1805), 90–2; and Kutuzov, 96–8; at Olmütz,

98–9; in peace parleys with Napoleon, 100–2; at battle of Austerlitz, 103, 106, 107, 108; after battle, 110–17; at war on two fronts (1806), 122; appoints Kamensky as commander-in-chief, 124; inspects garrison towns (1807), 150; promotes military colonies, 194; 346–7, 366, 384, 398; plans campaign (1811), 208–9, 213; inspects border fortresses, 210; joins army (1812), 214–15; at Volna, 216–26; in retreat, 226–32; leaves army for Moscow, 232–3, 234–6; his difficulties over appointment of commander-in-chief, 238–40 announces the news of Borodino, 245; refuses to consider peace, 247, 251; hears of French retreat, 254, 255; in Vilna (1813), 256, 257; appoints successor to Kutuzov as commander-in-chief, 259, 264, 265; satisfied with armistice, 266; asks for command of Allied forces, 271; battle of Leipzig, 273; presses for advance on Paris, 276, 277, 278–9; enters Paris (1814), 281–2; hears of Napoleon's escape (1815); puts Russian armies on war footing, 320, 321; at review on Plain of Vertus, 332–3; his attitude to Semeonovsky mutiny (1820), 373–4; prepares troops to assist Austria (1821), 376;

in internal affairs: his ideas of reform, 22–3, 35, 47–50; his Secret Committee, 50–4; some reforms initiated, 54–5; growing autocracy of, 64, 67; September Decrees for government reform (1802), 67–9; end of government by friends of, 117–20; his throne in danger? 147–51; sees Speransky's reforms as modernization of Tsardom (1808–9), 166, 168–70; consults his confidants on proposed Council of State, 172–4; his enthusiasm for reform declines, 175; dismisses Speransky (1812), 210–12; appoints Arakcheev to deal with breakdown of administration (1816), 343–4;

his attitudes to liberal ideas, 363–6; travels about Russia, 367, 384, 394, 402, 403–5; fails to live up to his reputation, 385;

in foreign affairs, 62–5, 71–2, 78–9; *see further under places and people involved;*

his religion: at church ceremonies, 206, 252, 352–3, 362, 388; turns to Bible for comfort and revelation, 253, 260, 380; has Bible translated into Russian, 352; interested in Society of Friends, 298–9, 300, 301, 335, 352, 380; his periods of mystical exaltation, 318–20, 323–4; his relations with the prophetess Julie von Krüdener, *see* Krüdener; receives monk Photius, 392, 393–4;

his personal relations and later days: and Queen Louise of Prussia, 88, 129, 157, 158, 363; his relations with his wife and with Maria Naryshkin, 73–6, 90, 120–2, 154–5, and with his sisters, 76–7; death of his baby daughter, 154, 155; and Grand Duchess Catherine's marriage, 181–2; and Napoleon's proposal for Grand Duchess Anna, 185–7; visits Grand Duchess Catherine in Tver, 193, 199, 202, 237; deaths of his daughters by Maria Naryshkin, 195, 391; death of Queen Louise, 195; falls ill, 247; rebuked by Grand Duchess Catherine (1812), 248, 249; visits his sisters, 361; death of Grand Duchess Catherine, 363; on Nicholas as future Tsar, 367–8; talks of abdicating, 368, 386; his reconciliation with Elizabeth during his illness (1824), 387–90; sees Neva floods, 395, 396; illness of Elizabeth, 397, leads to decision to spend winter at Taganrog, 398–9; prepares route for Elizabeth, 400–1; arranges to buy estate in Crimea, 403; succumbs to "Crimean fever", 405–9; death of, 409–10; rumours about death of, 412–13, 414–15; his funeral at cathedral of Peter and Paul fortress, 413; his tomb opened and found empty, 415; perhaps buried at Nevsky cathedral, 416

Alexander II, Tsar, reputed to have moved body of A from Peter and Paul fortress to Nevsky monastery, 416

Alexander Nevsky, St, 5, 245

Alexandra Feodorovna (Charlotte of Prussia), wife of Grand Duke Nicholas, 350, 362; on Arakcheev, 365; records A's intention that Nicholas should succeed him, 367–8

Alexandra Pavlovna, Grand Duchess (sister of A), 25; wife of Archduke Joseph; dies in childbirth, 76

Allen, William, of Society of Friends, 299; in Russia, 352, 354; at Verona, 382–3

Alsace and Lorraine, Prussian efforts to obtain, 329

Ambrose, Metropolitan, 206

Amiens, Treaty of (1802), between Britain and France, 70

Anglo-Russian Convention (1801), 63; Anglo-Russian Alliance (1805), 86

Anichkov Palace, St Petersburg, assigned to Grand Duchess Catherine and her husband, 181

Anna Feodorovna (of Saxe-Coburg), wife of Grand Duke Constantine, 31, 42; returns to Germany, 75; marriage annulled, 386

Anna Pavlovna, Grand Duchess (sister of A), 252; Napoleon offers to marry, 162, 185–7; married to Prince of Orange (1816), 303, 349; A visits, at Brussels, 361; sees flood at St Petersburg, 395

Ansbach; Prussian territory of, violated by Napoleon, 92, and ceded to France (1805), 112

Anstedt, Jean: envoy to Prague (1813), 269, 270; in Russian delegation at Vienna, 304

Arakcheev, Alexei, 23, 29; introduces A to military service, 23–4, 33–4, 35; dismissed by Tsar Paul, 40, 43; Paul tries to recall, 43; recalled by A to reform army, as Inspector-General of Artillery, 72–3, 111; with A at Olmütz, 98; head of commission to inquire into failure of artillery at Austerlitz, 116; A's reliance on, 147; appointed War Minister, 150; and Speransky's reforms, 166, 173–4; Chairman of Military Department, Council of State, 174; organizes military colonies, 194, 346–8, 365–6, 384; Secretary for Military Affairs to A (1812), 230, 232, 233; heads committee to appoint commander-in-chief, 239; Deputy Chairman of Committee of Ministers (1816), 344; administrative system of, 344–5; 365; in control of internal policy (1820), 272; involved in ousting of Golitsyn (1824), 391–2; puts forward Photius, 392; and murder of his mistress, 411

army, European, proposal for, 359

army, Russian: Prussian methods introduced by Tsar Paul into, 13–14, 33, 34; A summons Arakcheev to reform, 72–3, 111; levies of serfs for, 125, 132, 153, 236; slow to mobilize, 124, 355; strength of, during peace negotiations (1814), 287, 301; at A's death, declares for Constantine, 441n

artillery: Arakcheev and, 73; at Austerlitz, 108, 116; at Pultusk, 127; at Borodino, 244

Artois, Comte d', brother of Louis XVIII, 285

Auerstadt, battle of (1806), 124

Augereau, Marshal: A waltzes with widow of, 288

Austerlitz, battle of (1805), 103–10, 112, 113, 114, 115–16, 118, 361

Austria: Russia assists, against France (1790), 37–8; adheres to Anglo-Russian alliance (3rd Coalition, 1805), 87; and Poland, 89; at war with France (1805), 91; defeated, 96, 111; effect of Tilsit agreement on, 145; feeling against France in, 155, 156; Napoleon and, at Erfurt, 160, 161; challenges France and is defeated (1809), 182, 183, 184; A strengthens relations with, 201; signs commitment to France (1811), 208; concludes armistice with Russia (1813), 260; joins 4th coalition against France, 270; in Teplitz Treaties with Prussia and Russia, 272; in Quadruple Alliance, (1814), 278, (1815) 337; with Allies in advance westward, 273, 278; A and political influence of, 287, 301; Congress of Vienna and, 305, 314–15, 322; causes of friction between Russia and, 329, 398; entente between Britain and, 358; and unrest in Italy (1820–1), 371, 374, 376; see also Francis II, Metternich

Baader, Franz von, Catholic publicist, 335, 356
Baden: Napoleon and, 71; Duc d'Enghien abducted from, 81; Empress Elizabeth visits, 293, 300
Bagration, Prince: cavalry commander (1805), 99, 101, 102; at Austerlitz, 103, 104, 106, 108; feted in Moscow, 120; commands Russian rearguard (1806), 128n; Grand Duchess Catherine and, 149, 151, 249; idol of soldiery, 210; commands 2nd Army in 1812 campaign, 219, 224, 231, 238, 239; A's letter of rebuke to, 229–30; feud between Barclay de Tolly and, 229–30, 238; mortally wounded at Bordino, 244, 249
Bagration, Princess Katharina (widow of foregoing and cousin of A); A's visits to, in Vienna (1814–15), 308, 309–10, 314, 323; in Paris, 331
Bakhchisarai, A visits, 402, 404, 405
Bakounina, Ververa, on A's entry into Moscow, 234–5
Balashov, General: Minister of Police, 211; brings news of French invasion to A, 224; emissary from A to Napoleon, 225–6, 228; wants A to leave army, 232, 233
Balkans: French agents in, 80; Czartoryski favours forward policy in, 117–18; Napoleon and Russian policy in, 142–3; memorandum of Capodistrias on, 356; risings against Turkey in, 377, 378, 379, 380; A's proposals for, 394
Banbury: enthusiasm for Russians in (1814), 293
banks: failures of, in Germany and Paris (1810), 197, 198
Barante, C. de, French diplomat, on Capodistrias, 329
Barclay de Tolly, General: War Minister, 174, 194–5; commands 1st Army in 1812 campaign, 219, 225; made commander-in-chief, 226, 227, 231, 233, 237; feud between Bagration and, 229–30, 238; confirmed in command, 239, and as War Minister, 240; reappointed commander-in-chief (1813), 265, 276; in

Poland (1815), 322; opposes military colonies, 346
Bartenstein Convention, between Prussia and Russia (1807), 129, 138, 335
Basle, Allied sovereigns at (1814), 275
Bautzen, battle of (1813), 265
Bavaria: Austrian thrust into (1805), 90; thrust checked by Napoleon, 91; Napoleon concentrates forces in, 92; deserts Napoleon (1813), 273
Beauharnais, Eugene: made Viceroy of Italy (1805), 86; commands Italian corps of Grand Army (1812), 252, 260, 264; A's attentions to (1814), 288
Beauharnais, Hortense: A's attentions to (1814), 288; expelled from France (1815), 328
Benckendorff, Countess Sophia, governess to A, 8
Bennigsen, General: involved in murder of Tsar Paul (1801), 43, 44, 45; high appointments for, 56; commander-in-chief (1806), 124, 127, 128, 130, 131; at Tilsit, 135; decorated by Napoleon, 144; in 1812 campaign, 219; gives ball for A at his estate at Zakret, 223–4; considered for commander-in-chief; appointed chief-of-staff, 239
Berezina river, 254; French cross, 255
Berlin: A visits (1805), 93; Napoleon in (1806), 124; liberation of (1813), 260, 262
Bernadotte, Marshal: with Napoleon (1805), 92, 109; elected Prince Royal of Sweden, 208n; opposes French influence in Baltic, 208; meets A at Åbo, 240–1, 248; as possible commander of Allied forces, 270–1; as possible ruler for France, 276, 283, 285; halts his army in the Netherlands (1815), 282
Berri, Duc de, assassination of (1820), 370
Berthier, General, chief-of-staff to Napoleon, 133, 135
Bessarabia, ceded to Russia (1812), 231n
Bessières, Marshal, at Moscow, 250
Bialystok province, transferred from Prussia to Russia (1807), 142
Bible: A turns to, for comfort and revelation, 253, 260, 380; A persuades Holy Synod to have Russian translation of, 352
Blücher, General, Prussian commander: at battle of Dresden (1813), 264; considered for command of Allied forces, 271; in France (1814), 275, 276, 277, 278; at Oxford, 297; in 1815 campaign, 322, 327; at Russian review in Paris, 333
Borodino, battle of (1812), 244–5
Bouche, Mme, prophetess from Marseilles, 369
Bourbon dynasty: question of restoration of, 283; A's attitude to, 289, 329, 330; Mme von Krüdener foretells disappearance of, 320; Wellington and, 328; see also Louis XVIII
Boyen, General von, Prussian patriot, 259

Britain: Czartoryski and, 22; Tsar Paul at first allies Russia with, 37, and then puts an embargo on trade with, 41; Convention between Russia and (1801), 63; Treaty of Amiens between France and (1802), 70; resumes war with France (1803), 72; Russian mission to propose Grand Design to (1804), 83–5; counter-proposals by, 85–6; subsidies to Russia from, 86, 231, 268; Napoleon desires Russian alliance against 134, 136, 152–3; Russia committed to Continental System against, 140, 146; Russia breaks off relations with, 150; Russian need to trade with, 198; A uncertain about, 220; technical state of war between Russia and, ended by treaty (1812), 231; feeling in, warms to Russia (1813), 263; A gives assurance of no peace with France without consulting, 268; in 4th Coalition (1813), 270; in Quadruple Alliance, (1814) 278, (1815) 337; Louis XVIII's thanks to, 289; A's visit to, 291–301; at Vienna, 314–15, 322; entente between Austria and, 358; Cato Street conspiracy in, 370; suspects Russia of wanting naval bases in Spain, 370; sends observer to Troppau Congress, 371; deprecates interference by one State in affairs of another, 374; and Balkans, 380, 398

Bucharest Treaty, between Russia and Turkey (1812), 230–1, 235

Budberg, General Andrei: Foreign Minister, 119, 122, 167; at Tilsit, 130, 131, 138, 146; wishes to retire, 147

Bülow, General von, Prussian commander: at Waterloo, 327

Buxhöwden, General, Russian commander (1805), 98, 106, 108, 109, 110; in Finland (1808), 153

Canning, George, British Foreign Secretary, 146, 398

Canning, Stratford, British Minister in Constantinople, 231

Capel, Maria on A at Dover, 293–4

Capodistrias, John: in Russian delegation at Vienna, 304, 315, 316; and 2nd Treaty of Paris (1815), 329, 337; at Foreign Ministry: A's relations with, 355–7, 370, 380; at Aix Congress, 359, 360; Austrians distrust, 371; at Troppau Congress, 372–3, 374, 375; and Balkans, 377, 378–9

Carbonari, 369

Carlsbad Decrees, repressive measures (1819), 364, 366

Castlereagh, Viscount, British Foreign Secretary: on A, xv, 284; and war aims (1813), 267, 268; during advance into France, 275, 276, 277, 279, 282; disturbed by A's ascendancy, 284, 286, 300, 301; wants early settlement with France, 290; in Vienna, 310, 311, 312, 314; on Julie von Krüdener, 331, 332; and Holy Alliance, 334; and Quadruple Alliance, 337; A proposes disarmanent in letter to, 354–5; friendship of Metternich and, 358; proposes Aix Congress (1818), 358, 360; and Balkans, 379; and Spain, 381; suicide of, 382

casualties: at Austerlitz, 109, 111; at Borodino, 244; at Eylau, 128; of French in Russia, 255; of advancing Russians, 258

Cathcart, Lord, British Ambassador in St Petersburg, 241, 247, 267; on A and Metternich, 274

Catherine II of Russia (the Great), 2–6; reforms by, 4; and A, 6–11; and A's marriage, 13–16; visits Crimea, 12; question of successor to, 21, 24–6; last years of, 21–4; death, 27–9; burial, 30

Catherine Pavlovna, Grand Duchess (sister of A), 76–7; and Tilsit agreement, 139, 157; and Bagration, 149, 151, 249; suggested as bride for Napoleon, 162; marries George of Holstein-Oldenburg (1809), 163, 181, and settles at Tver, 181–2; dislikes Speransky, 166, 192, 212; as champion of conservatives, 170, 172; and Napoleon's proposal to her sister Anna, 186, 187; A visits at Tver, 193, 199, 202, 237; birth of son to, 197; against A as commander (1812), 221, 232, 239; birth of second son to, 237, 247, 248; reproves A, 247–8, 249; death of her husband, 261–2; at Teplitz, 264, 265; meets Metternich, 268; question of second marriage for, 292, 303, 317; in England (1814), 291–8 passim; in Vienna, 317, 323; married to William of Württemberg (1816), 348–9; A visits at Stuttgart, 361; death of (1819), 362–3

Cato Street conspiracy, London (1820), 370

Cattaro, ceded by Russia to France (1807), 142

Caucasus, Russians in, 179, 378

Caulaincourt, General Armand de: with Napoleon at Tilsit, 135; Ambassador in St Petersburg, 151, 153, 155, 157, 165, 178–9, 182, 183–4; on Grand Duchess Catherine, 162; on Queen Louise, 180; and Grand Duchess Anna as bride for Napoleon, 185–7; loses his privileged position in St Petersburg, 191, 199; recalled, 203, 205; with Napoleon at Vilna (1812), 228–9; declines to undertake mission to A from Moscow, 250; with Napoleon on journey to Paris, 255; sent to arrange armistice (1813), 266; at Prague Conference, 270; as Foreign Minister, conveys Napoleon's offer to negotiate peace (1814), 279; has alternate interviews with A and Napoleon, 284; conveys Napoleon's offer to abdicate, 284, 285, 286 censorship: by Tsar Paul, 29, 35; by Carlsbad Decrees, 364; in Russia (1819) 364, (1820) 366, (1823) 385

Chanpagny, J.-B. de, French Foreign Minister, 161, 183, 185

Charles, Archduke, 111, 183; as possible commander for Allied forces, 271; as possible husband for Grand Duchess Catherine, 292, 303, 317

Charlotte, Princess, daughter of Prince Regent, 293, 296, 303

Chatillon, peace negotiations at (1814), 277

Chaumont, Treaty of, between Austria, Britain, Prussia and Russia (1814), 278

Chernyshev, General, attached to Russian Embassy in Paris, 202, 213; reports on movements of French troops are sold to, 207

Chichagov, Admiral, 214; commanding in Moldavia, 230, 231n; advances on Minsk (1812), 254, 255

Christian, Prince of Anhalt-Zerbst, father of Catherine the Great, 2

civil service, new regulations for advancement in, (1809), 171

Clarence, Duke of (later William IV of Britain), 291; proposes to Grand Duchess Catherine, 292

Clarkson, Thomas, has interview with A, 336

Clausewitz, Col. Karl von, 209, 240

Coalitions against France: Second (1799), 38, 63, 81; Third (1805), 82, 84, 86; Prussia and Third, 82, 88–92 passim Fourth (1813), 270

Colditz, action at (1813), 264

comet of 1811, 206–7

Congress System, 337

Constantine, Grand Duke (brother of A), 3, 5, 11, 12; at death of Empress Catherine, 28; and Tsar Paul's military forces, 23, 30–1; married to Anna of Saxe-Coburg, 31, 75; allowed to join army in Italy, 38; on Tsar Paul's "war on common sense", 41; at Mikhailovsky Palace, 42; amorous vagaries of, 74, 151; at Austerlitz, 103, 109, 110; sent on mission to Berlin, 112; jealous of A, 116; at Tilsit, 130, 144; Empress Elizabeth on, 149; unpopular, 151, 367; at church ceremonies, 206, 252; pens bad advice to A, 238; in advance to Paris, 279, 280, 288; commands Polish Military Commission, Warsaw, 305, 323, 339, 341; renounces succession, 368, 386; marriage annulled; makes morganatic marriage, 386; informed of A's illness, 406; at A's death, proclaims Nicholas as Tsar, 410

Constantinople, Russian and Napoleonic dreams of, 143, 155

constitutionalism: indistinguishable from Jacobinism to Tsar Paul, 35; A's avowed faith in, 53; A's experiments with, in Poland, alarm

Metternich, 357; German states linked by marriage with A committed to projects of, 364; prospects of, in Russia, 364–5; in Italy, 369; in Spain, 370; A apologetic for sympathy with, 372

"Continental System", Napoleon's, 140, 152, 160, 189; economic ills produced by, 189, 197–8, 235; A takes Russia out of 197–9

Copenhagen, British naval action at (1801), 63

Corfu: Russians in (1804), 80–1, 87; ceded to France (1807), 142; British protectorate over (1815), 315

Council of State: Permanent, established by A, 50, 89, 172; proposals for new, 168, 169; A takes advice on new, 172–4; new, at work, 174–6, 198; disappearance of, 344

Cracow: surrendered by Austria to Russia (1809), 183; becomes Free City (1815), 315

Crimea: Empress Catherine visits, 12; A visits, 402, 403–5

Crimean fever, 406

Cruickshank, George, ridicules A, 301

Czartoryska, Princess Isabella, 339

Czartoryski, Prince Adam: confidant and mentor of A, 22–3, 24, 35, 36, 170; circle round, 33, 34; and Grand Duchess (Empress) Elizabeth, 39, 188, 316–17, 388; member of Secret Committee, 52, 53; on A's coronation, 59; and Prussia, 67; as Deputy Foreign Minister, 70, 79, 80, 81, 83, 156; growing influence of, 74, 82; and Grand Design, 83, 85–6, 87; schemes of, for restoration of Poland, 88–9, 126; with A on Austerlitz campaign (1805), 98, 107–8, 111, 116; on A, 117, 118; favours forward policy in Balkans, 117–18; resigns, 120; disapproved by aristocrats as a Pole, 167; consulted by A on Poland, 188–9, 200; in London, 291, 300; at Vienna as spokesman of Russian Poles, 304, 307; and Congress Poland, 305, 316, 341

Czartoryski, Prince Constantine, 22, 27, 305

Czartow, Galicia: annexed to Russia (1809), 184; returned to Austria (1815), 315

Czernowitz, A meets Francis II at (1823), 384

Danubian Principalities (Moldavia and Wallachia): Turkish pro-French action in, leads to war with Russia (1806), 122, 142, 152; Russian annexation of, recognized at Erfurt, 161; A offers to restore to Austria, in return for Polish lands, 201; left under Turkish rule by Treaty of Bucharest (1812), 231n; A against Capodistrias's scheme for Russian control of, 356; Ypsilanti leads revolt against Turkey in (1812), 377

Davout, Marshal: commands French 3rd Corps at Austerlitz, 101, 109; commands army in

Germany, 162, 200, 202; in 1812 campaign, 228, 229, 234; in retreat, 254

Decembrist Rising (1825), 411-12

Denmark: in League of Armed Neutrality, 63; British naval actions against (1801) 63, (1807) 146; in Tilsit settlement, 140

Diebitsch, General: commander under Wittgenstein, 259; military aide-de-camp to A, 402, 403, 404, 405, 409

Dimsdale, Dr Thomas, inoculates A against smallpox, 298

disarmament, A's proposals for, 354-5, 359

Docturov, General, Russian commander, 252

Dolgoruky, Prince Peter: leads opposition to Czartoryski, 89-90; as envoy to Berlin (1805), 91, 93; with A at Olmütz, 98, 99; as envoy to Napoleon, 102; and battle of Austerlitz, 104, 105, 106; sent to Berlin again, 112, 116

Dorpat, University of, 68

Dover: A visits, 293-4, 300

Dresden: Napoleon in (1812), 221; liberated (1813), 262; Napoleon returns to, 265, 269; battle of, 271, 272

Drissa, on R. Dvina: defensive encampment built at, 209, 219; A at 229, 230

Duroc, General: emissary from Napoleon to Bennigsen, 133, 134; at Tilsit, 135

dynastic principle: Napoleon and, 82; and throne of France, 276, 283

education: project for system of, 54; Ministry of, 68; need for reform of, 170; Golitsyn as Minister for (1817), 351

Elba: as place of exile for Napoleon, 286; Napoleon escapes from, 320

Elena of Württemberg, married to Grand Duke Michael, 387-8, 389; in Russian social history, 387n; and death of A's daughter, 390, 391

Elizabeth Alexievna (Louise of Baden), Grand Duchess and then Empress (wife of A), 16-21; and death of Empress Catherine, 31-2; birth and death of daughter of, 39; and Czartoryski, 39, 188, 316-17, 388; and murder of Tsar Paul, 45-6; her family visit Russia, 49n; at coronation, 58-61; and Prussia, 67; relations between A and, 73-6, 90, 120-2, 154-5, 387-8; and Grand Duchess Catherine, 77; appearance and dress, 77; after Austerlitz, 112, 113, 115; birth and death of second daughter ('Lisinka'), 122, 154-5; after Tilsit, 148-9; comments on reforms, 174; and Queen Louise, 179; and marriage of Grand Duchess Catherine, 181; takes holiday by sea (1810), 196-7; at church ceremonies, 206, 252; on departure of A for war, 215; during 1812 campaign, 238, 247, 253; war charities of, 238; Mme de Stael on, 243; visits her

mother in Baden (1814), 293, 300; in Vienna for Congress, 303, 317; interested in Julie von Krüdener, 319-20; in Munich with her sister, 323; in St Petersburg with A, 342, 350; at Moscow, 350-1; at Karlsruhe (1818), 361; and death of Grand Duchess Catherine, 363; on A's travels, 367, 381, and difficulties caused by his absence, 371-2; and Semeonovsky mutiny, 373; attends A in illness, 388-90; and death of A's daughter by Maria Naryshkin, 391; illness of, 397; recommended to go to Taganrog for winter, 398-8; travels after A, 401; at Taganrog, 402; during A's illness, 405, 406, 407, 408; and death, 409; remains in Taganrog until spring, 413-14; death of, 414

Enghien, Duc d', kidnapping and execution of (1804), 81, 101

Erfurt: Napoleon and A meet at (1808), 156-61; Treaty of, 161-2; Napoleon offers principality of, to Duke Peter of Oldenburg, 199n

Esterhazy, Marie, daughter of Metternich, 359

Eylau, battle of (1807), 128

Fain, Baron, secretary to Napoleon, 222

Ferdinand VII of Spain, 370

finance: Speransky and, 166, 168-9; decrees on, 174-5

Finland: Russia conquers, 152, 153-4; annexation of, recognized at Erfurt, 161, and by Peace of Friedrichsham, 208n; Norway offered to Sweden as compensation for loss of, 240, 315; A visits (1819), 367

Fontainebleau: Decrees of, on blockade against British goods (1810), 198; Treaty of (1814), 286

Fouché, Joseph, in French government (1815), 330

Fox, Charles James, 83, 84

France: treaty between Russia and (1801), 64, 65; Treaty of Amiens between Britain and (1802), 70; A breaks off relations with (1804), 81; Austria at war with (1805), 91, defeated by, 96, 111; treaty between Russia and, not ratified (1806), 123; treaties between Russia and (1807), 143; secret treaty between Russia and (1808), 161-2; Austria makes preventive war against (1809) 182, 183, 184; Rhine as "natural frontier" of, 274; campaign in (1814), 275-9; question of future government of, 282-6; generous peace settlement with (1814), 287, 290; position of, at Vienna, 310, 312, 314-15, 322; defeated at Waterloo (1815), 327, 349; peace settlement with, 337; at Congress of Aix, 358; end of army occupation, 359n; suggested intervention in Spain by, 376, is authorized, 382; see also Napoleon

Francis II, Emperor of Austria (Holy Roman Emperor to 1806), 71; in 1805 campaign, 90, 100; and battle of Austerlitz, 103, 106, 107, 110, 111; A confides anti-French scheme to (1811), 201; in 1813–14 campaign, 270, 274, 275, 279, 282; leaves Paris after peace treaty, 290; and Congress of Vienna, 306; visits Hungary with A and Frederick William, 312, 313; in 1815 campaign, 324, 327; and Holy Alliance, 333–4, 335; and Balkans, 379; meets A at Czernowitz, 384

Frankfurt entry of Allies into (1813), 274

Frederick II of Prussia (the Great), 6; A and Frederick William at tomb of, 94

Frederick Augustus of Saxony: comes down on Napoleon's side, 265; Talleyrand defends, 312; and Vienna settlement, 316

Frederick William III of Prussia: A visits in Memel (1801), 65–7; and 3rd Coalition, 88, 89, 90, 91; allows Russian troops to cross his territory, 92; meets A in Berlin (1805), 93–4; after Austerlitz, 112, 123; Napoleon sees correspondence between A and, 125; A visits in Memel (1807), 129–30; in background at Tilsit, 135, 137, 138; A reduces Napoleon's demands on, 141, 144; A visits in Königsberg (1808), 157; entertained in St Petersburg (1810), 179–80; A confides anti-French scheme to (1811), 201; meets Napoleon at Dresden (1812), 221; A offers alliance to (1813), 259; A joins at Breslau, 261; in 1813–14 campaign, 265, 272, 275, 279, 280; in Paris, 283, 286; in Britain, 293, 297; enters Vienna with A, 306; visits Hungary with Francis II and A, 312, 313; instructs Hardenberg not to negotiate on Poland and Saxony, 313; leaves Vienna, 324; in 1815 campaign, 327; and Holy Alliance, 333, 335; A entertains (1818), 359; abandons vestiges of liberalism, 364; at Troppau Congress, 372

Frederika, Princess of Baden (sister of Empress Elizabeth), 14, 17

Friedland, battle of (1807), 131, 132, 265

Friends, Society of: A and, 298–9, 300, 301, 335, 380; A asks for farming specialists from, 352

Galicia: A expects Austria to cede, 88; A plans to incorporate in Poland, 305, 311; retained by Austria (1815), 315

Gatchina: Grand Duke Paul's estate at, 8, 11, 20, 21, 23, 27, 28, 34, 37

Gentz, Friedrich von: secretary to Congress of Vienna, 310; on A at Aix, 360

George III of Britain: mental illness of, 40, 41, 42; letter to A from, 63

George, Prince of Holstein-Oldenburg, 199; marries Grand Duchess Catherine, 163;

Governor-General of Tver and other provinces, 181, 212; advice to A from, 239, 248; dies of fever (1812), 261

George, Prince of Wales (later George IV): Novosiltsov and, 84; A writes to, 231; ill feeling between A and (1813), 289n, 294–5, 298, 300; entertains A on royal yacht, 299–300; A exchanges letters with (1815), 332

Germany: France, and Russian interest in states of, 64, 65, 66, 71; proposals for confederation of, 84, 130; A and Napoleon discuss, 140–1; Napoleon incorporates coasts of, into France (1810), 199, 200; collapse of Napoleon's hold on (1813), 260; question of future of, 267; Teplitz Treaties and, 272; confederation of, agreed on, (at Chaumont) 278, (at Vienna) 317, 321, 324; Jewish communities in, 321, 360n; A sympathizes with smaller states in, 357

Goethe, J. W. von, A meets, 95

Gogol. N. V., The Government Inspector by, 345

Golitsyn, Prince Alexei: army commander, 183; in suite of Empress Elixabeth, 197n; old friend of A, 211, 253, 335; "devotional secretary" to A, 351–2, 363, 369, 375; Minister of Spiritual Affairs and Education (1817), 351; shares A's interest in Society of Friends, 253; blames A for his relations with Maria Naryshkin 353; as messenger between A and Julie von Krüdener, 379; presses A for declaration on succession, 386; impressed by monk Photius, 392; enemies force resignation of, 391–2, 393–4

Golitsyn, Princess Anna: A visits, in Crimea, 403

Golovina, Countess Varvara, 20

government: reform of administrative system of (1802), 54, 67–9

grain exports, 198, 378

Grand Design of A and Czartoryski (1804), 82–7

Greeks: Russia and fate of, 304; rebel against Turkey (1821), 377; A's dilemma over, 378–80; deputation of not allowed to meet A at Verona, 382; Ibrahim Pasha leads army against, 397

Gregorius, Patriarch, executed by Turks (1821), 378

Grellet, Stephen, of Society of Friends, 299; in Russia, 352, 354

Grey, Lord, on A, 298

Grimm, Melchior, friend of Rousseau, 6, 8, 9; Empress Catherine's letters to, 7, 12, 14, 15, 16, 25

Grudzinska, Joanna, morganatic wife of Grand Duke Constantine, 386

Guards regiments, 1; palace revolutions staged by, 3, 36, 150; and murder of Tsar Paul, 43; at coronation of A, 58; at Austerlitz, 109; mutiny of Semeonovsky Regiment of, 373

Hager, Baron, Austrian chief of police, 307; *for reports of spies to, see* spies

Hamburg: occupied by Russians (1813), 260; to be reconstituted as Free City, 269

Hanover: in military plans (1805), 87, 88; proposed cession to Prussia of, 94, 112, 123

Hardenberg, Prince Karl August von: Prussian representative at Teplitz, 272; wants European settlement (1814), 290; in Vienna, 310, 311, 312; at Troppau Congress, 372

Harrowby, Lord, British Foreign Secretary (1804), 84

Haugwitz, Count, Prussian envoy to Napoleon after Austerlitz, 111, 112

Heidelberg, A at (1815), 327

Heilbronn: A at (1815), 324; meets Julie von Krüdener at, 325-7

Helen Pavlovna, Grand Duchess (sister of A), wife of Prince of Mecklenburg-Schwerin, 65

Herder, J. G. von, A meets, 95

Hermitage, St Petersburg: A gives New Year ball at, 178; removal to safety of art treasures of (1812), 245, 247; collection at, includes gifts to A from Napoleon, 288

Hessler, Pauline, nurse to A, 7

Hobhouse, John Cam, on A, 288, 296

Hohenlinden, battle of (1800), 63

Holy Alliance, Treaty of (1815), 333-5, 336n; read in Russian churches, 342; A's intentions in, 354, 355; conspiracies against doctrines of, 369

Hungary, visit of Allied sovereigns to (1814), 312, 313

Ibrahim Pasha, commands army against Greeks (1825), 397

India, Franco-Russian invasion of: preliminaries for, ordered by Tsar Paul (1801), 41; proposed by Napoleon (1808), 152-3

Ionian Islands: Russia claims protectorate over, 81; ceded to France (1807), 142; become British protectorate, 315

Italy: Russian victories over France in (1799), 38; Napoleon conquers northern, 63, and crowns himself King of (1805), 86; plans for future of (at Chaumont), 278, (at Vienna) 315; unrest in (1820-1), 369, 371; A offers troops to suppress unrest, 371, 372; Austrian army to be sent to Naples, 374, 376

Jefferson, President, on A, xv

Jena, battle of (1806), 124; Napoleon and A visit field of, 159

Jerome Bonaparte, as King of Westphalia, 140, 141

Jersey, Countess of, partners A at balls, 296, 297

Jesuits, establish school in St Petersburg, 171

Jewish communities in Germany, civil rights of, 321, 360n

Joseph, Archduke, Palatine of Hungary, 313; death of wife of (A's sister Alexandra), 76

Josephine, wife of Napoleon: Napoleon's letters to, 137, 159, 160; divorce of, 162-3; 187; A's friendship with, 288-9, 328; death of, 289

Jung-Stilling, J. H., A meets, 335

Kalisch Treaty, between Prussia and Russia (1812), 261, 267

Kamensky, Marshal: nominal commander-in-in-chief (1806), 124, 127

Kamensky, P. General: takes Silistria (1810), 194

Kammionyi Island, St Petersburg: A's villa on, 121, 155, 169, 237, 247, 400; Maria Naryshkin's villa on, 121; Caulaincourt's villa on, 178, 185

Karaite Jewish community, near Sebastopol: A visits, 404-5

Karamzin, Nikolai: rebuked for translating Cicero, 35; and educational reform, 170; pleads for strong autocratic government, 212

Karazin, Vassili, and A's accession, 49-50

Kazan, university of, 68

Kazan Cathedral, St Petersburg, 206, 246; silence of crowd at (Sept. 1812), 216; rejoicing of crowd at (Oct. 1812), 252

Kharkov, university of, 50n, 68

Knights of St John, Malta: Tsar Paul as champion of, against French, 37, 37n-38n, 71

Kochubey, Count Victor, diplomat: and A, 23, 24; member of Secret Committee, 52, 53, 55; in charge of foreign affairs, 64, 65; with A at Memel, 65, 66, 67; Minister of the Interior, 69, 120, 147, 165; Speransky as deputy for, 166; on educational reform, 170; consulted on Council of State, 172; complains of Ministry of Police, 364

Königsberg: A meets Frederick William at (1808), 157; French evacuate (1812), 259

Kosciuszko, Tadeusz, Polish leader, 21, 22; A meets, 287

Koshelev, Rodion, Grand Master of Court, 253, 335, 369

Kotzebue, August, German dramatist, assassinated (1819), 363-4

Krasnoe Selo, Empress Elizabeth on domination of army at, 77

Kremlin, Moscow: Empress Catherine in residence at, 32; A at, 58, 235; Napoleon rides into (1812), 246; A's body at (1825), 413

Kronstadt dockyard, 396

Krüdener, Baroness Julie von, evangelical prophetess, 318; A hears of, 319, 320, 323, 324; A meets (1815), 325-7, 331-2; and Holy Alliance, 334-5; A loses faith in, 336-7, 351; A meets again (1819), 363, 369, 379, and sends messages to, 375; asks in vain for interview with A (1824), 393; retires to Crimea, 394; death of, 397; daughter and son-in-law of, in Crimea, 403

Kurakin, Prince: at Tilsit, 131, 138, 139, 143, 205; Ambassador in Vienna, 147; Speransky as secretary to, 165; Ambassador in Paris, 202, 204–5, 207; transmits to Napoleon A's proposals for a settlement (1812), 213, 214

Kusmich, Fyodor, Siberian *starets* (holy man), 415

Kutuzov, Mikhail, Prince and Marshal: in Paul's reign, 44; commands Russian advance-guard (1805), 90, 96; character and earlier career, 96, 97, 98; with A at Olmütz, 97–8; at Austerlitz, 103–10; recuperating in Kiev, 120; on Turkish Front (1811–12), 208, 223–4, 230; appointed commander against Napoleon (1812), 239–40, 242; at Borodino, 243–4; abandons Moscow, 245, 246; hostility of A towards, 248, 251, 255, 258; counter-offensive in 1812, 251–5; reluctant to advance into Germany, 255, 258; receives A at Vilna (Dec., 1812), 257–8; and 1813 Campaign, 259, 263–4, 267; death, 264.

La Harpe, Frederick Caesar: tutor to A, 8, 9, 10, 11, 17, 20, 366; A's letters to, 34–5, 275, 304; A invites to Russia, 50, 52; in Vienna, 311

Lafayette, Marquis de, A meets, 287

Laibach, meeting of sovereigns at (1821), 374, 375

Lamb, Lady Caroline: in Paris, 331; *Glenarvon* by, 381

Land Cadet Corps College, 171

landowning nobility: and Czartoryski, 70, 119; and Speransky's reforms, 171, 172, 175; and A's peace policies, 304–5

Langeron, Comte de, Russian commander, 98; at battle of Austerlitz, 103, 104

Lannes, Marshal, French commander, 156, 158

Lanskoy, Count Vassili, Russian Senator: made chairman of provisional Supreme Council for Poland, 305; objects to Poles having army, 341

Lauriston, Marquis de: French Ambassador in St Petersburg, 203, 204, 205, 207, 213, 214; sent to A to ask for peace (1812), 250

laws of Russia, codification of, 54, 168, 169, 175

League of Armed Neutrality (1801), 63

Lebzeltern, Ludwig von: Austrian envoy to St Petersburg, 201; in Vilna, 219; in Kalisch, 262; Ambassador in St Petersburg, 357–8, 399

Lee, Dr Robert, physician to Vorontsov, 403, 406, 409

Leipzig, battle of (1813), 89, 273

Liechtenstein, Prince Johann von: at Olmütz

(1805), 99; Austrian commander at Austerlitz, 106, 108; sent to Napoleon to seek peace, 111

Lieven, Dorothea: on death of Tsar Paul, 46; on Grand Duchess Catherine, 292–3; on A in London, 294; in Russia (1825), 398

Lieven, Paul, aide-de-camp to A at Tilsit, 135; ambassador in London, 294, 299

Lithuania, A considers proclaiming Grand Duchy of, 216

Liverpool, Lord: British Foreign Secretary (as Lord Hawkesbury), 63, 72; Prime Minister (1812–27), 292

Lobanov-Rotovsky, Prince Dmitri: as peace emissary to Napoleon (1807), 133, 134; at Tilsit, 135

Loewenstern, General, Prussian in Russian army, 232

London, banquet to Allied sovereigns given by City of, 297

Londonderry, Lady, at Verona, 382, 383

Lopukhin, Prince, consulted on Council of State, 173

Louis XVIII of France: called to throne (1814), 283; A and (1814), 289–90, 295; reaches Paris ahead of A (1815), 328; calls on A, 328–9; and Congress of Aix, 360, 361

Louise, Princess of Baden, 14, 15; takes name Elizabeth on marriage to A, 16; *see further under* Elizabeth Alexievna

Louise, Queen, wife of Frederick William III of Prussia, 65, 66, 67; A and 88, 129, 157, 158, 363; Napoleon and private correspondence of, 125; summoned to Tilsit, 138, 141, 144; in St Petersburg, 179–80, 180–1; meets Julie von Krüdener, 326; death of, 195

Lübeck, reconstituted as Free City, 269

Lützen, battle of (1813), 264

Macdonald, Marshal, and Napoleon's abdication, 285, 286

Maevsky, General, assistant to Arakcheev, 345

Magnitsky, M. L., publicist, involved in ousting of Golitsyn, 391–2, 393

Mahmud II, Sultan of Turkey, 378

Maistre, Joseph de, Sardinian Minister in St Petersburg, 150, 154, 171; on Speransky, 166; on A's return to St Petersburg, 342

Mallia, Joseph, agent of Speransky in Vienna, 191n

Maloyaroslavets, battle of (1812), 252

Malta: Tsar Paul and Knights of, 37, 37n–38n, 71; A and British occupation of, 71–2, 86, 87

Marat (brother of Jean Paul Marat), tutor in Saltykov family, 10

Marengo, battle of (1800), 63

Maret, H. B., French Foreign Minister, 205

Marie Feodorovna of Württemberg, Grand Duchess and then Empress (wife of Paul, mother of A), 5, 10, 12; and A's marriage, 15–16, 39; birth of children to, 20, 37; as Empress, 31, 32; fears mutiny of Guards, 36; distrusts Poles, 39, 85; at death of Tsar Paul, 46; her circle at Court, 55; her influence on A, 64; approves A's friendship with Frederick William, 67; takes precedence of Empress Elizabeth, 74–5, 151, 197; after Austerlitz, 113, 116; in internal affairs, 119, 120, 121, 149, 151, 170; and foreign affairs, 129, 139, 140, 147, 157, 180; Empress Elizabeth on, 148–9, 350, 381; and Grand Duchess Catherine, 162, 249; and proposed marriage of Grand Duchess Anna to Napoleon, 185, 186–7; at church ceremonies, 206, 252; gives banquet on A's return (1814), 302; and marriages of her daughters, 303, 349; visits her daughters, 362, and death of Grand Duchess Catherine, 362, 363; and state ceremonies in absence of A, 372; and Grand Duke Michael's wife, 387; informed of A's illness, 406; sees A's body, 413

Marie Pavlovna, Grand Duchess (sister of A), 44; married to Crown Prince of Saxe-Weimar, 95, 159; at Opotschna, 268; at Vienna, 323; A visits at Weimar, 361

Marie Louise, Archduchess of Austria: married to Napoleon, 188, 191; Metternich's part in marriage of, 268; future of (1814), 286; in Vienna, 317

maritime law, proposal for revised code of, 84

Marlborough, Duke of, entertains A at Blenheim, 297

Marmont, Marshal, French commander: corps of, goes over to Allies, 285; as envoy with Napoleon's offer to abdicate, 284, 285, 286

Masson, Frederic, tutor to A, 5, 9, 10; on Tsar Paul, 29

Mediterranean: French recognize Russian interest in, 64; A and French in, 71–2, 79; Russia in, 116, 142

Memel, A meets Frederick William at (1802), 65–7, (1807), 129

merchants: effects of Continental System on, 140, 148, 198; contributions to war expenses from (1812), 235–6

Metternich, Prince Clement von: on A, xv; as Austrian Ambassador in Berlin, 93; and Franco-Russian alliance, 145; as Ambassador in Paris, 204, 205; as Austrian Foreign Minister, 191n, 201; private plan of A and, to limit Russo-Austrian hostilities, 220; tries to mediate (1813), 260, 265; perplexed by A's evasiveness, 267; meets A, 268–9, and Napoleon, 269; at Prague Conference, 270; threatens withdrawal of Austria from Allies if A commands, 271; proposes offering generous terms to Napoleon, 274; has interview with A on Poland, 321–3; reports escape of Napo-

leon to A, 320; on Paris society (1815), 330; and Holy Alliance, 334, 336n; distrusts Capodistrias, 356; alarmed by A's Polish policy, 357; and Congress of Aix, 358, 359, 360; entertains A in Vienna, 361; his fear of Jacobin contagion, 364, 366; and Troppau Congress, 370–1, 372, 373, 374–5; profession of political faith by, 375; and Laibach Conference, 376; and Balkans, 377, 379, 380; at Verona Conference, 381, 382, 383; eager to avoid action in foreign affairs, 384–5

Meuse, free navigation on, 321

Michael, Grand Duke (brother of A): in Paris, 289; married to Elena of Württemberg, 387, 389; A dines with, 400; at A's death, 411

Michaud, General, aide-de-camp to Kutuzov, 246

Mikhailovsky Palace, St Petersburg, 37; built by Tsar Paul, 41–2; Paul murdered in, 44–5; Paul lies in state in, 47; "grace and favour" apartments in, 352

military colonies: first (1810), 194; large-scale (1816 onwards), 346–8, 384, 398; rising of soldiers and peasants of (Chuguev), 365–6

Miloradovich, General Mikhail, Russian commander, 99; at Austerlitz, 107, 108, 110; in 1812 campaign, 264; and Decembrist insurgents, 412

Ministers, Committee of, 68–9, 172; administration by, during A's absence, 342–3

Minsk, falls to Davout (1812), 229, 234

Mitford, Mary Russell, on A, 295–6

Moira, Lord and Novosiltsov, 84

Monferrand, R. de, designer of column in memory of A, 416–17

Morkov, Count Arkady, Russian Ambassador in Paris, 79–80

Moscow: coronations at Uspensky Cathedral in, 3, 32, 56–61; A's visits to, 58, 182, 185, 232–3, 234–5; French enter (1812), 246; burning of, 247; Russians retake, 251, 252; A and Elizabeth in residence at (winter 1817), 350–1; see also Kremlin

Mulgrave, Lord, British Foreign Secretary, 84, 85, 88

Murat, Marshal, French commander, 226; at Moscow, 250, 251

Muraviev, M. N., tutor to A, 9

Muraviev-Apostol, Catherine, maid-of-honour to Grand Duchess Catherine, 193

Naples: proposal for invasion of, 87; unrest in, 374, 376

Napoleon I: on A, xv; Tsar Paul and, 41; political methods of, appeal to A, 57, 63; and German princes, 66, 71; suggests mediation by A, but rejects his proposals (1803), 79; insults Russian Ambassador (Morkov), 79–80;

A is enraged by his execution of the Duc d'Enghien, and refuses to acknowledge him as Emperor, 81–2, 101; in abortive peace parleys (1805), 100–2; at battle of Austerlitz, 103, 106, 107, 108, 109; aims at alliance against Russia (1806), 122; creates Confederation of the Rhine, 123; defeats Prussia (1806), 124–5; condemned by Orthodox Church, 126–7, 138; on Eylau battlefield, 128; holds peace talks with A at Tilsit (1807), 133, 134–9, and makes settlement and alliance, 139–44; Empress Elizabeth on, 148, 243; proposes Russo-French advance into Asia (1808), 152–3; his proposal to meet A, 153, is postponed, 155, and takes place at Erfurt, 156–63, 164; Grand Duchess Catherine suggested as bride for, 162; sends Caulaincourt as Ambassador to St Petersburg, 177; offers marriage to Grand Duchess Anna, 185–7; marries Marie Louise of Austria, 188, 191; troubled by effects of Continental System, 197, 198; writes to A in pained surprise at war preparations (1811), 202; recalls Caulaincourt, 203; A on, 204; rebukes Russian Ambassador (Kurakin), 204–5; prepares for war on Russia, 205–6; will fight "in chivalrous spirit", 213–14; in 1812 campaign, exchanges letters with A, 221–2, 225–6, 228; crosses Niemen, 224; enters Vilna, 228; on Borodino, 244; in Moscow, 246; disclaims responsibility for burning Moscow, 247; plans to use Grand Duchess Catherine against A, 248; seeks peace, 250, 251; nearly captured, 254; leaves front for Paris: calls up new troops, 263; takes initiative again, 264; sends to A to arrange armistice, 266; has interview with Metternich, 269; at battle of Leipzig, 273; victories of, in campaign in France, 277; draws invaders away from Paris, 278–9; deposed by Senate, 283; question of Regency for son of, 283; A wishes to be generous to, 284; offers to abdicate in favour of Regency for his son, 284–5; abdicates, 286; social effects of reforms of, in occupied countries, 304; escapes from Elba, 320; reveals secret alliance against Prussia and Russia to A, 322; restoration of art treasures filched by, 331, 337n

Napoleon III: as a child meets A, 288

Narbonne, Count Louis de: envoy from Napoleon to A (1812), 221–2; and Mme de Staël, 242n

Naryshkin, Prince Alexander, in suite of Empress Elizabeth, 197n

Naryshkin, Maria, mistress of A, 60, 61, 74–5, 90; birth and death of daughter of, 76; renewed connection of A with (1806), 120, 121, (1808), 154; death of second daughter of (Zinaida), 195; in Vienna, 308; surviving

daughter of (Sophia), 353, dies (1824), 390–1; A breaks with, 353–4

Naryshkin family, Empress Elizabeth on, 350

navy, Russian: in Adriatic (1806), 117, 123, 304; Sultan refuses passage of Straits to, 123

Nelidova, Catherine, mistress of Tsar Paul, 31–2, 41

Nesselrode, Karl von, 261; commercial envoy to Paris, as agent of Speransky, 190, 198; warnings about war perparations from, 207; returns to St Petersburg, 211–12; as secretary to A at Vilna, 219–20, and Åbo, 240; in negotiations with Napoleon, 266, 267, 269; and Teplitz Treaties, 272; and terms for Napoleon, 274, 276; receives messages from Talleyrand, 278, 280; in Paris (1814), 283; in London, 291; State Secretary for Foreign Affairs, 304, 355, 358, 399; at Vienna Congress, 307, 310; out of sympathy with A on Polish question, 311, 314; in Paris (1815), 329, 330, 337; at Troppau Congress, 373, 375; A ceases to rely on, 380; favours passive policy in Balkans, 394–5

Netherlands, plans for future of, (at Chaumont) 278, (at Vienna) 315, 321

Neuchâtel, proposed cession to France of, 112

Neva river: Epiphany blessing of waters of, 362, 388; flooding by, 395–6

Nevsky Monastery: Tsar Peter III first buried at, 30, 416; Suvorov buried at, 39; A's baby daughters buried at, 155; theological seminary at, 165; A visits (1825), 400–1; A perhaps buried at, 416

Ney, Marshal, French commander, 130, 254, 277; as envoy with Napoleon's offer to abdicate, 284, 285, 286; A waltzes with wife of, 288

Nicholas, Grand Duke (brother of A, later Tsar Nicholas I): birth of, 20; in Paris, 289; and military colonies, 348n; marries Charlotte of Prussia (Alexandra Feodorovna), 350, 357; indicated by A as his successor, 367–8, 386; at Troppau Congress, 372; head of Council of Regency during A's absence at Taganrog, 399; on A's death, renounces succession, 410; reconciled to accession by fear of army revolt, 411; order firing on insurgents, 412; repressive policies of, 414

Norway: cession of, to Sweden, as compensation for loss of Finland, 240, 315

Novosiltsov, Nikolai, friend of A, 33, 35; visits Britain, (1797) 34, (1804), 83, 84–5; member of Secret Committee, 52; with A at Memel, 65; in Berlin, 90; with A at Olmütz, 98; resigns from administration, 120; and educational reform, 170; deputy chairman of provisional Supreme Council for Poland (1814),

306; Imperial Commissioner in Warsaw, 341; works on draft constitution for Russia, 364, 385

Odessa: 330, 378, 381, 406; A reluctant for Empress to visit, 399.
Oginski, Count, Polish nobleman, 224, 227
Oldenburg: Napoleon annexes, 199–200, 204, 226; question of compensation for, 204, 205, 214
Olmütz, A at (1805), 95, 97, 98
Opotschna, meeting of A and Metternich at (1813), 268
Orlov, Count Alexei, and Peter III, 30
Orlova-Chemenskaya, Countess Anna, patroness of Photius, 392, 393
Orthodox Church: at Moscow, 57; Holy Synod of, condemns Napoleon, 126–7, 138; schools of, 170; calendar used by, 217; bond between State and, 266; A and ceremonial of, 352–3
Oterbeck, Six d', Dutch Minister in St Petersburg, 186
Oubril, P. de, Russian emissary to Paris (1806), 119, 123
Oudinot, General, French commander, 158
Oxford, A given honorary degree at, 296–7

Pahlen, Count Peter von, military commandant of St Petersburg, 40; involved in murder of Tsar Paul, 42–5; resignation of, 55
Panin, Count Nikita, adviser on foreign affairs, 56, 63; and murder of Tsar Paul, 40, 41; granted leave of absence, 62, 64
Paris: A's vision of entering, 275; A presses for advance on (1814), 277; surrender of, 279; A enters, 280–1; A's ascendancy in, 282–6; peacemaking in 286–91; A at Elysée Palace in (1815), 328; A visits (1818), 361
Paris: First Peace of (1814), 290; Second Peace of (1815), 337
partisans (1812): raid French lines of communication, 250; harass retreating French, 255
Paul, Grand Duke and later Tsar (father of A), 2, 10, 12, 14, 18; tours Europe, 4–5; military interests of, 11, 13–14, 23; and succession to throne, 17, 19; and La Harpe, 20; at death of Catherine II, 27–9; succeeds as Tsar 29–32; his coronation, 32; makes tour of inspection, 33–4; mental vagaries of, 36, 39–40; and 2nd Coalition, 37–9; writes to Napoleon, 41; moves into Mikhailovsky Palace, 41–2; murder of, 42–6, 98; his body lies in state, 47; Talleyrand accuses Britain of complicity in murder of, 81
Paul, Prince of Württemberg, 363
peasant revolt (1773–4), 4, 245
Périgord, Countess Dorothea de, official hostess at Vienna, 309

Peter, Duke of Oldenburg, 199n, 213
Peter, Tsar of Russia (the Great), equestrian statue of, 2, 417
Peter III, Tsar of Russia, 2–3; reburial of, 30, 416; murder of, recalled by Tsar Paul, 43
Petrovsky Palace, Moscow, A at, 58
Pfuehl, General von, former chief-of-staff of Prussian army: in St Petersburg, 208–9, 219, 230
Photius, visionary monk: A interviews, 392, 393; hostile to Golitsyn, 393–4
Piedmont, unrest in (1821), 376
Pitt, William, British statesman: Simon Vorontsov a confidant of, 70; as Prime Minister, 82, 334; and Novosiltsov's mission, 84–5; death of, 118
Plaeswitz, armistice of (1813), 266, 309
Platon, Metropolitan of Moscow, at A's coronation, 59, 60
Poland; partitions of (1772, 1795), 6, 21, 33; interest of A in, 21, 89; Czartoryski's scheme for restoration of, 88–9, 92, 126, 189; Napoleon and, 126, 140, 141–2, 184, 186, 187, 188, 226; Russia awarded territory in (1807), 83, 142, (1809) 184; A offers to proclaim Kingdom of, with liberal constitution (1811), 200, 267; future of, not settled by Teplitz Treaties, 272–3; Britain and, 276, 300, 301; expatriates from, in Paris, 297, 290; A's provisional administration for (1814), 303; discussions on, at Vienna, 305; 310–11, 312–13; central part of, becomes Kingdom under Russia (Congress Poland); remainder goes to Austria and Prussia, 315–16, 321; Constitutional Charter for, 340; A uses as field for constitutional experiments, 341, 357, 365; see also Warsaw
Police, Ministry of, 175; abolished (1819); functions pass to Ministry of Interior, 364
Polotsk, Russian victory at (1812), 251
Pomerania, Swedish: Davout ordered to occupy (1812), 208n; A insists on French leaving, 214; Congress of Vienna and, 315
Poniatowski, Prince, 89; enters French service, 126; Polish brigades of, 182, 183, 197, 200, 202; killed at battle of Leipzig, 89
populations, of St Petersburg, Moscow, Vilna, London, Paris, 216n
Portugal, 140; risings against Napoleon in, 155
Potemkin, Prince Gregory, 6, 12–13; death of, 13
Potsdam Oath, between A and Frederick William (1805), 94, 123, 138, 335
Pozzo di Borgo, General: of Russian delegation at Vienna, 304; and Polish question, 311, 314; favours Franco-Russian accord, 329; Ambassador in Paris, 330, 355–6, 357; and 2nd Treaty of Paris, 337; at Aix Congress,

359; anti-liberal warnings from, 370; at Troppau Congress, 375

Prague Conference (1813), 269-70

primogeniture in inheritance of throne: abolished by Peter the Great (1722), 14; restored by Paul (1797), 32

Protassov, General, tutor to A, 9, 11, 13, 14, 16, 17, 18, 19

Prozorovsky, Marshal, 124

Prussia: in League of Armed Neutrality (1801), 63; army of, 66; and 3rd Coalition, 82, 88–92 passim; secret treaty between Russia and (1805) 93–4, 111; and Peace of Schönbrunn, 112; agreement between Russia and (1806), 123; defeated by French (1806), 124–6; Bartenstein Convention between Russia and (1807), 129, 138, 385; in Tilsit settlement, 140–1; French troops in, 144, 155; troops to be withdrawn under Erfurt agreement, 162; forced into alliance with France (1811), 207–8; French insist on retaining troops in, 213; A demands removal of troops, 214; Tauroggen military convention between Russia and, pledges neutrality of (1812), 259; liberated; enters war against France (1813), 260–2; Russian military alliance with (Kalisch Treaty), 260; in 4th Coalition, 270; in Teplitz Treaties with Austria and Russia, 272; in Quadruple Alliance, 278, 337; question of Saxony for, at Congress of Vienna, 305, 314, 315; obtains part of Saxony, 316; improved position of, after Waterloo, 327; greed of, 328, 329; troops of, in Paris, 331; links between Russia and strengthened by marriage of Grand Duke Nicholas, 357; last vestiges of liberalism abandoned in, 364; at Troppau Congress 371; see also Frederick William III

Publiciste, Le, on A's private life, 120–1

Pugachev, Emelian, leader of peasant revolt, 4, 245

Pulawy, Czartoryski estate: A at, 91–2, 305

Pultusk, battle of (1806), 127

Pushkin, Alexander: on A, xv; at Tsarskoe Selo school, 171; writes verse epistle to A, 343; banished to country, 385; on floods at St Petersburg, 396; welcomes accession of Constantine, 411n–412n

Quadruple Alliance of Austria, Britain, Prussia, and Russia (Chaumont, 1814), 278; renewed (1815), with provision for occasional meetings, 337, 358; validity of, re-affirmed at Congress of Aix, 360n

Quakers, see Friends, Society of

Radischev, Alexander, sent to Siberia for indictment of serfdom, 6

Radziwill, Princess, on A in Poland, 92

Radziwill family, 340

Razumovsky, Count Andrei: Russian delegate to Chatillon Conference, 277; Ambassador in Vienna, 304

Récamier, Mme, 331

Reichenbach Convention, between Austria, Prussia, and Russia (1813), 269, 270

Rhine: Confederation of the, 123, 267, 269, 272; as "natural frontier" of France, 274; Allies cross (1814), 275; free navigation on, 321

Ribas, Admiral, and murder of Tsar Paul, 40, 41

Richelieu, Duke of: returns from Russian service to become French Prime Minister, 330, 357

Rickman, Nathaniel and Mary, of Society of Friends, 300, 301

Rossi, Carlo, architect, 181

Rossini, G.; operas by, performed at Verona, 302

Rostopchin, Theodore: attached to Court of Grand Duke Paul, 27, 28; dismissed, 40, 43; Paul tries to recall, 44; on Budberg, 119; against Speransky, 212; made Governor-General of Moscow, 212, 225, 234, 235, 236, 237, 248; supports appointment of Kutuzov, 239; antipathy of A and Grand Duchess Catherine towards, 249

Rousseau, J. J., Empress Catherine and, 6, 7

Rumiantsev, Count Nikolai: Minister of Commerce (1802), 147–8, and Foreign Minister (1807), 148, 150, 153, 155; pro-French attitude of, 156–7, 173, 205; signs Erfurt Treaty, 161; Chancellor (1809), 172–3, 195, 242, 267; and Poland, 183, 184; and Continental System of Napoleon, 198, 202; suffers stroke and partial paralysis (1812), 220; wants last gesture of appeasement towards Napoleon, 225; with A at Åbo, 240; on A's mission to save Europe, 258; retires (1814), 303–4

Rumiantsev, General P. A., 96

Rumiantsev, Count S. P., 54

Russian Bible Society, 352

Sagan, Wilhelmine, Duchess of: and A in Vienna, 308, 309, 312; in Paris, 331

St Aignan, Baron de; Allied emissory (1813), 274

St Helens, Lord, British Ambassador in St Petersburg, 63, 64

St Peter and St Paul fortress church, St Petersburg, 18; A buried at, 413

Saltykov, General Nicholas: Governor to A, 9–10, 27; consulted on Council of State, 172; responsible for administration in St Petersburg (1812), 221, 225; and appointment of commander-in-chief, 239; Chairman of Committee of Ministers, 10, 343

Saltykov, Prince Serge, father of Tsar Paul?, 2

Samborsky, Andrei: tutor to A, 9, 16; Court chaplain, 167

Sardinia, A's instructions to envoy to (1811), 200

Savary, General: envoy from Napoleon to A (1805), 101, 102; envoy to St Petersburg (1807), 147, 149, 150, 151, 152

Saxony: allied with Napoleon, 200, 238; Russians and Prussians in (1813), 263, 264; deserts Napoleon, 273; A plans to compensate Prussia for losses in Poland by territory of, 305; objections to A's plan for 311, 312; administration of, transferred by A from Russian to Prussian army, 313; part of, passes to Prussia (1815), 316

Scharnhorst, General, Prussian commander, 262

Schönbrunn, Peace of (1805), 112

Schools: Directorate of, 50n, 68; Speransky as administrator of, 170

Schwarz, Col., of Semeonovsky Regiment, 373, 374

Schwarz, Mme, reputed mistress of A, 318

Schwarzenberg, Prince: at Olmütz (1805), 99; commander of Allied forces (1813), 271, 272, 274, 275; in campaign in France, 276, 277, 278, 279; in Paris, 283, 291; to concentrate army on right bank of Rhine (1815), 322, 327; at Russian review, 333

Scott, Walter, in Paris (1815), 332

Sebastopol, A in (1825), 404

Secret Committee, established by A, 52–5; favours peace with France, 63–4; A differs from, on foreign affairs, 64, 65; A does not invite resumption of meetings of, 67; and government reform, 68; A under pressure to cut himself free from, 117; final dispersal of, 120

secret societies, of liberals, 366, 374, 385; of Decembrists, 412

Semeonovsky Regiment of Guards: and murder of Tsar Paul, 43, 44; in Paris (1814), 284; mutiny of (1820), 373

Senate: A sets up Committee to review powers of, 50, 68; reformist elements in, 55

Senyavin, Admiral Dmitri: in Adriatic, 117, 123, 304; returns to Baltic, 146

Seraphim, Metropolitan: in ousting of Golitsyn, 391–2, 393; and insurgents at Nicholas's accession, 412

Serfdom, 6, 51, 53; A determined not to allow increase of, 61; A acknowledges need to abolish, 287, 385

serfs: A forbids advertisements for sale of, 52; amelioration of conditions of, 54; levies of, for militia, 125, 132, 153, 236; A encourages landowners to emancipate, 347; risings of, 365

Sevastionov, hermit, 90

Shelley, Lady Frances, on A, 332

Shishkov, Admiral: succeeds Speransky as State Secretary, 212; in Vilna with A, 221, 225, 226; on abandonment of Vilna, 227; wants A to leave army, 232, 233

Shuvalov, General Prince, 238

Shuvalova, Countess, lady-in-waiting to Empress Catherine, 14

Siberia: Speransky appointed Governor of, 365; A travels to west of (1824), 394, 395

Silesia: proposed as recompense to Austria for cession of Galicia, 88; proposed cession of, to Westphalia, 141

Silistria, fortress on Danube, falls to Russian army (1810), 194–5

slave trade, appeals for abolition of, 321, 360

Slobodsky Palace, Moscow, A at, 58

Smith, Horatio, writes verses on A, 263

Smolensk: modernization of fortifications of, 89; French army and (1812), 238, 240; Arakcheev and rebuilding of, 344

Soult, Marshal, French commander, 107, 108

Spain: risings against Napoleon in, 155, 197, 200; Wellington's victory in, 268; future of, discussed at Chaumont, 278; unrest in (1820), 370; suggestion of intervention in, 370, 376; French authorized to take military action in, 382

Speransky, Michael, 164–8; Minister of the Interior, 68; secretary to A at Erfurt, 164–5; Assistant Minister of Justice, 166; reforms suggested by, 168–72; and Arakcheev, 173; as State Secretary, 172, 176, 193, 195; as scapegoat for grievances about reforms, 175–6; A consults on Poland, 189–90; in contact with Talleyrand, 190–1; victim o intrigue; is exiled to Nizhni Novgorod (1812), 210–12, 242; Governor of Penza (1816), 348; Governor-General of Siberia (1819), 365

spies of Austrian police: reports of, during Congress of Vienna, 307–8, 309–10, 313, 314, 315, 317, 318, 323

Stackelberg, Count, in Russian delegation at Vienna, 304

Stadion, Count, Austrian diplomat, 268, 269

Staël, Mme de: on patriotism of Russians, 236; on A, 242–3

Stein, Baron vom, chief Minister of Prussia, 157–8; joins A at Vilna (1812), 214; urges Russian advance from Vilna, 258; appeals to Frederick William to break with Napoleon, 259; hopes for united German state, 267, 321; memorandum by, on Poland, 314

Stephens, Elizabeth, wife of Speransky, 167

Stoffregen, Dr, physician to Empress Elizabeth, 197n

Stourdza, Alexander, as secretary to A, 318, 319

Stourdza, Roxane, lady-in-waiting to Empress Elizabeth, 246; follower of Julie von Krüdener 318–19, 320, 325, 335; in Bavaria with Elizabeth, 323; A's letter to, 353; Capodistrias a friend of, 356; with Elizabeth at Taganrog, 413–14

Stroganov, Paul, friend of A, 33, 34, 35; member of Secret Committee, 52, 53, 55, 64; deputy Minister of the Interior, 69; with A at Olmütz, 98; in London, 116; resigns, 120; and educational reform, 170

subsidies, British: to Russia, 83, 86–7, 231, 268; to Prussia, 268

Sukhozanet, Major-General, and Decembrist insurgents (1825), 412

Sukhtelen, General, Quartermaster-General (1805), 98; in Finland, 153

Sussex, Duke of, proposes to Grand Duchess Catherine, 292

Suvorov, General, 12, 96, 99; made to retire by Tsar Paul, 36; reinstated (1799), 38, 63

Sveaborg: besieged, by Russians (1808), 153

Sweden: threatened invasion from (1786), 12; in League of Armed Neutrality, 63; troops of, in 3rd Coalition plans, 87, 88; in talks between Napoleon and A, 140; refuses to stop trade with Britain, 152; Russia at war with, over Finland, 153–4, 155, 179; limited alliance between Russia and (1811), 208; Russian agreement with (1812), 240; enters war against France (1813), 260; in 4th Coalition, 270

Switzerland: Suvorov's army in, 38, 99; A and affairs of, 71; A in (1814), 273; question of future of, (at Chaumont), 278, (at Vienna) 321; A travels in (1815), 338

Taganrog: A and Elizabeth winter at (1825), 398–9, 401–2; A's illness and death at, 405–10

Talleyrand-Périgord, C. M. de: French Foreign Minister, 81; in Vienna (1805), 111; and Haugwitz, 112; signs treaty with Oubril (not ratified), 123; prefers Austrian to Russian alliance, 134; summoned to Tilsit, 137, 143, 205; at Erfurt (as Grand Chamberlain); achieves understanding with A, 161; and Napoleon's marriage, 162; and Speransky, 164, 190–1, 211n; asks A for money, 198; lets Allies know they can advance (1814), 278; offers hospitality to A, 280–1; and Bourbon restoration, 283, 285; and Wilhelmine of Sagan, 309; objects to status of France at Congress of Vienna, 310; interviews A on Saxony, 312, 314; concludes secret defensive alliance with Austria and Britain, 314–15; temporary head of Ministry (1815), 330

Talma, François-Joseph, actor, 156, 159

Talytzin, General, of Semeonovsky Guard, 44

tariffs: high protectionist of 1797 relaxed by A, 52; changes in (1810) (Taxes on goods arriving overland, but not on goods arriving by sea), 199, 226; French puzzled by change in, 201; hints at modification of, to French advantage, 202, 204; A willing to modify, 214

Tarnopol district (Galicia): annexed to Russia (1809), 184; Austria demands return of (1814), 311, 314, and obtains, 315

Tatischev, Dmitri: Ambassador in Madrid, 370; Ambassador in Vienna, 380

Tauride Palace, St Petersburg: Potemkin entertains Empress Catherine at, 12–13; A and Czartoryski at, 22; made cavalry barracks by Tsar Paul, 30; A at 90; Empress Marie at, 185n

taxation: by Speransky's scheme, to be based on agricultural wealth, 168; by stamp duties, 175; mounting burden of, 212; see also tariffs

Teplitz: Grand Duchess Catherine at, 264, 265; Allied headquarters at (1813), 272; Treaties of, 272–3

Thomas à Kempis: Speransky translates, 167

Thurn-Taxis, Princess de (sister of Queen Louise of Prussia), at Erfurt, 161

Tiesenhausen, Countess: on A in Vilna, 217, 218, 223, 224, 227; on A's return to Vilna, 258

Tilsit: A at (1807), 130; Napoleon at, 133; A and Napoleon meet at, 134–6, conduct conversations, 136–9, and conclude treaty and alliance, 139–44, 199n

Tolstoy, Leo, on 1811 comet, 207

Tormassov, General: commands 3rd Army (1812), 224, 237; advances on Minsk, 254; resents appointment of Wittgenstein (1813), 264

Trianon Decrees, on blockade against British goods, 198

Troppau Congress (1820), 371, 372–3; Preliminary Protocol of, 374

Troschinsky, Dmitri, Procurator of the Senate, 49

Tsarskoe Selo Palace, St Petersburg: Empress Catherine at, 4, 7, 8, 9, 18; left empty by Tsar Paul, 30; school at, 171

Tuala Arms Works, 73, 250, 252

Turkey (Ottoman Empire): Empress Catherine's victories over, 12; Tsar Paul associated with, against France, 37; peace between France and, 70; French activities in, 80; proposals for eventual partition of, 84, 140, 143, 205; Russia at war with (from 1806), 122–3, 179, 194; in talks between A and Napoleon, 140, 142–3; Napoleon proposes Franco-Russian conquest of, 152–3; peace talks opened with (1811), 208, 223; peace terms agreed with, 230–1, 235; Balkan risings against, 377, 378, 379, 394

Tver: George of Oldenburg and Grand Duchess Catherine at, 181–2, 193; A visits, 193, 199, 202, 237

Ulm, battle of (1805), 96, 101
universities: foundation of, 68; purge of teachers in (1820), 366, 385
Uvarov, General, friend of A, 397

Valouiev, Catherine, friend of Roxane Stourdza, 319
Vauban, Marshal, 210
Vaughan, Dr, Warden of Merton College, Oxford, 296
Verona Conference (1822), 381, 382–3
Vertus, Plain of: military review and religious ceremony on (1815), 332–3
Viazemsky, Prince: and Tsar Paul, 43; complains of "government from a post-chaise", 367
Vienna: Napoleon in (1805), 91, 95; (1809), 183; A visits (1818), 361
Vienna Conference (1822), 381
Vienna Congress (1814–15); prospect of, 277, 290, 301, 302–6; activities of, 306–7, 310–16; Final Act of, 321, 324
Vilna: University of, 68; A in (1821), 216–26; abandoned to Napoleon, 227; Napoleon enters, 228; Kutuzov re-enters, 255; A in, 257
Vincent, Baron, representative of Austria at Erfurt, 160
Vistula: as boundary between Napoleon and Russia, 134, 142; A and French bases on, 214
Vitebsk: abandoned to French (1812), 237; retaken, 253
Vitrolles, Baron, Bourbon representative (1814), 285
Volkonsky, Prince Peter, 56; with A at Olmütz, 98; aide-de-camp to A, 239, 251, 325, 345; aide-de-camp to Empress Elizabeth on journey to Taganrog, 401; at Taganrog, 405, 406, 409
Voltaire, Empress Catherine and, 4, 10
Vorontsov, Alexander, 55; Foreign Minister and State Chancellor, 69–70, 79; his health fails, 80, 81
Vorontsov, Count Michael, Governor of "New Russia", 402, 403, 406
Vorontsov, Simon, 55; Ambassador in London, 65, 70; resents Novosiltsov's mission, 83
Vyazma, Napoleon takes (1812), 240
Vyazmitinov, General, War Minister: dismissed (1807), 150

Wagram, battle of (1809), 245
Walewska, Marie, Napoleon's Polish mistress, 126
War Ministry of, 68

Warsaw: as capital of "Southern Prussia", 88, 91; French in, 126; Grand Duke Constantine commands Military Commission in, 305, 323, 339, 341; in Congress Poland under Russia, 315; A visits, (1815) 339, (1818) 364; Imperial Commissioner in, 340, 341; A attends sessions of Diet in, 367, 371, 387
Warsaw, Grand Duchy of, set up by Napoleon, 142, 158; troops raised for Napoleon in, 182, 183, 197, 200; French refer to, as "Duchy of Poland", 188; to be dissolved (by Reichenbach terms) 269, (by Teplitz Treaties) 272
Waterloo, battle of (1815), 327, 349
Weimar: A visits his sister, in (1805) 95, (1808) 159, 160
Wellington, Duke of: in Spain, 268; at Congress of Vienna, 321; commands Anglo-Dutch force in Belgium (1815), 322, 327; and Bourbons, 328; receives sword from A, 329; in Paris (1815), 332, 333; and Holy Alliance, 334; at Congress of Aix, 359; objects to intervention in Spain, 382; at A's funeral, 413
Westphalia, Jerome Bonaparte as King of, 141, 142
Weyrother, General, Austrian chief-of-staff, 99; before Austerlitz, 103–4; during battle, 108
Wheeler, Daniel, farming member of Society of Friends: in Russia, 352
Whitworth, Lord, British Ambassador in St Petersburg, 40, 41
Wieland, C. M., A meets 95
Wilkinson, John, of Society of Friends, 299
William III of the Netherlands, 349n–350n
William, Prince of Orange, husband of Grand Duchess Anna, 303, 349
William, Prince of Prussia, in march on Paris (1814), 279
William of Württemberg, second husband of Grand Duchess Catherine, 303, 317, 348–9; becomes King, 349
Wilmot, Martha, on A and the Empress Elizabeth, 77
Wilson, General Sir Robert: attached to Russian army (1807), 146; sees fall of Smolensk (1812); carries message from Russian officers to A, 241–2; attached to Kutusov's headquarters (1813), 258
Winter Palace, St Petersburg: Empress Catherine at, 5, 10, 11; A and Elizabeth at, 18, 46; Tsar Paul at, 29, 37; A escapes from life at, 120; flood surrounds, 395
Wintzingerode, General, Russian commander, 98, 279
Wittgenstein, General, Russian commander, 231, 253; wins victory at Polotsk (1812), 251; at Vitebsk, 253, 254; on heels of French, 255, 259; approaches Oder, 260; meets

stiffening resistance over Elbe, 263–4; commands mainly Prussian force (1813), 264, 265; in France, 276

Wrankel, General: Prussian envoy to St Petersburg, 195; aide-de-camp to Frederick William, 262

Württemberg: Napoleon and, 71; deserts Napoleon, 273

Wylie, Dr James, 388n–389n; physician to Tsar Paul, 44, 46; physician to A, 111, 154, 390–1, and to Empress Elizabeth, 397, 398; in Crimea, 404; and A's last illness, 405, 406, 407, 408, 409

Yashvil, Prince, and Tsar Paul, 43

Yorck, General Hans von, Prussian commander: concludes convention of neutrality with Russia at Tauroggen, 259

Ypsilanti, Prince Alexander, leads rising against Turks (1821), 377

Zaionczek, General Joseph, Viceroy of Congress Poland, 341

Zherebzova, Countess, sister of the Zubovs, 44

Zubov, Nicholas, 27, 28, 43; involved in murder of Tsar Paul, 45

Zubov, Platon, favourite of Empress Catherine, 17, 27, 43